Lecture Notes in Computer Science 14483

Founding Editors

Gerhard Goos
Juris Hartmanis

Editorial Board Members

The series Lecture Notes in Computer Science (LNCS), including its subseries Lecture Notes in Artificial Intelligence (LNAI) and Lecture Notes in Bioinformatics (LNBI), has established itself as a medium for the publication of new developments in computer science and information technology research, teaching, and education.

LNCS enjoys close cooperation with the computer science R & D community, the series counts many renowned academics among its volume editors and paper authors, and collaborates with prestigious societies. Its mission is to serve this international community by providing an invaluable service, mainly focused on the publication of conference and workshop proceedings and postproceedings. LNCS commenced publication in 1973.

Regine Kadgien · Andreas Jedlitschka ·
Andrea Janes · Valentina Lenarduzzi ·
Xiaozhou Li
Editors

Product-Focused Software Process Improvement

24th International Conference, PROFES 2023
Dornbirn, Austria, December 10–13, 2023
Proceedings, Part I

 Springer

Editors
Regine Kadgien
FHV Vorarlberg University of Applied
Science
Dornbirn, Austria

Andreas Jedlitschka (iD)
Fraunhofer Institute for Experimental
Software Engineering
Kaiserslautern, Germany

Andrea Janes (iD)
FHV Vorarlberg University of Applied
Science
Dornbirn, Austria

Valentina Lenarduzzi (iD)
University of Oulu
Oulu, Finland

Xiaozhou Li (iD)
University of Oulu
Oulu, Finland

ISSN 0302-9743   ISSN 1611-3349 (electronic)
Lecture Notes in Computer Science
ISBN 978-3-031-49265-5   ISBN 978-3-031-49266-2 (eBook)
https://doi.org/10.1007/978-3-031-49266-2

This Springer imprint is published by the registered company Springer Nature Switzerland AG
The registered company address is: Gewerbestrasse 11, 6330 Cham, Switzerland

Paper in this product is recyclable.

Preface

On behalf of the PROFES Organizing Committee, we are proud to present the proceedings of the 24th International Conference on Product-Focused Software Process Improvement (PROFES 2023). The conference was held during December 11–13, 2022.

Following the previous editions, the main theme of PROFES 2023 was professional software process improvement (SPI) motivated by product, process, and service quality needs. The technical program of PROFES 2023 was selected by a committee of leading experts in software process improvement, software process modeling, and empirical software engineering.

This year, we received 82 submissions. After a thorough evaluation that involved at least three independent experts per paper, 21 full technical papers were selected together with 6 industrial papers, 8 short papers, and 1 poster paper. Each submission was reviewed by at least three members of the PROFES Program Committees.

Alongside the technical program, PROFES 2023 hosted a doctoral symposium, two workshops, and one tutorial. In total three papers were accepted for the doctoral symposium. The 2nd Workshop on Computational Intelligence and Software Engineering (CISE 2023) aimed to foster integration between the software engineering and AI communities, and to improve research results, teaching and mentoring, and industrial practice. 8 papers were selected for CISE 2023. The 2nd Workshop on Engineering Processes and Practices for Quantum Software (PPQS 2023) aimed to establish a community, fostering academic research and industrial solutions focused on quantum software engineering principles and practices for process-centric design, development, validation, and deployment and maintenance of quantum software systems and applications. 3 papers were selected for PPQS 2023.

We are thankful for the opportunity to have served as chairs for this conference. The Program Committee members and reviewers provided excellent support in the paper evaluation process. We are also grateful to all authors of submitted manuscripts, presenters, keynote speakers, and session chairs, for their time and effort in making PROFES 2023 a success. We would also like to thank the PROFES Steering Committee members for their guidance and support in the organization process.

December 2023

Regine Kadgien
Andreas Jedlitschka
Andrea Janes
Valentina Lenarduzzi
Xiaozhou Li

Organization

Organizing Committee

General Chairs

Regine Kadgien — FHV Vorarlberg University of Applied Sciences, Austria

Andreas Jedlitschka — Fraunhofer Institute for Experimental Software Engineering, Germany

Program Chairs

Andrea Janes — FHV Vorarlberg University of Applied Sciences, Austria

Valentina Lenarduzzi — University of Oulu, Finland

Short Paper and Poster Chairs

Javier Gonzalez Huerta — Blekinge Institute of Technology, Sweden

Matteo Camilli — Politecnico di Milano, Italy

Industrial Chairs

Jan Bosch — Chalmers University of Technology, Sweden

Ralph Hoch — FHV Vorarlberg University of Applied Sciences, Austria

Workshop and Tutorial Chairs

Helena Holmström Olsson — Malmö University, Sweden

Simone Romano — University of Salerno, Italy

Doctoral Symposium Chairs

Maria Teresa Baldassarre — University of Bari, Italy

Tommi Mikkonen — University of Helsinki, Finland

Journal First Chair

Sira Vegas   Universidad Politécnica de Madrid, Spain

Proceedings Chair

Xiaozhou Li   University of Oulu, Finland

Publicity Chairs

Dario Amoroso d'Aragona   Tampere University, Finland
Rahul Mohanani   University of Jyväskylä, Finland

Program Committee

Dario Amoroso d'Aragona   Tampere University, Finland
Fabio Calefato   University of Bari, Italy
Tomas Cerny   University of Arizona, USA
Marcus Ciolkowski   QAware GmbH, Germany
Maya Daneva   University of Twente, The Netherlands
Dario Di Nucci   University of Salerno, Italy
Michal Dolezel   Prague University of Economics and Business,
                                       Czechia
Matteo Esposito   University of Rome "Tor Vergata", Italy
Michael Felderer   German Aerospace Center (DLR), Germany
Xavier Franch   Universitat Politècnica de Catalunya, Spain
Carmine Gravino   University of Salerno, Italy
Helena Holmström Olsson   Malmö University, Sweden
Martin Höst   Malmö University, Sweden
Marcos Kalinowski   Pontifical Catholic University of Rio de Janeiro,
                                       Brazil
Terhi Kilamo   Tampere University, Finland
Michael Kläs   Fraunhofer IESE, Germany
Jil Klünder   Leibniz Universität Hannover, Germany
Marco Kuhrmann   Reutlingen University, Germany
Xiaozhou Li   University of Oulu, Finland
Tomi Männistö   University of Helsinki, Finland
Tommi Mikkonen   University of Jyväskylä, Finland
Sandro Morasca   Università degli Studi dell'Insubria, Italy
Sergio Moreschini   Tampere University, Finland
Maurizio Morisio   Politecnico di Torino, Italy

Juergen Muench	Reutlingen University, Germany
Rudolf Ramler	Software Competence Center Hagenberg, Austria
Simone Romano	University of Salerno, Italy
Nyyti Saarimaki	Tampere University, Finland
Darja Smite	Blekinge Institute of Technology, Sweden
Kari Systä	Tampere University of Technology, Finland
Davide Taibi	University of Oulu, Finland
Xiaofeng Wang	Free University of Bozen-Bolzano, Italy
Dietmar Winkler	ACDP & SBA Research & TU Wien, Austria

Program Committee Members (Poster and Short Papers)

Eduardo Guerra	Free University of Bolzen-Bolzano, Italy
Eriks Klotins	Blekinge Institute of Technology, Sweden
John Noll	University of Hertfordshire, UK
Giovanni Quattrocchi	Politecnico di Milano, Italy
Ehsan Zabardast	Blekinge Institute of Technology, Sweden
Panagiota Chatzipetrou	Örebro University, Sweden
Bogdan Marculescu	Kristiania University College, Norway
Davide Fucci	Blekinge Institute of Technology, Sweden
Sandro Morasca	Università degli Studi dell'Insubria, Italy
Francis Palma	University of New Brunswick, Canada
Fabian Fagerholm	Aalto University, Finland
Priscila Cedillo	Universidad de Cuenca, Ecuador
Kwabena Ebo Bennin	Wageningen University & Research, The Netherlands
Renata Carvalho	Eindhoven University of Technology, The Netherlands
Alessandro Marchetto	University of Trento, Italy

Program Committee Members (Industry Papers)

Anas Dakkak	Ericsson, Sweden
Hongyi Zhang	Chalmers University of Technology, Sweden
Torvald Mårtensson	Saab AB, Sweden
Aiswarya Raj	Chalmers University of Technology, Sweden
Benjamin Schwendinger	TU Wien, Austria
Daniel Rotter	University of Applied Sciences Vorarlberg, Austria
Daniel Ståhl	Ericsson, Sweden

Sandro Widmer	RhySearch, Switzerland
Rimma Dzhusupova	McDermott, USA
Simon Kranzer	Salzburg University of Applied Sciences, Austria
David Issa Mattos	Volvo Cars, Sweden

Contents – Part I

Machine Learning and Data Science

Software Analysis and Tools

Software Testing and Quality Assurance

Security, Vulnerabilities, and Human Factors

Contents – Part II

**2nd Workshop on Engineering Processes and Practices for Quantum
Software (PPQS'23)**

Doctoral Symposium

Software Development and Project Management

Virtual Reality Collaboration Platform for Agile Software Development

Enes Yigitbas[✉], Iwo Witalinski, Sebastian Gottschalk, and Gregor Engels

Paderborn University, Zukunftsmeile 2, 33102 Paderborn, Germany
{enes.yigitbas,iwo.witalinski,sebastian.gottschalk,gregor.engels}@upb.de

Abstract. Nowadays, most software teams use Scrum as their software development process framework. Scrum highly values collaboration and communication inside the team and aims to make them more flexible to spontaneous changes. However, due to the rise of working from home, many developers experienced a significant decrease in communication, social interactions, and a general feeling of social connectedness with their colleagues, which might impede the effectiveness of Scrum teams. To overcome these issues, we present a VR collaboration platform for Scrum meetings, called *Virtual Reality-based Agile Collaboration Platform* (VRACP). VRACP provides the visualization of and interaction with Scrum artifacts inside a realistic virtual office, the integration and synchronization of external data sources, remote collaboration, and human-like user representations. To evaluate whether VR can increase social connectedness in agile software development teams, we conducted a user study where our solution was compared to common web/desktop applications for Scrum meetings. The results suggest that although efficiency and effectiveness were reduced, it could indeed increase the feeling of being together, collaborating more naturally, and having more fun and motivation.

Keywords: Virtual Reality · Agile Software Engineering · Scrum

1 Introduction

Due to the rise of agile software development processes in modern software engineering, the value of collaboration and communication has massively increased. Software developers should not only have good programming skills but also distinctive soft skills like teamwork. The focus on communication is believed to enhance productivity and flexibility [25]. The most popular agile software development process framework is Scrum [12] with its variety of meetings/events, members, and artifacts[1]. All meetings have in common that (almost) every team member takes part and is motivated to bring in his opinions and ideas. However, due to the rise of home office, one consequence of the COVID-19 pandemic, companies are forced to mainly rely on remote collaboration tools for their meetings. Although these circumstances provide many advantages like saving time

---

[1] https://www.scrum.org/learning-series/what-is-scrum.

R. Kadgien et al. (Eds.): PROFES 2023, LNCS 14483, pp. 3–19, 2024.
https://doi.org/10.1007/978-3-031-49266-2_1

and money by not driving to the office, it was recently shown that employees, in general, often criticize the missing direct communication with their colleagues and an increased feeling of isolation [10]. In a user study focused on software development teams during the COVID-19 lockdown, Miller et al. [17] found out that 74% of the interviewees missed social interactions and 65% reported a decrease in feeling socially connected to their team. Furthermore, more than 50% noticed a decrease in the ability to brainstorm and their communication ease. This is a threat to the main principles of Scrum and its relevance to communication and team collaboration and might therefore affect the productivity and effectiveness of software engineering in a negative way. A potential solution for this problem could be provided by Virtual Reality (VR). Per definition, VR describes a computer-generated simulation or environment which allows the user to walk around and interact with its objects as if they were real [20], hence a way of collaboration that is more similar to being in the same room with others than sitting in front of the PC. In this paper, we explored the use of VR in the context of agile software engineering by investigating the following two research questions:

RQ1: *Can VR provide a solution for the missing social interaction in agile software engineering in a remote context?*
RQ2: *To what extent is such a VR application suitable for daily use?*

With *RQ1*, we investigate whether VR can substitute face-to-face meetings better than remote desktop-based collaboration tools concerning the user's feeling of social connectivity in the context of agile software engineering. With *RQ2*, we explore how suitable such an application is in the real world and which aspects must be necessarily improved. In order to answer these questions, we created a VR-based solution that tackled the following challenges: First, *Remote collaboration* (C1) encompasses several features that are needed to work remotely, including voice chat, proper visual representation, and movement synchronization so that one can see where the others are currently inside the virtual environment. Next, *Immersiveness* (C2) covers the variety of possibilities modern VR systems offer to create a real-world-like experience, especially referring to mirroring the movement of the physical body into the virtual one. With *Scrum meetings* (C3), the application should integrate the necessary features to hold the main Scrum meetings Daily, Sprint Planning, Sprint Review, and Sprint Retrospective. *Interoperability* (C4) denotes the feature of connecting the application to an existing source of data and synchronizing changes accordingly so that users do not have to manage two separate data sources. Although there were already several VR solutions in the context of software engineering, none fully covered these challenges (see Sect. 2). Thus, we developed our own VR-based solution called *Virtual Reality-based Agile Collaboration Platform* (VRACP) and evaluated it based on a user study.

The rest of the paper is structured as follows: Sect. 2 deals with work related to the topic. Section 3 shows a conceptual solution of the application while Sect. 4 provides its implementation. In Sect. 5, we show the results of the user study and finally, in Sect. 6, we conclude the paper and give an outlook for potential future work.

2 Related Work

In this section, works related to the paper's topic, categorized in Desktop, VR, and AR, are presented and discussed.

2.1 Desktop

With *dBoard*, Esbensen et al. [9] developed a digital scrum board for distributed software teams by using a large multitouch surface and integrating a scrum board on its surface. The people can see and talk to each other and simultaneously, they are able to move the different scrum artifacts on the screen. In 2013, Rodrigues et al. published *Virtual Scrum* [22] which is a teaching-oriented 3D environment for different scrum meetings. The users are represented as virtual characters and can walk through the environment and speak with each other. The user study on students shows the potential of such an application as they reported being more involved in the process and learning the different scrum meetings very fast. Next, Dawood et al. [5] proposed a web-based Scrum collaboration platform that includes many necessary functionalities for agile practices like project management, version control, coding environment, and online video meetings. With *SCRUM-X* [14], Lee developed an interactive single-player learning platform for teaching Scrum methodology in a chapter-based way, covering all necessary Scrum meetings. A similar approach was proposed by Seabra et al. with *SCRUMI* [6], a single-player 2D board game for teaching the Scrum framework. A user study was executed based on usability, motivation, and applicability and suggested the usefulness of the game. Zhang et al. [28] proposed a Scrum-based collaboration platform for managing project tasks, meant to be a training platform for students who are asked to participate in different projects and in different roles to gain insight into the different tasks he has to fulfill.

To conclude, it can be seen that there are several desktop-based solutions for holding Scrum meetings. However, many of them are teaching-oriented and therefore did not meet the challenges of *Remote Collaboration* (C1) and *Interoperability* (C4). As they are desktop-based, there was also only little potential to implement *Immersiveness* (C3). Additionally, in their user studies, the authors did not focus on the social aspects which are essential for answering the research questions.

2.2 Virtual Reality (VR)

In the book *Serious Games* [4], Pohlman and Göbel present a VR environment to learn the basic steps of the Scrum framework for people with little or no knowledge about it. In the application, the goal is to develop a small jump'n'run game based on Scrum methodology. For this, the player has to act as a scrum master and interact with other Non-Player-Characters (NPCs) representing developers and product owners. With *Scrum VR* [16], Mayor et al. published a similar approach to teaching Scrum interactively in a scenario-based environment. One acts as a software developer entering a new company and gets guided by an NPC Scrum master through the office while getting introduced to the meaning of agile, Scrum, Kanban, etc. In general, the authors received positive feedback for their approach. Similarly, Yilmaz published a paper [26] in which he examines the question of whether VR can help participants gain experience in daily scrum meetings. Therefore, he developed a VR daily scrum meeting environment with several scenarios and NPC characters representing different personalities. The user study suggests that those VR-based simulations could be helpful for training software practitioners. Radhakrishnan et al. [19] developed a VR sprint simulation with collaboration support which aims to teach students the basics of sprint meetings remotely. The users have to fulfill block-building tasks and manage the process with the help of a Kanban board placed in the environment. With *VIAProMa*, Hensen et al. [11] proposed a collaborative Mixed Reality environment for agile project management with integration of GitHub issues and Requirements Bazaar, enabling the users to hold Scrum meetings remotely. One restriction of the application is the missing native creation and editing of new issues and sprints with synchronization back to the data source. Another approach, dealing with the development phase of the software development lifecycle, is *VirtualDesk* by Dominic et al. [8], a VR-based remote collaboration platform for pair programming. Both developers sit in front of their computer, keyboard, and mouse and wear a Head-Mounted Display (HMD) that tracks the movement of their hands. A user study, comparing their solution to the desktop-based one, showed that the VR participants found and solved more bugs.

To conclude, similar to the Desktop-based related works, many VR-works have a teaching purpose and do not enable *Remote Collaboration* (C1) nor *Interoperability* (C4) which are necessary for our purpose. Additionally, none of the works examine the social aspects in their user studies.

2.3 Augmented Reality (AR)

With *ARPostIts*, Deva et al. [7] proposed a mobile application that uses AR to simplify agile paper-based task boards which might become very confusing due to their limited space. *ARPostIts* solves this problem by using encoded frames on the post-it notes that can be identified via smartphone and then be linked to further information. Similarly to VR, Reuter et al. [21] developed an AR UML Modeling application with which one can create UML classes and connect them together to a class diagram, even if it was designed for teaching purposes.

To summarize, it can be seen that there is only little AR-based work in the context of software engineering and none of them tackled the defined challenges entirely.

All in all, it can be seen that there are various different related works in the context of software engineering. However, as many of them were teaching-oriented, they could barely meet the challenges of *Remote Collaboration* and *Interoperability* entirely. Additionally, none of the work examined the social aspects in their studies. Because of this, we developed and evaluated our own solution which will be presented in the following chapters.

3   Conceptual Solution

In this section, the conceptual solution of *VRACP* is presented. We first give an overview of the components and then conceptualize each component separately.

3.1   Overview

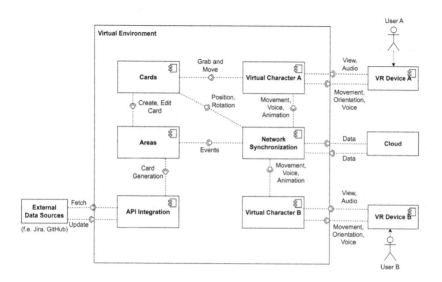

Fig. 1. Solution architecture of VRACP

At the top of Fig. 1, the Users interact with their VR Devices by moving the HMD and the hand controllers. Every user is represented by a Virtual Character which gets the movement, orientation, and voice information of the *User* and applies it to its corresponding components. For this, there must be a mapping between the real objects of the VR Device and the virtual ones of the Virtual Character. The Virtual Character sends his View and the Audio he receives from other users back to the display and speaker of the VR Device. Through the virtual character, the user interacts with the Artifacts inside the Virtual Environment. Here, an Artifact represents an issue or a sprint from the external data source. In the original definition of Scrum, artifacts denote i.a. Product and Sprint Backlog. However, in our context, we call them Areas. The issues and sprints are generated by their corresponding AREA component which handles the correct setting of card data he receives from the API INTEGRATION component. This component handles the REST API calls to and from the EXTERNAL DATA SOURCES and then proceeds with the result for its desired task. The last main component, the NETWORK SYNCHRONIZATION SERVICE, is required for sending the data to be synchronized from the local player to the others and applying remote data to the local player. This is done with the help of an external CLOUD.

3.2   Components

Virtual Environment. The VIRTUAL ENVIRONMENT is the place where the users move inside and interact with. We decided to use an office room as our virtual environment as, by this, the users move inside familiar surroundings without the need to adapt to new unknown circumstances.

Virtual Character. For representing a user in the virtual environment, i.e. the VIRTUAL CHARACTER, we opted to use a human-like realistic full-body avatar. Based on a study conducted in 2001 by Cassanueva et al. [3], human-like avatars yielded the most feeling of co-presence in comparison to unrealistic and cartoon-like ones. Similarly, based on the individual answers of the study executed by Yoon et al. [27] and the results of Zibrek et al. [29], we have chosen a realistic render style of the virtual character. According to [27], the choice of showing body parts yields a significant difference in social presence. As there were many positive opinions and a high level of social presence we decided to use the whole-body version. By providing more than one avatar for both males and females, we cover human diversity as well as possible and give the user more choices to select the one he/she can identify herself the most. This influences the sense of self-presence positively [24].

Concerning the movement of the virtual character, we decided to make use of the VR systems' provided possibilities: head movement is reached by moving the HMD while hand movement is simulated by the hand controllers. The user can continuously walk inside the virtual environment by using the left joystick. Finally, we decided to use *Inverse Kinematics*², a technique to address the difficulty of correct behavior of body parts depending on the position and rotation of the head and hand.

Network Synchronization. The NETWORK SYNCHRONIZATION component deals with synchronizing the following four types of data between all users: (1) Movement, (2) Animation, (3) Voice, and (4) Events. The first aspect refers to the movement of the players and the artifacts inside the virtual environment. The second one is about the animations of the virtual character when he is walking. The third type refers to the voice chat feature which also considers the positional condition where the voice is coming from. Finally, the last type encompasses all

---

² https://de.mathworks.com/discovery/inverse-kinematics.html.

events that may occur during a session, e.g. when a user changes the text of an artifact which must be updated on all users accordingly. It is important to mention that these EVENTS are not Scrum events but general events that occur occasionally. To establish connections, we conceptualized a basic room system that consists of a central server that holds a list of available rooms which the users can browse through. He is also able to create a new room which can then be joined by his/her colleagues. For this, we opted to create a separate environment, similar to the main environment, where the user can walk through, adapt to the new setting and do the actions described before.

Artifacts. The ARTIFACTS component consists of two subcomponents, ISSUES and SPRINTS, which must be visualized and represented in the virtual environment. As a first step, we collected the main data of each artifact. An issue usually consists of a title, description, creator, status, type, and key/ID, whereas a sprint consists of a title, start date, end date, status, list of related issues, and key/ID. As the second step, we conceptualized their visual representation. For the issues, we decided to use a card design with all the necessary information on the front, while the sprints are represented by three-dimensional boxes that contain several issues inside and their information on the front. The users take these objects and can place them everywhere inside the virtual environment, however, it makes the most sense to place them in the predefined AREAS of the room.

Areas. Based on the use cases of the Scrum process, we defined several AREAS inside the virtual environment with specific purposes: a *Backlog Area* which contains all the backlog issues, a *Board Area* for the issues of the current sprints separated by their current status, an *Issue Area* where the users can edit and create issues, a *Sprint Area* for managing sprints and finally a *Code Review Area* for conducting a code review. For their visual representations, we decided to mainly use bookshelves or tables as they are common in office rooms and provide a more three-dimensional impression than if placed on the wall.

Whenever a user takes an issue and places it into another AREA, an event is triggered to synchronize the change on all users and to send an API call to the external data source. An overview of the Scrum meetings, their required functionality, and the corresponding area is presented in Table 1.

API Integration and External Data Sources. The API INTEGRATION is needed to fulfill the *Interoperability* feature. It is responsible for making requests to the REST API of the *External Data Source*, fetching and proceeding with the result, and returning it to the component that called for it. We divided the component into three subcomponents, namely API ENDPOINTS, a list of necessary points for communication purposes, API CALLS, which uses the endpoints to make requests, and API CONTROLLER, dedicated to choosing the right calls and return the results to the caller. By creating a dedicated component for this purpose, we simplify exchanging the data source if another one should be added in the future.

Table 1. Overview of which scrum meeting was integrated by which area and functionality

Scrum Meeting	Required Functionality	Covered by?
Sprint Planning	Create Sprint	*Create Sprint Area*
	Create Issue	*Create Issue Area*
	Move Issue to Sprint	*Backlog* and *Sprint Issues Area*
Daily	Answer the 3 "W questions"	*Voice Chat*
	View current board	*Board Area*
Sprint Review	Present Software	Partially, *Code Review Area*
	Discuss	*Voice Chat*
Sprint Retrospective	Discuss last sprint	*Voice Chat*
Sprint	Manage Board	*Boards Area*
	Edit Issue	*Edit Issue Area*

4   Implementation

In this Section, we present the implementation of *VRACP* by motivating the choice of VR Device and Development Platform and presenting each component separately. The code of *VRACP* is publicly available via GitHub[3].

4.1   VR Device and Development Platform

Based on our conceptual decisions, we decided to use the *Oculus Quest 2* as our main VR device. It comes with one HMD and a pair of hand controllers, has integrated speakers and microphones, provides 6 degrees of freedom, and is not dependent on further external hardware like PCs. Concerning the development platform, we opted to use *Unity 3D* which is a very popular game engine for developing 2D, 3D, AR, and VR games. It comes with many freely available plugins to enhance productivity and simplify programming.

4.2   Components

Virtual Environment. Following the decision and design elements from Sect. 3, we designed a realistic-looking office room. We relied on free external models and objects from the Unity *Asset Store*[4], mainly furniture, tables, chair, decoration, plants, etc. The resulting office room can be divided into two areas: the first area contains the mentioned furniture without further functionality while the second area contains all the necessary areas to enable Scrum meetings and deals with its artifacts.

---

[3] https://github.com/iwowi-projects/VRACP.
[4] https://assetstore.unity.com/.

Virtual Character. For the visual representation of the users' VIRTUAL CHAR-ACTERS, we decided to integrate seven male and female pre-rigged avatars from *mixamo*[5], an online avatar library, as they were free, human-like, full-body, and came with walking animations. In order to synchronize the physical hardware (HMD and controllers) with their virtual correspondings, we made use of the *XR Interaction Toolkit* provided by Unity, a free package coming with pre-configured, platform-independent game objects to reduce development time. Concerning the interaction with the objects inside the environment, the package's *Ray Interactor* was used which shoots a ray (line) from the user's hand. Whenever the ray reaches a valid target, the user can interact with the object. By this, unnecessary movement inside the room is reduced and the user can more easily interact with UI elements.

For the movement of the user, we added the *Continuous move provider* and *Snap turn provider* to the character. The user uses the left joystick to move and the right one to turn. The Inverse Kinematics aspect of the body was mainly provided by the *Animation Rigging* package and its predefined components, where we only had to map the corresponding objects. For completion, each character has a nickname field above his head to better distinguish the people in the room and also a menu in front of the avatar where the user can make configurations, read a help text or leave the current room. Figure 2 shows one male avatar with a body, nickname, and menu.

Fig. 2. Male user represented through an avatar

Fig. 3. *Backlog Area*

Network Synchronization. We required a system to enable multiplayer browsable rooms, the synchronization of the user's movement, voice chat, and sporadic events. We decided to use Exit Games' *Photon Unity Networking* (PUN)[6], a free software package for creating multiplayer-based games in Unity as it provided all the necessary functionality to fit our needs. In order to implement

---

[5] https://www.mixamo.com/.
[6] https://www.photonengine.com/pun.

these features, according to the official documentation, it was only necessary to place specific predefined objects into the environment or attach them to the players (Fig. 3).

Artifacts. We opted to use three-dimensional interactable objects for representing issues and sprints which are shown in Figs. 4 and 5. We designed the objects from scratch and put a canvas with all the relevant information on it. In order to make them grabbable and synchronized, it was only necessary to attach the required components from the *XR Interaction Toolkit Package* and *PUN2*.

Fig. 4. 3D Issue Card   **Fig. 5.** 3D Sprint Box

Areas. The environment required different areas dedicated to a specific purpose for providing Scrum meetings and managing issues and sprints. These areas were either designed as a scrollable bookshelf with slots for issues/sprints or as a table on which the user can place an issue/sprint. The first design was used for the *Backlog Area, Board Area, Sprint Area* and *Sprint Issues Area*, whereas the second one was required by the *Edit Issue Area, Create Issue Area* and *Create Sprint Area*. Two areas are shown in Figs. 6 and 7.

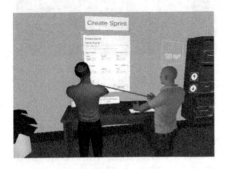

Fig. 6. Collaborative Sprint Creating in *Create Sprint Area*   **Fig. 7.** Collaborative Issue Editing in *Edit Issue Area*

5   Evaluation

This section deals with the evaluation of *VRACP*. First, the method and structure of the evaluation and then its main results are presented.

5.1   Method and Structure

The goal of the evaluation was to give an answer to our research questions **RQ1**, whether VR can provide a solution for the missing social interaction in remote agile software development, and **RQ2**, to what extent the prototype is suitable for daily use. For RQ1, it was necessary to compare a desktop-based remote meeting tool (MS Teams) and a project-management tool (Jira) to our VR-based solution *VRACP*. In order to gain enough qualitative information and feedback, we decided to make a within-subjects comparative user study where a group of 2–4 members executes specific tasks on both platforms. During the execution, we measured the execution time and observed the errors made. Afterward, the participants were handed a questionnaire that encompassed questions concerning presence, social interaction, user satisfaction, comparisons, and also open-ended questions to gain even further feedback (see Fig. 8). Concerning the participant groups, we invited 8 software developer employees from industrial companies and 4 computer science students with a mean age of 34,5 in total. All the participants had much experience with software development and ordinary experience with Scrum and project management. The tasks each group had to execute were designed to encompass all common Scrum meetings/events and actions.

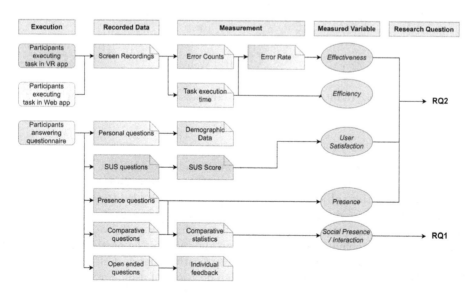

Fig. 8. Overview of the user study's measurements

5.2   Results and Analysis

Efficiency, Effectiveness and User Satisfaction. The efficiency, as the first part of usability, was analyzed by time measures for each group and system. Figure 9 presents the task execution times per platform by the box plots on the left side. In all groups, the task in VR needed longer than in the Web which might have several reasons like familiarity with keyboards and mouse, text input in VR which usually takes longer, or the general prior experience with VR. The effectiveness, as the second part of usability, was measured by errors per minute which is visualized in the middle of Fig. 9. Based on the definitions of [13,15], we regard an error as a missed, undesired, or failed interaction. It can be seen that the errors per minute are higher in the VR app than in the web app which could be again justified by familiarity with the use of mice and keyboards. In order to analyze user satisfaction as a third part of usability, we used the SUS questionnaire [2]. The average SUS score of *VRACP* is 70.4 which is slightly above the average of 68 [1]. From this, and referring to RQ2, we conclude that *VRACP* is already quite usable, however, there are still several aspects that need to be improved.

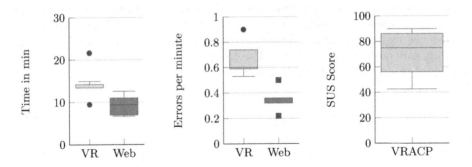

Fig. 9. Base results for efficiency, effectiveness, and user satisfaction

(Spatial) Presence. As virtual environments aim to create a high sense of presence, denoting the user's sense of "being there", we included several questions concerning this subject in our questionnaire. We decided to use the *iGroup Presence Questionnaire* by Schubert et al. [23] as our basis as it is a very well-known and popular questionnaire. From the results in Fig. 10, we can conclude that the feeling of being there was very high and most of the participants stated they were actually acting in a real environment rather than just sitting passively in front of pictures. This confirms our design decisions of using a realistic virtual office with which everyone is familiar.

In the computer-generated world, I had a sense of "being there".

Somehow I felt that the virtual world surrounded me.

I felt like I was just perceiving pictures.

I did not feel present in the virtual space.

I had a sense of acting in the virtual space, rather than operating something from outside.

I felt present in the virtual space.

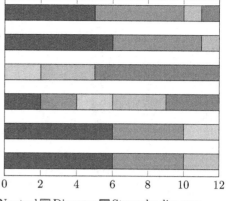

■ Strongly Agree ■ Agree ☐ Neutral ☐ Disagree ■ Strongly disagree

Fig. 10. Results of the Spatial Presence Questionnaire

Social Presence. The questions on social presence were needed to compare the sense of being together between the VR and Web App. We included 7 questions based on Nowak & Biocca's Social Presence questions from [18] and let the participants fill them out for both systems separately. In order to discover statistically significant differences between the two systems, we used the Wilcoxon-Signed-Rank test (WSR test) based on W-values and $\alpha = 0.05$ for ordinal, non-normally distributed data. The results of each question (SP1 to SP7) are visualized by box-plots in Fig. 11, where 1 means "Strongly Disagree/Not likely" and 5 "Strongly Agree/Very likely".

In general, from the results and analysis, it could be concluded that the VR solution often yielded better results, however only two of the 7 values were statistically significant. On the one hand, the users had a much higher feeling of sharing the same room with their partners (SP3) and a much more little feeling of being very far away (SP5). On the other hand, both systems yielded similar results concerning the ability to assess the partner's reactions (SP1), the partner's realness (SP4), and the feeling of being able to get to know somebody through the system (SP7). Next, when comparing the similarity to face-to-face meetings (SP2), VR had a higher median, however, the results were not enough to be significant according to the WSR test. Finally, the Desktop-based system is generally slightly preferred when having to choose a system for persuading others of something (SP6), although there was no significance to make it statistically relevant.

System Preference and Further Comparative Questions. In order to compare the participants' preferences for each (Scrum) meeting and actions, we included four questions regarding editing/creating issues, Sprint Planning, Daily, and Code Review. The results suggest that managing issues and conducting a code review are still much preferred on the Desktop/Web version, whereas Sprint

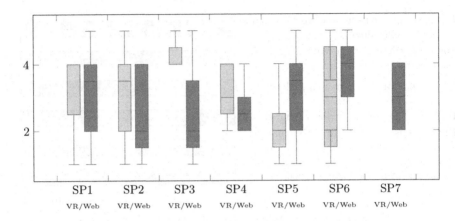

Fig. 11. Results of the Social Presence Questionnaire

Planning and the Daily are quite similarly distributed with no clear tendency. Based on the free-text answers, the main reason for this is the text input which takes more time compared to the keyboard text input on the Web. Although the time difference might decrease the more experience one has in VR, it is necessary to find alternative ways and overcome these hurdles. As 8 of the 12 participants stated that they could imagine using the VR App at least sometimes, we believe that such a VR solution has already much potential in being used more frequently, despite its current limitations.

Individual Feedback. To gain further textual and individual feedback, we included three questions on which aspects must be improved, which features must be added, and which aspects were already well done. The two most named aspects to be improved referred to the text input and movement inside the virtual environment. The participants criticized that text input lasted too long and there was no sign of whether another person was currently writing something in the same field. One possible alternative might be to include speech-to-text functionality. Concerning movement, it was suggested to also provide *teleportation movement*. Referring to the features to be added, participants often suggested improvements for the code review area, including highlighting of code and a laser-pointer functionality to see which part the partner is currently talking about. Finally, 6 of the 12 participants pointed out the visualization of the Scrum components positively, while three found the real-time collaboration features very well implemented. This confirmed our decision of using three-dimensional objects to represent the Scrum artifacts and features in the environment visually.

5.3 Threats to Validity

Although we conducted the user study with developer employees as well as computer science students, we gave the participant groups predefined tasks to do. Further research under "real" conditions would be necessary in the future. Another potential threat might be our decision to use the within-subjects study design which let the participants execute one task on each platform. By this, the provided answers and measured data might be influenced by the order in which the tasks were done on which platform. Although we tried to minimize this potential effect by varying the execution order, it would still be safer to have a between-subject study which we could not do due to the little number of participants.

6 Conclusion and Outlook

In this paper, we investigated the use of VR in the context of agile software development and, in particular, Scrum, which highly values communication and collaboration. However, these central values suffer due to the rise of working distributively and from home. For this problem, we conceptualized and implemented a VR collaboration platform for Scrum meetings, called *Virtual Reality-based Agile Collaboration Platform* (VRACP). We investigated the research questions of whether VR can provide a potential solution for the mentioned social-related problems in the agile context and to what extent the application is suitable for daily use. Therefore, we conducted a user study where participants compared the VR application to usual remote Scrum meetings on the Web/Desktop. The results suggest that such a VR application has high potential. The participants felt significantly more connected and perceived a higher sense of togetherness with their partners. The collaboration was more natural and yielded more fun and motivation, together with a high feeling of being present in the virtual environment. However, there are still aspects that need to be improved, for example, text input, movement, and the avatars. Based on these results, we concluded that VR can provide a solution for social-related problems in agile software development to a certain degree and is already usable for purposes without much interaction with user interfaces but with a higher focus on togetherness, collaboration, and motivation.

Considering possible future work, there is much improvement potential in the virtual character, especially its representation, facial expressions, and interaction possibilities. It would be interesting to see how this would affect the results, especially for social presence. Next, the virtual office might be further extended to a virtual house where each room is dedicated to a specific purpose - one for Scrum meetings, one for pair programming, etc.

References

1. Brooke, J.: SUS: a retrospective. J. Usability Stud. **8**(2), 29–40 (2013)
2. Brooke, J., et al.: SUS-A quick and dirty usability scale. Usability Eval. Ind. **189**(194), 4–7 (1996)
3. Casanueva, J., Blake, E.: Presence and co-presence in collaborative virtual environments (1999)

4. Caserman, P., Göbel, S.: Become a scrum master: immersive virtual reality training to learn scrum framework. In: Ma, M., Fletcher, B., Göbel, S., Baalsrud Hauge, J., Marsh, T. (eds.) JCSG 2020. LNCS, vol. 12434, pp. 34–48. Springer, Cham (2020). https://doi.org/10.1007/978-3-030-61814-8_3
5. Dawood, A.A., Mohammed, H.D., et al.: Scrum development platform, Ph. D. thesis, Sudan University of Science & Technology (2015)
6. De Souza, A.D., Seabra, R.D., Ribeiro, J.M., Rodrigues, L.E.d.S.: SCRUMI: a board serious virtual game for teaching the scrum framework. In: 2017 IEEE/ACM 39th International Conference on Software Engineering Companion (ICSE-C), pp. 319–321. IEEE (2017)
7. Deva, D., Lima, T., Werner, C., Rodrigues, C.: ARPostits: mobile application for agile software engineering using augmented reality. In: FEES 2014, p. 74 (2014)
8. Dominic, J., Tubre, B., Ritter, C., Houser, J., Smith, C., Rodeghero, P.: Remote pair programming in virtual reality. In: 2020 IEEE International Conference on Software Maintenance and Evolution (ICSME), pp. 406–417 (2020)
9. Esbensen, M., Tell, P., Cholewa, J.B., Pedersen, M.K., Bardram, J.: The dBoard: a digital scrum board for distributed software development. In: Proceedings of the 2015 International Conference on Interactive Tabletops & Surfaces, pp. 161–170. ITS 2015, Association for Computing Machinery, New York, NY, USA (2015)
10. Flüter-Hoffmann, Christiane / Stettes, O.: Homeoffice nach fast zwei jahren pandemie (2022)
11. Hensen, B., Klamma, R.: VIAProMa: an agile project management framework for mixed reality. In: De Paolis, L.T., Arpaia, P., Bourdot, P. (eds.) AVR 2021. LNCS, vol. 12980, pp. 254–272. Springer, Cham (2021). https://doi.org/10.1007/978-3-030-87595-4_19
12. Komus, A.e.a.: Status quo (scaled) agile 2020 (2020)
13. Lavery, D., Cockton, G., Atkinson, M.P.: Comparison of evaluation methods using structured usability problem reports. Behav. Inf. Technol. **16**(4–5), 246–266 (1997). https://doi.org/10.1080/014492997119824
14. Lee, W.L.: SCRUM-X: an interactive and experiential learning platform for teaching scrum. In: The 7th International Conference on Education, Training and Informatics (ICETI 2016) (2016)
15. Manakhov, P., Ivanov, V.: Defining usability problems. In: The 2016 CHI Conference Extended Abstracts, pp. 3144–3151 (2016). https://doi.org/10.1145/2851581.2892387
16. Mayor, J., López-Fernández, D.: Scrum VR: virtual reality serious video game to learn scrum. Appl. Sci. **11**, 9015 (2021)
17. Miller, C., Rodeghero, P., Storey, M.A., Ford, D., Zimmermann, T.: "how was your weekend?" software development teams working from home during COVID-19. In: 2021 IEEE/ACM 43rd International Conference on Software Engineering (ICSE) (2021)
18. Nowak, K., Biocca, F.: The effect of the agency and anthropomorphism on users' sense of telepresence, copresence, and social presence in virtual environments. Presence Teleoperators Virtual Environ. **12**, 481–494 (2003)
19. Radhakrishnan, U., Koumaditis, K.: Teaching scrum with a virtual sprint simulation: initial design and considerations. In: 26th ACM Symposium on Virtual Reality Software and Technology. VRST 2020, ACM, New York, NY, USA (2020)
20. Rebbani, Z., Azougagh, D., Bahatti, L., Bouattane, O.: Definitions and applications of augmented/virtual reality: a survey. Int. J. Emerg. Trends Eng. Res. **9**, 279–285 (2021)

21. Reuter, R., et al.: Using augmented reality in software engineering education? first insights to a comparative study of 2D and AR UML modeling. In: Proceedings of the 52nd Hawaii International Conference on System Sciences (2019)
22. Rodriguez, G., Soria, A., Campo, M.: Virtual Scrum: a teaching aid to introduce undergraduate software engineering students to scrum. Comput. Appl. Eng. Educ. **23**(1), 147–156 (2015)
23. Schubert, T., Friedmann, F., Regenbrecht, H.: The experience of presence: factor analytic insights. Presence Teleoperators Virtual Environ. **10**, 266–281 (2001)
24. Slater, M., Usoh, M.: Presence in immersive virtual environments. In: Proceedings of IEEE Virtual Reality Annual International Symposium, pp. 90–96 (1993)
25. Wagner, S., Ruhe, M.: A systematic review of productivity factors in software development. In: Proceedings of the 2nd International Workshop on Software Productivity Analysis and Cost Estimation (SPACE 2008). Technical Report ISCAS-SKLCS-08-08, State Key Laboratory of Computer Science, Institute of Software, Chinese Academy of Sciences (2018)
26. Yilmaz, M.: Virtual reality-based daily scrum meetings. In: Encyclopedia of Computer Graphics and Games, pp. 1–6 (2017)
27. Yoon, B., Kim, H.i., Lee, G.A., Billinghurst, M., Woo, W.: The effect of avatar appearance on social presence in an augmented reality remote collaboration. In: 2019 IEEE Conference on Virtual Reality and 3D User Interfaces (VR), pp. 547–556 (2019)
28. Zhang, Y., Li, Z., Liu, K.: Design and implementation of a scrum project training platform supporting virtual enterprise environment. In: 2020 IEEE 2nd International Conference on Computer Science and Educational Informatization (CSEI), pp. 130–134. IEEE (2020)
29. Zibrek, K., Kokkinara, E., Mcdonnell, R.: The effect of realistic appearance of virtual characters in immersive environments - does the character's personality play a role? IEEE Trans. Visual Comput. Graphics **24**(4), 1681–1690 (2018)

Effects of Ways of Working on Changes to Understanding of Benefits – Comparing Projects and Continuous Product Development

Sinan Sigurd Tanilkan[1,2](✉) 🆔 and Jo Erskine Hannay[1] 🆔

[1] Simula Metropolitan Center for Digital Engineering, Pb. 4 St. Olavs plass, 0130 Oslo, Norway
johannay@simula.no
[2] Norwegian Computing Center, Pb. 114 Blindern, 0314 Oslo, Norway
sinan@nr.no

Abstract. The practices of *benefits management* are designed to help development initiatives to identify and realize the benefits of a system under development. Although several benefits management frameworks and guidelines exist, practitioners experience challenges in applying the practices. In particular, practitioners experience challenges in that their understanding of what benefits the system should enable and how the benefits should be realized, changes during the course of a development effort. Since such benefits understanding is affected by experiences with the system in use, we conducted a survey to investigate if such changed understanding is affected by whether development is organized in *projects* (whose organization terminates after main deployment) or as *continuous product development* (whose organization persists throughout the lifecycle of the system). We find that (1) there is no difference in the occurrence of changes in understanding between the two, but that (2) practitioners in projects think that changed understanding could have been obtained earlier. There is (3) no difference in how one takes advantage of changes in benefits understanding, but (4) practitioners in continuous product development think that the use of changes in benefits understanding is more appropriate than do practitioners in projects. We also look at process models, where we do not find that agile facilitates early changes to understanding. We conclude that continuous product development seems to cater for changed benefits understanding better, but since the way one organizes work will vary depending on a host of factors, specific practices for handling changes to benefits understanding appropriately should be developed that span different ways of organizing work.

Keywords: Software project · Continuous Product Development · Changed Understanding of Benefits

1 Introduction

Foreseeing what the benefits of software investments will be, how large they are, who they will affect and what it takes to realize them, is challenging. Although

R. Kadgien et al. (Eds.): PROFES 2023, LNCS 14483, pp. 20–38, 2024.
https://doi.org/10.1007/978-3-031-49266-2_2

the discipline of benefits management provides sensible management models and guidelines, the benefits of a system under development often turn out to be different than anticipated in several aspects [2,16,27,42]. General approaches to managing uncertainty in software investments range from better planning (which is common for those advocating linear project approaches to software development [31]), to more dynamic approaches that advocate continuous learning and discovery [7], sometimes organized using continuous product development (CPD) [20,35].

In benefits management, which has a special emphasis on organizing to ensure the realization of benefits [22], managing uncertainty regarding benefits is primarily focused on better planning at the project level to ensure that sufficient understanding of the benefits is created prior to project execution. At the portfolio, or program, level, there is explicit mention of handling changes in understanding and discovery, but this is between projects – so during program execution rather than project execution [40]. Thus, approaches to software development that have been found to be advantageous to benefits realization, such as agile [19] and CPD [35], run contrary to the plan-based linear approaches advocated at the project level in benefits management.

With this somewhat incongruous backdrop, we wish to gain deeper insights into how different working approaches impact stakeholders' understanding of benefits and how they utilize this evolving comprehension. Specifically, we conducted a survey to investigate whether practitioners' changing understanding of benefits is affected by organizing work through projects versus CPD, using a linear work model (such as the waterfall model), agile, DevOps, BizDev or program organization.

2   Definitions

In this section, we provide definitions related to benefits and benefits management.

There is no consensus on the term *benefit* in the normative literature on benefits management, but there is a central core that is recurring between authors. Benefit is defined as "... an outcome of change which is perceived as positive by a stakeholder" [5], such as increased sales, improved customer satisfaction, reduced costs etc. While some authors suggests that benefits can be both tangible and intangible [23], others stress that benefits should be measurable [21,29]. If they are not measurable, claims can not be made of their realization [21].

The realization of benefits is termed *benefits realization*, which is the *raison d'être* for *benefits management* – defined as a "... process of organizing and managing such that potential benefits arising from the use of IT are actually realized" [41].

3   Background

The traditional project focus on delivering according to the agreed time, cost and scope, fits nicely with investment decisions, where there is a need for predictability of what will be delivered, at what cost, and when it will be delivered (which often represents the time when returns on investments begin to materialize).

Although focusing on time, cost and scope may provide predictability on the cost-side of investments, successfully delivering on time, cost and scope seems not to correlate with realization of benefits [32]; the latter being the primary reason for making an investment in the first place. A recent study found that although practitioners think that projects should focus on benefit and the ratio of benefit/cost, projects rather resort to time, cost and scope when major project decisions are to be made [34].

To understand better the priorities made when working in projects, Baccarini [4] suggests to consider two components of project success – *project management success* and *product success*. While project management success is concerned with delivering on time, cost and scope, which can be measured at project completion, product success is concerned with the realization of the benefits of a product, which often cannot be measured until later [22]. Projects have been criticized for having too much emphasis on project management success, with too little focus on product success [13].

Continuous product development is an alternative to projects [20]. In CPD, a team (often organized as a small solid line organization) is allocated to work continuously on a product for its entire lifecycle, in contrast to projects which are dismantled when the product is delivered. The team is allowed to isolate attention on the product and is empowered to create solutions that are measured by outcome [7]. Teams prioritize work according to product needs as changes arise. The success of the product and the team is thus the same thing, enabling professionals to limit focus on project management success and increase focus on product success. While projects might seem to provide more predictability by making promises on time, cost and scope, work organized as CPD has been found to outperform projects on benefits realization [35].

While projects and the frameworks for benefits management are phase-based, where the identification of benefits should happen within one phase, an in-depth study revealed that practitioners' understanding of benefits has a tendency to changes at different, often unpredictable, points in time, that do not necessarily coincide with the "right" project phase [33,36]. That study identified the following six types of changes to the understanding of benefits:

A: The identification of new benefits
B: The identification of new user groups
C: New understanding of known user groups
D: Changes in the need for the benefits
E: Changes in the value of the benefits
F: New understanding of what was required in order to realize the benefits

Now, agile is designed to handle change, but despite agile's ripe age and its success in adjusting time, cost and scope according to project learning, the management of benefits has lagged behind for a while [6]. There are methods for estimating and monitoring benefits, using benefit points [18] analogous to story points for cost, and similar methods [25, 26, 30], in agile settings, but organizations struggle to integrate these ideas into daily work. If agile itself is not sufficient for utilizing changes to the understanding of benefits, then maybe the explicit product focus of CPD might help.

A difference between projects and CPD that is especially relevant in the context of changing understanding of benefits, is how static versus dynamic the two ways of organizing are. Although even the most linear project models, such as the waterfall model, acknowledge that there might be a need to go back to a previous phase when new information becomes available [31], retrofitting changes to earlier phases incurs additional costs. CPD, on the other hand, is built on the assumption that there will be changes over the entire lifecycle of a product, which means that one can learn from changes in the understanding of the product's benefits over time, which can then be handled through continuous discovery and delivery [7], thus fitting in changes when and where they should be applied.

Other approaches that are relevant to handle changes in understanding is DevOps and BizDev. Both DevOps and BizDev were created to integrate different organizational units and contribute to communication and collaboration. In DevOps, the development teams and operations teams are integrated into cross-functional teams. [15]. By integrating development teams with operations teams, developers are brought closer to the users, where benefits are consumed. It is reasonable to assume that this move, could help developers with more frequent updates to their benefits understanding. Similarly to how DevOps integrates development teams and operations, BizDev integrates development teams with those making business decisions. It is reasonable to expect that BizDev-practices, such as continuous planning and continuous budgeting [17], will cater for practitioners' changing understanding of benefits.

4   Research Method

4.1   Research Questions

Based on the above deliberations, we pose the following research questions:

RQ1. Are there differences in the occurrence of changed benefits understanding when organizing work in different ways?

RQ2. Do practitioners perceive that changes to the understanding of benefits could have arrived earlier and how is this affected by different ways of working?

RQ3. Are there differences in the use of changed benefits understanding when organizing work in different ways?

RQ4. Are there differences in the appropriateness of the use of changed benefits understanding when organizing work in different ways?

4.2   Survey and Survey Questions

To address the research questions, we conducted a survey with an online questionnaire, in a webinar titled *Digitalization as Continuous Product Development*, in June 2021. In the webinar, IT-professionals shared reflections and insights on ways of organizing work, based on their experiences with digitalization efforts. The survey was conducted before the first presentation.

Table 1 shows the survey questions relevant for the research questions. A complete list of survey questions and responses is available at https://tinyurl.com/pvscpd.

Respondents were asked to base their answers on the latest IT product development effort they had been involved in, where the product (or part of the product) had been taken into use. During the first page of the survey (where demographic information was collected), respondents were asked to report how the product development effort was organized, selecting either project, CPD or other (free text). The questionnaire then proceeded to ask about occurrences of the change types (A–F) in Sect. 3.

Although participants in a webinar on CPD might differ from the population of digitalization-professionals (it is, for example, reasonable to assume that they have more interest in CPD than the population), they can provide valuable insights into the use of CPD.

4.3   Pilot

We conducted two rounds of pilot testing of the survey. First, with research colleagues at Simula Metropolitan Center for Effective Digitalization of the Public Sector (four pilot testers). Second, with professionals from the IT industry (six pilot testers). The pilot testers in the first group were given a link to the survey to go through the survey on their own time, and gave feedback orally or written. The second group of pilot testers tested the survey in an online meeting with the first author. The professionals went trough the survey during the meeting, and raised questions and provided feedback as they came up. Both rounds of pilot testing resulted in changes to the introduction to the survey, and to the wording of the questions and answer alternatives.

4.4   Respondents and Response Rate

A total of 140 people were present at the webinar (excluding the arranging committee and presenters), all of which were invited to participate in the survey. Out of these, $n_{partial} = 112$ people completed parts of the survey, while $n_{complete} = 94$ completed the entire survey.

The organizational size of the work effort, expressed as the maximum number of people (approx.) simultaneously allocated to the development effort, are grouped according to the categories used by [37]: 4% large (> 250 people), 20% medium (50–249 people), 55% small (10–49 people) and 20% micro (<10 people).

Table 1. Survey questions

Question	Answer options
SQ1 *How was this work organized?*	Select one: -Project -CPD -Other, explain: [text field]
SQ2 *Which ways of working/organizing was used?*	Multiple choice: -Linear model (waterfall, V-model, etc.) -Agile -DevOps -BizDev -Organized as program -Other: [text field]
SQ3 For each change type A-F, did you experience this?	Multiple choice: -Yes, during development -Yes, after functionality was taken into use -No, not experienced in this case
SQ4 For each change type A-F, do you believe the new understanding could have come earlier?	Multiple choice: -Yes, if we had done a better analysis -Yes, if we had organized the work differently -Yes, other -No, the new understanding could not have come earlier
SQ5 For each change type A-F, what was the new understanding used for?	Multiple choice: -Used to change the solution -Used to re-prioritize development work -The benefits were realized without needing to change the solution -The insight was used in a different project/work -We chose not to use this insight -Other
SQ6 For each change type A-F, was the new understanding used appropriately	Select one: -Yes -Partially -No -Don't know

Among the $n_{partial}$ respondents, 32% reported on products that were owned by the private sector, while 68% reported on products owned by the public sector. 40.2% reported on work organized using CPD, and 51.8% reported on work organized as projects. 8% reported on work organized as other (mostly some form of combination of project and CPD). The product developer side was

Table 2. Statistical power $(1 - \beta)$ of the tests performed for each RQ (min–max)

	Small effect size	Medium effect size	Large effect size
RQ1	.111–.115	.681–.706	.990–.993
RQ2 & RQ3	.101–.143	.503–.755	.906–.993
RQ4	.077–.100	.348–.591	.794–.972

represented by 49%, the product owner side was represented by 36% and both sides were represented by 15%. The numbers of respondents using the various ways of working appear in the results section. The number of people reporting to use BizDev is only 2, so no analysis is done for BizDev.

4.5   Analysis

For this analysis, we view all variables as categorical. In order to check for association between variables, we use the Chi-Square test for two-way tables [28]. In the Chi-Square test, expected values for each cell are calculated, assuming there is no association between the variables. The actual values are then compared to the expected values. Although early references on the Chi-Square test, such as [10], suggested that 80% of expected values should be five or more for the Chi-Square test to be reliable, more recent guidance suggests that for 2×2 tables (RQ1–RQ3), it is sufficient that all expected values are one or more [8] and for tables larger than 2×2 (4×2 for RQ4), it is sufficient that the average expected value is five or more and that the smallest expected value is one [28]. These conditions are met for most of the tests conducted here. When the conditions are not met, we use the more conservative Fischer-Irwin two-sided test [9] and mark the reported p-value with an asterisk.

We accept a significance level $p \leq \alpha = 0.05$ when testing for associations. We report the omnibus Chi-Square test for the overall association between two categorical variables, and use a two-tailed Independent Samples Z-Test [28] for post-hoc pair-wise tests between categories from each variable. We report post-hoc tests even when the omnibus test is not significant. In this study, we do not rely on rejecting multiple pairwise tests to reject a null hypothesis, and we do not Bonferroni-correct the p-values [1].

We express effect sizes with Cramér's V [24, p. 151], using Cohen's rules of thumb, which for Cramér's V "... varies with the size of the smaller of the table's two dimensions" [11, p. 221]. Here that dimension is two for all tests, hence we use the following rule of thumb: $0.100 - <0.300$ (small), $0.300 - <0.500$ (medium), $0.500 >$ (large).

As the number of survey respondents was determined by the number of seminar participants, there was no point in computing power *a priori* to calculate sample size. Instead, we calculated power *post hoc*, to check the power of the tests we had performed. Power $(1 - \beta)$ – where it is customary to accept $\beta \leq .2$ – is the probability that the sample does exhibit differences that are in fact there in the population [12]. Table 2 presents statistical power of the tests performed for each research question, for small, medium and large effect sizes. Since sample sizes varied for the different tests performed for each research question, Table 2 presents the corresponding minimum and maximum power values. We see that there is an estimated probability of 7.7% to 14.3% of detecting associations with small effect size, 34.8% to 75.5% for medium effect size, and 79.4% to 99.0% for large effect size. Hence, it is likely that our data does not exhibit significant associations of small and medium effect size.

Significance test were computed in IBM SPSS Statistics version 27, statistical power in G*Power version 3.1.9.7, and diagrams were generated in Microsoft Excel 2019.

Note that in SQ2 was a multiple choice question, while SQ1 only allowed to select one choice. In the analysis of responses to SQ1 we make comparisons between the responses (project VS CPD), while for SQ2 (multiple choice) we compare those reporting to use vs not use each way of working.

5   Results

RQ1: Are There Differences in the Occurrence of Changed Benefits Understanding When Organizing Work in Different Ways? To answer this research question, we use responses to SQ1 through SQ3. Figure 1(a) shows a simplified rendering of the relevant 2 × 2 table in terms of a comparison of proportions of those experiencing changes to understanding in, respectively, projects and CPD, for each change type (A–F). Visual inspection reveals that it is slightly more common in our sample that understanding changes for work organized as CPD than for projects, for some of the categories (A–D and F). The p-values show that the differences are not significant. Further, the effect sizes (V) are small. There is very little difference for change regardless of type (All).

Similarly, visual inspection of Fig. 1(b–e), does not reveal any pattern in the change types (A–F) when using, versus not using, different ways of working (linear model, agile, DevOps and program organization). However, in Fig. 1(d), we see that a significantly higher proportion ($p = .022$) of those organizing work using DevOps experience changes to the understanding of what was required in order to realize the benefits (F) compared to those not using DevOps.

In summary, there are no systematic differences in the occurrence of change in understanding of benefits.

RQ2: Do Practitioners Perceive that Changes to Understanding of Benefits Could have Arrived Earlier and How is This Affected by Different Ways of Working? To answer this research question, we use responses to SQ1, SQ2 and SQ4. Visual inspection of Fig. 2(a) indicates that it is more

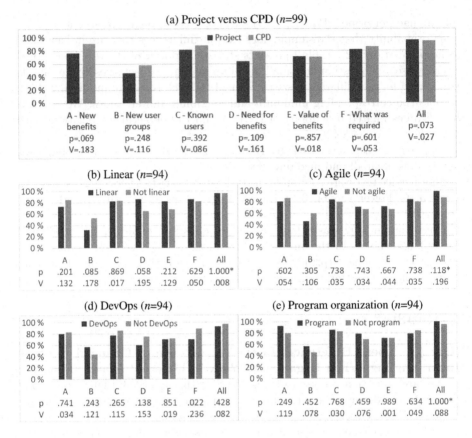

Fig. 1. Percentage of respondents reporting to have experienced the change types (A–F) in their last IT product development.

common among those who organize work using projects to think that new understanding of benefits could have come earlier than do those using CPD. Inspecting the *p*- and *V*-values, this association is significant for change types C–F and when looking at all changes as one (All). The effect size is small (for C, E and All) to medium (for D and F).

Visual inspection of Fig. 2(b–e) indicates that those organizing work using a linear model (such as the waterfall model, v-model or similar) are more likely to experience that the changed understanding for benefits could have come earlier, compared to those not using a linear model (Fig. 2(b)). Inspecting the *p*-values, we see that this association is significant for changes D–F and when looking at all changes as one (All), but the effect sizes (*V*) are small.

Contrary to what might be expected, a higher proportion of those using agile report that changed understanding of benefits could have occurred earlier compared to those not using agile (Fig. 2(c)). This association is not significant for any of the change types, but on the other hand, one would expect agile, with

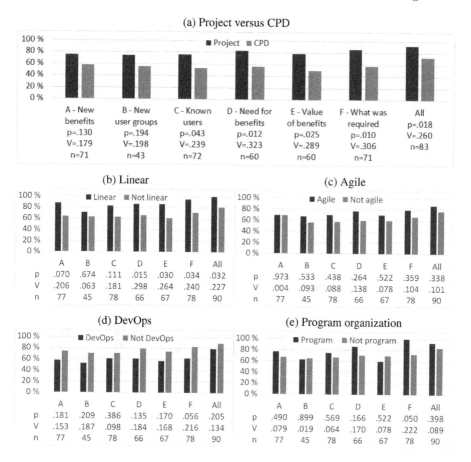

Fig. 2. Percentage of respondents reporting that changed understanding could have come earlier in their last IT product development.

its focus on "embracing change", to perform significantly better at catering for early changes in understanding.

A smaller proportion of those using DevOps report that changed understanding of benefits could have come earlier, compared to those not using DevOps, and this is consistent over all change types (A–F); see Fig. 2(d). Although this difference is not significant, DevOps might be a work practice that consistently outperforms not using the work practice in terms of obtaining early changes to understanding of benefits.

Only for program organization do results alternate between change types (A–F); see Fig. 2(e). All using program organization report that *changed understanding of what was required to realize the benefits* (F) could have come earlier. This is significantly higher than those not using program organization, but the effect is small.

In summary, respondents' perceptions of whether changed understanding of benefits could have come earlier or not, varies with how work is organized for some of the change types. While there is no significant variation in how early (A) *identifying new benefits* and (B) *identifying new user groups* could have happened, the other change types (C–F) vary with some of the ways of organizing and working. Specifically CPD enables earlier change to understanding of (C) *known users*, (D) *the need for the benefits*, (E) *the value of the benefits*, and (F) *what was required in order to realize the benefits*. Also, using a linear model has a negative effect on early changes to D–F.

RQ3: Are There Differences in the Use of Changed Understanding of Benefits When Organizing Work in Different Ways? To answer this research question, we use responses to SQ1, SQ2 and SQ5. Visual inspection of Fig. 3(a) reveals little difference between project and CPD on the use of changed

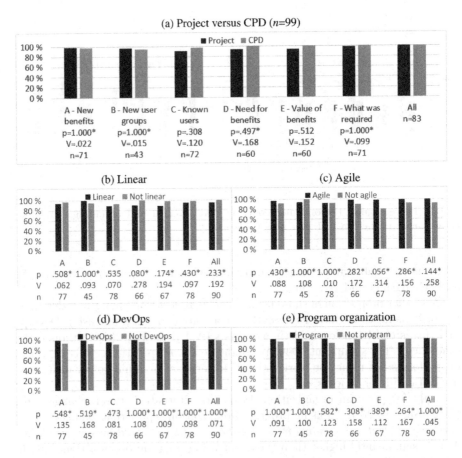

Fig. 3. Percentage of respondents reporting to use changed understanding of benefits in their last IT product development.

understanding. Most of the respondents both in projects and in CPD report that the changed understanding is utilized. All respondents, using either project or CPD, report to have used the changed understanding (Fig. 3(All)).

Figure 3(b–e) reveals no significant associations between ways of working and use of changed benefits understanding. Hence, the overall impression is that practitioners for the most part make use of the changed understanding of benefits, regardless of the type of change or how work is organized.

In summary, we find no difference in how one takes advantage of changes to understanding of benefits.

RQ4: Are There Differences in the Appropriateness of the Use of Changed Understanding of Benefit When Organizing Work in Different Ways? To answer this research question, we use responses to SQ1, SQ2 and SQ6.

Table 3 shows 4×2 tables for the appropriateness of the use of changed understanding against work organization (project/CPD), with response percentages, for each change type (A–F). For change type B, the data exhibits a significant medium-sized association ($p = .048$, $V = .429$) between appropriateness and project/CPD. Post hoc tests show specifically that a significantly larger proportion of those using CPD (50%) report their use of changed understanding as appropriate, than do those who use project organization (17%). This also holds for change type D (33% versus 12%); although the omnibus test is not significant (meaning that the other pairwise differences for D are so weak that they weaken the overall association). Visual inspection supports this trend for the other change types, although the data does not show significant differences. Similarly, a larger proportion of those using project organization in our sample report that their use of changed understanding was not appropriate, compared to those using CPD. Visual inspection of *Don't know* in Table 3 also reveals that those in our sample using CPD have a better understanding of the appropriateness of their use of changed understanding, compared to those using project organization.

Table 4 shows 4×2 tables for the appropriateness of the use of changed understanding against the use of linear model (used/not used), with response percentages, for each change type (A–F). For change type A, the data exhibits

Table 3. The appropriateness of the use of changed understanding of benefits – project versus CPD. Significant results in bold.

| Change type | A | | B | | C | | D | | E | | F | |
Work organization	Project	CPD	Project	CPD	Project	CPD	Project	CPD	Project	CPD	Project	CPD
Appropriate	33%	42%	**17%**	**50%**	29%	47%	**12%**	**33%**	31%	33%	31%	31%
Partially appropriate	48%	52%	44%	40%	36%	37%	55%	48%	42%	50%	48%	52%
Not appropriate	8%	3%	22%	10%	14%	10%	9%	7%	22%	4%	12%	10%
Don't know	13%	3%	17%	0%	21%	7%	24%	11%	22%	4%	10%	7%
n p V	71 .419 .200		43 **.048** .429		72 .227 .246		60 .199 .278		60 .239 .265		71 .972 .058	

a significant medium-sized association ($p = .017$, $V = .364$) between appropriateness and the use of a linear model. Post hoc tests show specifically that those using a linear model report significantly fewer occurrences (6%) of appropriate use of changed understanding than those not using a linear model (41%), and conversely, that those using a linear model report significantly more occurrences (19%) of inappropriate use of changed understanding than those not using a linear model (3%). Visual inspection supports these trends for the other change types as well, although the data does not show this significantly.

Table 4. The appropriateness of the use of changed understanding of benefits – Linear model: used versus not used. Significant results in bold.

Change type	A		B		C		D		E		F	
Linear model	used	!used	used	!used	used	!used	used	!used	used	!used	used	!used
Appropriate	**6%**	**41%**	14%	37%	33%	35%	5%	26%	17%	33%	26%	31%
Partially appropriate	63%	49%	29%	45%	39%	37%	63%	53%	50%	49%	42%	54%
Not appropriate	**19%**	**3%**	29%	13%	17%	12%	16%	4%	17%	6%	21%	9%
Don't know	13%	7%	**29%**	**5%**	11%	17%	16%	17%	17%	12%	11%	7%
n p V	77 **.017** .364		45 .094*, .359		78 .902 .086		66 .142 .287		67 .389 .212		78 .435 .187	

Table 5 reveals no significant association between agile and the appropriateness of use of changed understanding of benefits. However, pairwise tests indicate that for (E) *the value of benefits*, a larger proportion of those not using agile (30%) think that the use of this changed understanding is not appropriate than do those using agile (5%). On the other hand, those using agile seem more uncertain about whether their use of new understanding is appropriate compared to those not using agile, but this association is not found to be significant.For DevOps (Table 6), no significant differences were found.

Table 5. The appropriateness of the use of changed understanding of benefits – Agile: used versus not used. Significant results in bold.

Change type	A		B		C		D		E		F	
Agile	used	!used	used	!used	used	!used	used	!used	used	!used	used	!used
Appropriate	34%	31%	28%	56%	35%	33%	18%	30%	28%	30%	32%	17%
Partially appropriate	53%	46%	42%	44%	36%	42%	55%	60%	51%	40%	50%	58%
Not appropriate	5%	15%	16%	0%	12%	17%	7%	10%	**5%**	**30%**	11%	17%
Don't know	8%	8%	9%	0%	17%	8%	20%	0%	16%	0%	8%	8%
n p V	77 .458* .163		45 .314* .314		78 .872 .095		66 .414* .203		67 .082* .337		78 .657* .127	

Table 6. The appropriateness of the use of changed understanding of benefits – DevOps: used versus not used. Sign. results in bold.

Change type DevOps	A		B		C		D		E		F	
	used	!used	used	!used	used	!used	used	!used	used	!used	used	!used
Appropriate	38%	32%	35%	31%	39%	33%	28%	17%	38%	24%	29%	30%
Partially appropriate	58%	49%	53%	36%	39%	36%	56%	56%	52%	48%	57%	49%
Not appropriate	0%	9%	6%	21%	4%	16%	6%	8%	0%	13%	10%	12%
Don't know	4%	9%	6%	11%	17%	15%	11%	19%	10%	15%	5%	9%
n p V	77 .352 .206		45 .441 .245		78 .544 .166		66 .702 .146		67 .244 .249		78 .891 .089	

For program organization (Table 7), for change type E, the data exhibits a significant medium-sized association ($p = .030^*$, $V = .355$) between the use of program organization and appropriateness. Post hoc tests show specifically that those using program organization report significantly less appropriate use (0%) of changed understanding for change type E, than do those not using program organization (33%), but more occurrences (90%) of partially appropriate use of changed understanding for change type E than do those that do not use program organization (42%). This latter trend is also significant for change types A, B and D, although the omnibus test is not significant for those change types. Perhaps program organization puts practitioners in situations where they must compromise, reducing the most appropriate use of new information and limiting its inappropriate use.

In summary, those organizing work as CPD report that their use of changed understanding of benefits is more appropriate than those organizing work in projects.

Table 7. The appropriateness of the use of changed understanding of benefits – Program organization: used versus not used. Significant results in bold.

Change type Program organization	A		B		C		D		E		F	
	used	!used	used	!used	used	!used	used	!used	used	!used	used	!used
Appropriate	23%	36%	25%	35%	25%	36%	0%	24%	**0%**	**33%**	9%	33%
Partially appropriate	**77%**	**47%**	**75%**	**35%**	58%	33%	**91%**	**49%**	**90%**	**42%**	73%	48%
Not appropriate	0%	8%	0%	19%	17%	12%	0%	9%	0%	11%	18%	10%
Don't know	0%	9%	0%	11%	0%	18%	9%	18%	10%	14%	0%	9%
n p V	77 .292* .246		45 .271* .335		78 .219 .238		66 .094* .324		67 **.030*** .355		78 .195* .238	

6   Discussion

While RQ1 and RQ3 addresses the occurrences of events (changed understanding and actions based on those changes), RQ2 and RQ4 pertains to the quality of those events (could have occurred earlier and appropriateness of actions). One particularly interesting observation emerging from this characterization, is that the occurrence of events does not seem to be affected by how work is organized, but the quality of those events does. The understanding of benefits seems to change, for the most part, regardless of how work is organized, and practitioners tend to utilize that changed understanding regardless of work organization. When looking at whether changes in understanding could have occurred earlier and whether changed understanding was used appropriately, results differ with how work is organized.

These observations are interesting for several reasons. First, since changes to the understanding of benefits happens regardless of how we organize work, but the appropriateness of using that changed understanding varies according to work organization, questions arise as to (A) whether the changed understanding is usable in itself and (B) whether the way of working precludes appropriate use or even initiates inappropriate use, and if so, (C) what it is exactly that precludes appropriate use and forces inappropriate use. Understanding these aspects might be a first steps toward developing methods to utilize changed understanding better in, and across, various ways of working, and thereby updating outdated benefits management models to modern state of practice.

Second, while normative models and (governmental) guidelines for benefits management promote and require a substantial benefits plan in the inception phases – thereby, in effect, directing benefits management toward a linear way of thinking – changes to understanding of benefits seems to happen even when conducting a thorough analysis before project initiation [36]. An interesting question is, therefore, whether committing (too) early, to specifications of benefits based on information that is not yet available, might hinder appropriate use of updated and real information on benefits.

Third, although those investing in IS solutions might appreciate the perceived predictability provided in what amounts to linear models, at least when it comes to managing benefits, organizing to be predictably sub-optimal is not rational. The question then arises as to how one might think of investments in ways that optimizes the benefit/cost ratio, rather than optimizing project management success in terms of time, cost and scope. On that note, agile principles must explicitly be applied to foster learning on benefits and the appropriate use of that learning.

7   Limitations

Our primary concerns related to the validity of this study is statistical conclusion validity, external validity and construct validity [14,39].

7.1   Statistical Conclusion Validity

This study has a relatively low number of respondents ($n_{partial} = 112$ and $n_{complete} = 94$); a problem which is exacerbated when conducting tests on changes to understanding that not all respondents experienced ($n_{smallest} = 43$).

As we see in Table 2, this results in low statistical power – meaning that we have a low probability of detecting associations with small and medium effect size. A study with a larger sample might therefore identify further significant associations.

In SQ2, ways of working/organizing (linear model, agile, DevOps, BizDev and program organization) were given as multiple choice. This is in harmony with reality – that organizations combine multiple ways of working, but for analysis this poses additional threats to validity in our case, since we only made comparisons on those using versus not using each way of working. With a larger sample, combined effects of the ways of working can be examined.

7.2   External Validity

External validity concerns the extent to which the results obtained under this study's setting (including the respondents' respective work context) are valid in other settings. It is likely that people attending a seminar on continuous product development in Norwegian might not be representative of the population of IS development initiatives (they might, for example, be more positively inclined towards CPD). Nevertheless, the results should be transferable to other relevant settings according to the demographic information that was collected.

7.3   Construct Validity

In the context of this survey, construct validity concerns how well defined the concepts are and how well the survey questions reflects the concepts. Testing the constructs was an implicit part of the pilot test for the survey. Still, there are challenges with the precision of the constructs explored here. The word benefit, for example has more than one meanings in English [6]. And even for people who agree on the definition, perceptions about and understanding of the actual benefits tend to differ [3,36]. Although the change types (A–F) seem to be intuitively understood by the pilot study participants, they lack precision in attributes such as size and importance. While one respondent could have experienced identification of a new benefit that was very important, another respondent could have made a similar experience with little importance, but their response in the survey might have been the same. Similarly, how one organization uses a set of work practices is likely to differ from how other organizations use the same work practices [38]. The constructs are therefore not validated formally, but we rely on a degree of common understanding of the concepts and the wording in the questionnaire.

8   Conclusion and Further Research

The present paper provides evidence that changes to understanding of benefits happen regardless of how work is organized, but the timing of those changes seems to be affected by how work is organized. Similarly, practitioners' ability to take action seems (mostly) to happen regardless of how work is organized, but the appropriateness of those actions does seem to be affected by how work is organized.

We suggest that future research should focus on understanding the interplay between the fact that understanding changes, but that it is not straightforward how to use that updated understanding appropriately. As part of this endeavour, one should investigate combinations of process models with work organized as, respectively, projects and continuous product development to uncover patterns and anti-patterns for appropriate use of changed benefits understanding.

Acknowledgments. The authors are grateful to Berit Benjaminsen, Hans Dragnes, Andrea Halvorsen, Adam Lawson, Camilla Brynhildsen, Alexandra Leisse, Magne Jørgensen, Casper Lassenius, Jefferson Seide Mólleri and Leif Knutsen for feedback on the questionnaire. Further, the authors are grateful to the survey respondents.

References

1. Armstrong, R.: When to use the Bonferroni correction. Ophthalmic Physiol. Opt. **34**(5), 502–508 (2014)
2. Ashurst, C., Doherty, N.F., Peppard, J.: Improving the impact of IT development projects: the benefits realization capability model. European J. Inform. Syst. **17**(4), 352–370 (2008)
3. Aubry, M., Boukri, S.E., Sergi, V.: Opening the black box of benefits management in the context of projects. Proj. Manag. J. **52**(5), 434–452 (2021)
4. Baccarini, D.: The logical framework method for defining project success. Proj. Manag. J. **30**(4), 25–32 (1999)
5. Bradley, G.: Benefit Realisation Management: A Practical Guide to Achieving Benefits Through Change. Routledge (2016)
6. Breese, R., Jenner, S., Serra, C.E.M., Thorp, J.: Benefits management: lost or found in translation. Int. J. Project Manage. **33**(7), 1438–1451 (2015)
7. Cagan, M.: Inspired: How to Create Tech Products Customers Love, 2nd edn. Wiley (2017)
8. Campbell, I.: Chi-squared and Fisher-Irwin tests of two-by-two tables with small sample recommendations. Stat. Med. **26**(19), 3661–3675 (2007)
9. Campbell, J.P.: Modeling the performance prediction problem in industrial and organizational psychology. In: Dunnette, M.D., Hough, L.M. (eds.) Handbook of Industrial and Organizational Psychology, vol. 1, pp. 687–732. Consulting Psychologists Press, Inc. (1990)
10. Cochran, W.G.: Some methods for strengthening the common χ^2 tests. Biometrics **10**(4), 417–451 (1954)
11. Cohen, J.: Statistical Power Analysis for the Behavioral Sciences, 2nd edn. Routledge (1988)
12. Cohen, J.: Statistical power analysis. Curr. Dir. Psychol. Sci. **1**(3), 98–101 (1992)
13. Collins, A., Baccarini, D.: Project success - a survey. J. Constr. Res. **5**(2), 211–231 (2004)
14. Cook, T.D., Campbell, D.T.: Quasi-Experimentation. Design & Analysis Issues for Field Settings. Houghton Mifflin (1979)
15. Ebert, C., Gallardo, G., Hernantes, J., Serrano, N.: Devops. IEEE Softw. **33**(3), 94–100 (2016)

16. Farbey, B., Land, F., Targett, D.: The moving staircase - problems of appraisal and evaluation in a turbulent environment. Inform. Technol. People **12**(3), 238–252 (1999)
17. Fitzgerald, B., Stol, K.J.: Continuous software engineering: a roadmap and agenda. J. Syst. Softw. **123**, 176–189 (2017)
18. Hannay, J.E.: Benefit/Cost-Driven Software Development with Benefit Points and Size Points. In: Simula Springer Briefs. Springer, Cham (2021). https://doi.org/10.1007/978-3-030-74218-8
19. Holgeid, K.K., Jørgensen, M.: Benefits management and agile practices in software projects: how perceived benefits are impacted. In: Proceedings of 22nd IEEE Conference Business Informatics (CBI), pp. 48–56 (2020)
20. Huang, W.: The Management of Continuous Product Development: Empirical Research in the Online Game Industry. Springer, Singapore (2022). https://doi.org/10.1007/978-981-19-4679-0
21. Infrastructure and Projects Authority (UK): Guide for effective benefits management in major projects. Guidance to practitioners, Infrastructure and Projects Authority (2017)
22. Jenner, S.: Managing Benefits: Optimizing the Return from Investments. The Stationery Office, 2nd revised edn. (2014)
23. Jenner, S.: Realising benefits from government ICT investment: A fool's errand? Academic Conferences Limited (2009)
24. Kline, R.B.: Beyond Significance Testing: Reforming Data Analysis Methods in Behavioral Research. American Psychological Association (2004)
25. Larman, C., Vodde, B.: Practices for Scaling Lean & Agile Development: Large, Multisite, and Offshore Product Development with Large-Scale Scrum. Addison Wesley (2010)
26. Leffingwell, D.: Agile Software Requirements: Lean Requirements Practices for Teams, Programs and the Enterprise. Addison Wesley (2011)
27. Lin, C., Pervan, G.: The practice of IS/IT benefits management in large Australian organizations. Inform. Manage. **41**(1), 13–24 (2003)
28. Moore, D.S., McCabe, G.P.: Introduction to the Practice of Statistics. W. H. Freeman and Company (2001)
29. Payne, M.: Benefits Management: Releasing Project Value into the Business. Project Manager Today (2007)
30. Reinertsen, D.: Principles of Product Development Flow: Second Generation Lean Product Development. Celeritas Publishing (2009)
31. Royce, W.W.: Managing the development of large software systems: concepts and techniques. In: Proceedings of 9th International Conference Software Engineering (ICSE), pp. 328–338 (1987)
32. Shenhar, A.J., Dvir, D., Levy, O., Maltz, A.C.: Project success: a multidimensional strategic concept. Long Range Plan. **34**(6), 699–725 (2001)
33. Tanilkan, S.S., Hannay, J.E.: Perceived challenges in benefits management–a study of public sector information systems engineering projects. In: Proceedings of 24th IEEE Conference Business Informatics (CBI 2022), pp. 156–165 (2022)
34. Tanilkan, S.S., Hannay, J.E.: Benefit considerations in project decisions. In: Proceedings of International Conference Product-Focused Software Process Improvement (PROFES 2022), pp. 217–234 (2022)
35. Tanilkan, S.S., Hannay, J.E.: Projects vs continuous product development - does it affect benefits realization? In: Proceedings of International Conference Advances and Trends in Software Engineering (SOFTENG), pp. 20–25 (2023)

36. Tanilkan, S.S., Hannay, J.E.: Managing the changing understanding of benefits in software initiatives. J. Syst. Software (accepted)
37. The European Commission: User guide to the SME definition (2020)
38. Thummadi, B.V., Lyytinen, K.: How much method-in-use matters? a case study of agile and waterfall software projects and their design routine variation. J. Assoc. Inform. Syst. **21**(4), 863–900 (2020)
39. Trochim, W.M.K.: The Research Methods Knowledge Base, 2nd edn. Atomic Dog Publishing (2001)
40. Ward, J., Daniel, E.: Benefits Management: How to Increase the Business Value of Your IT Projects, 2nd edn. Wiley (2012)
41. Ward, J., Taylor, P., Bond, P.: Evaluation and realisation of IS/IT benefits: an empirical study of current practice. Eur. J. Inform. Syst. **4**, 214–225 (1996)
42. Williams, T., et al.: A cross-national comparison of public project benefits management practices - the effectiveness of benefits management frameworks in application. Prod. Plan. Control **31**(8), 644–659 (2020)

To Memorize or to Document: A Survey of Developers' Views on Knowledge Availability

Jacob Krüger[1]([✉])[iD] and Regina Hebig[2][iD]

[1] Eindhoven University of Technology, Eindhoven, The Netherlands
j.kruger@tue.nl
[2] University of Rostock, Rostock, Germany
regina.hebig@uni-rostock.de

Abstract. When developing, maintaining, or evolving a system, developers need different types of knowledge (e.g., domain, processes, architecture). They may have memorized (but potentially not documented) the knowledge they perceive important, while they need to recover knowledge that they could not memorize. Previous research has focused on knowledge recovery, but not on what knowledge developers consider important to memorize or document. We address this gap by reporting a survey among 37 participants in which we investigated developers' perspectives on different types of knowledge. Our results indicate that the developers consider certain types of knowledge more important than others, particularly with respect to memorizing them—while all of them should be documented, using specific means. Such insights help researchers and practitioners understand developers' knowledge and documentation needs within processes, thereby guiding practices and new techniques.

Keywords: Human Memory · Forgetting · Knowledge · Documentation

1 Introduction

Developing, maintaining, and evolving a software system requires knowledge regarding various of that system's properties, such as its domain, used technologies, architecture, or development processes [2,9,17]. Consequently, developers need to learn, memorize, and recover knowledge about a system if needed, which often leads to expensive program comprehension [15,20]. To facilitate this cognitively challenging activity, researchers and practitioners are concerned with various related concepts, for instance, onboarding practices [22], providing reliable documentation [1], or reverse engineering information [8].

In this context, a particularly important problem is to understand what knowledge developers need during their tasks and how they obtain it. Previously, we [9] have reviewed 14 studies that elicited hundreds of questions developers ask during their work, spanning different areas like the source code, architecture,

© The Author(s), under exclusive license to Springer Nature Switzerland AG 2024
R. Kadgien et al. (Eds.): PROFES 2023, LNCS 14483, pp. 39–56, 2024.
https://doi.org/10.1007/978-3-031-49266-2_3

testing, collaborators, or processes. Despite some of the studies investigating how important or challenging it is for developers to answer certain questions, these studies are typically concerned with very context-specific questions (e.g., "What are the implications of this change?" [14]). Similarly, research has been conducted on understanding how developers memorize and forget knowledge [7,13,17].

Surprisingly, little research has aimed to connect the two areas, essentially asking: **What knowledge do developers consider important to memorize or document?** Addressing this question promises important insights for research and practice alike. For instance, knowledge developers consider important to remember may be documented well due to its importance, but based on empirical findings [1,9,16] it seems more likely that developers do not document it properly because they are certain to remember it. Since developers forget or may leave a project, such tacit and undocumented knowledge can cause severe problems, and recovering it is expensive. Regarding documentation, developers may trust or mistrust specific types, for example, because it is not maintained properly. So, there is an important link between what knowledge developers aim to memorize, what they document, and how much they trust their memory or the documentation.

In this paper, we shed light into this link by reporting the results of a questionnaire survey with 37 participants. We asked our participants for five types of knowledge whether they consider that knowledge important (to memorize), how it should be documented, and how they recover it. Our results highlight that developers consider various types of knowledge as important for their work. However, they do not think that all of it should be memorized, and value available information sources to recover knowledge very differently. In detail, we contribute:

- We present the results of our survey to describe what knowledge developers consider important and how they recover it from what sources.
- We discuss our results to help practitioners deal with tacit knowledge in their processes and about their systems, thereby sketching directions for research.
- We publish the anonymous responses to our survey in a persistent repository.[1]

Overall, we contribute to a better understanding of developers' knowledge needs, memory, and documentation preferences—helping practitioners and researchers tackle the connected challenges.

2   Related Work and Motivation

For any task (e.g., fixing a bug) they perform on a system, developers require knowledge regarding, for instance, the goal of the task, the source code they need to change, and how their change may impact the remaining system. We [9] have previously collected studies that identified questions that developers may have during their tasks. Some of these and similar works aim to provide supportive

---

[1] https://doi.org/10.5281/zenodo.8391861.

techniques that help developers recover the required knowledge. Particularly, such techniques aim to reverse engineer information directly from a system to provide reliable documentation [1,8]. Other researchers have proposed ways to deal with knowledge-sharing processes, intending to improve the provisioning of information in an organization and decreasing sharing barriers [2].

Still, developers primarily rely on *program comprehension* to recover knowledge they are missing, which is the cognitively challenging activity of understanding what a certain piece of code does and how it relates to the remaining system by reading through the actual code [15,19,20]. Developers focus on the code rather than other documentation, because it is the most reliable piece of information about the system: The code exactly specifies what the system does, while any other documentation may be outdated or wrong [1,5,9,16]. While there are various barriers when it comes to sharing and documenting knowledge, it is widely agreed on that documenting a system beyond its source code is helpful and important. Specifically, reliable documentation can help developers obtain or recover knowledge faster, for instance, when they forgot it [7,10,13,17] or are onboarding [4,6].

While such works are related to and motivate our study, we are focusing on a complementary goal that links these areas: understanding what knowledge developers aim to memorize or document in what forms. As a concrete example, the onboarding of developers must be scoped based on the available documentation. If the developers of a system do not reliably document their system and processes, but trust their knowledge instead, newcomers can only learn from other developers. However, this takes time away from the experts, and thus the additional effort of reliably documenting could have been worth the investment. To research such directions and understand the link between what developers aim to memorize or document, it is first necessary to understand developers' perceptions of these two options. We aim to move into this direction and provide a better understanding of what knowledge developers consider important to memorize or document. So, we complement the related work with novel insights.

3 Design of the Questionnaire

Research Questions. To achieve our goal, we conducted an exploratory survey. Particularly, we designed a questionnaire in which developers rated the importance of different types of knowledge as well as of memorizing or documenting it. Through open questions on how they typically recover each type of knowledge, we aimed to obtain in-depth insights into the connections between knowledge and documentation. To guide our study, we defined four research questions (RQs):

RQ₁ *What knowledge do developers consider important?*
RQ₂ *What knowledge do they consider important to memorize or document?*
RQ₃ *What information sources help recover knowledge?*
RQ₄ *How do developers recover knowledge from the sources?*

Answering these RQs contributes to understanding developers' perceived value of memorizing and documenting knowledge. This, in turn, guides future research and practice in designing new techniques, recommendations, as well as studies for managing knowledge in development processes and on systems.

Questionnaire Design. Using an exploratory questionnaire survey allowed us to combine open-ended with closed questions that we could easily distribute to developers. We started the design by analyzing related [7,17] and our own previous work [9,11–13] on developers' memory and knowledge needs. At first, each author derived types of knowledge they considered most relevant based on the related work. In three sessions (one hour each), we merged these types into a single classification, derived questions we wanted to ask for our RQs, and defined what background information we would need about the participants. Then, we re-iterated twice through the questionnaire ourselves, merging and removing questions or changing the answering options. For instance, we redesigned question $<K>_2$ (cf. Table 1) into its final matrix structure—before this step, each entry was an individual question. At this point, we focused on narrowing down the questionnaire to the key questions and types of knowledge, aiming to limit the time developers would need to answer them. We transferred the questionnaire into the SUNET[2] instance hosted by the University of Gothenburg, and conducted test runs ourselves as well as with colleagues. After fixing a few typos and comprehension problems, we ended up with the questions in Table 1.

As we show in Table 1 ("sections on knowledge"), we ended up with five (merged from nine) types of knowledge. We decided to focus on knowledge about a developer's system rather than its domain or technologies to shed light into software development and maintenance processes. The five final types are:

General Code (GC) Knowledge is concerned with the intentions, rationales, and features of the source code. So, this type of knowledge helps developers understand what the code actually does on an abstract level (i.e., the features implemented) and why it has been implemented. Examples: *What is the purpose of this code? Why was this code implemented this way? Why is this code needed?*

Detailed Code (DC) Knowledge is concerned with the code details, such as variables, methods, and other implementation details. So, this type of knowledge is more detailed than the first one and helps developers understand a specific part of the code. Examples: *Where is this method defined? Is this library code? How overloaded are the parameters to this function?*

Quality and Testing (QT) Knowledge is concerned with bugs and design flaws in the code, as well as the methods how to test, debug, and thus quality assure the code (but not tools). Examples: *Is this tested? Is this entity or feature tested? What are hidden (correlated) code issues that may be affecting quality?*

---

[2] https://www.sunet.se/services/samarbete/enkatverktyg.

Static and Dynamic Structure (SD) Knowledge is concerned with the general structure of a program, for example, in terms of class diagrams or flow charts, relating to its design and dependencies. Examples: *How does this code interact with libraries? How is this functionality organized into layers? What depends on this code or design decision?*

Collaboration (CO) Knowledge is concerned with understanding how the program evolves and by whom. Examples: *When has a file last been changed? Who made a particular change and why? Who is working on similar issues?*

These are the precise definitions we provided in our questionnaire, including the example questions to improve the comprehensibility of each definition.

Questionnaire Structure. We started our questionnaire with a general introduction into our research, the goal of the survey itself, and that it would take approximately 20 min to complete (based on our test runs). Due to missing funding and ethical concerns, we did not use incentives. Instead, we motivated that our survey helps reflect on perceptions and practices, while also guiding research intended to facilitate developers' work. At the end of the welcome page, we informed each participant that their participation is voluntarily and asked for their consent. We noted that they could withdraw at any point, that all responses were anonymous (except what they revealed themselves and B_{12}), and that the data would be used as well as published (in anonymous form) for research.

In the first actual section (IS_i in Table 1), we asked two questions. First (IS_1), we elicited how valuable each participant perceives common information sources, also providing an option to add important ones we did not list ($\mathbf{RQ_3}$). Second (IS_2), we asked how much each developer agrees that it is important to know where to find relevant knowledge ($\mathbf{RQ_2}$, $\mathbf{RQ_4}$). We asked these questions first to avoid biases by participants reflecting on their knowledge and processes in the following sections, aiming to elicit their unbiased opinions first. For both questions, we used Likert scales as an intuitive means to indicate preferences. We allowed participants to select a neutral state in case they do not have a strong opinion about a statement or are not too familiar with the specific topic.

Then, we defined one section for each knowledge type ($<K>_i$ in Table 1), asking the exact same three questions for each. In this paper, we replace $<K>$ in the label of the questions with the abbreviation of the respective type of knowledge (i.e., GC_1 refers to $<K>_1$ for *general code knowledge*). Through the first question ($<K>_1$), we compared the developers' perceptions regarding knowing or documenting knowledge ($\mathbf{RQ_2}$). Then, we asked ($<K>_2$) how the respective knowledge should be available ($\mathbf{RQ_3}$) and ($<K>_3$) how the developer typically recovers their knowledge ($\mathbf{RQ_4}$). We again used Likert scales and single-choice selections to identify participants' preferences in the first two questions. For the last question, we used free text to allow for detailed descriptions of activities.

After a developer iterated through each type of knowledge, we asked (IK_1) them in the last section to rank the types according to importance ($\mathbf{RQ_1}$). We put this question last to allow each participant to understand the different types first and to reflect on how they build on it during their daily work. In this case,

Table 1. Questions and answering options in our questionnaire.

id	questions & answering options
section on information sources (IS)	
IS$_1$	How valuable do you consider the following information sources? Likert scale < ∘ not valuable at all ∘ not valuable ∘ neutral ∘ valuable ∘ very valuable> for each • *own knowledge* • *knowledge of collaborators* • *source code* • *documentation* • *version control system* • *analysis tools (e.g., debuggers)* free text for • *Are we missing any information source you consider valuable or very valuable?*
IS$_2$	How much do you agree with the following statement: *It is important to remember where to search for necessary information.* Likert scale < ∘ strongly disagree ∘ disagree ∘ neutral ∘ agree ∘ strongly agree>
sections on knowledge (<K>), one for each:	
	general code (GC); detailed code (DC); quality and testing (QT); static and dynamic structure (SD); collaboration (CO)
<K>$_1$	How much do you agree with the following statements: single-choice selection < ∘ strongly disagree ∘ disagree ∘ neutral ∘ agree ∘ strongly agree> for each • *It is important to know about <K> knowledge out of memory.* • *It is important to have <K> knowledge available in some other form, e.g. within source code, via supporting tools, or as documentation.*
<K>$_2$	According to your preference, information should be available in the following form: single-choice selection < ∘ yes ∘ no> for each • *source code (e.g. code logic or identifier names)* • *additional information in source code (e.g. comments or annotation)* • *documentation (e.g. manuals or models)* • *version control system (e.g. commit)* free text for • *other*
<K>$_3$	How do you normally familiarize yourself with <K> knowledge regarding one of your programs? free text
section on importance of knowledge	
IK$_1$	How important do you consider the different types of knowledge compared to each other? ranking from < 1st – most important> to < 5th – least important> for • *general code* • *detailed code* • *quality and testing* • *static and dynamic structure* • *collaboration*

we anticipated that this comprehension is needed and that the reflection on the own practices does not induce biases, but rather improves the trust in the rankings.

We asked 13 questions on the participants' background (not in Table 1, but in our repository[1]), building on guidelines for empirical studies [21] and recommendations by our universities for designing inclusive questions. Specifically, we asked for the country participants work in (B$_1$), their programming experiences (B$_{2-4}$), the domains (B$_5$) and example projects (B$_6$) they have worked with, their mostly used programming languages (B$_7$), typical team (B$_8$) and system sizes (B$_9$), as well as gender (B$_{10}$) and age (B$_{11}$). Finally, we asked whether the participants wanted to receive the results of the survey (B$_{12}$) and for additional comments (B$_{13}$).

Data Handling. The survey responses were automatically stored on internal servers of the University of Gothenburg to ensure data security. We used a private repository to share the data between both authors. For our analysis, we used only complete responses and discarded dropouts, meaning that the participants answered each question except for background questions they preferred not to answer. However, there is one exception: One participant answered all questions, but put only a single character for all versions of $<K>_3$. We decided to include this otherwise complete survey.

Inviting Developers. We aimed to target developers focusing on different aspects of software engineering, such as programming, testing, or architecting, and with varying backgrounds. It is challenging to define the size of this target population and design an appropriate sampling, due to missing information. Moreover, it is problematic to contact a larger number of potential candidates without spamming them or causing other ethics concerns [3]. For these reasons, we designed the following strategy to contact potential participants.

First, each author listed (open-source) projects that they knew and perceived as having a strong connection to research (intending to increase the response rate), such as the Linux Kernel, Mozilla, Debian, Apache, Rust, or Eclipse. We merged these lists and investigated each project's websites to identify details on research collaborations or contact information for such inquiries. Then, we drafted individual mails motivating why our research may be interesting for them and asking whether there would be any option to invite developers of the project to our questionnaire. In some cases, we received no response (we sent no follow-up mails) or were informed that this would not be possible. In a few cases, we were informed about alternative means (e.g., blog postings), which we tried but were mostly rejected. Fortunately, several project managers were positive about our survey and sent our invitation to developers or mailing lists they deemed interested. Using this process, we aimed to get responses by experienced developers of established systems, while not spamming uninterested developers.

To expand the pool of candidates, we used two more channels to distribute our survey. First, we posted a short invitation on feasible discussion platforms for software developers, such as DanniWeb and Reddit. Second, we submitted our survey to professional participant recruitment platforms, for instance, SurveyCirlce and clickworker. We identified the respective platforms through an unstructured search. In our questionnaire, we did not ask participants how they got into contact with it, and thus we cannot specify how many participants each channel resulted in. One of our participants commented to have found it on DanniWeb, while the participant recruitment platforms indicated that we received only one response—likely due to its members lacking the required background. So, these two channels did unfortunately not really work out.

Participants. At least 83 individuals started our survey to the point that they agreed to the consent statement. Of these, 37 (44.58 %) provided answers to all questions, and are thus included in our analysis. These 37 participants worked in different countries (B_1), specifically Germany (16), Sweden (4), UK (4), USA (2), Switzerland (2), Poland, Russia, Norway, Austria, Mexico, Turkey, Ireland, Brazil, and The Netherlands. Their programming experiences varied: None of the participants had less than a year of general programming experience (B_2), while eight had 1–5, four 6–10, and 25 more then ten years of experience. Regarding industry (B_3), five participants had less than a year of experience, while 12 of them had 1–5, nine 6–10, and 11 more than 10 years of experience. The industrial experiences spanned various domains (B_5), such as transportation, healthcare, robotics, finance, and telecommunications. Nine participants indicated less than a year of experience with open-source systems (B_4; 1–5: 8; 6–10: 6; >10: 14), for which mostly Debian (13 times), but also Linux Kernel, Eclipse, Mozilla, and Apache projects were mentioned (B_6). Consequently, the participants also worked with various programming languages (B_7), such as C/C++ (20), Python (20), Java (15), JavaScript (11), and many others (e.g., Ruby, Rust, Perl, Bash). Similarly, the sizes of the teams (B_8) they typically worked in (1: 3; 2–4: 13; 5–8: 16; 9–15: 2; >15: 3) and of the systems (B_9) varied (<10,000 LoC: 10; <100,000 LoC: 10; <1,000,000 LoC: 12; >1,000,000 LoC: 5). Regarding their gender (B_{10}), 25 participants indicated to be male, one to be female, and all others preferred not to tell. Finally, (B_{11}) 17 participants were 36–45, four 18–25, three 46–55, and two 66–75 years old (the rest preferred not to tell). Overall, this sample of participants spans a variety of characteristics and backgrounds (except for gender, a typical problem in software engineering), representing different experiences in developing software. So, we argue that our participants are representative of typical software developers.

Data Analysis. We downloaded the data for all 37 responses as a spreadsheet. Using R [18], we derived summarizing statistics and plots (e.g., Fig. 3) for all questions that had fixed answering options (i.e., Likert scales, single-choice selection, ranking) to analyze the distribution of our data. For the free-text answers and "other" options, we used methods for qualitative document analyses. Specifically, we employed open coding to identify important information related to developers' activities, documentation, and knowledge. Then, we employed open-card sorting [23] to derive higher-order themes from our codes. We used the statistics, plots, and insights from the "other" options to answer RQ_1, RQ_2, and RQ_3. By reflecting on the statistics, plots, and free-text analysis, we answered RQ_4.

4 Results and Discussion

Next, we report and discuss the results we obtained for each RQ.

4.1 RQ_1: Important Knowledge

Results. In Fig. 1, we summarize our participants' responses to IK_1, how important they would rank each type of knowledge. As we can see, the ranking of the individual types is rather clear. GC knowledge is perceived as most important with a majority of 24 participants ranking it in first place. The SD knowledge follows in second place with nine participants ranking it first and 16 ranking it second. For DC knowledge, the rankings are tending towards third place (12 responses), and it was ranked almost equally as more (12) and less important (13). QT knowledge was most often put into fourth place (17), and rarely into one of the first two places (5). Finally, the least important is the CO knowledge, with 16 and 11 participants ranking it last and fourth, respectively.

Discussion. From our data, we can derive that our participants perceive more abstract knowledge (GC, SD) about their system as more important. This finding is in line with our other works [9,10], underpinning such findings and also improving our trust in the results of our survey. For researchers as well as practitioners, this implies that techniques and supportive means for documenting, maintaining, and recovering more structural or conceptual knowledge about a system is important to support developers, for instance, during their onboarding in a project.

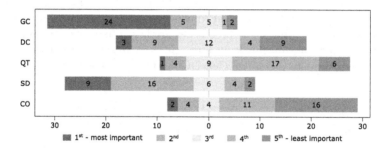

Fig. 1. IK$_1$: Ranking the types of knowledge.

Interestingly, QT and CO knowledge are perceived least important. The former may rank lower because our participants perceive it as the task of others and not themselves, to quote one of them: *"QA's job, not mine."* However, considering that many participants mentioned test cases as artifacts they look into when recovering knowledge (cf. Sect. 4.4), it seems unlikely that this is the primary cause. Similarly, while CO knowledge is ranked last, collaborators and version-control data are regularly mentioned as means for recovering knowledge. So, we consider it more likely for both types of knowledge that they are simply perceived as less important by our participants compared to the other types. This aligns with our results for **RQ$_2$** (cf. Sect. 4.2): On average, all types of knowledge receive strong agreement that respective information should be available, while the more important ones should also be memorized. This also matches with DC knowledge ranking third. It can be recovered during program comprehension and is mostly relevant for a specific task, during which it can be recovered and does not need to be memorized. This implies that, while perceived as less important, supporting developers with relevant information about QT, CO, and DC knowledge can still facilitate their tasks.

RQ$_1$: Important Knowledge

Developers perceive more abstract knowledge (GC, SD) as more important.

4.2 RQ$_2$: Memorizing and Documenting

Results. In Fig. 2, we display the agreement of our participants with question <K>$_1$ regarding to what extent they consider it important to memorize knowledge or to have it available. We can see that a majority perceives it important to have information available across all types of knowledge. This is further underpinned by the answers to IS$_2$, with 20 participants strongly agreeing and 13 agreeing that it is important to remember where to search for information. Only three responses to IS$_2$ are neutral and one disagrees with the statement.

Contrary to the availability, we can see a clear difference in Fig. 2 when considering memory, which aligns to our previous results for **RQ$_1$**: The two more abstract types of GC and SD knowledge are rated more important to memorize. In contrast, the other three types are less often considered important to memorize. More specifically, only four, six, and ten participants consider it somewhat important to memorize CO, DC, and QT knowledge, respectively.

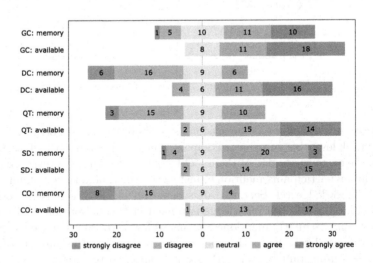

Fig. 2. K>$_1$: How much do you agree that it is important to know <K> out of **memory** and to have <K> **available** in some other form?

Discussion. Developers consider it more important to memorize abstract (GC, SD) knowledge about their system, which helps them obtain an overarching understanding of a system. Based on this knowledge, they would be capable of narrowing down what parts of a system are relevant for a task. In our previous research, we have hypothesized that developers may focus on remembering more abstract knowledge and recover details during program comprehension [9,13]. Our new results provide supportive evidence that this is indeed the case. For researchers, this insight can help design techniques for reverse engineering information and guiding system explorations. A particular challenge for researchers and practitioners is to document tacit knowledge of developers to make it available to others and identify the experts for a specific piece of a system.

It is not surprising that a majority of our participants perceives it important to have information available across all types of knowledge. We argue that this reflects that any type of knowledge can become important for a task or process. For any task in which knowledge may not be available and must be recovered, additional, reliable information about it can facilitate the developers' work. Also, we argue that the responses show that important knowledge developers aim to memorize should still be documented in case it is forgotten, and that detailed knowledge that is not considered important to memorize is more challenging to recover. In either case, having information available is helpful for the developers.

> **RQ$_2$**: Information Sources
>
> Developers' knowledge and source code are perceived as most valuable source, but other sources (e.g., documentation) should not be neglected.

4.3   RQ$_3$: Information Sources

Results. In Fig. 3, we display how valuable our participants consider different information sources. We can see that especially own knowledge, knowledge of collaborators (despite the low ranking of CO knowledge), and source code are perceived as highly valuable, with each receiving 34 valuable or highly valuable scores. Documentation and the version control system are also perceived valuable, but to a slightly lesser extent. Interestingly, 18 of our participants consider analysis tools neutrally, while 19 think these are (very) valuable information sources.

In addition to the information sources we listed, our participants mentioned several others as important. Via our open coding (codes and multiple occurrences in parentheses) and card sorting (bold label), we derived seven categories:

Online resources (discussion forums: 3; Q&A sites: 2; web search: 2; blog posts; video tutorials) have been mentioned repeatedly. Typically, such resources provide examples or discuss concrete problems of a system. This is valuable information, but does only exist for more prominent systems.

Stakeholders (product owner; users) can provide valuable information, particularly on the intended use of a system and its requirements.

Test cases (test case: 2) have been mentioned as a specific piece of source code with particular value. Specifically, test cases (ideally) serve as descriptions of the code's intended use, and provide examples of how to use the code.

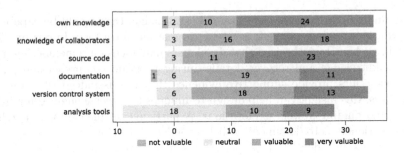

Fig. 3. IS_1: How valuable are these information sources?

Specifications (use case, standard, formal specification) are helpful means to understand what a piece of software has to fulfill.

Packages (dependencies, library authors) are structural elements as well as reusable components within a system. Their dependencies can help understand the structure of a system, while their authors are experts to ask for help.

Issues (tickets, issue histories) provide insights into what requirements a system should fulfill, and their history reveals how this changed over time.

Monitoring data (monitoring data) can provide insights into the actual behavior of the system at runtime.

Note that we consider some of the codes to overlap with the sources we listed. For instance, we would expect specifications to be part of or being referenced in documentation and stakeholders involved in a system to be considered collaborators.

In Table 2, we summarize our participants' opinions on how information for each type of knowledge should be available. We highlight large majorities (i.e., at least 80 % / 30 responses) with green (agreement) and red (disagreement) background. In the last column, we list the additional information sources we derived via our open coding. As we can see, most combinations of type of knowledge and information source are somewhat balanced, with several developers considering it relevant while others do not. In contrast, a majority of our participants agrees that GC and DC knowledge should be documented directly in the source *code*, for instance, following clean-code principles. A majority of our participants does not agree that CO knowledge should be available in the source code or *add*itional code elements (e.g., author tag in comments), but all of them agree that the version-control system (*vcs*) should be used for that. Regarding SD knowledge, particularly *docu*mentation is perceived as a relevant information source whereas the version-control system is not. Note that these ratings align to the results of our open coding for RQ_4 in Sect. 4.4 (cf. Table 3).

Discussion. The differences in how important our participants' perceive a certain information source (Fig. 3) for a type of knowledge (Table 2) is likely caused

Table 2. $<K>_2$: In what form should information be available? We use colors to highlight cases in which at least 80% of the participants agreed (i.e., at least 30).

$<K>$	code		add.		docu.		vcs		others (open coding)
	yes	no	yes	no	yes	no	yes	no	
GC	30 / 7		25 / 12		25 / 12		18 / 19		collaborator, homepage, architecture diagrams, readme, tickets
DC	34 / 3		23 / 14		9 / 28		16 / 21		test cases, coding tools, tickets
QT	21 / 16		15 / 22		19 / 18		11 / 26		test cases, tools, test reports
SD	28 / 9		23 / 14		32 / 5		4 / 33		collaborator, tools
CO	4 / 33		1 / 36		9 / 28		37 / 0		tickets, collaborator, communication, tools

by their individual experiences. Consequently, we expected the outcome that many different sources exist and will be mentioned, and that our abstracted sources will mostly receive mixed ratings. However, the strong tendencies in Table 2 in which at least 80 % of our participants agree, highlight clear preferences.

It is not surprising that developers value their own and collaborators' knowledge as well as source code the most. The former two build the cognitive understanding of the system, while the latter is exactly representing the system's behavior. Similarly, we are not surprised that the developers see value in the version control system, since it documents all changes automatically and provides additional information by collaborators (e.g., commit messages, issues). In contrast, we are surprised by how valuable our participants perceive documentation, since it is often considered unreliable and outdated (cf. Sect. 4.4). Also, the even split between neutral and (very) valuable for analysis tools is interesting, which we take as an indicator that such tools are sparsely used by our participants. Reflecting on the perceived value of information sources, we argue that further research is needed to understand the reliability of developers' knowledge.

Considering Table 2, it is intuitive that our participants agree that particularly GC and DC knowledge should be available directly in the source code. Interestingly, and aligning to our previous discussion, documentation is perceived particularly important to make SD structure knowledge available. Arguably, it is more challenging to recover such structural information from the source code, and documentation can severely reduce the effort. We are a bit surprised that almost all participants agree that neither source code nor code additions (e.g., annotations, comments) should be used to make CO knowledge available, since author and contributor tags are often used in code comments. Finally, the version control system itself is unsurprisingly not considered for making SD knowledge available, but all participants agree that it is the primary source for CO knowledge. Considering the other forms in which knowledge should be made available, these align with our previous categorization, including collaborators, test cases, tools, or tickets. Overall, we can see from these results that our participants seem to perceive different strength and weaknesses regarding individual information sources. For researchers and practitioners, it is important to reflect on these perceptions to design useful techniques and management strategies.

Table 3. Codes we extracted from the responses to <K>$_3$.

code	# occurrences for					
	GC	DC	QT	SD	CO	$\sum$
code	23	27	10	18	—	78
documentation	20	9	5	19	4	57
vcs	4	8	1	1	34	48
colleagues	10	7	2	8	9	36
execution	6	5	4	7	—	22
test cases	1	1	19	1	—	22
tools	—	6	7	7	2	22
comments	9	7	3	2	—	21
test reports	—	—	4	—	—	4
search engine	2	1	—	—	—	3
directory structure	2	—	—	2	—	2
change logs	1	—	—	—	1	2
examples	1	—	—	—	—	1
bug injection	—	—	1	1	—	1
logging messages	—	—	—	1	—	1

RQ$_3$: Recovering Knowledge

While source code represents the ground truth, developers actually perceive many other information sources as valuable for recovering knowledge.

4.4 RQ$_4$: Recovering Knowledge

Results. For <K>$_3$, our participants provided highly varying levels of details. Some explained in great detail the processes of how they recover what type of knowledge. In a few cases, they left individual descriptions empty or listed only a few information sources they typically look at. To answer **RQ$_4$**, we read the descriptions and coded the mentioned information sources, which we summarize in Table 3. We can see how often each (card sorted) source is mentioned for each type of knowledge, and the sum of all mentions in the last column. In the following, we report the participants' descriptions and Table 3 in more detail.

For **GC knowledge**, most of our participants analyze the source code (23) and documentation (20)—with some explicitly mentioning comments in the code (9), too. Interestingly, most participants indicate to actually start with looking for documentation (e.g., on APIs, readme files) and only afterwards they (may) look at the source code. Investigating the source code typically means that the developers move from a higher level (e.g., classes, header files) down to code details if necessary. Specifically, one participant mentions that *"the high level should be explained in the documentation,"* and another one that the documentation should be the right point to start: *"I start with the documentation looking for overall information like architecture, design patterns etc. (which is usually missing, outdated or incorrect)."* Due to documentation being apparently often unreliable, our participants typically move towards analyzing the source code, but also ask colleagues (10) and execute the system (6), for instance, using debuggers. However, while *"code is always more accurate and up to date than docs, [it is] usually harder to get an overview from [it],"* which is why two of our participants consider *"the code [only] if there is nothing else."* There are some other information sources that developers use when recovering GC knowledge, including test cases, online search engines, directory structures, change logs, or examples. Some developers investigate the version control system to understand why and how code evolved, for instance, by reading commit messages.

For **DC knowledge**, it is not surprising that this type is almost exclusively recovered from the source code itself (27). Specifically, aligning to existing research and the responses above, one participant stated that *"the code is the ground truth, everything else is outdated by definition."* Consequently, it is logical that none of the other information sources is considered particularly often when investigating details of the source code. However, we found two interesting strategies for recovering DC knowledge in those. First, one participant stated that pair sessions are helpful, arguably because the two developers involved explain the code to each other to improve their comprehension. Second, another participant mentions to actually execute test cases to see how the source code behaves.

For **QT knowledge**, we can see that the source code receives less attention (10). Instead, our participants explain to focus on reading and running test cases (19) and looking at (historical) test reports (4), which is not surprising. Note that we list test cases despite the overlap with code and execution because these have been explicitly mentioned various times. Some other information sources are used to enrich knowledge recovery, but none sticks out in terms of occurrences—even though some a very interesting. For instance, one participant stated to essentially inject bugs into the system to actually understand the quality of the tests (i.e., mutation testing). Some others mention to investigate particularly tools, scripts, and test cases in continuous integration pipelines, bug trackers, and documented testing instructions. Moreover, one participant highlights that *"[...] testing knowledge often needs a synchronization between developers, testers and the business. This knowledge should be shared somewhere [...]."* We consider this a very important reflection that puts the statement we refer to in Sect. 4.1 into context: Even if it is not the responsibility of the developers, testing and quality assuring is a collaborative effort and to facilitate the tasks of everyone involved, a place to share, manage, and maintain knowledge is essential.

For **SD knowledge**, our participants primarily investigate documentation (19) and match it to the source code (18). This aligns with our previous insights for **RQ$_3$** that documentation is perceived particularly helpful to document a general architecture and overview of the system, for instance, using diagrams. One developers states that *"this is either part of the project documentation and/or usually presented as part of the project onboarding."* Again, some other information sources are used somewhat, such as asking colleagues, executing the system, or analysis tools (especially dependency analyses). Again, one participant each stated to use bug injections and to check logs to understand the program flow.

For **CO knowledge**, our investigation into how our participants' recover it clearly shows that they are investigating almost exclusively the version control system (34). Particularly, one participant described: *"Whenever I'm curious about a certain code change (e.g. it looks wrong), I almost always use git blame to see why a certain line was changed."* In fact, we found that typical version control systems seem to provide all means needed to recover CO knowledge, such as issue trackers and commit logs. Some other information sources, such as asking colleagues (9) or consulting documentation (4) and change logs (1), seem to rather be used to gain a general understanding of collaboration practices: *"[...] Almost all interesting result[s] of such interaction will be recorded in the git repository graph as contributed work and can be easily queried, but hints about non-documented design choices can still sometimes be learned from studying the code review interaction, as well as learning about what the project maintainers' care about in terms of code quality and architecture."* So, while a version control system is the most relevant source, it still seems reasonable to extend it with further documentation.

Discussion. Our participants indicated different processes and preferred information sources for recovering certain types of knowledge. The mapping between source and consequent knowledge is intuitive, but we identified some interesting practices. In fact, we believe that in most cases the full potential for documenting and recovering knowledge is not exploited, yet. Also, how to combine the different information sources to recover a reliable knowledge base remains an open issue. So, our results imply various important research directions to facilitate developers' tasks by providing new techniques—or by improving the adoption of existing ones.

Again, it is clear that source code is the most reliable information source. Still, other sources are used extensively across various (e.g., documentation) or for specific (i.e., test cases) types of knowledge. Seeing how many developers rely on documentation and consider it important (RQ_3), we argue that the problem of outdated documentation may rather be a self-fulfilling prophecy today. So, it is an important challenge to improve the management and maintenance of information sources; and to convince developers to engage with these. Finally, we identified interesting practices for recovering knowledge that are not explored in research (e.g., bug injection) or lack practical value at the moment (e.g., tools).

> **RQ_4: Recovering Knowledge**
> While source code represents the ground truth, developers actually perceive many other information sources as valuable for recovering knowledge.

4.5   Threats to Validity

Our questionnaire design (e.g., wording, length) may have caused misunderstandings, not motivated participation enough, or biased participants. To mitigate such threats, we discussed the order and phrasing of questions; and conducted test runs with colleagues to identify and resolve confusions. Second, our sample of participants may have introduced bias, for instance, because they were more connected to open-source systems or because we did not perform demographic analyses. Still, our participants' backgrounds varied, they have also industrial experiences, and their answers mostly hint in the same directions—which is why we argue that this threat is minimal. Finally, our data analysis (e.g., open coding) may have introduced bias due to our interpretation. This is an inherent threat, but we contribute our data to allow others to replicate and validate our study.[1]

5 Conclusion

In this paper, we reported a questionnaire survey with 37 developers regarding the availability, memorization, and documentation of knowledge. Overall, we learned:

- Developers consider abstract knowledge the most important (Sect. 4.1).
- Developers consider it important to have all types of knowledge available, and aim to memorize abstract knowledge (Sect. 4.2).
- Developers consider their own knowledge and source code as the most important information sources, but other sources are also valuable (Sect. 4.3).
- Developers use various information sources as complements; particularly documentation even though its quality is typically poor (Sect. 4.4).

Our findings link different research areas and provide empirical insights that guide future work, for instance, on recording, maintaining, and sharing knowledge.

References

1. Aghajani, E., et al.: Software documentation: the practitioners' perspective. In: ICSE. ACM (2020)
2. Anquetil, N., de Oliveira, K.M., de Sousa, K.D.: Batista Dias. Software Maintenance Seen as a Knowledge Management Issue. Inf Softw Technol, M.G. (2007)
3. Baltes, S., Diehl, S.: Worse than spam: issues in sampling software developers. In: ESEM. ACM (2016)
4. Dominic, J., Ritter, C., Rodeghero, P.: Onboarding bot for newcomers to software engineering. In: ICSSP. ACM (2020)
5. Fluri, B., Würsch, M., Gall, H.C.: Do code and comments co-evolve? on the relation between source code and comment changes. In: WCRE. IEEE (2007)
6. Ju, A., Sajnani, H., Kelly, S., Herzig, K.: A case study of onboarding in software teams: tasks and strategies. In: ICSE. IEEE (2021)
7. Kang, K., Hahn, J.: Learning and forgetting curves in software development: does type of knowledge matter? In: ICIS. AIS (2009)
8. Koschke, R.: Architecture reconstruction: tutorial on reverse engineering to the architectural level. In: ISSSE. Springer (2009)

9. Krüger, J., Hebig, R.: What developers (care to) recall: an interview survey on smaller systems. In: ICSME. IEEE (2020)
10. Krüger, J., Hebig, R.: What data scientists (care to) recall. In: PROFES. Springer (2023)
11. Krüger, J., Mukelabai, M., Gu, W., Shen, H., Hebig, R., Berger, T.: Where is My Feature and What is it About? A Case Study on Recovering Feature Facets, J Syst Softw (2019)
12. Krüger, J., Nielebock, S., Heumüller, R.: How Can I Contribute? A Qualitative Analysis of Community Websites of 25 Unix-Like Distributions. In: EASE. ACM (2020)
13. Krüger, J., Wiemann, J., Fenske, W., Saake, G., Leich, T.: Do you remember this source code? In: ICSE. ACM (2018)
14. LaToza, T.D., Myers, B.A.: Developers ask reachability questions. In: ICSE. ACM (2010)
15. von Mayrhauser, A., Vans, A.M.: Program comprehension during software maintenance and evolution. Computer **28**, 44–55 (1995)
16. Nielebock, S., Krolikowski, D., Krüger, J., Leich, T., Ortmeier, F.: Commenting source code: is it worth it for small programming tasks? Empir. Softw. Eng. **24**, 1418–1457 (2019)
17. Parnin, C., Rugaber, S.: Programmer information needs after memory failure. In: ICPC. IEEE (2012)
18. R Core Team: R: A language and environment for statistical computing. R Foundation for Statistical Computing (2023). https://www.R-project.org
19. Roehm, T., Tiarks, R., Koschke, R., Maalej, W.: How do professional developers comprehend software? In: ICSE. IEEE (2012)
20. Schröter, I., Krüger, J., Siegmund, J., Leich, T.: Comprehending studies on program comprehension. In: ICPC. IEEE (2017)
21. Siegmund, J., Kästner, C., Liebig, J., Apel, S., Hanenberg, S.: Measuring and modeling programming experience. Empir. Softw. Eng. **19**, 1299–1334 (2014)
22. Steinmacher, I.F., Graciotto Silva, M.A., Gerosa, M.A., Redmiles, D.F.: A systematic literature review on the barriers faced by newcomers to open source software projects. Inf. Softw. Technol. **59**, 67–85 (2015)
23. Zimmermann, T.: Card-sorting: from text to themes. In: Perspectives on Data Science for Software Engineering, pp. 137–141. Elsevier (2016)

Facilitating Security Champions in Software Projects - An Experience Report from Visma

Anh Nguyen-Duc[1,2(✉)], Daniela Soares Cruzes[1], Hege Aalvik[1], and Monica Iovan[3]

[1] Norwegian Univeristy of Science and Technology, Trondheim, Norway
daniela.s.cruzes@ntnu.no, hegeaal@stud.ntnu.no
[2] University of South Eastern Norway, Bø i Telemark, Norway
angu@usn.no
[3] Visma, Timisoara, Romania
monica.iovan@visma.com

Abstract. The role of security practices is increasingly recognized in fast-paced software development paradigms in contributing to overall software security. Security champions have emerged as a promising role in addressing the shortage of explicit security activities within software teams. Despite the growing awareness of general security practices, there remains limited knowledge regarding security champions, including their establishment, effectiveness, challenges, and best practices. This paper aims to bridge this gap by presenting insights from a survey of 73 security champions and 11 interviews conducted within a large Norwegian software house. Through this study, we explore the diverse activities undertaken by security champions, highlighting notable differences in motivations and task descriptions between voluntary and assigned champions. We also reported challenges with onboarding, communication, and training security champions and how they can be better supported in the organization. Our insight can be relevant for similar software houses in establishing, implementing, and improving their strategic security programs.

Keywords: Security Champion · Agile · Experience Report · Security Training

1 Introduction

As software security becomes increasingly important in our modern society, most organizations have their initiatives to ensure the quality of their products and services through the implementation of processes and frameworks. An increasing number of companies are employing the role so-called security champion in their software teams. A security champion is a member of the development team who serves as an advocate for security [23]. The champion is typically a developer

R. Kadgien et al. (Eds.): PROFES 2023, LNCS 14483, pp. 57–72, 2024.
https://doi.org/10.1007/978-3-031-49266-2_4

with security interest who volunteers for the role [22]. Typical tasks can be to show the team how to use cryptography libraries, authentication functions, key management, and most importantly be a source of support for security functionality [16]. Because the security champion is a part of the development team, he/she can serve as an important liaison between the security specialists and the development team [23]. Having a security champion on a development team is proven to be an effective strategy for creating a better security culture within the team, and thus more secure software [14].

In theory, a security champion is considered a boundary-spanner who can work across organizational, cultural and expertise boundaries. As the field and profession of boundary spanning develop, a lack of clarity of who boundary spanners are and what they do can potentially challenge their effectiveness and contribute to ambiguity in their career paths. Previous research in software project management has explored the role of project managers, project owners, business analysts, etc., in spanning through project boundaries. However, it is little known about security champions as boundary spanners, their roles, their contributions, and their best practices [15,16]. This study investigates the role of security champions, especially looking at the practical introduction and operation of security champions. We derive from the objective two main research questions:

- RQ1 - How security champion roles are recruited and established in Visma?
- RQ2 - How does Visma facilitate the effective functions of Security Champions?

The paper's structure is as follows: Sect. 2 presents related research, Sect. 3 outlines the research methodology, Sect. 4 presents the findings of the search, and Sects. 5 and 6 delve into discussions and concluding remarks.

2   Related Work

2.1   The Champion Role and Security Champions

Several definitions of *champions* have been proposed in the literature. Jenssen et al. propose the following definition: "A champion is an individual that is willing to take risks by enthusiastically promoting the development and/or implementation of an innovation inside a corporation through a resource acquisition process without regard to the resources currently controlled" [17]. An *innovation* is defined as "the introduction of new things, ideas, or ways of doing something" [3]. Due to increased turbulence, complexity, and global competition in organization environments, there is a need for innovation to achieve competitiveness, survival, and profitability [19]. The goal of the champion is to draw attention to new ideas, needs, and possibilities and make organization members appreciate them [24]. Therefore the presence of a champion can be essential for successful innovations, and thus company competitiveness [17].

To better understand the security champion's work, typical tasks found in case studies are listed in Table 1.

Table 1. Typical security champion tasks found from literature

Typical security champion tasks	Source
Motivate developers to write safe code and fix the security problems founds	[23]
Contribute to security awareness	[12,13,16]
Help developers follow the security policies given by their company	[13]
Organise security briefings in their teams	[13]
Ensure that security is not a blocker on active development or reviews	[16]
Help integrate security into the software development life cycle	[16]
Show developers how to use security libraries, authentication functions, and key management	[16]
Help team report phishing emails and scam phone calls	[12,13]
Participate in peer reviews	[16,23]
Help with quality assurance and testing	[16]
Assist in making security decisions for their team	[16]
Gather information on upcoming changes or questions to the company's Security Program	[16]
Report back valuable insights to the security team	[12,13]
Engage and introduce non-security people into security	[16]

3 Methodology

A case study is an appropriate methodological choice as we aim to explore the roles and practices of security champions in their organizations. In addition, it is suitable for theory testing and produces data close to people's experiences. Visma was selected as the subject of the case study due to its convenience. However, its organization and engineering process can be found similar to the typical middle to large-size software development houses in Nordic and European countries. The security engineer program in Visma is regarded as a typical security champions program and does not, to the best of our knowledge, contain any extreme cases. Generalizing the data from the case study makes it possible to test the existing theory and make conclusions that apply to all similar situations. Data collection was done via two approaches: a digital survey and semi-structured interviews. The research process can be seen in Fig. 1.

3.1 Data Collection

Before we started collecting data, we got feedback from other researchers on the research plan, which is known to reduce the risk of missing relevant data sources and questions [21]. Both questionnaire and interview were used as a part of the case study (as shown in Fig. 1), which forms a triangulation by creating different angles towards the studied objects and thus a broader picture [21]. Survey data provides an opportunity to obtain standardized data from many people, making a more general view of the practices at the studied generalization. Given that the respondents are a group of tech-savvy, it is reasonable to assume that they will be able to read and understand the questions and possible replies, justifying the questionnaire being self-administered. The survey questionnaire was created according to the guidelines in B. Oates's book [20] and consisted of a set of fixed

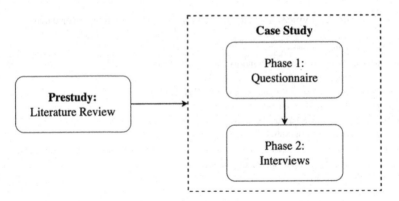

Fig. 1. The case study research process.

questions in a pre-established order with standardized wording. The questions were identified using the results from the literature review [11] and the research questions. The questionnaire was distributed using Google Forms.

The subject group for the questionnaire was anyone with security competence or interest at Visma Global offices, which is ca. 250 people. The questionnaire was first presented at the bi-weekly Security Guild Meeting. After the meeting, the presentation was followed up by posting reminders on the Security Guild Slack Channel (600+ members). We sent four reminders, and the Visma Security Team sent one. In the third reminder, we included some results from the questionnaire, hoping to engage more SE. In addition to this, we contacted the Chief Information Security Officer in the Benelux countries. She agreed to promote the questionnaire in a more intimate meeting with the Benelux area's SE. The questionnaire ended up getting 73 respondents.

To gain more detailed information about the program, we conducted semistructured interviews. The interview guide consisted of six categories containing, in total, 17 questions. Semi-structured interviews were chosen because they allow for improvisation and exploration of the studied objects [21]. We selected people randomly from these two lists and sent them a Slack direct message asking if they would like to participate in an interview. Then we asked a person in the security team if she could suggest some possible candidates. Through this method, we were able to get three more interviews. We also asked the security officers in Finland if they could recommend any potential candidates, which gave us two more interviewees. Lastly, we asked some of the more active members of the Security Engineer Slack channel if they would like to participate. Information about the interviewees is presented in Table 2. We were able to conduct 11 interviews. Each interview lasted from 30 min to one hour.

All the interviews were conducted online using Microsoft Teams because the interviewees were located all over Europe. We saved video recordings and a generated transcription from each interview. Each transcript was then manually checked and cleaned up to ensure correct data. The data was also anonymized.

Table 2. Interviewee's demographic information

Main roles	Software developer (6), full-time SE (3), architect (2)
Prior security competence	None/low (5), medium (4), high (2)
Time in the role	<1 year (3), 1–2 years (2), 3–4 years (4), >4 years (2)
Locations	Finland (4), Sweden (2), Lithuania, Latvia, Netherlands, Norway, Romania
Gender	Female (5), Male (6)

We collected the consent for data processing orally at the beginning of each interview, where we also clarified the purpose of the research and ensured confidentiality and anonymity. After we had checked the transcripts, they were sent back to the participants to enable the correction of the raw data.

3.2   Data Analysis

The quantitative data were analyzed using Microsoft PowerBI. We conducted descriptive and correlation analyses and analyzed the data separately to prevent bias. The results were then presented and discussed with two additional researchers. The respondents were asked to answer several questions using the Likert scale [18]. When analyzing the data, responses were, in some cases, reduced to disagree, neutral, and agree, rather than including all five steps on the scale. Agree included Strongly Agree and Agree, and disagree included Strongly Disagree and Disagree. The neutral results remained the same. This was done to make the graphs more understandable and less overwhelming.

The qualitative data was analyzed using MaxQDA [4]. The data was divided into 11 different codes, with, in total, 45 sub-codes, which also contained sub-sub-codes. The codes were developed to categorize the data to make it possible to answer the research question and thus verify the steps.

3.3   The Case

Visma Group is one of the top five software companies in the EU, providing software and services that help businesses in both the private and public sectors simplify and digitalize their processes [10]. Their customers range from small businesses to large corporations and municipalities and include all sectors from plumbing to banking. The Visma Group consists of more than 200 companies and operates in 20 countries worldwide [10]. In Europe, they specifically operate in the Nordic region, Benelux, and central and Eastern Europe. According to recent numbers, the company has more than 14000 employees, including 6500 developers [10].

In order to provide appropriate security and data protection across their products and services, Visma has created a program called the VASP as a part of their security program [9]. The program aims to improve the security and privacy of services as well as raise the security awareness in the teams. This includes ensuring that the product is managed, developed, and operated in a secure and compliant manner in terms of application security, data protection, and privacy. As a part of this, every team gets a dedicated "Security Engineer", or a Security Champion. A Security Champion receives additional security and data protection training and act as the teams' specialist and primary point of contact on security and data protection issues while maintaining their original role, typically as a Developer or System Architect [9]. There were approximately 250 Security Champion scattered across Visma's over 200 companies at the time of this study. Because the SE are working in different companies, the experience of working as a SE might vary, even though they all officially work within the Visma Group.

As defined by Visma, typical tasks for a Security Champion include improving security, following up on issues found during testing, assessing the priority and severity of security issues, and translating them into team context [9]. Tools and resources available to help the SE at Visma include a Security Awareness Program, Slack channels, a Secure coding training platform, self-studies, Visma internal security event, internal guidelines, security conferences, and Security Engineer Guild meetings [9].

4   Results

We present our findings for RQ1 and RQ2 in Sect. 4.1 and Sect. 4.2 correspondingly.

4.1   RQ1 - How Security Champion Roles are Recruited and Established in Visma?

In Visma, the security champion role is formed in one of two ways: officially assigned or asking for volunteering from development teams. Figure 2 displays the number of appointed security champions compared to the number of volunteered ones in Visma.

When asking for the motivation for doing this role, the result is interestingly different between two groups. Almost 91 percent of those who volunteered state that they are motivated for their role as a SE, compared to 57 percent for appointed ones. All of the security champions who said they volunteered for the position in the interviews indicated they did so because they were interested in security. Security was identified as a trending direction, and people were curious about the field. Trying something new and getting a variation from everyday work tasks was also a motivation: "I felt that having that role and making a difference in security would be cool and not as grinding as just the normal development work." Another interviewee voiced: "I do not have any security-related background, so it was a chance to try something new."

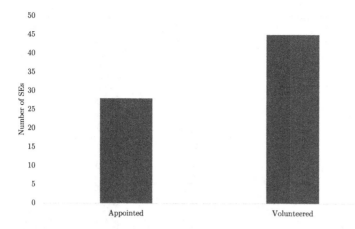

Fig. 2. Number of SEs who were appointed compared to the number of SEs who volunteered.

Overall, we find that security champions in Visma have a relatively clear view of what is expected from them as security champions. Figure 3 shows the number of SEs that think they were given a realistic view of what was expected from them as a SE during recruitment. However, most of the survey participants found that the onboarding process for the role is somewhat unclear.

In official offers, role description is found to be difficult to find and comprehend. One of the interviewees noted that: "When we read it, we did not think it fit us very well because Visma is a large company with many products. So what we did, we just started with the roles that Visma has provided and made our own based on those."

To better understand the role of Security Champions, we collected data about typical tasks and time usage. Typical tasks are presented in Table 3. The responsibilities and tasks that belong to the role also seemed unclear to many: "There are some things that came as a surprise because I did not have a list or anything I could follow." Another SE stated: "I have no deep understanding about what I should do, what are my main tasks?" Several SEs mentioned a list of tasks or responsibilities to improve this issue: "It would be nice to have a formal list of responsibilities that I had to do because sometimes there was something that I thought, 'OK, wait, I have to do this as well? I did not know that'". A common theme among interviewees was a lack of comprehension of the whole picture: "I could have had more like the big picture view." Another interviewee noted: "Also to understand what it is really about. I think that is one of the sections that maybe could be improved."

We also documented a great difference in completion time among these tasks. The average seemed to be one or two days per week, but several Security Champions said that time spent varied from week to week. Some people also found it difficult to declare time dedicated for security tasks because the tasks overlapped with their regular responsibilities. One Security Champion stated: "I feel like it

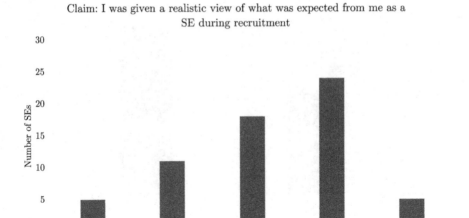

Fig. 3. Number of SEs who say they were given realistic expectations for the role.

is a way of working aligned with the development role." Another said: "I think most things we do are highly related to security."

When asked whether they found it challenging to fit the security tasks into daily tasks, most answered no. A majority of the interviewees highlighted prioritizing urgent security tasks and the need to be flexible about it. Known security issues take precedence over other tasks, and they considered themselves as Security Champion first and developer second. Having an understanding product owner and team leader was also emphasized.

4.2 RQ2 - How Does Visma Facilitate the Effective Functions of Security Champions?

In Visma, the functions of security champions are facilitated in several ways, including (1) self-study, (2) available resources, (3) communication, (4) mentoring, and (5) organized training. We reported the positive sides of these practices, but also the problems reported by interviewees.

Self-study. Many interviewees talk about self-studying as their primary form of training. "I think it was mostly off to ourselves how we wanted to work with the security things." Multiple resources for self-studying were recorded, as presented in Table 4.

Numerous interviewees had used online tools to learn about security and hacking. The tools appeared to be something with which they were very satisfied. Many preferred to learn practically: "In my experience, getting your hands dirty is the best way to learn. So getting an example application and having to try to hack it works best." Self-study is beneficial because it is something you can log

Table 3. Typical SE tasks discovered through interviews.

ID	Task
T1	Filling out security assessments (SSA)
T2	Working with security risks and data protection issues
T3	Using and checking code scanners
T4	Using Coverity [1] (static code analysis tool)
T5	Triage vulnerabilities
T6	Checking new libraries and packages
T7	Testing and finding new vulnerabilities
T8	Keeping track of the security issues in the backlog and making sure they are properly labeled
T9	Making sure there are security-related cases in the Sprint
T10	Ordering tests from the security team
T11	Assisting the rest of the team in security matters
T12	Showing and explaining found vulnerabilities to the team
T13	Delegating security tasks
T14	Developing knowledge, self-learning
T15	Be up to date with security

Table 4. Resources for self-study discovered in the interviews.

Practical learning	
L1	Secure Code Warrior [7]
L2	Pluralsight [6]
L3	TryHackMe [8]
L4	HackTheBox [2]
L5	Cybersecurity course offered by a private company
Theoretical learning	
L6	Different security Slack channels
L7	Googling
L8	Security news
L9	Conferences
L10	Visma Career Website
L11	OWASP [5]
L12	Articles received from the security team

in and do from time to time. Also, you can do things at your own pace and look things up while you are going.

Available Resources. Figure 4 illustrates what resources the se are familiar with. Most interviewees seemed satisfied with the provided support and tools: "I think those [the tools] are great because they help us in the real world. And it's also more documented now how you get onboarded on all of these."

Another interviewee mentioned: "I think we have very good services for testing and surveillance."

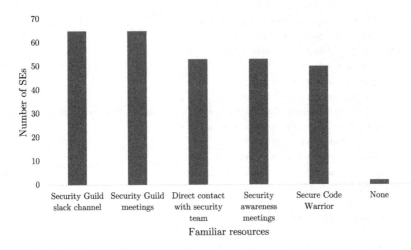

Fig. 4. Number of SEs that are familiar with various coaching and support provided by Visma.

However, one se mentioned that it can be a bit overwhelming with all the tools available: "Basically, there are a lot of tools, but the problem is when there are too many of them, it gets quite tedious to follow every single channel and participate in every meeting." There is also some confusion about what tools are available, what they are used for, and who has access to them: "(...) that is something I do not have access to, and I do not know if I can have access to it [the tool] or not." Another interviewee stated: "I am not aware of all the available tools for us as a team in the company."

Communication. Slack and email are the most used communication tools. When asked if the available support tools and channels are effective for sharing information and raising awareness, more than 74% answered agree or strongly agree. Slack channels have helped the communication between the ses a lot. One interviewee mentioned it as the best thing about the whole se program: "I think the part that might be the best part of the security engineer program is that we have one place in Slack where we can raise questions and get answers to them." The Slack channel is also helpful for learning reasons: "The Slack channel, I personally have not asked any questions, but I read quite a lot of questions. So I think at least a few a day, and when I read the answers, they are very informative and good."

A problem with communication is that it tends to be decreased over time. Many of the people interviewed said they usually do not communicate with other Security Champions. Some of them communicated a bit, but it decreased after the people had been in the role for a while. A reason for the lack of communication is that each team is dealing with different things: "At the moment, I think that each team is mainly concentrated on dealing with their own problems. So, for some time, there is no frequent communication". The ses responsible for projects of different sizes also have different responsibilities. One of the interviewees works in a small team and can focus on making small improvements and details. However, another se in the company has a product with more than 100 people in the development team and is, therefore, more focused on delegating and having control over the project. "For him, he does not have that much time to deal with those small improvements. I would say he is more focused on delegating stuff (...)". In conclusion, they would have little in common to discuss. It is also a problem that the ses in the same company are unaware of each other. When asked if there were many ses in the company, one of the interviewees responded that they did not know.

Mentoring. Almost all of the interviewees mentioned mentoring unsolicited. The interviewees who had a mentor spoke positively about it, while those who did not have it said it was something they were missing: "To have a person delegated for me to ask, like a mentor, that would have been really nice." When asked if there is any tool or document that could have replaced a mentor, the answer was no: "I do not think so, just a dedicated person." A mentor could be helpful because some of the problems the new ses run into are very specific and hard to solve. "You can read all the technical papers you want. But if you have specific questions, it is hard to find the answer in the documentation." Another interviewee remarked: "I would spend much less time and resources if someone could guide me. It would be much more productive."

One interviewee stated that while he did not have a dedicated mentor, he did have certain colleagues to whom he could turn for advice. However, this was not a good solution as he felt he was taking up too much of his colleague's time: "I had someone I could ask, but at some point, I felt like I was taking too much of their time because it was not part of their work responsibilities."

One interviewee also talked about alternatives to individual mentoring. However, they were hostile to having mentored in groups because they were not comfortable asking questions in big groups of unknowns. "I think the security Engineer Guild meetings show that people are not keen on asking questions in big groups. (...) If I do not know anyone in a big group of people, I would not ask questions most of the time."

One of the interviewees talked a bit about who could be a mentor: "It is easier if they are in the same company and I can meet him or her in person. But yeah, in our company, we do not have, at least, I do not know of anyone who could be a mentor. So it could also be not someone who is not on the premises."

Organized Training. Training is the part of the security engineering program where the highest dissatisfaction was recorded. Figure 5 depicts security program activities that our respondents think they need improvement. Besides the onboarding process mentioned above, training is negatively perceived by both appointed and volunteering champions.

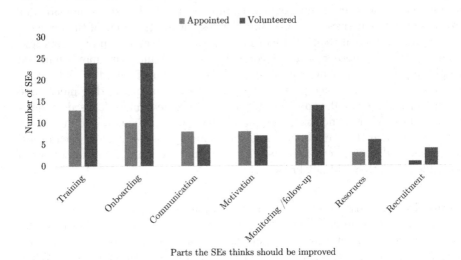

Fig. 5. Perceived improvement area across Visma' security champion program

Most of the security champions did not have a lot of organized security training, which seemed to be the main problem. Some had a previous experience they could consult, but otherwise, not anything specific. One of the interviewees stated: "It would be nice to have some structure to organize some courses to, at least, get some basics." The organized training we recorded is presented in Table 5.

Table 5. Organised training recorded in the interviews.

ID	Training	Relevance to S.C.
Tr1	Application security training organized by Visma as a part of a bigger security event	No
Tr2	Other security engineers held cyber security training within the company	No
Tr3	Small workshop with other SEs	Yes
Tr4	Instant courses on how to detected and hack a server set up for the course	No
Tr5	Theoretical presentation on data protection and information related to that	No
Tr6	Presentation with real examples from the OWASP Top Ten [5]	No
Tr7	Security Conferences	No

The interviewee reported that they need more guidance on how to acquire security knowledge. Even though they have time to do self-studies, they struggle to find information and where to start: "I can imagine that it can be cumbersome for new Security Engineers that get appointed to figure out where to start and

what to focus on." Another statement suggests that the field is too broad and hard to navigate:
"Developing security skills and gaining more knowledge has been a goal for the past two years. (...) it [the field] is so wide, and I am lost. I do not know what to do or where to start. This failure to gain more knowledge in this field is mostly because I do not know where to look or what to do."

Some suggestions for topics the SEs think could be suitable for basic security training were recorded. The suggestions are presented in Table 6.

Table 6. Topics for basic security training mentioned in the interviews.

ID	Topic
Tp1	OWASP cheat sheet series
Tp2	Defensive training
Tp3	Offensive training
Tp4	How to deal with an issue; how to look into it, how to prioritize it
Tp5	Threat modelling
Tp6	Penetration testing
Tp7	How to teach their teams to always think of security
Tp8	How to delegate tasks efficiently

Getting a certification is also mentioned. "(...) it would be nice to get some kind of certification. It would like, feel better."

The interviewees also mention the need of group training: "Two people think differently. So even though you are stuck on this task, the other person might not, which makes you understand a little bit more, and you can move on to the next one instead of being stuck on one task." One Security Champion also mentioned that working in groups is more fun: "(...) It was very fun. And that is also very important for training. If you are having fun, you are learning better. At least that is my experience.". Those who already have some experience with workshops or other group training seemed to be satisfied: "It would be really nice to have those hacking workshops for the developers again. We have a lot of new people who could really benefit from that kind of experience. Just getting a little hands-on experience seeing for themselves that this is how a service gets hacked."

Another thing mentioned is that it is easier to carry out the training when it is scheduled: "I think it should be done in classrooms because if you have a document, you will just do it later." Another interviewee stated: "When you are on a scheduled training, you have the whole day for that, and it is booked in your calendar. You know you will do it; you will not miss it." It was also mentioned that justifying the training to your superior is easier when something is scheduled: "If Visma says, 'On this date, all our security engineers in Oslo need to take this time', then I can go to my manager and say 'OK, this day I need to set aside because I have a course' and that is much easier than to say 'OK, I need to read this 20-page document and I need to take time for it."'

5   Discussion

To answer RQ1, we found that security champions emerge more than officially appointed. While knowledge and experience are commonly insufficient in the beginning, and self-interest and motivation are important factors that impact the effective functions of the security champion role. There is also a mismatch in how security champions' tasks are described for volunteers and assigned ones. To answer RQ2, our case showed that the functions of security champions can be supported at organizational levels. Self-study and utilizing resources can be done at individual levels. However, mentoring and organized training should be aligned with the actual needs of security champions.

Our insights from Visma agree with many practices found in the literature. It is essential to get support from managers and stakeholders to establish a security champions program successfully. This means that it is not only important to increase developers' attention to security issues but also for organizations to develop routines and reward the security work that developers do. The security champion should have clear expectations about what the champion's role involves. Besides, Communication between champions should occur on both formal and informal channels.

Regarding the assigned role of a boundary spanner, our case shows that the volunteered champion is effective due to the clear interest and motivation of the champions to fulfill the role successfully. As seen in the general results, a security champion should be enthusiastic and have a particular security interest. If an employee who does not want to become a security champion is forced to take the role, he or she might show little enthusiasm and hence, somehow reduce the interest of his or her team on security issues.

While our case study offers valuable insights into the specific context and experiences of Visma, we acknowledge that the applicability of our findings to other software development settings may be limited. The unique organizational culture, resources, and security landscape at Visma might not be directly transferable to organizations with different product portfolios, organizational structures, ways of working and security practices. To mitigate this limitation, future research efforts could involve conducting similar studies in a diverse set of software development organizations to facilitate a more comprehensive understanding of the challenges and opportunities associated with fostering Security Champions.

6   Conclusions

A security champion program bridges the gap between security and development teams. Security champions have attracted significant interest from the software industry recently. This work presents the state-of-the-art about security champions in software development projects, including Agile teams. We found that implementing a security champions program requires significant expertise, as well as continuous time, effort, and funding. Despite finding multiple actions for building and maintaining security champions, we can not come up with clear recommendations to practitioners due to the lack of details and relevancy of the reported experience. In future work, one can conduct case studies on the role of security champions and their connections to the team, managers, and other stakeholders in specific types of software projects.

References

1. Coverity scan - static analysis. https://scan.coverity.com
2. Hack the box. https://www.hackthebox.com
3. Innovation. https://www.oxfordlearnersdictionaries.com/definition/american_english/innovation
4. MAXQDA. https://www.maxqda.com
5. OWASP top ten. https://owasp.org/www-project-top-ten/
6. Pluralsight. https://www.pluralsight.com
7. Secure code warrior. https://www.securecodewarrior.com
8. TryHackMe. https://tryhackme.com
9. VASP VCDM. https://www.visma.com/trust-centre/security/vasp-vcdm/
10. Who we are. https://www.visma.com/organisation/
11. Aalvik, H., Nguyen-Duc, A., Cruzes, D.S., Iovan, M.: Establishing a security champion in agile software teams: a systematic literature review. In: Arai, K. (eds.) Advances in Information and Communication. FICC 2023. LNNS, vol. 652. Springer, Cham (2023). https://doi.org/10.1007/978-3-031-28073-3_53
12. Alshaikh, M.: Developing cybersecurity culture to influence employee behavior: a practice perspective. Comput. Secur. **98**, 102003 (2020)
13. Alshaikh, M., Adamson, B.: From awareness to influence: toward a model for improving employees' security behaviour. Pers. Ubiquit. Comput. **25**(5), 829–841 (2021)
14. Gabriel, T., Furnell, S.: Selecting security champions. Comput. Fraud Secur. **2011**(8), 8–12 (2011)
15. Haney, J.M., Lutters, W.G.: The work of cybersecurity advocates. In: Proceedings of the 2017 CHI Conference Extended Abstracts on Human Factors in Computing Systems, pp. 1663–1670 (2017)
16. Jaatun, M.G., Cruzes, D.S.: Care and feeding of your security champion. In: 2021 International Conference on Cyber Situational Awareness, Data Analytics and Assessment (CyberSA), pp. 1–7. IEEE (2021)
17. Jenssen, J.I., Jørgensen, G.: How do corporate champions promote innovations? Int. J. Innov. Manag. **8**(01), 63–86 (2004)
18. Likert, R.: A technique for the measurement of attitudes. Arch. Psychol. **22**(140), 55 (1932)
19. Morgan, G.: Riding the waves of change. Imaginization Inc. (2013)
20. Oates, B.J., Griffiths, M., McLean, R.: Researching information systems and computing. Sage (2022)
21. Runeson, P., Höst, M.: Guidelines for conducting and reporting case study research in software engineering. Empir. Softw. Eng. **14**(2), 131–164 (2009)

22. Ryan, I., Roedig, U., Stol, K.J.: Understanding developer security archetypes. In: 2021 IEEE/ACM 2nd International Workshop on Engineering and Cybersecurity of Critical Systems (EnCyCriS), pp. 37–40. IEEE (2021)

23. Thomas, T.W., Tabassum, M., Chu, B., Lipford, H.: Security during application development: an application security expert perspective. In: Proceedings of the 2018 CHI Conference on Human Factors in Computing Systems, pp. 1–12 (2018)

24. Van de Ven, A.H.: Central problems in the management of innovation. Manage. Sci. **32**(5), 590–607 (1986)

Benefits and Challenges of an Internal Corporate Accelerator in a Software Company: An Action-Research Study

Vanessa Lopes Abreu, Anderson Jorge Serra Costa, André Coelho Pinheiro, and Cleidson R. B. de Souza[✉]

Faculdade de Computação, Universidade Federal do Pará, Belém, Pará, Brazil
andersonjsc@uepa.br, andre.pinheiro@icen.ufpa.br, cleidson.desouza@acm.org

Abstract. To maintain a competitive advantage and adapt to the rapid changes in both the market and technology, organizations need to continuously innovate. As a result, internal corporate accelerators have been implemented as a means to internalize external innovation and promote corporate innovation. However, research on internal corporate accelerators is still limited, and there is a need for a more detailed analysis of both the positive and negative consequences of their implementation. In this paper, we employ the action research methodology to define and implement an internal corporate accelerator within a Brazilian software development company. We describe the accelerator phases, selection criteria, and provided services. We also present the advantages and challenges of implementing this accelerator. The benefits encompass the stimulation of creativity and the evolution of knowledge, while the challenges are tied to participants' time constraints and the limitation of virtual communication.

Keywords: corporate accelerator · internal startup · innovation · technology · software company

1 Introduction

Startups are commonly perceived as drivers of innovation, offering new products and business models with agility and cutting-edge technology [10]. However, they often face challenges such as limited resources and a lack of expertise at scale. Thus, in an increasingly competitive and globalized business landscape, the synergy between the agile innovation of startups and the infrastructure and resources of established organizations has been sought after to create an environment conducive to value creation and technological advancement [20]. In this context, corporate accelerators act as a bridge between established companies and startups [18]. Their primary objective is to internalize *external* innovation and promote corporate innovation through partnerships with entrepreneurial startups [10]. Another approach used by established organizations involves the implementation of *internal* corporate accelerators so that it is possible to

R. Kadgien et al. (Eds.): PROFES 2023, LNCS 14483, pp. 73–88, 2024.
https://doi.org/10.1007/978-3-031-49266-2_5

invest in their own employees as a means to stimulate innovation through intrapreneurship, enabling the collaborative development of new ventures between the company and internal startups, resulting in mutual advantages [20].

Despite the existence of many studies related to corporate accelerators, these studies are more focused on accelerators targeting external audiences and are generally applied in a broader context. Regarding internal corporate accelerators applied in specific contexts, such as software development, this approach is only beginning to emerge [9, 24]. Additionally, most studies on this topic focus on developed countries, leaving a gap in developing or low-income countries [3]. Another existing gap is the lack of in-depth analyses of outcomes and their consequences, considering both the benefits and challenges of internal accelerator implementation [3]. In this context, understanding these impacts is crucial to guide corporate practices and direct future projects.

This research aims to address the limitations of previous studies by presenting (1) a proposal for an internal corporate accelerator defining its stages, selection criteria, and offered services, and (2) the outcomes of implementing this accelerator in a software company, highlighting both the benefits and challenges of this implementation. This was achieved through action research [23] conducted with a mid-sized Brazilian software company. Specifically, we answer the following research questions:

- RQ1: How to implement an internal corporate accelerator in an established technology-focused organization?
- RQ2: What are the main benefits arising from the implementation of an internal corporate accelerator?
- RQ3: What are the primary challenges encountered during the implementation of an internal corporate accelerator?

The findings of this study indicate that the implementation of the internal corporate accelerator resulted in benefits such as fostering creativity, facilitating knowledge creation and evolution, and nurturing the development of ideas proposed by intrapreneurs. However, challenges related to exclusively virtual communication and time constraints were identified, leading intrapreneurs to report a sense of overload.

2 Background

We conducted a literature search using the snowballing technique [19] to identify studies addressing the development and implementation of internal corporate accelerators. The results indicate that there are several different approaches to promoting innovation within organizations. One of these approaches is through corporate accelerators [10, 20]. These accelerators are time-limited programs supported by private companies that help a group of startups during the process of creating a new business, offering mentorship, education, and specific resources from the parent company [10]. Some characteristics of these corporate acceleration programs include an open and selective application process; limited-duration support; mentorship; and ultimately, investment offerings, sometimes in exchange for equity [10]. Corporate accelerators can either focus on external audiences, in which case companies seek innovations from external sources, or they can target internal audiences. In the latter case, an employee or a group of employees are tasked with developing innovations [10].

Internal corporate accelerators are being adopted more frequently [10, 24]. They typically emerge within established companies due to the need to enter new markets or create new products and services. The creation and acceleration of new businesses within established organizations enable better utilization of opportunities, increased profitability, knowledge production, competitive advantage, support for organizational transformation, and the generation of new skills, knowledge, or businesses [21].

A study conducted by Edison [5] within a major European software company introduced Lean-ICV, a 3-stage conceptual framework combining internal corporate venturing and lean startup [14]. The results revealed two main challenges: the lack of training and management strategies for the new ventures, and the absence of an organizational champion, i.e., an employee dedicated to improving a specific area within the company. Meanwhile, Selig et al. [20] conducted a study by interviewing internal accelerator teams in two German high-tech companies. Their results indicate that certain aspects such as limited time for intrapreneurial projects, lack of adequate monitoring structures, and conflicting objectives pose obstructive potential. On the other hand, mentorship, full project dedication, and access to shared services are supportive resources for intrapreneurial teams in the accelerator. In contrast to our study, Selig et al.'s [20] study did not describe the phases of the accelerator.

While these studies provide a framework for internal corporate accelerators, it is noteworthy that they focused on *developed* countries. This reinforces Crisan's et al. [3] observation highlighting the scarcity of research in *developing* countries.

Another initiative adopted by organizations to stimulate innovation is running corporate hackathons [10]. These events bring together different participants into small teams, to collaboratively create innovative solutions and develop specific skills [16]. They share some characteristics with internal corporate accelerators, such as a focus on external or internal (employees) audiences; and they both involve a selection process, stages for idea development, and culminate in a demonstration event [25]. However, there are fundamental differences between these approaches. Internal corporate accelerators are structured and ongoing programs [10]. Their main objective is to create an environment conducive for employees to develop innovative ideas and projects that can add value to the organization [25]. Meanwhile, corporate hackathons are intensive short-duration events designed to address specific problems faced by the company [10, 25]. They are designed to quickly generate solutions and promote collaboration within a very limited timeframe. Thus, while internal corporate accelerators seek to create a long-term innovation environment, corporate hackathons are more agile and focused on immediate solutions.

3 Methodology

3.1 Action Research

To address the proposed research questions, the action research methodology was adopted. Action research aims to clarify and solve problems in the observed reality, involving the active participation of all participants and a close monitoring of their decisions and actions [22]. It is conducted within a specific context.

The choice of action research as a method to implement an internal corporate accelerator in a software company aims for a participatory and practical approach, allowing direct intervention and concrete results. This approach enables the combination of theory and practice, introducing changes in the context while also contributing to the development of theories [22]. The objective was to plan and execute an acceleration cycle to assess its benefits and challenges, involving active participation from employees and adaptation of existing organizational practices.

Action research typically involves cycles with well-defined phases that relate continuously [22]. In this study, four stages of action research were used, and each cycle consists of the following steps: (1) *diagnosis*, aimed at exploring and identifying problems and characteristics of the situation, (2) *planning* to define the activities necessary for the execution of the research, (3) *execution*, with the goal of carrying out the activities defined in the previous stage, and finally, (4) *evaluation*, which aims to identify the results of actions in the organizational context of the research.

3.2 The Company Under Study

The studied company is a private software company headquartered in Belém, Pará, Brazil. It currently operates two branches, one in São Paulo and one in Florianópolis. With over 10 years of existence, this company has delivered more than 600 software projects. Presently, it boasts a workforce of over 150 employees in Brazil.

Upon founding its branch in Florianópolis, the company encountered challenges in establishing itself within the local highly innovative ecosystem. Consequently, the company sought to develop new initiatives to foster innovation. In this context, the authors collaborated with the company to define the structure of the accelerator and execute one acceleration cycle. Although the initial plan was to carry out two acceleration cycles, feasibility issues arose due to ongoing internal projects within the company, and only one cycle was conducted.

3.3 Data Collection and Analysis

As the action research methodology was adopted, this research employed a qualitative approach seeking to understand the perspectives of participants within the investigated context. Qualitative approaches are particularly suitable for data derived from interviews, observations, and documents [7]. Indeed, data collection was carried out through meetings and semi-structured interviews [4] conducted during the construction and execution of the acceleration program.

Regarding the data analysis, the following techniques from grounded theory [4] were used: (i) initial coding; (ii) axial coding; and finally, (iii) selective coding. During the selective coding stage, themes indicating the benefits and challenges of implementing the corporate accelerator emerged.

4 The Action Research Process

This section describes the results of each of the stages of the action research applied within the studied software development company.

4.1 The Diagnosis Stage

In the diagnosis stage, a semi-structured interview was conducted by the action team with the Director of New Businesses to identify the problems and characteristics of the company. The interview lasted 50 min and was conducted online. During the interview, this director mentioned the challenges faced by the company in creating innovative new businesses, as quoted below: *"We identified that we needed to seek knowledge in the product development area... we made several attempts to create products, and I can say that they failed in a certain way."* To address this issue, the company initially sought to implement a process of selecting technology startups in the validation or early operational stage. The goal was to identify promising startups for a partnership, where the company could invest technical resources in the development of software products. However, the company encountered challenges in finding startups that aligned with the organization's strategic objectives: *"We saw that it was very complicated to identify profiles outside the company that had a fit with what we were looking for."* Faced with these difficulties, the company redirected its focus to its internal context, meaning that its own employees could present business idea proposals. This work was conducted in this context.

In addition to the initial interview, five other meetings were held between the research team and the Director of New Businesses, and one meeting was conducted with a founder of the studied company. These meetings provided more details about the initiative previously adopted by the company. Furthermore, the project focus was defined, as well as the team responsible for executing the action research.

The defined acceleration process primarily focuses on the development of innovative ideas with the potential to generate new products. The team responsible for executing the action research cycle was defined following the example proposed by Staron [22]: (i) *the action team,* which consists of two external researchers not affiliated with the company who are responsible for planning and executing the research project, and (ii) *the reference group,* which is composed of an external researcher not affiliated with the company. The role of the reference group is to provide feedback to the action team to mitigate potential biases and identify situations where bias could negatively impact the study's results. Finally, (iii) *the company management* is represented by the Director of New Businesses overseeing and guiding the project within the organization. This structure ensures a well-rounded and unbiased approach to the research and acceleration process, involving both internal and external perspectives to achieve meaningful results.

4.2 The Planning Phase

This phase took place between January and May 2022 and encompassed the planning of activities, teams, and schedules necessary for the execution of the action research. During this phase, five planning meetings were conducted, involving the action team, the reference group, and the company management, including one of the company's founders. Additionally, a meeting was held with the company's marketing team to plan the launch of the corporate accelerator. The established timeline encompassed the following activities: (1) defining the accelerator stages, (2) setting the selection criteria, (3) defining the offered services, (4) determining the communication strategy, (5) conducting the acceleration cycle, and (6) evaluating the accelerator.

Due to the COVID-19 pandemic, the acceleration program was structured to be executed entirely remotely, with all communication taking place through various online tools including Microsoft Teams for video calls, Google Drive for storing and distributing supporting materials, Slack platform for communication with participants, among others.

4.3 The Execution Stage

During this phase the research was carried out in accordance with the schedule established in the previous phase. To accomplish this, twenty-two meetings involving the action team, the reference group, and the company management were conducted.

Table 1 outlines the stages of the corporate acceleration program, which were established based on the literature and aligned with the company's needs. The defined stages are as follows: planning, promotion, submission, acceleration, and post-acceleration. In addition to the stages of the internal corporate accelerator, the selection criteria, tools, and services to be provided were also defined in this stage.

Table 1. Stages of the Accelerator

Stages	Authors who influenced the definition of the stages
Planning	Mohammadi. and Sakhteh [13]; Ghorashi. and Asghari [8]
Promotion	Mohammadi. and Sakhteh [13]; Ghorashi. and Asghari [8]; Barrehag et al. [2]
Submission	Mohammadi. and Sakhteh [13]; Prexl et al. [17]
Acceleration	Mohammadi. and Sakhteh [13]; Ghorashi. and Asghari [8]; Prexl et al. [17]; Barrehag et al. [2]
Post-acceleration	Mohammadi. and Sakhteh [13]; Ghorashi. and Asghari [8]; Barrehag et al. [2]

Selection Criteria

Based on the literature [26, 27] and the organizational structure of the parent company, twenty-four criteria were defined to construct a selection model for the acceleration program. The criteria were divided into two categories: those assessed by the intrapreneurial teams and those assessed by the evaluators (action team). The criteria assessed by the intrapreneurial teams served as a self-assessment to align the team's understanding with their reality. The criteria assessed by the evaluators are those analyzed by the research team; in other words, the intrapreneurial team informs their level of knowledge on a specific item, and the research team evaluators analyze the quality of the reported response. Each criterion was assessed on a scale from one to five, where one indicated low idea maturity in that criterion and five indicated the highest maturity. Some of the defined criteria included: level of problem knowledge, knowledge of competitors, and experience level in the business idea's market.

Services Offered

To be attractive, an accelerator should offer services its target audience [12]. In our study, in partnership with the parent company, the following services were defined:

- **Mentorship:** The mentorship sessions were conducted with the aim of guiding and answering questions related to the tasks carried out by the intrapreneurial teams. Mentorship meetings took place remotely in two formats: (i) group mentorships, which included all participating intrapreneurs, and (ii) individual mentorships, which could be requested by each team individually.
- **Learning Environment:** The learning environment aims to serve as support for intrapreneurial teams, providing a knowledge base for them to access the concepts used during the acceleration process. This environment consists of an online repository on Google Drive, containing videos, articles, and blog posts from trustworthy sources.
- **Reward System:** During the acceleration process, a scoring scheme and ranking system were used. Points were allocated based on the following criteria: participation in meetings, task execution, punctuality in delivery, and presentation of results. As a reward system, the company used an exclusive internal currency, which employees could accumulate and later exchange for items provided by the company.

Promotion Phase

During this stage, which took place in June 2022 and lasted for fifteen days, the entire marketing strategy for the promotion of the acceleration program was executed. Within this period, the first announcement was released, and the official notice for the launch of the acceleration program occurred at an event attended by most employees. That same month, two remote entrepreneurship events were organized to encourage employee participation in the acceleration program. These events featured external entrepreneurs from the local innovation ecosystem.

Submission Phase

During the idea submission phase, candidates for the acceleration program completed their registration and each proposal was subsequently evaluated. The registration form contained both objective and descriptive questions that covered contact information, the number of team members, details about the proposed business idea and the problem it aimed to solve, issues related to the market the idea was set in, as well as aspects about the team profile, such as skills and experience.

For a fifteen-day period, the registration form was available only to employees of the parent company. Five intrapreneurial teams submitted their ideas, and after evaluation, were invited to the selection interviews, which lasted an average of forty minutes. All registered teams were selected for the acceleration stage since the proposed ideas met the defined selection criteria. Another factor influencing the number of selected teams was the capacity that the program's organization had based on the available resources, that is, there were sufficient resources to accelerate all five proposals. Subsequently, participants from two teams were assigned to strategic internal company tasks and therefore could no longer participate in the corporate accelerator. Thus, the acceleration process took place with three teams. For confidentiality reasons, we can not provide more information about the business ideas. As for the roles of the participants, three participants were project managers and one was a junior software developer.

Acceleration Phase

In the context of the parent company, the acceleration cycle lasted 13 weeks, beginning in August 2022 and concluding in November 2022. Each week introduced different topics appropriate to the acceleration phase. The acceleration stage was based on lean, agile principles and customer development [18]. The executed acceleration activities were divided into three categories: (i) problem immersion, where activities were conducted to help the team identify and validate the defined problem, (ii) solution immersion, where based on the identified problem, the team performed activities to help pinpoint the product's objective and determine if it genuinely addressed the issue set in the previous phase, and, finally, (iii) business immersion, where the team developed and validated its business model and, in the end, constructed the *pitch*. The pitch presentation was carried out on the demo day or demonstration day [8].

Each of these categories (immersion in the problem, in the solution, and in the business) consisted of weekly tasks that participants needed to submit during the mentorship meetings. Throughout this period, activities such as problem hypothesis definition, validation interviews with potential customers, prototypes, and value proposition canvases were carried out [14]. In total, there were ten collective mentorship sessions and six individual ones. Mentorships generally took place on a set day and time. However, on a few occasions, meetings were postponed due to participants' challenges in balancing work commitments with the acceleration program.

Post-acceleration Phase

Lastly, during this stage, the "Demo Day" event took place in November 2022 with all three teams presenting their pitches to the company founders. At the end of the presentations, the teams were rewarded with a monetary value provided by the parent company. After the entire process concluded, a feedback session was conducted with the program participants to gather their feedback on the acceleration process. This meeting was recorded and lasted approximately two hours. Data from this meeting was later analyzed, highlighting both the benefits and challenges of the program.

4.4 Evaluation Phase

In this phase, the objective was to discern the results from implementing the action research within the company's context, focusing on the benefits and challenges of the corporate accelerator's implementation. For this, five interviews were conducted with various stakeholders involved in the acceleration process. One interview was with the mentor in charge of the process, two were with participants of the acceleration program, and another two were with the founder, who also acted as a manager of the acceleration program participants. Each interview followed a semi-structured interview script, crafted specifically to capture the diverse perspectives of each individual. The average duration of each interview was 40 min, and all were conducted virtually. All interviews were transcribed and recorded, with the participants' permission, for a more detailed analysis later. From the data analysis, it was possible to identify eleven central codes that were grouped into the following categories: benefits and challenges, which are discussed in the subsequent section.

5 Benefits and Challenges of Internal Corporate Accelerators

Table 2 presents a summary of the benefits and challenges associated with the implementation of an internal corporate accelerator in a Brazilian software company.

Table 2. Benefits and Challenges

Categories	Codes
Benefits	Support from management
	Services provided
	Diversity of participants
	Stimulation of creativity
	Creation and evolution of knowledge
	Evolution of proposed ideas
Challenges	Time availability
	Program infrastructure
	Exclusively virtual communication
	Lack of clarity about investment
	Resistance to the program format

5.1 Benefits

Within the Benefits category, the following points were identified: (i) support from top management, (ii) services offered by the accelerator; (iii) professional diversity in the program; (iv) stimulation of creativity; (v) creation and evolution of knowledge; and (vi) development of the proposed ideas. Each of these aspects will be described below.

Support from Senior Management: In the context of the company studied, it can be said that although the company's top management did not actively participate in mentoring sessions, they still encouraged the accelerator by providing resources such as mentors, a learning environment, tools used, and a reward system, as well as access to company departments such as marketing and human resources. This can be observed in the following excerpt mentioned by one of the mentors: *"They made some departments available for the program like communications, and some other departments* *when needed ... mainly the communication and HR sectors since they also provided some reward tokens for participants which is an internal currency in the company, (...) so from this point of view they gave support".* One of the interviewed participants mentioned: *"I find it interesting and very positive that the company offers this, because in other companies where I worked there was no such process".*

Services Offered by the Accelerator: Regarding the services offered, participants emphasized the importance of the availability and feedback from mentors and the importance of the learning environment. The active presence of the mentors and the weekly feedback received were regarded as essential for the participants' progress throughout the program, as stated by an employee: *"The availability for mentoring was positive, especially for those to whom this process is new [...] the feedbacks were fundamental for the development* [of the work]*".* Moreover, the support materials and tools used in the learning environment facilitated the learning process: *"The material used was very enlightening [...] it presented startup and entrepreneurship tools more practically for those who participated".*

Participant Diversity: Although no diversity policies were set, there was a noticeable presence of significant professional plurality among the participants in the acceleration process. Indeed, one of the main benefits mentioned by the interviewed founder was: *"One thing I found cool was the diversity, having an equal number of men and women, having the diversity of senior and junior roles, diversity of leadership roles ... [it] was really nice in that regard".* In this scenario, in addition to gender diversity, the acceleration program had significant professional diversity (specialization, founding experience, and executive positions) [1]. The founder also mentioned that it would be interesting to include other employees in the final evaluation event, as this diversified participation could lead to better feedback: *"perhaps if there were 140 people from the company where there are women, people of different colors, different sexual genders, the idea might have a breadth of perspectives and even a breadth of contributions."* In short, the company's management recognized the importance of involving other employees to promote diversity and inclusion within the organizational context.

Stimulation of Creativity: When asked about the benefits perceived in the implementation of the accelerator, the founder mentioned an improvement in the employees' creativity: *"we managed to see that everyone was engaged with creativity, another point that we feel converged well was that we noticed an improvement in people's day-to-day creativity, which is cool."*

Creation and Evolution of Knowledge: At the beginning of the acceleration program, participants stated they did not have solid knowledge about concepts related to entrepreneurship and innovation. One of the mentors mentioned: *"some people had never followed such a process and didn't have knowledge about these tools."* Thus, by engaging in the program, participants had the opportunity to learn and apply new techniques and methodologies, which resulted in expanding their knowledge, as mentioned by a participant: *"It was positive to bring in a more practical way the tools of startups and entrepreneurship for those who participated, getting to know the tools and acceleration processes, which were new to me".*

Development of Proposed Ideas: At the beginning of the program the participants had limited knowledge about startups, the proposed ideas were in an early stage, without having undergone any type of validation, for instance. According to the interviewed mentor: *"There were ideas that initially didn't even seem like a business and evolved into a real business possibility"*. The interviewed partner also mentioned that the expectation was for the ideas to evolve to a more professional level, as illustrated: *"And the expectation regarding the participants was that they could get there, and we could see an idea not just in a draft tone, but we could see an idea in a pitch tone and be something more professional"*. By participating in the accelerator and having access to the provided knowledge, and carrying out the proposed tasks, participants managed to improve the proposed ideas. This allowed one of the interviewed participants to apply the idea developed during the acceleration to a real project: *"Look, what we did with the idea, which was that queue application and so on. Now, recently, I even used it for a client who wanted something in that direction. So, I kind of took what I had put there* [in the acceleration program], *and we created a proposal for him* [a client]*"*.

5.2 Challenges

The main challenges identified in this research were: (1) limited availability of participants; (2) lack of clarity regarding investments; (3) resistance to the program's format; (4) exclusively virtual communication; and finally, (5) some aspects related to the program's infrastructure, such as exceeding meeting times.

Time Availability: Time availability was a point of concern during the implementation of the accelerator due to the difficulty some employees had in reconciling the program's activities and their regular tasks in the company. Due to limited time availability, employees' attendance at the weekly meetings became less frequent, which impacted team performance, as stated by one of the employees: *"I had problems reconciling my personal routine with the timing of the talks [from the acceleration program], which might have affected my performance"*. Moreover, some employees found the given timeline for the program's activities insufficient due to the time constraints they had to deal with: *"Very tight deadlines at the beginning, especially considering that people are involved with many other activities"*. Given this difficulty in juggling tasks, and adopting an action-research perspective, at times the delivery deadlines were adjusted to minimize participants' challenges.

Program Infrastructure: Further due to limited time availability (see previous challenge), some team members could not attend live meetings. Therefore, a cited weak point was the lack of availability of recordings for some of the mentoring meetings so that they could be watched later. This limitation was due to the short storage period for the files in the tool used, representing a constraint. Moreover, some points mentioned regarding the mentoring meetings were related to the overrunning of time in some meetings, i.e., they took longer than expected, as stated by an employee, *"Lack of time control when teams present. Sometimes it ran way over time."* This was detrimental since participants already had a limited time for their participation in the meetings.

Exclusive Virtual Communication: The fact that communication between participants and mentors was conducted solely through online tools, such as corporate email and Slack, was pinpointed as a challenge. For instance, the mentor noted, *"we had no direct contact, only through corporate email, communication tools, and weekly meetings, so there was no direct contact, which I think hindered a bit"*. In other words, the lack of other communication opportunities with the participants was perceived as a weak point, as the interaction occurred solely through corporate tools. As a result, there was limited exchange with employees during the execution of the program.

Lack of Clarity on Investment: Regarding contractual matters, the lack of clarity on the rules of a potential investment in a business idea under acceleration was highlighted: *"(...) how will the company's founders invest? Will a new company be created? How will the partnership with the idea owner be structured? What resources from the company will be committed to the ideas?"*. In this case, these issues were entirely up to the company, where they would be discussed between the founders and participants, if, according to the founders, the idea was suitable for potential investment.

Resistance to the Program Format: One of the main challenges mentioned by the interviewed founder was related to the format of the program, as described in the following passage, *"Perhaps the program could have a format not necessarily something very strict, it was more a process that helped them to validate ideas in a demo day ... lighter"*. The founder also mentioned that, during the idea evaluation, the participation of the company's senior management was not necessary, as it generated a high cost: *"In the end, who had to validate was the board* [of founders] *and stopping the company's board is an expensive business, involving people who are at a very high decision-making level is an expensive business"*. In other words, (s)he recognized the benefits of the program, however, (s)he questioned the need for the board in a particular stage, suggesting the possibility of involving other employees.

6 Discussion

Based on our results, we argue that the senior management played a pivotal role in the implementation of the corporate accelerator, providing crucial resources such as access to strategic sectors of the company, a learning environment, tools, and a reward system. This result aligns with previous research that emphasizes senior management's involvement by providing resources to encourage entrepreneurial activities [12]. In this context, for a company to take on an innovative role, it is essential to construct a structured innovation process involving senior management. This structure provides the necessary conditions for the continuous development of ideas [9]. Thus, it's vital that senior management understands the importance of getting involved in the accelerator's innovative activities, bringing their strategic vision, experience, and knowledge to validate the ideas being discussed in the accelerator [12]. Furthermore, promoting an organizational culture that values innovation and encourages participation from employees regardless of hierarchical levels is fundamental [24].

Mentoring sessions played a crucial role in the acceleration program, as they provided ongoing guidance through the mentors. The support offered through mentoring can accelerate the learning curve of startups, fostering the creation of an entrepreneurial mindset, making it possible to transfer the different areas of knowledge present in the internal corporate accelerator to the organization [20].

Meanwhile, time availability was one of the main challenges for participants. According to Kurakto et al. [12], this availability is essential for generating innovations, and its absence can hinder the development of new opportunities, especially when work routines demand stringent commitments. Therefore, it is vital for a company to find time management strategies, allowing accelerator participants to engage in innovative activities without overburdening their work responsibilities. A possible approach is adopting the 20% rule, in which employees have 20% of their weekly working time reserved for dedicating themselves to innovation projects [6].

Another challenge was the exclusively virtual format of the acceleration program. This constrained the communication between participants and mentors. Kohler [10] suggests that a combination of face-to-face and virtual meetings might be an alternative to improve communication. Although it was not feasible to have in-person meetings due to the COVID-19 pandemic and the geographical distance between participants and mentors, the accelerator's organization can explore the use of other communication tools to bridge the gap between mentors and participants. It is also worth noting the importance of informal and spontaneous interactions - which occur more easily when people are in the same physical environment - in the innovation process. In other words, casual encounters have been recognized since the 70s as vital for a culture of communication, collaboration, and innovation [12].

Another issue to be addressed is clarity regarding investment possibilities. It is essential for the accelerator to establish from the outset how investments will occur if a proposed idea is selected for a partnership with the parent company. By defining and communicating these aspects clearly, the internal accelerator contributes to a more transparent and trustworthy relationship with its participants.

To mitigate the challenges faced during the implementation of the internal corporate accelerator, another initiative that can be considered to promote internal innovation is hackathons. Some benefits identified in the literature from the implementation of hackathons were also identified as results in this research and include: the use of tools that are not typically part of the organization's context resulting in a significant increase in available knowledge [25]; participant diversity [15]; knowledge creation [15]; encouragement of a creative mindset [25] and increased confidence among participants [15]. Meanwhile, a common challenge in the implementation of both internal corporate accelerators and hackathons is the lack of post-event activities designed to sustain an entrepreneurial environment [25]. The absence of these follow-up initiatives can be an obstacle to fostering a culture of ongoing innovation [15].

Regarding the challenges faced during the implementation of an internal corporate accelerator, such as the issue of time availability, hackathons have a significant difference in that they have a shorter duration. This allows employees to focus exclusively on developing their ideas without the need to split their time with regular company tasks [24]. However, it is essential to highlight that the choice between an internal corporate accelerator and hackathons depends on the company's strategic objectives. These initiatives can be complementary and tailored to the organization's specific needs. Therefore, the company should reflect on its goals and available resources when deciding which innovation approach to adopt [10].

Overall, the creation of an environment conducive to continuous innovation using the an internal acceleration program, with appropriate resources, enabled employees to develop their projects, skills, and entrepreneurial mindset, and insights to solve problems within the company. However, to ensure participants' productivity and quality of life, it is crucial for the company to seek ways to allocate resources adequately to avoid overburdening and stressing participants.

7 Conclusions and Future Work

Using an action-research process in partnership with a Brazilian software development company, we implemented an internal corporate accelerator to engage employees in the company's innovation process. Through interviews and meetings, we structured the accelerator into five stages, established the selection criteria, and defined the services provided. During the execution of the acceleration cycle, we identified the benefits and challenges of the accelerator's implementation. Based on these results, we present a set of recommendations for companies wishing to implement their own accelerators:

- Ensure clarity regarding potential investments in selected ideas, transparently defining how the investment will occur;
- Encourage senior management's participation in the program, actively involving them in idea evaluation and support for participants;
- Provide high-quality support materials and tools to facilitate participants' learning and development;
- Establish realistic deadlines for program activities, considering participants' time constraints and the complexity of tasks;
- Promote effective interaction and contact with employees, aiming to create an environment of collaboration and knowledge exchange among participants, mentors, and program staff;
- Value mentoring as a crucial element of the program, ensuring that mentors are available to provide appropriate guidance;
- And promote knowledge transfer throughout the organization, encouraging the dissemination of the learnings acquired during the acceleration program.

By adopting these recommendations, a company can create an environment conducive to innovation, develop internal talents, and boost the growth and success of the participating startups.

For future work, we plan to conduct a new acceleration cycle taking into account the results reported here. Furthermore, an investigation can be conducted on the long-term effects of the internal corporate accelerator in software development companies, analyzing whether the benefits persist and how challenges are mitigated. Finally, individual case studies can be conducted on the specific results of this work, allowing for a comparison of the experience gained in this study with other companies.

References

1. An, H., Chen, C.R., Wu, Q., Zhang, T.: Corporate innovation: do diverse boards help? J. Fin. Quant. Anal. **56**(1), 155–182 (2021)
2. Barrehag, L., Fornell, A., Larsson, G., Mårdström, V., Westergård, V., Wrackefeldt, S.: Accelerating success: a study of seed accelerators and their defining characteristics. Bachelor thesis TEKX04-12-10 Chalmers University, Sweden (2012)
3. Crişan, E.L., Salanţă, I.I., Beleiu, I.N., Bordean, O.N., Bunduchi, R.: A systematic literature review on accelerators. J. Technol. Transfer **46**(1), 62–89 (2021)
4. Charmaz, K.: Constructing Grounded Theory: A Practical Guide Through Qualitative Analysis. Sage, New York (2006)
5. Edison, H.: A conceptual framework of lean startup enabled internal corporate venture. In: Abrahamsson, P., Corral, L., Oivo, M., Russo, B. (eds.) PROFES 2015. LNCS, vol. 9459, pp. 607–613. Springer, Cham (2015). https://doi.org/10.1007/978-3-319-26844-6_46
6. Leppänen, M., Hokkanen, L.: Four patterns for internal startups. In: Proceedings of the 20th European Conference on Pattern Languages of Programs, July 2015
7. Dybå, T., Prikladnicki, R., Rönkkö, K., Seaman, C., Sillito, J.: Qualitative research in software engineering. Empirical Soft. Eng. **16**, 425–429 (2011)
8. Ghorashi, H., Asghari, R.: Minimum viable accelerator: planning, starting and improving startup accelerator programs under a lean approach. Am. J. Manag. **19**(2), 10–25 (2019)
9. Kemell, K.K., Risku, J., Strandjord, K.E., Nguyen-Duc, A., Wang, X., Abrahamsson, P.: Internal software startups–a multiple case study on practices, methods, and success factors. In: 46th Euromicro Conference on Software Engineering and Advanced Applications (SEAA), pp. 326–333, August 2020
10. Kohler, T.: Corporate accelerators: building bridges between corporations and startups. Bus. Horiz. **59**(3), 347–357 (2016)
11. Kraut, R., Egido, C., Galegher, J.: Patterns of contact and communication in scientific research collaboration. In: Proceedings of the 1988 ACM Conference on Computer-Supported Cooperative Work, pp. 1–12. ACM, New York, NY, USA (1988)
12. Kuratko, D.F., Hornsby, J.S., Covin, J.G.: Diagnosing a firm's internal environment for corporate entrepreneurship. Bus. Horiz. **57**(1), 37–47 (2014)
13. Mohammadi, N., Sakhteh, S.: Start-up accelerator value chain: a systematic literature review. Manag. Rev. Q. **73**, 661–694 (2022)
14. Peralta, C.B.D.L., Echeveste, M.E., Lermen, F.H., Marcon, A., Tortorella, G.: A framework proposition to identify customer value through lean practices. J. Manuf. Technol. Manag. **31**(4), 725–747 (2020)
15. Pe-Than, E.P.P., Nolte, A., Filippova, A., Bird, C., Scallen, S., Herbsleb, J.: Corporate hackathons, how and why? A multiple case study of motivation, projects proposal and selection, goal setting, coordination, and outcomes. Hum.-Comput. Interact. **37**(4), 281–313 (2022)
16. Porras, J., et al.: Hackathons in software engineering education: lessons learned from a decade of events. In: Proceedings of the 2nd International Workshop on Software Engineering Education for Millennials, pp. 40–47, June 2018
17. Prexl, K.M., Hubert, M., Beck, S., Heiden, C., Prügl, R.: Identifying and analysing the drivers of heterogeneity among ecosystem builder accelerators. R&D Manage. **49**(4), 624–638 (2019)
18. Ries, E.: The Lean Startup, p. 27. Crown Business, New York (2012)
19. Molléri, J.S., Petersen, K., Mendes, E.: Survey guidelines in software engineering: an annotated review. In: Proceedings of the ACM/IEEE International Symposium on Empirical Software Engineering and Measurement (2016)

20. Selig, C.J., Heinzelmann, N., Kohlhase, S., Baltes, G.H.: Fostering Intrapreneurship through the Implementation of Internal Corporate Accelerators. HTWG Konstanz (2018a)
21. Selig, C.J., Gasser, T., Baltes, G.H.: How corporate accelerators foster organizational transformation: an internal perspective. In: 2018 International Conference on Engineering, Technology and Innovation, pp. 1–9. IEEE, June 2018b
22. Staron, M.: Action research as research methodology in software engineering. In: Action Research in Software Engineering. Springer, Cham (2020). https://doi.org/10.1007/978-3-030-32610-4_2
23. Susman, G.I., Evered, R.D.: An assessment of the scientific merits of action research. Adm. Sci. Q. **23**(4), 582–603 (1978)
24. Tkalich, A., Moe, N.B., Sporsem, T.: Employee-driven innovation to fuel internal software startups: preliminary findings. In: Gregory, P., Kruchten, P. (eds.) XP 2021. LNBIP, vol. 426, pp. 145–154. Springer, Cham (2021). https://doi.org/10.1007/978-3-030-88583-0_14
25. Valença, G., Lacerda, N., de Souza, C.R.B., Gama, K.: A systematic mapping study on the organization of corporate hackathons. In: Euromicro Conference on Software Engineering and Advanced Applications, pp. 421–428. IEEE (2020)
26. Yin, B., Luo, J.: How do accelerators select startups? Shifting decision criteria across stages. IEEE Trans. Eng. Manage. **65**(4), 574–589 (2018)
27. Yusubova, A., Andries, P., Clarysse, B.: Entrepreneurial team formation and evolution in technology ventures: looking beyond the top management team. J. Small Bus. Manage. **58**(5), 893–922 (2020)

A Process for Scenario Prioritization and Selection in Simulation-Based Safety Testing of Automated Driving Systems

Fauzia Khan[✉][iD], Hina Anwar[iD], and Dietmar Pfahl[iD]

University of Tartu, Narva mnt 18, 51009 Tartu, Estonia
{fauzia.khan,hina.anwar,dietmar.pfahl}@ut.ee

Abstract. Simulation-based safety testing of Automated Driving Systems (ADS) is a cost-effective and safe alternative to field tests. However, it is practically impossible to test every scenario using a simulator. We propose a process for prioritizing and selecting scenarios from an existing list of scenarios. The aim is to refine the scope of tested scenarios and focus on the most representative and critical ones for evaluating ADS safety. As a proof-of-concept, we apply our process to two pre-existing scenario catalogs provided by the Land Transport Authority of Singapore and the Department of Transportation. After applying our process, we prioritized and selected six scenario groups containing 51 scenarios for testing ADS in the CARLA simulator.

Keywords: Autonomous Driving System (ADS) · Simulation-based Testing · Safety Testing · Scenario Prioritization · Scenario Selection Process

1 Introduction

Several accidents[1,2] with Automatic Driving Systems (ADS) as well as the ADS accident statistics released by the National Highway Traffic Safety Administration - (NHTSA)[3] have made authorities more determined than ever to gain trust and a deeper understanding of real-world safety issues before fully embracing autonomous driving. To gain the necessary trust, it is necessary that the safety of ADS is sufficiently tested in all relevant driving scenarios. ADS encounter a wide range of scenarios based on the combination of scenery, traffic, road objects, environment, road geometry, and maneuvers [2,4]. The complexity of driving tasks and the uncertainty of the driving environment grows exponentially, translating into infinite scenarios that ADS could encounter.

Testing all driving scenarios in real life is time-consuming, risky, and costly [9,24]. Simulation-based testing is a cost-effective alternative to traditional field

---

[1] Uber Self-driving Crash.

[2] Tesla Autopilot Crash.

[3] NHTSA.

© The Author(s), under exclusive license to Springer Nature Switzerland AG 2024
R. Kadgien et al. (Eds.): PROFES 2023, LNCS 14483, pp. 89–99, 2024.
https://doi.org/10.1007/978-3-031-49266-2_6

tests [3,25]. However, it is practically impossible to test every scenario using a simulator. The safety testing of ADS should be based on a feasible number of test scenarios, and the critical ones should be prioritized [17]. A critical scenario involves potential accidents or hazardous situations, such as sudden obstacles or collisions, which can challenge the ADS's ability to react and avoid accidents. Thus, it leads to an interesting question: How to prioritize and select the critical scenarios for the safety testing of ADS?

In this paper, we present a process for prioritizing and selecting scenarios for simulation-based safety testing of ADS. The proposed process aims to help researchers and developers ensure a comprehensive evaluation of ADS safety in a simulated environment to regain and improve public trust in ADS safety.

2   Background

This section explains foundational concepts and context related to the ADS.

Automated Driving Systems (ADS) - An ADS refers to a technology that enables vehicles to operate autonomously without human intervention. It must possess real-time functionality to operate safely and efficiently, navigate various driving scenarios, avoid obstacles, follow traffic rules, and react to changing road conditions [11,20].

Level of Automation - ADSs are classified into six automation levels based on their capabilities, as defined by the Society of Automotive Engineers -(SAE). These levels, ranging from no automation (level 0) to full automation (level 5), represent different degrees of automation. The term *ADS* applies to automation levels 3 to 5 [20].

Operation Design Domain (ODD) - refers to the specific conditions and environments under which a particular driving automation system is designed to operate [6]. The scope of ODD is defined but not limited to spatial, temporal, and environmental conditions. Spatial conditions refer to geographical area (city, suburb, rural), road type (urban roads, rural roads, highways, etc.), lane configuration (single-lane roads or multi-lanes), and speed limit ranges. Temporal conditions refer to the specific time frames during which the ADS is designed to function, e.g., day or night time. Environmental conditions refer to weather conditions such as snow, fog, rain, and sunshine [12,20,23].

3   Related Work

One group of studies [7,14,16] focuses on comprehending the behavior of ADS in lane change scenarios, analyzing factors like lane position, proximity to other vehicles, and lane delineation from road lines and edges. Other studies [1,8,21, 22,26] report on safety testing of ADS in a car following scenario, where one vehicle follows another while maintaining a defined distance. Any collision in such scenarios is referred to as a rear-end collision. Moreover, a group of studies [1,7,8,22,27] conducted tests of the car following scenario with the inclusion of static objects like lane markings, traffic signs, pedestrian crossings, and drive-by billboards. Several studies [1,7,14,22] explore the safety aspects of ADS in scenarios with dynamic objects such as traffic lights, pedestrians, and other vehicles. Furthermore, another group of studies [1,5,18,19,21,26,27] tested ADS in different weather conditions, including rain, fog, sun, snow, overcast, cloud, and wind. Lastly, several studies [8,16,19,21,26,27] considered the effects of different lighting conditions, such as daylight and night, in the safety testing of ADS.

Together, these studies have significantly contributed to understanding how ADS perform in various scenarios, helping to enhance the safety and reliability of ADS in real-world situations. However, to our knowledge, the existing literature lacks clarity on the scenario selection process.

4   Methodology

In this section, we describe the process to prioritize and select scenarios for the simulation-based safety-testing of ADS. The flow chart showing the complete process and external material (Tables and Results of each step of the method in an Excel sheet is available at https://shorturl.at/BFNV0).

Select scenario catalog(s) - This step involves choosing a publicly available scenario catalog that is comprehensive and published by a reputable organization. Several reputable authorities have published catalogs that consist of compiled scenario lists. For example, the National Highway Traffic Safety Administration - (NHTSA)[4], Euro NCAP[5], Land Transport Authority of Singapore[6]. Academic researchers [13,15] also have generated scenario catalogs using various methodologies. Once the catalog(s) are chosen, assign a unique identifier to the catalog(s) and scenarios within, as in Eq. 1.

$$C = [C_{i,j} | i \in \{1, 2, \ldots, n\}, j \in \{1, 2, \ldots, m\}] \tag{1}$$

In Equ. 1, C is the list of chosen scenario catalogs, $C_{i,j}$ represents an individual scenario in the list, i ranges from 1 to n representing the catalog index, j ranges from 1 to m representing the scenario index within each catalog.

Enumerate ODD conditions - Parallel to selecting a scenario catalog(s), chracterize the ODD in terms of spatial, temporal, and environmental conditions, e.g., based on design specifications provided by the ADS developers. An example worksheet template that could be used to list ODD conditions is available at https://shorturl.at/BFNV0.

Filter scenarios - This step excludes scenarios that do not fall within the ODD enumerated in the previous step. This filtering helps narrow down the list of scenarios to those aligned with the specified ODD of the ADS.

---

[4] List of Pre-Crash Scenario for Crash Avoidance Research.
[5] Test Scenarios- European New Car Assessment Programme.
[6] List of Scenario Categories for the Assessment of Automated Vehicles.

From each of the chosen scenario catalogs C_i, assess each scenario to ascertain its alignment with the ODD of the ADS. Begin by examining spatial conditions (road types, number of lanes, junctions), followed by temporal conditions (time), and finally, environmental conditions (weather). If a scenario falls within the ODD of the ADS, include it in the list of scenarios for further processing.

Group scenarios - This step involves categorizing the scenarios into groups based on similar critical actions of the ego vehicle or the target object, such as pedestrians, cyclists, animals, etc. To form groups, identify the text describing the critical action of the ego vehicle and mark it as a key term. If the critical action of the ego vehicle is not described in the scenario, consider the text describing the target object from the scenario's description. If both critical action and target object are included in the scenario, only the text describing the critical action of the target user should be considered as a key term. Once these key terms are identified, formulate high-level terms by applying the bottom-up merging technique. Assign the high-level term as the name for the group. Corresponding scenarios tied to identifying critical action terms are placed within their respective groups. In scenarios that lack information about the critical action of the ego vehicle and the target object, form a group "Miscellaneous".

As an example consider two scenarios where the critical action of the ego vehicle is described, e.g., $C_{i,j}$ (*The Ego vehicle performs* <u>lane change</u> *with vehicle behind.*) and $C_{i,j+1}$ (*The Ego vehicle observes traffic slowing* <u>in the curb lane</u>. *The Ego vehicle decides to* <u>change lanes</u> *and go around the slowing traffic. The ego vehicle* <u>changed lanes</u> *to* <u>the inside lane</u> *only to find vehicle B stopped directly in front. The* <u>driver in</u> *the ego vehicle cannot stop and hits B in the rear.*). In both scenarios the critical action of the ego vehicle is underlined. After applying the bottom-up merging technique on these terms, the resulting high-level term is "lane change". Subsequently, a group called "Lane Change" is formed, encompassing all scenarios in which the key terms signify lane change as the critical action. Accordingly, scenarios $C_{i,j}$ and $C_{i,j+1}$ are placed within this group.

Remove duplicates within scenario group - This step focuses on identifying within scenario groups scenarios with identical or similar descriptions and retaining the most comprehensive one.

Prioritize scenarios groups - The objective of ADS safety testing could be to test corner cases, common crash scenarios, or behavior competencies. In this study, our focus is to prioritize the scenario based on common crash scenarios. Common crash scenarios involve driving situations where crashes frequently occur. To prioritize scenario groups formed in the previous step, assess the potential risk associated with each scenario by considering the frequency of crash occurrence based on real world statistics. Such statistics can be obtained from the National Highway Traffic Safety Administration[7], European Road Safety Data Portal[8], Department for Transport - United Kingdom[9] or Transport Canada's

---

[7] NCSA Tools, Publications, and Data (Traffic Safety facts Annual Report Tables).

[8] European Road Safety Data Portal - European Union.

[9] Statistics at DfT - United Kingdom.

National Collision Database[10]. In these datasets, tables present the statistics for the predominant accident scenarios. Based on the numbers of the most frequent accidents in specific scenarios, prioritize the scenario groups for testing.

Filter simulators based on their limitations - Choose a simulator that is capable of accurately replicating real-world conditions such as dynamic traffic, weather conditions, vehicle sensors, road types, and junctions. Additionally, the simulator should be able to collect and analyze data on performance metrics such as travel time, crashes, violation of safety distances, and compliance with traffic rules. After selecting the simulator, remove those scenarios that cannot be implemented due to simulator limitations, as they could result in unreliable results or simulation crashes.

Prioritize and select scenarios for testing - This step involves prioritizing the scenarios within the remaining groups using a scoring system. To achieve this, we create a scoreboard and assign points according to count of scenario elements, including actors, ego vehicle maneuver, road topology, lighting, and weather condition. The points are assigned based on the number of occurrences of each scenario element in the relevant crash statistics. We used crash statistics provided by NHSTA[11,12,13,14].

In our study, we developed the scoreboard by assigning points to scenario elements based on their number of occurrence. Each element's least common value received 1 point, with subsequent values getting an additional point based increasing occurrence. Table 1 shows the calculated scores for each scenario element and value. We used statistics from the years 2000 to 2020. Table 1 only shows the score points for scenario elements "actors". The complete Table containing scores for additional scenario elements, such as "Driving Maneuvers", "Weather", and "Lightning", are available at https://shorturl.at/BFNV0.

Table 1. Scoreboard

Sr.#	Elements	Possible Value	Points
01	Actors	Movable objects - (vehicles)	05
		Movable objects - (pedestrians)	04
		Movable objects - (cyclists)	03
		Movable objects - (others)	02
		Static Object	01

---

[10] Canadian Motor Vehicle Traffic Collision Statistics: 2021.

[11] Stat. for collision with dynamic & fixed objects: Ch. 3→Passenger Cars→ Table 42.

[12] Stat. for weather and lighting conditions: Goto: Chap. 2→Time →Table 26.

[13] Stat. for occupants, non-occupants killed & injured in traffic crashes:Goto:Chapter 1:Trends → General→ Table 3.

[14] Stat. for crashes by vehicle driving maneuver: see table "Vehicles Involved in Single - and Two-Vehicle Fatal Crashes by Vehicle Maneuver", State: USA, Year: 2020.

Using the scoreboard, one can assign a score to each scenario within the prioritized scenarios groups. For example, consider a scenario description *The ego vehicle is approaching a slower lead vehicle*. In this scenario, the dynamic actor involves *vehicle*, and the driving maneuver is *driving straight*. However, the weather condition and lightning information are not mentioned. In such cases, assume the weather to be *clear/normal* and the lightning to be *daylight*, i.e., the default values. Using Table 1, the total score for this scenario is calculated as: Total score = movable objects vehicles+driving maneuver+weather+lightning. Using values from the scoreboard: Total score = $(05+14+04+02) = 25$.

Based on calculated scores, one can prioritize scenarios within their respective groups in descending order. Scenarios with a higher score are selected first. If two scenarios share identical scores, either option may be considered.

5   Application Example

In this section, we present proof-of-concept example of our process for prioritizing and selecting scenarios for simularion-based safety testing of ADS. In the following, we refer to the ADS under test as the *ego vehicle*.

Results of scenario catalog selection - We selected two publicly available catalogs to form a comprehensive list of scenarios. The first catalog has been published by the Land Transport Authority of Singapore[15] and contains 67 real-world traffic scenarios. The second catalog has been published by the US Department of Transportation[16] and contains 44 pre-crash scenarios specifically capturing the situations and conditions leading up to an accident or collision.

We assigned a distinct identifier to each scenario within the catalogs using the format C_i, j as described in Equ. 1. The total of scenarios from both catalogs is 111, with i ranging from 1 to 2 and j from 1 to 111. The consolidated list of scenarios from catalogs and their unique identifiers is available at https://shorturl.at/BFNV0 (Sheet 1 of the Excel worksheet)

Results of enumerating ODD of ADS - We chose a level 4 ADS as the ego vehicle, representing a high level of automation where the vehicles can operate independently without requiring driver intervention in unsafe traffic conditions. The ego vehicle can stop and go, change lanes, pass through a signalized intersection, turn at an intersection, and detect road objects like pedestrians, traffic lights, vehicles, etc. Moreover, the ego vehicle is designed to function on highways and urban roads, including signalized junctions during daytime in sunny and cloudy weather. Table 2, showing the ODD of the ego vehicle and the excluded scenarios based on the ODD of the ego vehicle, is available at https://shorturl.at/BFNV0 (Sheet 2 of the Excel worksheet).

Results of filtering scenarios based on ODD of ADS - We match each scenario with the ego vehicles' ODD regarding spatial, temporal, and environmental conditions and excluded the scenarios that do not fall within the ego vehicle ODD. The excluded scenarios and the reasons for exclusion are available

---

[15] List of scenarios - Land Transport Authority of Singapore.
[16] List of scenarios - US Department of Transportation - Table 1.

Table 2. ODD for ego vehicle

ODD	Values
Spatial Condition	*Road type*: Urban roads and Highways
	Number of lanes: 2–3
	Junctions: Signalized intersection only
Temporal Condition	*Time*: Daytime
Environmental Condition	*Weather*: Sunny and Cloudy

at https://shorturl.at/BFNV0. The remaining number of scenarios is 90. The full list of scenarios is available at https://shorturl.at/BFNV0 (Sheet 3 of the Excel worksheet).

Results of scenario grouping - We derived 15 groups by examining the scenario descriptions and identifying critical actions of the ego vehicle or the target object. The groups and their corresponding key terms and the distribution of the scenarios over groups are available at https://shorturl.at/BFNV0.

Results of removing duplicates within a scenario group - We identified nine duplicates reducing the total number of scenarios to 81. The list of duplicates and that of scenarios after duplicate removal is available at https://shorturl.at/BFNV0 Sheets 5 and 6 of the Excel worksheet, respectively).

Results of prioritizing scenarios groups - We prioritized the remaining scenarios using the previously developed scoreboard, focusing on the most common pre-crash scenarios. We refer to crash statistics provided by the National Crash Data for the period of 2011–2015[17]. These statistics provide insights into different scenarios involving vehicles before a crash. Based on these statistics, the prioritized groups are *Following lead vehicle* group followed by *Crossing Path, Lane change, Control Loss, Animal Interaction, Opposite direction, Pedestrian Interaction, and Cyclist Interaction*. After this step, the total number of scenarios within the prioritized groups is 58. The corresponding data is available at https://shorturl.at/BFNV0 (Sheet 7 of the Excel worksheet).

Results of filtering scenarios based on simulator limitations - We chose CARLA[18] simulator as it can closely replicate real-world conditions as well as collect and analyze data of many performance metrics [10]. However, some scenarios involve complex real-world situations or events that are beyond CARLA's capabilities. For example, scenarios involving extreme weather conditions, e.g., snow and hurricanes, large-scale disasters, e.g., earthquakes, or highly dynamic and unpredictable elements might not be replicable in CARLA. Additionally, scenarios requiring interactions with certain behavior of non-vehicle entities, e.g., animals, or scenarios in which the component of the vehicle is not working, e.g., brakes failing, are not present in CARLA. In addition, we excluded $C_{1,38}, C_{2,95}$ as they could not be executed in CARLA. We also excluded scenarios related to

---

[17] GES Crash Statistics - See Table 5: All crashes.
[18] https://carla.org/.

the *Control Loss* group as control loss events cannot be directly input to an ADS. After this step, the remaining number of scenarios is 51. All data is available at https://shorturl.at/BFNV0 (Sheet 8 of the Excel worksheet).

Results of prioritizing and selecting scenarios for testing - We prioritized scenarios within each priority scenario group based on our scoreboard and rearranged the scenarios within each prioritized scenario group in descending order based on their scores as shown in Table 3 with scenario group G3 having the highest priority. Testing will start with the top-scoring scenario in the G3 group, followed by scenarios within the same group in descending order. Group G5 has the second highest priority. Once all the scenarios in G3 are tested, the scenarios in G5 will be tested in descending order. This process will continue until all the scenario groups are covered in testing. The complete data is available at https://shorturl.at/BFNV0 (Sheet 9 of the Excel worksheet).

Table 3. Selected Scenarios for Safety Testing of ADS

Sr. #	Groups	Scenario Name	Identifier	Score
G3	Following Lead Vehicle	Ego vehicle approaching slower lead vehicle	$C_{1,13}$	25
		Turning lead vehicle	$C_{1,65}$	23
		Inattentive, Rear	$C_{2,92}$	20
		Stutter Stop	$C_{2,93}$	20
G5	Crossing Path	Oncoming vehicle turns right at signalized junction	$C_{1,27}$	26
		Sirens	$C_{2,82}$	25
		...	...	...
		Ego vehicle turns right with oncoming vehicle at signalized junction	$C_{1,28}$	18

6   Discussion

The selection of scenario catalogs is deliberately kept flexible, leaving the choice to the testers. Optimal results may emerge from the utilization of multiple catalogs making the starting set of scenarios as comprehensive as possible.

If the ODD of an ADS becomes more complex, it influences the selection process by imposing more complex scenarios which, in turn, enhances trust and confidence in the ADS. ADS developers must clearly communicate the ODD to help ensure comprehensive and appropriate safety testing. If the ODD is not communicated effectively, it can influence the selection process, which may lead to potential gaps in assessing the performance and safety of the ADS in real-world conditions, reducing the overall confidence in the system's capabilities.

For the formulation of scenario grouping, accurate identification of critical actions is important. We have shown examples of the process for identifying critical actions from scenario descriptions. We recommend using scenario catalogs with clear and comprehensive scenario descriptions. Inside each scenario group, the prioritization of scenarios relies on the scoreboard, which is constructed using a trustworthy data set. Over time, the scoreboard might need to be updated based on new data. In the future, more versions of the prioritization process can be introduced for testing corner cases. We have excluded the scenario element "road topology" due to the unavailability of data. This limits our study.

The choice of the simulator is very important. An inadequate simulator could misrepresent real-world scenarios, potentially affecting the validity of the test results. However, one can check the reliability of the simulator with the help of known real-world reference behavior.

7 Conclusion and Future Work

Given the impracticality of on-road testing for every scenario, our study introduces a method to prioritize and select scenarios for simulation-based safety testing of ADS. We apply our process to two publicly accessible scenario catalogs encompassing 111 scenarios. As a result, we successfully identified and prioritized six distinct scenario groups, containing 51 scenarios for ADS testing. In the future, we plan to simulate the selected scenarios in the CARLA simulator to compare ADS behavior with that of human drivers.

Acknowledgements. This research was partly funded by the Austrian BMK, BMAW, and State of Upper Austria under the SCCH competence center INTEGRATE [(FFG grant 892418)], the Estonian Research Council (grant PRG1226), Bolt Technology OÜ, and the Estonian state stipend for doctoral studies.

References

1. Abdessalem, R.B., Nejati, S., Briand, L.C., Stifter, T.: Testing vision-based control systems using learnable evolutionary algorithms. In: Proceedings of the 40th International Conference on Software Engineering, pp. 1016–1026 (2018)
2. Chen, Z., He, F., Yin, Y., Du, Y.: Optimal design of autonomous vehicle zones in transportation networks. Transp. Res. Part B: Methodological **99**, 44–61 (2017)
3. Chen, Z., He, F., Zhang, L., Yin, Y.: Optimal deployment of autonomous vehicle lanes with endogenous market penetration. Transp. Res. Part C: Emerging Technologies **72**, 143–156 (2016)
4. Duarte, F., Ratti, C.: The impact of autonomous vehicles on cities: a review. J. Urban Technol. **25**(4), 3–18 (2018)
5. Huang, X., Kwiatkowska, M., Wang, S., Wu, M.: Safety verification of deep neural networks. In: Majumdar, R., Kunčak, V. (eds.) CAV 2017. LNCS, vol. 10426, pp. 3–29. Springer, Cham (2017). https://doi.org/10.1007/978-3-319-63387-9_1
6. Iso, I.: Pas 21448-Road Vehicles-Safety of the Intended Functionality. Int, Organization for Standardization (2019)
7. Jha, S., et al.: ML-based fault injection for autonomous vehicles: a case for Bayesian fault injection. In: 2019 49th Annual IEEE/IFIP International Conference on Dependable Systems and Networks (DSN), pp. 112–124. IEEE (2019)
8. Jha, S., et al.: Kayotee: A fault injection-based system to assess the safety and reliability of autonomous vehicles to faults and errors (2019). arXiv preprint arXiv:1907.01024

9. Karunakaran, D., Worrall, S., Nebot, E.: Efficient statistical validation with edge cases to evaluate highly automated vehicles. In: 2020 IEEE 23rd International Conference on Intelligent Transportation Systems (ITSC), pp. 1–8. IEEE (2020)
10. Kaur, P., Taghavi, S., Tian, Z., Shi, W.: A survey on simulators for testing self-driving cars. In: Fourth International Conference on Connected and Autonomous Driving (MetroCAD). IEEE (2021)
11. Komzalov, A., Shilov, N.: Driver assistance systems: state-of-the-art and possible improvements. In: Proceedings of the 20th Conference of Open Innovations Association FRUCT, LETI University, St. Petersburg, Russland (2014)
12. Mercedes-Benz: Safety first for automated driving (SaFAD) (2019). https://group. mercedes-benz.com/innovation/case/autonomous/safety-first-for-automated-driving-2.html. Accessed 19 Jul 2023
13. Nitsche, P.: Safety-critical scenarios and virtual testing procedures for automated cars at road intersections. Ph.D. thesis, Loughborough University (2018)
14. O'Kelly, M., Abbas, H., Gao, S., Shiraishi, S., Kato, S., Mangharam, R.: APEX: Autonomous vehicle plan verification and execution (2016)
15. Park, S., Park, S., Jeong, H., Yun, I., So, J.: Scenario-mining for level 4 automated vehicle safety assessment from real accident situations in urban areas using a natural language process. Sensors 21(20), 6929 (2021)
16. Pei, K., Cao, Y., Yang, J., Jana, S.: DeepXplore: automated whitebox testing of deep learning systems. In: Proceedings of the 26th Symposium on Operating Systems Principles, pp. 1–18 (2017)
17. Ponn, T., Gnandt, C., Diermeyer, F.: An optimization-based method to identify relevant scenarios for type approval of automated vehicles. In: Proceedings of the ESV-International Technical Conference on the Enhanced Safety of Vehicles, Eindhoven, The Netherlands, pp. 10–13 (2019)
18. Ramanagopal, M.S., Anderson, C., Vasudevan, R., Johnson-Roberson, M.: Failing to learn: autonomously identifying perception failures for self-driving cars. IEEE Robot. Autom. Lett. 3(4), 3860–3867 (2018)
19. Rubaiyat, A.H.M., Qin, Y., Alemzadeh, H.: Experimental resilience assessment of an open-source driving agent. In: 2018 IEEE 23rd Pacific Rim International Symposium on Dependable Computing (PRDC), pp. 54–63. IEEE (2018)
20. SAE: 3016-taxonomy and definitions for terms related to on-road motor vehicle automated driving systems (2021). https://www.sae.org/standards/content/ j3016_202104/. Accessed 15 Jul 2023
21. Tian, Y., Pei, K., Jana, S., Ray, B.: DeepTest: automated testing of deep-neural-network-driven autonomous cars. In: Proceedings of the 40th International Conference on Software Engineering, pp. 303–314 (2018)
22. Tuncali, C.E., Fainekos, G., Ito, H., Kapinski, J.: Simulation-based adversarial test generation for autonomous vehicles with machine learning components. In: 2018 IEEE Intelligent Vehicles Symposium (IV), pp. 1555–1562. IEEE (2018)
23. Waymo: Waymo safety report: on the road to fully self-driving (2018). https://downloads.ctfassets.net/sv23gofxcuiz/4gZ7ZUxd4SRj1D1W6z3rpR/ 2ea16814cdb42f9e8eb34cae4f30b35d/2021-03-waymo-safety-report.pdf. Accessed 18 July 2023
24. Xinxin, Z., Fei, L., Xiangbin, W.: CSG: critical scenario generation from real traffic accidents. In: 2020 IEEE Intelligent Vehicles Symposium (IV), pp. 1330–1336. IEEE (2020)
25. Yamamoto, D., Suganuma, N.: Localization for autonomous driving on urban road. In: 2015 International Conference on Intelligent Informatics and Biomedical Sciences (ICIIBMS), pp. 452–453. IEEE (2015)

26. Zhang, M., Zhang, Y., Zhang, L., Liu, C., Khurshid, S.: DeepRoad: GAN-based metamorphic testing and input validation framework for autonomous driving systems. In: Proceedings of the 33rd ACM/IEEE International Conference on Automated Software Engineering, pp. 132–142 (2018)
27. Zhou, H., et al.: DeepBillboard: systematic physical-world testing of autonomous driving systems. In: Proceedings of the ACM/IEEE 42nd International Conference on Software Engineering, pp. 347–358 (2020)

The Journey to Serverless Migration: An Empirical Analysis of Intentions, Strategies, and Challenges

Muhammad Hamza(✉) , Muhammad Azeem Akbar , and Kari Smolander

Department of Software Engineering, LUT University, Lappeenranta, Finland
{Muhammad.hamza,Azeem.akbar,Kari.smolander}@lut.fi

Abstract. Serverless is an emerging cloud computing paradigm that facilitates developers to focus solely on the application logic rather than provisioning and managing the underlying infrastructure. The inherent characteristics such as scalability, flexibility, and cost efficiency of serverless computing, attracted many companies to migrate their legacy applications toward this paradigm. However, the stateless nature of serverless requires careful migration planning, consideration of its subsequent implications, and potential challenges. To this end, this study investigates the intentions, strategies, and technical and organizational challenges while migrating to a serverless architecture. We investigated the migration processes of 11 systems across diverse domains by conducting 15 in-depth interviews with professionals from 11 organizations. We also presented a detailed discussion of each migration case. Our findings reveal that large enterprises primarily migrate to enhance scalability and operational efficiency, while smaller organizations intend to reduce the cost. Furthermore, organizations use a domain-driven design approach to identify the use case and gradually migrate to serverless using a strangler pattern. However, migration encounters technical challenges i.e., testing event-driven architecture, integrating with the legacy system, lack of standardization, and organizational challenges i.e., mindset change and hiring skilled serverless developers as a prominent. The findings of this study provide a comprehensive understanding that can guide future implementations and advancements in the context of serverless migration.

Keywords: Legacy application · Serverless Computing · Migration · Empirical Study

1 Introduction

Serverless has emerged as a disruptive cloud computing paradigm that revolutionized the way software applications are developed and deployed. Companies utilizing a serverless paradigm can solely focus on developing the application logic rather than maintaining and provisioning the underlying cloud infrastructure [1]. Function-as-a-service (FaaS), an implementation serverless pattern, enables developers to create an application function in the cloud that automatically triggers in response to an event or request [1].

© The Author(s), under exclusive license to Springer Nature Switzerland AG 2024
R. Kadgien et al. (Eds.): PROFES 2023, LNCS 14483, pp. 100–115, 2024.
https://doi.org/10.1007/978-3-031-49266-2_7

Companies in serverless computing are only charged for the resources their applications consume. This pricing model contrasts traditional cloud computing, where resources are persistently leased, irrespective of whether the application is running. Seeking the potential of this computing paradigm, major cloud providers such as AWS Lambda, Google Cloud Functions, Microsoft Azure have rolled out their serverless platforms with well-defined features and pricing.

According to recent reports, the serverless market will substantially grow from $3 billion in 2017 to an approximate value of $22 billion by 2025 [2]. Moreover, it is estimated that 50% of enterprises worldwide are expected to adopt serverless computing by 2025 [3]. However, the distinct features of serverless computing also bring new challenges (e.g., statelessness, short-lived functions) for companies developing greenfield projects or migrating existing legacy applications. Legacy applications face a myriad of technical challenges (e.g., excessive coupling, maintenance complexities) and business-related challenges (e.g., longer release time, low developers' productivity). Therefore, embracing a migration to serverless computing offers a compelling solution to address current challenges while improving system scalability and faster releases to the market.

Significant research has been done on the various aspects of serverless computing, including serverless architectural design [4], development features, technological aspects, performance characteristics of serverless platforms [5], etc. For instance, Lin et al. [6] extensively discussed serverless architecture, presenting its associated concepts, advantages, and disadvantages while exploring various architectural implications. Taibi et al. [7] conducted a thorough multivocal literature review to identify a set of patterns (common solutions to solve common problems) and classified them based on the benefits and issues. Similarly, Wen et al. [8] conducted a systematic literature review and highlighted the benefits of serverless computing, its performance optimization, commonly used platforms, research trends, and promising opportunities in the field. Another study by Taibi et al. [9] discussed the increasing popularity and adoption of serverless architecture, its evolution, benefits, and challenges associated with this new cloud computing paradigm. However, to the best of our knowledge, no study empirically investigates why companies migrate to serverless architecture, how they refactor their legacy applications, and what technical and organizational challenges they face during migration to serverless.

To this end, we conducted 15 in-depth interviews with industrial practitioners from 11 organizations in different countries. All the practitioners were involved in the migration or development of serverless applications. Thus, the main objective of this study is to uncover the intentions of migrating applications to serverless, refactoring strategies, and technical and organizational challenges. Furthermore, we talked about 11 serverless-based systems, two being during migration, eight having migrated over the past two years and one greenfield development. The research question addressed in this study are:

RQ1: What are the intentions of migrating legacy applications to serverless architecture?
RQ2: What are the migration strategies that companies employ?
RQ3: What technical and organizational challenges do companies face during migration to serverless architecture?

The rest of paper is structured as follows: Sect. 2 covers related serverless work; Sect. 3 outlines our research method; Sect. 4 details the interview cases; Sect. 5 discusses results, and Sect. 6 concludes the study.

2 Related Work

Serverless computing represents a paradigm shift in the way applications are developed and deployed, eliminating the need to manage underlying infrastructure. The unique nature of this architecture has led researchers and practitioners to explore its facets, seeking to optimize it for future use. Existing studies have discussed different aspects of serverless computing, including architectural design, performance improvement, technological aspects, testing and debugging [10, 11], and empirical investigations.

For instance, Wen et al. [12] mined and manually analyzed 619 discussions from the stack overflow. The study finds the challenges that developers face when developing the serverless application. Our study is methodologically different from this as we analyzed the migration process of 11 systems by conducting 15 interviews from 11 organizations. We believe that developers do not fully share their migration experiences on these Q&A sites; instead, they share their problems and get feedback from community members.

Similarly, Eskandani and Salvaneschi [13] provided insight into the FaaS ecosystem by analyzing the 2k real-world open-source applications developed using a serverless platform. The study collected open-source applications from GitHub. The study explores aspects like the growth rate of serverless architecture, architectural design, and common use cases. Another similar study by Esimann et al. [14] revealed various aspects, including implementation, architecture, traffic patterns, and usage scenarios. The study is slightly different from Eskandani and Salvaneschi [13]. Both studies analyze the serverless open-source applications developed by the greenfield approach. These studies did not discuss the migration process to serverless, intentions, and technical and organizational challenges.

Taibi et al. [15] identified the bad practices among the practitioners while developing serverless applications and proposed a solution to those practices. They identified seven concerns, derived five bad practices, and proposed solutions to address them. Our work is completely different from this study as we investigated the migration process of legacy applications to serverless. Leitner et al. [16] conducted a mixed-method empirical study highlighting the need for a different mental model when adopting serverless and prevalent application patterns. However, the study did not investigate the migration processes. Moreover, the study was conducted in 2018, and since then serverless computing has evolved rapidly, and many companies have migrated their systems between 2019 to date [2]. To the best of our knowledge, no existing study investigated the serverless migration processes. This study explores migration processes by investigating the intention of migration, strategies, and challenges (technical and organizational) when migrating legacy applications to serverless.

3 Research Method

We employed a qualitative research method, specifically semi-structured interviews, to fulfill the objective of this study. Qualitative approaches aim to understand real-world situations, deal directly with complex issues, and are useful in answering "how" questions in the study [17]. The interviews were undertaken with industrial practitioners with recent experience developing or migrating their legacy applications to serverless.

3.1 Interviews

Interview Instruments: The semi-structured interview guide was developed based on the research questions following the guidelines of Robinson [18]. The interview guide covers demographic information, migration intentions, strategies followed during the migration, and technical and organizational challenges. All the authors were involved in developing the interview questions by conducting regular meetings. The interview guide can be found in our replication package [19].

Recruiting Participants: The first and third authors attended several technology innovation industrial meetups where companies participated to share their success stories. Both authors randomly contacted industrial practitioners and asked whether they employed serverless computing in their industry. In addition, the second author contacted the targeted population by leveraging social media platforms (e.g., LinkedIn, ResearchGate, Facebook). A total of 38 participants were contacted, of which 15 were selected for the interview. We adopted a defined set of acceptance criteria for selecting our interviewees and case organizations. Mainly, our participants are (a) professionals in software engineering who (b) have either participated in or closely observed a serverless migration project within their professional scope.

We shared the interview script with the practitioners beforehand to familiarize them with the study. The interviewees were informed that ethical standards would be maintained by ensuring the confidentiality of their recordings and transcriptions. We interviewed 15 professionals from 4 countries (Finland, The Netherlands, UAE, and Pakistan) that have worked at medium to large companies in different business domains. The first author conducted all the interviews online using Zoom and Microsoft Teams platforms. The interviews lasted for ~40 to ~55 min on average. The recorded interviews were transcribed for further analysis. However, we omitted the interview transcripts from the replication package to ensure confidentiality [19].

3.2 Data Analysis

This study used a thematic analysis approach to identify, analyze, and report the findings [20]. The thematic analysis enabled us to identify motivations, strategies, and challenges subsequently mapped into themes. We utilized NVivo qualitative data analysis tool to identify and categorize the codes into themes. Initially, we meticulously read the interview transcriptions and made observational notes without establishing codes. After familiarization, we began coding the transcriptions, subsequently scrutinizing, and categorizing the resultant codes under main themes. The main themes were intentions, strategies, and technical and organizational challenges. The coding part was revisited repeatedly, and statements with similar meanings but different phrasing were connected (Fig. 1).

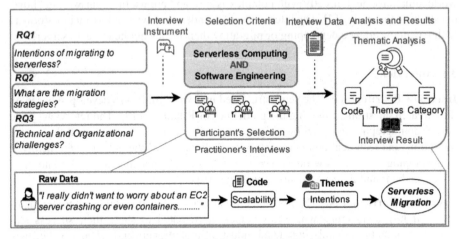

Fig. 1. Overview of the research methodology

4   Interview Case Descriptions

In this section, we describe the interview cases of systems that have been migrated to serverless or developed greenfield. To understand the systems, we only selected the participants involved in the migration process or development. All the interview participants were professional in their technical roles (e.g., lead engineer, architect, software engineer) with significant experience in the software industry and a minimum of 2 years of experience in serverless. We also interviewed participants having managerial roles in their organization to understand the organizational changes that happened due to the migration to serverless. We recruited participants from multiple countries (Finland, The Netherlands, UAE, and Pakistan) to generalize the study results. The detail of participating companies (C1–C11) of different sizes and domains are shown in Table 1. Altogether we investigated 11 systems with 15 practitioners from 11 organizations. We have presented all the migration intentions, strategies, and technical and organizational challenges reported in the interviews in our replication package [19]. However, due to the page limitation, we only present the most common intentions, strategies, and challenges in this paper. The details of the systems are discussed in the following case descriptions based on the interviews.

C1-S1 Logistic Management System: C1 is a large-scale enterprise providing logistic services such as mail and parcel delivery and e-commerce solutions at domestic and international levels. The has big monolithic systems to handle logistic services with physical servers. The company realized that running data centers and managing servers and operations were not aligned with its core business. It spent lots of time managing underlying infrastructure rather than focusing on business logic. Similarly, the system faced scalability, flexibility, and high-cost issues due to the high request volume, mainly in the peak season. According to P1, *"we leveraged the serverless computing as we are determined to enhance our operational efficiency, elevate customer experiences, and faster release to the market"*. The company closely analyzed the nature of the system as it was responding to several internal and external events as P1 stated *"So, a consumer might want to send a parcel and they register that parcel with one of our APIs that is an event parcel registered then we pick it up with the van and that's an event parcel picked up[...] you can think of a million other events in that system. So, personnel should build an event driven application landscape because it's the best fit to our business"*. They extracted the functionality using the bounded context of the domain-driven approach and decomposed it into more granular microservices. This allowed them to isolate and manage different functionalities independently. Following the strangler pattern approach, they gradually migrated the system to the serverless. However, they faced testing the event-driven architecture challenging due to the distributed nature of applications and the difficulty in estimating functional timeouts for long event-driven chains. Furthermore, implementing schema validation and versioning in a distributed, event-driven system, integrating with the legacy system *"Somebody has had to make a plan on where it's going and where it needs to be and which [...]"* appeared as a challenge. However, they apply contract testing, unit, integration, service, and end-to-end testing depending on the need of use case. Among organizations, changing the mindset is challenging for existing developers *"Well, there's a lot of organization and a lot of cultures that you need to build around serverless"*. However, P1 stated that migrating to serverless significantly reduced their operational overhead, improved scalability, led to faster time to market and reduced cost.

C2-S2 Financial Service Management: The company offers a Software as a Service (SaaS) system for banks, asset managers, and other financial institutions to handle savings, current accounts, loans, mortgages, and investment products. The system can be integrated with a bank's existing systems through APIs to use its services. Initially, the system was a monolithic system hosted on AWS EC2. However, the system faced scalability issues and released new features to the market due to massive access through the API. To mitigate this, they initially understood that the nature of the system is event-driven, so the serverless architecture would be the best option in their case. They migrated their monolithic systems to monolithic Lambda using lift and shift approach as P2 stated, *"So, what we did is slowly transition to Lambda and Fargate for massive workload. [...], I think it's called shift and lift. Essentially this approach embeds a whole Web API within a Lambda [...]"*. The company soon realized that having a single lambda function to handle all the operation makes the system more complex to manage. However, they migrated using strangler pattern by understanding the function domain.

Furthermore, to handle substantial workloads that exceeded the service limitations of the platform, such as memory and timeout constraints, they employed a combination of Lambda functions and serverless containers (AWS Fargate) approach. The system faces several technical challenges, such as integration to an existing system, event contract validation, maintaining events order, and cold start due to the tech stack, such as .Net. Due to performance issues of other programming languages, they decided to use JavaScript and Python. They faced organizational challenges such as regulatory compliance, learning new technologies, and serverless mindset. However, migration to serverless improved scalability, faster time to market, and reduced cost.

Table 1. Company and participants demographics

Comp*	Domain	Emp*	Par*	P.Role	Exp* (Ser*)	ID
C1	Logistics services	37365	P1	Architect	18(5)	S1
C2	Financial Services	17500	P2	Lead Engineer	13(4)	S2
C3	E-commerce	15000	P3	Architect	16(5)	S3
C4	Web Services	14500	P4	Architect	9(3)	S4
C5	E-commerce	9500	P5	Architect	13(5)	S5
C6	E-commerce	700	P6 P7	Developer Lead Engineer	8(3) 12(4.5)	S6
C7	Financial Services	536	P8	Architect	15(4)	S7
C8	Consultancy	20	P9 P10	Lead Engineer Architect	5(2) 10(4)	S8
C9	AI & Security Services	300	P11	Software Engineer	5(2)	S9
C10	Financial Services	280	P12 P13	Team Manager Developer	5(2) 4(3)	S10
C11	Media Services	350	P14 P15	Software Engineer Architect	6(2) 12(3)	S11

C3-S3 E-commerce: The company provides e-commerce services mainly for ordering food and grocery items. Initially, the company had a big monolithic system that faced, scalability issues in the peak seasons as their traffic was unpredictable, faster time to market, and high operation overhead (e.g., managing EC2 instances). The P3 stated that *"We were determined to build something that we could own and iterate on quickly. However, there was a specific part of the system that concerned me regarding scalability. [...] EC2 server crashing or managing containers and similar backend complexities"*. They decided to identify the main functions of their system using domain driven design and gradually migrated functionalities to serverless 'strangler pattern'. *"Our strategy closely follows the 'strangler pattern,' where we begin with a low-risk component and then gradually tackle other parts of the system [...]"*. They identified the low-risk components and migrated to serverless, eventually continuing to mission-critical components upon success. The company decided to go with the serverless-first mindset for all the new applications and rewriting some of the existing tools *"is a system we designed to* *supplant any of these older ETL tools"*. They faced various technical challenges such as lack of standardization, platform constraints (memory or timeout), and organizational challenges like hiring serverless experts. However, migration to a serverless improved the scalability, reduced operational overhead, and cost.

C4-S4 Pitch Decker: The company helps other startups with various aspects, such as pitching to investors and getting up and running the startups. Initially, they used AWS EC2 instances for hosting but encountered scalability and maintenance issues. They then switched to Elastic Beanstalk, which offered some scalability features. However, as the system grew, the scalability issue raised, so they embraced serverless architectures as P4 stated, *"that initially got us up and running, but we soon encountered issues with scalability and server maintenance, which became a significant hassle"*. The company tested components with serverless and rewrote their application. They leveraged GraphQL and GraphQL Federation to distribute the backend logic across different microservices. However, complex workflow orchestration, testing, and debugging became challenging for the organization.

C5-S5 Online Real Estate System: An intelligent home decision system that aims to help people determine the value of their homes, find their next place, and sell their current homes. Initially, the system was built monolithic but faced the scalability issues stated by P5 *"as the company grew and the volume of data it handled increased; it became clear that a more scalable, flexible solution was needed"*. Then the company explored the possibility of serverless architecture and gradually migrated to new technology. P5 stated, *"The transition to serverless was not an overnight change but a gradual process. we started by experimenting with AWS Lambda for small, non-critical tasks [...] the company began to shift more of its operations to serverless platforms"*. They face integrating the new system with its legacy one as a main pain point, *"having serverless side by side to legacy systems for example or to non-serverless systems for example is always a bit of a tricky"*. The migration improved the scalability, performance, and reduced the operational overhead *"The move not only improved scalability and performance but also reduced operational costs and complexity"*.

C6-S6 E-commerce: The company specializes in providing custom apparel and accessories to their customers, where they can design their own t-shirts, sweatshirts, and other items using the design tools. The company was facing the high cost of managing the servers and scalability issues as they received unpredictable workloads during and of seasonal time; stated by P6, *"we needed to transition to a more performant, scalable system, where scaling up EC2 instances was no longer a constant requirement"*. To this end, the company started exploring more scalable solutions. Initially, they did a lift and shift to cloud *"around three or four years ago, when we undertook our significant lift-and-shift migration into the cloud"* and then gradually migrating to serverless *"I've gradually been adopting and learning serverless techniques to optimize many of our more demanding workloads, particularly those under stress as we begin extracting them from larger applications"*. According to P6, *"it has always been good for us to start with monolithic serverless application and then gradually migrating to microservices serverless"*. From microservices they identified the use cases to be migrated to serverless *there's never a single approach, and I tend to favor small apps over monoliths, breaking things up only when business success indicates the need to do so"*. However, the system faces technical challenges such as testing system, event validations, integration to legacy application stated by P7: *"....and then, how did that kind of integrate back into the rest of the application"*. Similarly, changing the mindset of existing developers has seen significant organizational challenges. The application is still transitioning to be fully serverless, saving up to 90% of running application cost by improving scalability.

C7-S7 Financial Services Provider: The system provides financial services, including life and non-life insurance, retirement services, investments, and banking, to individual, corporate, and institutional clients. Their main intention was to make their system more secure, reliable, scalable, and performance *"you know, in this financial industry, it is important to take care of the data of our customers, make sure that we don't lose them, that they can always access their data when they need it. So, reliability super important performance is important"*. The system is still in migration process toward embracing fully serverless. According to P8, they tried new functions building with serverless first mindset *"We started in 2019 and started playing around with serverless with just one or two teams trying things out, but now we already have with it 20 to 25 teams actively using serverless. We are pretty much, you know, Serverless first and trying to do as much serverless as possible"*. They gradually migrated legacy systems to serverless by decomposing and testing the functionalities with serverless. Their main challenge was identifying the use case that can be migrated to serverless and enabling their existing team to adopt serverless architecture. Integrating with the existing system and evaluating the different tech stacks for better performance is also challenging. However, embracing and migrating to serverless has reduced cost, time to market, and operational overhead.

C8-S8 Reinsurance System: The small size company provides consultancy to other companies that tend to do greenfield development and migrate their legacy systems to serverless architecture as stated by P9: *"The projects we undertake are mostly greenfield developments, while a significant portion involves migrating large, legacy workloads to serverless platforms"*. The company recently migrated a system that provides reinsurance and insurance services, focusing on risk management and quick claim settlements. The system also creates investment opportunities aligning with their risk selection and portfolio management capabilities. The system was developed on-premises and does high performances computing problems by doing a lot of statistical modeling jobs. The system was growing fast, and it tended to improve its scalability. The existing system was taking hours to compute the business functionalities, as stated by P10: *"When we were in a position where like they were running on-prem their workload was taking quite a long time to run, but their business was growing. So, they're really talking about massive scale that are on prem servers wouldn't really handle"*. So, initially, the company started with an approach called lift and shift to migrate the workload to AWS. The company analyzed the use cases of the system and identified the domains of the system, and gradually migrated it to serverless. They faced technical challenges such as a lake of serverless job scheduling services for managing highly intensive computing, concurrency issues, debugging, and distributed logging and tracing. To mitigate these, they built several local tools. The migration to serverless architecture resulted in several benefits, including running roll-ups in under an hour, increased scalability with no limits on the number of runs, reduced code base by about 70%, improved cost efficiency, and decreased operational overhead.

C9-S9 Smart Mobility System: The startup company developed the smart mobility data generation system. This system involves collecting data from mobile phones and sending it to the startup's backend infrastructure. The startup wants to develop a system where they reduce the cost of the system and manage the underlying infrastructure, as stated by P11: *"The need for scalability and flexibility in their operations was paramount. We want to get rid of like the time we spent on managing servers"*. The company evaluated that the nature of its system is event-driven and will grow exponentially, so it decided to go with a serverless first mindset. They initially developed the monolithic serverless system. As the monolithic system reached complexity, they migrated to microservices serverless to reduce the system's complexity. They decomposed the system using a domain-driven design approach and delegating the Lambda microservices by teams. However, the startup faces the testing and debugging of an event-driven application challenging. The application solved the scalability and cost issues by embracing serverless.

C10-S10 Financial Services Management: The system provides bookkeeping, invoicing, and banking functions, enabling small and medium-sized businesses to streamline their financial operations and improve overall business functions. Initially, they had a big monolithic system that handled all the operations. However, over time, the system started facing scalability issues and reduced time to market for new features. The system is still in transition from monolithic to microservices. They initially evaluated the uses cases that were best suitable for serverless and rewrote the entire use case as stated by P12: *"We are basically rewriting some parts of our system. We are of course trying not to directly, you know, cut out pieces, but moreover rethinking of serverless"*. The new use cases are then integrated with the system through API. The company rethinks the purpose of the new features and works on them separately to ensure smooth integration with the current infrastructure.

Furthermore, they utilized the Fargate and Lambda as a combination for massive workloads. Testing and integrating with existing systems are noted as significant challenges. The adoption of serverless reduced operational overhead, improved scalability, and the ability to focus on business logic rather than infrastructure management.

C11-S11 Digital Media Services: The company provides several media services, including television, radio, and digital media. Among many applications, the digital media services system distributes formats and content to other media companies and social media platforms. Initially, the system was developed using a monolithic approach on EC2 machines. Sooner, the system started facing scalability issues as the number of users increased stated by P14: *"The problem at that time was that the team was constantly firefighting the system. It couldn't scale, and every time we adjusted something, it would break something else in the distributed monolithic world"*. They started evaluating the use cases and ended up with serverless. The company gradually migrate to serverless using strangler pattern P15: *"We employ the strangler pattern, incrementally replacing components of the legacy system with a serverless model, aiming to complete the transition within a six-month timeframe."* Serverless architecture greatly helped them by simplifying rules, designing functions with single responsibilities, and improving flow with Step Functions. The main challenge was to migrate the data from the existing monolithic database to microservices. Instead of rewriting the entire system, they updated the legacy system to emit events; when some change happens to the database, it emits the event and stores the events in the new database. This way, they migrated the database. They gradually created parallel microservices to handle specific functionalities previously performed by the monolith. Over time, they redirected requests from the monolith to the new microservices, repeating the process gradually. However, migrating to serverless reduced the cost significantly. The team experienced significant speed improvements, delivering features in weeks rather than months, with reduced bugs and improved testing practices.

5 Results and Discussion

This section describes the aggregated results of our study. All the results of our research questions are presented in Fig. 2. We only presented the common findings in more than two systems. However, all the findings from the participants and migration cases are presented in our replication package [19].

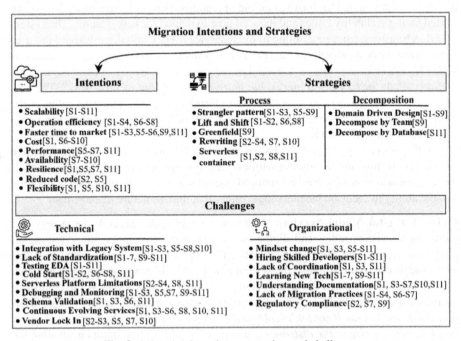

Fig. 2. Migration intentions, strategies, and challenges

5.1   Migration Intentions (RQ1)

The Fig. 2 presents the intention to migrate systems, strategies, and challenges (technical and organizational) to a serverless architecture.

Drivers for Migrating Legacy Systems: Our study reveals that large-scale enterprise systems face scalability issues. Participants (P3, P6, P8, P9, P11, P12, P13) stated that their systems were receiving unpredictable traffics, mainly on seasonal days, causing delays in response. They spent most of the time provisioning the underlying infrastructure rather than focusing on the business logic. This leads them to migrate to serverless architecture *"We were determined to build something that we could own and iterate on quickly. However, there was a specific part of the system that concerned me regarding scalability. I didn't want to have to worry about issues like an EC2 server crashing or managing containers and similar backend complexities"*. Apart from these, the companies were facing issues such as a lack of system overview (P1), downtime during updates (P13), and costly changes (P15).

Similarly, time to market was the main driver for most of the large-scale organizations. New features take over 6 months for several organizations to go into production. However, for small-scale organizations, the main driver for adopting serverless is to reduce the cost and operational overhead. Participant P4 stated: *"I had my own startup where every dollar counted"*. Apart from these main drivers of migrating the legacy system to serverless, (P3) resilience, (P5) reliability, (P2) flexibility, (P6, P7) performance, (P9, P10) reduced code base and increased agility, (P12, P13) maintainability are considered the main drivers for migrating legacy system to serverless architecture.

5.2   Migration Strategies and Decomposition (RQ2)

The prevalent migration strategy in our investigated systems was identifying the use case that had the best fit to the serverless. Seven participants identified that their systems have an event-driven nature and has unpredictable workloads. They extracted the use cases from the existing system, built and tested it with a serverless system, and integrated it with the legacy system. This process leads them to gradually migrate their entire system to serverless using strangler pattern as in P5: *"We started in 2019 and started playing around with serverless with just one or two teams trying things out, but now we already have with it 20 to 25 teams actively using serverless"*. All the interviewed participants stated that they built new functionality with the serverless first mindset and integrated it with the legacy system. They were more focused on developing new projects with the serverless first mind set.

Furthermore, we investigated two high-computing systems doing a lot of statistical computation. The systems were not the best fit for serverless due to the resource limitations of serverless platforms. Thus, they used a combination of serverless and containers to compute the massive workload *"So, we used Fargate for long-running massive workloads due to its improved scalability characteristics. On the other hands, Lambda was used for near real-time analytics where quick response times was crucial"*. Five participants were involved in rewriting the existing functionality with serverless architecture.

Similarly, four participants said they made a lift and shift approach from on-premises to cloud serverless. One system was developed with a greenfield development approach where the participant predicted that their system would receive a high workload in the coming years, and they wanted to reduce the cost and time of managing the underlying infrastructure. Companies start with monolithic lambda functions for greenfield projects to offer the application's functionalities. However, the complexity of managing monolithic functions increases as the function grows. Therefore, the best practice is to identify and split the monolithic serverless to serverless microservices, as reported by participants. Most of the systems were migrated in two years, and new functionality was released in hours.

For the migrated system to serverless architecture, identifying the use case and boundaries of the services was challenging for many companies. Nine out of eleven companies adopted the domain-driven design approach for identifying the boundaries and splitting it into Lambda microservices. Two companies decomposed their systems based on database complexity or API integration. One system decomposed the system by teams. The participant revealed that there are no automatic tools to identify the use cases and boundaries from existing systems.

5.3 Challenges (RQ3)

The third section of the figure presents the technical and organizational challenges companies face when migrating their legacy systems to a serverless architecture.

Technical Challenges: The migration journey poses several technical challenges. Identifying the use cases best fit for the serverless architecture and splitting the system was challenging for organizations. Furthermore, integration with legacy systems is reported as a significant challenge. P5 stated, *"If you want Greenfield, then take this toolbox and go ahead. But now we also have lots of like legacy bits in our system [......] to integrate all these systems is a technical challenge"*. Similarly, lack of standardization, testing event-driven architecture, validating the events, building the central event broker, and managing different accounts are also prevalent challenges.

Furthermore, financial systems are more concerned with vendor lock-in problems due to regulatory compliance. Companies utilizing the old tech stack are more prone to face performance issues due to the cold start problem of serverless. Programming languages like Java, Python, and Typescript hold fewer cold start problem than other languages such as C# and .Net. Therefore, choosing the right tech stack is becoming challenging for organizations that are using old programming languages, i.e., C#, .Net. Moreover, handling the long-running process becomes a challenge due to serverless platforms' resource and time limitations. Most organizations built a charter to standardize the use of technology stack. They standardize around dev, test, and observability *"We standardized around a dev, test, acceptance, and production workflow and currently, we're looking at standardizing around observability tooling"*.

Organizational Challenges: Our study revealed that organizations face several changes when migrating their legacy systems to serverless. The transition from traditional to more agile development needs a change in the organization's mindset. Convincing developers to develop the application serverless is sometimes challenging as they are stuck to the traditional way of development, as stated by P4: *"You know, this served as the first mindset, partly because it's really difficult to get buying from so many developers who are used to building things traditionally"*. To convince more developers to adopt serverless, the serverless evangelist started testing new components with a few team members and presented the success within other teams of the project *"first year, we were tasked with doing all of these corporate startup projects and we did something around 10 to 20 projects with serverless first mindset, we started in a very small corner of our company in innovation and then we presented the success with others"*. Some organizations hire serverless evangelists and develop a serverless implementation guide to follow the process. Learning new technology and enabling ops mindset in the development team for serverless is also challenging for many organizations *"So really bringing the DevOps mentality that you build it, you run it in team is challenging"*. For this, organizations encourage attending serverless workshops, taking courses, and participating in serverless success stories. Furthermore, hiring skilled serverless developer (P1–P13), lack of understanding the platform documentations (P3, P6, P7, P9, P13), lack of existing migration practices (P1, P3, P6, P7, P9, P15) and lack of coordination (P2, P4, P11) also seen as a challenge in the organizations.

6 Threat to Validity

Several potential threats could impact the validity of the results of this study. These threats are typically categorized into four primary categories: internal validity, construct validity, external validity, and conclusion validity [21].

Internal Validity: refers to the degree to which specific factors influence methodological robustness. The first threat to this study is the understanding of the interview questions by participants. We mitigated this threat by conducting the pilot interviews with other professionals of our contacts and by sharing the questions beforehand to ensure the interview questions' understandability and readability. Only participants having knowledge of the migration process or serverless greenfield projects are included in the final interviews.

Construct Validity: refers to the degree to which the research constructs are adequately substantiated and interpreted. The core constructs are the interview participants' viewpoints on the migration or adoption of serverless technology and the associated challenges in the context of this study. The verifiability of the construct is considered the limitation of qualitative studies. Therefore, we followed a rigorous and step-by-step research method process and gave examples in quotations from the collected data (e.g., interviews). This shows how a well-planned research process and the findings we reported (RQ1, RQ2, RQ3) help prove the verifiability of the study construct.

External validity refers to generalizing the conducted study to another context. The sample size and sampling approach in the study may not allow generalizing the findings. Also, serverless architecture and migration of the legacy applications to serverless is not yet well established in practice. Therefore, finding a large sample was challenging to us. However, we mitigated this threat by using all possible sources to find the potential population. We collected data from 4 countries across two continents from participants with diverse experience in various industrial domains. In the future, we plan to extend our study findings by mining the Q&A platforms and conducting industrial surveys and interviews.

Conclusion Validity: refers to the factors that impact the trustworthiness of the study conclusion. To mitigate this threat, all the authors conducted weekly meetings to develop the interview instruments and data analysis process. The first author conducted the interviews via Zoom and Microsoft Teams. All other authors reviewed the data and provided feedback to improve the analysis. Finally, all the authors conducted a brainstorming session to draw the findings and conclusion of this study.

7   Conclusion and Future Work

In this study, we investigated 11 systems from 11 organizations by conducting interviews with 15 participants having diverse professional experiences in various domains. We mainly investigated intentions, strategies, and challenges (technical and organizational) during migrating legacy applications to serverless. The results revealed scalability was the main challenge for large-scale enterprises due to unpredictable traffic. They were spending much of the time managing underlying infrastructure rather than focusing on the business logic, which hindered them from releasing features faster in production. On the other hand, smaller organizations tended to reduce the cost and operational overhead.

The study revealed that most systems were migrated gradually using strangler patterns to serverless, while new components were developed with a serverless first mindset. However, legacy monolithic systems were decomposed into microservices and migrated to serverless by applying domain driven design approach, decomposition by database, and decomposition by teams. Integration into the existing system, testing event-driven architecture, and validating the event schema were reported as the main technical challenge. The organizations face severe mindset changes of existing developers toward the new technology, hiring the serverless evangelist, and lack of existing migration practices as the main organizational challenge during migration.

In future work, we plan to expand our research to various industry domains to uncover more practical challenges and solutions related to serverless migration. We also aspire to holistically chart the decision-making process on all the dimensions of migration to serverless. Furthermore, we will develop a multicriteria decision-making (MCDM) framework for platform selection in the industry.

References

1. Jonas, E., et al.: Cloud programming simplified: a Berkeley view on serverless computing. arXiv preprint arXiv:1902.03383 (2019)
2. Datadog: The state of serverless (2022). https://www.datadoghq.com/state-of-serverless/. Accessed 12 July 2023
3. Katie Costello: The CIO's guide to serverless computing. Accessed 12 July 2023. https://www.gartner.com/smarterwithgartner/the-cios-guide-to-serverless-computing

4. Hamza, M.: Software architecture design of a serverless system. In: Proceedings of the 27th International Conference on Evaluation and Assessment in Software Engineering, pp. 304–306 (2023)
5. Yussupov, V., Breitenbücher, U., Leymann, F., Wurster, M.: A systematic mapping study on engineering function-as-a-service platforms and tools. In: Proceedings of the 12th IEEE/ACM International Conference on Utility and Cloud Computing, pp. 229–240 (2019)
6. Lin, C., Khazaei, H.: Modeling and optimization of performance and cost of serverless applications. IEEE Trans. Parallel Distrib. Syst. **32**(3), 615–632 (2020)
7. Taibi, D., El Ioini, N., Pahl, C., Niederkofler, J.R.S.: Patterns for serverless functions (function-as-a-service): a multivocal literature review (2020)
8. Wen, J., Chen, Z., Jin, X., Liu, X.: Rise of the planet of serverless computing: a systematic review. ACM Trans. Softw. Eng. Methodol. **32**, 1–61 (2023)
9. Taibi, D., Spillner, J., Wawruch, K.: Serverless computing-where are we now, and where are we heading? IEEE Softw. **38**(1), 25–31 (2020)
10. Lenarduzzi, V., Panichella, A.: Serverless testing: tool vendors' and experts' points of view. IEEE Softw. **38**(1), 54–60 (2020)
11. Rinta-Jaskari, E., Allen, C., Meghla, T., Taibi, D.: Testing approaches and tools for AWS lambda serverless-based applications. In: 2022 IEEE International Conference on Pervasive Computing and Communications Workshops and other Affiliated Events (PerCom Workshops), pp. 686–692. IEEE (2022)
12. Wen, J., et al.: An empirical study on challenges of application development in serverless computing. In: Proceedings of the 29th ACM Joint Meeting on European Software Engineering Conference and Symposium on the Foundations of Software Engineering, pp. 416–428 (2021)
13. Eskandani, N., Salvaneschi, G.: The uphill journey of FaaS in the open-source community. J. Syst. Softw. **198**, 111589 (2023)
14. Eismann, S., et al.: The state of serverless applications: collection, characterization, and community consensus. IEEE Trans. Software Eng. **48**(10), 4152–4166 (2021)
15. Taibi, D., Kehoe, B., Poccia, D.: Serverless: from bad practices to good solutions. In: 2022 IEEE International Conference on Service-Oriented System Engineering (SOSE), pp. 85–92. IEEE (2022)
16. Leitner, P., Wittern, E., Spillner, J., Hummer, W.: A mixed-method empirical study of Function-as-a-Service software development in industrial practice. J. Syst. Softw. **149**, 340–359 (2019)
17. Benbasat, I., Goldstein, D.K., Mead, M.: The case research strategy in studies of information systems. MIS Q. **11**, 369–386 (1987)
18. Robinson, O.C.: Sampling in interview-based qualitative research: a theoretical and practical guide. Qual. Res. Psychol. **11**(1), 25–41 (2014)
19. The Journey to Serverless Migration: An Empirical Analysis of Intentions, Strategies, and Challenges. Zenodo (2023). https://doi.org/10.5281/zenodo.8233478
20. Braun, V., Clarke, V.: Using thematic analysis in psychology. Qual. Res. Psychol. **3**(2), 77–101 (2006)
21. Zhou, X., Jin, Y., Zhang, H., Li, S., Huang, X.: A map of threats to validity of systematic literature reviews in software engineering. In: 2016 23rd Asia-Pacific Software Engineering Conference (APSEC), pp. 153–160. IEEE (2016)

On the Role of Font Formats in Building Efficient Web Applications

Benedikt Dornauer[1,2]([envelope]) [ORCID], Wolfgang Vigl[1] [ORCID], and Michael Felderer[1,2,3] [ORCID]

[1] University of Innsbruck, 6020 Innsbruck, Austria
{benedikt.dornauer,wolfgang.vigl}@uibk.ac.at
[2] University of Cologne, 50923 Cologne, Germany
[3] German Aerospace Center (DLR), Institute for Software Technology,
51147 Cologne, Germany
michael.felderer@dlr.de

Abstract. The success of a web application is closely linked to its performance, which positively impacts user satisfaction and contributes to energy-saving efforts. Among the various optimization techniques, one specific subject focuses on improving the utilization of web fonts. This study investigates the impact of different font formats on client-side resource consumption, such as CPU, memory, load time, and energy. In a controlled experiment, we evaluate performance metrics using the four font formats: OTF, TTF, WOFF, and WOFF2. The results of the study show that there are significant differences between all pair-wise format comparisons regarding all performance metrics. Overall, WOFF2 performs best, except in terms of memory allocation. Through the study and examination of literature, this research contributes (1) an overview of methodologies to enhance web performance through font utilization, (2) a specific exploration of the four prevalent font formats in an experimental setup, and (3) practical recommendations for scientific professionals and practitioners.

Keywords: front-end development · font formats · web typography · performance evaluation · energy-efficiency

1 Introduction

To ensure the success of websites and achieve optimal user satisfaction, it is crucial to consider usability and various other design criteria [31,34]. According to Took [40], users' interaction with websites with a higher-than-normal user experience was significantly associated with improved web performance. The importance of performance was also stated by Google's March 2016 data showing that more than half of mobile site visits are abandoned if the site takes longer than three seconds to load [1]. Besides that, improving performance also contributes to energy-saving efforts, reducing the time and resources required for rendering and displaying content [36]. Consequently, comprehensive research is in progress

© The Author(s), under exclusive license to Springer Nature Switzerland AG 2024
R. Kadgien et al. (Eds.): PROFES 2023, LNCS 14483, pp. 116–131, 2024.
https://doi.org/10.1007/978-3-031-49266-2_8

to enhance the efficiency of web applications with different approaches, including specific considerations related to the utilization of fonts.

In an article from 2022, Google experts Hempenius and Pollard [18] explore the potential performance enhancements of different web page font settings. They identify potential bottlenecks for web performance and provide insights into mitigation opportunities. One of their mentioned bottlenecks was the improper choice of suitable font formats.

Usually, fonts are utilized in computer systems and other text presentation systems to represent glyphs visually. Most computers have various fonts available preinstalled for creating documents and graphics. This availability and flexibility of fonts are the culmination of over three decades of gradual advancements in computer font science [45]. Nowadays, fonts also play a pivotal role in impactful web designs, as font features convey feelings and reactions that text alone cannot achieve. Hence, fonts are often chosen that match the corporate design [39].

Unfortunately, these specific font styles are often not preinstalled on the devices by default [46]. In order to solve this requirement (using a non-standard font), web developers use a @font-face declaration in Cascading Style Sheet (CSS) file to declare the new fonts. The declaration also includes an URL to the online font-file resource (e.g., Google Fonts), a file holding information about the specific custom font [32].

Among the various font file formats, the predominant options encompass the system font formats, TrueType Font (TTF) and OpenType Font (OTF), as well as the web font formats, Web Open Font Format (WOFF) and its second generation WOFF2. Most of web browsers widely support TTF, OTF, and WOFF, whereas WOFF2 is comparatively supported only by newer browser versions. TTF and OTF hold particular significance due to their extensive availability, serving as standard font formats developed by Adobe, Microsoft, and Apple. While TTF and OTF are font formats designed for system fonts, WOFF and the newer version WOFF2 are web fonts optimized for loading from a web server. WOFF is a container format that embeds TrueType or OpenType fonts and compresses them. The second version of WOFF can show a significantly reduced file size, according to Buhler et al. [6]. Following the transmission of web fonts to the client, the browser undertakes data decompression to facilitate font loading and display. Although the diminished file size contributes to decreased transfer time, this advantage is anticipated to be accompanied by heightened CPU and memory utilization [22,33].

This study investigates how the choice of font format in web applications affects the client's device performance. Therefore, we conducted a benchmark experiment to investigate the effects during the loading of web content of **different font formats (independent variable)** on the **clients' performance-related metrics (dependent variable)**. Therefore, the research question is:

[RQ] How do different web font formats compare in terms of their impact on performance improvement in web applications?

In order to evaluate the performance-related metrics, the following null-hypothesis are defined:

H_1 The font format does not influence the required **Document Loading Time**.
H_2 The font format does not affect the **Processor Cycles**.
H_3 The font format does not impact the **Allocated Amount of Memory**.
H_4 The font format overall does not influences the **Energy Consumption**.

After providing the necessary context and motivation for this experiment, the subsequent sections of this paper are organized as follows. Section 2 provides background information on font optimization techniques and related work, including grey literature. Section 3 describes the conducted methodology. Subsequently, in Sect. 4, the implications of these findings are then discussed in Sect. 5 and followed by Sect. 6, which addresses study limitations and potential Threats to Validity. Finally, Sect. 7 concludes the overall study.

2   Related Work

Prior studies on web font optimization have followed two distinct methods. The first perspective focuses on identifying improved visual representations that enhance task performance, promote better text comprehension, and ultimately increase user satisfaction (Sect. 2.1 *Aesthetic Optimization*). The second viewpoint revolves around optimizing computational performance, such as by reducing the load time, which is the perspective that is considered mainly in this paper (Sect. 2.2 *Performance Optimization*).

2.1   Aesthetic Optimization

Ling et al. [26] have presented the results of two experiments in which the influence of font and line length on several task performance and subjective measures was investigated. The authors showed that the effect of line length was significant on performance, but the effect of font type had an insignificant small impact.

Similarly, Bhatia et al. [4] have conducted a study to investigate the effects of font size, italics, and color count on three web usability dimensions: effectiveness, efficiency, and satisfaction. While the effectiveness and efficiency of the participants were measured via tasks, satisfaction was determined using a survey instrument. The study showed that font size and number of colors had no significant effect on any variable. However, using italics had a statistically significant effect on performance but not on efficiency and satisfaction.

In 2016, Rello et al. [35] examined the font size and line spacing in more detail regarding objective and subjective legibility and showed a continuous improvement in both up to a size of 18 points. From 22pt, there was again a decrease in subjective legibility. The effects of line spacing on objective legibility were insignificant, but participants indicated that their subjective legibility was impaired at extreme values (0.8 and 1.8). The authors summarized that increasing the font size is an efficient way to improve legibility.

2.2   Performance Optimization

Improving a web application's energy efficiency, related to many other performance metrics, requires a deep understanding of various optimization techniques. Therefore, for instance, Wagner [43] collated several performance improvement techniques that were also addressed in research. Such as optimizing CSS as well as JS content (e.g., [7]), tackling the problem of media-related optimization (e.g., [44]), considered different transmission protocols (e.g., [16]), covering design-effective aspects (e.g., [23]) and also mentioned the optimization of web fonts considering mainly the application layer of the Open Systems Interconnection model (OSI). Riet et al. [42] further advanced these techniques by incorporating some of them into a replicable performance engineering plan consisting of 13 interventions for the desktop and mobile web. Appropriating those to a sample case study showed significant performance improvement opportunities. One of those was "Intervention 10: Preload Fonts", also known as lazy-loading. Besides the papers mentioned above, we also reviewed some gray literature that described other font-related techniques, as follows:

Font Subsetting: It is a technique for reducing the size of a font file. Here, only the characters needed in a font file are selected, and the rest is discarded. One often-used example is subsetting a font by language, e.g., to provide a font with only Latin characters for English-language pages. Using this technique, the loading time of the fonts can be improved by more than 200% [43]. The widely used Google Web Fonts API is able to automatically create a subset for many font families by providing an additional attribute. There is also the possibility to create a subset specifically for custom purposes by modifying the file [2]. Last but not least, the CSS *unicode-range* property of a `@font-face` Definition specifies the characters for which, if any, the font is to be loaded [43].

Font Hosting: There are two ways to load fonts: Self-Hosting or Third-Party Hosting. While self-hosting stores the files on your own web server, third-party hosting uses a font service such as Google Fonts [28]. While using Third-Party-Hosting is generally considered easier, it requires additional communication with an external resource, resulting in a decreased loading speed and a dependency on the service provider [24].

Font Loading: Another option is using `<link rel="preload">` so that the font is not loaded when it is encountered in the external stylesheet but already when this tag appears. Another variant is to use the Font Loading API in the JavaScript code. This way, the process can be followed precisely, and user-defined steps can be initiated [15].

Font Rendering: The *font-display* CSS attribute determines what happens until the external font file is loaded: Should the browser wait until it is loaded or render the text in a fallback font? Besides these two options, there are others to choose from. The default behavior varies from browser to browser. The attribute affects the *Largest Contentful Paint*, the *First Contentful Paint*, and the stability of the layout [18].

General Optimizations: Furthermore, the use of general optimization strategies is often suggested, such as enabling client-side caching [15] or enabling server-side compression using algorithms such as GZIP or Brotli. The latter should only be used for TTF and OTF formats, as WOFF and WOFF2 already use built-in compression [21].

Many studies have been conducted, focusing on several aspects of performance improvement or improving the visual perception of fonts. However, we have not identified any scientific literature yet examining the performance of font formats in terms of several efficiency criteria. Also, the grey literature in this field has no benchmarking tests available. The present study attempts to fill this gap.

3   Experimental Methodology

To assess the influence of various font formats on the performance of web applications and address the research questions as well as the hypothesis (see Sect. 1), we have outlined the following proposed experimental framework, simplified in Fig. 1.

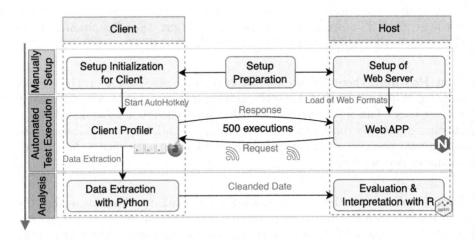

Fig. 1. Overview of experimental setup.

3.1   Environmental Setup

The web client (Windows 11; AMD Ryzen 5 5500, 32 GB) and web server (Ubuntu 22; i7-6700HQ, 16 GB) are hosted on two different machines inside the same Wireless Local Area Network (WLAN). The web server uses NGINX to handle the requests and deploy the web application containing the different web formats.

The web application consists of a single web page containing several headings together with textual paragraphs and a footer. In total, three different fonts are used as this is a common practice for designing interfaces [39]. The following combination, based on a selection of common Google Fonts, was selected:

- *Raleway Extrabold v3.000* for the headings,
- *SourceSans Regular v3.052* for the paragraphs, and
- *Montserrat Semibold v3.100* for the footer.

Each of the fonts is provided in each of the considered font formats: *True-Type Font (TTF)*, *OpenType Font (OTF)*, *Web Open Font Format Version 1.0 (WOFF)*, and *Web Open Font Format Version 2.0 (WOFF2)*. While all of the required formats of Montserrat are downloaded directly from the official Github repository [41], the repositories of Raleway [27] and SourceSans [19] did only provide TTF and OTF versions. For obtaining the WOFF and WOFF2 formats, which contain the same information as their counterparts, two prevalent NPM conversion tools *ttf2woff version 3.0.0* [37] and *ttf2woff2 version 5.0.0* [13] are used to convert from TTF to WOFF as well to WOFF2. Both packages claim over $150K$ weekly installations.

Performance measurements are subject to fluctuations on the client device due to other processes running on the same client machine. These processes have different resource consumption at different times. To mitigate this specific threat, some common practices [10] were considered. First, the client device is restarted before each bunch of repeated trials to minimize the influence of processes running and ensure the trials are independent. After the reboot, all heavy background processes are shut down, including collaboration tools, synchronization software, antivirus software that might perform arbitrary security scans, and background browser processes. These measures are intended to put the computer into a "low idle energy fluctuations" state before profiling is started.

3.2   Automated Test Execution

A total of 500 individual trials were conducted for each font format, wherein the resource consumption was meticulously profiled. To measure the performance of the web application, a commonly used tool was applied, the *Firefox Profiler* [12]. Specifically, the developmental version *Firefox Nightly* (version 115.0a1) is used, as memory usage analysis is only available in the respective Firefox Profiler. In this way, we were able to analyze and measure various performance metrics of the entire browser process or specific threads. It provides insights into CPU, memory, as well as energy consumption. This study did not consider other browsers, as they lack support for the aforementioned performance metrics.

The selected profiler takes samples at a desired interval and writes the result to a buffer, overwriting old values when complete. The sampling rate in this experiment was set to 0.5 ms, with a buffer size of 2 GiB. In addition, the following manual settings are applied to all experimental runs in order the retrieve the specific metrics: any additional threads have been disabled, Browser Cache deactivated, only CPU Utilization has been enabled in the "Features" section, and the experimental features "Process CPU Utilization" and "energy Use" have been switched on.

The repeated trials are conducted automatically using AutoHotkey [14]. The respective script launches Firefox Nightly, starts the Firefox Profiler, navigates to the web application, stops the Profiler, saves the result as JSON, and shuts down Firefox before the next run starts.

Some actions have been performed to minimize skewed results in the runs. Causes of such distortions include, for example, the Profiler recording the resource consumption of other processes and tasks or the runs influencing each other. For this reason, the following delays are built into the AutoHotkey script: an 8-second delay after Firefox Nightly is started and an 8-second delay after it is closed.

Each batch of runs, where each font is provided with the same format, is automatically profiled 500 times, and the results are used for evaluation.

3.3 Data Evaluation Process

The data provided by one run of the Firefox Profiler includes performance metrics, events, and other actions that happened during the recorded time frame. The Profiling was started before the request and stopped after it finished. While each metric covers the entire recorded period, only a fraction of that period is necessary for examining performance. To focus on the font acquisition process, including decoding, conversion, and display, the data series of each performance metric is trimmed accordingly. The starting point is determined by extracting the time in milliseconds when the "DOMContentLoaded" event occurs. This event indicates that the HTML file has been downloaded, parsed, and external resources are being fetched [29]. Similarly, the end time is determined by the millisecond timestamp when the *Load Event* is triggered. At this point, all resources, including fonts, have been successfully loaded and rendered [30].

The profile of one run provides many measurement values, specifically yielding information about the performance. Some of these metrics are expressed as related to a particular thread. This allows a targeted analysis of that specific thread in the browser process, which particularly processes the request to the test web application, and further excludes any values of other threads. However, other measurements, such as the energy consumption are provided per core and in total. When evaluating the performance, the metrics given in Table 1 are extracted using a Python script and considered in the evaluation.

Although a sampling rate of 0.5 ms was set, the distances between the individual samples are not always uniform. For this reason, the values are first converted to *per milliseconds* to allow for comparability. Subsequently, for each data

Table 1. Performance-related metrics overview.

Metric	Description	Unit
Load Time	The time in Milliseconds between the events *DOMContentLoaded* and *Load*.	Milliseconds [ms]
CPU Cycles	The Profiler's JSON output provides a data series for each thread, indicating the number of processor cycles required between each sampling point. For each run, the sum of this data series between the two events considered is extracted.	CPU Cycles [Count]
Average memory allocation changes	This metric provides the number of relative changes in the allocated memory. The size of the allocated memory at a given sampling point in time can be calculated by the cumulative sum of the changes. However, since an investigation of the performance is primarily concerned with the development of memory usage, absolute values are not required and the 10% trimmed mean of the series of relative values is sufficient for analysis.	MegaByte [MB]
Energy Consumption	The energy consumption provided by an implementation of RAPL (Running Average Power Limit) is used [17] and is specified in picowatt-hours by the Firefox Profiler. The sum of all data series values within the two events is considered.	Milli-Watt-hours [mWh]

series provided, only the values that lie within the desired observation period, i.e., between the two events, are considered.

Following this, a one-way ANOVA was used, along with the Tukey HSD post-hoc test, to assess the significance of differences in font formats for various hardware-related metrics. To meet ANOVA preconditions, both the Brown-Forsythe test for variance equality [5] and the Lilliefors-Test for normality testing [25] (with transformation using outlier exclusion by Tukey's Outer Fence and Box-Cox-Transformation mentioned by [20]) were conducted, combined with graphical interpretation. According to Blanca et al., the one-way ANOVA is relatively robust against violations of the normality assumption. Therefore, the transformation mentioned seems justifiable. For details, we point out the replication package published on Zenodo [11].

4 Results

The forthcoming analysis provides a comprehensive evaluation of hardware resource consumption, encompassing load times, processor cycles, memory allocations, and energy consumption. For each metric, the Brown-Forsythe test confirmed equal group variances among font formats, ensuring the validity of the homogeneity of variance assumption for one-way ANOVA. Additionally, the Kolmogorov-Smirnov-Lilliefors test verified the normality of the data.

Format	Load Time [ms]	Processor Cycles [Count]
otf	196.0 (189.1, 205.1)	32667944 (31923896, 33319052)
ttf	210.0 (203.5, 219.1)	32217562 (31500902, 32846721)
woff	172.0 (164.9, 180.1)	28661862 (28039596, 29193426)
woff2	161.5 (155.8, 169.3)	27888552 (27333156, 28507697)

Format	Memory Allocations [Mb]	Energy Consumption [mWh]
otf	2264.5 (1953.7, 2634.3)	3.13 (2.99, 3.26)
ttf	2727.5 (2306.4, 3152.3)	3.27 (3.15, 3.42)
woff	6235.8 (5157.0, 7540.5)	2.72 (2.57, 2.88)
woff2	5746.6 (4877.8, 6779.1)	2.59 (2.47, 2.73)

(a) Values given as: median(1st quartile, 3rd quartile)

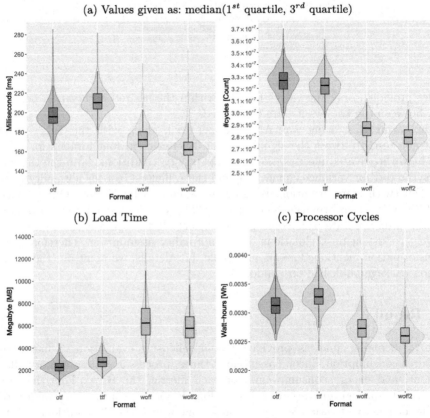

(b) Load Time

(c) Processor Cycles

(d) Average memory allocation changes

(e) Energy Consumption

Fig. 2. Comparison of performance metrics (b)–(d) across the four **web font formats**.

4.1 Load Times

First, a look at the differences in the length of the time frame between each of the font formats is provided. The length of this specifies how much time has been spent after the HTML has been parsed to download further, parse, and render external resources [29].

As illustrated in Fig. 2b, there are clear differences in the individual font formats considering the web page speed. TrueType Fonts had the lowest performance in terms of the speed at which the fonts are loaded, parsed, and rendered, with a median of 209 ms. OpenType fonts already had a slightly shorter length between the two window events considered, with a median of 195 ms. Fonts provided in the Web Open Font Formats were significantly faster in the analysis, with version one yielding a median of 171 ms and its extension WOFF2 showing the best performance with a median of 161 ms.

Also evident in Figs. 2b is the skewness of the distributions. The skewness of each format is positive, indicating a right-skewed distribution ranging from TrueType with a skewness of 1.11 to WOFF2 with a value of 1.95. These values suggest that more values on the upper end show a longer loading time than the median. Similarly, all four distributions show a positive kurtosis, ranging from 7.00 (TrueType) to 11.2 (WOFF), indicating leptokurtic distributions. This signalizes the required time between both events to contain more extreme outliers than a normal distribution, especially at the upper end.

The results of the one-way ANOVA revealed that there was a statistically significant difference in the document loading time between at least two formats $(F(3, 1996) = 1138, p < 2.2e^{-16})$. Thus, the null hypothesis H_0 can be rejected. A Tukey HSD test shows a significant difference $(p_{adj} = 0)$ between all pairwise format comparisons. With η^2 value (and partial η^2 value) equals 0.631, the effect size of format on load time is considered as high [8].

4.2   Processor Cycles

As a metric of resource consumption, the results of the processor cycles are presented. An overview of the sum of required processor cycles is shown in Fig. 2c. As illustrated, the variations depend on the font format. In terms of the required processor cycles, using WOFF2 results in the lowest CPU consumption, with a mean of 27.89 million cycles. The second-best performance was achieved by using the WOFF font format, with a median of 28.66 million cycles. This is followed by TrueType fonts (32.21 M) and OpenType fonts (32.67 M). With a correlation coefficient of 0.736, the correlation between the length of the time frame and the required processor cycles is high.

Considering the skewness of the processor cycles concerning the format, very symmetrical distributions are observed, as the values range from -0.064 (WOFF) to 0.177 (TrueType). Furthermore, the kurtosis of the distributions is similar to those of a normal distribution, as all values are within the range of 2.97 (WOFF) and 3.45 (OpenType).

The null hypothesis associated with H_2 can be rejected, stating that the format does not influence the processor utilization measured in the number of cycles required. The results revealed that there is a statistically significant difference in the processor cycles between at least two formats $(F(3, 1996) = 2903, p < 2.2e^{-16})$. The Tukey HSD test indicates that there are significant differences between all pairs $(p_{adj} = 0 < 0.01)$. According to the calculated η^2 value of 0.813, the effect size of the format on the processor cycles required is considered high [8].

4.3   Memory Allocation

The profiler results regarding the required memory allocations are presented. An overview of the relative changes to the allocated memory is shown in Fig. 2d. It is noted that the values provided are the 10% trimmed means of the relative memory allocation changes. The distribution of the metric differs depending on the format. While OpenType fonts and TrueType fonts show few additional memory allocations with medians of 2264 and 2728 allocated bytes, respectively, the web fonts have significantly more memory allocations with medians of 6236 (WOFF) and 5747 (WOFF2) allocated bytes.

The allocation of memory is symmetric for all formats with skewnesses in the range of 0.493 (TrueType) to 0.874 (WOFF2). Similarly, the kurtosis of the distributions is similar to those of a normal distribution, ranging from 3.43 (TrueType) to 4.19 (WOFF2).

Furthermore, a clear difference in the spread between system fonts and web fonts is illustrated. While system fonts have a standard deviation of 545 (Open-Type) and 630 (TrueType) bytes, a greater dispersion is shown for WOFF and WOFF2, whose average deviation from the mean varies by 1846 and 1540, respectively.

Again, a one-way ANOVA test is performed. The H_3 associated null hypothesis states that the format has no effect on the memory allocations required. The results revealed that there was a statistically significant difference in memory consumption between at least two formats ($F(3, 1996) = 1381, p < 2.2e^{-16}$). Further analysis with Tukey HSD shows a significant difference between all pairwise groups. Similarly to the prior resource metrics, the effect sizes are considered as high according to an η^2 value of 0.678.

4.4   Energy Consumption

Finally, the energy consumption of each of the formats is analyzed by specifying the watts per hour consumed in the considered time frame, i.e., between the two events. A violin plot in Fig. 2e is provided.

By only looking at the required watts per hour, web fonts can show a better performance related to energy consumption. WOFF2 formats required the least energy with a median of 2.59 Milliwatts per hour (mWh), followed by the older version WOFF with 2.72 mWh and OTF with 3.13 mWh. The lowest performance in terms of energy consumption was achieved by using TrueType fonts, with a median of 3.27 mWh.

To test H_4, whether the font format affects the energy consumption while the document is loaded, a one-way ANOVA is conducted. The results of this test revealed that there was a statistically significant difference in energy consumption between at least two formats ($F(3, 812) = 1381.p < 2.2e^{-16}$). The Tukey HSD test shows a significant difference between all pairwise font formats. The effect size is strong according to the η^2 value of 0.55. Therefore, the associated null hypothesis is rejected, stating that the font format does not influence energy consumption.

5   Discussion

Fonts play a crucial role in design and typography. In the competitive market of web applications, they need to have a distinctive appeal and value proposition. Consequently, it has become customary to employ custom-designed fonts in one of the four prevalent formats: TTF, OTF, WOFF, and WOFF2. However, incorporating these font formats can introduce performance challenges that potentially compromise user satisfaction, particularly in regions with limited data bandwidth, such as developing countries. Thus, the selection of an appropriate format assumes paramount importance. Through the analysis, we can reject the null hypotheses associated with H_1 to H_4, as compelling evidence has emerged highlighting a significant impact of the font format on all four dependent variables.

H1: The results confirm the recommendations mentioned by the gray literature [18,38] about the usage of the font formats. The web fonts are able to show a faster loading time in contrast to the system fonts. Usage of the newest Web Open Font Format version 2 resulted in the best loading time, followed by WOFF, OpenType and TTF.

H2: The process utilization results were contrary to the expectations since a higher CPU utilization was expected for web fonts due to the necessary decompression. The possible reason for these contradictory results is assumed to be the longer network connection, which leads to a longer observation period for system formats with respect to the processor cycles (idle time). The longer network connection may require additional processing cycles, compensating for decompression's necessary disadvantage.

H3: An examination of the performance of the different formats concerning the allocated memory resulted in the conclusion that system fonts (TrueType and OpenType) require significantly less memory than web fonts. Although the observation period is longer for system fonts, OpenType fonts were able to minimize the required allocated memory, with TrueType fonts following closely with 1.2 times more allocations. Using WOFF2 resulted in 2.53 times more memory allocations on average; for WOFF the factor increases to 2.75. To prioritize memory consumption, it is advisable to specify fonts with fallback formats in this order.

H4: The last performance metric examined is the energy consumption required to load the web page with respect to the font formats used. The results show that the usage of font formats with fallback formats in the following order can reduce energy consumption: WOFF2, WOFF, OpenType, and TrueType. Web developers with a high prioritization of energy efficiency are recommended to use this order.

To sum up, we suggest the following key takeaways to both researchers and practitioners:

---

1. TTF and OTF fonts have been established for a considerable period, making them widely adopted and offering an extensive range of styles.
2. Overall, WOFF2 is the favored font format due to its superior performance, as predicted by gray literature (e.g., [18,18,38]). Hence, a wrapper like ttf2woff2 seems to be appropriate and recommended.
3. It must be noted that WOFF2 might face limited support in specific browsers. As a result, it is advisable to consider using WOFF as a fallback option to ensure broader compatibility.

---

6   Threats to Validity

Threats to Validity refer to factors that may undermine the reliability and generalizability of this study. We split those into four types based on Cook and Campbell [9] that we want to discuss further:

Internal Validity: In order to mitigate this risk, we took into consideration the requirements for reliable benchmarking from Beyer et al. [3]. Concretely this means we decided to completely automate the test execution using AutoHotkey, which also allows independent replication and verification of the experiment. Similarly, we have used common practices in order to keep the performance measurement stable using, for instance, a timeout window between the runs, a specific configuration to avoid external influences, and conducted 500 test runs per web font format to recognize potential outliers.

External Validity: As there exist many font styles, we combined three font styles as this is a typical design principle [39]. Nonetheless, while our combination encompasses a variety of font styles, it is worth considering the inclusion of further styles as a potential avenue for future research. Moreover, to retrieve the targeted performance metrics, our study was constrained to a concrete experimental setup (described in Sect. 3). This limitation adversely impacts the generalizability of our findings, given the multitude of alternative browsers and client devices available in the market. However, it is noteworthy that our results confirm prevailing assumptions documented in the grey literature, lending support to their relevance across different experimental configurations.

Construct Validity: In terms of the construct design and poor operationalization, we outlined the design process. We selected the performance metric in a way that direct impacts to hardware effects were identifiable. Specifically, CPU cycles, allocated and deallocated memory, and the loading time. For a general metric, we selected the energy consumption as an overall is expected to provide a good overview of how efficient the website is in providing the expected outcome.

Statistical Conclusion Validity: This threat is addressed by using statistical hypothesis tests, namely *one-way ANOVA* and *Tukey HSD*, such that the conclusions drawn from this study are founded on common data analysis practices. Furthermore, the results are checked against grey literature, which was selected by specific inclusion criteria. Furthermore, we have fully disclosed all findings and test materials in Zenodo [11] obtained by our experiments.

7   Conclusion and Future Work

Loaded via CSS, font formats give web developers the opportunity to individualize their visual representation, with the drawback of performance downturns. Hence, the selection of an appropriate font format is essential. This study aims to provide insights into the prevailing font formats, TTF, OTF, WOFF, as well as its second generation. Our benchmarking shows that WOFF2 surpasses all other types, albeit with a higher memory allocation. Thus, we conclude that practitioners should employ WOFF2 and consider converting other formats to WOFF2 when feasible. Other optimization options mentioned in Sect. 2, such as font subsetting or the hosting method used, also influence the web application's performance and could be part of further elaboration.

Acknowledgment. This work has been supported by and done in the scope of the ITEA3-SmartDelta project, which has been funded by the Austrian Research Promotion Agency (FFG, Grant No. 890417).

References

1. An, D.: Find out how you stack up to new industry benchmarks for mobile page speed. Think with Google-Mobile, Data and Measurement, p. 24 (2017)
2. Barashkov, A.: Advanced web font optimization techniques - Pixel Point (2022)
3. Beyer, D., Löwe, S., Wendler, P.: Reliable benchmarking: requirements and solutions. Int. J. Softw. Tools Technol. Transfer **21**(1), 1–29 (2019). https://doi.org/10.1007/s10009-017-0469-y
4. Bhatia, S.K., Samal, A., Rajan, N., Kiviniemi, M.T.: Effect of font size, italics, and colour count on web usability. Int. J. Comput. Vision Robot. **2**(2), https://doi.org/10.1504/IJCVR.2011.042271 (2011)
5. Brown, M.B., Forsythe, A.B.: Robust tests for the equality of variances. J. Am. Stat. Assoc. **69**(346), 364–367 (1974). https://doi.org/10.1080/01621459.1974.10482955
6. Bühler, P., Schlaich, P., Sinner, D., Bühler, P., Schlaich, P., Sinner, D.: Schrifttechnologie. Typografie: Schrifttechnologie-Typografische Gestaltung-Lesbarkeit, pp. 73–84 (2017)
7. Cao, B., Shi, M., Li, C.: The solution of web font-end performance optimization. In: 2017 10th International Congress on Image and Signal Processing, BioMedical Engineering and Informatics (CISP-BMEI), pp. 1–5. IEEE, Shanghai (2017). https://doi.org/10.1109/CISP-BMEI.2017.8302083
8. Cohen, J.: Statistical Power Analysis for the Behavioral Sciences. Lawrence Erlbaum Associates (1988)

9. Cook, T.D., Campbell, D.T.: Quasi-Experimentation: Design & Analysis Issues for Field Settings. Houghton Mifflin, Boston (1979)
10. Dornauer, B., Felderer, M.: Energy-saving strategies for mobile web apps and their measurement: results from a decade of research. In: 2023 IEEE/ACM 10th International Conference on Mobile Software Engineering and Systems (MOBILE-Soft), pp. 75–86. IEEE, Melbourne, Australia (2023). https://doi.org/10.1109/MOBILSoft59058.2023.00017
11. Dornauer, B., Vigl, W., Felderer, M.: On the role of font formats in building efficient web applications - replication package (2023). https://doi.org/10.5281/zenodo.8391883
12. Firefox, M.: Firefox profiler (2023)
13. Froidure, N.: Ttf2woff2 - npm (2022)
14. Gray, S., Mallet, C.: AutoHotkey. https://www.autohotkey.com/
15. Grigorik, I.: Optimize WebFont loading and rendering (2020)
16. Gupta, P., M, I.O.P.: A survey of application layer protocols for internet of things. In: 2021 International Conference on Communication Information and Computing Technology (ICCICT), pp. 1–6. IEEE, Mumbai, India (2021). https://doi.org/10.1109/ICCICT50803.2021.9510140
17. Hackenberg, D., Ilsche, T., Schone, R., Molka, D., Schmidt, M., Nagel, W.E.: Power measurement techniques on standard compute nodes: a quantitative comparison. In: IEEE International Symposium on Performance Analysis of Systems and Software (ISPASS 2013), pp. 194–204. IEEE Computer Society (2013). https://doi.org/10.1109/ISPASS.2013.6557170
18. Hempenius, K., Pollard, B.: Best practices for fonts. Optimize web fonts for Core Web Vitals. (2022)
19. Hunt, P.: Adobe-fonts/source-sans: Sans serif font family for user interface environments (2023)
20. Johansen, M.B., Christensen, P.A.: A simple transformation independent method for outlier definition. Clin. Chem. Lab. Med. (CCLM) **56**(9), 1524–1532 (2018). https://doi.org/10.1515/cclm-2018-0025
21. Kaleev, N.: 8 font loading strategies to improve your core web vitals (2022) (2023)
22. Kew, J., van Blokland, E., Leming, T.: WOFF file format 1.0. W3C recommendation, W3C (2012)
23. Li, Z.: Cross-Layer Optimization for Video Delivery on Wireless Networks. Princeton University, Doctor (2023)
24. Liew, Z.: The best font loading strategies and how to execute them — CSS-Tricks - CSS-Tricks (2021)
25. Lilliefors, H.W.: On the Kolmogorov-Smirnov test for normality with mean and variance unknown. J. Am. Stat. Assoc. **62**(318), 399–402 (1967). https://doi.org/10.1080/01621459.1967.10482916
26. Ling, J., van Schaik, P.: The influence of font type and line length on visual search and information retrieval in web pages. Int. J. Hum Comput Stud. **64**(5), 395–404 (2006). https://doi.org/10.1016/j.ijhcs.2005.08.015
27. McInerney, M.: Impallari/Raleway: Raleway fonts (2016)
28. Morey, R.: A guide to web font optimization (2022)
29. mozilla: Window: DOMContentLoaded event - web APIs MDN (2023)
30. mozilla: Window: Load event - web APIs MDN (2023)
31. Nielsen, J.: Designing Web Usability: The Practice of Simplicity. New Riders Publishing, USA (1999)
32. Olsson, M.: Font. CSS3 quick syntax reference: a pocket guide to the cascading style sheets language, pp. 67–70 (2019)

33. Ouyang, J., Luo, H., Wang, Z., Tian, J., Liu, C., Sheng, K.: FPGA implementation of GZIP compression and decompression for IDC services. In: 2010 International Conference on Field-Programmable Technology, pp. 265–268 (2010). https://doi.org/10.1109/FPT.2010.5681489

34. Pearrow, M.: Web Site Usability Handbook with Cdrom. Charles River Media Inc, USA (2000)

35. Rello, L., Pielot, M., Marcos, M.C.: Make it big! the effect of font size and line spacing on online readability. In: Proceedings of the 2016 CHI Conference on Human Factors in Computing Systems, pp. 3637–3648. CHI '16, Association for Computing Machinery, New York, NY, USA (2016). https://doi.org/10.1145/2858036.2858204

36. Rodriguez Fernandez, M., Zalama Casanova, E., Gonzalez Alonso, I.: Review of display technologies focusing on power consumption. Sustainability 7(8), 10854–10875 (2015)

37. Semykin, V.: Ttf2woff2 - npm (2021)

38. Stein, B.: The 2022 Web Almanac: Fonts. Tech. Rep. 5, HTTP Archive (2022)

39. Tidwell, J., Brewer, C., Valencia, A.: Designing Interfaces: Patterns for Effective Interaction Design. O'Reilly Media, Sebastopol, CA, third edition edn. (2020)

40. Took, R.: Putting design into practice: Formal specification and the user interface. In: Formal Methods in Human-Computer Interaction, pp. 63–96. Cambridge University Press, USA (1990)

41. Ulanovsky, J.: Montserrat/Montserrat-SemiBold.otf at master · JulietaUla/Montserrat · GitHub (2021)

42. Van Riet, J., Malavolta, I., Ghaleb, T.A.: Optimize along the way: an industrial case study on web performance. J. Syst. Softw. 198, 111593 (2023). https://doi.org/10.1016/j.jss.2022.111593

43. Wagner, J.L., Marcotte, E.: Web Performance in Action: Building Fast Web Pages. Manning Publications Co, Shelter Island, NY (2017)

44. Willis, M., Hanna, J., Encinas, E., Auger, J.: Low power web: legacy design and the path to sustainable net futures. In: Extended Abstracts of the 2020 CHI Conference on Human Factors in Computing Systems, pp. 1–14. CHI EA '20, Association for Computing Machinery, New York, NY, USA (Apr 2020). https://doi.org/10.1145/3334480.3381829

45. Wright, T.: History and technology of computer fonts. IEEE Ann. Hist. Comput. 20(2), 30–34 (1998). https://doi.org/10.1109/85.667294

46. Zhao, N., Cao, Y., Lau, R.W.: Modeling fonts in context: font prediction on web designs. In: Computer Graphics Forum. vol. 37, pp. 385–395. Wiley Online Library (2018)

Web Image Formats: Assessment of Their Real-World-Usage and Performance Across Popular Web Browsers

Benedikt Dornauer[1,2]([✉]) [iD] and Michael Felderer[1,2,3] [iD]

[1] University of Innsbruck, 6020 Innsbruck, Austria
[2] University of Cologne, 50923 Cologne, Germany
benedikt.dornauer@uibk.ac.at
[3] German Aerospace Center (DLR), Institute for Software Technology,
51147 Cologne, Germany
michael.felderer@dlr.de

Abstract. In 2023, images on the web make up 41% of transmitted data, significantly impacting the performance of web apps. Fortunately, image formats like WEBP and AVIF could offer advanced compression and faster page loading but may face performance disparities across browsers. Therefore, we conducted performance evaluations on five major browsers - Chrome, Edge, Safari, Opera, and Firefox - while comparing four image formats. The results indicate that the newer formats exhibited notable performance enhancements across all browsers, leading to shorter loading times. Compared to the compressed JPEG format, WEBP and AVIF improved the Page Load Time by 21% and 15%, respectively. However, web scraping revealed that JPEG and PNG still dominate web image choices, with WEBP at 4% as the most used new format. Through the web scraping and web performance evaluation, this research serves to (1) explore image format preferences in web applications and analyze distribution and characteristics across frequently-visited sites in 2023 and (2) assess the performance impact of distinct web image formats on application load times across popular web browsers.

Keywords: web applications · image formats · web scarping · performance evaluation · web browsers

1 Introduction

Images are one of the critical elements that can make a web application more appealing and competitive, as they can attract and engage users with the content. The rationale behind this is simple: Users tend to focus on images before they read the textual content, which makes them a powerful tool for capturing user interest [27]. Moreover, images can illustrate stories, are used to display ads, or simply represent products or services.

These positive effects come with the drawback that often more data must be transmitted, which leads to higher energy demand [18]. As shown in Fig. 1,

R. Kadgien et al. (Eds.): PROFES 2023, LNCS 14483, pp. 132–147, 2024.
https://doi.org/10.1007/978-3-031-49266-2_9

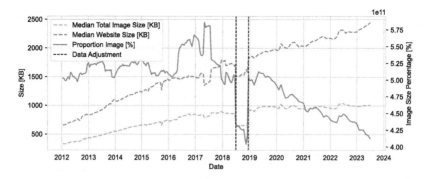

Fig. 1. Total transfer size in kilobytes for all website resources, as well as separately requested images [2].

an analysis of the data traffic shows that the median request size of the total website has increased over the decade, reaching 2449.4 KB in July 2023. Similarly, the total image file size has risen to 1010.6 KB in July 2023, although the percentile has slightly declined in recent years. Nevertheless, images still account for nearly 41% of the total website request size, making it a big contributor to the environmental footprint of webpages [13]. This issue is caused not only by data transfer but also by image rendering. According to Thiagarajan et al. [13], the "amount of energy used to render images is proportional to the number and size of images on the page."

For web apps, various image formats can be used, such as Portable Network Graphics (PNG), Joint Photographic (Expert) Group format (JPEG), Scalable Vector Graphics (SVG), or Graphics Interchange Format (GIF), which are well-established and widely supported. However, newer image formats, such as Web Picture format (WEBP) and AV1 Image File Format (AVIF), have emerged as alternatives that could offer better compression and faster loading times than older formats, leading overall to better performance. Due to length limitations, we refer the reader to [9] for a detailed explanation of the image formats. Until recently, these newer image formats often lacked browser support, as shown in Table 1, and might not often be used as expected.

Table 1. First support year of image format in different browsers

Browser	Chrome	Safari	Firefox	Edge	Opera
WEBP	2014 (v32)	2022 (v16)	2019 (v65)	2018 (v18)	2014 (v19)
AVIF	2020 (v20)	2023 (v16.4)	2021 (v93)	Support (not off.)	2020 (v71)

The primary objective of this study is to compile and present an overview of the current utilization of images on the World Wide Web. To accomplish this, we applied web scraping techniques to gather data from the top 100,000 popular websites as of July 2023. Leveraging the collected website characteristics, we conducted a performance analysis focusing on raster-based image formats: PNG, JPEG, WEBP, and AVIF. This analysis underscores the potential performance improvements associated with these formats, considering a wide range of browsers. The specific contributions of this study are as follows:

1. Investigation of prevalent image format preferences within web applications, accompanied by an analysis of their distribution and intrinsic characteristics across frequently-visited websites.
2. Systematic assessment of the impact of various web image formats on application performance across a range of popular web browsers.

After providing the necessary context and motivation for this research, the succeeding sections of this paper are organised as follows. Subsequently, we discuss in Sect. 2 the findings of related studies and emphasise the differentiation from our work. In Sect. 3, we outline the methodology employed in conducting Web Scraping and Web Performance Measurement, including the specific research questions. These questions are subsequently addressed in Sect. 4, where we present the findings. The implications of these findings are then discussed in Sect. 5. In Sect. 6, we address the potential threats to validity that may have influenced the results of the review and conclude with Sect. 7.

2   Related Work

In order to streamline the incorporation of images into web applications, Zheng et al. [29] discuss the role of *computer image processing* for manipulating and optimizing images to meet specific requirements. Specifically, they highlight common computer image processing steps to address web images. These steps encompass controlling image size, manipulating image shapes, adopting colors as well as transforming those into specific image formats. On the one hand, this can be done in a way that leads to optimal user satisfaction as well as can impact the performance of web applications.

One specific study was done by Thiagarajan et al. [25], interested in the energy consumption of websites of mobile browsers. In the study conducted, the researchers have shown that rendering JPEG images is considerably cheaper and more energy-efficient than other formats, i.e., GIF and PNG, for equivalent-size 1600×1200 images. They claim that GIFs were mainly used for small images like arrows and icons, while PNGs were used for larger images like banners and logos. Moreover, JPEG images were used for handling even bigger images. The last mentioned, JPEG seems to outperform the other formats due to its efficient encoding.

In 2021, Öztürk and Altan [19] examined the encoding process in more detail considering the lossless compression performance of the algorithms developed by the JPEG group (JPEG-LS, JPEG 2000, JPEG XR, JPEG XT, and JPEG XL), WEBP, as well as PNG. Regardless of the image size, JPEG XL exhibited the best compression ratios, along with satisfactory compression and decompression speeds. However, when it comes to decompression time, done on the client side, PNG images take less time compared to WEBP and PNG.

Focusing on low-cost mobile hardware, Singh and Zaki [24] examined in their report 1300 web pages (e.g., page size, economic context of the country of origin, and web page popularity). Furthermore, they have examed the performance impact of the "newly" image formats WEBP and AVIF in order to show the positive effect for low-cost hardware devices. They come to the conclusion that switching to these formats offers a simple optimization that significantly enhances web page agility and competitiveness in low-income countries.

Expanding on the aforementioned related work, we have incorporated web scraping into our methodology to understand the current image format landscape comprehensively. Building upon the insights from previous studies, our experiments were conducted across all commonly used browsers on two distinct client devices, offering a more holistic perspective.

3   Experimental Methodology

In this research, we conducted an exploratory study to examine how images are currently used in web applications and analyzed the hardware-related performance of various image formats on the web. To accomplish this, we formulated three research questions, used web scraping techniques and data analysis, and performed automated performance tests. To better illustrate the overall strategy, Fig. 2 provides an overview of the general approach as well as shows the specific steps involved, described in the following subsections.

3.1   Research Questions

The objective of the research questions are to understand the usage of images on the web (RQ1, RQ2) and analyze the impact of specific image formats on the performance on the web (RQ3).

RQ1: What are the prevailing image formats utilized across the most popular website on the World Wide Web?
Over the last few years, several image formats have been common that are pixel-based with quite long-existing formats PNG and JPEG, "newer" AVIF and WEBP or the vector-based format SVG. This research question aims to investigate the prevalence of various formats among a data set comprising 100 000 websites, already used by previous research. Specifically, we seek to determine whether WEBP, despite being in existence for 13 years [17], is not that popular compared to other formats.

RQ2: What are the predominant image characteristics found on popular websites, and how do these characteristics vary across different image formats?
Building upon the results obtained from the analysis presented in RQ1, this research question seeks to delve deeper into the discourse surrounding additional image characteristics. The attributes considered for investigation within this section include the following:

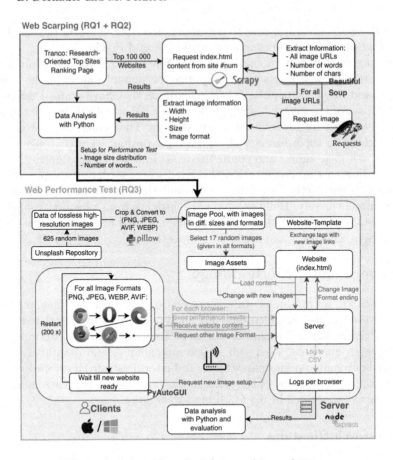

Fig. 2. Overview of methodology and its techniques.

- Bits per Pixel (BPP) per Image Format
- Image File Size (Width & Height) Distribution
- Textual Findings

RQ3: What is the comparative impact of different web image formats and common web browsers on performance improvement in web applications?

This research question is dedicated to investigating and contrasting the effects of raster-image formats, consisting of the established options PNG and JPEG, as well as newer alternatives WEBP and AVIF. Non-raster formats like infinitely scalable SVGs and (multi-image) GIFs are excluded from consideration due to their structural disparities from raster-based image formats. The central objective is to examine the difference between these formats and prominent web browsers (i.e., Chrome, Edge, Safari, Opera, and Firefox) and their consequential influence on the loading speed of web content.

3.2 Web Scraping for Image Information

In order to address the research questions designated as RQ1 and RQ2, we have commenced the utilization of Web Scraping, a technique also identified as web extraction or harvesting. This approach enables the systematic retrieval of relevant data from diverse online sources [28]. To automate the process *Scrapy*[1], an open-source and collaborative Python framework is used. To feed Scrapy with a list of relevant 100 000 websites, we used the *Tranco* data set [14], claiming to be a research-oriented top site ranking, already used by several other studies. Websites, including limiting access by `robots.txt` or without any images included, were excluded. In the initial phase, we scraped through the `index.html` of each website, analyzing relevant data from the raw HTML code. Using *Beautiful Soup*[2], we extracted all image URLs and also gathered information about the text (i.e., number of words and characters) visible for users. For all extracted image URLs, we started a second run, extracting relevant information about the images used. Therefore, we used *Request* to download the images and extract the necessary information (for details, see replication package [8]).

3.3 Web Performance Measurements

The second stage of the methodology involves a performance evaluation to investigate the effectiveness of different image formats in conjunction with a range of web browsers. Initially, we created a website with a simple design that avoids unnecessary features. This ensures any performance issues are primarily due to differences in web browsers and image formats. Leveraging the insights garnered from web scraping of real-world sites (see Sect. 4.1), we created a website with structured content that comprises 792 words and the integration of 17 image tags `<!-- Image #nb -->` which were substituted with their corresponding images. The rationale for choosing the image distribution is based on the following assumptions:

1. Image aspect ratios of 17 images:
   - Landscape: 57% (9 images)
   - Symmetric: 32% (6 images)
   - Portrait: 11% (2 images)
2. Common image dimensions (e.g., 1280×720, 64×64, ...), see Table 5c
3. One prominent large image [20]
4. One invisible tracking 1×1 pixel

Based on these assumptions, we derived a set of image formats, given in Table 2. This collection of images counts a total of 1 732 621 pixels, which closely matches the median pixel count found on the scraped webpages (1 735 713).

In our image sampling, we randomly picked 625 high-resolution lossless images from Unsplash[3]. The data set contained images that covered a wide spectrum of visual content. The photos were then trimmed to the different image

---

[1] https://scrapy.org.

[2] https://www.crummy.com/software/BeautifulSoup/.

[3] https://unsplash.com.

dimensions and converted to the four image formats PNG, JPEG, WEBP, and AVIF. For this purpose, we selected the Python Imaging Library *Pillow*[4], with over 11K GitHub stars, and also used by other scientific papers such as [6,11]. To ensure consistent image quality, we adjusted the compression levels of each image format accordingly. Therefore, we used Structural Index Similarity (SSIM) equal to 0.95 (compared to PNG) as the criterion, as this implies almost perfect similarity [10,23] among the other image formats.

Table 2. Selection of image sizes in pixels, based on RQ2

Landscape	Symmetric	Portrait
3 x (240, 180), 2 x (300, 225)	1 x (1, 1), 1 x (32, 32)	1 x (225, 300)
2 x (320, 180), 1 x (640, 360)	1 x (64, 64), 1 x (120, 120)	1 x (300, 420)
1 x (1280, 720)	1 x (150, 150), 1 x (200, 200)	

The test automation setup consisted of a server (Express 4.18.2), a router (Netgear WNDR 4300), and two client machines (1) MacBook Pro 2019 16 Zoll (2.3 GHz 8-Core Intel Core i9, 16 GB) with MacOS 13.5 as well as (2) ThinkPad T490 (1,80 GHz, Intel Core i7, 16 GB) with Windows 11.

Besides hosting the website, the web server additionally had the ability to randomly choose images (using the same configuration) and alternate between their respective image formats. Furthermore, it collected measurements from the client machines. These machines were connected via WAN in an isolated environment, i.e. with no access to the internet or other clients.

The setup for each client machine is based on the default settings provided by the operating system supplier, excluding any third-party software. We proceeded to install a selection of the most up-to-date and widely used web browsers on each machine, guided by the browser usage data from July 2023 as presented by *StatCounter* [1]: Chrome (63.33%), Safari (19.95%), Edge (5.14%), Opera (2.98%), Firefox (2.79%) and Others (5.81%). It's important to note that Safari was exclusively employed on MacOS due to the specific OS prerequisites. Additionally, Python 3.11 was installed on all machines, along with the *PyAutoGUI*[5] and *Keyboard*[6] libraries, enabling us to automate the execution of the tests.

An automated test run consisted of three steps for each browser. First, the Incognito/Private Browser was launched to eliminate the influence of cookies and caching. Second, the URL was entered, and the webpage was loaded while its performance was measured. Third, the browser was closed, terminating the session and initiating a cooldown period before the next run. A test cycle comprised 20 (for Windows: 16) experimental iterations, each employing a distinct

---

[4] https://pillow.readthedocs.io/.
[5] https://pyautogui.readthedocs.io.
[6] https://pypi.org/project/keyboard/.

set of images randomly selected from a pool. The test cycle systematically traversed 5 (for Windows: 4) different browsers in sequence and then transitioned to the subsequent four image formats. We focused on the metrics

- **Page Load Time (PLT)**: time from the start of page loading to the display of any part of the page's content on the screen, and
- **First Contentful Paint (FCP)**: which measures the time from the start of page loading to the end of page rendering

to measure the performance of each test run. These metrics reflect how well a web application performs, as shown by [5,21]. However, other metrics are also available but not considered for this evaluation. For these measurements, we used the *PerfumeJS*[7] performance profiler with the latest stable release v8.4.0. It leverages the latest Performance APIs to collect field data for cross-browser testing and was used in previous publications [15,16].

The experimental design employed in this study follows a 4–5 (for Windows: 4–4) Factorial Design principle, wherein the combinations of two independent variables, namely browser types and image formats, are systematically manipulated to investigate their joint impact on web page loading performance. By utilizing the *Scheirer-Ray-Hare test* [22], a non-parametric version of two-way ANOVA based on ranks, on this factorial arrangement, we gain an understanding of how each variable independently and collectively contributes to the observed variations in the measured metrics.

4 Results

To address the aforementioned research questions, we have employed web scraping techniques to gather relevant data. The results obtained from the web scraping analysis are presented in the following Subsect. 4.1 (RQ1 and RQ2). Moreover, we address RQ3 in Subsect. 4.2, presenting the results of the web performance test.

4.1 Results Using Web Scraping

We scraped the 100 000 most frequently visited websites listed in Tranco [14], which focuses on research-oriented top-site ranking. After filtering out websites that were blocked by `robot.txt` or have not contained any images, we were able to analyze 58 057 sites. This resulted in a total of 2 662 548 images in 10 formats, namely JPEG, PNG, SVG, GIF, WEBP, Bitmap file (BMP), Microsoft Icon (ICO), Multi Picture Object (MPO), Photoshop Document (PSD), and Tagged Image File Format (TIFF) formats, with a median of 25 images per site (17 unique images - duplicates are images with same URL).

---

[7] https://zizzamia.github.io/perfume/.

Image Format Distribution: Considering the different formats, we calculated the distribution of the images regarding their image format, illustrated in Fig. 3. Thereby, we found that JPEG and PNG formats are the most commonly used, with each format making up almost one-third of all images. SVG comes in third place at 19.90%, followed by GIF at 11.34%. It's worth noting that WEBP format only makes up 3.01% of occurrences, indicating it is not as commonly used. All other formats BMP, ICO, MPO, PSD, BMP, AVIF and TIFF were not that popular by web developers, in total 0.05% of all images. An interesting observation to consider is that some images occur multiple times. This specifically includes the formats SVG and GIF.

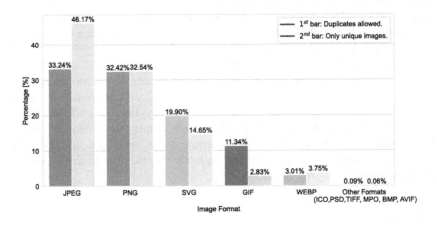

Fig. 3. Distribution plot of image formats among the 2 662 548 images collected from crawled websites.

Bits per Pixel: We have depicted the distribution of BPP for the image formats JPEG, PNG, and WEBP, as shown in Fig. 4. The distribution is presented using discrete bins with an interval of 0.025 BPP, along with the Kernel Density Estimate (KDE). Within the BPP range of [0.0, 0.25], it is observed that WEBP exhibits the highest frequency of occurrences, suggesting that a larger proportion of images, as compared to JPEG and PNG, possess a smaller file size per pixel. In general, the majority of PNG images utilize the highest file size per pixel when compared to the other image formats studied in this analysis.

Width and Height Properties: Due to their resolution independence and infinite scalability, SVG images were excluded from the analysis, focusing solely on raster images (PNG, JPEG, GIF, and WebP) to assess width and height. The units employed in our analysis are denoted in pixels.

As an initial point, we removed the extreme outliers using Tukey's Outer Fence equally for the width and height of the images, which led to the inclusion of 97.31% of all images. Using the data, we started to illustrate the density

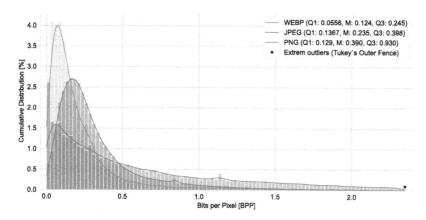

Fig. 4. Distribution of the BPP for the image formats JPEG, PNG, and WEBP. The extreme outliers are not illustrated, based on Tukey's Outer Fence [26] and checked to justify their exclusion. The related quartiles 1,3 (Q1, Q3) and median (M) are given as (Q1, M, Q3).

of the frequency of specific widths (Fig. 5b) in the range of $[0, 1872]$ as well as the density of heights (Fig. 5a) in the range of $[0, 1254]$ for the image formats independently.

Overall, we discern that nearly all image dimensions are well-represented. Additionally, conspicuous patterns emerge, highlighting certain values that appear with higher frequencies. Specifically, for width, the prominent values are 1, 300, 200, 100, 320, 600, while for height, they are 1, 200, 300, 100, 180, 150, 400. These values are presented in descending order of their prevalence. Notably, we observed a prevalence of sizes multiples of a hundred.

Notably, the top ten dimensions comprise 1×1 (Invisible Pixels (tracking) [3]), 100×100, 150×150, 320×180, 16×16, 320×180, and other symmetric dimensions such as (16, 300, 64, 32).

It appears that widths are more frequently longer ($Q1 : 96px$, $M : 262px$, $Q3 : 540px$) compared to heights ($Q1 : 64px$, $M : 180px$, $Q3 : 380px$), as shown by Table 5d. Our observations reveal that 57% of the images exhibit a Landscape orientation, wherein their width exceeds their height horizontally. In contrast, 31.22% of the images possess a symmetric aspect ratio, while a smaller proportion, constituting only 11.78%, are in Portrait mode, where their height surpasses their width vertically (ref. Fig. 5).

Textual Findings: In addition to conducting image-related analyses, we also compiled data regarding the textual content present on the examined websites. The median word count per site was determined to be 792 words, with $Q1 = 407$ and $Q3 = 1397$.

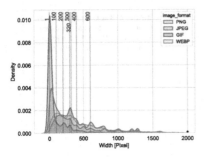
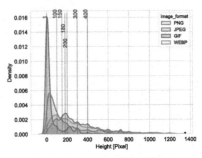

(a) Density of **Width** per image format.   (b) Density of **Height** per image format.

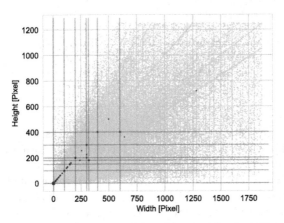

	Density	
Pixel	Width	Height
[0, 100]	28.3%	36.8%
(100, 200]	15.9%	20.5%
(200, 300]	14.9%	14.0%
(300, 400]	11.2%	9.1%
(400, 500]	6.1%	6.3%
(500, 600]	5.4%	4.8%
(600, 700]	3.8%	2.5%
(700, 800]	4.3%	2.5%
(800, 900]	1.9%	1.2%
(900, 1000]	1.9%	1.0%
(1000, 1100]	1.5%	0.7%
(1100, 1200]	1.7%	0.5%
(1200, ∞)	3.1%	0.1%

(c) Scatter plot, using width and height. The dark-blue dots indicate the 30 most frequent image sizes.

(d) Density distribution per 100 chunks.

Fig. 5. The plots depict width density (Fig. 5a), height density (Fig. 5b), and their correlation (Fig. 5c). Extreme outliers are excluded using Tukey's Outer Fence (*). Standard normalization is applied to each font format for Figs. 5a and 5b.

4.2   Results of the Web Performance Tests

To evaluate the performance, we conducted 200 test runs on two different client devices and were able to measure the FCP and PLT metrics using PerfumeJS, supported by all browsers.

First Contentful Paint: The FCP metric measures the time from the start of page loading to the display of any part of the page's content on the screen. We found no significant effect of the image formats on this metric, as the p-value was greater than 0.05. However, we observed a significant effect of the browsers on the FCP metric, indicating that different browsers render the page content at different speeds.

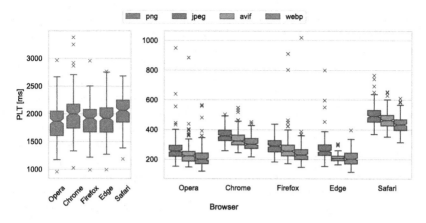

Fig. 6. PLT for different browsers and image formats on the Mac client. The results for the Windows client draw a similar picture.

Page Load Time: Considering the PLT metric, which measures the time from the start of page loading to the end of page rendering (including loading and displaying all the content), we found that both the browser and the image formats had a significant effect on this metric, based on the results of the *Scheirer-Ray-Hare test* [22], a non-parametric version of two-way ANOVA. The PNG format had the highest median PLT of 1943 ms, which was much longer than the other formats: JPEG (312 ms), AVIF (271 ms), and WEBP (258 ms) for all browsers on the Mac. Figure 6 shows the breakdown of PLT for each browser and image format. From this figure, we can notice that the performance gains from using different formats are consistent across different browsers. However, the browser itself also has a large influence on the PLT, with Safari being the slowest and Opera being the fastest. The results for the Windows client show a nearly similar picture, demonstrating the independence of results from the client device.

5 Discussion

Images have a significant impact on human perception as they capture user attention more effectively than text [27]. By using web scraping techniques (RQ1 &RQ2) , we have observed that the median number of images on websites was 25 (including header images, logos, and tracking pixels), showing their relevance for web apps.

To dispaly raster-based images, two formats are commonly utilized: PNG for smaller images and JPEG for larger images. These findings are in line with research from previous years conducted by HTTP Archive [2]. However, we found that WEBP and AVIF are still uncommon in July 2023. This situation might arise due to the fact that support for WEBP was lacking for certain browsers in the last years, specifically in the case of Safari. The picture for AVIF is even worse (see Table 1).

However, images constitute a large fraction of the data transfer - up to 41% - on the web, and the novel formats WEBP and AVIF offer potential benefits in reducing data consumption. Singh [24] showed that replacing images on real-world websites with WEBP and AVIF resulted in a median decrease of 25% (websites high-income countries) and 35 % (websites low-income countries), in terms of page size. Considering the findings of our performance test (RQ3), we similarly identify a clear performance improvement, which comprises the transmitting, rendering, and displaying of content in a benchmark setup. The PLT improves by a factor of 1.21 using WEBP and by 1.15 using AVIF compared to the JPEG format. These findings are relevant not only for Chromium-based browsers (Chrome, Edge, Opera) but also for Safari and Firefox.

Considering the situation with image format support and how they affect how fast websites load, we strongly suggest using the WEBP format. WEBP works well across the board, leading to increased website performance and a better user experience.

Besides that, newer image formats also extend the battery life of devices. This may seem insignificant, but it has a significant impact on energy conservation [18] considering a worldwide perspective. For example, if we assume savings of 5% through the new image formats for mobile devices, we would be able to shut down one of the Fukushima nuclear power plants [7].

6   Threats to Validity

Threats to Validity are potential sources of error or bias that may compromise the quality and applicability of a study. Following Cook and Campbell [4], we organised our threats into the four types:

Internal Validity: To mitigate this risk, we conducted our experiment in a controlled and isolated environment, with consistent hardware and software configurations throughout all experimental runs. In addition, we automated the test execution using PyAutoGUI, allowing independent replication. Performance measurement stability was ensured through timed intervals, specific configurations to minimize external effects (e.g., disabled cache or turning off third-party software), and 200 test runs per image combination for outlier detection. One important threat is the influence of image attributes like color depth, distortion, and sharpness [12] on the image format efficiency. Thus, we employed a randomized selection strategy. From a pool of images, we randomly selected 17 images of various sizes, representing typical website diversity, based on results from RQ2 for each test run. Furthermore, we fall back to the SSIM metric to ensure comparable image quality across all formats.

External Validity: The study examined a relatively small fraction of the existing websites, which may limit the generalizability of the results. However, the sample size of 58 057 websites, selected from the 100K most popular sites based on a representative dataset Tranco [14], should mitigate this threat. A comparison with gray literature [20] showed a consistent pattern of the findings. Regarding the comprehensive conclusion drawn that WEBP and AVIF are recommended today for use in web applications, we conducted our study on two different operating systems and the five most popular web browsers (latest versions). We believe exploring the potential combinations of image formats could be another aspect worth investigating in more detail.

Construct Validity: The study's approach involves webpage design to isolate browser and format-related performance issues. An image dataset is utilized, and images are randomly selected, ensuring a wide range of visual content representation. The analysis employs a factorial design to dissect the interplay between browser types and image formats on the loading performance, employing common metrics for evaluation such as FCP or PLT. A detailed description is provided in the replication package on Zenodo [8].

Statistical Conclusion Validity: Employing a factorial design, we systematically manipulated both web browsers and image formats. This approach facilitated the isolation and thorough analysis of the distinct and combined impacts they exert on the loading performance of web pages. Consequently, the *Scheirer-Ray-Hare test* [22] was employed as the chosen statistical method for our analysis.

7   Conclusion

Web images are pivotal for optimizing websites and enhancing user satisfaction by captivating their attention. However, they can prolong a website's loading time due to bandwidth and rendering demands. Our analysis of popular websites highlights a predominant use of traditional image formats like PNG and JPEG. Based on performance tests across widespread browsers, we recommend adopting modern image formats, particularly WEBP and AVIF. Of these, WEBP is preferable due to its broad compatibility and more efficient performance advantages.

Acknowledgment. This project received support from ITEA3-SmartDelta and funding from the Austrian Research Promotion Agency (FFG, Grant No. 890417).

References

1. Browser Market Share Worldwide. https://gs.statcounter.com/browser-market-share

2. HTTP archive. https://httparchive.org/
3. Bekos, P., Papadopoulos, P., Markatos, E.P., Kourtellis, N.: The Hitchhiker's guide to facebook web tracking with invisible pixels and click IDs. In: Proceedings of the ACM Web Conference 2023, pp. 2132–2143. WWW '23, Association for Computing Machinery, New York, NY, USA (2023). https://doi.org/10.1145/3543507.3583311
4. Cook, T.D., Campbell, D.T.: Quasi-Experimentation: Design & Analysis Issues for Field Settings. Houghton Mifflin, Boston (1979)
5. Amjad, M., Tutul Hossain, Md., Hassan, R., Rahman, M.A.: Department of computer science & engineering, stamford university bangladesh, bangladesh, web application performance analysis of ecommerce sites in bangladesh: an empirical study. Int. J. Inform. Eng. Electron. Bus. **13**(2), 47–54 (2021). https://doi.org/10.5815/ijieeb.2021.02.04
6. Dhanawade, A., Drode, A., Johnson, G., Rao, A., Upadhya, S.: Open CV based Information Extraction from Cheques. In: 2020 Fourth International Conference on Computing Methodologies and Communication (ICCMC), pp. 93–97 (Mar 2020). https://doi.org/10.1109/ICCMC48092.2020.ICCMC-00018
7. Dornauer, B., Felderer, M.: Energy-saving strategies for mobile web apps and their measurement: results from a decade of research. In: 2023 IEEE/ACM 10th International Conference on Mobile Software Engineering and Systems (MOBILESoft), pp. 75–86. IEEE, Melbourne, Australia (May 2023). https://doi.org/10.1109/MOBILSoft59058.2023.00017
8. Dornauer, B., Felderer, M.: Web Image Formats: Assessment of Their Real-World Usage and Performance across Popular Web Browsers - Replication Package (2023). https://doi.org/10.5281/zenodo.8395044
9. Frain, B.: Responsive Web Design with HTML5 and CSS: Build Future-Proof Responsive Websites Using the Latest HTML5 and CSS Techniques. Birmingham Mumbai, fourth edition edn, Packt (2022)
10. Horé, A., Ziou, D.: Image quality metrics: PSNR vs. SSIM. In: 2010 20th International Conference on Pattern Recognition, pp. 2366–2369 (2010). https://doi.org/10.1109/ICPR.2010.579
11. Hu, J., Song, S., Gong, Y.: Comparative performance analysis of web image compression. In: 2017 10th International Congress on Image and Signal Processing, BioMedical Engineering and Informatics (CISP-BMEI), pp. 1–5 (2017). https://doi.org/10.1109/CISP-BMEI.2017.8301939
12. Inouri, L., Tighidet, S., Azni, M., Khireddine, A., Harrar, K.: A fast and efficient approach for image compression using curvelet transform. Sens. Imag. **19**(1), 26 (2018). https://doi.org/10.1007/s11220-018-0212-0
13. Jones, N.: How to stop data centres from gobbling up the world's electricity. Nature **561**(7722), 163–166 (2018). https://doi.org/10.1038/d41586-018-06610-y
14. Le Pochat, V., Van Goethem, T., Tajalizadehkhoob, S., Korczynski, M., Joosen, W.: Tranco: a research-oriented top sites ranking hardened against manipulation. In: Proceedings 2019 Network and Distributed System Security Symposium. Internet Society, San Diego, CA (2019). https://doi.org/10.14722/ndss.2019.23386
15. Malavolta, I., et al.: A framework for the automatic execution of measurement-based experiments on Android devices. In: Proceedings of the 35th IEEE/ACM International Conference on Automated Software Engineering Workshops, pp. 61–66. ACM, Virtual Event Australia (2020). https://doi.org/10.1145/3417113.3422184
16. Malavolta, I., et al.: JavaScript dead code identification, elimination, and empirical assessment. IEEE Trans. Softw. Eng. **49**(7), 3692–3714 (2023). https://doi.org/10.1109/TSE.2023.3267848

17. Matijević, M., Mikota, M., Čačić, M.: Impact of JPEG-WebP conversion on the characteristics of the photographic image. Tehnicki vjesnik - Technical Gazette **23**(2) (2016). https://doi.org/10.17559/TV-20141208110946
18. Morley, J., Widdicks, K., Hazas, M.: Digitalisation, energy and data demand: the impact of Internet traffic on overall and peak electricity consumption. Energy Res. Soc. Sci. **38**, 128–137 (2018). https://doi.org/10.1016/j.erss.2018.01.018
19. Öztürk, E., Mesut, A.: Performance Evaluation of JPEG standards, WebP and PNG in terms of compression ratio and time for lossless encoding. In: 2021 6th International Conference on Computer Science and Engineering (UBMK), pp. 15–20 (2021). https://doi.org/10.1109/UBMK52708.2021.9558922
20. Portis, E., Ranganath, A.: The 2022 Web Almanac: Media. Tech. Rep. 6, HTTP Archive (2022)
21. Pourghassemi, B., Amiri Sani, A., Chandramowlishwaran, A.: What-if analysis of page load time in web browsers using causal profiling. Proceedings of the ACM on Measurement and Analysis of Computing Systems **3**(2), 1–23 (2019). https://doi.org/10.1145/3341617.3326142
22. Scheirer, C.J., Ray, W.S., Hare, N.: The analysis of ranked data derived from completely randomized factorial designs. Biometrics **32**(2), 429 (1976). https://doi.org/10.2307/2529511
23. Setiadi, D.R.I.M.: PSNR vs SSIM: imperceptibility quality assessment for image steganography. Multimed. Tools Appl. **80**(6), 8423–8444 (2021). https://doi.org/10.1007/s11042-020-10035-z
24. Singh, S.: A Comparative Evaluation of Next-Generation Image Formats on Low-Cost Mobile Hardware. Tech. Rep. 2, New York University Abu Dhabi, Abu Dhabi, UAE (2023)
25. Thiagarajan, N., Aggarwal, G., Nicoara, A., Boneh, D., Singh, J.P.: Who killed my battery?: analyzing mobile browser energy consumption. In: Proceedings of the 21st International Conference on World Wide Web, pp. 41–50. ACM, Lyon France (2012). https://doi.org/10.1145/2187836.2187843
26. Tukey, J.W.: Exploratory data analysis. Addison-Wesley Series in Behavioral Science, Addison-Wesley Pub. Co, Reading, Mass (1977)
27. Wang, P.: Visual design of web interface based on computer image processing technology. J. Phys: Conf. Ser. **1915**(2), 022030 (2021). https://doi.org/10.1088/1742-6596/1915/2/022030
28. Zhao, B.: Web scraping. In: Schintler, L.A., McNeely, C.L. (eds.) Encyclopedia of Big Data, pp. 1–3. Springer International Publishing, Cham (2017)
29. Zheng, Y., Li, H., Ren, A.: Research on application of computer image processing in web design. In: 2020 IEEE International Conference on Power, Intelligent Computing and Systems (ICPICS), pp. 405–409 (2020). https://doi.org/10.1109/ICPICS50287.2020.9202235

Machine Learning and Data Science

Operationalizing Assurance Cases for Data Scientists: A Showcase of Concepts and Tooling in the Context of Test Data Quality for Machine Learning

Lisa Jöckel[1]([⊠]), Michael Kläs[1], Janek Groß[1], Pascal Gerber[1], Markus Scholz[2], Jonathan Eberle[3], Marc Teschner[3], Daniel Seifert[1], Richard Hawkins[4], John Molloy[4], and Jens Ottnad[3]

[1] Fraunhofer Institute for Experimental Software Engineering IESE, Kaiserslautern, Germany
{lisa.joeckel,michael.klaes,janek.gross,pascal.gerber,
daniel.seifert}@iese.fraunhofer.de
[2] NovelSense, Karlsruhe, Germany
scholz@novelsense.com
[3] TRUMPF Se + Co. KG, Ditzingen, Germany
{jonathan.eberle,marc.teschner,jens.ottnad}@trumpf.com
[4] University of York, York, UK
{richard.hawkins,john.molloy}@york.ac.uk

Abstract. Assurance Cases (ACs) are an established approach in safety engineering to argue quality claims in a structured way. In the context of quality assurance for Machine Learning (ML)-based software components, ACs are also being discussed and appear promising. Tools for operationalizing ACs do exist, yet mainly focus on supporting safety engineers on the system level. However, assuring the quality of an ML component within the system is commonly the responsibility of data scientists, who are usually less familiar with these tools. To address this gap, we propose a framework to support the operationalization of ACs for ML components based on technologies that data scientists use on a daily basis: Python and Jupyter Notebook. Our aim is to make the process of creating ML-related evidence in ACs more effective. Results from the application of the framework, documented through notebooks, can be integrated into existing AC tools. We illustrate the application of the framework on an example excerpt concerned with the quality of the test data.

Keywords: Testing · Dependability · Artificial Intelligence · Python · Data Analysis Notebook · Safety

1 Introduction

Assurance Cases (ACs) are a systematic approach to ensure quality in safety engineering. They are defined as "a reasoned and compelling argument, supported by a body of evidence, that a system, service or organization will operate as intended for a defined

R. Kadgien et al. (Eds.): PROFES 2023, LNCS 14483, pp. 151–158, 2024.
https://doi.org/10.1007/978-3-031-49266-2_10

application in a defined environment" [1]. Most commonly, they are implemented in a tree structure with the quality claim as the root. The claim is iteratively broken down into subclaims until these are modular enough for evidence supporting the claim to be generated.

Quality assurance for software systems with Machine Learning (ML) components is currently a significant area of research and the argumentation of safety and dependability of ML components via ACs is also being discussed (e.g., as possible basis for evidence-based standards for AI certification) [2–4].

There already exist several tools and frameworks for operationalizing ACs, mainly aimed at supporting safety engineers on the system level [5–9]. These tools could also be applied for quality assurance of ML components within a software system. However, data scientists are seldom familiar with these tools. Data scientists often use Python and data analysis notebooks like Jupyter Notebook [10], which is a web-based computing environment for usage in a web browser. One of the distinguishing features of Jupyter Notebook is the combination of textual elements, executable code blocks, and computational output, allowing for documents that include textual or visual explanations as well as interaction via executable code. This makes it easier to create reproducible and understandable routines since the code is embedded within the document itself. Notebooks are portable between different users or operating systems and support several programming languages, including those popular with data scientists, such as Python and R.

In this work, we propose the framework pyAC, which is based on Python and Jupyter Notebook. The framework supports data scientists by enabling them to operationalize ACs for ML components in their familiar developing environments. This eliminates the need for them to learn other AC tools in depth. pyAC allows integrating the resulting evidence into external AC tools. This is possible in two ways: (A) First, the claims for the ML component are completely refined in the external tool. Then evidence is generated using pyAC, and finally, the evidence is provided to the external tool. (B) Further refinement of the claims for the ML component is done in pyAC. The evidence is generated for all subclaims and then accumulated evidence is provided to the external tool.

There are three main *contributions* in this work. First, we introduce the tooling framework pyAC, which is specifically designed for data scientists to support them in operationalizing ACs for ML components. We present how to integrate this framework into existing AC tools. Second, we describe how the elements and the structure of an AC can be implemented in Jupyter Notebook and Python. Third, we illustrate how to apply the framework on an example AC excerpt where the quality of test data is assured.

The paper is structured as follows: Sect. 2 provides background and related work on ACs. Section 3 introduces the concept of the tooling framework pyAC. Section 4 illustrates the application of pyAC on test data quality. Section 5 presents future directions and concludes the paper.

2 Background and Related Work on Assurance Cases

ACs are an established approach to assure the safety of a software system but are also discussed to assure other qualities, e.g., fairness [11]. They are predominantly implemented in a graphical form as a tree structure, which starts at a *claim* about a system property in its related operating *context*. Based on the iterative application of suitable *strategies*, with their related *assumptions* and *justifications*, a (complex) claim is decomposed into *subclaims* until *evidence* can be provided to justify the validity of the subclaims [12]. ACs can be structured based on, e.g., the Claims-Argument-Evidence (CAE) or the Goal Structuring Notation (GSN) [1] approach, which primarily differ in the designation of their structuring elements [12, 13]. The concept of ACs also appears promising for application in systems containing ML-based components [3, 4, 14].

Various tools supporting the creation of ACs exist [15], such as ASCE [5], ISCaDE [6], Astah GSN [7], from Confiance.ai [8], or safeTbox [9], which are mainly designed to support safety engineers in assuring system-level safety. With these tools, ACs can be created from scratch in a flexible manner for a specific system. Some of them are based on proprietary software platforms, which additionally require a certain amount of expertise. The AMLAS Tool [16] already gives guidance by providing patterns for assuring the ML component that need to be instantiated for a use case. However, to the best of our knowledge, no tools exist that specifically focus on supporting data scientists in creating evidence for the quality assurance of ML components in a development environment that they use on a daily basis.

For the Open Dependability Exchange (ODE) metamodel, which aims at tool-independent exchange of safety-related artifacts, extensions for enabling the integration of ML assurance-related artifacts are intended [17]. Tools that are compatible with the ODE metamodel, such as safeTbox, could complement pyAC by providing the AC on the comprehensive system level.

3 Tooling Framework for Operationalizing Assurance Cases for ML

This section describes the concept of the pyAC framework and how it operationalizes the AC structure and elements using Python and Jupyter Notebook. The framework supports three purposes: (A) It provides guidance for data scientists to implement the AC; (B) it can be applied to a use case to generate evidence for the claimed quality of the ML component; and (C) it can be used for validation of the AC by an (external) assessor, thus providing auditability and reproducibility. An overview of the framework architecture together with the three purposes is shown in Fig. 1.

The framework contains *claims, measures,* and *blueprints* as **assurance case elements (AC elements)**, which are instances of their respective Python class (i.e., `Claim`, `Measure`, or `Blueprint`). They inherit from `AssuranceCaseElement`, which provides basic functionalities like storing/loading/deleting a class instance, versioning, or providing an HTML-formatted summary of information on this element. AC elements are created, described, and adjusted in Jupyter Notebook. Notebooks can be stored as *documentation* in HTML or PDF format.

Claims are either inner nodes or leaves of the tree-like structure of ACs. As inner nodes, they contain a *strategy* for refinement into subclaims, as well as a reference to their *subclaims*. As leaves, claims are not further refined by subclaims and get a reference to the *evidence* supporting the claim, which are *realized blueprints*. A *conclusion* can be added as a *justification* over the evidence, i.e., if and how the evidence from one

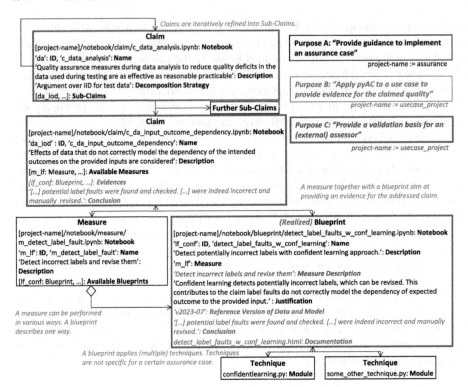

Fig. 1. Framework architecture for operationalizing ACs illustrated on the example of detecting label faults. AC elements, techniques, and their relations are depicted for the three different purposes of the framework (indicated by color).

or multiple realized blueprints shows that the claim holds. A claim can contain one or multiple *contexts* or *assumptions* described in textual form. Furthermore, a claim contains a list of references to available measures. A quality *measure* together with a blueprint is intended to provide evidence for a claim. A measure can be performed in various ways. For example, a measure for detecting outliers in the dataset might either apply one selected outlier detection technique or apply multiple techniques and combine the outliers found. A *blueprint* is a concrete way to implement a measure and provides step-by-step guidance to apply it for a specific use case, which we refer to as a *realized blueprint*. Measures contain a list of references to available blueprints that implement the measure. Blueprints contain a *justification* that they have the ability to sufficiently address the corresponding claim. Moreover, the applied blueprint keeps information on the model and data versions used, which can also be updated to create a new documentation. A *conclusion* is added to describe the contribution of the generated evidence to the corresponding claim.

All notebooks contain a *summary section* loading a previously stored AC element and providing summarized information on the AC element, an overview of generated documentation versions (i.e., the exported HTML/PDF versions of the notebook), and the most recently added conclusion (in the case of claims and blueprints). This section

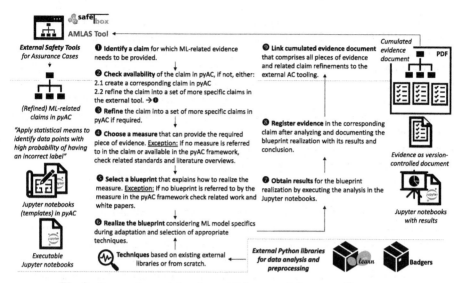

Fig. 2. Process for applying the pyAC framework for a specific use case.

mainly targets the purpose of providing a validation basis for an assessor. The *management section* creates a new AC element, manages its versions, and stores it. Measures provide an overview of available blueprints, while claims provide an overview of available measures. Claims further reference their contributing evidence and the justifications over them. Blueprints contain an additional *blueprint section* describing the steps to generate the evidence when applying the blueprint for a specific use case.

Besides AC elements, the framework contains **techniques**, which are implemented in Python modules and inherit from the class `Technique`. They are compliant with the estimator interface of the Machine Learning package scikit-learn [18]. Techniques are either based on existing packages like scikit-learn or are implemented as custom techniques. They can be used in the blueprint Jupyter notebooks; e.g., a technique using scikit-learn's isolation forest might be applied as part of a measure to detect outliers.

The framework in its bare form is intended to provide a basic collection of AC elements and techniques that are not realized and adapted for a specific use case yet. The **process for applying the framework for a use case** is depicted in Fig. 2. For a use case, already available AC elements can be assembled and applied. If further AC elements or techniques are needed, respective notebooks (or Python modules in the case of techniques) can be added, which will extend the framework over time. Elements and documentation are only stored when the AC elements are applied for a use case.

4 Quality Assurance of Test Data

In this section, we illustrate the application of the framework (using the process depicted in Fig. 2) on an excerpt of the AC that is concerned with the quality assurance of the test data. Data is used during the whole lifecycle of the ML component, e.g., for fitting the model parameters as well as for validating and testing the ML component. Hence, data quality assurance is an important part of the overall quality assurance of the ML component [3]. Compared to traditional software testing, different concepts are used for ML testing, which are mainly based on determining the performance of the ML component on a test dataset using statistical evaluation metrics [19]. Hence, deriving dependable test results strongly depends on the quality of the test data [20]. Three key quality characteristics for test data were derived from the property of random samples that they are independent and identically distributed (IID): The test data (1) was unseen during model development, (2) provides model inputs that are representative of the intended application scope of the ML component, and (3) models the relation between model inputs and intended outcomes correctly [20].

Each dataset is associated with a data lifecycle starting with the specification of requirements on the data (i.e., data specification). Data construction includes data collection and data preparation. Data analysis aims at finding weak points in the dataset in order to improve it. Data testing estimates the amount of remaining weak points to be considered in the test result of the ML component. Data operation refers to the application of the data for training, validation, or testing of the ML component. The key characteristics of test data need to be addressed by various measures during different lifecycle phases of the test data. E.g., representativity can be addressed by appropriate sampling approaches to collect data combined with approaches to enhance the data with realistically occurring quality issues (e.g., [21, 22]). A common problem regarding the correctness of the input-outcome relationship are incorrect labels, i.e., annotated ground truth information. In the following, we will illustrate the application of the presented framework on the example of detecting incorrect labels during data analysis and revising them, thereby reducing the risk arising from a test result derived from unreliable

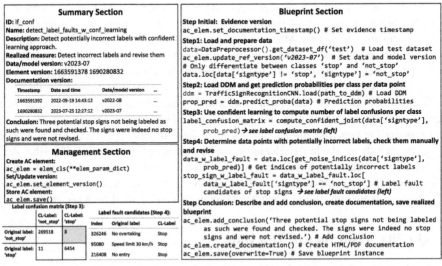

Fig. 3. Overview of a realized blueprint notebook for dealing with incorrectly labeled data points on the example of traffic sign images annotated with their traffic sign type, illustrating the three sections and example code snippets.

data. From a safety perspective, this contributes to the risk acceptance criterion ALARP, which states that the risk remaining after the application of the quality measures is *As Low As Reasonably Practicable* [23].

In Fig. 1, the framework architecture is illustrated on the example of detecting incorrect labels. The claim regarding quality measures applied during data analysis is based on the ALARP criterion and is divided into subclaims for each key characteristic of the test data. The quality measure for detecting and revising incorrect labels is implemented by a blueprint using confident learning [24] to identify potentially incorrect labels, which are then checked and revised if necessary. An overview of the blueprint is shown in Fig. 3, showing the summary, management, and blueprint section together with some code snippets.

5   Conclusion and Future Directions

We have proposed a lightweight Python-based framework named pyAC for operationalizing ACs to assure qualities of ML components, focusing on smooth integration into the daily work of data scientists. We introduced how AC claims can be refined in pyAC and how evidence supporting the subclaims is implemented by quality measures and blueprints. By applying pyAC on an example in the context of test data quality, we illustrated the process of using the framework for a use case. We further presented three main purposes of pyAC: providing templates for data scientists, instantiating them for a use case, and providing a validation basis for assessors.

We also outlined the possibilities of integrating pyAC-generated artifacts into existing AC tools that assure the software system. One possibility is for claims regarding ML components to be completely refined using the external AC tool and pyAC-generated evidence addressing the refined subclaims. Another possibility provides a higher-level claim regarding the quality of the ML component and pyAC further refines this claim in addition to generating evidence.

In future work, we plan to integrate the pyAC-generated artifacts into existing tools such as AMLAS, which already provides an argumentation structure for ML components, or safeTbox, which focuses on assuring the safety of the overall system. Integration of pyAC into external AC tools supports combining capabilities concerning data science and classical software and systems engineering.

pyAC is a step towards the assurance of AI systems, and seems promising in terms of simplifying the verification and validation of these systems by providing support and guidance for data scientists. We hope that our contribution will facilitate the development of more robust and reliable AI systems, and we look forward to further exploration and development of our framework and its potential applications.

Acknowledgments. Parts of this work have been funded by the German Federal Ministry of Education and Research (BMBF) in the project "DAITA", by the project "LOPAAS" as part of the internal funding program "ICON" of the Fraunhofer-Gesellschaft, by the project "AIControl" as part of the funding program "KMU akut" of the Fraunhofer-Gesellschaft, and by the German Federal Ministry for Economic Affairs and Energy in the project "SPELL".

References

1. GSN Community Standard Version 1 (2011). https://scsc.uk/r141:1?t=1. Accessed 28 July 2023
2. Feather, M.S., Slingerland, P.C., Guerrini, S., Spolaor, M.: Assurance guidance for machine learning in a safety-critical system. In: WAAM 2022 (2022)
3. Kläs, M., Adler, R., Jöckel, L., Groß, J., Reich, J.: Using complementary risk acceptance criteria to structure assurance cases for safety-critical AI components. In: AISafety 2021 (2021)
4. Hawkins, R., et al.: Guidance on the assurance of machine learning in autonomous systems (AMLAS). arXiv preprint arXiv:2102.01564 (2021)
5. ASCE Software Overview. https://www.adelard.com/asce/. Accessed 28 July 2023
6. Integrated Safety Case Development Environment. http://www.iscade.co.uk/. Accessed 28 July 2023
7. Astah GSN. https://astah.net/products/astah-gsn/. Accessed 28 July 2023
8. Adedjouma, M., et al.: Engineering dependable AI systems. In: SOSE 2022 (2022)
9. Moncada, V., Santiago, V.: Towards proper tool support for component-oriented and model-based development of safety critical systems. Commer. Veh. Technol. (2016)
10. Kluyver, T., et al.: Jupyter Notebooks-a publishing format for reproducible computational workflows. In: ElPub 2016 (2016)
11. Hauer, M.P., Adler, R., Zweig, K.: Assuring fairness of algorithmic decision making. In: ITEQS 2021 (2021)
12. Rushby, J.M., Xu, X., Rangarajan, M., Weaver, T.L.: Understanding and evaluating assurance cases. NASA Technical Report No. NF1676L-22111 (2015)
13. Wei, R., Kelly, T.P., Dai, X., Zhao, S., Hawkins, R.: Model based system assurance using the structured assurance case metamodel. J. Syst. Softw. (2019)
14. BSI, Fraunhofer HHI, Verband der TÜV. Towards Auditable AI Systems (2021)
15. Maksimov, M., Fung, N.L.S., Kokaly, S., Chechik, M.: Two decades of assurance case tools: a survey. In: Gallina, B., Skavhaug, A., Schoitsch, E., Bitsch, F. (eds.) SAFECOMP 2018. LNCS, vol. 11094, pp. 49–59. Springer, Cham (2018). https://doi.org/10.1007/978-3-319-99229-7_6
16. AMLAS Tool. https://www.york.ac.uk/assuring-autonomy/guidance/amlas/amlas-tool/. Accessed 28 July 2023
17. Zeller, M., Sorokos, I., Reich, J., Adler, R., Schneider, D.: Open dependability exchange metamodel: a format to exchange safety information. In: RAMS 2023 (2023)
18. Pedregosa, F., et al.: Scikit-learn: machine learning in python. J. Mach. Learn. Res. (2011)
19. Jöckel, L., Bauer, T., Kläs, M., Hauer, M.: Towards a common testing terminology for software engineering and data science experts. In: PROFES 2021 (2021)
20. Kläs, M., Jöckel, L., Adler, R., Reich, J.: Integrating testing and operation-related quantitative evidences in assurance cases to argue safety of data-driven AI/ML components. arXiv preprint arXiv:2202.05313 (2022)
21. Jöckel, L., Kläs, M.: Increasing trust in data-driven model validation – a framework for probabilistic augmentation of images and meta-data generation using application scope characteristics. In: SafeComp 2019 (2019)
22. Siebert, J., Seifert, D., Kelbert, P., Kläs, M., Trendowicz, A.: Badgers: generating data quality deficits with python. arXiv preprint arXiv:2307.04468 (2023)
23. IEC. IEC 61508-5:2010 – Functional Safety of Electrical/Electronic/Programmable Electronic Safety-related Systems (2021)
24. Northcutt, C.G., Jiang, L., Chuang, I.L.: Confident learning: estimating uncertainty in dataset labels. Artif. Intell. Res. (2021)

Status Quo and Problems of Requirements Engineering for Machine Learning: Results from an International Survey

Antonio Pedro Santos Alves[1], Marcos Kalinowski[1(✉)], Görkem Giray[2],
Daniel Mendez[3], Niklas Lavesson[3], Kelly Azevedo[1], Hugo Villamizar[1],
Tatiana Escovedo[1], Helio Lopes[1], Stefan Biffl[4], Jürgen Musil[4],
Michael Felderer[5,6], Stefan Wagner[7], Teresa Baldassarre[8], and Tony Gorschek[3]

[1] Pontifical Catholic University of Rio de Janeiro (PUC-Rio), Rio de Janeiro, Brazil
kalinowski@inf.puc-rio.br
[2] Istanbul, Turkey
[3] Blekinge Institute of Technology (BTH), Karlskrona, Sweden
[4] Vienna University of Technology (TU Wien), Vienna, Austria
[5] German Aerospace Center (DLR), Cologne, Germany
[6] University of Cologne, Cologne, Germany
[7] University of Stuttgart, Stuttgart, Germany
[8] University of Bari, Bari, Italy

Abstract. Systems that use Machine Learning (ML) have become commonplace for companies that want to improve their products and processes. Literature suggests that Requirements Engineering (RE) can help address many problems when engineering ML-enabled systems. However, the state of empirical evidence on how RE is applied in practice in the context of ML-enabled systems is mainly dominated by isolated case studies with limited generalizability. We conducted an international survey to gather practitioner insights into the status quo and problems of RE in ML-enabled systems. We gathered 188 complete responses from 25 countries. We conducted quantitative statistical analyses on contemporary practices using bootstrapping with confidence intervals and qualitative analyses on the reported problems involving open and axial coding procedures. We found significant differences in RE practices within ML projects. For instance, (i) RE-related activities are mostly conducted by project leaders and data scientists, (ii) the prevalent requirements documentation format concerns interactive Notebooks, (iii) the main focus of non-functional requirements includes data quality, model reliability, and model explainability, and (iv) main challenges include managing customer expectations and aligning requirements with data. The qualitative analyses revealed that practitioners face problems related to lack of business domain understanding, unclear goals and requirements, low customer engagement, and communication issues. These results help to provide a better understanding of the adopted practices and of which problems exist in practical environments. We put forward the need to adapt further and disseminate RE-related practices for engineering ML-enabled systems.

G. Giray—Independent Researcher

Keywords: Requirements Engineering · Machine Learning · Survey

1   Introduction

Companies from different sectors are increasingly incorporating Machine Learning (ML) components into their software systems. We refer to these software systems, where an ML component is part of a larger system, as ML-enabled systems. The shift from engineering conventional software systems to ML-enabled systems comes with challenges related to the idiosyncrasies of such systems, such as addressing additional qualities properties (*e.g.*, fairness and explainability), dealing with a high degree of iterative experimentation, and facing unrealistic assumptions [21, 25]. Furthermore, the non-deterministic nature of ML-enabled systems poses challenges from the viewpoint of software engineering [7].

Literature suggests that Requirements Engineering (RE) can help to address problems related to engineering ML-enabled systems [1, 25, 28]. However, research on this intersection mainly focuses on using ML techniques to support RE activities rather than exploring how RE can improve the development of ML-enabled systems [4]. The state of empirical evidence on how RE is applied in practice in the context of ML-enabled systems is still weak and dominated by isolated studies.

In order to help addressing these issues, we conducted an international survey with the aim to understand the current industrial RE practices and problems that practitioners face when developing ML-enabled systems. In total, 188 practitioners from 25 countries completely answered the survey. Based on practitioners' responses, we conducted quantitative and qualitative analyses, providing insights into (i) what role is typically in charge of requirements, (ii) how requirements are typically elicited and documented, (iii) which non-functional requirements typically play a major role, (iv) which RE activities are perceived as most difficult, and (v) what RE-related problems do ML practitioners face. We share our findings on the state of practice and problems of RE for ML with the community to help steer future research on the topic.

The remainder of this paper is organized as follows. Section 2 provides the background and related work. Section 3 describes the research method. Section 4 presents the results. Sections 5 and 6 discuss the results and threats to validity. Finally, Sect. 7 presents our concluding remarks.

2   Background and Related Work

ML involves algorithms that analyze data to create models capable of making predictions on new, unseen data [20]. Unlike traditional systems, ML-enabled systems learn from data instead of being programmed with predefined rules. However, poor-quality data can lead to inaccurate results. This supposes a change in the way of designing and developing this type of system. On the other hand, RE constitutes approaches to address challenges that are amplified by the use of ML, e.g., understanding the problem space, aligning interdisciplinary teams, and dealing with stakeholder expectations.

RE and ML have a special connection. According to Kästner [10], an ML model can be seen as a requirements specification based on training data since the data can be seen as a learned description of how the ML model shall behave. In this manner, when developing ML models, we need to identify relevant and representative data, validate models, and balance model-related user expectations (*e.g.*, accuracy versus inference time); just as in RE for traditional systems where we need to identify representative stakeholders, validate specifications with customers, and address conflicting requirements.

Current theoretical SE research has identified many challenges with RE for ML [3,18,19]. Some studies have proposed new methods or adapted existing ones to handle requirements on such systems [9,26,27]. While these research contributions are valuable, gathering empirical evidence from the industry is essential to bridge the gap between theory and practice. Collecting practitioners' insights becomes imperative to identify real-world challenges and current practices accurately. Such studies can provide a better understanding of the practical problems that can guide the advancement of new RE for ML techniques and their effective implementation in real-world scenarios. In the following, we present studies conducted within industry settings involving practitioners to understand RE for ML.

Vogelsang and Borg [28] conducted interviews with four data scientists to find out the current practices and what should be done to handle and surpass the challenges regarding requirements. They suggest the need for new RE for ML solutions or at least the adaptation of existing ones. Habibullah *et al.* [8] conducted interviews and a survey to understand how Non-Functional Requirements (NFRs) are perceived among ML practitioners. They identified the degree of importance practitioners place on different NFRs, explored how NFRs are defined and measured, and identified associated challenges.

Recently, Nahar *et al.* [21] identified challenges in building ML-enabled systems through a systematic literature survey aggregating existing studies involving interviews or surveys with practitioners of multiple projects. With respect to RE, they reported challenges related to unrealistic expectations from stakeholders, vagueness in ML problem specifications, and additional requirements such as regulatory constraints. Scharinger *et al.* [22] revealed the worries at Siemens regarding problems that any ML project is susceptible, listing *ML Pitfalls*, such as lack of decision quality baselines and underestimating costs. They believe that RE is the key to avoid this pitfalls and to ripen ML development.

We complement the valuable research discussed above with additional empirical evidence on current practices and problems regarding RE for ML-enabled systems, obtained from an industrial survey on ML-enabled systems.

3 Research Method

3.1 Goal and Research Questions

The goal of this paper is to characterize the current practices and problems experienced by practitioners in the requirements life cycle stage of ML-enabled system projects. From this goal, we established the following research questions:

- **RQ1. What are the contemporary practices of RE for ML-enabled systems?** This question aims at revealing how practitioners are currently approaching RE for ML, identifying trends, prevalent methods, and the extent to which the industry aligns with established practices. We refined *RQ1* into more detailed questions as follows:
  - RQ1.1 Who is addressing the requirements of ML-enabled system projects?
  - RQ1.2 How are requirements typically elicited in ML-enabled system projects?
  - RQ1.3 How are requirements typically documented in ML-enabled system projects?
  - RQ1.4 Which NFRs do typically play a major role in ML-enabled system projects?
  - RQ1.5 Which activities are considered to be most difficult when defining requirements for ML-enabled system projects?
- **RQ2. What are the main RE-related problems faced by practitioners in ML-enabled system projects?** Identifying these challenges is crucial as it informs the development of strategies to mitigate difficulties, helping to steer future research on the topic in a problem-driven manner. For this research question, we applied open and axial coding procedures to allow the problems to emerge from open-text responses provided by the practitioners.

3.2 Survey Design

We designed our survey based on best practices of survey research [30], carefully conducting the following steps:

- **Step 1. Initial Survey Design.** We conducted a literature review on RE for ML [25] and combined our findings with previous results on RE problems [6] and the RE status quo [29] to provide the theoretical foundations for questions and answer options. Therefrom, the initial survey was drafted by software engineering and machine learning researchers of PUC-Rio (Brazil) with experience in R&D projects involving ML-enabled systems.
- **Step 2. Survey Design Review.** The survey was reviewed and adjusted based on online discussions and annotated feedback from software engineering and machine learning researchers of BTH (Sweden). Thereafter, the survey was also reviewed by the other co-authors.
- **Step 3. Pilot Face Validity Evaluation.** This evaluation involves a lightweight review by randomly chosen respondents. It was conducted with 18 Ph.D. students taking a Survey Research Methods course at UCLM (Spain) (taught by the second author). They were asked to provide feedback on the clearness of the questions and to record their response time. This phase resulted in minor adjustments related to usability aspects and unclear wording. The answers were discarded before launching the survey.

– Step 4. Pilot Content Validity Evaluation. This evaluation involves subject experts from the target population. Therefore, we selected five experienced data scientists developing ML-enabled systems, asked them to answer the survey, and gathered their feedback. The participants had no difficulties in answering the survey and it took an average of 20 min. After this step, the survey was considered ready to be launched.

The final survey started with a consent form describing the purpose of the study and stating that it is conducted anonymously. The remainder was divided into 15 demographic questions (D1 to D15) followed by three specific parts with 17 substantive questions (Q1 to Q17): 7 on the ML life cycle and problems, five on requirements, and five on deployment and monitoring. This paper focuses on the demographics, the ML life cycle problems related to problem understanding and requirements, and the specific questions regarding requirements. The excerpts of the substantive questions related to this paper are shown in Table 1. The survey was implemented using the Unipark Enterprise Feedback Suite.

Table 1. Research questions and survey questions

RQ	Survey No	Description	Type
-	...	...	...
RQ2	Q4	According to your personal experience, please outline the main problems or difficulties (up to three) faced during the Problem Understanding and Requirements ML life cycle stage.	Open
-	...	...	...
RQ1.1	Q8	Who is actively addressing the requirements of ML-enabled system projects in your organization?	Closed (MC)
RQ1.2	Q9	How were requirements typically elicited in the ML-enabled system projects you participated in?	Closed (MC)
RQ1.3	Q10	How were requirements typically documented in the ML-enabled system projects you participated in?	Closed (MC)
RQ1.4	Q11	Which Non-Functional Requirements (NFRs) typically play a major role in terms of criticality in the ML-enabled system projects you participated in?	Closed (MC)
RQ1.5	Q12	Based on your experience, what activities do you consider most difficult when defining requirements for ML-enabled systems?	Closed (MC)
-			

3.3 Data Collection

Our target population concerns professionals involved in building ML-enabled systems, including different activities, such as management, design, and development. Therefore, it includes practitioners in positions such as project leaders, requirements engineers, data scientists, and developers. We used convenience sampling, sending the survey link to professionals active in our partner companies, and also distributed it openly on social media. We excluded participants that informed having no experience with ML-enabled system projects. Data collection was open from January 2022 to April 2022. In total, we received responses from 276 professionals, out of which 188 completed all four survey sections. The average time to complete the survey was of 20 min. We conservatively considered only the 188 fully completed survey responses.

3.4 Data Analysis Procedures

For data analysis purposes, given that all questions were optional, the number of responses varies across the survey questions. Therefore, we explicitly indicate the number of responses when analyzing each question.

Research questions $RQ1.1$ - $RQ1.5$ concern closed questions, so we decided to use inferential statistics to analyze them. Our population has an unknown theoretical distribution (i.e., the distribution of ML-enabled system professionals is unknown). In such cases, resampling methods like bootstrapping, have been reported to be more reliable and accurate than inference statistics from samples [17,30]. Hence, we use bootstrapping to calculate confidence intervals for our results, similar as done in [29]. In short, bootstrapping involves repeatedly taking samples with replacements and then calculating the statistics based on these samples. For each question, we take the sample of n responses for that question and bootstrap S resamples (with replacements) of the same size n. We assume n as the total valid answers of each question [5], and we set 1000 for S, which is a value that is reported to allow meaningful statistics [15].

For research question $RQ2$, which seeks to identify the main problems faced by practitioners involved in engineering ML-enabled systems related to problem understanding and requirements, the corresponding survey question is designed to be open text. We conducted a qualitative analysis using open and axial coding procedures from grounded theory [24] to allow the problems to emerge from the open-text responses reflecting the experience of the practitioners. The qualitative coding procedures were conducted by one PhD student and reviewed by her advisor at one site (Brazil) and reviewed independently by three researchers from two additional sites (two from Sweden and one from Turkey).

The questionnaire, the collected data, and the quantitative and qualitative data analysis artifacts, including Python scripts for the bootstrapping statistics and graphs and the peer-reviewed qualitative coding spreadsheets, are available in our open science repository[1].

4 Results

4.1 Study Population

Fig. 1 summarizes demographic information on the survey participants' countries, roles, and experience with ML-enabled system projects in years. It is

---

[1] https://doi.org/10.5281/zenodo.8248332.

possible to observe that the participants came from different parts of the world, representing various roles and experiences. While the figure shows only the ten countries with the most responses, we had respondents from 25 countries. As expected, our convenience sampling strategy influenced the countries, with most responses being from the authors' countries (Brazil, Turkey, Austria, Germany, Italy, and Sweden).

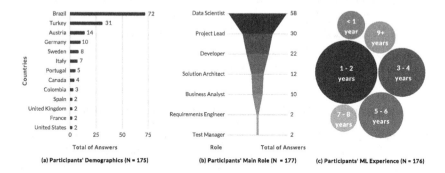

Fig. 1. Demographics: countries, roles, and years of experience.

Regarding employment, 45% of the participants are employed in large companies (2000+ employees), while 55% work in smaller ones of different sizes. It is possible to observe that they are mainly data scientists, followed by project leaders, developers, and solution architects. It is noteworthy that only two participants identified themselves as requirements engineers. Regarding their experience with ML-enabled systems, most of the participants reported having 1 to 2 years of experience. Following closely, another substantial group of participants indicated a higher experience bracket of 3 to 6 years. This distribution highlights a balanced representation of novice and experienced practitioners. Regarding the participants' educational background, 81.38% mentioned having a bachelor's degree in computer science, electrical engineering, information systems, mathematics, or statistics. Moreover, 53.72% held master's degrees, and 22.87% completed Ph.D. programs.

4.2   Problem Understanding and Requirements ML Life Cycle Stage

In the survey, based on the nine ML life cycle stages presented by Amershi *et al.* [2] and the CRISP-DM industry-independent process model phases [23], we abstracted seven generic life cycle stages and asked about their perceived relevance and difficulty. The answers, presented in Fig. 2, revealed that ML practitioners are extremely worried about requirements. The *Problem Understanding and Requirements* stage is clearly perceived as the most relevant and most complex life cycle stage.

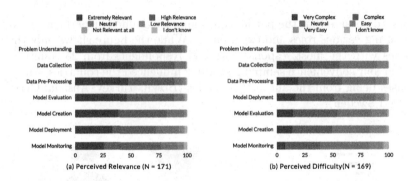

Fig. 2. Perceived relevance and complexity of each ML life cycle stage

4.3   Contemporary RE Practices for ML-Enabled Systems

[RQ1.1] Who is Addressing the Requirements of ML-Enabled System Projects? The proportion of roles reported to address the requirements of ML-enabled system projects within the bootstrapped samples is shown in Fig. 3 together with the 95% confidence interval. The N in each figure caption is the number of participants that answered this question. We report the proportion P of the participants that checked the corresponding answer and its 95% confidence interval in square brackets.

It is possible to observe that the project lead and data scientists were most associated with requirements in ML-enabled systems with **P = 56.439 [56.17, 56.709]** and **P = 54.71 [54.484, 54.936]**, while Business Analysts (**P = 29.518 [29.288, 29.749]**) and Requirements Engineers (**P = 11.202 [11.061, 11.342]**) had a much lower proportion. Several isolated options were mentioned in the "Others" field (*e.g.*, Product Owner, Machine Learning Engineer, and Tech Lead), altogether summing up 11% and not significantly influencing the overall distribution (**P = 11.021 [10.865, 11.177]**).

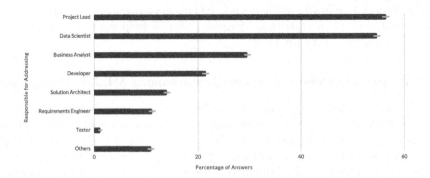

Fig. 3. Roles addressing requirements of ML-enabled systems (N = 170)

[RQ1.2] How Are Requirements Typically Elicited in ML-Enabled System Projects? As presented in Fig. 4, respondents reported interviews as the most commonly used technique (**P = 55.795 [55.567, 56.022]**), followed (or complemented) by prototyping (**P = 43.953 [43.711, 44.195]**), scenarios (**P = 43.065 [42.834, 43.297]**), workshops (**P = 42.708 [42.483, 42.933]**), and observation **P = 36.838 [36.613, 37.063]**.

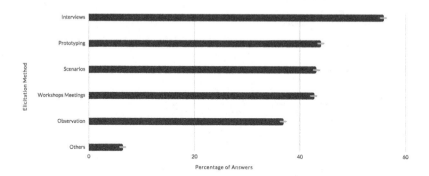

Fig. 4. Requirements elicitation techniques of ML-enabled systems (N = 171)

[RQ1.3] How Are Requirements Typically Documented in the ML-Enabled System Projects? Figure 5 shows Notebooks as the most frequently used documentation format with **P = 37.357 [37.149, 37.564]**, followed by User Stories (**P = 36.115 [35.875, 36.356]**), Requirements Lists (**P = 29.712 [29.499, 29.925]**), Prototypes (**P = 23.957 [23.748, 24.166]**), Use Case Models (**P = 21.617 [21.412, 21.822]**), and Data Models (**P = 19.92 [19.724, 20.117]**). Surprisingly, almost 17% mentioned that requirements are not documented at all with **P = 16.955 [16.767, 17.143]**. Several isolated options were mentioned in the "Others" field(*e.g.*, Wiki tools, Google Docs, Jira) with **P = 8.877 [8.744, 9.011]**.

[RQ1.4] Which Non-Functional Requirements (NFRs) Do Typically Play a Major Role in Terms of Criticality in the ML-Enabled System Projects? Regarding NFRs (Fig. 6), practitioners show a significant concern with some ML-related NFRs, such as data quality (**P = 69.846 [69.616, 70.075]**), model reliability (**P = 42.679 [42.45, 42.907]**), and model explainability (**P = 37.722 [37.493, 37.952]**). Some NFRs regarding the whole system were also considered important, such as system performance (**P = 40.789 [40.573, 41.006]**), and usability (**P = 29.589 [29.36, 29.818]**). A significant amount of participants informed that NFRs were not at all considered within their ML-enabled system projects (**P = 10.617 [10.465, 10.768]**). Furthermore, in the "Others" field (**P = 1.814 [1.745, 1.884]**), a few participants also mentioned that they did not reflect upon NFRs.

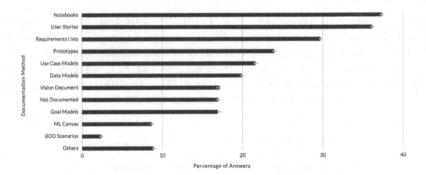

Fig. 5. Requirements documentation of ML-enabled systems (N = 171)

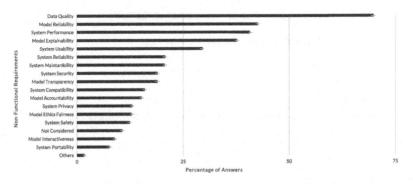

Fig. 6. Critical non-functional requirements of ML-enabled systems (N = 169)

[RQ1.5] Which Activities are Considered Most Difficult When Defining Requirements for ML-Enabled Systems? We provided answer options based on the literature on requirements [29] and requirements for machine learning [25], leaving the "Other" option to allow new activities to be added. As shown in Fig. 7, respondents considered that managing customer expectations is the most difficult task (**P = 66.804 [66.575, 67.032]**), followed by aligning requirements with data (**P = 57.306 [57.066, 57.546]**), resolving conflicts (**P = 38.582 [38.341, 38.824]**), managing changing requirements (**P = 35.62 [35.395, 35.846]**), selecting metrics (**P = 33.95 [33.723, 34.176]**), and elicitation and analysis (**P = 29.036 [28.824, 29.248]**).

4.4   Main RE-Related Problems in ML-Enabled System Projects

Regarding the main problems faced by the participants during the Problem Understanding and Requirements stage, they emerged from open coding applied to free text answers. Participants could inform up to three problems related to each ML life cycle stage. In total, 262 open-text answers were provided for problems related to problem understanding and requirements.

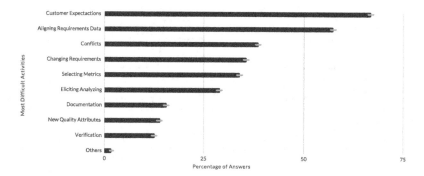

Fig. 7. Most difficult RE activities in ML-enabled systems (N = 171)

We incorporated axial coding procedures to provide an easily understandable overview, relating the emerging codes to categories. We started with the sub-categories *Input*, *Method*, *Organization*, *People*, and *Tools*, as suggested for problems in previous work on defect causal analysis [11]. Based on the data, we merged the *Input* and *People* categories, as it was difficult to separate between the two, given the concise answers provided by the participants. We also renamed the *Tools* category into *Infrastructure* and identified the need to add a new category related to *Data*. It is noteworthy that these categories were identified considering the overall coding for the seven ML life cycle stages, while in this paper, we focus on the problem understanding and requirements stage.

Figure 8 presents an overview of the frequencies of the resulting codes using a probabilistic cause-effect diagram, which was introduced for causal analysis purposes in previous work [12,13]. While this representation provides a comprehensive overview, the percentages are just frequencies of occurrence of the codes (*i.e.*, the sum of all code frequencies is 100%). Also, the highest frequencies within each category are organized closer to the middle.

It is possible to observe that most of the reported problems are related to the *Input* category, followed by *Method* and *Organization*. Within the *Input* category, the main problems concern difficulties in understanding the problem and the business domain and unclear goals and requirements. In the *Method* category, the prevailing reported problems concern difficulties in managing expectations and establishing effective communication. Finally, in the *Organization* category, the lack of customer or domain expert availability and engagement and the lack of time dedicated to requirements-related activities were mentioned. While we focus our summary on the most frequently mentioned problems, it is noteworthy that the less frequent ones may still be relevant in practice. For instance, computational constraints or a lack of data quality (or availability) can directly affect ML-related possibilities and requirements.

5 Discussion

The survey findings reveal an intriguing aspect within ML contexts: the distribution of roles in RE activities. Contrary to conventional expectations, the

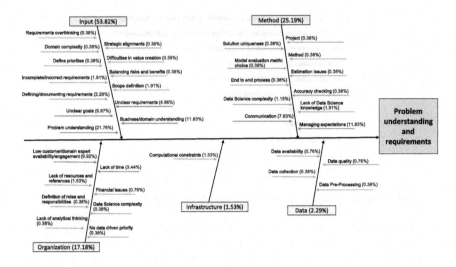

Fig. 8. Main problems faced during problem understanding and requirements

role of requirements engineers and business analyst appears to be less prominent. Instead, a notable shift is observed, with project leaders and data scientists taking the lead in RE efforts. As the literature suggests that RE can help address problems related to engineering ML-enabled systems, this could point to the fact that software engineering practices are not yet well established within this domain. Nevertheless, the involvement of project leaders and data scientists as key RE contributors could reflect the nature of ML projects, where domain expertise and data-driven insights are pivotal. This shift in responsibilities raises questions about the evolving dynamics of cross-functional collaborations within ML endeavors and prompts further exploration into how such roles influence the shaping of ML-enabled systems.

The survey also revealed that practitioners typically use traditional requirements elicitation techniques (interviews, prototyping, scenarios, workshops, and observation). Comparing the results to the elicitation techniques reported for traditional RE [29], an observable difference is that requirements workshops are slightly less commonly used in ML contexts. This could be related to the absence of the requirements engineer, who is typically familiar with conducting such workshops, or to the lack of specific adaptations on such workshop formats for ML-enabled systems.

With respect to requirements documentation, notebooks, which are interactive programming environments that can be used to process data and create ML models, appear as the most used tool for documenting requirements. Again, this could be a symptom of the absence of a requirements engineer and the lack of awareness of RE specification practices and tools. Furthermore, a proportion of almost 17% mentioned that requirements were not documented at all. Given that in conventional contexts problems related to requirements are common causes of overall software project failure [6], this apparent lack of RE-related maturity may also be causing pain in ML contexts. Traditional artifacts, such as user stories, requirements lists, prototypes, and use case models, are also used in the ML context, but significantly less than in the conventional software context [29]. Even specific approaches, such as the ML Canvas, do not relevantly represent a current practice for documenting the requirements of ML-enabled systems.

Regarding NFRs, practitioners express considerable concerns with specific ML-related NFRs, such as data quality, model reliability, and model explainability, while also recognizing the significance of overall system-related NFRs. Nevertheless, more than 10% of practitioners do not even consider NFRs in their ML-enabled system projects. Again, given the potential negative impacts of missing NFRs on software-related projects [6], this can be seen as another indicator of the lack of overall awareness of the importance of RE in the industrial ML-enabled systems engineering context.

The survey also revealed the most difficult activities perceived by practitioners in defining requirements for ML-enabled systems. The difficulties reported by practitioners includes managing customer expectations and aligning requirements with data, highlight the importance of effective communication, a deep understanding of customer needs, and domain and technical expertise to bridge the gap between aspirations and technological feasibility.

Finally, we contributed to the RE-related problems faced by practitioners in ML-enabled system projects. The main issues relate to difficulties in problem and business understanding, managing expectations, and low customer or domain expert availability or engagement. These issues clearly have comparable counterparts in the conventional RE problems [6]. As comparable problems may have comparable solutions, adopting established RE practices (or adaptations of such practices) may help improve ML-enabled system engineering.

6 Threats to Validity

We identified some threats while planning, conducting, and analyzing the survey results. Hereafter we list these potential threats, organized by the survey validity types presented in [16].

Face and Content Validity. Face and content validity threats include bad instrumentation and inadequate explanation of constructs. To mitigate these threats, we involved several researchers in reviewing and evaluating the questionnaire with respect to the format and formulation of the questions, piloting it with 18 Ph.D. students for face validity and with five experienced data scientists for content validity.

Criterion Validity. Threats to criterion validity include not surveying the target population. We clarified the target population in the consent form (before starting the survey). We also considered only complete answers (*i.e.*, answers of participants that answered all four survey sections) and excluded participants that informed having no experience with ML-enabled system projects.

Construct Validity. We ground our survey's questions and answer options on theoretical background from previous studies on RE [6, 29] and a literature review on RE for ML [25]. A threat to construct validity is inadequate measurement procedures and unreliable results. To mitigate this threat we follow recommended data collection and analysis procedures [30].

Reliability. One aspect of reliability is statistical generalizability. We could not construct a random sample systematically covering different types of professionals involved in developing ML-enabled systems, and there is yet no generalized knowledge about what such a population looks like. Furthermore, as a consequence of convenience sampling, the majority of answers came from Europe and South America. Nevertheless, the experience and background profiles of the subjects are comparable to the profiles of ML teams as shown in Microsoft's study [14]. To deal with the random sampling limitation, we used bootstrapping and only employed confidence intervals, conservatively avoiding null hypothesis testing. Another reliability aspect concerns inter-observer reliability, which we improved by including independent peer review in all our qualitative analysis procedures and making all the data and analyses openly available online.

7   Conclusions

Literature suggests that RE can help to tackle challenges in ML-enabled system engineering [25]. Recent literature studies (*e.g.*, [1, 21, 25]) and industrial studies (*e.g.*, [22, 28]) on RE for ML-enabled systems have been important to help to understand the literature focus and industry needs. However, the studies on industrial practices and problems are still isolated and not yet representative.

We complement these studies, aiming at strengthening empirical evidence on current RE practices and problems when engineering ML-enabled systems, with an industrial survey that collected responses from 188 practitioners involved in engineering ML-enabled systems. We applied bootstrapping with confidence intervals for quantitative statistical analysis and open and axial coding for qualitative analysis of RE problems. The results confirmed some of the findings of previous ML-enabled system studies, such as the relevance NFRs related to data quality, model reliability, and explainability [8, 28], and challenges related to customer expectation management and vagueness of requirements specifications [21, 25]. However, we also shed light on some new and intriguing aspects. For instance, the survey revealed that project leaders and data scientists are taking the reins in RE activities for the ML-enabled systems and that interactive Notebooks dominate requirements documentation. With respect to the problems, the main issues relate to difficulties in problem and business understanding, difficulties in managing expectations, unclear requirements, and lack of domain expert availability and engagement.

Overall, when comparing RE practices and problems within ML-enabled systems with conventional RE practices [29] and problems [6], we identified significant variations in the practices but comparable underlying problems. As comparable problems may have comparable solutions, we put forward a need to adapt and disseminate RE-related practices for engineering ML-enabled systems.

References

1. Ahmad, K., Bano, M., Abdelrazek, M., Arora, C., Grundy, J.: What's up with requirements engineering for artificial intelligence systems? In: 2021 IEEE 29th International Requirements Engineering Conference, pp. 1–12. IEEE (2021)
2. Amershi, S., et al.: Software engineering for machine learning: a case study. In: 2019 IEEE/ACM 41st International Conference on Software Engineering: Software Engineering in Practice, pp. 291–300. IEEE (2019)
3. Challa, H., Niu, N., Johnson, R.: Faulty requirements made valuable: on the role of data quality in deep learning. In: 2020 IEEE 7th International Workshop on Artificial Intelligence for Requirements Engineering, pp. 61–69. IEEE (2020)
4. Dalpiaz, F., Niu, N.: Requirements engineering in the days of artificial intelligence. IEEE Softw. **37**(4), 7–10 (2020)
5. Efron, B., Tibshirani, R.J.: An Introduction to the Bootstrap. Chapman & Hall/CRC (1993)
6. Fernández, D.M., et al.: Naming the pain in requirements engineering: Contemporary problems, causes, and effects in practice. Empir. Softw. Eng. **22**, 2298–2338 (2017)
7. Giray, G.: A software engineering perspective on engineering machine learning systems: state of the art and challenges. J. Syst. Softw. **180**, 111031 (2021)
8. Habibullah, K.M., Gay, G., Horkoff, J.: Non-functional requirements for machine learning: understanding current use and challenges among practitioners. Requirements Eng. **28**(2), 283–316 (2023)
9. Ishikawa, F., Matsuno, Y.: Evidence-driven requirements engineering for uncertainty of machine learning-based systems. In: 2020 IEEE 28th International Requirements Engineering Conference, pp. 346–351 (2020). https://doi.org/10.1109/RE48521.2020.00046
10. Kaestner, C.: Machine learning is requirements engineering-on the role of bugs, verification, and validation in machine learning. Medium post. Accessed June 25 (2020)
11. Kalinowski, M., Card, D.N., Travassos, G.H.: Evidence-based guidelines to defect causal analysis. IEEE Softw. **29**(4), 16–18 (2012)
12. Kalinowski, M., Mendes, E., Card, D.N., Travassos, G.H.: Applying DPPI: a defect causal analysis approach using bayesian networks. In: Ali Babar, M., Vierimaa, M., Oivo, M. (eds.) Product-Focused Software Process Improvement, pp. 92–106. Springer, Berlin, Heidelberg (2010). https://doi.org/10.1007/978-3-642-13792-1_9
13. Kalinowski, M., Mendes, E., Travassos, G.H.: Automating and evaluating probabilistic cause-effect diagrams to improve defect causal analysis. In: Caivano, D., Oivo, M., Baldassarre, M.T., Visaggio, G. (eds.) Product-Focused Software Process Improvement, pp. 232–246. Springer, Berlin, Heidelberg (2011). https://doi.org/10.1007/978-3-642-21843-9_19
14. Kim, M., Zimmermann, T., DeLine, R., Begel, A.: Data scientists in software teams: State of the art and challenges. IEEE Trans. Software Eng. **44**(11), 1024–1038 (2017)
15. Lei, S., Smith, M.: Evaluation of several nonparametric bootstrap methods to estimate confidence intervals for software metrics. IEEE Trans. Software Eng. **29**(11), 996–1004 (2003)

16. Linaker, J., Sulaman, S.M., Höst, M., de Mello, R.M.: Guidelines for conducting surveys in software engineering v. 1.1. Lund University 50 (2015)
17. Lunneborg, C.E.: Bootstrap inference for local populations. Therapeut. Innov. Regulatory Sci. 35(4), 1327–1342 (2001)
18. Lwakatare, L.E., Raj, A., Crnkovic, I., Bosch, J., Olsson, H.H.: Large-scale machine learning systems in real-world industrial settings: a review of challenges and solutions. Inform. Softw. Technol. 127 (2020). https://doi.org/10.1016/j.infsof.2020.106368
19. Martínez-Fernández, S., et al.: Software engineering for AI-based systems: a survey. ACM Trans. Softw. Eng. Methodol. 31(2), 1–59 (2022)
20. Mitchell, T.M.: Machine learning (1997)
21. Nahar, N., Zhang, H., Lewis, G., Zhou, S., Kästner, C.: A meta-summary of challenges in building products with ml components-collecting experiences from 4758+ practitioners. arXiv preprint arXiv:2304.00078 (2023)
22. Scharinger, B., Borg, M., Vogelsang, A., Olsson, T.: Can re help better prepare industrial AI for commercial scale? IEEE Softw. 39(6), 8–12 (2022)
23. Schröer, C., Kruse, F., Gómez, J.M.: A systematic literature review on applying crisp-dm process model. Proc. Comput. Sci. 181, 526–534 (2021)
24. Stol, K.J., Ralph, P., Fitzgerald, B.: Grounded theory in software engineering research: a critical review and guidelines. In: Proceedings of the 38th International Conference on Software Engineering, pp. 120–131 (2016)
25. Villamizar, H., Escovedo, T., Kalinowski, M.: Requirements engineering for machine learning: a systematic mapping study. In: 2021 47th Euromicro Conference on Software Engineering and Advanced Applications, pp. 29–36 (2021)
26. Villamizar, H., Kalinowski, M., Lopes, H.: Towards perspective-based specification of machine learning-enabled systems. In: 2022 48th Euromicro Conference on Software Engineering and Advanced Applications, pp. 112–115. IEEE (2022)
27. Villamizar, H., Kalinowski, M., Lopes, H., Mendez, D.: Identifying concerns when specifying machine learning-enabled systems: a perspective-based approach (2023)
28. Vogelsang, A., Borg, M.: Requirements engineering for machine learning: Perspectives from data scientists. In: 2019 IEEE 27th International Requirements Engineering Conference Workshops, pp. 245–251 (2019)
29. Wagner, S., et al.: Status quo in requirements engineering: a theory and a global family of surveys. ACM Trans. Softw. Eng. Methodol. 28(2) (2019)
30. Wagner, S., Mendez, D., Felderer, M., Graziotin, D., Kalinowski, M.: Challenges in survey research. Contemporary Empirical Methods in Software Engineering, pp. 93–125 (2020)

A Stochastic Approach Based on Rational Decision-Making for Analyzing Software Engineering Project Status

Hannes Salin[1,2(✉)] [iD]

[1] Swedish Transport Administration, Borlänge, Sweden
hannes.salin@trafikverket.se
[2] School of Information and Engineering, Dalarna University, Borlänge, Sweden
hasa@du.se

Abstract. This study presents a novel approach to project status prediction in software engineering, based on unobservable states of decision-making processes, utilizing Hidden Markov Models (HMMs). By establishing HMM structures and leveraging the Rational Decision Making model (RDM), we encoded underlying project conditions; observed project data from a software engineering organization were utilized to estimate model parameters via the Baum-Welch algorithm. The developed HMMs, four project-specific models, were subsequently tested with empirical data, demonstrating their predictive potential. However, a generalized, aggregated model did not show any sufficient accuracy. Model development and experiments were made in Python. Our approach presents preliminary work and a pathway for understanding and forecasting project dynamics in software development environments.

Keywords: Project status · Software engineering · Hidden Markov Model · Decision making · Project status prediction

1 Introduction

Effective decision-making plays a crucial role in steering software projects towards success, as it directly impacts time management, resource allocation, and quality control. Sound decisions can ensure that a project remain within budget and deadlines while maintaining the expected level of quality [12]. Hence, the ability to accurately predict project statuses through the understanding of project decision-making processes, could ultimately contribute to more efficient data-driven decision-making for project managers [1,7]. Addressing the complexities of project status prediction is challenging due to the inherent hidden processes of decision making. Our focus is thus to develop a predictive model being able to forecast project status by capturing these underlying, unseen decision-making processes. One approach to analyze non-observable processes in a stochastic system is to use Markov models. Such models have been studied in many different areas within the software engineering context [9], e.g., software test result prediction [15] and system reliability analysis [2]. Also, specifically in

© The Author(s), under exclusive license to Springer Nature Switzerland AG 2024
R. Kadgien et al. (Eds.): PROFES 2023, LNCS 14483, pp. 175–182, 2024.
https://doi.org/10.1007/978-3-031-49266-2_12

IT-projects, Markov models have been used, e.g., risk prediction [5], developer learning [13] and bug-fix prediction [3]. The aim of this study then, is to provide preliminary results of modelling hidden decision-making processes in software engineering projects, based on observed project status data. Our results will provide for future interdisciplinary research where we can combine qualitative approaches to better understand project decision-making, and fusing it into predictive models. The paper proceeds as follows: Sect. 2 explains hidden Markov models, followed by our research method in Sect. 3. Our model is elaborated in Sect. 4, and experimental results are showcased in Sect. 5. Finally, Sects. 6 and 7 discuss and conclude the results, respectively.

2   Hidden Markov Models

We briefly introduce the concept of a *Hidden Markov Model* (HMM), which is a stochastic model used for representing a system that follows a Markov process with unobserved states [6]. It defines a system where transitions between states occur with certain probabilities and these transitions are inherently time-discrete. The model have a set $S = \{s_1, s_2, ..., s_N\}$ of N states, which are hidden but can be inferred through a sequence of observable outputs from the set $\mathcal{O} = \{o_1, o_2, ..., o_M\}$ of M possible outputs. To transition between two hidden states s_i and s_j, the first-order Markov property must hold, i.e. the probability of moving to the next state s_j only depends on the current state s_i and not on the sequence of previous states. If q_t denotes the state at time t, the transition probability from state s_i to state s_j is expressed as:

$$a_{ij} = P(q_{t+1} = s_j | q_t = s_i) \tag{1}$$

where each a_{ij} are the elements of a state transition matrix $\mathbf{A}$ which relates to the emission probabilities:

$$b_{ij} = P(o_j \text{ at time } t | q_t = s_i) \tag{2}$$

referring to the probability of observing the j-th observation at time t, when the system is in the i-th hidden state. These are collected into the emission matrix $\mathbf{B}$. These matrices are thus of the form:

$$\mathbf{A} = \begin{bmatrix} a_{11} & a_{12} & \cdots & a_{1N} \\ a_{21} & a_{22} & \cdots & a_{2N} \\ \vdots & \vdots & \ddots & \vdots \\ a_{N1} & a_{N2} & \cdots & a_{NN} \end{bmatrix} \quad \mathbf{B} = \begin{bmatrix} b_{11} & b_{12} & \cdots & b_{1M} \\ b_{21} & b_{22} & \cdots & b_{2M} \\ \vdots & \vdots & \ddots & \vdots \\ b_{N1} & b_{N2} & \cdots & b_{NM} \end{bmatrix}$$

We denote a model as $\lambda = (\mathbf{A}, \mathbf{B})$. There are three fundamental problems to solve when dealing with a HMM, formulated by Rabiner [10]. Let $O_s = o_1...o_k$ be a sequence of k observations from the observation set $\mathcal{O}$, then the problems are: to compute the likelihood of a sequence of observations O_s given λ (i.e. $P(O_s)|\lambda)$), to identify the optimal sequence of hidden states for a provided sequence of observations O_s and a HMM $\lambda = (\mathbf{A}, \mathbf{B})$, and to infer the probabilities in $\mathbf{A}$ and $\mathbf{B}$ of the model for a specific sequence of observations O_s and the state set within the HMM. The first problem can be solved by the Forward-algorithm, the second by the Viterbi algorithm and the third can be estimated using the Baum-Welch algorithm [6].

3   Method

Our study is an experimental model evaluation study, based on real data from the Swedish Transport Administration (STA). Hence, the results may not lead to general conclusions. We used recorded project status data from a subset of STA's software engineering organization. The studied projects were similar in scope and size (deliver software systems, between 4–7 team members), and all included software development and agile practices. Each project had a project manager and an annually planned budget.

Our study consists of two phases: develop the model, and experimental testing of the model. We first establish the structure of our HMM:s, involving the definition and probability estimations of the hidden states and the observable outputs of our model. These states represent underlying conditions or factors that drive the observed data but are not directly measurable. The hidden states are based on the Rational Decision Making model as described in [14], which includes seven different stages, whereas our model only consider four of them. The observable output definitions are derived through an analysis of the company's project tracking system and the specific project status data that is stored. After developing the HMM we then tested the model using a subset of the observed data that was not used for training, by computing the probability of observing a specific sequence of emissions given the parameters of the model [6]. During data extraction from the project tracking tool, we anonymized the project meta data by listing all projects and then randomly assigning identities P_i for $i = 1, 2, ..., n$. For each P_i, a CSV file containing the numerical encoding of the observed output was created where each row consisted of k, t_k, c_k, q_k where k is the reporting date, and t_k, c_k, q_k representing the reported values of time, cost and quality at date k. From these CSV files, the parameter estimation, i.e. estimating $\mathbf{A}$ and $\mathbf{B}$, were derived using the Baum-Welch algorithm. We used Python and the `hmmlearn` package [4] for encoding the collected data, building the HMM proof of concept implementation and prediction testing.

3.1   Rational Decision Making

Rational decision-making, as defined by Scott and Bruce [11], includes a thorough investigation for data and a logical analysis of various alternatives, emphasizing systematic, goal-oriented decision processes. It underscores planning and verification of information sources to ensure accurate facts. Rational decision-making presumes that with complete information, individuals can discern all potential solutions and choose the one maximizing their outcome [8]. In the context of the company we studied, this model is notably relevant as their projects largely revolve around long-term, standard activities, although adopting agile best practices, rather than innovative or research-oriented activities.

We have chosen four essential stages of decision making, derived from the seven stages of the Rational Decision-Making (RDM) model in [14]. The chosen stages are *"Identifying the Solution"*, *"Information Gathering and Analysis"*, *"Evaluate Options"*, and *"Implementing Decision"*. The rationale for selecting these specific stages is twofold. Firstly, they provide the core of decision-making, simplifying the process while ensuring systematic considerations. Secondly, they include the logical steps in project decision-making by identifying solutions upfront, conducting thorough analysis, evaluating potential options, and implementing the chosen decision. These stages thus highlight the essence of software engineering project management: discerning issues and making informed decisions.

We work under the assumption that decision-making, especially as demonstrated in agile software engineering projects [1,8], strongly influences project performance and therefore should effectively define the hidden states of project progression. The decision-making process with four simplified stages is then established as a single influential factor for project success, setting the initial step towards a project status prediction model based on empirical data. We firmly believe that future expansions of this model should take into account multiple influencing parameters such as organizational culture and other socio-psychological aspects. Although this may necessitate qualitative and mixed-method approaches, it holds the potential to significantly enhance our model's effectiveness.

4   Model Development

Our collected data consisted of project status reports from 4 different projects $P_1, ..., P_4$, spanning over 36 months, ending in May 2023. The projects were chosen out of 11 available projects, but the remaining 7 projects did not have historical data more than 14 months. The projects had an increasing status fluctuation where P_1 changed between 3 states in long cycles (up to 8 months), and P_4 changed between 7 states with cycles between 1 and 4 months. There is no information of any change of decision states in the projects between these 4 weeks. Therefore, we need to consider a HMM due to the non-observable states in-between reporting of the project status. The project tracking tool uses traffic-light encoding on the three dimensions time, cost and quality, where red equals *"Bad status"*, yellow equals *"Acceptable status"*, and green equals *"Good status"*. We encode these into numerical values 0 (bad), 1 (acceptable) and 2 (good). Thus, our model have 27 different observable outputs where observation is defined as follows:

Definition 1. *Let $o = (\tau_T, \tau_C, \tau_Q)$ be a tuple, representing an observation of the model where the dimensions τ_T is time, τ_C is cost, and τ_Q is quality. Each dimension has a discrete value of either 0,1 or 2.*

The set of states for our HMM is $S = \{s_1, s_2, s_3, s_4\}$, defined as *identify, analyze, evaluate* and *implement*, respectively, hence representing the project's decision-making status. Each observation o is represented as a tuple in Definition 1, with a date stamp k, thus allowing for records of temporal sequences of the observations for a project P_i. This setup results in 27 possible observations each project can inhabit and 4 different states. The emission matrix **B** is thus of size 4×27.

4.1 Parameter Estimation

The notion of *parameter estimation* is the third problem stated by Rabiner, i.e. of computing suitable state transition probabilities for **A** and **B**. Several different methods are used in practice, but the Baum-Welch method is one of the more commonly used one [6]. We implemented a HMM $\lambda = (\mathbf{A}, \mathbf{B})$ using the Baum-Welch algorithm for estimating the transition probabilities, using the hmmlearn Python package. Each project P_i's CSV file with project status data was fed into the HMM via an encoding function we wrote for encoding each entry (c_k, t_k, q_k) into a corresponding integer representing the observation. The mapping is in increasing order where $(0, 0, 0) \rightarrow 0$ up to $(2, 2, 2) \rightarrow 26$. The HMM was then computed using the hmm.CategoricalHMM model, and the parameters were estimated using the model.fit() function. In total we used extracted data from the projects P_1–P_4, each project containing 36 rows of data points.

5 Experimental Results

We conducted two separate experiments. First, each project P_i was trained into a separate HMM $\lambda_i = (\mathbf{A}_i, \mathbf{B}_i)$, using the above described parameter estimation. These were then tested for status prediction. In the testing phase, the parameter estimations were updated in iterations, until the best fit was found, i.e. the model that gave the most accurate prediction when executing the model.predict() function. Next, we aggregated each λ_i into one large model λ to compare a more generalized model with the project specific models. This was done by using weights w_i from each model, based on the accuracy from the testing phase. For a better readability, we created heat maps for each emission matrix. The developed models λ_1–λ_4 had the following transition matrices and the corresponding emission matrices are shown as heat maps in Fig. 1:

$$\mathbf{A}_1 = \begin{bmatrix} 0.09 & 0.00 & 0.36 & 0.55 \\ 0.00 & 0.47 & 0.01 & 0.52 \\ 0.01 & 0.16 & 0.83 & 0.00 \\ 0.82 & 0.11 & 0.02 & 0.07 \end{bmatrix} \quad \mathbf{A}_2 = \begin{bmatrix} 0.21 & 0.00 & 0.60 & 0.19 \\ 0.31 & 0.69 & 0.00 & 0.00 \\ 0.11 & 0.61 & 0.26 & 0.12 \\ 0.00 & 0.00 & 0.09 & 0.91 \end{bmatrix}$$

$$\mathbf{A}_3 = \begin{bmatrix} 0.00 & 1.00 & 0.00 & 0.00 \\ 0.21 & 0.78 & 0.01 & 0.00 \\ 0.38 & 0.24 & 0.00 & 0.38 \\ 0.42 & 0.54 & 0.00 & 0.04 \end{bmatrix} \quad \mathbf{A}_4 = \begin{bmatrix} 0.87 & 0.00 & 0.00 & 0.13 \\ 0.03 & 0.00 & 0.42 & 0.55 \\ 0.12 & 0.00 & 0.00 & 0.88 \\ 0.03 & 0.84 & 0.13 & 0.00 \end{bmatrix}$$

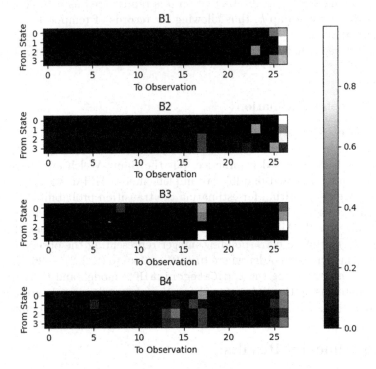

Fig. 1. The computed emission matrices $\mathbf{B}_1, ..., \mathbf{B}_4$ for models $\lambda_1, ..., \lambda_4$, represented as heat maps. The bar shows probability measure.

Note that due to readability, we rounded each probability into two decimals, hence some entries with 0.00 might be a non-zero probability but lower than 0.01. Each model was tested on the observed states $o_{27}, ..., o_{31}$ from the collected observations of each project, letting the model predict the 5 next future observations using the model.predict() function. We compared these with the actual observations $o_{32}, ..., o_{36}$, computing the model's accuracy. The resulting accuracy for each model were 0.8, 0.5, 0.8 and 0.9 respectively. The accuracy was computed as the frequency the model successfully predicted the output, where 1.0 means 100% accuracy. For the aggregated model we computed the weights w_i for each HMM: $w_i = \frac{\alpha_i}{\sigma}$ where α_i is the accuracy of λ_i and $\sigma = \sum_{j=1}^{4} \alpha_j$. These were used in the weighted calculation of the aggregated matrix $\mathbf{A} = \sum_{i=1}^{N} w_i * \mathbf{A}_i$. The same procedure was made for the aggregated matrix $\mathbf{B}$. Due to space constraints we only show $\mathbf{A}$:

$$\mathbf{A} = \begin{bmatrix} 0.32 & 0.26 & 0.25 & 0.17 \\ 0.12 & 0.45 & 0.13 & 0.30 \\ 0.15 & 0.21 & 0.27 & 0.37 \\ 0.33 & 0.43 & 0.06 & 0.18 \end{bmatrix}$$

To compute the matrices we used the weights $w_1 = 0.267, w_2 = 0.167, w_3 = 0.267$ and $w_4 = 0.300$. The aggregated model $\lambda = (\mathbf{A}, \mathbf{B})$ was then tested on a sequence $o'_{27}, ..., o'_{31}$ selected from a random project P_i. The computed accuracy was only 0.2 with the aggregated models, and we did not get any better result trying other models with lower accuracy.

6 Discussion

The increasing fluctuation of observable states of the projects (from the extracted project data) are reflected by the emission matrices, where P_1 had the least jumps between project status states (stable project) and P_4 had most jumps (unstable project). In models λ_1 and λ_2, there is a strong tendency to remain in the *evaluate* state, indicating a process that relies on evaluation and adjustment. However, λ_2 also shows a tendency for the *analyze* state to transition back to *identify*, suggesting a cycle of redefining problems during the analysis phase. λ_3 shows an immediate transition from *identify* to *analysis* and has a significant likelihood of identifying new problems during the analysis and decision implementation stages. λ_4 depicts a fast-track decision-making process that often bypasses the *evaluate* stage, with a strong tendency to revisit the *analyze* stage during implementation, suggesting iterative refinement or correction. Together, these models suggest a range of decision-making behaviors, from reflective and evaluative to direct and iterative. The aggregated model λ had a very low accuracy and it would be a natural consequence due to the largely different sub models. We interpret this as the need for customized project models are necessary, given the proposed, yet simple, model development. Most importantly, future research must validate and refine these suggestions, and we propose qualitative methods to cross-check these findings with the decision-makers.

7 Conclusion

The models were trained on relative small data sets, but were still able to perform sufficient predictions in most cases, i.e. better than random guessing. Due to its simple implementable nature, the project specific models can serve as a basis for further development of project status prediction using sophisticated and novel approaches in fine-tuning the parameters further. There is no fruitful effect of aggregate the models, thus keeping them project specific is the most efficient approach. The anonymized data sets for training and testing, and the developed boiler plate code can be found at github.com/hannessalin/research-code.

References

1. Drury-Grogan, M.L., O'Dwyer, O.: An investigation of the decision-making process in agile teams. Int. J. Inf. Technol. Decis. Making **12**(06), 1097–1120 (2013)
2. Farahani, A., Shoja, A., Tohidi, H.: Chapter 6 - Markov and semi-Markov models in system reliability. In: Garg, H., Ram, M. (eds.) Engineering Reliability and Risk Assessment, pp. 91–130. Advances in Reliability Science, Elsevier (2023). https://doi.org/10.1016/B978-0-323-91943-2.00010-1. https://www.sciencedirect.com/science/article/pii/B9780323919432000101
3. Habayeb, M., Murtaza, S.S., Miranskyy, A., Bener, A.B.: On the use of hidden Markov model to predict the time to fix bugs. IEEE Trans. Softw. Eng. **44**(12), 1224–1244 (2018). https://doi.org/10.1109/TSE.2017.2757480
4. hmmlearn developers: hmmlearn (2023). https://hmmlearn.readthedocs.io/en/latest/
5. Jiang, G., Fu, Y.: A two-phase method based on Markov and TOPSIS for evaluating project risk management strategies. In: The 27th Chinese Control and Decision Conference (2015 CCDC), pp. 1994–1998 (2015). https://doi.org/10.1109/CCDC.2015.7162248
6. Mattila, R.: Hidden Markov models: identification, control and inverse filtering. Ph.D. thesis, KTH Royal Institute of Technology (2018)
7. Mendes, E., Rodriguez, P., Freitas, V., Baker, S., Atoui, M.A.: Towards improving decision making and estimating the value of decisions in value-based software engineering: the value framework. Softw. Qual. J. **26**, 607–656 (2018)
8. Moe, N.B., Aurum, A., Dybå, T.: Challenges of shared decision-making: a multiple case study of agile software development. Inf. Softw. Technol. **54**(8), 853–865 (2012). https://doi.org/10.1016/j.infsof.2011.11.006. https://www.sciencedirect.com/science/article/pii/S0950584911002308. Special Issue: Voice of the Editorial Board
9. Mor, B., Garhwal, S., Kumar, A.: A systematic review of hidden Markov models and their applications. Arch. Comput. Methods Eng. **28**, 1429–1448 (2021)
10. Rabiner, L.: A tutorial on hidden Markov models and selected applications in speech recognition. Proc. IEEE **77**(2), 257–286 (1989). https://doi.org/10.1109/5.18626
11. Scott, S.G., Bruce, R.A.: Decision-making style: the development and assessment of a new measure. Educ. Psychol. Measur. **55**(5), 818–831 (1995)
12. Simon, H.A.: Rational decision making in business organizations. Am. Econ. Rev. **69**(4), 493–513 (1979)
13. Singh, P.V., Tan, Y., Youn, N.: A hidden Markov model of developer learning dynamics in open source software projects. Inf. Syst. Res. **22**(4), 790–807 (2011)
14. Uzonwanne, F.C.: Rational model of decision making. In: Farazmand, A. (ed.) Global Encyclopedia of Public Administration, Public Policy, and Governance, pp. 1–6. Springer, Cham (2016). https://doi.org/10.1007/978-3-319-31816-5_2474-1
15. Whittaker, J., Rekab, K., Thomason, M.: A Markov chain model for predicting the reliability of multi-build software. Inf. Softw. Technol. **42**(12), 889–894 (2000). https://doi.org/10.1016/S0950-5849(00)00122-1. https://www.sciencedirect.com/science/article/pii/S0950584900001221

CAIS-DMA: A Decision-Making Assistant for Collaborative AI Systems

Diaeddin Rimawi[1]([✉]) [iD], Antonio Liotta[1] [iD], Marco Todescato[2] [iD],
and Barbara Russo[1] [iD]

[1] Faculty of Engineering, Free University of Bozen-Bolzano, 39100 Bolzano, Italy
{drimawi,antonio.liotta,barbara.russo}@unibz.it
[2] Fraunhofer Italia, 39100 Bolzano, Italy
marco.todescato@fraunhofer.it

Abstract. A Collaborative Artificial Intelligence System (CAIS) is a cyber-physical system that learns actions in collaboration with humans in a shared environment to achieve a common goal. In particular, a CAIS is equipped with an AI model to support the decision-making process of this collaboration. When an event degrades the performance of CAIS (i.e., a disruptive event), this decision-making process may be hampered or even stopped. Thus, it is of paramount importance to monitor the learning of the AI model, and eventually support its decision-making process in such circumstances. This paper introduces a new methodology to automatically support the decision-making process in CAIS when the system experiences performance degradation after a disruptive event. To this aim, we develop a framework that consists of three components: one manages or simulates CAIS's environment and disruptive events, the second automates the decision-making process, and the third provides a visual analysis of CAIS behavior. Overall, our framework automatically monitors the decision-making process, intervenes whenever a performance degradation occurs, and recommends the next action. We demonstrate our framework by implementing an example with a real-world collaborative robot, where the framework recommends the next action that balances between minimizing the recovery time (i.e., resilience), and minimizing the energy adverse effects (i.e., greenness).

Keywords: Greenness · Resilience · Software Development Process · Collaborative Artificial Intelligence System · Cyber-Physical System

1 Introduction

A Cyber-Physical System (CPS) has heterogeneous hardware-software components that collaborate to deliver real-time services, [13]. The complexity of CPS varies from one domain to the other. A Collaborative Artificial Intelligence System (CAIS) is an example of a CPS that works together with humans to achieve a common goal, [1]. The core component of CAIS responsible for decision-making is its Artificial Intelligence (AI) model. The AI model is responsible for making decisions to control the collaboration between the system and the human. In

R. Kadgien et al. (Eds.): PROFES 2023, LNCS 14483, pp. 183–199, 2024.
https://doi.org/10.1007/978-3-031-49266-2_13

general, AI model's training can be either from historical data (offline learning) or iterative during run-time (online learning), [15]. In CAIS context, the AI model learns from the human in an online learning mode. Online learning can be affected by environmental changes (i.e., disruptive events) that may hamper the ability of the system to take real-time decisions. For instance, disruptive events may affect the learning data, and thus, it may affect the AI model prediction accuracy and the reliability of the system, [2]. Therefore, it is of paramount importance to provide CAISs with a recovery instrument that automatically supports the decision-making process in case of disruptive events. The instrument needs to monitor the system performance, detect performance degradation, mitigate the cause through feasible recovery actions, and recover the system performance to an acceptable performance level, [4,6,15].

In this paper, we introduce our framework the *Collaborative Artificial Intelligence System Decision-Making Assistant (CAIS-DMA)*, which automatically orchestrates the decision-making process between CAIS and humans when CAIS's performance degrades. The framework is developed to be equipped as a CAIS component, monitors its performance under a disruptive event, and automatically intervenes when a performance degradation occurs. The framework intervention aims to recover CAIS from performance degradation to an acceptable performance level. The recovery is achieved by supporting CAIS's AI model in restoring its accuracy as fast as possible, to ensure the real-time service delivery of CAIS. To this aim, CAIS-DMA is equipped with three extendable components: i) Simulator, ii) Actuator, and iii) Monitoring component. The simulator simulates the run-time environment of CAIS's AI model and the human role in an online learning dataset. Then, it allows us to enforce the disruptive event effect on the dataset, and stream the data to the AI model in the expected structure. On the other hand, the actuator monitors CAIS's performance and invokes the measurement mechanism to recommend the next action in case of performance degradation. Finally, the monitoring component provides a toolbox for CAIS's managers to tune the framework components' configurations, and illustrates CAIS's behavior through a visual analysis representation.

Additionally, we demonstrate CAIS-DMA in a real-world demonstrator, in which we implement CAIS-DMA to assist a collaborative robot in recovering from performance degradation after a disruptive event occurs. In this demonstration, CAIS-DMA will assist the robot in taking the next action that ensures fast recovery from the disruptive event (*resilience*). However, this implies additional energy consumption, which increases the energy adverse effects and lowers CAIS's *greenness*. Thus, we leverage our approach that balances the two properties. Our approach is *GResilience* [13,15], a measurement mechanism to find the action that best trade-off between greenness and resilience. GResilience is equipped with two independent techniques: i) a weighted sum optimization model, and ii) a game theory model leveraging "The Battle of Sexes" game.

Our major contribution in this paper can be summarized as follows:

1. We introduce CAIS-DMA our novel framework to assist CAIS's managers in simulating, actuating, and monitoring their systems. CAIS-DMA simulator supports creating a working environment with potential disruptive

events, which allows testing CAIS's AI model responsible for the collaboration between the system and the human, without risking draining CAIS's resources. Additionally, the framework actuator automatically supports CAIS's decision-making by recommending the next action that achieves the selection criteria (through the selection mechanisms). Finally, CAIS-DMA provides a visual analysis monitoring component to monitor CAIS's performance.

2. We design CAIS-DMA components to be extendable, where the developers can customize the framework components to represent different CAISs. The simulator can simulate different CAISs environments including the disruptive events they may be exposed to. Additionally, the actuator can be extended with new selection mechanisms and new recovery actions to recommend from. As for the monitoring component, it can tune the framework configurations to run different environmental settings.

3. We show how CAIS-DMA can be equipped with CAIS, by demonstrating the development process with a real-world collaborative robot. In our application, we support action selection by recommending the action that best trade-off between greenness and resilience. Specifically, we wrap the GResilience [13,15] as the measurement mechanism, to automatically support decision-making.

The rest of this paper is structured as follows. In Sect. 2 we provide a background about the performance states, resilience, greenness, and the GResilience approach. In Sect. 3 we discuss CAIS-DMA architecture. In Sect. 4 we discuss how CAIS-DMA can automatically support the decision-making process in online-learning-based CAIS. In Sect. 5 we demonstrate the development process of equipping CAIS-DMA with CAIS. In Sect. 6 we discuss the paper threats to validity. In Sect. 7 we discuss the related work. Finally, in Sect. 8 we state our conclusion and discuss our future work.

2   Background

By principle, the online learning model eventually readjusts to the environmental changes after enough training, [15]. Thus, CAIS's AI model, which is an online-learning-based model, learns based on accumulated data between normal and disruptive environmental settings. Hence, when fixing the disruption event CAIS's performance will face another performance degradation, due to the training data used while being under disruption. Figure 1, shows the performance behavior of CAIS under disruption. The system starts with a *Steady State*, in which the *Performance Threshold* is defined as the lowest performance point. When the *Disruptive Event* occurs it leads to performance degradation entering the *Disruption State*. At this point, CAIS will try to adjust to the disruption, and with enough data from the *human*, it manages to enter a *Recovered State*. The system will continue living in disruption until a new environment change occurs (*Fix Event*), then it enters the *Final State*, starting with a second *Disruptive State* due to the historical data, and then recover back to a second *Steady State*.

CAIS-DMA aims to recommend actions based on decision criteria that are concerned with restoring the system performance from performance degradation to an acceptable performance level. Thus, it is important to define how to measure performance in order to understand what state the system is in. In this paper, we focus on CAIS's AI model's ability for autonomous decision-making, and we consider the autonomous decision-making ratio in a windows of time as our performance measurement. As a result, we search for the action that both minimizes the time to restore the autonomous decision-making ratio from degradation to an acceptable level and minimizes the energy adverse effect. Thus, we consider two non-functional properties of CAIS: *resilience* and *greenness*. The rest of this section discusses what they represent based on the GResilience measurement mechanism leveraged in our demonstration.

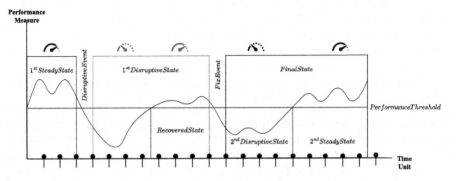

Fig. 1. CAIS Under Disruptive Event Performance States

2.1   Resilience

We consider resilience as a non-functional property that is concerned about recovering the system performance from a performance degradation to an acceptable performance level. Thus, we measure it by the action's *Estimated Time (ET)*. Equation (1), uses the *exponential smoothing* as an estimation technique to find the next iteration $i + 1$ *ET* for action a (ET_a^{i+1}), where ($DT_a^i - ET_a^i$) is the error with the actual time from the previous iteration i, and α is the smoothing constant.

$$ET_a^{i+1} = ET_a^i + \alpha \cdot (DT_a^i - ET_a^i) \tag{1}$$

2.2   Greenness

System greenness is a non-functional property concerned with the efficient usage of energy while minimizing its adverse effects, [8]. One of the energy adverse effects we consider to measure CAIS greenness is the CO_2 footprint, which may increase

Table 1. The GResilience Game General Payoff Matrix

		P_g		
		$a_1(p)$	$a_2(1-p)$	P_r **Expected Payoff**
P_r	$a_1(q)$	$P_r^2(a_1), P_g^2(a_1)$	$P_r^1(a_1), P_g^1(a_2)$	$pP_r^2(a_1) + (1-p)P_r^1(a_1)$
	$a_2(1-q)$	$P_r^1(a_2), P_g^1(a_1)$	$P_r^2(a_2), P_g^2(a_2)$	$pP_r^1(a_2) + (1-p)P_r^2(a_2)$
	P_g **Expected Payoff**	$qP_g^2(a_1) + (1-q)P_g^1(a_1)$	$qP_g^1(a_2) + (1-q)P_g^2(a_2)$	

when the CAIS's AI makes decisions to autonomously operate while still under disruption. On the other hand, we can not drain human resources all the time by continuously moving to the learning mode. Thus, we constrain the human measurements with a maximum number of human iterations. To compute the system greenness we consider two variables: i) *Estimated CO$_2$ Footprint (ECF)* of an action, and ii) the human labor cost as *Number of Human Interactions (NHI)* remaining for the action. As for ET, the ECF is estimated using the exponential smoothing, Eq. (2). ECF_a is the ECF for action a for an iteration i, DCF_a is the actual carbon footprint of an iteration, and α is the smoothing constant. Equation (3) shows the NHI_a which is the NHI for an iteration, NHI_{max} is the maximum allowed NHI, and NHI_a is the NHI required to complete action a.

$$ECF_a^{i+1} = ECF_a^i + \alpha \cdot (DCF_a^i - ECF_a^i) \tag{2}$$

$$NHI_a^{i+1} = NHI_{max} - NHI_a^i - NHI_a \tag{3}$$

2.3 GResilience Measurement Mechanism

The GResilience (GR) approach [13,15] provides CAIS with an automated instrument to support decision-making during disruption. GR aims to find the action that best trade-off between greenness and resilience. It solves the trading off problem by forming the problem into two independent mechanisms:

1. Multi-Objective Optimization using the *Weighted Sum Model* (GR-WSM): Where it combines both the resilience and the greenness measures into a single score per action. Then the model chooses the action with the highest score. Equation (4), shows the global score equation ($S()$) for the action a, where w_R and w_G are the weights of resilience and greenness respectively. ϵ is the confidence level of the AI model ($\epsilon \in [0,1]$): the higher the value the more we trust the AI to continue operating. Thus, ϵ multiplies the inverse of the resilience measure, and $1 - \epsilon$ multiplies the summation of the greenness measures. Each resulting measure is then normalized ($N()$). Finally, we search for the action that maximizes $S(a)$.

$$S(a) = w_R \cdot \epsilon \cdot N(ET^{-1}) + w_G \cdot (1 - \epsilon) \cdot \{N(NHI) + N(ECF^{-1})\} \tag{4}$$

2. Game Theory by leveraging "The Battle of Sexes" game into building *The GResilience Game* (GRG): A collaborative game where each of the players has a preferred option, while they share a common goal (i.e., recovering the

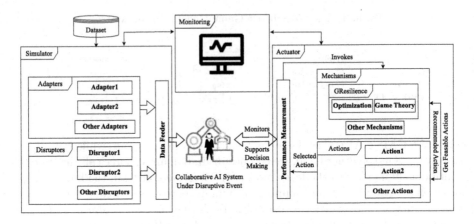

Fig. 2. CAIS-DMA Architecture

system). The game treats resilience and greenness properties as two game players (P_r the resilience player and P_g the greenness player), and each of the players has an independent way to measure its payoff. Same as "The Battle of Sexes" the GRG has two Pure Strategies Nash Equilibria (PSNE), in which the two players agree on the same action. GRG may have another Mixed Strategy Nash Equilibrium (MSNE) based on the probability of each player's action. Equation (5) shows the expressions to find the P_r and P_g payoffs, where α is the matching factor that is a smaller value in case the players land on different actions and a larger value in case they match. Table 1, shows two PSNEs where both players choose the same action and a possible MSNE based on the probability of each player's action, [13,16]. In the MSNE, P_r chooses a_1 with probability q and a_2 with probability $1 - q$, while P_g chooses a_1 with probability p and a_2 with probability $1 - p$, which results to the *expected payoff* described in Table 1. Thus, to find the probability q (resp. p) with MSNE, we equal the expected payoffs of P_g (resp. P_r) for a_1 and a_2 and solve the resulting equation for q (resp. p).

$$P_r^\alpha(a) = \epsilon \cdot \alpha \cdot ET^{-1}, \; P_g^\alpha(a) = (1 - \epsilon) \cdot \alpha \cdot NHI^{-1} \cdot ECF^{-1} \qquad (5)$$

3   Framework Architecture - CAIS-DMA

The CAIS-DMA operates as an assistant to support CAIS's AI model responsible for the collaboration actions between the system and the human during the first disruptive state (Fig. 1). It aims to assist the AI model until it reaches the recovered state. The framework consists of three components: i) a data simulator, ii) a decision-making actuator, and iii) a monitoring component. Figure 2, shows the three components interacting with the CAIS under the disruptive event. The rest of the section will discuss each of CAIS-DMA's components.

3.1   Simulator

The goal of the simulator component is to simulate the learning data of CAIS's AI model, editing the data to represent a specific disruptive event effect and structure it as expected by the AI model. To this aim, the simulator consists of two packages:

1. *Adapters*: An extendable package that contains the adaptation classes. These classes prepare the dataset and restructure it to adapt the AI model's expected input. Moreover, it adds a data field for human representation. The human field is assumed to be the ground truth of the specific data instance. This field is important to simulate the human action for the specific data instance.
2. *Disruptors*: The disruptors package is an extendable package, where it allows multiple disruptors. Each disruptor aims to simulate a disruptive event effect on the data, and it is important to note that the disruptors affect only the data and not the system itself.

After data preparation, the simulator streams the data instances to the AI model using the *Data Feeder*. The data feeder is responsible for sorting the data and streaming them over to the AI model. It streams the data in three states: i) Steady State, where it streams the data without disruptions, ii) Disruption State, where it streams the data with the disruptive effect, and iii) Final State, where it streams again the data without disruptions (to simulate the disruptive event fix). By default, the data are split into thirds, unless defined otherwise in the framework configurations.

3.2   Actuator

The actuator component has two main functionalities: i) Monitoring the AI model performance, and ii) Supporting the AI model decision-making. The following summarizes these functionalities:

1. *Performance Monitor.* This package monitors the AI model's decisions and measures its performance based on the autonomous decisions made for a window of time. Algorithm 1, shows the algorithm we use to measure CAIS's AI model performance. The algorithm first initializes the variables, measures the performance, invokes CAIS-DMA decision mechanisms, and executes the final decision (recommended action). Where ADR is the autonomous decision ratio, $ADRT$ is the ADR threshold that defines what an acceptable performance level, D is the AI's decision (chosen/recommended action), ϵ is the AI model confidence level towards the decision D, W is the time window size, Q is a queue that stores the last W decisions.
2. *Support Decision-Making.* In case of performance degradation the performance monitor invokes a decision-making mechanism to recommend the action to be executed. All feasible actions are defined in the *actions package* including their properties, for example, their execution time. The decision-making mechanisms represent different techniques for decision-making, such

as the GResilience measurement mechanism which recommends the action that best trade-off between greenness and resilience. Other measurement mechanisms can be defined in this package to support the different nature of CAIS under test.

Algorithm 1. Performance Measurement Algorithm

```
 1: W ← WindowSize                                              ▷ Variables Initialization
 2: ADRT ← ADRThreshold
 3: Q ← Queue()
 4: for i = 0 → W do
 5:     Q.enqueue(0)
 6: end for
 7: while True do                                   ▷ Keep Monitoring The CAIS's AI Decisions
 8:     D, ε ← ReadDecisionAndProbability()              ▷ D: AI Decision, ε: Confident Level
 9:     Q.dequeue()                                                    ▷ Update the Queue
10:     switch D do
11:         case "Autonomous": Q.enqueue(1)
12:         case "Human": Q.enqueue(0)
13:     ADR ← Q.sum()/W                                               ▷ Calculate ADR
14:     if ADR < ADRT then                              ▷ Check for Performance Degradation
15:         D ← InvokeDecisionMechanism(D, ε)                    ▷ Recommend Decision D
16:     end if
17:     ExecuteDecision(D)                                   ▷ Proceed with the Decision D
18: end while
```

3.3   Monitoring Component

The monitoring component is a web-based application, which provides a toolbox for the framework users to visually analyze CAIS performance during runtime, and tunes the framework variables to run experiments over CAIS under test. Through visual analysis, we can monitor the performance anomalies caused by the disruptive event(s), where for each experiment it plots the performance behavior per each window of time. While through the experiment tuning, we can customize an experiment by setting the experiment configurations, like the *number of iterations*, the *dataset*, the *adapters* to use, the *disruptors*, what *decision-making mechanism* to apply, and the *actions set* to recommend from.

4   Support Decision Making Process with CAIS-DMA

The AI model of CAIS is responsible for controlling the collaboration between the human and the system. It decides whether to run autonomous actions by the system or ask the human to perform the action and update the AI model with the new learning. Figure 3, shows the online learning flow diagram of CAIS, where it starts by receiving a new data stream, preprocessing the data, and then estimating the prediction probability (i.e., the confidence level ϵ, where $\epsilon \in [0, 1]$) using the AI model to perform a specific task. If the prediction probability is more than the predefined minimum probability ($min(prob)$), the decision will be to perform autonomous actions, through predicting and performing the task by the system itself. Otherwise, it asks the human to perform the task, by entering into a learning mode and updating the AI model with the new data.

To support the decision-making process, CAIS-DMA monitors the estimated probability of the online learning process to measure CAIS's performance. This measurement helps CAIS-DMA to automatically detect disruptive events that lead to performance degradation. If performance degradation is detected, CAIS-DMA calls the decision measurement mechanism, which, in turn, considers ϵ with the feasible actions to measure the action that best trade-off between the predefined non-functional properties. In online learning, CAIS-DAM selects between requesting human intervention or proceeding autonomously. Requesting human intervention simply means continuing with the original flow. While proceeding autonomously, means moving forward with CAIS tasks by allowing predictions.

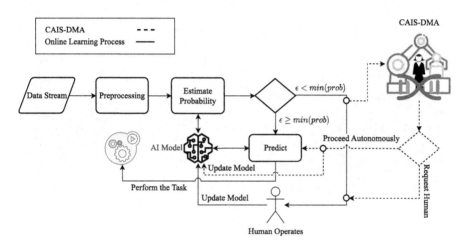

Fig. 3. Online Learning with CAIS-DMA

Finally, CAIS managers have the flexibility to update the AI model with the new prediction or not. If they decide to update the AI model, this reduces CAIS dependability on CAIS-DMA, allowing the system to live under disruption without the framework support, however, it causes a higher probability to face another disruptive state after fixing the disruptive event, due to the accumulative learning. While, if they avoid updating the AI model, this means discarding learning from disruptive data, which reduces the chances of being disrupted again after fixing the disruptive event, but increases the dependability over CAIS-DMA during the disruptive state.

5 First Application and Evaluation

To understand if CAIS-DMA supports the decision-making of CAIS to recover from performance degradation caused by disruptive events, we aim to answer the following research questions:

- **RQ1**: *What is the software development process of CAIS-DMA to automatically support the decision-making of CAIS?* To answer this question, we will demonstrate development process decisions to successfully design an application of CAIS-DMA, using both its simulator and actuator to automatically support the decision-making of CAIS.
- **RQ2**: *What are the extendable components of CAIS-DMA that allow wider support for decision-making?* To answer this question, we will consider CAIS-DMA architecture with the online learning process to reflect on a real-world demonstrator, showing the framework components to be extended in order to complete a full application.

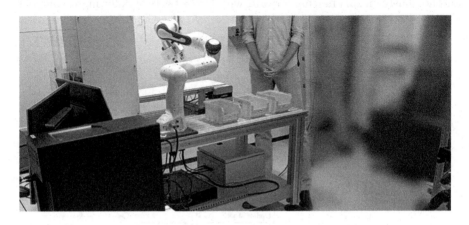

Fig. 4. Collaborative Robot Learning from Demonstrations - CORAL

5.1   Application Context - CORAL

Our demonstrator is a collaborative robot named "CORAL[1]". Figure 4, shows CORAL, which consists of a robotic arm installed above a conveyor belt that transfers objects of multiple colors. The robot detects the objects using an RGB camera installed on top of the conveyor belt. The detected object is streamed to an *online learning model* to be classified based on its color. The classifier monitors human movements by tracking the human skeleton. The human movement helps the classifier to label the object class with the target box.

5.2   Equipping CORAL with CAIS-DMA

CAIS-DMA framework is built using *Python3*, and its available on *GitHub[2]*. Figure 5, shows CORAL online learning associated with CAIS-DMA. The online

---

[1] CORAL is developed by Fraunhofer Italia Research in the context of ARENA Lab.
[2] https://github.com/dmrimawi/CAIS-DMA.

learning of CORAL starts when a new object is detected, the detected object is streamed to the preprocessing step. The preprocessor extracts the object histogram and passes it to estimate the class probability. If $\epsilon \geq min(prob)$ ($min(prob) = 0.4$ in the case of CORAL) the classifier predicts the object's box and asks the robotic arm to pick the object to the predicted box. Otherwise, the classifier notifies the human to classify the object and update the model with the new labeled object. To the aim of building a successful application using CAIS-DMA, we illustrate the software development process of building a green resilient CORAL. The process milestones are: i) Defining the performance measurements, ii) Understanding the dataset structure the AI model expects, iii) Listing the disruptive events that may lead to performance degradation, iv) Creating a set of all feasible recovery actions, v) Defining the non-functional properties the actions have to balance, vi) Setting the decision-making measurement mechanisms, vii) Storing the collected decisions, and finally, viii) Updating the AI model with the decision.

The rest of this section summarizes the decisions with respect to CORAL:

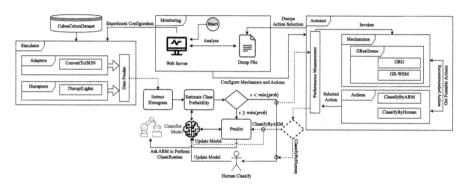

Fig. 5. Equipping CORAL with CAIS-DMA, Simulate Cubes Colors Dataset, Support Decision Making using GResilience Mechanism, and Analyze Performance

Performance Measurements. In our application, we monitor the estimated classification probability from CORAL's AI model, to count the number of autonomous operations against the number of human operations. Then we compute the autonomous classification ratio in a window of time (W-consecutive operations). CAIS-DMA supports running experiments with a range of values for W, allowing CAIS managers to tune the value to what suits their systems.

Cubes Colors Dataset. As illustrated CORAL's learning starts when a new object is detected over the conveyor belt. The detected object is streamed into a JSON-structured instance. This instance is then processed by the learner preprocessing step. CAIS-DMA simulator's goal is to simulate the input data (i.e., the cube images in this case), thus, we created the *Cubes Colors Dataset*, a set of cubes images taken from the RGB camera installed above the conveyor belt of CORAL, to have a real-world dataset from the application itself. Finally, we create an adapter that prepares the images to be streamed in the same structure CORAL's AI model expects.

Disruptive Event. One of the disruptive events that lead to performance degradation for online learners depending on computer vision to produce the learning data, is disrupting the vision itself. Thus, in this application, we simulate the environmental effect of losing the lights above the conveyor belt, which, in turn, leads to darker images. As we are using the simulator to produce images' darkness, this gives us the flexibility to simulate the disruptive event effect from dimming the lights to losing the lights completely. The effect of darkness hampers online learning as it produces different histograms than the training data before the disruptive event, which disrupts the decision-making and eventually leads to performance degradation (low autonomous classification ratio).

Recovery Actions. The online learning classifier of CORAL is moving between two states: i) the learning state, where it asks the human to classify the object, and ii) the operating state, where it predicts the cube box and places it using the arm. Both of these states are considered as the decision actions, and the iterative execution of these actions will eventually lead to recovery from the performance degradation. However, choosing which action to execute will depend on the action that best trade-off between the non-functional properties selected in the measurement mechanism. To summarize, in our application we consider two feasible recovery actions from the light disruption: *action1*) ask the arm to classify the cube, and *action2*) learn from the human classification of the cube.

Greenness and Resilience. The main goal of this application is to restore CAIS performance from degradation to an acceptable performance state. In other words, ensure the *resilience* property of CAIS. Although choosing the *fastest action* all the time may restore CAIS performance faster, it leads to higher energy consumption, which increases the energy adverse effects. Increasing the energy adverse effects reduces CAIS *greenness*, thus, it is important to find the action that balances CAIS's greenness and resilience. Hence we use ECF and NHI to measure greenness and ET to measure resilience.

GResilience Measurement Mechanism. The GResilience approach aims to recommend the next action that best trade-off between greenness and resilience to restore CAIS's performance to an acceptable performance state. The approach defines two techniques to find the next action, either by recommending the action with the highest combined score of resilience and greenness through optimization, or by considering the two properties as game theory players in a collaborative game of common goal (Sect. 2).

Storing the Results. To be able to revisit the results, analyze them, and support CAIS's managers in making decisions based on these results, it is important to structure these results in a readable and productive way. In our application we dump the decisions into a Comma-Separated Values (CSV) structure, in which we record timestamped data that contains the selected action, the measurements

(ET, ECF, and NHI), and if this decision is made autonomously by CORAL, or it is overridden through CAIS-DMA.

Update the AI Model. Finally, CAIS managers need to decide whether to update the AI model with CAIS-DMA results or not. Based on our observation, updating the AI model leads to faster recovery during the disruption state, in other words, CAIS learns to *live in the darkness*. However, this leads to a second disruptive state after fixing the disruptive event. On the other hand, not updating the AI model, leads to higher dependency on CAIS-DMA during a disruptive state, making it difficult to learn to live in the darkness. While, after fixing the disruptive event it is faster to return to the steady state again. We recommend running both options under simulation and taking the decision of updating the AI model or not based on the CAIS under test.

5.3   Takeaways

In this application, we equipped our real-world demonstrator (CORAL) with CAIS-DMA. The implementation process of our application helps address our research questions as follows:

Answer to RQ1. The answer to this research question aims to demonstrate the development process for CAISs managers. In particular, the managers need to define the measures that are relevant to observing CAIS's performance, and what are the events that may lead to performance degradation. Then, they have to address the feasible recovery actions, and the recommendation criteria for the next action. In this application, we show an application of the development process decisions based on CORAL, where we used CAIS-DMA to simulate CORAL's working environment and the effect of losing the light on the vision sensor of CORAL. Then we implemented CAIS-DMA actuator to recover CORAL by balancing between greenness and resilience, and finally, we monitored CORAL behavior to understand the performance behavior during the different states.

Answer to RQ2. This question provides CAIS's developers with the main extendable packages to consider during implementation. Starting with the simulator, in our application, we created a dataset of images to simulate CORAL's environment, however, the developers can customize the simulator to simulate their own dataset. They just need to provide the adapter class and the disruptor to feed the data to CAIS under test. Additionally, the mechanisms and the recovery action packages in the actuator component are also extendable to different measurement mechanisms and recovery actions. Finally, CAIS-DMA is full of utilities and toolboxes to automate running experiments, visual analysis, and sorting the dataset instances.

6   Threats to Validity

Wieringa *et al.* [17] define validity as the support degree to a fallible inference. Our paper introduces an architectural explanation of CAIS-DMA, to automatically support decision-making of CAIS during disruptive state. The threats to the *internal validity* in our paper are represented in the degree of support to the architectural explanation, where we have selected the GResilience approach throughout the explanation. In this respect, we did not consider the human cost and energy in the overall measurement, which left to future work.

Threats to *external validity* are related to the degree of support for the generalization of the architectural explanation to a theoretical population. Which in our case is related to the application implementation that has been applied to the specific domain of CAIS, and CORAL robot. However, the framework itself is designed to be general.

Finally, *conclusion validity*, which represents the degree of support of a statistical inference from a sample to a study population. It is important to state that the nature of our framework is mainly exploratory, and generalization beyond the CORAL application is needed for consolidating our claims. Thus, we plan to run more experiments with another real-world demonstrator we have in-house and with simulators.

7   Related Work

We have reviewed existing literature according to three lines of research: i) The non-functional properties to balance, specifically resilience and greenness, ii) The trading off techniques using optimization and game theory, iii) The decision-making support framework in CAIS context. In the following, we illustrate a brief overview of them.

Resilience and Greenness. Methods and frameworks aim to build a resilient system have been discussed extensively by the literature, like using a multi-agent model by Januário et al. [7], tri-optimization model by Liu et al. [9], and deep learning model by Zarandi et al. [19], to mention a few. The major goal of these methods is to restore the system performance from degradation caused by disruptive events to acceptable performance. The disruptive events are different depending on the system itself, for example, the disruptive event can be a security vulnerability of the system [9,19], a defect in the software or hardware parts [7], or caused by humans [15]. In this paper, we add an additional requirement to restore the system's performance. We are interested in restoring the performance while monitoring and controlling the energy adverse effects, which is how Kharchenko et al. [8] define greenness. Studies have discussed greenness as a default result of building a resilient system, such as, Pandey et al. [11]. Other studies seek to find a trading-off between greenness and resilience, [10,15].

Optimization and Game Theory. In the greenness and resilience context, Mohammed et al. [10], propose a solution to optimize supply chain network distribution using the eco-gresilient model, which trades off between three objectives, specifically economical, green, and resilient. They used the proposed solution to find the best number of facilities in the supply network section. Game theory is a decision-making process with multiple actors. For instance, Xu et al.

[18], defined a collaborative game to support the decision process for a recommendation system for users' satisfaction. To the best of our knowledge, using game theory to trade off non-functional properties is a novel idea that we have sketched in our previous work, [15]. In this current paper, we have built a novel framework that operationalizes our initial idea and we have exemplified it to CORAL. We have further worked on a case study on CORAL, which is now under submission, [14].

Decision-Making Assistant. Various studies handle the automatic support of decision-making frameworks in CAIS context, by considering humans as the ground truth of the system's actions. They build specific knowledge about human actions and then use the knowledge to support decision-making by inferring human actions. For example, Chen *et al.* [3], build a computation model to assess the human trust in CAIS autonomous actions, and then it uses this assessment to automatically support decision-making with the action that maximizes the trust value. Other studies predict human actions using AI-based techniques, such as Ghadirzadeh *et al.* [5], using deep reinforcement learning, and Quintas *et al.* [12], who built an AI-agent that monitors human actions and generates descriptive scenarios to automatically support CAIS's decisions. As there are several frameworks to support decision-making, to our knowledge none of these frameworks provide extendable components backed with the toolbox and utilities needed, to first, simulate the system environment, second, automatically support decision-making through different decision-making mechanisms, and third visually analyze different experimental configurations, which make our framework (CAIS-DMA) a novel framework in that sense.

8 Conclusion and Future Work

Conclusion. In this paper, we introduce our novel extendable framework *CAIS-DMA* to automatically support CAIS decision-making in an online learning process. CAIS-DMA aims to deal with different learning situations, for this reason, it contains a simulator, actuator, and monitoring component. The framework simulates CAIS environment and represents the potential disruptive events that face the specific CAIS. It monitors CAIS's performance to detect any performance degradation to automatically support the decision-making to recommend the actions that help in restoring the performance to an acceptable level. CAIS-DMA monitors the decision made by CAIS's AI model and overrides the selected action, by the action that best trade-off between the non-functional properties defined through measurement mechanisms. Additionally, CAIS-DMA supports running different experiments on CAIS's AI model through different experiment configurations and provides a visual analysis of the performance behavior. Finally, we demonstrate the framework through a real-world demonstrator, showing the implementation steps and the framework's extendable components.

Future Work. This framework allows us to conduct a wider range of experiments with simulated data. Thus, we plan to run an experiment to compare the results from the simulation and the real-world case. Secondly, we plan to extend the framework in order to explore other non-functional properties such as safety. For instance, we can create a disruptive event that simulates an attack that alters the safe distance between the human and the robotic arm. In this case, we will study the actions that trade-off between human safety and system performance. Moreover, we plan to use the measurement mechanism results as reinforcement learning of the system that rewards recommended decisions.

References

1. Camilli, M., et al.: Risk-driven compliance assurance for collaborative AI systems: a vision paper. In: Dalpiaz, F., Spoletini, P. (eds.) REFSQ 2021. LNCS, vol. 12685, pp. 123–130. Springer, Cham (2021). https://doi.org/10.1007/978-3-030-73128-1_9
2. Camilli, M., Guerriero, A., Janes, A., Russo, B., Russo, S.: Microservices integrated performance and reliability testing. In: IEEE/ACM International Conference on Automation of Software Test, AST@ICSE 2022, Pittsburgh, PA, USA, 21–22 May 2022, pp. 29–39. ACM/IEEE (2022)
3. Chen, M., Nikolaidis, S., Soh, H., Hsu, D., Srinivasa, S.: Trust-aware decision making for human-robot collaboration: model learning and planning. ACM Trans. Hum.-Robot Interact. (THRI) 9(2), 1–23 (2020)
4. Colabianchi, S., Costantino, F., Gravio, G.D., Nonino, F., Patriarca, R.: Discussing resilience in the context of cyber physical systems. Comput. Ind. Eng. 160, 107534 (2021)
5. Ghadirzadeh, A., Chen, X., Yin, W., Yi, Z., Björkman, M., Kragic, D.: Human-centered collaborative robots with deep reinforcement learning. IEEE Robot. Autom. Lett. 6(2), 566–571 (2020)
6. Henry, D., Ramirez-Marquez, J.E.: Generic metrics and quantitative approaches for system resilience as a function of time. Reliab. Eng. Syst. Saf. 99, 114–122 (2012)
7. Januário, F., Cardoso, A., Gil, P.: A distributed multi-agent framework for resilience enhancement in cyber-physical systems. IEEE Access 7, 31342–31357 (2019)
8. Kharchenko, V., Illiashenko, O.: Concepts of green IT engineering: taxonomy, principles and implementation. In: Kharchenko, V., Kondratenko, Y., Kacprzyk, J. (eds.) Green IT Engineering: Concepts, Models, Complex Systems Architectures. SSDC, vol. 74, pp. 3–19. Springer, Cham (2017). https://doi.org/10.1007/978-3-319-44162-7_1
9. Liu, Z., Wang, L.: A distributionally robust scheme for critical component identification to bolster cyber-physical resilience of power systems. IEEE Trans. Smart Grid 13, 2344–2356 (2022)
10. Mohammed, A., Harris, I., Nujoom, R.: Eco-Gresilient: coalescing ingredient of economic, green and resilience in supply chain network design. In: Parlier, G.H., Liberatore, F., Demange, M. (eds.) Proceedings of the 7th International Conference on Operations Research and Enterprise Systems, ICORES 2018, Funchal, Madeira, Portugal, 24–26 January 2018, pp. 201–208. SciTePress (2018)
11. Pandey, P., Basu, P., Chakraborty, K., Roy, S.: GreenTPU: predictive design paradigm for improving timing error resilience of a near-threshold tensor processing unit. IEEE Trans. Very Large Scale Integr. Syst. 28(7), 1557–1566 (2020)

12. Quintas, J., Martins, G.S., Santos, L., Menezes, P., Dias, J.: Toward a context-aware human-robot interaction framework based on cognitive development. IEEE Trans. Syst. Man Cybern. Syst. **49**(1), 227–237 (2018)
13. Rimawi, D.: Green resilience of cyber-physical systems. In: 2022 IEEE International Symposium on Software Reliability Engineering Workshops (ISSREW), pp. 105–109. IEEE (2022)
14. Rimawi, D., Liotta, A., Todescato, M., Russo, B.: GResilience: Find a Trade-off between Greenness and Resilience in Collaborative AI Systems (2023). Under Submission
15. Rimawi, D., Liotta, A., Todescato, M., Russo, B.: GResilience: trading off between the greenness and the resilience of collaborative AI systems. In: Bonfanti, S., Gargantini, A., Salvaneschi, P. (eds.) ICTSS 2023. LNCS, vol. 14131, pp. 266–273. Springer, Cham (2023). https://doi.org/10.1007/978-3-031-43240-8_18
16. Stowe, C.J., Gilpatric, S.M.: Cheating and enforcement in asymmetric rank-order tournaments. Southern Econ. J. **77**(1), 1–14 (2010)
17. Wieringa, R., Daneva, M.: Six strategies for generalizing software engineering theories. Sci. Comput. Program. **101**, 136–152 (2015)
18. Xu, L., Jiang, C., Chen, Y., Ren, Y., Liu, K.R.: User participation in collaborative filtering-based recommendation systems: a game theoretic approach. IEEE Trans. Cybern. **49**(4), 1339–1352 (2018)
19. Zarandi, Z.N., Sharifi, I.: Detection and identification of cyber-attacks in cyber-physical systems based on machine learning methods. In: 2020 11th International Conference on Information and Knowledge Technology (IKT), pp. 107–112 (2020)

Comparing Machine Learning Algorithms for Medical Time-Series Data

Alex Helmersson[1]([✉]), Faton Hoti[1], Sebastian Levander[1], Aliasgar Shereef[1],
Emil Svensson[1], Ali El-Merhi[2,3][iD], Richard Vithal[2,3][iD],
Jaquette Liljencrantz[2,3][iD], Linda Block[2,3][iD], Helena Odenstedt Hergès[2,3][iD],
and Miroslaw Staron[1][iD]

[1] Department of Computer Science and Engineering, Chalmers University
of Gothenburg, Gothenburg, Sweden
a.helmersson@outlook.com
[2] Institute of Clinical Sciences, Sahlgrenska Academy, University of Gothenburg,
Gothenburg, Sweden
[3] Department of Anesthesia and Intensive Care, Sahlgrenska University Hospital,
Gothenburg, Sweden

Abstract. Medical software becomes increasingly advanced and more mission-critical. Machine learning is one of the methods which is used in medical software to tackle a diversity of patient data, problems with data quality and providing the ability to process increasingly large amounts of data from medical procedures. However, one of the challenges is the lack of comparisons of algorithms in-situ, during medical procedures. This paper explores the potential of performing real-time comparisons of algorithms for early stroke detection during carotid endarterectomy. SimSAX, DTW (dynamic time warping), and Pearson correlation were compared based on the real-time data against medical specialists in clinical evaluations. The analysis confirmed the general feasibility of the approach, though the algorithms were inadequate in extracting significant information from specific signals. Interviews with physicians revealed a positive outlook toward the system's potential, advocating for further investigation. Despite their limitations, the algorithms and the prototype application provides a promising foundation for future development of new methods for detecting stroke.

Keywords: Machine learning · stroke · SimSAX · dynamic time warping

1 Introduction

In medical software development, the integration of machine learning has witnessed a notable surge, aimed at assisting physicians in achieving swift diagnoses and correspondingly prompt responses. Particularly the case of cerebral ischemia, a critical condition demanding rapid evaluation of minute fluctuations within various high-frequency signals, this technology-healthcare synergy

R. Kadgien et al. (Eds.): PROFES 2023, LNCS 14483, pp. 200–207, 2024.
https://doi.org/10.1007/978-3-031-49266-2_14

becomes more important for dealing with critical situations. Cerebral ischemia is a condition characterized by reduced blood flow to a specific region of the brain, causing damage and death of brain cells. Cerebral ischemia can arise from various disorders, with stroke being the most prevalent and critical among them. Stroke is a disorder that occurs when the blood supply to part of the brain is interrupted leading to the death of brain tissue, i.e. infarction. Quick diagnosis and clinical treatment are crucial for the outcome of recovering from a stroke, both with respect to mortality but also to permanent disabilities [6]. In 2022, stroke was the second-leading cause of death worldwide, and the third cause of death and disability combined [7].

There is today no effective way to detect cerebral ischemia in patients who are unconscious, whether due to disease or anesthesia. In medicine, there is an unfulfilled need for continuous, machine learning-based analysis of high-frequency data. Conventional methods to diagnose cerebral ischemia such as clinical examination are not always possible in unconscious patients. Furthermore, while these methods offer good sensitivity, their temporal resolution is insufficient, making them incapable of continuous monitoring. Since these patients are often monitored with several non-invasive and continuous parameters, it is hypothesized that cerebral ischemia can be detected by analyzing the data generated from the patient monitors [3]. Non-invasive continuous monitors that can be used to indicate cerebral ischemia are electroencephalography (EEG), near-infrared spectroscopy (NIRS), and electrocardiography (ECG). There are several studies done or ongoing aiming to develop models able to detect ischemia using physiological data. Megjhani et al. retroactively analyzed physiological data averaged to 1 h in order to classify ischemia in a cohort being treated in the ICU for a type of brain hemorrhage, namely subarachnoid hemorrhage (SAH), and achieved an area under the receiver operating curve (AUROC) of 0.86 [10]. Another study conducted used only HRV parameters to train classifiers to detect ischemia in patients with SAH [13]. The models performed with high sensitivity but low specificity. While most research in this domain utilizes classifiers, another approach would be comparing time-series data of patients with those of other patients with known incidences of specific events, e.g. cerebral ischemia [4]. The purpose of this study is to use different algorithms to compare time-series data from different monitors collected during surgery and compare the results against the assessments of specialized physicians.

2 Methods

2.1 Data Collection

Data was collected from four patients undergoing surgery on the carotid artery. The carotid artery is one of the blood vessels that supply blood to the brain. During this surgery, the artery is clamped to minimize bleeding during the procedure, effectively reducing the blood flow to the brain. This surgery was used as an experimental model of stroke since clamping the artery may cause cerebral ischemia. The timing of the clamping and release is known, so the data is labeled accordingly.

EEG records brain electrical activity non-invasively using scalp electrodes [6,9]. Interpretation is complex and typically done by neurophysiology specialists. Quantifying EEG can aid interpretation in some cases. The waveform includes alpha, beta, gamma, delta, and theta frequency bands, reflecting different consciousness levels.

EEG is simple to set up and useful for continuous monitoring during operations. It can indicate post-stroke changes that persist [6], potentially contributing to stroke diagnosis [8].

NIRS is a technique for monitoring regional tissue oxygenation by transmitting near-infrared light and recording wavelength absorption variations. It estimates oxygen ratios between oxygenated hemoglobin and total hemoglobin [11], displayed as regional oxygen saturation (rSO2). rSO2 is affected by blood flow changes, therefore, it is used as a surrogate for blood flow e.g. during neurovascular surgery. NIRS, placed bilaterally on the forehead, tracks superficial frontal brain parts.

The interbeat interval, the time between heartbeats, varies continuously in a healthy heart. Even during seemingly stable heart rates, adjacent interbeat intervals differ in length. This heart rate variability (HRV) can be analyzed in time or frequency domains. Controlled by the brain, HRV is influenced by stress and disease, with reduced HRV linked to higher mortality in certain diseases [5]. HRV-variables are derived from an ECG, and research indicates its potential for monitoring patients at risk of cerebral ischemia [2].

2.2   Algorithms Utilized in This Project

Symbolic Aggregate ApproXimation (SAX) and Similarity-Based SAX (SimSAX). SAX transforms continuous time series into discrete symbols for analysis [14]. It standardizes data through z-normalization, dividing the series into bins. Each bin is represented categorically based on its mean, producing a sequence of categories. Parameters n-bins and n-letters control bin count and categorization. Figure 1 illustrates the algorithm.

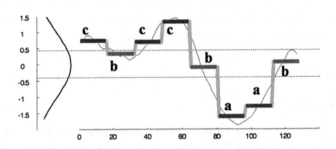

Fig. 1. SAX algorithm representing each divided part as categories depending on the value of the parts mean.

SimSAX, initially for project similarity [12], builds on SAX [14]. It segments time series into overlapping windows, representing each with SAX. SimSAX compares sequences between series, marking shared indexes. The result is the marked index percentage, providing a single value for each series.

Dynamic Time Warping (DTW). DTW is a time series comparison algorithm used in fields such as economics and medicine. DTW has shown promising results in finding correlations in medical data of for example post-stroke patients and is widely used as a similarity metric of general data [16].

The algorithm is generally used for determining alignment between series, and also calculating a score based on the distance between the series. The algorithm's goal is to map the indexes of two separate time series to each other. If the algorithm finds it more optimal to map an index to an already mapped index, it will do so. However, it has to take into consideration that all indexes have to be mapped at least once. As such, the algorithm might get one extra index to map each time it chooses an already mapped index. The algorithm is visualized in Fig. 2.

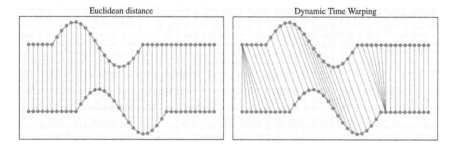

Fig. 2. DTW mapping in comparison to Euclidean distance [15].

Pearson Correlation Coefficient (PCC). PCC refers to the standard correlation metric calculated by:

$$P = \frac{\text{cov}(X, Y)}{\sigma_X \cdot \sigma_Y}$$

where X and Y are random variables [1]. The algorithm returns a number between -1 and 1. A positive value means there is a positive correlation, while a negative value means there is a negative correlation.

2.3   The Artifact StrokeSAX

StrokeSAX is a prototype web application developed using modern web technologies and frameworks. Its design allows for displaying and comparing patient signals from various sources, such as previously recorded data or real-time data collected using a Moberg monitor. StrokeSAX offers both online and offline inter-patient comparison functionality, as well as intra-patient comparison capabilities. The frontend is constructed using React and Typescript, while the backend is developed with Python and utilizes the FastAPI web framework. FastAPI provides a contemporary, high-speed, and user-friendly toolkit, ideal for swiftly prototyping APIs. The database is established using MongoDB, allowing the capability to save monitoring sessions from patients as reference data.

One of the key features of StrokeSAX is its ability to display patient signals from a single patient to n patients, where n represents all the patients collected in the system. The user can choose which signals to display in the UI. The available options are created dynamically, based on the unique data for each patient. For instance, if a patient has three signals in their data, the user can simply select these three signals in the interface. When two or more patients are selected, the application displays the union of their available signals. When two patients are selected, StrokeSAX activates its bidirectional similarity scoring. The application displays a percentage score for each selected signal, indicating the mutual similarity between Patient X's and Patient Y's signals. Additionally, it shows an overall percentage score representing the total bidirectional similarity between the two patients, calculated using the SimSAX algorithm.

3   Results

The data collected from patients consisted of time-series datasets with values from different signals from 5 min prior to the clamping of the carotid artery, which is the event that can lead to cerebral ischemia, to 5 min after releasing the clamp. The artifact StrokeSAX was used to analyze and present the data. Two pairs of patients were chosen, and 5 signals were analyzed for similarity using the three algorithms. The signals were also displayed for two specialist physicians and they were asked to rate their similarity using the five-point Likert scale. Before evaluating each signal separately, the two specialist physicians were asked to provide an account of whether each of the pairs (A and B) could be considered similar or different based on their medical conditions, e.g., age, and the severity of the disease. Pair A was considered to be two different patients and the Pair B was considered to include two similar patients.

Results obtained from these comparisons are presented in Table 1. The column with the SimSAX algorithm shows generally a higher degree of similarity compared to the two specialists, while the Pearson Correlation Coefficient is the least similar. The DTW is in-between, although generally showing a stronger correlation than the other two methods.

For both patients' data, the Pearson Correlation Coefficient is the worst as it indicated a very weak correlation (0.15) or no correlation at all (0). Although it is suggested by the data, it is not clinically correct. Even for Pair A (two different patients), there should be some correlation as they undergo the same procedure and therefore some of the physiological signals are similar – e.g., C3 Theta (which is one of the EEG signals).

Table 1. Evaluation results for patient pairs A and B. The possible values for Sim-SAX and DTW ranges from 0–1, where 1 corresponds to a 100% similarity between the patient signals. The table shows physicians' five-point Likert ratings and algorithm's similarity scores. For SimSAX and DTW, the data contains similarities between patients (patient 1 to patient 2, patient 2 to patient 1). For Pearson Correlation Coefficient these numbers are the same and thus reported only once.

Pair	Signal	Phys. 1	Phys. 2	SimSAX	DTW	PCC
A	NIRS right	2	2	(0.3, 0.27)	(0.5, 0.32)	0.25
A	NIRS left	4	4	(0.35, 0.41)	(0.43, 0.22)	-0.13
A	Blood pressure	5	4	(0.4, 0.68)	(0.91, 0.88)	-0.02
A	C3 theta	5	5	(0.4, 0.34)	(0.98, 0.98)	0.03
A	HR mad	2	2	(0.44, 0.54)	(0.88, 0.83)	-0.14
A	**Total**	3	3	(0.38, 0.45)	(0.74, 0.65)	0
B	NIRS right	3	4	(0.84, 0.85)	(0.93, 0.91)	0.56
B	NIRS left	4	4	(0.71, 0.51)	(0.95, 0.93)	0.26
B	Blood pressure	2	2-3	(0.58, 0.6)	(0.84, 0.78)	-0.01
B	C3 theta	4	4	(0.39, 0.51)	(0.79, 0.73)	0.02
B	HR mad	1	1	(0.77, 0.68)	(0.76, 0.68)	-0.05
B	**Total**	4-5	4-5	(0.66, 0.63)	(0.85, 0.81)	0.15

There are signals where more studies are needed, though. For example, in the HR Mad (Heartrate Variability Mean Average Deviation), the specialists rated the signals to be rather different while the algorithms considered them to be moderately or highly similar (depending on the patient pair). Although this could be caused by the difference in the base amplitude of the signal, we need more studies to explain it.

The physicians' scores in the total column correspond to their evaluation of how similar the compared patients were in terms of clinical relevance, based on the patients' health conditions. When considering the total similarity, we can see that both SimSAX and DTW shows that the more similar pair (Pair B) has a higher degree of similarity than Pair A. Although the magnitude of the difference (the effect size) needs to be studied further, this is a positive result as it allows the clinicians to get the first impression of the physiological similarity between the patients.

4 Discussion

This study finds that analyzing physiological time-series data with SimSAX, DTW, and PCC is feasible, but agreement with physician assessments varies due to differences in signal time-series and algorithm properties. The primary strength of SimSAX lies in its ability to find common patterns in two separate time series. However, it does not take the amplitudes of the graphs into account, which is a significant part of determining similarities in certain signals, such as blood pressure or EEG. Looking at NIRS for example, which is usually a stable signal, it is expected that SimSAX returns high similarity scores. DTW rated most of the measurements quite high but had difficulties differentiating between signals that are clinically similar from those that are not. DTW's similarity score is largely dependent on the amplitude difference of connected data points. This could also be a limitation since it does not take into account where on the x-axis these differences occur, whereas when physicians analyze these signals, the timing of amplitude shifts and differences are of great importance. These two dynamic algorithms SimSAX and DTW agreed more with the physicians compared to PCC which acted as a partially static algorithm baseline.

From the evaluation, it seems to be preferred that the algorithm can spot sequences. In some signals, the amplitude is important while in others they are not, at least to some degree where they start to get important. Capturing this versatility of amplitude importance is hard using these algorithms. It is also reasonable to think that using different algorithms to quantify similarity in different signals would give an accuracy enhancement, as there are different characteristics that are more or less important in different signals.

Knowing more about which sequences are important in developing cerebral ischemia, a possibility could be to take certain parts from previous stroke patients and use them as reference sequences to match against a live patient's data. If it detects similarity, the system could alarm the physicians.

The prototype full-stack application developed for this study provides a foundation for further research, and the results indicate that time series analysis in real-time can be a useful tool in the early detection of cerebral ischemia.

This study contributes to the growing body of research in the field of cerebral ischemia detection and gives insights into analyzing time-series data instead of classifiers. It also highlights the potential applicability of software engineering algorithms in the medical domain.

5   Conclusion

This study explores the use of algorithms for comparing physiological time-series data during carotid artery surgery to detect cerebral ischemia. SimSAX, DTW, and PCC were evaluated for signal similarity and compared with expert physicians' ratings. The results of the study demonstrated that while the general concept of the system is feasible, there were limitations in the ability of the algorithms to extract significant information from specific signals. Nonetheless, the study's evaluation by physicians showed that there is potential for the system's clinical application. Further research is needed with larger amounts of data, i.e. more patients, to further evaluate this method and specify when and how it can be used to help detect cerebral ischemia.

References

1. Benesty, J., Chen, J., Huang, Y., Cohen, I.: Pearson correlation coefficient. In: Cohen, I., Huang, Y., Chen, J., Benesty, J. (eds.) Noise Reduction in Speech Processing. Springer Topics in Signal Processing, vol. 2, pp. 1–4. Springer, Heidelberg (2009). https://doi.org/10.1007/978-3-642-00296-0_5

2. Wenneberg, S.B., et al.: Heart rate variability monitoring for the detection of delayed cerebral ischemia after aneurysmal subarachnoid hemorrhage. Acta Anaesthesiol. Scand. **64**(7), 945–952 (2020)

3. Block, L., El-Merhi, A., Liljencrantz, J., Naredi, S., Staron, M., Hergès, H.O.: Cerebral ischemia detection using artificial intelligence (CIDAI)-a study protocol. Acta Anaesthesiol. Scand. **64**(9), 1335–1342 (2020)

4. Tak chung Fu: A review on time series data mining. Eng. Appl. Artif. Intell. **24**(1), 164–181 (2011)

5. Task Force of the European Society of Cardiology the North American Society of Pacing Electrophysiology. Heart rate variability: standards of measurement, physiological interpretation, and clinical use. Circulation **93**(5), 1043–1065 (1996)

6. Fagius, J., ten-Magnus Aquilonius, S.: Chapter 9 Cerebrovaskulära sjukdomar. Stockholm Liber (2006)

7. Feigin, V.L., et al.: World stroke organization (WSO): global stroke fact sheet 2022. Int. J. Stroke **17**(1), 18–29 (2022)

8. Foreman, B., Claassen, J.: Quantitative EEG for the detection of brain ischemia. Crit. Care **16**(2), 1–9 (2012)

9. Martini, F., Nath, J.L.: The Brain and Cranial Nerves. Stockholm Liber (2006)

10. Megjhani, M., et al.: Dynamic detection of delayed cerebral ischemia. Stroke **52**(4), 1370–1379 (2021)

11. Moerman, A., Wouters, P.: Near-infrared spectroscopy (NIRS) monitoring in contemporary anesthesia and critical care. Acta Anaesthesiol. Belgica **61**, 185–94 (2010)

12. Ochodek, M., Staron, M., Meding, W.: SimSAX: a measure of project similarity based on symbolic approximation method and software defect inflow. Inf. Softw. Technol. **115**, 131–147 (2019)

13. Hergès, H.O., Vithal, R., El-Merhi, A., Naredi, S., Staron, M., Block, L.: Machine learning analysis of heart rate variability to detect delayed cerebral ischemia in subarachnoid hemorrhage. Acta Neurol. Scand. **145**(2), 151–159 (2022)

14. Song, K., Ryu, M., Lee, K.: Transitional sax representation for knowledge discovery for time series. Appl. Sci. **10**(19), 6980 (2020)

15. Tavenard, R.: An introduction to dynamic time warping (2021). https://rtavenar.github.io/blog/dtw.html

16. Tormene, P., Giorgino, T., Quaglini, S., Stefanelli, M.: Matching incomplete time series with dynamic time warping: an algorithm and an application to post-stroke rehabilitation. Artif. Intell. Med. **45**(1), 11–34 (2009)

What Data Scientists (Care To) Recall

Samar Saeed[1], Shahrzad Sheikholeslami[1], Jacob Krüger[2(✉)] [iD],
and Regina Hebig[3] [iD]

[1] University of Gothenburg, Gothenburg, Sweden
{gussaesaa,gussheish}@student.gu.se
[2] Eindhoven University of Technology, Eindhoven, The Netherlands
j.kruger@tue.nl
[3] University of Rostock, Rostock, Germany
regina.hebig@uni-rostock.de

Abstract. To maintain and evolve a software system, developers need
to gain new or recover lost knowledge about that system. Thus, program
comprehension is a crucial activity in software development and maintenance processes. We know from previous work that developers prioritize
what information they want to remember about a system based on the
perceived importance of that information. However, AI-based software
systems as a special case are not developed by software developers alone,
but also by data scientists who deal with other concepts and have a different educational background than most developers. In this paper, we
study what information data scientists (aim to) recall about their systems. For this purpose, we replicated our previous work by interviewing
11 data scientists, investigating the knowledge they consider important
to remember, and whether they can remember parts of their systems correctly. Our results suggest that data scientists consider knowledge about
the AI-project settings to be the most important to remember and that
they perform best when remembering knowledge they consider important. Contrary to software developers, data scientists' self-assessments
increase when reflecting on their systems. Our findings indicate similarities and differences between developers and data scientists that are
important for managing the processes surrounding a system.

Keywords: Program Comprehension · Human Memory ·
Remembering · Data Scientists · Maintenance

1 Introduction

Development, maintenance, and evolution (we refer to *engineering*) processes
surrounding software systems require the involved developers to obtain extensive knowledge about various properties. In particular, they must know details
about the system and its engineering, such as the system architecture, the
employed engineering processes, or the intended system behavior. Aiming to
facilitate developers' work, researchers and practitioners continue to investigate
and develop techniques for recovering and documenting the respective knowledge. Such activities are key, but also expensive, within engineering processes.

R. Kadgien et al. (Eds.): PROFES 2023, LNCS 14483, pp. 208–224, 2024.
https://doi.org/10.1007/978-3-031-49266-2_15

Past studies on these activities have focused on program comprehension and knowledge recovery, but little on whether, how, and what knowledge the involved developers aim to memorize [8]. Moreover, the focus has been on software developers and similar roles (e.g., testers, architects) that are closely connected to software development.

However, software systems are typically engineered by involving various different stakeholders and domain experts. Particularly with the rise of artificial intelligence (AI) and AI-based systems, data scientists have become more and more involved in engineering processes. Data scientists can have considerably different backgrounds and tasks compared to typical software developers [1,14,18,19], focusing on, for example, data collection, data cleansing, training AI models, or improving the performance of such a model. Unfortunately, research on AI-based systems focuses mainly on data quality, algorithms, performance, and similar technicalities, while the human aspects within the respective engineering processes have received less attention. In parallel, the findings of studies on developers' knowledge needs and what knowledge they consider important may not be fully transferable.

Overall, there are two gaps we aim to tackle in this paper: First, little research has focused on understanding what knowledge different stakeholder roles consider important, and thus aim to memorize. Second, none of these studies has focused on data scientists as a new, but more and more important, role. We address these gaps by replicating our previous interview survey on software developers' knowledge needs and memory performance [8] with 11 data scientists. So, in this paper, we investigate the information needs, memory, and perceived importance of knowledge of data scientists, contributing to a better understanding of their needs and characteristics in engineering processes. Our results can help researchers and practitioners alike, for instance, for developing novel techniques that are focused on helping data scientists with their specific AI-related knowledge needs.

2   Related Work

Developers need to continuously comprehend the system they are working on during an engineering process. This may include learning new things or recovering knowledge they have forgotten over time. Consequently, there has been extensive research on program comprehension, the activity of recovering knowledge about the source code a developer is working on [3,15,20,21]. Research in this area investigates how developers comprehend code, what constructs (e.g., code comments [17], identifier names [4]) facilitate or complicate program comprehension, and proposes novel techniques for supporting developers. However, program comprehension is concerned with recovering detailed knowledge about the code and consequent system behavior, not tackling other knowledge issues like developers' memory or forgetting that we are concerned with. In our own previous works, we have been focusing on such issues, specifically developers' memory regarding source code [7,11] and how to recover knowledge from different artifacts [10]. Most importantly, we [8] have previously investigated the relationship between developers' information needs and their memory decay in a two-fold study. We collected questions that developers asked during their work by reviewing existing studies, classifying these questions into three themes: architecture, code, and meta. Then, we conducted a qualitative interview survey with 17 experienced developers working mostly on smaller systems, asking questions about their systems based on the three themes. We aimed to understand what knowledge developers consider important to recall from memory, assess their actual ability to remember such knowledge, and understand how they assess themselves in terms of memorizing. The results of our study imply that developers working on smaller systems tend to consider architecture and abstract knowledge about the code more important to remember, with meta knowledge being considered the least important to remember. For this paper, we replicated the interview part of our study with a different population: data scientists. Recently, in another study building on that previous work, we [9] have conducted a questionnaire to understand what knowledge developers consider important to memorize or document. So, we contributed complementary insights into how developers would prefer to document knowledge they may forget over time.

Differentiating between typical software developers and data scientists is important, since engineering AI-based systems exhibits different processes and consequent knowledge. For instance, Liu [14] performed interviews in which they identified 25 tasks covering various engineering phases that must be added to processes for AI-based systems. As a result, the types of knowledge that are relevant, their perceived importance to know from memory, and data scientists' ability to actually remember these may deviate compared to typical software developers—highlighting an important research gap. This gap has not been tackled in previous work on engineering AI-based systems. However, several other studies on such systems showcase the differences in terms of engineering processes [1], reasoning about or explaining AI-based systems [16,23], or guiding end users [22]. Lastly, researchers have investigated the challenges for data scientists in engineering AI-based systems [18,19]. All these works highlight the differences between data scientists and software developers, but do not investigate their knowledge needs and memory, which we study in this paper.

3   Methodology

For this paper, we replicated the interview part of our previous work [8] and built on systematic survey procedures [13]. Due to the different domains (software developers in the original versus data scientists in this study), we implemented some changes in the design that we explain in this section.

3.1   Research Questions (RQs)

With our study, we aimed to elicit what types of knowledge data scientists consider important to remember about their system (RQ_1), how well they perform at remembering these (RQ_2), and how their self-assessment matches their actual ability to remember knowledge (RQ_3). For this purpose, we defined four RQs:

RQ$_1$ What knowledge about their system do data scientists consider important to memorize and remember?

RQ$_2$ Can data scientists correctly answer questions about their system based on their memory?

RQ$_3$ To what extent does a data scientist's self-assessment of their familiarity with a system align with their actual knowledge about that system?

RQ$_4$ What are the similarities and differences between data scientists and software developers?

We adapted the first three RQs from our previous study, and defined **RQ$_4$** to compare between both studies.

3.2 Interview Instrumentation

Identically to our previous study, we performed face-to-face interviews administered by the interviewer. An interviewer-administered interview limits the risk of misunderstandings and allowed us to gather more reliable data compared to a questionnaire. For our interview guide, we aimed to keep or adopt the questions from our previous study, since (1) these questions were established through a systematic literature review and (2) this allows a comparison of the outcomes for data scientists to those for software developers. We adjusted and added questions to account for the different artifacts data scientists work with, for which we built on the main practices of data scientists described by Burkov [2].

Questions. We provide an overview of the questions we asked during our structured interviews in Table 1. As we show, the questions align to five sections:

Overall Self-Assessment (OS): This section involves four questions on the interviewees' self-assessments regarding their memorized knowledge. These questions are identical to our previous study and we asked them four times: once at the beginning and once after each knowledge section (A, M, C). We did this to identify whether an interviewee's self-assessment would change after reflecting on their system.

AI-Project Setting (A): With these seven questions, we investigated our interviewees' memory of the project setting used for the AI-based part of their system. This section did not exist in our previous work and substitutes the questions about architecture that we asked the software developers.

Meta Knowledge (M): Next, we asked five questions on collaboration and system evolution, adapting one question (M$_5$) to the specifics of AI engineering.

Code Knowledge (C): In this last knowledge section, we asked four questions on code and AI-modeling details. Particularly, we adapted two questions (C$_3$, C$_4$) to AI engineering. Note that we adapted C$_3$ depending on the learning algorithm our interviewees used within their systems, differentiating between the types (e.g., supervised, unsupervised) and changing the respective details we asked for (e.g., labels, output).

Importance of Knowledge (IK): To wrap up, we asked the same five questions on the perceived importance of knowledge as in our previous study.

Table 1. Overview of our interview questions. Those questions fully unchanged compared to our previous study [8] are asterisked (*).

id	questions and answering options (AOs)
	section: overall self-assessment (repeated after sections A, M, and C)
OS_1 *	How well do you still know your system?
OS_2 *	How well do you still know the architecture of your system?
OS_3 *	How well do you know your code in the system?
OS_4 *	How well do you know file *<three>*?
	. AO *<for each OS_i>*: 0–100 %
	section: AI-project setting (A)
A_1	What are the learning algorithms used in your system?
	AO: free text
A_2	Where did you get your data from?
	AO: ○ provided by customer ○ generated from another algorithm ○ others (free text)
A_3	Did you continue collecting data? If yes, did you retrain your model?
A_4	Did you use a validation set or test sets? How did you split your training dataset?
A_5	Did you apply any feature engineering to your dataset? If yes, what techniques did you use?
A_6	Did you do any hyperparameter tuning? If yes, what techniques did you use?
A_7	Did you combine different models in your system? If yes, what techniques did you use?
	AO *<for each A_{3-7}>*: ○ yes (free text) ○ no
	section: meta (M)
M_1 *	Can you point out an old file that has especially rarely/often been changed?
	○ Yes (free text for file name) ○ No
M_2 *	How old is this file in the project life-cycle and how often has it been changed since its creation?
M_3 *	Who is the owner of file *<one>*?
M_4 *	How big is file *<two>*?
	AO *<for each M_{2-4}>*: free text
M_5	Did your model have any overfitting or underfitting? If yes, how did you fix it?
	○ Yes (free text) ○ No
	section: code (C)
C_1 *	What is the intent of the code in file *<three>* and *<four>*?
C_2 *	Is there a code smell in the code of file *<three>* or *<four>*?
	AO *<for each file in C_{1-2}>*: free text
C_3	If you use *<learning>*, can you describe your *<X>*?
	AO: free text *<for each>*
	<supervised learning>: *<feature vector & labels>*
	<semi-supervised learning>: *<feature vector & labels & data mostly labeled/unlabeled>*
	<unsupervised learning>: *<feature vector & types of output>*
	<reinforcement learning>: *<feature vector>*
C_4	How did you assess your model's performance? What techniques did you use?
	AO: free text
	section: importance of knowledge
IK_1 *	Which part of your system do you consider important?
	AO: free text
IK_2 *	Which type of the previously investigated types of knowledge do you consider important?
	AO: ○ architecture ○ meta ○ code
IK_3	Which of the previous questions do you consider important or irrelevant when talking about familiarity?
	AO: free text
IK_4 *	What do you consider/reflect about when making a self-assessment of your familiarity?
IK_5 *	Do you have additional remarks?
	AO *<for each file in IK_{4-5}>*: free text

In contrast to our previous study, we did not ask our interviewees to report their perceived importance of each individual question, but to only mention those questions they considered particularly important or relevant. Our main motivation for this adaptation was to limit the time needed for each interview.

The first and last sections ask for opinions and experiences, while the other three (knowledge) sections ask for details about the systems we could verify afterwards.

Data-Science Adaptations. Initially, we planned to use all of our previous questions and to only add data-scientist-specific ones. However, this drastically increased the time needed for each interview (≈ 2 h). Based on our test runs and potential interviewees raising the issue that this would be too long and not focused on their actual tasks, we decided to refocus the interviews on AI engineering.

For this reason, we exchanged the section on software architecture from our previous study with the section on AI-project settings, namely on the AI algorithms used (A_1), data sources (A_2), and similar strategical decisions relevant for engineering an AI. Note that we initially called this section "architecture" during the interviews as well. However, as several interviewees pointed out, this name was not the best fit to describe the type of questions we asked.

Similarly, we exchanged questions in the section code knowledge to refocus it from code details (e.g., return types, exceptions) towards the coding details of an AI. Specifically, we added a question about feature vectors and labels (C_3) as well as a question about the assessment of model performance (C_4). We also reduced the number of files about which we asked such questions from three to two to save time. In the section on meta knowledge, we removed the questions about the last changes to a file and instead added a question on whether there had been overfitting/underfitting and how this has been fixed (M_5).

Finally, we initially wanted to assess the importance of knowledge as we did before, namely for each individual question. However, to reduce the interview length, we decided to assess the importance of the knowledge sections only, and to depend on the qualitative analysis results that we obtained from the answers to IK_3. In the end, we limited the time of each interview to around 1 h. Of course, this means that our new study is not an exact replication, but the focus on the specifics of AI engineering also promises more important insights into data scientists' knowledge needs.

Evaluation. Due to our adaptations, we needed to verify that our interview survey remained valid and reliable. Besides test runs and checks among ourselves, we asked particularly our first interviewee to give us their opinion about the questions and if there were any irrelevant or difficult-to-follow questions. According to that first interviewee, all questions made sense in the context of AI-based systems and did not need to be changed. We continued to ask all of our interviewees about the quality of the questions to reflect on potential threats to validity (part of IK_5). None of our interviewees indicated that our questions were hard to comprehend or irrelevant for data scientists.

3.3   Interview Conduct

Initially, we planned to conduct the interviews in person. However, most of our potential interviewees preferred online sessions, we were restricted in traveling due to the COVID-19 pandemic, and we ended up interviewing data scientists in different countries. For such reasons, we decided to conduct the interviews via online meetings using Zoom. This resulted in the structure and assessment of each interview as we describe in the following.

Interview Structure. We started each interview by introducing the interview protocol, checking for the interviewee's consent, and asking some background questions (cf. Table 2). Since most of our interviewees' systems were closed-source, we could not investigate those beforehand to prepare our questions (i.e., questions asking about specific files). To solve this problem, we asked each interviewee to write down four code files in the beginning, to which we then referred to in the respective questions (cf. Table 1). We aimed to avoid potential threats in the file selection by asking each interviewee to open their system and navigate to a file based on our suggestions. Specifically, we asked how many folders their repository involved and then randomly picked a number to select a folder, and we repeated the same for the files (or folders) in that folder. Using this method, we aimed to avoid our interviewees selecting a file they were particularly familiar with. Note that we ensured that the interviewee had worked on the file to ensure that we were not asking questions about a completely unknown piece of the system. Then, we continued with iterating through our questions without the interviewee looking into their system.

Rating Correctness. As in our previous study, we aimed to understand to what extent our interviewees could answer our questions correctly based on their memory. Unfortunately, we were not allowed to investigate the systems together with the interviewees, since the systems were closed source. For this reason, each interviewee had to re-iterate through the questions and assess themselves whether the question was correct or not—this time being allowed to look at the system's code and artifacts to compare their answers against the actual implementation.

While this strategy may have introduced bias, we trusted our interviewees to provide truthful assessments, since there were no negative consequences and they could check to what extent they could trust their memory. Moreover, while some questions can be easily self-corrected (e.g., M_{1-4}), others require a detailed reflection about various parts of the system and involve subjective opinions anyway (e.g., C_1, A_{2-4}). This problem is inherent to program comprehension, since two individuals may have different perceptions about the same concept. To mitigate potential threats, we asked the interviewees to explain their reasoning for each assessment to us, which we considered to improve the fairness. For instance, to compare their answers to C_1 and C_2 against the actual code, two interviewees explained to us in detail what they thought the intention of each file was after looking at it again and what they considered to represent a code smell within each file. Note that we followed a similar strategy as in our previous study to deal with such inherently more subjective questions, which we found to yield reliable results and to connect better to an interviewee's memorized knowledge (which is based on their subjective perception, too).

Table 2. Overview of the 11 included interviewees.

id	degree	exp.	domain	devs.
I_1	master	<1	finance	7
I_2	bachelor	15	telecommunications	3
I_3	master	2	machine learning	15
I_4	master	4	finance	6
I_5	master	10	healthcare	3
I_6	master	5	agriculture	4
I_7	PhD	5	software engineering	1
I_8	master	10	image processing	2
I_9	master	5	image processing	2
I_{10}	master	7	real estate	2
I_{11}	master	4	biomedicine	1

exp.: years of experience
devs.: number of developers involved

Rating Scheme. To make it possible that we could compare the findings of our previous to this study, we employed the same rating scheme. Specifically, we awarded 0 points for incorrect, 0.5 points for partially correct, and 1 point for correct answers. We considered an answer partially correct if we and the interviewee noticed that an answer was missing important details that were relevant to the question. Identically, we awarded half a point if an interviewee was not completely sure about or confident in their answer.

3.4   Target Population and Sampling

We characterized our target population based on characteristics recommended in established guidelines [5,13]. Namely, we targeted data scientists, initially those located in Sweden or working for Swedish companies. We did not put limitations on the educational level, gender, age, or years of experience in data science when recruiting interviewees. Due to time constraints, a lack of direct contacts, and other restrictions (e.g., COVID-19), finding interviewees within Sweden was challenging. Therefore, we decided to interview any data scientist who accepted our interview request, regardless of whether they worked in Sweden or for Swedish companies. In the end, we interviewed 12 data scientists of different genders, with varying years of experience, and working in various countries (e.g., Sweden, Germany) as well as domains. However, similar to our previous study, most of them have been working on smaller systems. Note that we excluded one interview during a quality check. The interviewee worked on a system at a very early development stage. As a consequence, seven out of 18 questions in the knowledge sections were not applicable and we could not assess the respective correctness. To improve the trust into our results, we decided not to use the respective interview data for our analysis. We provide an overview of the included interviews in Table 2.

We used judgment and snowballing sampling to recruit interviewees. Both are non-probabilistic sampling strategies, which we chose because we assume that the target population is rather large but its actual size and the respective individuals are unknown to us—which is why we cannot employ probabilistic sampling [13]. Specifically, we employed judgment sampling by contacting data scientists that we identified through searching on public company websites and Linked-In profiles. On Linked-In, we searched for data scientists who are working in Sweden. Then, we contacted the data scientists we could find via email and asked them to introduce us to any other data scientists that they thought may be interested to participate (i.e., snowballing). We also used our personal networks (convenience sampling), which yielded four additional interviewees from different countries.

3.5   Data Analysis

To answer RQ_1, we analyzed the interviewees' responses to the questions within the section importance of knowledge qualitatively and quantitatively. We used open coding on the free texts and computed the number of times each knowledge section was chosen as important or not important. To answer RQ_2, we quantitatively analyzed the correctness of the answers to the three knowledge sections. Specifically, we computed the average of the overall correctness for each question within the knowledge sections in Table 1 individually as well as for the knowledge sections combined. To answer RQ_3, we compared the interviewees' self-assessments to their correctness. Finally, to answer RQ_4, we compared our previous findings on software developers to those we obtained during this study for data scientists.

4   Results

Next, we present the results for each of our RQs individually.

4.1 RQ_1: Importance of Memorizing

To answer RQ_1, we asked our interviewees to choose the knowledge sections they think are important (I_2 in Table 1) while reflecting on the questions that we had in the questionnaire. Not surprisingly, considering their background, 10 out of the 11 interviewees chose AI-project setting knowledge as an important knowledge type, and seven out of the 11 interviewees chose code knowledge. Only one out of the 11 interviewees chose meta knowledge (cf. Fig. 1). This interviewee selected all three types of knowledge as important.

To obtain more detailed insights, we also analyzed the answers to question I_3 to understand what questions we asked target knowledge that the interviewees consider important or irrelevant for reflecting on their familiarity with a system. Note that the interviewees chose what questions they wanted to make statements about. AI-project setting questions were mentioned by six of the interviewees as being important when talking about familiarity. Most of them mentioned all questions in the AI-project setting section. One specified in more detail that they considered knowledge about the learning algorithms (A_1), data collection (A_3), feature engineering (A_5), and hyperparameter tuning (A_6) as important.

When it comes to code knowledge, three interviewees elaborated about what knowledge they consider important. One of them made a general statement that code is important for detailed knowledge. The second interviewee said that knowledge about code smells (C_2) and feature vectors/labels (C_3) is important.

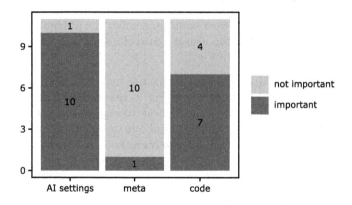

Fig. 1. IK_2: Importance of types of knowledge.

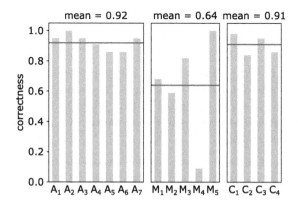

Fig. 2. Assessed correctness of our interviewees for each question on average.

Lastly, the third interviewee only mentioned that feature vectors/labels (C_3) are important. Interestingly, another interviewee referred to knowledge about code smells (C_2) explicitly as not important. Lastly, six interviewees chose meta questions as not important, stating that questions about, for instance, the size of a file (M_4) are irrelevant to remember. Another interviewee mentioned explicitly that remembering whether an old file has been rarely or frequently changed (M_1) is not important.

Observations RQ$_1$ • The majority of our interviewees believes that AI-project setting knowledge is important to remember. • A little more than half of the interviewees thinks that code knowledge is important to remember. • The majority of the interviewees mentioned meta knowledge as not important when talking about familiarity with a system. •

4.2   RQ$_2$: Correctness of Memory

To assess how well our interviewees could remember the different parts of their systems (**RQ$_2$**), we calculated the average correctness of each question. We display a summary of the results in Fig. 2.

AI-Project Settings. Most interviewees have scored noticeably high in the AI-project settings section. As we can see in Fig. 2, the average correctness for the AI-project settings section is 92%. The highest average correctness is actually at 100% and it was scored for A_2, which asks about the source of the data used in the system. In contrast, the lowest average correctness is 86% and it was scored for two questions: A5, which asks about feature engineering, and A6, which asks about hyper-parameter tuning.

Meta. Our interviewees had the lowest correctness when it comes to meta knowledge. We can see in Fig. 2 that the average correctness of the meta section is 64%. However, our interviewees scored 100% on question M_5 about whether the model in the system had an overfitting or underfitting. For question M_4, about the size of a file in terms of lines of code (approximated), our interviewees had an average correctness of only 9%.

Code. Similar to the AI-project settings, our interviewees scored a considerably high correctness of 92% for code knowledge. They scored on average 98% correctly for question C_1 about the intent of two different files in the system. The lowest average correctness score is 84% for question C_2 about the presence of code smells in selected files.

Overall Average. On average, our 11 interviewees reached a correctness score of 83%, with one interviewee scoring a correctness of 100% and the interviewee with the lowest correctness scoring 66%.

Observations RQ₂ • Only one interviewee could remember all details we asked about correctly. • All interviewees could remember the source of their data and whether their model had an overfitting or underfitting. • Interviewees seem to remember the intent of their files, as well as their feature vector and labels better than code smells and the model-performance assessment techniques used. • Interviewees remember AI-project setting knowledge and code knowledge equally well. •

4.3   RQ₃: Self-assessments Versus Correctness

To answer **RQ₃**, we compared the interviewees' average correctness to their initial and final self-assessments, which we display in Fig. 3. We used Kendall's τ [6] on this data to test for rank correlations. The results indicate no significant correlation between the overall self-assessment and the average correctness of the interviewees (both p-values > 0.05, initial $\tau = 0.242$, final $\tau = 0.061$). We also looked into how the results of the initial and final overall self-assessments changed during the interview. In particular, five interviewees increased and three interviewees decreased their overall self-assessment during the interview. Three interviewees left their self-assessments unchanged during the interview.

When analyzing the interviewees' responses to IK₄, we found that many of them reflect on their AI-project settings or architectural knowledge when making a self-assessment of how well they know their system. Namely, six of the interviewees described that they reflected on the pipeline flow and model training, their ability to explain the system structure or architecture, and the idea of the implementation. Three of these six interviewees also talked about reflecting on code knowledge. Other reflections were on what aspects are relevant in a system (two interviewees) and on the confidence in the own memory regarding the sys-

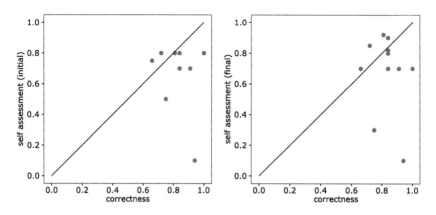

Fig. 3. Participants' self assessment in the beginning (left, some points overlap) and end (right) compared to their correctness. The diagonals serve as indicators only.

tem (one interviewee). Lastly, one of the interviewees mentioned that they were not considering anything in particular, because the system was small and fairly recent and they were the only developer.

> **Observations RQ$_3$** • There is no correlation between interviewees' self-assessment of their familiarity and the correctness of their answers from memory. • The most mentioned aspect interviewees consider when making a self-assessment is their AI-project settings knowledge. •

4.4   RQ$_4$: Data Scientists Versus Software Developers

In Table 3, we compare the perceived importance that interviewees assigned to the different types of knowledge in this study (data scientists) and in our previous one [8] (software developers). We found that the results from both studies are similar with regard to the following aspects: The perceived importance is similar. AI-project settings knowledge is, identically to architectural knowledge, considered most important. Note that data scientists assign even higher importance to AI-project settings knowledge than software engineers do to architectural knowledge. The importance that is assigned to code knowledge and meta knowledge is comparable for both populations, too. We can observe that in both cases abstract knowledge, such as the intent of code [12], was considered more important. Also, both populations considered meta-knowledge to be the least important.

> **Observations RQ$_4$** • The order of perceived importance of knowledge types by data scientists and software engineers is similar: AI-project settings knowledge and architecture knowledge are followed by code knowledge and, lastly, meta-knowledge. •

Table 3. Comparison of the perceived importance of different types of knowledge.

type of knowledge	software developers [8]	data scientists
architecture	76.5%	n.a.
ai-project settings	n.a	90.9%
code	52.9%	63.6%
meta	11.8%	9.1%

5 Discussion

In the following, we summarize our findings' implications for researchers and practitioners, before discussing threats to the validity of our results.

5.1 Implications for Researchers

Be Careful with Using Self-assessments of Familiarity. Just as for software developers [8], researchers should be careful when using data scientists' self-assessments of their familiarity with a system. Our results indicate no correlation between self-assessments and the actual correctness of answers.

Plan Comparisons Between Data Scientists and Software Developers Carefully. Comparing between data scientists and software developers needs to account for differences in the way of thinking and working. Specifically, we formulate the following conjectures that should be investigated in future work:

- *A different intensity of knowledge use?* We observed that data scientists are specifically good at remembering answers to questions that are data-science specific (answering each question added to this study compared to our previous work with >80% correctness). In contrast, they answered only one of the questions we also asked to developers with this high level of correctness. Thus, it does not seem reasonable to assume that they are simply better at remembering things. Another logical interpretation is that data scientists use individual pieces of knowledge about the data science-specific questions more often during their daily work. In contrast, software developers may have to switch contexts more often, recovering the same knowledge less frequently.
- *A different way to structure knowledge?* Data scientists seem to structure their knowledge about a system less in terms of files than software engineers would. This is supported by the observation that questions on meta knowledge that concern files (M_{1-4}) were answered with lower correctness by data scientists than by software developers.
- *A different notion of "big picture?"* In our previous study [8], software developers have indicated that the architectural knowledge is considered the big picture of a software system, with all interviewees agreeing on the importance of being able to draw a high-level architecture of the system. Even though we did not explicitly ask about architecture in this study, we collected some input from interviewees that indicate a different idea about what the "big picture" of an AI-enabled system is. One of the interviewees remarked that they are not too fond of software engineers who are *"always thinking about code"*, and that they—as a data scientist—prefer to always think about design and the solution on a "higher level". We can only guess whether this higher level refers to AI-project settings knowledge or to a different type of knowledge that we did not capture here.

In future work, we need to investigate such questions in more detail.

5.2   Implications for Practitioners

Focus on AI-Project Settings During Documenting and Onboarding.
Knowledge related to AI-project settings received the highest vote of importance, even compared to the importance software developers put on architectural knowledge. Thus, the respective pieces of information seem to be crucial for data scientists to perform their work, which is confirmed by their very high ability to answer these questions correctly without looking at their system (i.e., from memory). In practice, documenting an AI-system and onboarding new data scientists to an existing project should focus on these questions.

5.3   Threats to Validity

Internal Validity. The individual characteristics of our interviewees like their age, gender, or memory performance may have impacted their perceptions and responses. Due to the limited number of interviewees, we could not perform population analyses, which are subject to future work. Also, there is the risk that some questions may have been misunderstood by an interviewee. To mitigate this risk, we performed test runs among ourselves and at least one interviewer was present in each interview to explain questions and clarify potential confusions.

As we have mentioned before, we added and modified some questions to focus on knowledge relevant to data scientists. These new questions have a weaker foundation in empirical evidence compared to our original study for which we elicited the questions via a systematic literature review. However, to the best of our knowledge, there is currently no comparable data basis that we could have built on for data scientists. To still mitigate this threat, we derived our questions from the main practices of AI-based systems that are described by Burkov [2].

While we did not inform the interviewees in our previous study about the interviews' exact purpose to avoid biases, we had to briefly explain our motivation for this study to gain the interest of the data scientists. This may have caused a threat to the internal validity, because the interviewees may have prepared for our interviews by investigating their system beforehand or proposing to work on a system they know particularly well. While this is unlikely since all of them are working in practice, we further aimed to mitigate this threat. For this purpose, we did only share a short motivation for our interviews without details on the types of questions we would ask. Moreover, we asked rather different questions and chose files at random. On a related matter, there is the risk that an interviewee looked at their system while answering our questions, since the online setting limited our control at that point. However, this is very unlikely and we did not observe any behaviors that would hint at such a case.

As indicated in Sect. 3, we used the term "architecture knowledge" for the AI-project settings section during the interviews. Some interviewees pointed out that the term "architecture" is not the best description for that type of knowledge. In the end, we renamed the section for this paper using a term that was suggested by one of the interviewees: "project settings". It is possible that the use of the term architecture confused some interviewees and influenced their judgment of the importance of knowledge. We would assume that such confusion would decrease their rating of importance, and thus the values we present may be an underestimate. Moreover, among us authors, we discussed whether the placement of question C_4 (assessment of the model's performance) in the code knowledge section is appropriate, or whether the question should have been placed in the AI-project settings section. It is possible that the placement changed the perceived importance of the code knowledge section.

External Validity. The primary external threat to this study is the small sample size. We analyzed only 11 interviews, which means that it is not clear to what degree the results can be generalized. This uncertainty holds especially with regard to data scientists working on larger systems, since we mostly studied data scientists working on smaller systems. Furthermore, after interviewing data scientists who are working in different companies, it became clear that the tasks assigned to data scientists in such companies vary. This may cause individuals with the same title (data scientist) to have very different responsibilities, which eventually leads to varying perceptions. Such threats are partly inherent to interview surveys as well as human cognition, and thus we cannot fully overcome them. Still, we aimed to mitigate such threats by involving a diverse sample of data scientists to cover broader experiences and perceptions.

6 Conclusion

In this paper, we presented an interview survey with 11 data scientists, investigating what knowledge they consider important, aim to remember, and how they perform when recalling it from memory. For this purpose, we replicated parts of our previous work with software developers [8], against which we also compared our results. Among others, our results indicate that data scientists (identical to software developers) consider more abstract knowledge more important to remember, and perform quite well at recalling it from memory. Also, we highlighted differences between data scientists and software developers, particularly with respect to what constitutes "more abstract" knowledge. Based on these findings, we have discussed concrete recommendations and steps for future work to improve our understanding of data scientists' knowledge needs and to facilitate their work.

References

1. Amershi, S., et al.: Software engineering for machine learning: a case study. In: ICSE-SEIP. IEEE (2019)
2. Burkov, A.: The Hundred-Page Machine Learning Book. Andriy Burkov (2019)
3. Haiduc, S., Aponte, J., Marcus, A.: Supporting program comprehension with source code summarization. In: ICSE. ACM (2010)
4. Hofmeister, J., Siegmund, J., Holt, D.V.: Shorter identifier names take longer to comprehend. In: SANER. IEEE (2017)

5. Kasunic, M.: Designing an effective survey. Technical report CMU/SEI-2005-HB-004, Carnegie Mellon University (2005)
6. Kendall, M.G.: A new measure of rank correlation. Biometrika **30**(1/2), 81–93 (1938)
7. Krüger, J., Çalıklı, G., Berger, T., Leich, T.: How explicit feature traces did not impact developers' memory. In: SANER. IEEE (2021)
8. Krüger, J., Hebig, R.: What developers (care to) recall: an interview survey on smaller systems. In: ICSME. IEEE (2020)
9. Krüger, J., Hebig, R.: To memorize or to document: a survey of developers' views on knowledge availability. In: Kadgien, R., et al. (eds.) PROFES 2023. LNCS, vol. 14483, pp. 39–56. Springer, Cham (2023)
10. Krüger, J., Mukelabai, M., Gu, W., Shen, H., Hebig, R., Berger, T.: Where is my feature and what is it about? A case study on recovering feature facets. J. Syst. Softw. **152**, 239–253 (2019)
11. Krüger, J., Wiemann, J., Fenske, W., Saake, G., Leich, T.: Do you remember this source code? In: ICSE. ACM (2018)
12. Krüger, J., Li, Y., Zhu, C., Chechik, M., Berger, T., Rubin, J.: A vision on intentions in software engineering. In: ESEC/FSE. ACM (2023)
13. Linåker, J., Sulaman, S.M., Höst, M., de Mello, R.M.: Guidelines for conducting surveys in software engineering. Technical report, Lund University (2015)
14. Liu, H., Eksmo, S., Risberg, J., Hebig, R.: Emerging and changing tasks in the development process for machine learning systems. In: ICSSP. ACM (2020)
15. Maalej, W., Tiarks, R., Roehm, T., Koschke, R.: On the comprehension of program comprehension. ACM Trans. Softw. Eng. Methodol. **23**(4), 1–37 (2014)
16. Montavon, G., Samek, W., Müller, K.R.: Methods for interpreting and understanding deep neural networks. Digit. Signal Process. **73**, 1–15 (2018)
17. Nielebock, S., Krolikowski, D., Krüger, J., Leich, T., Ortmeier, F.: Commenting source code: is it worth it for small programming tasks? Empir. Softw. Eng. **24**, 1418–1457 (2019)
18. Pereira, P.: Towards helping data scientists. In: VL/HCC. IEEE (2020)
19. Pereira, P., Cunha, J., Fernandes, J.P.: On understanding data scientists. In: VL/HCC. IEEE (2020)
20. Roehm, T., Tiarks, R., Koschke, R., Maalej, W.: How do professional developers comprehend software? In: ICSE. IEEE (2012)
21. Schröter, I., Krüger, J., Siegmund, J., Leich, T.: Comprehending studies on program comprehension. In: ICPC. IEEE (2017)
22. Winkler, J.P., Vogelsang, A.: "What does my classifier learn?" A visual approach to understanding natural language text classifiers. In: Frasincar, F., Ittoo, A., Nguyen, L.M., Métais, E. (eds.) NLDB 2017. LNCS, vol. 10260, pp. 468–479. Springer, Cham (2017). https://doi.org/10.1007/978-3-319-59569-6_55
23. Yosinski, J., Clune, J., Nguyen, A., Fuchs, T., Lipson, H.: Understanding neural networks through deep visualization. arXiv (2015). arXiv:1506.06579

Software Analysis and Tools

Using AI-Based Code Completion for Domain-Specific Languages

Christina Piereder[1](✉), Günter Fleck[2], Verena Geist[1], Michael Moser[1], and Josef Pichler[3]

[1] Software Competence Center Hagenberg GmbH, Hagenberg, Austria
{christina.piereder,verena.geist,michael.moser}@scch.at
[2] Siemens Energy Austria GmbH, Wien, Austria
guenter.fleck@siemens-energy.com
[3] University of Applied Sciences Upper Austria, Hagenberg, Austria
josef.pichler@fh-hagenberg.at
http://www.scch.at, https://www.siemens-energy.com,
https://pure.fh-ooe.at

Abstract. Code completion is a very important feature of modern integrated development environments. Research has been done for years to improve code completion systems for general-purpose languages. However, only little literature can be found for (AI-based) code completion for domain specific languages (DSLs). A DSL is a special-purpose programming language tailored for a specific application domain. In this paper, we investigate whether AI-based state-of-the-art code completion approaches can also be applied for DSLs. This is demonstrated using the domain-specific language TTI (Thermal Text Input). TTI is used for power transformer design specification in an industrial context, where an existing code completion shall be replaced by an advanced machine learning approach. For this purpose, implementations of two code completion systems are adapted to our needs. One of them shows very promising results and achieves a top-5 accuracy of 97%. To evaluate the practical applicability, the approach is integrated into an existing editor of a power transformer manufacturer.

Keywords: AI-based Code Completion · Domain-Specific Languages · Industrial Transformer Construction Domain · Experiences and Lessons Learned · Applied Research

1 Introduction

The use of integrated development environments (IDEs) has become an indispensable part of modern software development. These tools efficiently support developers in their daily work and all of them offer code completion to facilitate writing source code. Thus, typing effort and syntax errors can be avoided during the development phase by suggesting class names, variables, methods, fields or keywords based on the already existing code. Research has been done for

R. Kadgien et al. (Eds.): PROFES 2023, LNCS 14483, pp. 227–242, 2024.
https://doi.org/10.1007/978-3-031-49266-2_16

years to improve code completion features however, the implementations vary in their level of sophistication. Approaches range from traditional approaches using static code analysis [7,16,18] to more recent ones using machine learning models (e.g., Tabnine[1], Github Copilot[2]).

While code completion for many general-purpose languages is already very mature, little literature can be found on code completion for domain-specific languages (DSLs). DSLs are special-purpose programming languages that are tailored for a specific application domain [12]. This makes them easier to learn, especially for domain experts without extensive programming expertise, compared to general-purpose programming languages. For DSLs, which are developed using a language workbench [4], the generated editors only include basic code completion that is derived from language grammars; for DSLs that are developed from scratch like in the present industry context, code completion is often missing at all. However, in order to facilitate the writing of programs in DSLs and to improve the usability of domain-specific code editors, modern machine learning-based completion of user input is needed. Similar to code completion in conventional source code editors, the provided solution should offer context-sensitive suggestions and prioritize the suggestions. However, since DSLs are typically used for specific application domains and often by a limited number of developers, only small data sets are available. This small amount of training data poses a challenge for machine learning approaches.

In this paper, we investigate whether machine learning-based approaches for code completion applied to general-purpose languages are also suitable for DSLs. This is demonstrated using the TTI language, which is used for product engineering in transformer construction. We, therefore, developed a machine learning-based approach for completing TTI code and integrated the novel solution into an existing editor. In the main part of the paper, we report on our applied solution and the results of the developed code completion approach for an industrial transformer manufacturer. This development was driven by specific business needs and requirements and was performed in close cooperation with domain experts, electrical engineers, etc. who are typically no experts in software development. Finally, we also present the challenges, insights, and lessons learned from prototyping, development, and evaluation of the AI-based code completion approach applied to the DSL in the presented industrial context.

This paper is structured as follows. In Sect. 2, we outline the context of the applied research project and present specific industry needs and our research objective. Section 3 highlights the current state of the art of AI-based code completion approaches. Section 4 summarizes the activities in developing the AI-based approaches for a DSL used in transformer construction. We present our results in Sect. 5 and discuss challenges, insights as well as experiences structured along the defined research questions in Sect. 6. Section 7 states threats to validity and Sect. 8 concludes the paper and gives an outlook on future work.

---

[1] https://www.tabnine.com.

[2] https://copilot.github.com.

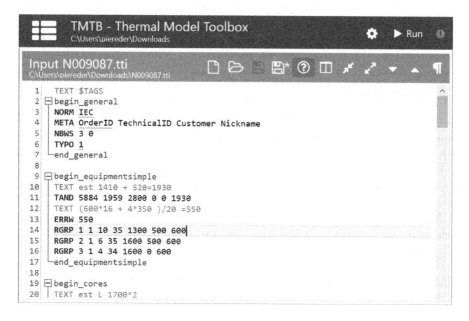

Fig. 1. The TMTB editor.

2   Industrial Context and Research Objective

2.1   Project Goal

The work reported in this paper has been done within an applied research project conducted in an industrial application context. As preliminary work for the code completion approach discussed in this paper, a domain-specific code editor, i.e., the Thermal Model Toolbox editor (TMTB), for writing and parsing TTI input files has been developed. This editor is in productive use at *Siemens Energy*, a manufacturer of large power transformers. With the help of TMTB it is possible to run calculation programs, load and edit input files, display calculation results, and visualize the current input. TMTB not only processes the format of input files on a textual level but also transforms the input into an abstract internal representation that is used to check the correctness of input files on a syntactic and semantic level. To further improve the usability of editing input files, a basic code completion approach was implemented. This simple approach is hard-coded and supports the insertion of keywords and groups of keywords into sections of the input files. Figure 1 shows two complete TTI code sections, i.e., *general* and *equipmentsimple*, and a starting *cores* section. All sections contain specific keywords, e.g., NORM, META or NBWS, which are followed by certain parameters.

In order to ease writing of TTI programs and to improve the overall usability of the domain-specific TMTB editor, automatic completion of user input is required. The existing, simple code completion mechanism is now to be replaced by a machine learning-based approach. It is the aim of this applied research (i) to develop the AI-based code completion approach, (ii) to integrate code completion into the existing editor, and (iii) to evaluate whether the novel approach meets the defined business needs in practice.

2.2   The TTI Language

Siemens Energy develops Fortran programs to calculate properties of power transformers, e.g., thermal development of isolation oil in transformers. These Fortran programs mostly focus on individual components, e.g., windings or core, and calculate the properties of these components on different levels of detail. To run calculations, comprehensive program-specific input data need to be provided in the company-specific format TTI.

TTI supports the specification of transformer components and calculation constraints by the definition of sections, keywords and their parameters. Figure 2 illustrates the overall structure of TTI files. A keywordfile contains one to many sections. Keywords are placed inside of these sections. TTI precisely defines which keywords may appear in which sections. Keywords, in turn, have their own parameters.

An example of the TTI language is shown in Listing 1. Sections are code blocks that start with begin_<sectionname> and end with end_<sectionname>. Some sections depend on each other. Currently, eight possible types of sections are defined. For example, the *windingdetail* section in Listing 1 models detailed information on the geometry of every winding and its sub-components. *Windingdetail* sections are referenced by their id. Keywords used in this section are, e.g., ALLG, BASB, BAST and DISC which define geometric properties for disc windings and their isolation components. Parameters are of simple types like string, double or sequence. The DISC keyword in line 7 of Listing 1 has a list parameter. TTI supports to write parameters in expanded as well as in compact version. For example, the expanded versions DISC [B] [A] [A] [A] and DISC [B] DISC [A] DISC [A] DISC [A] are equivalent to the compact version DISC [B] 3*([A]).

```
 1 begin_windingdetail PW
 2 ALLG   1122 1336
 3 STICK 44 14.5 6 6
 4 SPAC 71*25 8 3*6 2*5 5*4 6 2*5 7*4 8 3*4 6 4 8 3*4 /
 5      2*(6 3*5) 6 3*4 8 4 6 3*4 8 7*4 6 4 6 5*4 2*5 4*6
 6 WIRE   A 18.35 23.50 1.1 25   8.5 1.56 2 0.14
 7 DISC   10*([A 4 A 4 A 4 A])
 8 CAPT   21
 9 CAPB   21
10 BAST   S 6 B 49.6 20.4 S 10 C 96.3 0
11 BASB   S 6 0 8.75
12 end_windingdetail
```

Listing 1. Example of the TTI language (excerpt): TTI is interpreted line by line. Every line starts with a keyword. Specific keywords belong to specific sections.

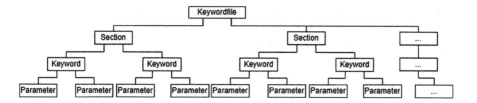

Fig. 2. Overall structure of the TTI language.

2.3 Requirements

To decide whether the new code completion approach proposed in this paper meets expectations, functional requirements were defined by major stakeholders at *Siemens Energy*. These requirements refer to the AI-based prediction of language elements on different levels of granularity, i.e., sections, keywords, and parameters. The requirements can be summarized as follows:

1. **Predict sections:**
   R-1.1 Context-sensitive prediction of sections. Predict sections in the outer context of TTI files.
   R-1.2 Consider unique sections. For sections that can only occur once in a file proposals should only be provided if sections do not exist yet.
   R-1.3 Consider optional sections. Distinguish between optional and non-optional sections.
   R-1.4 Rank sections according to context. Order predicted sections by probability.
   R-1.5 Recommend groups of sections. Predict groups of sections that fit together.
2. **Predict keywords:**
   R-2.1 Context-sensitive prediction of keywords. Predict keywords within a section and consider dependencies, e.g., suggest CAPT before BAST.
   R-2.2 Consider unique keywords. If a keyword that can only occur once in a section already exists, don't suggest it anymore.
   R-2.3 Consider cross-section dependencies of keywords. Suggest keywords that correspond with keywords of other sections.
   R-2.4 Rank keywords according to context. Order predicted keywords by probability.
   R-2.5 Recommend groups of keywords. Predict a group of keywords inside a section.
3. **Predict parameters:**
   R-3.1 Prediction of enumerations. Only suggest string values supported by the enumeration.
   R-3.2 Prediction of sequences. Suggest realistic values for sequences. Ideally based on already existing keywords in other sections.

R-3.3 Context-sensitive prediction of parameters. Suggest correct parameter type and value for current cursor position.

R-3.4 Consider optional parameters. Distinguish between optional and non-optional parameters.

2.4 Research Questions

The project aims to provide advanced code completion using machine learning techniques and by this to improve the usability of code completion for TTI. From a research perspective, the following questions should be addressed:

RQ1 What are the differences in applying machine learning techniques between DSLs and general-purpose languages?

RQ2 Are learning-based approaches suitable for DSLs for which only a small amount of training data is available?

RQ3 Can learning-based code completion approaches for general-purpose languages be applied to DSLs in practice?

3   Related Work

This paper relates to work in the field of AI-based code completion and more specifically to code completion for domain-specific languages (DSLs). Code completion has been targeted by research for a long time and approaches are integrated with core components of development environments (IDEs). Early work on code completion that goes beyond exploitation of static type information includes analysis of usage and change frequencies [18] and developer preferences [7,16]. Bruch et al. [2] implemented code completion systems that learned completions from existing source code repositories using frequency analysis, rule mining or a *k-nearest neighbor* based algorithm. Statistical language models learn a probability distribution over a text. N-gram models [9] have been used for code completion in the past. An N-gram consists of N consecutive fragments. Depending on the use case, these fragments can be letters, phonems or words. CACHECA [5], an Eclipse IDE plugin, combines a cache language model with Eclipse's existing code completion mechanism. Their $-gram model consists of an N-gram and a cache component. The N-gram stores the probabilities extracted from the training data whereas the cache component represents the N-grams from current source code. This can be used to improve the handling of out-of-vocabulary tokens. Another approach, i.e., SLANG [17], based on N-grams is trained to fill in holes in source code.

Other approaches use neural networks to model source code. They further make use of pointer networks [14] and attention mechanisms [1]. In order to address long range dependencies, Bahdanau et al. [1] proposed an attention technique. Vinyals et al. [14] proposed pointer networks as an adaption of the attention mechanism. For instance, Li et al. [10] use pointer networks together with neural attention to improve performance on the code completion task. An approach presented in more detail in the subsequent section is by Svyatkovskiy et al. [19]. They implemented a code completion system based on a model architecture that consists of stacked long short-term memory models (LSTM) trained on partial abstract syntax trees (AST). Current industry-ready approaches on neural code completion intensively build upon large language models (LLM) and include GitHub Copilot[3], Tabnine[4], AlphaCode[5], or CodeWhisperer[6]. All these approaches go far beyond the classic code completion task but are capable of generating code from natural language description or contextual information available from source code context. Ziegler et al. [20] report on productivity assessment of neural code completion in the case of Github Copilot, i.e., that users on average accept completions by 27% and that productivity assessment of developers correlates with acceptance rates.

To the best of our knowledge their is no scientific work that discusses (AI-based) code completion for domain-specific languages. Availability of code completion for DSLs is strongly coupled with the use of language workbenches [15]. If available, code completion systems in language workbenches infer predictions from grammatical language structure and static type information. Examples for language workbenches with such support include Jetbrains Meta Programming System[7], Eclipse XText[8], and Rascal[9].

4   Applied Solution Approach

In this section, we describe the approach chosen to apply code completion for DSLs. First, a model has to be selected. Then, training data need to be provided. In our case, very little training data were available. So we investigated several methods to overcome this issue. The available training files are processed by converting, shuffling and expanding keywords, sections and parameters respectively. Finally, the selected model is trained, integrated into the existing editor and evaluated using different metrics. To facilitate further research, we provide the sources of our implementation[10]. Please note that we are not allowed to publish the dataset from our industry context due to confidential information.

4.1   Model Selection and Design

We investigated machine learning architectures and adapted two architectures to fit TTI input files. The first one is Pythia [19]. Pythia is currently part of the

---

[3] https://github.com/features/copilot.

[4] https://www.tabnine.com.

[5] https://www.deepmind.com/blog/competitive-programming-with-alphacode.

[6] https://aws.amazon.com/de/codewhisperer.

[7] https://www.jetbrains.com/mps.

[8] https://www.eclipse.org/Xtext.

[9] https://www.rascal-mpl.org.

[10] https://github.com/software-competence-center-hagenberg/DSL-Code-Completion.

IntelliCode extension for Visual Studio Code IDE. Pythia was developed for the completion of Python code. Pythia was chosen because at time of writing it is state-of-the-art, provides promising results, and has a publicly available reference implementation. Second, we evaluated Code Completion with Neural Attention and Pointer Networks (NAPN) [10]. NAPN was developed for the code completion of dynamically typed programming languages like Python or JavaScript. For selection, we initially evaluated these models in two steps. First, throughout training using metrics like accuracy and loss score. In a second step, we explored inference performance for both models. Evaluation was done manually by two experts of both TTI format and electrical power transformer engineering following a structured procedure. During the second evaluation step, the adapted Pythia model showed the best results. In the second step, NAPN showed very poor results for sections and keywords, moreover, inference time was not acceptable. Therefore, we did not consider this model for the final integration into the editor. The sections below will therefore refer to the adapted Pythia model only. We use an already existing Pythia implementation[11] and adapt, e.g., preprocessing of input sources to fulfill requirements of TTI. In addition, we provide a model export functionality to ONNX (Open Neural Network Exchange) after training. The training logic itself is reused as is. The architecture is based on [19]. Pythia consists of a stacked LSTM. Pythia supports the specification of different neural network architectures, i.e., GRU, LSTM and LSTM with Attention as hyperparameter. Code snippets are serialized to files and feed into the neural network.

4.2   Prototypical Implementation

Preprocessing. To bring the input files into a more abstract representation, an adapted version of the existing TTI parser processes the whole file corpus and converts the files into a JSON representation. We differentiate between sections, keywords and its parameters by adding suffixes. These are *Section* for sections, *Call* for keywords and *Parameter* for parameters. The generated JSON files also contain several metadata on parameters (e.g., type, index, value, optional parameters, whether a parameter is an enumeration).

Generating the Dataset. The data set is created from 82 TTI input files. Several data augmentation steps are used to increase the amount of training data to finally 9582 input files. Keywords are converted to equivalent ones. List parameters are generated in expanded as well as in compact version. Sections are randomly shuffled all over the document. Keywords are randomly distributed inside of every section. As for conventional datasets, the input files are first converted into a JSON representation. From this, terminal symbols and non-terminal symbols are extracted. Sections and their entries are mapped to terminal symbols. Parameters are mapped to non-terminal symbols in most of the cases. Terminal and non-terminal symbols are associated with numbers. Partial ASTs, i.e., parts of section and keyword entries, are serialized to CSV files. The resulting CSV files

---

[11] https://github.com/motykatomasz/Pythia-AI-code-completion.

contain the actual token, the input length and the following tokens depending on the input length. Tokens that occur in TTI files are mapped to numbers. We also add an out-of-vocabulary token and a padding token to the vocabulary. The padding token is ignored during training. Padding tokens are necessary, because words need to be mapped to equally sized vectors. The resulting CSV files are processed during training.

Model Training and Hyperparameter Tuning. LSTM, GRU and LSTM with attention are considered and implemented in different Python classes. The model training is done using the PyTorch framework. In order to find the best fitting training parameters, hyperparameter tuning is applied. We use the distributed framework Ray [13] and its library Tune[12] [11]. The complete hyperparameter tuning process lasted 29 h. To speed up the hyperparameter tuning process, a maximum of 5 epochs were trained per run. Additionally, Ray Tune aborts bad performing runs early. The training of the finally chosen model on a Linux 64-bit distribution with a GeForce GTX 1060 GPU took 0.5 h. Hyperparameters chosen for training are whether or not to use attention, batch size, clip norm, dropout, embedding dimension, gamma, hidden dimension, l2 regularization, the number of lookback tokens, the initial learning rate, the number of layers and the kind of neural network. Samples are split into a training (70%) and a validation set (30%).

Model Test. To measure the accuracy of the recommendations, we apply two metrics, namely top-k-accuracy and loss. Loss is the distance between expected and actual tokens, i.e., the distance between actual tokens and the ones extracted from the CSV files. We use the *CrossEntropyLoss* function from PyTorch to calculate the loss. Top-k-accuracy means that the top k predictions match with tokens in the generated CSV files. For code completion, top-1-accuracy and top-5-accuracy are often used. Evaluation is done for the completion inside a section, inside an entry and outside of sections and entries.

4.3   Editor Integration

After training, the resulting model is converted to the ONNX file format, an exchange format for machine learning models, since PyTorch models can currently not be loaded using C# and the .Net platform. For the integration into .Net, we use several Nuget packages. Microsoft.ML.OnnxRuntime[13] is needed to run the ONNX model. OnnxRuntime requires models to have a batch size of one, which does not lead to optimal results. This is the reason why it is necessary to change the batch size in the exported ONNX graph. We use the Nuget package OnnxSharp[14] to achieve that.

When code completion is triggered, tokens are extracted from the current cursor position and fed into the model. After calculation, a softmax operation

---

[12] https://docs.ray.io/en/latest/tune/index.html.
[13] https://github.com/Microsoft/onnxruntime.
[14] https://github.com/nietras/OnnxSharp.

is applied to the result to get a probability distribution for the next tokens. Then the tokens with the best probability are chosen and mapped back to their vocabulary name.

4.4   Evaluation

Evaluation is done after integration into the editor and include (i) model size on disk, (ii) quality of recommendations, (iii) memory consumption and (iv) inference speed. The model size on disk is important as the model needs to be parsed by the editor in order to serve predictions. A too large model might influence the inference speed. The quality of recommendations is evaluated using top-1 and top-5 accuracy outside of sections, inside of sections and inside of entries. Memory consumption of the code completion process is determined using the Jetbrains dotMemory Profiler[15]. Jetbrains dotTrace[16] measures how long the code completion process takes.

5   Results

To select the best model for code completion for TTI two factors are considered: The accuracy on the one hand, and the number of trainable parameters on the other hand. The accuracy evaluates the quality of the recommendations. The number of trainable parameters affects the model size on disk and the inference speed. Inference speed affects latency during code completion.

In the course of hyperparameter tuning, we determined the best working configuration to train our final model. Table 1 shows that the best results were achieved with LSTM + Attention and GRU model architectures. Both show similar accuracy, e.g., top-5 accuracy between 95.7 and 95.8% for validation, and loss scores between 0.76 and 0.77. The GRU architecture has less trainable parameters (almost factor 12) and is therefore far smaller (1.1 versus 12 MB). Therefore, this configuration is selected, trained over 20 epochs and the resulting model is integrated into the TMTB editor.

When training the best model over 20 epochs, it achieves a top-1 accuracy of 86% and a top-5 accuracy of 97% (see Fig. 3). Compared to this, the original Pythia model [19] shows a top-1 accuracy of 71 and a top-5 accuracy of 92% on the validation set. This can be explained by the simpler syntax of the DSL.

---

[15] https://www.jetbrains.com/dotmemory.

[16] https://www.jetbrains.com/profiler.

Table 1. Best results per model achieved during hyperparameter tuning per model class.

	LSTM	LSTM + Attention	GRU
top-1 accuracy train [%]	69.334	71.535	71.163
top-5 accuracy train [%]	93.883	95.704	95.768
top-1 accuracy validation [%]	71.385	71.874	71.385
top-5 accuracy validation [%]	93.945	95.808	95.693
train loss	0.87427	0.76068	0.77256
validation loss	0.85935	0.75131	0.77118
model size [MB]	12.1	12.0	1.1
trainable parameters	2,755,364	3,006,650	252,338

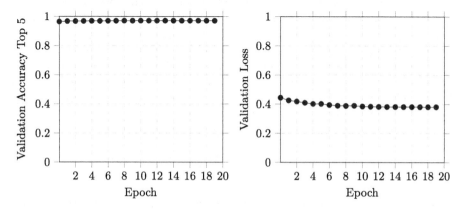

Fig. 3. The model is created using the best hyperparameters obtained during hyperparameter tuning and trained over 20 epochs.

Table 2. Comparison of prediction speed and memory consumption of original approach and machine learning approach.

	Prediction speed [ms]	Memory consumption [KB]
original approach	3	0 (does not show up)
Pythia approach	326	151.578

Another important aspect of code completion systems is that the latency is as low as possible. Therefore, also the memory consumption should be in an acceptable range. Table 2 compares the prediction speed and memory consumption when the cursor is positioned inside a *windingdetail* section. It compares the originally implemented, hard-coded approach with the machine learning approach. The tests were made using a lookback size of 100 tokens and a batch size of 128. The most important factor that influences the memory consumption and prediction speed is the model size on disk. Additionally, the model input needs to be created and an inference session needs to be started, which adds additional costs. The finally chosen model which uses GRU, shows a slightly higher memory consumption, but it does not negatively influence the code completion process concerning latency. Although the AI-based approach has longer latency times, it outperforms the previous simple approach to code completion in terms of desired functionality.

Evaluation of user requirements in test sessions showed the following results: According to requirement R-1.1, sections are only recommended outside of sections. The current solution is able to suggest sections outside of entries and order them by probability (R-1.4). Keywords are proposed inside of sections (R-2.1) and ordered by probability (R-2.4). Keywords that appear close to each other are ranked higher. Parameters are suggested inside of entries (R-3.1 - R-3.3). It currently works best for enumerations. For all other types the model suggests datatypes (e.g., doubleType for double). For given datatypes, we suggest default values (e.g. 0.0 for double). Optional and non-optional sections (R-1.5), entries (R-2.5) and parameters (R-3.4) are currently not captured by the machine learning approach. This also applies to the optional sections (R-1.3) and keywords (R-2.3), although this information would be available from training data. The current implementation does not consider unique sections (R-1.2) and keywords (R-2.2). The original code completion implementation is able to correctly recommend sections, keywords in sections and enumerations as well. However, it only provides hard-coded, context-insensitive ranking of predictions.

6   Discussion

In the following, we present the encountered challenges, gained insights and lessons learned during the development of the AI-based code completion approach for an industrial transformer manufacture. We structure our discussion according to the defined research questions.

6.1   What are the Differences in Applying Machine Learning Techniques Between DSLs and General-Purpose Languages? (RQ 1)

One difference between general-purpose languages and DSLs is that DSLs usually have a much simpler syntax. Thus, the vocabulary size is also smaller. The smaller the vocabulary size is, the fewer possibilities are for predicting the next token. Therefore, high accuracy can be achieved more quickly. Our results further show that models with fewer trainable parameters perform as good as or even better than more complex architectures for TTI. Also the amount of training data needed is related to the complexity of a DSL. TTI is a relatively simple DSL, which essentially consists of sections, entries or keywords and its parameters.

A further difference concerns the chunk size, which specifies how many different samples are written into a CSV file. The original Pythia implementation works with a chunk size of 10000, which is not practicable for code completion in TTI, where many sections are much shorter. In our experiments, chunks of size one work best. Another factor related to preprocessing is the lookback size. The authors of Pythia suggest a lookback size of 100 to 1000. Because of the simplicity of TTI, a lookback size of 100 has turned out to work well.

While for general-purpose languages established frameworks with code completion features are available, for DSLs there are no such frameworks out of the box. One possibility might be to design a DSL directly using the Jetbrains Workbench and make use of the extracted metamodel. Otherwise, the preprocessing has to be implemented by hand. For DSLs, there are typically no ready-made datasets. Parsers also may need to be programmed. Furthermore, some kind of classification of the characters has to be done. For example, whether they are terminal or non-terminal symbols and whether they are sections, entries or parameters. The training itself then works the same for DSLs and general-purpose languages.

6.2 Are Learning-Based Approaches Suitable for DSLs for Which only a Small Amount of Training Data is Available? (RQ2)

The small amount of training data is a major challenge in the development of an AI-based code completion system for DSLs. DSLs are often developed only for a selected domain or even only for a single company. In our case, there is only a small number of users. This results in a small amount of training data. Also the variation in the training files is not that big. An obstacle may also be that companies may not want to release training data for confidentiality reasons.

Another issue is the quality of the training data provided. For general-purpose languages such as C++, Java, or C#, there are thousands of Github repositories available that can be easily analysed. Nowadays, well curated datasets for learning on code are available, e.g., CodeSearchNet [8]. For enterprise-specific DSLs, the dataset has to be created and the quality needs to be checked manually.

To compensate for the lack of training data, several approaches can be used. First, slightly modifying the training data, which is commonly referred to as data augmentation. Another approach would be the use of Generative Adversarial Networks (GAN) [6] to generate training data. They consist of two components, one to generate samples and one to evaluate these. Using data augmentation only, the number of training data was increased from an initial amount of 82 to 9582. Last but not least, the choice of the machine learning model is also crucial for answering this question. From our results it can be deduced that for a DSL like TTI, GRU performs as good or even better than LSTM. This is also consistent with the literature. Chung et al. [3] have shown that GRU often perform better on smaller data sets.

6.3 Can AI-Based Code Completion Approaches for General-Purpose Languages Also Be Applied to DSLs in Practice? (RQ 3)

The chosen Pythia model focuses on method completion and leverages the paths to function calls. We modified this approach, since there are no methods and method calls in TTI. To generate the samples, whole sections, parts of sections and parts of entries were extracted and serialized in a numeric form. This approach is very generic and can therefore be applied in a language-independent manner. It turned out, that the general idea of using partial ASTs for training also works very well for TTI.

Regarding the integration of a PyTorch model into a .NET environment additional effort is needed, as models need to be converted to ONNX first to be useable from C#. ONNX is a very powerful exchange format, but not every operation is yet supported. In this case, a mathematically equivalent version must be provided for any missing operation. This can lead to wrong inference results in case of mistakes. To be able to execute inference, many Nuget packages are necessary. Each additional dependency increases the maintenance effort, since the versions of the individual Nuget packages must fit together.

To sum up, generic approaches are well suited also for DSLs. Which model to choose depends on several factors. Also additional aspects regarding preprocessing and inference times need to be considered for applying AI-based code completion to DSLs in practice. Especially, maintaining the machine learning approach is more complex. In case new keywords are added, a completely new training of the code completion model needs to be started. Another difficulty is the lack of training data containing the new keyword. It will be necessary to generate such training files. To make this process efficient, a completely automated pipeline is required.

7   Threats to Validity

Internal Validity. Threats to internal validity relate to the dataset we used to train and test code completion. To mitigate the limited number of TTI samples we applied data augmentation, yielding 9582 files, however this may deliver limited and artificial knowledge for model generalization.

External Validity. Threats to external validity relate to the generalization of results. We based our work on the TTI DSL only. Obviously, preprocessing of input data is specific for the industry case and will not work in the general case.

8   Conclusion

To improve a code completion system of a DSL used in industry, we investigate and adapt two AI-based code completion approaches used for code completion of general-purpose programming languages. The approach reused for in-depth analysis in the presented industry context, i.e. Pythia, shows promising results with respect to accuracy and performance of model inference. As Pythia supports the specification of different neural network architectures as hyperparameter, we showed that GRU has similar results than LSTM and LSTM with Attention, but with a much smaller number of trainable parameters and associated model size. Therefore, GRU was ultimately chosen for integration into the existing editor. The chosen model achieves a top-5 accuracy of over 97%. The comparison with the existing code completion mechanism in TMTB revealed very positive user feedback from the domain experts. Our approach currently covers 7 of the 14 defined requirements. It is able to predict sections, keywords and parameters in the respective context and rank them by probability. By this the code completion system helps to make writing of DSLs easier, lowers the threshold for new TTI developers and helps to improve acceptance of the presented DSL.

Limitations. The used machine learning models only calculate the probability for a token at a certain position. Additional domain knowledge is needed to filter out senseless tokens in specific contexts. The best approach to solve this issue is to return a score for each token, to calculate the probabilities and not to suggest senseless tokens in the respective context. As with other code completion systems, the out-of-vocabulary problem also comes into play here. If a token was not extracted during the training, it can of course not be suggested. This especially applies to the suggestion of enumerations. Regions and comments are currently not part of the vocabulary.

Future Work. Next steps will address the realization of yet missing requirements. From the user's perspective, it would also be desirable to include documentation for sections, entries and parameters in the popup of the editor. This information is mainly contained in help files but could also be extended by users themselves. This additional data could then be stored and loaded in the form of JSON files, for example. For this, it will also be necessary to increase the amount of training data, e.g., by using GAN or fuzzers. Especially the out-of-vocabulary problem can be addressed in this way.

References

1. Bahdanau, D., Cho, K., Bengio, Y.: Neural machine translation by jointly learning to align and translate. arXiv, Computation and Language **1409** (2014)
2. Bruch, M., Monperrus, M., Mezini, M.: Learning from examples to improve code completion systems. In: Proceedings of the 7th Joint Meeting of the European Software Engineering Conference and the ACM SIGSOFT Symposium on The Foundations of Software Engineering, ESEC/FSE 2009, pp. 213–222. Association for Computing Machinery, New York (2009). https://doi.org/10.1145/1595696.1595728
3. Chung, J., Gulcehre, C., Cho, K., Bengio, Y.: Empirical evaluation of gated recurrent neural networks on sequence modeling. In: NIPS 2014 Workshop on Deep Learning (2014)
4. Erdweg, S., et al.: The state of the art in language workbenches. In: Erwig, M., Paige, R.F., Van Wyk, E. (eds.) SLE 2013. LNCS, vol. 8225, pp. 197–217. Springer, Cham (2013). https://doi.org/10.1007/978-3-319-02654-1_11
5. Franks, C., Tu, Z., Devanbu, P., Hellendoorn, V.: Cacheca: a cache language model based code suggestion tool. In: Proceedings of the 37th International Conference on Software Engineering, ICSE 2015, vol. 2, pp. 705–708. IEEE Press (2015). https://dl.acm.org/doi/10.5555/2819009.2819143
6. Goodfellow, I.J., et al.: Generative adversarial nets. In: NIPS 2014, pp. 2672–2680. MIT Press, Cambridge (2014)

7. Hou, D., Pletcher, D.: Towards a better code completion system by API grouping, filtering, and popularity-based ranking. In: Proceedings of the 2nd International Workshop on Recommendation Systems for Software Engineering, RSSE 2010, pp. 26–30. Association for Computing Machinery, New York (2010)

8. Husain, H., Wu, H.H., Gazit, T., Allamanis, M., Brockschmidt, M.: CodeSearch-Net challenge: evaluating the state of semantic code search. arXiv preprint arXiv:1909.09436 (2019)

9. Jurafsky, D., Martin, J.H.: N-gram language models. In: Speech and Language Processing. Prentice-Hall Inc., Upper Saddle River (2009). https://web.stanford.edu/jurafsky/slp3/3.pdf. Accessed 08 Oct 2023

10. Li, J., Wang, Y., King, I., Lyu, M.R.: Code completion with neural attention and pointer networks. In: Proceedings of the 27th International Joint Conference on Artificial Intelligence, IJCAI 2018, pp. 4159–4165. AAAI Press (2018). https://dl.acm.org/doi/10.5555/3304222.3304348

11. Liaw, R., Liang, E., Nishihara, R., Moritz, P., Gonzalez, J.E., Stoica, I.: Tune: a research platform for distributed model selection and training. arXiv preprint arXiv:1807.05118 (2018)

12. Mernik, M., Heering, J., Sloane, A.M.: When and how to develop domain-specific languages. ACM Comput. Surv. 37(4), 316–344 (2005). https://doi.org/10.1145/1118890.1118892

13. Moritz, P., et al.: Ray: a distributed framework for emerging AI applications. In: Proceedings of the 13th USENIX Conference on Operating Systems Design and Implementation, OSDI 2018, pp. 561–577. USENIX Association, USA (2018). https://dl.acm.org/doi/10.5555/3291168.3291210

14. Oriol Vinyals, M.F., Jaitly, N.: Pointer networks. In: Proceedings of the 28th International Conference on Neural Information Processing Systems, NIPS 2015, pp. 2692–2700. MIT Press, Cambridge (2015)

15. Pfeiffer, M., Pichler, J.: A comparison of tool support for textual domain-specific languages. In: Proceedings of the 8th OOPSLA Workshop on Domain-Specific Modeling, pp. 1–7. Citeseer (2008)

16. Pletcher, D.M., Hou, D.: BCC: enhancing code completion for better API usability. In: 2009 IEEE International Conference on Software Maintenance, pp. 393–394. IEEE (2009). https://doi.org/10.1109/ICSM.2009.5306289

17. Raychev, V., Vechev, M., Yahav, E.: Code completion with statistical language models. In: ACM SIGPLAN Notices, PLDI 2014, vol. 49, pp. 419–428. Association for Computing Machinery, New York (2014). https://doi.org/10.1145/2666356.2594321

18. Robbes, R., Lanza, M.: How program history can improve code completion. In: 2008 23rd IEEE/ACM International Conference on Automated Software Engineering, ASE 2008, pp. 317–326. IEEE Computer Society, USA (2008). https://doi.org/10.1109/ASE.2008.42

19. Svyatkovskiy, A., Zhao, Y., Fu, S., Sundaresan, N.: Pythia: AI-assisted code completion system. In: Proceedings of the 25th ACM SIGKDD International Conference on Knowledge Discovery & Data Mining, KDD 2019, pp. 2727–2735. Association for Computing Machinery, New York (2019). https://doi.org/10.1145/3292500.3330699

20. Ziegler, A., et al.: Productivity assessment of neural code completion. In: Proceedings of the 6th ACM SIGPLAN International Symposium on Machine Programming, MAPS 2022, pp. 21–29. Association for Computing Machinery, New York (2022). https://doi.org/10.1145/3520312.3534864

Assessing IDEA Diagrams for Supporting Analysis of Capabilities and Issues in Technical Debt Management

Sávio Freire[1,2]($\boxtimes$) [iD], Verusca Rocha[1] [iD], Manoel Mendonça[1] [iD],
Clemente Izurieta[3] [iD], Carolyn Seaman[4] [iD], and Rodrigo Spínola[5] [iD]

[1] Federal University of Bahia, Salvador, Bahia, Brazil
`manoel.mendonca@ufba.br`
[2] Federal Institute of Ceará, Morada Nova, Ceará, Brazil
`savio.freire@ifce.edu.br`
[3] Montana State University, Bozeman, MT, USA
`clemente.izurieta@montana.edu`
[4] University of Maryland Baltimore County, Baltimore, MD, USA
`cseaman@umbc.edu`
[5] Virginia Commonwealth University, Richmond, VA, USA
`spinolaro@vcu.edu`

Abstract. *Context.* Technical debt management (TDM) comprises activities such as prevention, monitoring, and repayment. Current technical literature has identified, for each of these TDM activities, several applicable practices as well as practice avoidance reasons (PARs). This body of knowledge (practices and PARs) is available in the literature only in widely spread text and tables, and is not organized into artifacts, hindering the use of current knowledge on TDM. Previously, we organized these practices and PARs into IDEA (Impediments, Decision factors, Enabling practices, and Actions) diagrams. However, an empirical evaluation of these diagrams is still missing. *Aims.* To empirically assess the IDEA diagrams with respect to their ease of use, usefulness, potential future use, and support for TDM activities. *Method.* We conduct two complementary empirical studies. Firstly, we applied the technology acceptance model (TAM) with 72 participants in academic contexts. Afterwards, we interviewed 11 experienced software practitioners. *Results.* In the TAM study, 92% of the participants indicated that they could use the diagrams. Also, the diagrams were considered easy to learn and use. Through the interviews, participants indicated that the diagrams are easy to read and follow, can influence decisions on how to manage debt items, and could be used to support their daily activities. *Conclusion.* Both studies provided positive evidence that IDEA diagrams can be useful for supporting TDM activities.

Keywords: Technical Debt · Technical Debt Management · IDEA Diagrams

R. Kadgien et al. (Eds.): PROFES 2023, LNCS 14483, pp. 243–258, 2024.
https://doi.org/10.1007/978-3-031-49266-2_17

1 Introduction

Technical debt (TD) emerges from intentional shortcuts or even mistakes taken by software practitioners in their projects [1, 2]. Incurring debt can bring short-term benefits, usually in terms of high productivity, but also long-term drawbacks, making the software difficult to evolve [3–5]. By performing TD management activities, a software team can make TD items visible and under control, allowing it to balance benefits and drawbacks of debt presence [6].

TD management comprises several activities, such as prevention, monitoring, and repayment [6, 7]. By performing TD prevention, software teams can avoid potential TD items, while TD monitoring follows the identified TD items to measure their cost/benefits along with their elimination. This elimination is performed during the repayment activity. Knowing the practices to prevent, monitor, and repay debt items can support software teams in choosing the most appropriate practices in their context. On the other hand, and for different reasons, teams sometimes avoid the application of these practices. Having information of these reasons (herein called *practice avoidance reasons* - PARs) can aid software teams in increasing their ability in TD management, revealing internal or external factors resulting in TD non-prevention, non-monitoring, and non-repayment.

Related work has investigated TD prevention, monitoring, and repayment practices and PARs [6, 8–17]. For instance, Bomfim Jr and Santos [9] identified TD repayment practices and PARs considered in the agile software development process. Rios et al. [15] identified prevention and repayment practices for managing documentation debt items, while Aragão et al. [16] investigated prevention, monitoring, and repayment practices for test debt items. Despite the valuable contributions of the current literature in the area, there is still a need to organize the current body of practices and PARs into artifacts that can effectively be applied to support the management of TD in software projects. Such an artifact could provide guidance on how to understand and select the practices or PARs in isolation as well as in combination. In the absence of this guidance, development teams rely on textual information spread through several tables, thus hindering the use of current knowledge on TD management.

We propose to help fill this gap by using IDEA (Impediments, Decision factors, Enabling practices, and Actions) Diagrams to organize information on TD prevention, monitoring and repayment practices and PARs [17]. Loosely inspired by SWOT (strengths, weaknesses, opportunities, and threats) analysis [18], the IDEA diagrams organize TD management practices and PARs into quadrants: capabilities (actions and enabling practices) and issues (decision factors and impediments). To populate them, we use the practices and PARs reported by 653 practitioners who responded to the InsightTD survey, which is a globally distributed family of industrial surveys on TD [19].

In this work, we go further and investigate to what extent the IDEA diagrams can support software teams in increasing their capability for preventing, monitoring, and repaying the debt. The main contribution of this paper is to investigate if the diagrams are useful, their ease of use, whether they can influence decisions about how to manage debt items, whether they can be used in daily project activities, and their potential future use. Then, we empirically investigate IDEA diagrams through two complementary studies. Initially, we applied the Technology Acceptance Model (TAM) [20] with 72 students enrolled in a software engineering course. Results indicate that the diagrams can positively support TD management, making it easier to identify practices and PARs associated with TD prevention, monitoring, and repayment activities. Also, 92% of the participants stated that they could use the IDEA diagrams to manage TD items. Subsequently, we conducted an interview-based case study with 11 software practitioners. The participants pointed out that the IDEA diagrams are easy to read and follow, can influence the decisions on TD management, and could provide useful guidance if used. The results from both studies indicate that the IDEA diagrams are sound and can be used to increase the capability of software teams to manage debt items.

Beyond this introduction, this paper has six more sections. Section 2 discusses related work on TD prevention, monitoring, and repayment, and the IDEA diagrams. Next, Sects. 3 and 4 present the TAM and interview study we performed to assess the diagrams, respectively. We discuss the results in Sect. 5. Section 6 discusses the threats to validity. Finally, Sect. 7 presents the final remarks and future work.

2 Background

In this section, we initially discuss related work on TD prevention, monitoring, and repayment. We then present the IDEA diagrams.

2.1 Related Work on TD Prevention, Monitoring and Repayment

Technical literature reveals investigations into the prevention, monitoring, and repayment of debt items. By performing a systematic literature review, Li et al. [6] identified a set of categories for TD prevention, TD monitoring, and TD repayment, while Behutiye et al. [10] recognized a set of monitoring practices and categories for TD payment in agile software development processes.

By conducting case studies in industrial settings, Yli-Huumo et al. [8] identified some TD prevention practices (e.g., *coding standards*) and one practice (*used data collected from (management or TD measuring) tools*) for monitoring the debt. Bomfim Jr and Santos [9] identified a set of TD prevention (e.g., *using coding standards*), monitoring (e.g., *including TD tasks in product backlog*), and repayment (e.g., *refactoring older code*) practices in agile software development processes. The authors also identified the reasons (e.g., *low impact for business* and *high effort*) which hamper the application of those practices. Toledo et al. [11] identified 13 repayment practices used to eliminate architecture debt in microservices, such as *rewrite the communication layer*.

Silva et al. [12] ran a survey and identified TD prevention (e.g., *retrospective meetings*) and repayment (e.g., *redesign*) practices. Two replications of this survey were performed [13, 14], finding the same preventive practices previously reported and confirming the repayment practices. Rios et al. [15] recognized preventive (e.g., *comment the code*) and repayment (e.g., *review outdated documentation*) practices for documentation debt items. Lastly, Aragão et al. [16] identified a set of TD prevention (e.g., *present already identified debts*), monitoring (e.g., *changes in the test process*), and repayment (e.g., *change test cases by analyzing defects*) practices for test debt items.

Although these studies revealed practices used to prevent, monitor, or repay TD, most of them did not provide an artifact that organizes these practices and supports software practitioners in effectively managing TD items. Without an artifact, software practitioners rely on textual information spread through several tables. Only Rios et al. [15] and Aragão et al. [16] defined artifacts, but they are specific to documentation and test debt items, respectively. To deal with this gap, we proposed the IDEA diagrams, which are presented in next subsection.

2.2 The IDEA Diagrams

IDEA diagrams are inspired by SWOT (strengths, weaknesses, opportunities, and threats) analysis [18] to organize issues (decision factors and impediments) and capabilities (actions and enabling practices) related to TD management into four quadrants. Unlike SWOT, the scope of the IDEA diagrams is not organizational planning but is to support software teams in increasing their ability to manage the debt [17]. The diagrams can be defined for any TD management activity and their practices and PARs can be specialized considering the types of debt (such as code, design, and requirements) and project context variables, such as process model. We presented a set of IDEA diagrams for agile software development processes in [17].

Figure 1-A presents the diagram's structure and how the quadrants are related to each other. Each quadrant is depicted by a specific color and contains a set of practices or PARs. On the left side of the diagram, practices are concentrated in the actions and enabling practices quadrants. Actions (in the upper left quadrant) are practices or techniques that, when employed, will have a direct effect on TD management. Enabling practices (lower left), on the other hand, have an indirect effect on a team's ability to effectively manage TD by enabling a culture that promotes TD management or providing resources that are important for effective TD management. On the right side, the diagram presents the PARs in the decision factors and impediments quadrants. The decision facts (in the upper right quadrant) represent factors that led to decisions explicitly made by the team itself to incur TD or to not pay off TD. Impediments (lower right) are conditions or decision originating from an external agent (i.e., a customer or organization) who are outside the control of the project team, but that make it difficult or impossible to manage TD effectively. In all quadrants, the practices and PARs are ordered by a criterion that can be defined by software teams. For example, a sorting criterion could be how frequently practices and PARs have been used in the project in the past.

We used data from the InsighTD project to define IDEA diagrams for TD prevention, monitoring, and repayment. Also, we specialized them for design and documentation debt. Figure 1-B shows the IDEA diagram for design debt repayment with the five most cited elements per quadrant. The complete version is available here. The percentages with practices and PARs inform how frequently they were used in the InsighTD participants' software projects.

IDEA diagrams can support the selection of TD management strategies by analyzing one or two quadrants at time. When looking at isolated quadrants, software teams can identify the actions used to manage the debt (actions quadrant) and the practices that support these actions (enabling practices quadrant) shown in the left of the diagram. Further, software teams can identify the issues that hamper TD management through decisions made by the team (decision factors quadrant) or by external factors (impediments quadrant).

Analyzing the relationships between quadrants can support software teams in boosting their TD management initiatives. Looking at (Fig. 1-B):

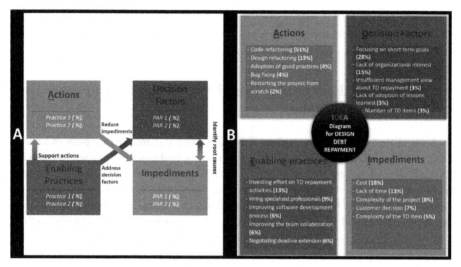

Fig. 1. (A) The IDEA diagram's structure. (B) A summarized version of the IDEA diagram for design debt repayment.

- **Actions and Enabling practices quadrants** can provide teams with a way to increase their TD management capacity by suggesting enabling practices that could support actions they already employ. For example, suppose a software team already uses *code refactoring* and *design refactoring* actions to repay design debt items, but not as often as they could. By discussing potential enabling practices, they could realize that *investing effort on TD repayment activities* and *negotiating deadline extension* would enable them to employ their successful refactoring tasks more often.
- **Decision factors and Impediments quadrants** can support teams to understand why they are not managing TD. For example, a software team might identify that they often decide against repaying TD because they are *focusing on short term goals*. By digging a bit deeper and discussing items in the impediments quadrant, they might realize that the *team overload* impediment is the primary reason for the short-term focus, and thus for not repaying design debt items. This could help equip them to take steps with their customers to argue for easing the load on the team.
- **Enabling practices and Decision factors quadrants** can reduce weak areas related to TD management. Suppose a team realizes that the *lack of adoption of lessons learned* decision factor is often the reason for design debt non-repayment. Then, the team could examine enabling practices that could counter their tendency to fail to apply lessons learned in TD decision-making, such as *improving software development process* and *improving the team collaboration*.
- **Actions and Impediments quadrants** can help teams to reduce the impediments for TD management. For example, if a team identifies that *complexity of the project*

impediment hampers the payment of design debt, the team can apply *code refactoring* or *design refactoring* actions for reducing the complexity of the project, reducing the external factors in TD repayment decisions.

For assessing the IDEA diagrams in terms of their support of TD prevention, monitoring, and repayment activities, we performed two empirical studies which are presented in Sects. 3 and 4.

3 Assessing the Ease of Use, Usefulness, and Potential Future Use of the IDEA Diagrams

The goal of this study was to **analyze** the IDEA diagrams **for the purpose of** characterizing them **with respect to** ease of use, usefulness, and potential future use **from the point of view of** undergraduate students enrolled in a software engineering course **in the context of** software development projects. As our intention was to investigate the perception on the use of a new technology (IDEA diagrams), we applied the technology acceptance model (TAM) [20]. It captures the opinion of the participants on three constructs (perceived usefulness, ease to use, and self-predicted future use), measured through a set of questions.

3.1   Project Context

The study consisted of analyzing the ease of use, usefulness, and potential future use of the IDEA diagrams through the simulation of TD management activities, whose objective was to identify, from a list of TD items, the prevention, monitoring and repayment practices and PARs that could be applied for the project. The list of debt items was extracted from a real software project called National Transplantation System (NTS), developed by a partner organization (the Fraunhofer Project Center at the Federal University of Bahia).

The NTS is responsible for the control and monitoring of transplants of organs, tissues and parts of the human body for therapeutic purposes in Brazil. The product consists of a medium-large database-driven web application. It includes several modules distributed through 212 use cases. The application was written in Java and based on the MVC framework. It includes 365K lines of code in 1377 domain classes. The project was developed with the following infrastructure: Eclipse IDE, Subversion, and Trac. The development team was composed of 1 project manager, 1 technical leader, 3 requirements analysts, and 8 developers. The project followed a Scrum-like development process to continuously integrate features and deliver working versions to the customer. The project team manually identified TD items and organized them into a spreadsheet, which constituted the list of TD items used in this study.

3.2   Procedure and Instrumentation

Initially, the participants filled in a characterization and consent form. Then, the first author trained the participants on TD and its concepts associated with the case study, such as, TD definition, design and documentation debt, and TD prevention, monitoring, and repayment activities. An example of identification of practices and PARs related to those activities was also explained (**step 1**). As we wanted to reduce bias during the identification of TD management practices and PARs step of the study, we used an example in the context of house maintenance. For instance, a repayment practice for *the kitchen drain is showing a slow flow of water* could be *using a plunger*.

In **step 2**, the participants, individually, analyzed in an *ad hoc* manner a design debt item and a documentation debt item (see Table 1) to suggest practices and PARs associated with the TD prevention, monitoring, and repayment of those items. We chose particular debt items that were described in detail in the list of TD items provided by our industry partner. Participants only analyzed **Actions and Enabling practices** and **Decision factors and Impediments** quadrants.

Step 3 focused on the training on the IDEA diagrams, explaining how to use them to support the analysis of practices and PARs associated with TD prevention, monitoring, and repayment. We presented an example of how to analyze a debt item using the diagram, but also in the context of the house maintenance scenario.

Table 1. TD items used in the case study.

Step	TD type	TD item description
2	Documentation	The allocation module does not have a req. specification document
2	Design	A verification with the name of the activity is necessary when it is required to identify a type of service or bill. This information is fixed in the code and can bring errors when some update is performed, or the data in the database has incorrect names
4	Documentation	The documentation should be up-to-date and requirements gathering should be conducted in accordance with the customer's needs. Frequent changes to these modules caused a lot of rework
4	Design	The invoice printing functionality need to be simplified. The functionality is working correctly but needs to be adjusted in the future to be more adherent to the system design

In **step 4**, the participants received two new TD items, shown in Table 1, and analyzed them using the IDEA diagrams to suggest practices and PARs associated with the prevention, monitoring, and repayment of those items. The participants received a set of IDEA diagrams for the types of analyzed debt items (documentation or design) for each TD management activity.

Lastly, the participants individually completed the evaluation form, containing a set of questions associated with the three constructs (perceived usefulness, ease to use, and self-predicted future use) considered in the TAM (**Step 5**). The evaluation form is available here. To answer the questions in the form, the participants indicated the option that best represented their point of view on the IDEA diagrams, according to the following 5-point scale: (1) I totally agree; (2) I agree partially; (3) Neutral; (4) Partially disagree; and (5) Strongly disagree. At the end of the form, the participants also described the positive and negative aspects of the diagrams and suggestions for improvements and indicated whether the diagrams helped them to identify practices and PARs that they would not have identified without using them.

3.3 Data Analysis

All answers were validated by following three criteria: (i) the participant filled in the consent and characterization forms, (ii) the participant performed the two activities of analysis of TD elements (steps 2 and 4), and (iii) the participant filled in the evaluation form.

For the closed questions, we calculated the share of participants choosing each option to obtain a better understanding of the data. For open-ended questions, we applied a coding process to identify the central idea described in the answers [21, 22]. For example, a participant indicated the following positive aspect of the IDEA diagrams: "items properly separated and placed, easy to locate." As this answer is related to the diagram representation, we coded it as *adequate representation structure*. The coding process was performed by the first author and revised by the last author. Divergences were resolved in a consensus meeting. In the end, we had a list of codes and their respective number of occurrences.

3.4 Results

The participants were undergraduate students enrolled in a software engineering course. In total, 72 participants completed all required steps. About 19% of them indicated that have at least one year of experience with software development. Participants also indicated their level of experience in nine areas related to the software development process. We present the results in Table 2. We can notice that there are participants with experience in all areas of software engineering. Lastly, most of the participants had some level of knowledge on TD ranging from low (53%) to good (10%) and expert (3%).

Participants' Point of View on IDEA Diagrams for TD Prevention, Monitoring, and Repayment. The TAM statements for the **perceived usefulness** construct asked each participant whether they are able to (U1) identify practices or PARs more quickly, (U2) improve their performance in identifying practices or PARs, (U3) improve their effectiveness in identifying practices or PARs, and (U4) make easy to identify practices or PARs, compared to carrying out these tasks without the IDEA diagram. These constructs are related to each TD management activity. Most of the participants agreed with the affirmations for IDEA diagrams for TD prevention (more than 86% of the participants), TD monitoring (more than 81%), and TD repayment (more than 89%). Thus, comparing the task execution with and without IDEA diagrams, the participants had high productivity (U1), increased performance (U2 and U4), and efficacy (U3). Moreover, 90% of the participants agreed with the following statements: "using the diagrams, I would increase my productivity in identifying practices and PARs" (strongly agree: 65%, agree: 25%, and neutral: 10%) and "I believe the proposed diagrams would be useful to support technical debt management" (strongly agree: 72%, agree: 18%, and neutral: 10%). All detailed results are available here.

Table 2. Level of Experience of Participants.

Knowledge area	Level of experience*				
	1	2	3	4	5
Project management	23	33	8	2	6
Monitoring and correction of software defects	29	27	4	4	8
Software maintenance	31	22	5	5	9
Software architecture	28	28	5	6	5
Software design	22	28	5	9	8
Software documentation	27	34	2	2	7
Requirement specification	20	40	7	1	4
Implementation	19	16	5	22	10
Software testing	22	28	6	8	8

*Levels of experience: (1) none, (2) studied in class, (3) practiced in classroom projects, (4) used in personal projects, and (5) used in projects in the industry

Figure 2 presents TAM statements for the **ease-of-use** construct. At least 80% of the participants agreed with the statements associated with the benefits: easy to learn (E1), clear and understandable (E2), easy to use for particular tasks (E3-E8), easy to become skillful (E9), easy to remember (E10), and easy to use (E11).

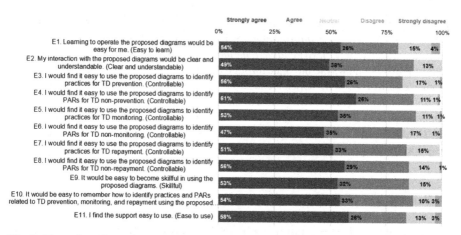

Fig. 2. Ease-of-use items for IDEA Diagrams for TD Prevention, Monitoring, and Repayment.

The participants also provided their opinion for the **self-predicted future use** construct. We found that (i) 92% of the participants agreed with "Assuming the proposed diagrams would be available to manage technical debt, I would use them in the future" (strongly agree: 63% and agree: 29%) and (ii) 63% of the participants agreed with "I would prefer to use the proposed diagrams to identify practices and PARs associated with TD prevention, monitoring and repayment activities than in the usual way (without the diagrams). Only 15% of the participants disagreed with this statement (strongly agree: 45%, agree: 18%, neutral: 22%, disagree: 7%, and strongly disagree: 8%).

Lastly, most of the participants indicated that using the diagrams helped them identify (i) TD prevention, monitoring, or repayment practices (93% of the participants) and (ii) PARs for TD non-prevention, non-monitoring, and non-repayment (94% of the participants) that they would not have identified without the diagrams.

Positive Points Reported. The participants indicated that the IDEA diagrams allow an *easy identification of practices and PARs* (number of occurrences 'NO' = 34), as described in the participant's quote "it is easier to identify reasons and practices for prevention, monitoring, and repayment..." The participants also explained that the IDEA diagrams have an *adequate representation structure* (NO = 25), for instance, "detailed, items properly organized, easy to locate." Lastly, participants argued that the diagrams *facilitate the decision making* (NO = 6; e.g., "better performance and effectiveness in decisions."). Other mentioned positive points are *ease of use, provide a variety of practices and PARs,* and *facilitate the understanding.*

Negative Points Reported. Participants indicated that *it is possible that practitioners only consider the practices/PARs in the diagram* (NO = 10), as illustrated in "it can create a false impression that everything has been listed and cause a lack of interest in identifying other elements". Also, the participants affirmed that *the diagrams have many practices or PARs* (NO = 5; e.g., "it contains a lot of information..."). Other negative points mentioned were *they do not present all practices and PARs* and *lack of dynamic manipulation of the diagram.*

Improvement Points Reported. The participants suggested the following improvements: (i) *better organize information* (NO = 10; "better distribution of data in the space in each quadrant."), (ii) *enable dynamic manipulation of the diagram* (NO = 4; "there could be some way to navigate through the diagrams..."), (iii) *enable the inclusion of new elements* (NO = 4; "Open a checkbox with the option to include new reasons."), (iv) *simplify the diagram* (NO = 3; "use diagrams as simple as possible."), (v) *remove redundant practices and PARs* (NO = 1; "some items can be merged as long as they look similar."), and (vi) *better explain percentages* (NO = 1; "explain the percentages present in the diagrams.").

4   Perception of Software Practitioners

The goal of this study is to **analyze** the IDEA diagrams **with the purpose of** characterizing them **with respect to** their support to TD management activities **from the point of view of** software practitioners **in the context of** software development projects.

4.1   Procedure and Instrumentation

We conducted semi-structured individual interviews composed of three steps. In the first step (**opening**), we presented the consent form and the concept of TD. Then, the participant answered questions on their expertise in TD management, such as the level of experience with TD management and the strategies and tools they have used to manage debt. In the second step (**perception about the IDEA diagrams**), we presented the IDEA diagrams and provided some examples of using the diagrams for supporting TD management considering all relationships among their quadrants. Then, we asked participants whether the diagrams (i) would be easy to use and follow, (ii) could influence their decision about how to manage the debt, and (iii) could be used in their daily activities. In the last step (**closing**), we asked participants if they have anything more to say about the diagrams and asked them to fill in a characterization form. The interview script and the participant characterization form are available here.

The first author conducted all interviews remotely. Each of them lasted around 30 min and were recorded with the interviewee's permission.

4.2 Data Analysis

We transcribed the interviews and organized the answers by question. Then, we coded the transcripts to identify the main idea presented in each answer [21, 22]. For example, a participant explained why IDEA diagrams can be used in daily activities: "you can communicate better with your team to avoid future problems." We coded it as *assist team communication*. This process was performed by the first author and revised by the last author. Divergences were resolved in a consensus meeting. Finally, we had a list of codes and their respective number of occurrences.

Concerning the characterization questions, we calculated the share of participants choosing each option of the characterization form to obtain a better understanding of the data. The characterization form is available here.

4.3 Results

We invited 11 practitioners from our contacts in the software industry. Most of them work in medium-sized companies (organizations with 51 to 1000 employees; 6 participants), followed by large (more than 1000 employees; 4 participants) and small (up to 50 employees; 1 participant). The participants identified themselves as project manager or leader (3 participants), developer (2), product owner (2), process analyst (1), agile coach (1), tester (1), and software architect (1). Regarding the participants' experience level, we interviewed 5 experts (authoritative knowledge of discipline and deep tacit understanding across area of practice), 5 proficient (depth of understanding of discipline and area of practice), and 1 competent (good working and background knowledge of area of practice). The participants mostly adopted agile software development (7) and the others followed hybrid methodologies.

Three participants did not have previous experience on TD management, while eight of them have experience by participating in projects in which they have identified TD items or have tried to actively manage them. The identified debt items are commonly registered in the product backlog or in managerial tools.

Easy to Read and Follow. Most of the participants (nine participants) affirmed that the IDEA diagrams are easy to read and follow to support decisions on TD management because the diagrams: (i) *facilitate TD decision making* ("Because you can extract data from their topics (actions, impediments, decisions…). They are very visible in aiding decision making"), (ii) *are succinct and clear* ("Yes, because I think they are very succinct and clear"), (iii) *can be understood by all stakeholders* ("I also clearly see how to use them in a very didactic way, even the product owner could understand"), (iv) *present in a summarized way both internal and external issues* ("I can see how I can get an x-ray of internal and external issues that are still not leading me to manage well debt items"), (v) *can be used in reviewing and planning meetings* ("…artifact to be considered at each review and backlog planning meeting"), and (vi) *facilitate TD items identification* ("It makes it easier to perceive the TD"). Lastly, three of these participants warned that the diagrams are *easy to use but are not self-explanatory* ("…Having the explanation is very useful to have visibility and put them into practice").

Influence Decision About How to Manage the Debt. Only one participant indicated that the diagram would not influence his/her decisions ("…in my case not so much. I have already implemented some of the practices you mentioned there"). The other participants reported that the diagrams could influence their decisions. They explained that the diagrams (i) *facilitate the communication between stakeholders* ("even with people who are not part of the team, you can take a picture of the situation and try to negotiate strategies to improve it."), (ii) *support the decision making on TD items* ("…from that diagram, make decisions about what would be relevant to do"), (iii) *support to identify problems* ("I would have clarity of the reasons that prevent me from managing them."), (iv) *have a customizable catalogue of practices used in the software industry* ("A catalog of best practices could be customized for each team."), and (v) *allow an effective risk management* ("As if it was an effective risk management, but for debt management. I can map impediments and internal factors and at the same time put together this action plan to improve management").

In addition, almost all participants (nine) indicated that the percentages would be useful for choosing a practice or a PAR, highlighting that they *support the practices and PARs prioritization, present the most representative elements*, and *are based on previous experience*. The other two participants mentioned that percentages can be difficult to calculate. Lastly, one participant was unsure about the usefulness of the percentage because it represents the consensus of other organizations, which not necessarily is related to her/his current context. However, the same participant indicated that the diagrams could be adapted to her/his context.

Can be Used in Daily Activities. All participants indicated that they could use the IDEA diagrams to support TD management activities. The participants explained that the diagrams (i) *enable continuous improvement of TD management actions* ("I see very clearly their use within a team, having a complete view of management and allowing us to set up a continuous improvement plan of actions to improve management"), (ii) *assist in tracking TD items*, (iii) *indicate possible problems and solutions to resolve them*, and (iv) *assist team communication*.

Most of the participants (six) indicated that the diagrams could be adapted to their current context because they *would assist in negotiating project constraints* and *highlight the problems*. The participants also indicated the following necessary adjustments in the diagrams: (i) *remove practices that do not fit the developer's scope* ("I have a programmer's point of view. I am not on the manager side. I would cut some things out to make the set of actions more streamlined"), (ii) *include arrows between quadrants to indicate how the analysis should be done*, and (iii) *make it automated by suggesting relationships between quadrants.*

5 Discussion

From the TAM study conducted with undergraduate students, we sought to collect initial evidence on the usefulness of IDEA diagrams. We found that 92% of the participants indicated that they could use the diagrams. Most of the participants also agreed that, by using them, they can see productivity gains in performance, and effectiveness in performing the task proposed in the study. Also, the diagrams were considered easy to learn and use. Based on the positive results, we decided to approach software practitioners. In the interviews, most of the participants indicated that the diagrams would be easy to read and follow, could influence decisions on how to manage debt items, and could be used to support daily activities.

In summary, the TAM study and the interviews provided positive evidence that the IDEA diagrams can be useful for supporting TD management activities. By identifying the actions and enabling practices, practitioners can define strategies for boosting their TD management activities, while having information on decisions factors and impediments can support practitioners in defining strategies for reducing the internal and external factors that result in TD non-management. By analyzing the relationships between quadrants, diagrams can assist practitioners in defining these strategies.

Results also provide initial evidence that the IDEA diagrams can be used by practitioners with or without experience in managing TD items. For software teams who want to start managing TD, the ranked lists of practices and PARs organized in each of the IDEA diagrams can provide guidance on what to employ (practices) or curb (PARs) based on experience from other development teams. If a team already has experience in managing TD, it can identify other commonly used practices or other PARs faced and can also identify enabling activities (enabling practices) that will improve the team's ability to manage TD. In other words, teams can create their own IDEA diagrams.

As a communication device, results also suggest that IDEA diagrams could be used in meetings to discuss TD items, explaining the factors that lead to non-management of TD and presenting possible solutions to minimize the effects of these factors.

For researchers, our findings can guide new investigations on TD management, considering the IDEA diagrams as a starting point. For example, practices and PARs could be further investigated to refine them according to different software contexts. The IDEA diagrams can be automatized as a plugin of an issue tracking tool, such as Jira or Asana. Lastly, there is still a need of conducting further industrial empirical investigations to evaluate IDEA diagrams as a supporting tool for TD management activities.

6 Threats to Validity

As in any empirical study, there are threats to validity in this work [23]. We attempt to remove them when possible, and mitigate their effects when removal is not possible.

6.1 TAM Study

Construct Validity. A threat emerges from the material used to perform the TAM study because the TD items analyzed by the participants can influence their perceptions about the IDEA diagrams. Although we have used actual TD items provided by an industry partner, only the replication of our study with variation in the material can reduce this threat. Another threat arises from the TAM questionnaire due to its questions and length. The participants could misunderstand the questions, and the number of questions could fatigue participants. To mitigate this threat, we conducted two internal validations to identify improvements in study design and its material (questionnaire and training materials). We then piloted the questionnaire before its execution. None of these participants reported issues in answering the questionnaire.

Conclusion Validity. The primary threat is that the participants were not allowed to participate in the software project that provided the TD items used in the study nor to talk to the project members. Therefore, it can affect the analysis of practices and PARs conducted by the participants. We assumed this threat as a limitation of the study. As we are not evaluating the final list of practices and PARs, but the use of the diagrams, the participants are able to simulate the work of identification of TD management practices and PARs based on the description of each TD item. Besides, as we did not obtain 100% agreement on the statements of the self-predicted future use construct, we believe that the participants were able to analyze the effort in performing the tasks with and without the diagrams.

External Validity. A threat arises from the fact that the study participants were chosen by convenience and were all students (some with industry experience in software development). Thus, although the results are not as generalizable as they could have been with a more representative sample, they provide initial evidence on the investigated topic.

6.2 Interview Study

Construct Validity. A threat emerges from the interview script in that the participants could misunderstand its questions. To mitigate this threat, we performed two internal validations and piloted the interviews with two participants with distinct levels of experience. Our goal was to identify the time necessary to run interviews (the mean time was about 30 min) and collect impressions about the questions and improvement points. All was considered fine during the validations and pilot.

Conclusion Validity. The primary threat arises from our coding process to analyze the interview transcripts. As this process is subjective, the first author coded the transcripts, and the last author reviewed the extracted codes. These authors conducted a meeting to resolve eventual disagreements.

External Validity. A threat arises from the small number of participants that may not be representative of a population. It did not allow us to perform more specific analysis, for example, if different practitioner roles who have different points of view on software projects, also have different perceptions of IDEA diagrams. We assumed this threat as the main limitation of this study. Another threat is related to the fact that study participants were chosen by convenience because we invited only practitioners from our network in the software industry. We decided to use this method because we had truly little control over the availability of subjects, resulting in inviting only practitioners via existing contacts in software organizations. To mitigate this threat, we tried to ensure that our sample was reasonably representative and not strongly biased. For this, we tried to carefully select practitioners from distinct roles, with experience in their roles, and from different organizations.

7 Concluding Remarks

This study presents the assessment of the IDEA diagrams, which provide support for TD prevention, monitoring, and repayment activities. We conduct a TAM study with 72 students enrolled in a software engineering course and an interview study with 11 software practitioners. The results from both studies are positive, complementary, and confirmatory, revealing that the data embedded into the IDEA diagrams and the diagrams themselves are useful for TD prevention, monitoring, and repayment initiatives.

As future work, we intend to: (i) specialize the diagrams considering project variables, such as process mode and company size, (ii) automate the diagrams to provide dynamic manipulation of data, (iii) define how practices and PARs can be collected by software teams to automatically feed the diagram, and (iv) conduct case studies in the software industry to investigate when and how the IDEA diagrams can be used as part of project activities.

References

1. Avgeriou, P., Kruchten, P., Nord, R., Ozkaya, I., Seaman, C.: Reducing friction in software development. IEEE Softw. **33**(1), 66–73 (2016)
2. Falessi, D., Kazman, R.: Worst smells and their worst reasons. In: Proceedings of the IEEE/ACM International Conference on Technical Debt, pp. 45–54. IEEE, Madrid (2021)
3. Izurieta, C., Vetrò, A., Zazworka, N., Cai, Y., Seaman, C., Shull, F.: Organizing the technical debt landscape. In: Proceedings of the International Workshop on Managing Technical Debt, pp. 23–26. IEEE, Zurich (2012)
4. Seaman, C., et al.::: Using technical debt data in decision making: potential decision approaches. In: Proceedings of the International Workshop on Managing Technical Debt, pp. 45–48. IEEE, Zurich (2012)
5. Spínola, R., Zazworka, N., Vetrò, A., Shull, F., Seaman, C.: Understanding automated and human based technical debt identification approaches-a two-phase study. J. Braz. Comput. Soc. **25**(5), 1–21 (2019)
6. Li, Z., Avgeriou, P., Liang, P.: A systematic mapping study on technical debt and its management. J. Syst. Softw. **101**, 193–220 (2015)
7. Rios, N., Mendonça, M., Spínola, R.: A tertiary study on technical debt: types, management strategies, research trends, and base information for practitioners. Inf. Softw. Technol. **102**, 117–145 (2018)
8. Yli-Huumo, J., Maglyas, A., Smolander, K.: How do software development teams manage technical debt? - An empirical study. J. Syst. Softw. **120**, 195–218 (2016)

9. M. Bomfim, M., A. Santos, V.: Strategies for reducing technical debt in agile teams. In: Silva da Silva, T., Estácio, B., Kroll, J., Mantovani Fontana, R. (eds.) WBMA 2016. CCIS, vol. 680, pp. 60–71. Springer, Cham (2017). https://doi.org/10.1007/978-3-319-55907-0_6

10. Behutiye, W., Rodríguez, P., Oivo, M., Tosun, A.: Analyzing the concept of technical debt in the context of agile software development: a systematic literature review. Inf. Softw. Technol. **82**, 139–158 (2017)

11. Toledo, S., Martini, A., Przybyszewska, A., Sjøberg, D.: Architectural technical debt in microservices: a case study in a large company. In: Proceedings of the International Conference on Technical Debt, pp. 78–87. IEEE, Montreal (2019)

12. Silva, V., Jeronimo Junior, H., Travassos, G.: A taste of the software industry perception of technical debt and its management in Brazil. J. Softw. Eng. Res. Develop. **7**(1:1), 1–16 (2019)

13. Apa, C., Solari, M., Vallespir, D., Travassos, G.: A taste of the software industry perception of technical debt and its management in Uruguay: a survey in software industry. In: Proceedings of the 14th ACM/IEEE International Symposium on Empirical Software Engineering and Measurement, pp. 1–9. ACM, New York (2020)

14. Apa, C., Jeronimo, H., Nascimento, L., Vallespir, D., Travassos, G.: The perception and management of technical debt in software startups. In: Nguyen-Duc A., Münch J., Prikladnicki R., Wang X., Abrahamsson P. (eds). Fundamentals of Software Startups. Springer, Cham (2020). https://doi.org/10.1007/978-3-030-35983-6

15. Rios, N., et al.: Hearing the voice of software practitioners on causes, effects, and practices to deal with documentation debt. In: Madhavji, N., Pasquale, L., Ferrari, A., Gnesi, S. (eds.) REFSQ 2020. LNCS, vol. 12045, pp. 55–70. Springer, Cham (2020). https://doi.org/10.1007/978-3-030-44429-7_4

16. Aragão, B., Andrade, R., Santos, I., Castro, R., Lelli, V., Darin, T.: TestDCat 3.0: catalog of test debt subtypes and management activities. Softw. Quality J. **30**, 181–225 (2022)

17. Freire, S., et al.: Pitfalls and solutions for technical debt management in agile software projects. IEEE Softw. **38**(6), 42–49 (2021)

18. Shahir, H., Daneshpajouh, S., Ramsin, R.: Improvement strategies for agile processes: a SWOT analysis approach. In: Proceedings of the International Conference on Software Engineering Research, Management and Applications, pp. 221–228. IEEE, Prague (2008)

19. Rios, N., Spínola, R., Mendonça, M., Seaman, C.: The practitioners' point of view on the concept of technical debt and its causes and consequences: a design for a global family of industrial surveys and its first results from Brazil. Empir. Softw. Eng. **25**, 3216–3287 (2020)

20. Davis, F.: Perceived usefulness, perceived ease of use, and user acceptance of information technology. MIS Quarterly 319–340 (1989)

21. Seaman, C.: Qualitative methods in empirical studies of software engineering. IEEE Trans. Software Eng. **25**(4), 557–572 (1999)

22. Strauss, A., Corbin, J.: Basics of Qualitative Research: Techniques and Procedures for Developing Grounded Theory, p. XIII. Sage Publications, Thousand Oaks (1998).

23. Wohlin, C., Runeson, P., Höst, M., Ohlsson, M.C., Regnell, B., Wesslén, A.: Experimentation in Software Engineering. Springer, Heidelberg (2012). https://doi.org/10.1007/978-3-642-29044-2

Automatic Fixation of Decompilation Quirks Using Pre-trained Language Model

Ryunosuke Kaichi[(✉)], Shinsuke Matsumoto[(✉)], and Shinji Kusumoto[(✉)]

Graduate School of Information Science and Technology,
Osaka University, Osaka, Japan
{r-kaichi,shinsuke,kusumoto}@ist.osaka-u.ac.jp

Abstract. Decompiler is a system for recovering the original code from bytecode. A critical challenge in decompilers is that the decompiled code contains differences from the original code. These differences not only reduce the readability of the source code but may also change the program's behavior. In this study, we propose a deep learning-based quirk fixation method that adopts grammatical error correction. One advantage of the proposed method is that it can be applied to any decompiler and programming language. Our experimental results show that the proposed method removes 55% of identifier quirks and 91% of structural quirks. In some cases, however, the proposed method injected a small amount of new quirks.

Keywords: decompiler · fine-tuning · deep learning · quirk · grammatical error correction

1 Introduction

Decompiler is one of the reverse engineering systems that translate low-level program representation (e.g., binary or bytecode) to human-readable language (e.g., source code) [2]. Decompiler is expected to be applied to various purposes. One of the major applications is to understand the program behavior in an environment where source code cannot be accessed. Famous IDE tools, such as Eclipse and IntelliJ, have a decompiler feature in default. This feature helps developers to analyze the inside of dependent libraries without their source code. Furthermore, a decompiler is one of the important techniques for binary security analysis [3]. Several decompiler-based malware detection methods have been proposed for Android applications [1,11].

A critical challenge in decompilers is that the decompiled code contains differences from the original code. This paper calls these difference *quirk*. Low-level program languages do not contain identifier information written in the original code. So, the complete identifier reconstruction is fundamentally impossible [8]. It is known that source code identifiers play an important role in source code comprehension [6]. Therefore, identifier quirks become obstacles to applying decompiler for the scenario of program comprehension. Decompilation quirks occur not in identifiers but rather in program structure. It is because a single program

© The Author(s), under exclusive license to Springer Nature Switzerland AG 2024
R. Kadgien et al. (Eds.): PROFES 2023, LNCS 14483, pp. 259–266, 2024.
https://doi.org/10.1007/978-3-031-49266-2_18

instruction in low-level language does not always correspond to high-level language instruction. For example, iteration instruction in low-level language can be translated to both `for` and `while` statements. This translation is considered an inference problem. Harrand et al. [5] have reported that the decompiled code sometimes behaves differently from the original code by the structural quirks.

The study aims to provide a method to fix decompilation quirks. We propose a deep learning-based quirk fixation method that adopts grammatical error correction (GEC) to achieve this goal. GEC is a well-known technique for detecting and fixing grammatical errors, including in natural language sentences. Our method assumes quirks in the decompiled code, one of the grammatical errors against the original code. The proposed method has a significant advantage in applicability, which can be applied to any decompilers and programming languages. Also, the method has high compatibility with deep learning. A large learning dataset (i.e., a set of pairs of decompiled and original code) can be easily generated with a fully automated. We apply our method to ReCa [10], a program competition dataset, as an evaluation. Evaluation results show that the proposed method removes 55% of identifier quirks and 91% of structural quirks.

2   Decompilation Quirk

This section illustrates decompilation quirks with concrete source code examples. Figure 1 shows quirk examples with famous Java decompilers, CFR. We can see various quirks in decompiled code. This paper broadly classifies quirks into two types: identifier quirk and structural quirk.

There are two identifier quirks for local variables. As explained in the first section, bytecode does not contain identifier information, especially in local and temporal variables. So, the reconstruction of local variable identifiers is a challenging task. Only the loop index `i` is reconstructed correctly. Probably, CFR has a specific reconstruction rule that follows common sense in which loop indexes should be named `i`, `j`, and `k`. However, we lost almost identifiers, such as `occurrence` and `numbers`, that help program comprehension.

Next, we focus on structural quirks. The `final` modifier for the method parameter has been lost. We cannot grasp the programmer's intent that the parameter is immutable from the decompiled code. Those variables and method modifiers are used to declare constraints for the compiler. So, bytecode does not contain this information. The guard clause to find a sentinel in a loop is merged into the loop condition in `for` statement. This merge causes a further quirk: the sentinel condition is reversed from `==` to `!=`. Postfix operator `++` becomes prefix operator. In summary, though overall behavior is the same as the original code, the decompiled code is slightly difficult to read to grasp its intent.

3   Proposed Quirk Fixation Method

3.1   Overview

This paper proposes an automated fixation method for decompilation quirks. The fundamental idea of our method is to adopt deep learning-based GEC

Original code	Decompiled code (CFR)
```int count(final int[] numbers) { int occurrence = 0; for (int i = 0; i < numbers.length; i++) { if (numbers[i] == -1) { // found sentinel break; } occurrence++; } return occurrence; }```	```int count(int[] arrn) { int n = 0; for (int i = 0; i < arrn.length && arrn[i] != -1; ++i) { ++n; } return n; }``` ▢ Identifier quirk ▢ Structure quirk

Fig. 1. Example of decompilation quirks in Java (Color figure online)

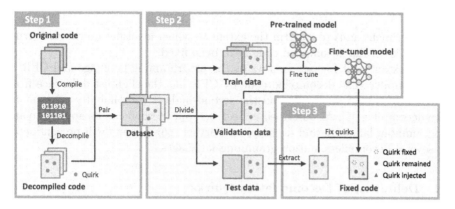

Fig. 2. Flow of quirk fixation by the proposed method

by assuming a decompilation quirk as a syntax error. Our method leverages CodeT5 [13], a Transformer-based pre-trained model, applying fine-tuning as a translation task using decompiled and original code pairs. The generated model attempts to translate code with quirks to code without quirks.

3.2 Procedure

Figure 2 shows the overall procedure of quirk fixation by the proposed method. The method consists of the following three steps.

Step 1. Dataset Generation: In this step, we create a learning dataset of original and decompiled code pairs. First, we obtain source code from an arbitrary data source such as GitHub or a public dataset. Next, all source code is compiled to generate byte code or machine code, depending on the language. Then, we recover the source code from the bytecode using a decompiler. At this point, decompiled code contains certain quirks. Finally, original and decompiled codes are paired as a dataset.

Step 2. Fine-Tuning: Next, we generate a quirk fixation model by fine-tuning. First, we divide the dataset generated in Step 1 into three types: training data, validation data, and test data. The split rates are 80%, 15%, and 5%, respectively. Then, CodeT5 is fine-tuned by using training data and validation data. The learning task is a translation task using a paired dataset. Finally, we obtain a model that considers quirks as grammatical errors and corrects them.

Step 3. Quirk Fixation: Finally, we attempt to fix decompilation quirks using the generated model. The input to the model generated by fine-tuning is decompiled codes contained in test data. As a result, the model generates fixed codes with certain quirks removed.

4   Experimental Setup

4.1   Purpose

The experiment aims to confirm the extent to which identifier quirks and structural quirks in the decompiled code have been fixed.

This experiment focuses on Java as the programming language and CFR as the decompiler. The decompiled code by CFR has the slightest difference from the AST of the original code and the second-highest compilability rate among Java decompilers [5]. As described in Sect. 3.1, our method can be applied to any programming language and decompiler. Further experiments will be conducted for several decompilers and programming languages.

4.2   Definition of Decompilation Quirks

We define quirks as differences in the AST between the original code and the decompiled code. Quirk is defined as the following two types.

Identifier Quirks: Identifier quirks are differences related to changes in identifier names. We classify the updates of nodes whose labels are SimpleName or QualifiedName in the AST as identifier quirks. Quirks highlighted in yellow in Fig. 1 are one of the identifier quirks. Since identifier names are lost at compile time, it is difficult for the decompiler to recover them. Even if the variables have meaningful names in the original code, the names are changed after decompiling. It leads to a decrease in program comprehension.

Structural Quirks: Structural quirks are differences related to changes in the syntax of the source code. All differences excluding identifier quirks, are classified as structural quirks. The reversal of the finding sentinel condition presented in Fig. 1 is one of the structural quirks. Structural quirks lead to reduced readability as with identifier quirks. It could also affect the behavior of the program.

4.3   Quirk Evaluation

As an experiment procedure, we first detect the difference in AST between the original code and the decompiled code and between the original code and the fixed code. These differences are considered a set of quirks. Then, we confirm how

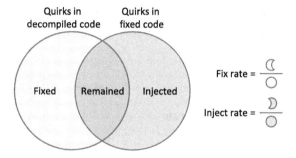

Fig. 3. Inclusion relation of two quirk sets

many quirks in the decompiled code have been fixed by analyzing the inclusion relationship between the two quirk sets. We use GumTree [4] to detect differences in AST. GumTree is a tool that can identify changes between two programs.

Figure 3 shows a Venn diagram representing the inclusion relationship between the set of quirks in the decompiled code and the set of quirks in the fixed code. We define the fix rate as the percentage of fixed quirks in the decompiled code. The fix rate is calculated as fixed/fixed+remained. The proposed method may inject new quirks. The percentage of injected quirks among the quirks in the fixed code is defined as the inject rate. The inject rate is calculated as injected/injected+remained.

4.4 Dataset

In the experiment, we use ReCa [10], a program competition dataset. ReCa contains source code for four programming languages, C, C++, Python, and Java, but we only use Java. The bytecode generated by the compiler is required to obtain the decompiled code. Therefore, we extracted only compilable source code. Furthermore, only codes with a file size of 2 KB or less were subjected to the experiment. Initially, the experiment was conducted without selection by file size. As a result, the fine-tuning of the model stopped halfway through due to memory problems. We considered both whether it would not cause memory problems and whether the number of data used for fine-tuning was sufficient. Finally, the experimental target was set to 2 KB or less source code. As a result of extracting codes that satisfy the above conditions, the number of source codes gathered was 17,220. These were divided in the ratio of 80:15:5 and used as training, validation, and test data, respectively.

4.5 Pre-trained Model

As the pre-trained model, we use CodeT5 [13], proposed by Wang et al. CodeT5 is a Transformer-based model pre-trained on the CodeSearchNet [7] dataset. It can multitask, including code generation, transformations, and modification. CodeT5 has several models of different sizes. We use CodeT5-small due to memory problems. Fine-tuning took approximately 90 min.

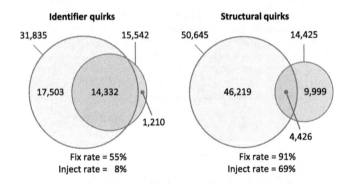

Fig. 4. Venn diagram of identifier quirks and structural quirks

5   Results and Discussion

5.1   Results

Figure 4 shows Venn diagrams for the set of identifier quirks and the set of structural quirks. The numbers in the Venn diagram represent the total quirk of all 861 source codes in test data. Focusing on identifier quirks, the total number in the decompiled code was 31,835. Of these, 17,503 were removed by the proposed method, and the fix rate of identifier quirks was about 55%. On the other hand, the proposed method injected a relatively small number of identifier quirks, with an inject rate of 8%. Next, the total number of structural quirks in the decompiled code was 50,645. The proposed method removed 46,219, which is about 91%. On the other hand, new structural quirks injected by the proposed method were 9,999. The inject rate was 69%, which was higher than identifier quirks.

A more detailed analysis can be shown in Fig. 5. This figure represents an actual example of quirk fixation by the proposed method. A part of the source code has been abbreviated to make it easier to understand the fixation's effect. The structural quirks highlighted in pink is the most important one to focus on. The original code uses a variable of type `boolean` as a flag, determining the final output. In contrast, the decompiled code uses the value of the variable n of type `int` as a flag. The role of variable n is difficult to understand intuitively, reducing readability. Furthermore, the conditional expression of the `if` statement in the `for` statement is reversed. Usually, humans code differently. It is precisely the cause of reduced readability. In contrast, the fixed code uses variables of type `boolean` as flags, making their role clear. The `if` statement has also been fixed to be written in the same way as the original code, which is easier to understand and more readable.

Next, note the identifier quirks highlighted in yellow. The variable names for arrays and flags in the fixed code have been changed to intuitively understandable names. Since it is not the same name as the original code, it is a modification failure in this definition. However, the fixed code is relatively superior in terms of readability. It is one of the strengths of the proposed method.

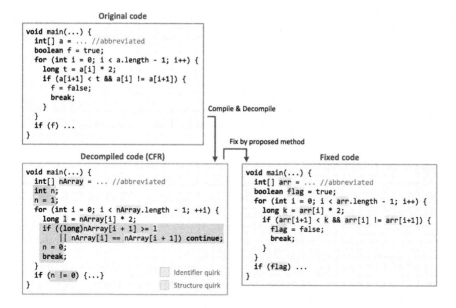

Fig. 5. Example of quirk fixation in a subject with ReCa (Color figure online)

5.2 Discussion

We discuss why the fix rate of structural quirks was significantly higher than that of identifier quirks. The pre-trained model used in this study was pre-trained and fine-tuned on a dataset consisting of source code created by multiple developers. The naming of identifiers is highly dependent on the developer, although there is a certain degree of shared understanding. Variables with the same meaning are often given different names, so the correct answer to identifier quirks can vary widely from data to data. However, since the syntax is developer-independent, the correct answer to structural quirks is almost uniquely determined. For these reasons, we consider that the fix rate of structural quirks was significantly higher than that of identifier quirks.

6 Conclusion

We proposed an automated fixation method for two types of quirks in the decompiled code. As a result, we confirmed that the proposed method could fix 55% of identifier quirks and 91% of structural quirks in the decompiled code.

For future work, we first try to conduct experiments with multiple decompilers. The proposed method can fix quirks without depending on decompilers or programming languages. Using more evaluation metrics is also an important task. For practicality, it is necessary to evaluate the fixed code in terms of whether it can be compiled and whether it passes the test cases of the original code. Finally, we will compare with existing methods focusing only on identifier quirks [9,12].

Acknowledgements. This research was partially supported by JSPS KAKENHI Japan (Grant Number: JP21H04877, JP20H04166, JP21K18302, and JP21K11829)

References

1. Cen, L., Gates, C.S., Si, L., Li, N.: A probabilistic discriminative model for android malware detection with decompiled source code. Trans. Dependable Secure Comput. (TDSC) **12**(4), 400–412 (2014)
2. Cifuentes, C., Gough, K.J.: Decompilation of binary programs. Softw. Pract. Experience **25**(7), 811–829 (1995)
3. Cifuentes, C., Waddington, T., Van Emmerik, M.: Computer security analysis through decompilation and high-level debugging. In: Working Conference on Reverse Engineering (WCRE), pp. 375–380 (2001)
4. Falleri, J., Xavier Blanc, F.M., Martinez, M., Monperrus, M.: Fine-grained and accurate source code differencing. In: International Conference on Automated Software Engineering (ASE), pp. 313–324 (2014)
5. Harrand, N., Soto-Valero, C., Monperrus, M., Baudry, B.: The strengths and behavioral quirks of java bytecode decompilers. In: International Working Conference on Source Code Analysis and Manipulation (SCAM), pp. 92–102 (2019)
6. Hofmeister, J., Siegmund, J., Holt, D.: Shorter identifier names take longer to comprehend. In: International Conference on Software Analysis, Evolution and Reengineering (SANER), pp. 217–227 (2017)
7. Husain, H., Wu, H.H., Gazit, T., Allamanis, M., Brockschmidt, M.: Codesearchnet challenge: evaluating the state of semantic code search. arXiv preprint arXiv:1909.09436 (2019)
8. Jaffe, A., Lacomis, J., Schwartz, E.J., Goues, C.L., Vasilescu, B.: Meaningful variable names for decompiled code: a machine translation approach. In: International Conference on Program Comprehension (ICPC), pp. 20–30 (2018)
9. Lacomis, J., et al.: Dire: A neural approach to decompiled identifier naming. In: International Conference on Automated Software Engineering (ASE), pp. 628–639 (2019)
10. Liu, H., Shen, M., Zhu, J., Niu, N., Li, G., Zhang, L.: Deep learning based program generation from requirements text: are we there yet? Trans. Softw. Eng.(TSE) **48**(4), 1268–1289 (2022)
11. Milosevic, N., Dehghantanha, A., Choo, K.K.R.: Machine learning aided android malware classification. Comput. Electr. Eng. **61**, 266–274 (2017)
12. Nitin, V., Saieva, A., Ray, B., Kaiser, G.: Direct: a transformer-based model for decompiled identifier renaming. In: Workshop on Natural Language Processing for Programming (NLP4Prog), pp. 48–57 (2021)
13. Wang, Y., Wang, W., Joty, S., Hoi, S.C.: Code T5: identifier-aware unified pretrained encoder-decoder models for code understanding and generation. arXiv preprint arXiv:2109.00859 (2021)

Log Drift Impact on Online Anomaly Detection Workflows

Scott Lupton[1,2]([✉]) [iD], Hironori Washizaki[1] [iD], Nobukazu Yoshioka[1] [iD],
and Yoshiaki Fukazawa[1] [iD]

[1] Waseda University, Tokyo, Japan
scott.lupton@toki.waseda.jp, {washizaki,fukazawa}@waseda.jp,
nobukazuy@acm.org
[2] Nomura Securities Co., Ltd., Tokyo, Japan
scott.lupton@nomura.com
https://www.waseda.jp, https://www.nomura.co.jp

Abstract. Traditional rule-based approaches to system monitoring have many areas for improvement. Rules are time-consuming to maintain, and their ability to detect unforeseen future incidents is limited. Online log anomaly detection workflows have the potential to improve upon rule-based methods by providing fine-grained, automated detection of abnormal behavior. However, system and process logs are not static. Code and configuration changes may alter the sequences of log entries produced by these processes, impacting the models trained on their previous behavior. These changes result in false positive signals that can overwhelm production services engineers and drown out alerts for real issues. For this reason, log drift is a significant obstacle to utilizing online log anomaly detection approaches for monitoring in industrial settings. This study explores the different types of log drift and classifies them using a newly introduced taxonomy. It then evaluates the impact these types of drift have on online anomaly detection workflows. Several potential mitigation methods are presented and evaluated based on synthetic and real-world log data. Finally, possible directions for future research are provided and discussed.

Keywords: anomaly detection · logs · monitoring · drift · feedback

1 Introduction

Production service engineers depend on monitoring systems to support their system estate. They utilize preemptive alerts to resolve issues before they occur and mitigate the impact of problems that have already occurred through remedial actions and repair. Alerts are necessary for revealing system issues that would result in significant business impact if left unmanaged. This is why monitoring tools are essential: they provide visibility for overall system health. However,

Supported by organization Nomura Securities Co., Ltd.

this visibility is only as valuable as it is reliable, making the performance of monitoring methods mission-critical for the industries that depend on them.

Log anomaly detection workflows can significantly improve system reliability by better detecting anomalous behavior. Current rule-based systems are useful, but rules are time-consuming to maintain, and their ability to detect unforeseen issues is limited [10]. Industry system logs are not static. Changes to monitored processes can result in log drift, significantly impacting the ability to monitor those processes properly. Log drift can be defined as the change in log entry behavior over time due to internal or environmental factors (including load, system releases, resource contention, etc.). In the case of supervised log anomaly detection, log drift can be considered closely synonymous with concept drift.

Kabinna *et al.* found that from their studied applications, 20–45% of the logging statements changed at least once in their lifetime [9]. Such changes could significantly impact log anomaly detection workflows. This is the motivation for this study: to analyze the impact of log drift variations and offer preliminary suggestions on mitigating their effects. Through this analysis, we hope to support the industrialization of log anomaly detection methods for industry system monitoring and promote better overall system reliability.

The rest of this paper is organized as follows: Sect. 2 analyzes a real-world industry example of log drift and introduces a taxonomy of log drift types. Section 3 presents our component-based encoder/detector pipeline framework and a new synthetic log dataset incorporating log drift examples. It uses these examples to assess the impact of different types of log drift (as defined by our taxonomy) on anomaly detection workflows. Section 4 implements event-based and sequence-based feedback mechanisms and assesses their ability to mitigate the impact of log drift. Section 5 discusses related work, and Sect. 6 presents our conclusions, including suggestions for future research direction.

1.1   Contributions

The primary contributions of this study are as follows:

- We define and classify the different types of log drift using a new taxonomy developed from the analysis of a real-world industry example
- We introduce a new synthetic log dataset for use with our component-based encoder/detector pipeline for log drift impact analysis
- We assess the impact of different log drift types on log anomaly detection method performance
- We introduce and assess preliminary log drift mitigation techniques
- We provide direction for future research on better managing log drift

1.2   Research Questions

This study aims to address the following research questions:

RQ1. What types of log drift exist, and how can they be classified? To answer this question, we created a taxonomy of log drift types by analyzing a real-world industry example.

RQ2. How do these log drift types affect online log anomaly detection workflows? To answer this question, we extended our component-based encoder/detector pipeline (introduced in previous work). We built a collection of synthetic log data representing the different types of log drift as defined through our taxonomy. We then used this data to perform experiments assessing the impact of the different types of log drift on anomaly detection methods.

RQ3. To what extent do feedback mechanisms mitigate the impact of log drift? We implemented feedback mechanisms for our encoder/detector pipeline detector components to answer this question. We assessed the ability of these methods to mitigate the impact of log drift using synthetic and real-world industry process log data.

2   Taxonomy of Log Drift

To address **RQ1**, we analyzed a real-world industry process log containing known log drift. Using the results of this analysis, we developed a taxonomy of log drift types that can be used for categorization. Finally, we discuss these categories, their interrelationship, and their potential causes.

2.1   Industry Log Drift Analysis

For this investigation, we utilized a front-office system log provided by Nomura Securities Co., Ltd. The log contains one year of data covering the period of one production incident and one system change. The change had two main components. First, the minor version of the OS and resource allocation for the virtual host were upgraded. Second, the command-line options used for launching the process were modified.

We compared the process log entries produced before and after implementing these changes. There were six newly introduced log entries, two altered entries, and two log parameter value differences. Due to confidentiality, we have included only a sample of each difference type in Table 1.

Note that the template change example listed in Table 1 could also technically be considered a parameter change. This command-line option alteration increased the maximum memory allocation pool for the Java Virtual Machine (JVM) by specifying a larger memory size. However, as the key and value for this setting are domain-specific and consist of a non-delimited sequence of numbers and letters, it would be challenging for a generic log parser to properly detect this value as a parameter (as is the case when using Drain3).

Table 1. Examples of log entry differences before and after a real-world system release.

Before Change	After Change	Difference Type
Running on: <:IP:>, **8** cpu(s)	Running on: <:IP:>, **12** cpu(s)	Parameter Change
-Xms**500m**	-Xms**1G**	Template Change[†]
	-verbose:gc	New Template[†]

[†] Results also in log entry sequence differences

Along with log entry differences, we also discovered timing changes. The duration between process launch and system initiation was reduced from approximately 18 to 15 s. This difference is reflected in the timestamps of the relevant log entries and thus can also be considered another distinct type of log drift.

Based on this analysis, we have developed a taxonomy of possible log drift types (Fig. 1). In subsequent sections, we will discuss these taxonomy nodes in more detail, including their potential causes. Finally, we will use these categories to assess the impact of different forms of log drift on anomaly detection methods (in Sect. 3.3).

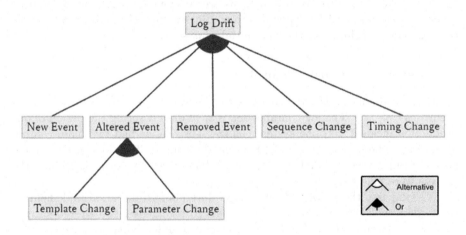

Fig. 1. Taxonomy of log drift types.

2.2 Log Drift Impact Types

We have defined five primary types of log drift in our taxonomy. These types are discussed in detail below:

New Events. New events result from process code changes that add log statements to new or preexisting code branches. It isn't always immediately apparent that new events have been added. Error and exception handling, for example, will not typically be triggered during regular system operations. These events are non-disruptive as their detection will produce true positive results. However, new log entries during normal systems operations (e.g., additional informational log checkpoints) are problematic. These new entries can trigger alerts even though the monitored system functions as expected. Note that new events will also result in sequence changes (as discussed below) and, in extreme cases, can also cause detectable changes in log entry timing.

Altered Events. Altered log events take two forms: template changes and parameter changes. Note that both of these change types can exist simultaneously. Template changes occur when the static text of a log entry is modified. Parameter changes occur when the log entry parameters' location, type, or count have been altered. Note that parameter changes can also include changes in value, such as when the variable used for an output parameter is swapped with a different variable.

While it is tempting to think of altered events as a combination of new and removed log statements, there is merit in considering this category as a separate, distinct case. Modifications to preexisting templates can be trivial or significant, and this difference can result in very different anomaly detection workflow results. For example, semantic vectorization workflows are generally more robust to small perturbations [4]. Trivial modifications such as spelling corrections may not significantly impact the model performance, while more considerable changes may be more likely to.

Removed Events. Log events can be removed as part of system code changes and releases. Removing regularly occurring log entries will result in sequence changes. These changes can significantly impact log anomaly detection models and result in false positives. Anomaly detection workflows that utilize statistics of event occurrence (such as ADR) can also be affected [12].

Sequence Changes. Sequence changes are caused by the addition, removal, or template alteration of preexisting events, changes in procedural execution timing (resulting from code or performance changes), and the reordering of logging statements. As mentioned, log sequence changes can significantly impact log anomaly detection workflows that detect anomalies using event sequence prediction. Anomaly detection workflows that utilize event frequency in session windows are generally unaffected. However, these changes can still impact models that depend on fixed windows if the reordering occurs across the window boundaries.

Timing Changes. Timing changes describe mutations in log innovation timing, both for individual log entries and for those resulting in altered intervals between events. These changes may occur for several reasons, including system load fluctuations, resource contention, and differences in thread synchronization. Note that log entry timing differences often result in sequence changes, but they do not necessarily have to. Also, timing changes near fixed window boundaries are likely to result in model impact even without changes in sequence. Anomaly detection models that incorporate event timing as part of their input features (e.g., LogNL, Drain, etc.) would be the most susceptible to these differences [3,14].

2.3   Log Drift Causes

The two leading causes of log drift are system and performance changes. We present a description of these below:

System Changes. As demonstrated in Sect. 2.1, system changes are one primary cause of log drift. It is common for developers to add new log entries for error handling and informative log checkpoints for debugging when performing bug fixes and minor enhancements. Removing superfluous log entries and altering preexisting entries is also common. However, code changes can indirectly impact log output even when the entries are untouched. For example, log statement invocation may be nullified due to deactivated code branches. Log sequence and timing differences may also arise as code logic is added, altered, and deleted.

Process configuration changes are another cause of log drift. They can result in performance changes and impact the timing and sequence of log entry output. Sometimes, the configuration is output directly as template parameter values, resulting in direct changes to log entries. Infrastructure changes can also cause log drift. Modifying hardware specifications (CPU speed and count, memory, and disk space, for example) can significantly impact performance, leading to log output differences (via parameter output in logs and performance changes as discussed below).

Performance Changes. Performance changes can result in log drift as well. This was seen with the process initiation time difference in the industrial log example analyzed in Sect. 2.1. Increased system load is another potential cause of timing differences. System load can result in larger time deltas between log events. As discussed previously, these timing differences may also result in event sequence changes.

Differences in execution time can impact parameter values. For example, the duration of request processing time is often recorded for debugging purposes in the form of log entry parameters. Execution delays can result in the execution of timeout or retry logic that hasn't been triggered previously, producing log entries not seen during model training. In some cases, these entries may be considered true positive anomalies and will have minimal effect on detection methods. They also may be regarded as noise if system performance remains in the range of acceptability (from the perspective of end-users and production service engineers), and result in what is considered false positives.

RQ1. What types of log drift exist, and how can they be classified? **Log drift types include new events, altered events (in the form of template or parameter changes), removed events, event sequence changes, and timing changes. Log drift can occur as a combination of these types and can be classified using our newly introduced taxonomy (Fig. 1).**

3   Log Drift Impact on Anomaly Detection Workflows

To address **RQ2**, we performed experiments using our component-based encoder/detector pipeline introduced in previous work [10]. We first created a collection of synthetic log data that contains each type of log drift as defined by our newly introduced taxonomy (Fig. 1). We then used this synthetic data to assess the impact of different log drift types on rule-based, event-based, and sequence-based anomaly detection methods.

3.1   Component-Based Encoder/Detector Pipeline

In previous work, we introduced a component-based encoder/detector pipeline that can be utilized for online log anomaly detection [10]. This pipeline feeds log entries through a series of configurable *Encoder* and *Detector* components (Fig. 2). *Encoder* components inherit from an Encoder parent class and implement the *encode* function. Within this design, log parsers are treated as encoder types. *Detector* components inherit from the Detector parent class and implement the *detect* function. The details of this implementation are provided in the UML class diagram in Fig. 3.

3.2   Synthetic Log Dataset

We created a collection of synthetic data logs consisting of the different types of log drift presented in our taxonomy. First, we created a control log that imitates a typical request/response execution flow. It includes a series of five ordered log entries representing a successful request and return sequence. Three of these log entries contain a dynamic parameter, and one entry contains two dynamic parameters. The control log includes 10 of these sequences overall. The final sequence contains one anomaly representing a request failure. We used this control log to create six other synthetic log files, introducing one type of log drift into each. The details of these logs are summarized in Table 2.

3.3   Log Drift Impact Assessment

Using our component-based encoder/detector pipeline and synthetic log dataset, we performed experiments to assess the impact different forms of log drift have on log anomaly detection models. The results of these experiments are presented below.

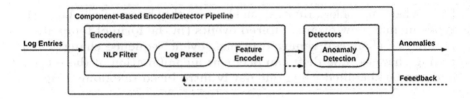

Fig. 2. Component-based encoder/detector pipeline for online log anomaly detection.

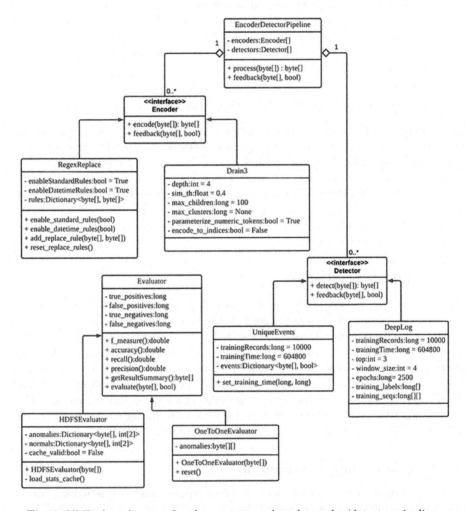

Fig. 3. UML class diagram for the component-based encoder/detector pipeline.

Table 2. Synthetic log data summary.

Log	Drift Type	Altered Lines	Total
Control.log	None	0	50
New.log	New Event (Sequence Change)	2	52
AlteredTemplate.log	Altered Event (Sequence Change)	2	50
AlteredParameter.log	Parameter Change	2	50
Removed.log	Removed Event (Sequence Change)	2	48
Sequence.log	Sequence Change	2	50
Timing.log	Timing Change	5	50

Impact on Rule-Based Detection To assess the impact of log drift on rule-based detection methods, we configured our component-based encoder/detector pipeline to use a rule-based detector with a regex replacement encoder. The rule engine was configured to detect keyword instances from a standard error keyword set (including the tokens "failed," "exception," and "error") using case-insensitive matching on log tokens. The regex replacement encoder was configured to use its default behavior: replacing date, time, IP addresses, hexadecimal tokens, and numeric tokens with static placeholders. Note that rule-based approaches to detection do not require training. Thus, the detection phase for these experiments was performed using all log entries.

The results of this experiment showed that the six different log drift types had no impact on the accuracy of detection for the rule engine. This demonstrates that rule-based detection methods are highly robust to log drift. However, the risk of influence is not zero. Detection rules generally target generic error conditions. Because of this, newly detected signals are more typically true positives resulting from additional error handling. However, false positives can be introduced with poor rule definition or logging practices (when dealing with log drift in the form of new or altered templates).

Impact on Event-Based Detection Event-based anomaly detection methods highlight abnormalities in individual log event signatures or behavior. We performed an identical experiment assessing the impact of log drift on such methods by configuring our component-based encoder/detector pipeline to use a unique event detector. The detector was configured to train on the first 40 log entries (i.e., the first eight request/response sequences before log drift and anomalies were introduced). We again used a regex replacement component with default settings but added the Drain3 log parser for template extraction in the encoder pipeline.

The results of our first experiment were surprising: we found no impact on the accuracy of detection for any of the log drift types. However, upon closer inspection, we found a significant impact on the output of the Drain3 parser. Newly introduced and altered entries were not detected due to the erroneous clustering of these entries with preexisting templates. Table 3 presents an example of this erroneous clustering. The two static tokens from the original and new entries were incorrectly combined into parameter placeholders. This resulted in a generic template that will match any info severity level log entry with three tokens in the future, regardless of whether the tokens are parameters or not.

Table 3. Example of Drain3 erroneous template derivation due to log drift.

Normal Entry	2023.07.02 18:49:15 [INFO] Using Mode: INT16
New Drift Entry	2023.07.02 20:39:15 [INFO] Preprocessed Input (5s)
Erroneous Template	<:DATE:> <:TIME:> [INFO] <*> <*> <*>

To extend this experiment, we adjusted the default similarity threshold of Drain3 from 0.4 to 0.6 and performed evaluations again using the synthetic log dataset. The results are shown in Table 4. As can be seen, removing the parsing error caused the log drift impact to propagate down to the detector pipeline. This reduced accuracy for new and altered log template drift types. Modified parameters had no impact as the Drain3 parser correctly replaced them with wildcards (and the current model doesn't perform anomaly detection on event parameter sequences). Sequence, timing, and event removal changes also did not result in impact as the model utilizes per-event detection (in contrast to window-based anomaly detection approaches).

Table 4. Impact of log drift types on event-based anomaly detection (Drain3 sim_th = 0.6).

Log	Precision	Recall	Accuracy	F-measure	TP	FP
Control.log	1	1	1	1	1	0
New.log	.3333	1	.9615	.5000	1	2
AlteredTemplate.log	.3333	1	.9600	.5000	1	2
AlteredParameter.log	1	1	1	1	1	0
Removed.log	1	1	1	1	1	0
Sequence.log	1	1	1	1	1	0
Timing.log	1	1	1	1	1	0

Impact on Sequence-Based Detection Sequence-based anomaly detection methods attempt to detect abnormal sequences by predicting subsequent events from prior ones as input. To test the impact of log drift on these methods, we replaced the unique event detector in our previous experiment with an LSTM-based anomaly detection model (keeping the Drain3 similarity threshold set to

0.6 and all other component parameters the same). Using this configuration, we repeated the experiment. The evaluation results are shown in Table 5.

Table 5. Impact of log drift types on sequence-based anomaly detection (LSTM).

Log	Precision	Recall	Accuracy	F-measure	TP	FP
Control.log	1	1	1	1	1	0
New.log	.2000	1	.9231	.3333	1	4
AlteredTemplate.log	.2000	1	.9200	.3333	1	4
AlteredParameter.log	1	1	1	1	1	0
Removed.log	.3333	1	.9583	.5000	1	2
Sequence.log	.3333	1	.9600	.5000	1	2
Timing.log	1	1	1	1	1	0

From these results, it can be seen that sequence-based anomaly detection methods are much more susceptible to varying forms of log drift. New and altered log templates cause detection errors due to their absence during training. However, they can also trigger further prediction errors due to their inclusion in subsequent window input sequences. The new and altered template synthetic log file evaluations illustrate this case: there were more false positives (four) than changed events (two). Due to this phenomenon, larger window sizes will likely run a higher risk of impact than shorter ones when using sequence-based methods.

Removed log entries also negatively impacted accuracy. This is because of the removal's effect on entry sequencing. Timing and parameter alterations were the only two types of log drift that did not negatively impact detection results. However, workflows that build parallel parameter detection models and incorporate time deltas (such as DeepLog [3]) would likely be susceptible to these categories as well.

RQ2. How do these log drift types affect online log anomaly detection workflows? **Unless poor logging practice is used when adding or altering entries, rule-based monitoring systems are generally unaffected by log drift. However, event-based log anomaly detection methods are susceptible to new or altered event types. Sequence-based anomaly detection methods are even more sensitive to log drift, being impacted by newly introduced entries, modified entries, removed entries, and sequence changes. Parameter and timing changes generally do not affect detection methods unless those methods incorporate functions targeting those characteristics (i.e., using parameter sequence models or log event time delta features).**

4   Feedback Mechanisms

Feedback mechanisms allow for corrective adjustments to models through output validation. To address **RQ3**, we implemented such mechanisms for our event-based and sequence-based detector components. We then used them to provide corrective feedback for the first occurrences of log drift in real-world and synthetic datasets. The results of these experiments are presented below.

4.1   Event-Based Method Feedback

To assess the ability of feedback mechanisms to mitigate the impact of log drift on event-based models, we implemented the encoder/detector framework *feedback* methods for Drain3 and the unique event detector component. For Drain3, the method acts as a simple pass-through function to generate templates for the raw log event input. The unique event detector's feedback method updates the component's event cache using the input log data and an associated anomaly flag (true values indicating true anomalies and false values indicating false positives). We performed an experiment assessing these methods using the real-world system log introduced in Sect. 2.1. The results of this experiment are shown below in Table 6.

Table 6. Event-based feedback method performance on real-world log drift.

Feedback Type	Precision	Recall	Accuracy	F-measure	TP	FP
None	.9902	.8320	.9820	.9042	4938	49
1 Day (8 Updates)	.9970	.8320	.9825	.9071	4938	15

As can be seen, event-based feedback mechanisms can significantly improve log anomaly detection performance. Providing feedback for all drift statements (eight updates) resulted in a 31% reduction in false positives. Precision, accuracy, and f-measure scores also improved. Eight of the 15 remaining false positives came from the first indications of log drift. The remaining seven were caused by parsing errors introduced after the occurrence of a true anomaly.

Note these parsing errors are an interesting phenomenon: the anomaly caused the further abstraction of a preexisting log template, and this abstraction resulted in false positives for all subsequent matching log entries (due to the template's absence during training). This reveals an unexpected weakness of using incremental log parsers for log anomaly detection. In the future, termination of incremental template derivation for anomalies should be considered.

4.2   Sequence-Based Method Feedback

To assess the ability of feedback mechanisms to mitigate the impact of log drift using sequence-based anomaly detection methods, we implemented a feedback mechanism for the encoder/detector pipeline's LSTM detector component. This implementation proved very challenging. First, while event-based feedback mechanisms can function using false positive events as input, sequence-based methods require the window of events preceding that event to perform model updates. As we had very high false positive rates using sequence-based detection on the real-world industry process log introduced in Sect. 4.1, we instead used our synthetic log dataset for this experiment ("New.log" from Table 2). The results are shown in Table 7.

Table 7. Sequence-based feedback method (LSTM) performance on synthetic (new entry) log drift data.

Feedback Type	Precision	Recall	Accuracy	F-measure	TP	FP
None	.2000	1	.9231	.3333	1	4
New Entry Prediction	.2000	1	.9231	.3333	1	4
New Entry Sequence	.1667	1	.9038	.2857	1	5

As can be seen, we could not mitigate the impact of log drift in any meaningful way using this mechanism. When providing feedback for incorrect predictions of the newly introduced log entry (i.e., the "New Entry Prediction" feedback type), future predictions for this event were corrected. However, other input sequences that included the new entry continued to result in incorrect predictions. We also attempted to apply feedback for all inaccurate predictions that had the new event in the input sequence (i.e., the "New Entry Sequence" feedback type). This resulted in correct predictions for subsequent sequences after the feedback was applied. However, we discovered some impact on other sequences that did not include the new entry. Overall, this assessment revealed that using incremental updates to mitigate log drift impact on sequence-based models is very challenging. Exploring other potential mitigation methods in future research would be beneficial.

RQ3. To what extent do feedback mechanisms mitigate the impact of log drift? **Implementing and using feedback mechanisms for event-based models is both simple and effective. Using a real-world log drift example, we reduced the false positive rate by 31%, performing only eight feedback updates (i.e., using only the first occurrence of each log drift event). Sequence-based feedback mechanisms are much more challenging. They require using the incorrectly predicted events and their surrounding events to perform incremental model updates properly. Furthermore, we have found that correcting incorrect sequences through feedback can negatively impact the predictive power of other sequences with shared elements.**

5   Related Work

5.1   Log Drift

A search for "log drift" in Scopus[1] (as of August 1st, 2023) produced seven articles, all of them unrelated to the intended topic except for one: Pal and Kumar's introduction to DLME, a distributed log mining approach using "a weighted ensemble learning algorithm for predicting network faults" [11]. This paper describes a method of managing log drift by reducing the weights of classifiers found to be using drifted log features (identified via approximated Kullback Leibler Divergence) [7]. Zhang *et al.* also touch upon log drift in discussing the broader topic of log instability [13]. They cite the evolution of log messages as one of the two leading causes for instability and show that semantic vectorization can improve the robustness of anomaly detection models against it.

5.2   Concept Drift

Log drift is closely related to concept drift. However, unlike log drift, concept drift is a well-covered concept. Gama *et al.* define concept drift as "an online supervised learning scenario when the relation between the input data and the target variable changes over time" [6]. They provide a survey on the topic focusing heavily on adaptive learning algorithms. Iglesias Vázquez *et al.* evaluated how different data characteristics (including concept drift) impact the algorithm accuracy of outlier detection mechanisms for streaming data [8]. Ahmad *et al.* present the Numenta Anomaly Benchmark (NAB), providing a scoring methodology designed for streaming applications [1]. When defining their ideal characteristics of real-world anomaly detection algorithms, they include the ability to adapt to dynamic environments and concept drift as one of them. They show that the "ability of each algorithm to learn continuously and handle concept drift is one of the contributing factors to obtaining a good NAB score."

5.3   Feedback Mechanisms

Du *et al.* introduced DeepLog, an LSTM-based anomaly detection method that includes a feedback mechanism [3]. This mechanism uses input sequences resulting in false positives to train model weights with corrected labels incrementally. Chen *et al.* include a similar mechanism in their dual LSTM-based anomaly detection method [2]. They train their model using 1% of regular sequences from the BGL dataset and achieve significant increases in accuracy after performing continual feedback updates on false positives (increasing the initial training F-score value from 29.89% to 80.94%). They do not, however, describe how many feedback updates were used to achieve this result. QLLog, a log anomaly detection method using Q-learning, uses a different type of feedback mechanism [5]. It implements an abnormal level table that can be updated to filter anomalous events based on operations feedback. Both DeepLog and QLLog, unfortunately, do not include evaluations of their feedback mechanisms' effectiveness.

---

[1] https://www.scopus.com.

6   Conclusion and Future Work

In this study, we categorized the different types of log drift using a newly introduced taxonomy (Fig. 1). The taxonomy was created by analyzing a real-world, industrial case of log drift. We assessed the impact different log drift types have on different monitoring approaches. Rule-based monitoring is generally robust to log drift except when rule definitions or logging practices are poor. Event-based anomaly detection methods are susceptible to new and altered log events. Sequence-based anomaly detection methods are the most sensitive to log drift, being impacted by all types except parameter and timing changes (unless parameter models or time delta input features are utilized). The continued presence of the drift effect over input sequence windows compounds this impact. It makes mitigating the impact of log drift on sequence-based methods especially challenging.

We explored some preliminary log drift mitigation techniques using feedback mechanisms. We found that event-based feedback mechanisms are straightforward to implement and highly effective. Sequence-based mechanisms are more complicated, requiring entire event sequences to train and necessitating incremental model weight updates. Our experiment found sequence-based feedback methods incapable of mitigating log drift impact satisfactorily, at least with the implementation utilized.

This study highlights several areas that would benefit from future exploration. First, our impact analysis of log drift on anomaly detection methods revealed that drift can significantly impact log parsers as well. Further research on the extent of this impact using different parser types would be informative. Introducing and assessing mitigation strategies for this impact would also be beneficial. Our experiments discovered that parser template abstraction post-training can result in false positive signals. Implementing a feature to lock down incremental template updates past the training phase may help to resolve this issue. Finally, an in-depth study of log drift mitigation strategies would be helpful. We have addressed preliminary approaches to mitigating log drift through feedback mechanisms, but a more thorough examination is needed. Surveying, for example, how general concept drift mitigation techniques could be utilized against log drift would be a worthy endeavor. Ultimately, our analysis of the types of log drift and their impact on detection models can serve as the basis for future experiments to manage log drift better, improving the performance of log monitoring methods and supporting their practical use in industrial settings.

Acknowledgments. The authors thank Xingfang Wu from the Polytechnique Montréal and the Data Science Initiative (DSI), Nomura Securities Co., Ltd. members for their support in preparing and completing this research. This work was partially supported by the JST-Mirai Program (Grant Number JPMJMI20B8).

References

1. Ahmad, S., Lavin, A., Purdy, S., Agha, Z.: Unsupervised real-time anomaly detection for streaming data. Neurocomputing **262**, 134–147 (2017). https://doi.org/10.1016/j.neucom.2017.04.070, https://www.sciencedirect.com/science/article/pii/S0925231217309864, online Real-Time Learning Strategies for Data Streams

2. Chen, Y., Luktarhan, N., Lv, D.: LogLS: research on system log anomaly detection method based on dual LSTM. Symmetry **14**(3), 454 (2022). https://www.mdpi.com/2073-8994/14/3/454

3. Du, M., Li, F., Zheng, G., Srikumar, V.: Deeplog: anomaly detection and diagnosis from system logs through deep learning. In: Proceedings of the 2017 ACM SIGSAC Conference on Computer and Communications Security, pp. 1285–1298. CCS '17, Association for Computing Machinery, New York, NY, USA (2017). https://doi.org/10.1145/3133956.3134015

4. Du, Q., Zhao, L., Xu, J., Han, Y., Zhang, S.: Log-based anomaly detection with multi-head scaled dot-product attention mechanism. In: Strauss, C., Kotsis, G., Tjoa, A.M., Khalil, I. (eds.) DEXA 2021. LNCS, vol. 12923, pp. 335–347. Springer, Cham (2021). https://doi.org/10.1007/978-3-030-86472-9_31

5. Duan, X., Ying, S., Yuan, W., Cheng, H., Yin, X.: QLLog: a log anomaly detection method based on Q-learning algorithm. Inf. Process. Manag. **58**(3), 102540 (2021). https://doi.org/10.1016/j.ipm.2021.102540, https://www.sciencedirect.com/science/article/pii/S0306457321000479

6. Gama, J.A., Žliobaitundefined, I., Bifet, A., Pechenizkiy, M., Bouchachia, A.: A survey on concept drift adaptation. ACM Comput. Surv. **46**(4) (2014). https://doi.org/10.1145/2523813, https://doi-org.waseda.idm.oclc.org/10.1145/2523813

7. Hershey, J.R., Olsen, P.A.: Approximating the Kullback Leibler divergence between gaussian mixture models. In: 2007 IEEE International Conference on Acoustics, Speech and Signal Processing - ICASSP '07, vol. 4, pp. IV-317-IV-320 (2007). https://doi.org/10.1109/ICASSP.2007.366913

8. Iglesias Vázquez, F., Hartl, A., Zseby, T., Zimek, A.: Anomaly detection in streaming data: a comparison and evaluation study. Expert Syst. Appl. **233**, 120994 (2023). https://doi.org/10.1016/j.eswa.2023.120994, https://www.sciencedirect.com/science/article/pii/S0957417423014963

9. Kabinna, S., Shang, W., Bezemer, C.P., Hassan, A.E.: Examining the stability of logging statements. In: 2016 IEEE 23rd International Conference on Software Analysis, Evolution, and Reengineering (SANER), vol. 1, pp. 326–337 (2016). https://doi.org/10.1109/SANER.2016.29

10. Lupton, S., Yu, L., Washizaki, H., Yoshioka, N., Fukazawa, Y.: Assessment of real-world incident detection through a component-based online log anomaly detection pipeline framework. In: The 10th International Conference on Dependable Systems and Their Applications (DSA 2023), pp. 1–2. Tokyo, Japan (2023)

11. Pal, A., Kumar, M.: DLME: distributed log mining using ensemble learning for fault prediction. IEEE Syst. J. **13**(4), 3639–3650 (2019). https://doi.org/10.1109/JSYST.2019.2904513

12. Zhang, B., Zhang, H., Moscato, P., Zhang, A.: Anomaly detection via mining numerical workflow relations from logs. In: 2020 International Symposium on Reliable Distributed Systems (SRDS), pp. 195–204 (2020). https://doi.org/10.1109/SRDS51746.2020.00027

13. Zhang, X., et al.: Robust log-based anomaly detection on unstable log data. In: Proceedings of the 2019 27th ACM Joint Meeting on European Software Engineering Conference and Symposium on the Foundations of Software Engineering, pp. 807–817. ESEC/FSE 2019, Association for Computing Machinery, New York, NY, USA (2019). https://doi.org/10.1145/3338906.3338931, https://doi-org.waseda.idm.oclc.org/10.1145/3338906.3338931

14. Zhu, B., Li, J., Gu, R., Wang, L.: An approach to cloud platform log anomaly detection based on natural language processing and LSTM. In: 2020 3rd International Conference on Algorithms, Computing and Artificial Intelligence. ACAI 2020, Association for Computing Machinery, New York, NY, USA (2020). https://doi.org/10.1145/3446132.3446415

Leveraging Historical Data to Support User Story Estimation

Aleksander G. Duszkiewicz[1], Jacob G. Sørensen[2], Niclas Johansen[1],
Henry Edison[3]👤, and Thiago Rocha Silva[2(✉)]👤

[1] Morningtrain ApS, Odense, Denmark
{alek,nj}@morningtrain.dk
[2] The Maersk Mc-Kinney Moller Institute, University of Southern Denmark, Odense,
Denmark
jacso18@student.sdu.dk, thiago@mmmi.sdu.dk
[3] Blekinge Institute of Technology, Karlskrona, Sweden
henry.edison@bth.se

Abstract. Accurate and reliable effort and cost estimation are still challenging for agile teams in the industry. It is argued that leveraging historical data regarding the actual time spent on similar past projects could be very helpful to support such an activity before companies embark upon a new project. In this paper, we investigate to what extent user story information retrieved from past projects can help developers estimate the effort needed to develop new similar projects. In close collaboration with a software development company, we applied design science and action research principles to develop and evaluate a tool that employs Natural Language Processing (NLP) algorithms to find past similar user stories and retrieve the actual time spent on them. The tool was then used to estimate a real project that was about to start in the company. A focus group with a team of six developers was conducted to evaluate the tool's efficacy in estimating similar projects. The results of the focus group with the developers revealed that the tool has the potential to complement the existing estimation process and help different interested parties in the company. Our results contribute both towards a new tool-supported approach to help user story estimation based on historical data and with our lessons learned on why, when, and where such a tool and the estimations provided may play a role in agile projects in the industry.

Keywords: User Stories · Agile Estimation · Natural Language Processing

1 Introduction

Effort and cost estimation is still one of the critical activities of agile software development [26]. A fair amount of developers' time is spent on understanding, discussing, and establishing a consensus on an accurate estimate for user stories.

© The Author(s), under exclusive license to Springer Nature Switzerland AG 2024
R. Kadgien et al. (Eds.): PROFES 2023, LNCS 14483, pp. 284–300, 2024.
https://doi.org/10.1007/978-3-031-49266-2_20

Such activity is even costlier for companies that need to budget a software project before gaining a development contract. In the agile context, the adoption of Planning Poker [15], despite being one of the most popular estimation techniques [27], remains a challenge for teams that lack the time, expertise, and domain knowledge to accurately estimate the user stories at hand, especially when there is no previous experience from similar tasks [16]. Moreover, estimates can easily be misjudged, and the development takes longer than first anticipated, leading to project loss.

Analogy-based estimation has been investigated for a long time as a strategy to overcome some of these challenges [24]. In the agile context, however, despite previous work has already demonstrated the benefits of Planning Poker to get better estimates [16,18,20], it is yet to know whether having access to the actual effort spent on similar user stories in the past could help developers to estimate user stories for new projects better. In practice, it is not trivial to identify similar stories from past projects, and many agile teams do not leverage this asset [3].

In this paper, we investigate to what extent user story information retrieved from a database of past agile projects can help developers estimate more easily the effort needed to develop new similar projects. Specifically, we seek to answer three research questions:

RQ1. How appropriate is the inference of user story similarity based on text similarity?

RQ2. To what extent can the actual effort spent on past user stories help developers estimate new similar user stories?

RQ3. What role an estimation tool can play to support the agile estimation process based on historical data?

To answer these questions, we followed design science principles to develop a software tool that employs Natural Language Processing (NLP) to identify and retrieve similar user stories from past projects. The tool was then evaluated in a focus group with key stakeholders. The contributions of this paper include the key findings of a focus group with an agile team that used the tool to estimate user stories for a new project in a real setting, as well as our lessons learned regarding the role of such a tool on agile projects in the industry.

We outline background and related work in Sect. 2 and our method in Sect. 3. In Sect. 4, we present our initial results, which are then discussed in Sect. 5 and concluded in Sect. 6.

2   Background and Related Work

As user stories are textual representations of features that need to be implemented, this work relies on text-based parameters to score story similarities. Text similarities can be literal or semantic. Literal similarity refers to looking at two strings and measuring how close or far from each other they are. Levenshtein distance, also called "edit distance" [31], is an example of such an algorithm. The output of the algorithm is the minimum number of character edits (replace, insert, or delete) to transform one string into another. The fewer edits, the more similar. Literal similarity, however, would only yield a high similarity score for stories close to the same phrasing, meaning that many stories would never be caught. On the other hand, semantic similarity is a branch of NLP that goes beyond looking at the literal text. It instead utilizes machine learning to figure out similarities in text. For example, spaCy [1] is an open-source Python library that enables people who are not necessarily machine learning experts to conduct NLP tasks on words and sentences. spaCy comes with basic pre-trained models but can also be used with other models to achieve better scoring, such as the Universal Sentence Encoder (USE) [5] trained by Google. This allows for a deeper semantic analysis since, as long as the words carry the same meaning, two strings do not have to be worded the same way to achieve a high score.

The use of NLP to support Requirements Engineering (RE) activities is a long-term research topic for the RE community. For example, Zhao et al. [32] present a comprehensive literature review in this area. The identification of requirements similarities is one of the NLP applications on RE. Abbas et al. [2] have recently evaluated different NLP models to study the correlation between requirements similarity and software similarity. These studies ultimately aimed to allow for code reuse based on requirements similarities in past and current projects. Other authors have investigated requirements similarity to identify the relationship between requirements and software architecture [11], and also possible redundancies and inconsistencies in the requirements specification to improve the quality of requirements sentences [21].

Raharjana et al. [23] investigated how NLP techniques have been applied to requirements specified in the context of user stories. The authors argue that NLP studies on user stories are broad, ranging from discovering defects, generating software artifacts, identifying the key abstraction of user stories, and tracing links between model and user stories. In the context of agile planning, a study reported by Barbosa et al. [4] employs requirements similarity to suggest the existence of duplicate user stories in the product backlog. Many other previous works have reported using different NLP models to support the agile estimation process.

Choetkiertikul et al. [6] propose a prediction model named Deep-SE for estimating story points based on a combination of two deep learning architectures. According to the authors, their model learns from the team's previous story point estimates to predict the size of new issues. The authors expect the resultant estimates to be used in conjunction with existing estimation techniques practiced by the team. A different model is proposed by Fu & Tantithamthavorn [13] based on a transformer architecture. Their model, GPT2SP, differs from Deep-SE by explaining the suggested estimates. The authors also suggest the estimates provided by GPT2SP on a project can also be transferred to other projects. Results of a small survey conducted by the authors with agile practitioners suggested that explainable estimates are indeed more useful in this context. A good overview of contributions in this area is provided by Alsaadi & Saeedi [3] with a recent systematic literature review (SLR) on data-driven effort estimation techniques of agile user stories.

These contributions, however, are heavily focused on the performance of their respective prediction models. Besides providing a concrete software tool to support the agile estimation process (as opposed to prediction models), our contribution in this paper primarily differs from theirs by focusing on the qualitative data obtained in a real setting regarding the role that this kind of tool may play in agile projects in the industry. The findings of the SLR conducted by Alsaadi & Saeedi [3] also confirm the lack of studies focused on understanding the concrete usefulness of these solutions in real-world agile projects.

3   Research Methodology

Our overall research approach is oriented towards design science [29], which provides a concrete framework for dynamic validation in an industrial setting [14]. Design science is a problem-solving paradigm which creates artefacts to solve a problem in a certain context [29]. The artefacts may be represented in various structured forms, e.g. software, formal logic, method, technique, or conceptual structure [29]. Each problem is rooted in a certain context so that the artefacts can be designed to understand the context. Following the design science principle, our research method comprised a design task cycle: problem investigation, treatment design, and treatment validation.

3.1   Case Organization

Morningtrain ApS is a Danish medium-sized, full-service digital agency specializing in web design, programming, and online marketing. A large amount of developers' time in the company is currently spent on estimating the effort needed to complete projects, as each requirement has to be analyzed, refined, and estimated individually before a price can be proposed to the client. It is a critical phase. Even though a lot of resources are spent on this activity, there is no guarantee of success given the uncertainty of the estimation process. This research aimed at developing a solution that utilizes historical data to improve the estimation process, making it faster, more reliable, and more accurate.

3.2   Problem Investigation

We started investigating the problem by interviewing the company's head of development. During the interview, we were provided with a description of the current process in the company. Morningtrain has employed so far a weighted three-point estimation technique based on PERT [19] and would like to keep using it. It was also revealed that the company is currently trying to adopt Planning Poker more extensively and that estimates for user stories are mainly based on time rather than story points. We also did a workshop with the relevant stakeholders to get a complete picture of the problem. Open-ended questions were used to understand documents and processes currently in use. To elaborate on the process, the company shared its current requirements spreadsheet and information on how this document is used on a daily basis for effort and cost estimation. It was revealed that the company would like to transfer this process to a new system, which should be able to generate a project on Jira based on the entered requirements, as well as provide historical data to support the process.

The way the company currently tracks effort is through its own internal hub with a tool where developers can register the time spent on a task. A Jira ID is provided during the process so the internal system matches the current Jira project and automatically updates the time-tracking field on that particular Jira issue. The time registered on previous Jira issues is expected to be used as ground truth effort estimates in the proposed solution. The proposed solution should also be able to support upfront planning and estimation at the beginning of the project, as well as ongoing estimation in each iteration, as they are both part of the challenges currently faced by the company. The ultimate purpose of the solution is to help reduce uncertainty as much as possible during the estimation process.

At the end of the aforementioned workshop, both functional and non-functional requirements for the system were identified. The non-functional requirements concerned maintainability and performance. The functional requirements included that the system should: *(i)* provide relevant historical data from similar user stories, *(ii)* keep the weighted three-point estimate technique, and *(iii)* be integrated with Jira providing a two-way communication of project data. Another particular characteristic identified in the company's process is that it deals with a lot of data when creating user stories for a new project. Part of this data is used as a customer's assurance that there is a mutual understanding of the features. Another part is used to describe the technical steps required to implement the stories, and another part describes the feature itself. Not all entries on a story follow a specific format or rule set. For example, the technical description for one story may include a detailed description of classes and patterns to follow, while for others, it may be completely empty. Most feature descriptions, however, follow the Connextra template for user stories [7].

3.3   Treatment Design

To address the investigated problems, we co-designed a solution with the company. The whole process, from the first interviews until the product evaluation, took seven months and consisted of three main steps. First, we conducted the interviews and workshops described above. Next, we did an informal literature review of the existing methodologies for scoring user stories, namely literal and semantic similarity. During this step, we also reviewed the existing tools and applications that had the potential to partially or fully address the problem.

Finally, the third step consisted of reviewing existing technologies based on the current set-up available in the company and implementing the tool according to the functional and non-functional requirements [12]. The tool employs semantic analysis to score semantic similarity among user stories. Semantic similarity analysis has been implemented using spaCy, which compares two strings through its similarity function that uses cosine similarity to calculate a similarity score. While spaCy comes with a selection of standard models that can be directly used, when tested with our database, the similarity scores were mostly in the high end, regardless of the actual similarity. This made us opt for USE [5], a pre-trained model developed by Google. USE was trained with a large variety of text, which makes it a good choice for general-purpose tasks. During our tests, the similarity scores with USE were closer to what we expected based on a manual analysis of the stories in the database.

The system compares a new story against all other stories marked with the status of "done" in the database. During the comparison process, the user stories are pre-processed to remove the template skeleton (i.e., the sub-strings *"As a"*, *"I want"*, and *"So that"*) since we noticed this actually improves the parsing. We set our similarity threshold as 60% (i.e., any user story with a similarity score of 0.6 or above is returned to the user) as higher thresholds were not returning enough results in our pilot studies. After finding similar stories, we use the actual effort spent on the highest-scoring user story returned as the most likely estimate for a new similar story. Overall, the system workflow is not linked to any estimation process or technique in particular, so the tool could be used to support teams employing different estimation strategies.

3.4   Treatment Validation

Through action research, we proposed an intervention in the company by using the tool to estimate a new project that was about to start. We wanted to observe how the tool would affect the developers' work in a real-life context. After using the tool to estimate the user stories for a new project, the developers participated in a focus group to share their experiences. From conception to execution, the intervention took about a month. The new project to be estimated was a website to sell courses online. For the study, the tool's database was seeded with five past projects previously developed by the company. These projects included B2B systems, shipbroking services, subscription management, business websites, and services for distribution platforms. In total, 250 user stories have been used in the study. The study included 6 participants, as shown in Table 1.

After a brief introductory training about the tool, the participants were instructed to use it independently for a couple of days to explore the features and get estimates for the new user stories at hand. The focus group that followed was held on the company premises with the participation of two researchers as moderators. After signing an ethical agreement explaining the nature of the study and giving permission for the discussion to be recorded and anonymously transcribed, the participants answered a demographic questionnaire. During the session, the moderators asked for feedback on each feature, including the accuracy of the estimates provided, its usefulness, the choice of techniques employed, the adopted classification threshold, its performance compared to a manual approach, and the role and practical use of the tool on future projects. After the session, two researchers independently transcribed the recording, codified the main topics, and classified the findings by themes [9].

Table 1. Background information of the participants.

ID	Role	E[a]	E[b]	E[c]	E[d]
P1	Software Developer	1–3 years	1–3 years	<1 years	<1 years
P2	Software Developer	5–10 years	5–10 years	<1 years	1–3 years
P3	Software Developer	5–10 years	5–10 years	<1 years	<1 years
P4	Software Architect	5–10 years	1–3 years	<1 years	<1 years
P5	Software Developer	3–5 years	3–5 years	<1 years	<1 years
P6	Software Developer	5–10 years	5–10 years	1–3 years	<1 years

[a]Overall professional experience, [b]Experience in the current role,
[c]Exp. in writing user stories, [d]Exp. in estimating user stories.

4   Results

In this section, we report the findings of our study. The findings are structured based on the research questions.

4.1   RQ1. How Appropriate is the Inference of User Story Similarity Based on Text Similarity?

During the validation stage with the developers, they agreed that inferring user story similarity based only on text similarity is not enough, as user stories can be similar but might describe a whole different context.

> "I don't think it's enough on its own. I think we need way more context, like tags, keywords, titles." – P6

> "It's a good way but it needs more ways to make sure that it's actually what we're looking for." – P2

The participants also highlighted the fact that the tool returned few similar stories. They explicitly mentioned that lowering the similarity threshold to return more stories (even the less similar ones) would be more useful than returning just the most similar ones.

> "I think the threshold might need to be lower because most of us didn't really find much, but I think rather than just have a threshold, you should also maybe just be shown the best matches, even if the numbers are only like 20 or 13. Because sometimes there might actually be something you can find. ... so you have like the list that kind of matches and then you go maybe this one actually is useful, OK then I can look at that one. So don't withhold information is what I'm trying to get at." – P5

One of the participants suggested being more specific when writing user stories in the first place. Another participant, however, raised a concern that it would be hard to find similar user stories if they become too specific and oriented towards a specific project.

"It would be hard to find matches because you become specific about the project and the task, and then suddenly it'll be like, "oh but these don't match", and then we actually can't find anything." – P5

Furthermore, there was a discussion about finding similar stories using keywords (tags), which extrapolates the use of tags we had previously anticipated while developing the tool (i.e., for pre-filtering stories) and later abandoned.

"Instead of having to write the user story as a whole, you could actually search using the keywords. So I want something to do with navigation, for example, I can just look up navigation, user stories written before." – P1

"I think you might be on to something there because if you like to have repeat or whatever you just insert keywords you feel like and then you can actually use those to match up against other previous stories that have like maybe similar keywords...because maybe I'm like OK, I need to make I don't know "WordPress contact form seven", with like some fields and it needs to sync up, so I just write in "context form 7", "WordPress", "confirmation mail", etc. and then that'll already basically describe any similar task with the keywords alone." – P5

Key Findings: Information should not be withheld. Even if no stories pass the threshold, the top-scoring stories should be displayed regardless. Alternative search techniques like tag search could supplement the textual similarity search in order to provide more context for the model, but also for the returned stories.

4.2   RQ2. To What Extent Can the Actual Effort Spent on Past User Stories Help Developers Estimate New Similar User Stories?

The participants also agreed that looking at the user story alone is not enough to judge whether the work required to implement such a story would be the same as the work required to implement another story deemed semantically similar by the model. An example of this came from two different participants, a back-end and a front-end developer. Both found the same past user story when trying to estimate a new similar one. The back-end developer agreed to the suggested most likely effort, while the front-end developer would have used much more time on it.

"I did the same like I found the same navigation user story and its estimates, and like as a front-end developer, I would have used a lot more time spent on that assignment. I think it is usually like 6 to 10 hours we use on that, and it was below 1...I'm not sure if it was like a back-end user story estimate or a front-end one" – P3

The participants also found that the technologies involved with the implementation of different user stories have a large impact on the effort spent. Without the information about the technology stack on the historical user story, it is hard for the developers to judge whether or not an estimate is realistic.

"The big thing here for me is Laravel, is it WordPress? Because there's no similarity basically, in the implementation in the end, it would be completely useless to me knowing that it took five hours in WordPress if I'm doing it in Laravel." – P6

"What is the actual stack for this particular project? Because the whole stack has something to say as well. If it's Blade there is one way to do it, if it's React, it's another way to do it, so it's very important to know the whole stack." – P4

> **Key Findings:** The context of the stories is crucial. An estimate cannot be reused if the tech stack is not similar or if the work is not done in the same part of the system, i.e., front-end or back-end.

4.3   RQ3. What Role an Estimation Tool Can Play to Support the Agile Estimation Process Based on Historical Data?

Even though the participants perceived the tool as being useful, they would rather use it alongside the Planning Poker sessions because these sessions help to bring context to an estimate.

"We would probably estimate faster because now we get more inputs on the actual time spent before on the previous task, which we can use to get the most accurate estimates, but I would probably not stop using Planning Poker" – P1

"With Planning Poker we actually get like some face-to-face sparring, with the tool you basically automate sparring. You will get a number, but you don't really know why it received those numbers. With Planning Poker, we actually get to the reason why." – P5

One of the participants disagreed with using the tool alongside the Planning Poker sessions.

"But I don't want to be biased by the system. My point is because if you do that, then the Planning Poker part is useless." – P6

A participant also emphasised the importance of monitoring their own accuracy while estimating stories.

"I think I need to get feedback on the accuracy we are actually doing at the moment because if we do not get better at estimating by using the tool I am probably not seeing the use of the tool" – P1

The participants also pointed out the need to expand the database of past projects as it would provide more stories and improve the estimation process.

"I think the only thing that's holding me back is not finding similar stories. I mean, I look at it I'm gonna write this story so I might as well copy and paste it into the tool and see what it gives me. But if it keeps giving me nothing, then it's obviously not useful, but if it gives me something at least have something to compare my thoughts with something else so I don't see why I wouldn't use it." – P6

Regarding the Jira integration, participants suggested the tool should not only provide a two-way communication, but developers should also be able to add projects from Jira, in a plug-and-play setting.

"I think the way we would do it would probably be like adding the Jira board and the project manager doing all the setup and then like using this as a support tool to like log all the user stories and estimates coming over, so if it could be like a seamless sync where you can just plug and play on an existing project..." - P3

The participants also had thoughts of who would benefit the most from the tool within the company, e.g., the Customer Care department. This department could search for related stories, receive the proposed estimate, and then consult it with a developer whether this would be a real effort to use.

"I actually see more usage for this tool in the Customer Care department. I think it would benefit having one or two Product Owners sitting with the tool and doing this for all the assignments they would get in the Customer Care department and then just dividing it out, and then we would more or less be the technical consultant on the estimates that we look at and see if this is anywhere near what we would think and such. So I think that would work well." - P1

"If they (Customer Care department) could put in the user story and find the matching user story and then ask a developer to sign off on the estimate then yeah it would already have an estimate that was roughly written, but we could double-check it and see that this actually match, that could be very nice." - P2

> **Key Findings**: The tool could be used as support for the Planning Poker sessions, either before as preparation help or after to see if the estimates are off. A Jira plug-and-play setting would also be useful to constantly feed the system with new stories and estimates. The tool could also be used to provide rough estimates before developers can provide real ones. Finally, it has also a role as a support to help developers improve their own accuracy while estimating.

5   Discussion

This section discusses and makes sense of the findings of our study. It is composed of three main parts. The first part discusses the lessons learned, followed by the implications to practice. The third part discusses the limitations of this study.

5.1   Lessons Learned

One of the critical concerns raised by the developers is searching for similar user stories only based on textual similarity. They mentioned that even if they found a similar story, they would not be able to make a qualified decision on whether to use the actual effort, as they could not base it on an actual context. Here, it was mentioned that the stories should include more context, such as categorization, who has made the story, and the relationship with the requirements and projects. During the study, it became evident that the required effort cannot be compared even if two stories are similar if they were developed for different development environments. Thus, to improve on the concern, we will need to make sure that retrieved stories include more context to help the decision process during the estimation.

An important issue raised by the participants was the amount of data that would be required for the tool to start returning more similar user stories. This also has an impact on the accuracy of the user story identification. We hypothesize whether it would be valuable to train a model specifically for the purpose of finding similarities between user stories. We did not do this initially due to the very limited data available in the company to perform training on. While previous research shows that some datasets of user stories from industry exist (e.g., [10]), they are still in a very small number for properly training NLP models.

On another front, an interesting feature suggested by the developers was to include real-time feedback on how well they estimate new stories. Currently, the tool does not support any form of feedback as suggested by the participants. If the feature were to be implemented to make the tool more useful, it should be able to give feedback on whether the estimation is accurate. This could help the developers get better at estimating, which could also reduce the time spent on estimating new stories.

Another lesson learned refers to the Jira integration. Participants mentioned the tool should also be able to add projects from Jira. This suggests a seamless plug-in-play integration with Jira that would, over time, help improve the tool's usefulness as data can be added more easily. Such a feature would expand the integration currently provided by the tool and possibly raise the flow of user stories into the system, ultimately providing more stories for analysis.

There are also lessons learned regarding the role of the tool during the estimation process. Participants had conflicting views on how the tool should be used alongside Planning Poker. While some participants suggested it might replace the sparring that is normally observed during Planning Poker (since it would only require them to search for similar stories and use the actual effort from a match), others stated that it would be more interesting to use the tool before the session, which could make the whole session useless. Other participants mentioned that they would not want to be biased by the tool, as they would like to have their thoughts on what estimate to give and not let the tool tell them exactly how long a story would take. This can be viewed both as a benefit and a drawback. On the one hand, the tool could be used to find a similar story, get the actual effort from that story, and then they could sign off on that estimate. On the other hand, it could also be a drawback since it removes the sparring that would normally be part of a Planning Poker session, where each developer could give his own estimate and explain their rationale. Thus, there might be some more considerations on improving the tool in this area to be more supportive and not completely remove the sparring the developers would normally have.

Lastly, the participants suggested this tool could play a role in different departments of the company. They explicitly mentioned that the Customer Care department would be a suitable place, as they suggested that the tool could support incoming change requests when a project is set into production. It was pointed out that the Customer Care team should also be able to use this tool to get a rough estimate based on past stories, and then they could consult the estimate with a developer who would sign off on that estimate. This suggests the tool has the potential to evolve to support more processes inside the company, which involve not only the start phases of the software development processes but also the last phases (maintenance and production) when new incoming change requests can be estimated more accurately with the help of the tool along with developer consultation.

5.2   Implications for Practice

Based on the results we discussed above, we provide a set of actionable recommendations for teams considering the use of automated estimates in their processes.

Lower Thresholds (RQ1). Lower similarity thresholds are more useful as developers could still be able to match their own stories to the found ones and evaluate whether a higher or a lower percentage would be a match for them. In addition, not only stories marked as "done" should be shown, but also those that are ongoing because developers would still be able to find these stories useful even if they are not finished yet.

Context Is Paramount (RQ2). More context should be added to the retrieved stories as developers found it difficult to evaluate the actual effort used on a story without any context. It was suggested to implement a form of categorization that could help them better evaluate a story.

Keywords Are Important for Search (RQ1). Searching similar stories based on specific keywords (or tags) would be helpful. Different methodologies could be applied with keywords to search similar stories. For example, developers could search for a specific keyword, and then the tool would return stories related to that specific keyword. To further assist the search process, a user story field could be added for the developer to insert the user story that s/he is currently working on. Whenever the developer searches with a keyword and a specific user story, the NLP similarity process can be used as an addition to score these stories and return the best matching stories back to the developer.

Jira in a Seamless, Plug-and-Play Integration (RQ3). Currently, projects can be created inside the tool and transferred to Jira, where changes from both systems are reflected afterwards in two-way communication. However, the tool does not support the other way around, i.e., transferring projects from Jira to the tool. This feature would greatly help to accommodate changes, as project managers and Product Owners would no longer have any trouble adding stories by transferring Jira projects directly into the tool. Additionally, this seamless feature would also help with the concern regarding the lack of data.

Automated Feedback on Accuracy Is a Plus (RQ3). The tool should provide some feedback on how accurately developers estimate new stories. This would help them to get better at estimating, which would give greater value to the customer. The tool should give feedback throughout the process, i.e., from when developers receive the story after it has been estimated using the tool and finally after delivering the accomplished purpose of that story to the customer. Through this accuracy cycle, the tool should be able to show figures based on the story estimation process so the company can see this data as feedback on that process cycle.

5.3   Threats to Validity

Reliability Validity. Reliability validity concerns the extent to which the data and analysis depend on the specific researchers [30]. Another researcher with more extensive knowledge and experience in design science research was also engaged in the review of the design and execution of the study. In addition, the focus group transcript used for the data analysis was sent back to the participants for review and shared among all authors. These practices helped to reduce biases during data collection and analysis.

Internal Validity. The retrospective analysis nature of this study makes it vulnerable to historical types of internal validity threats [30]. A company representative with extensive knowledge of the user story estimation process helped identify the key processes and their efficacy. All focus group participants had extensive knowledge about the company's user story-based effort estimation process. However, our interview is still vulnerable to internal validity threats. We acknowledge that the number of participants is a limitation of this study. Nonetheless, the vast years of experience that the participants have (i.e., four are about ten years) and the use of company documentation should reduce the threat to validity.

Construct Validity. Construct validity refers to the extent to which the operational measures, e.g., the construct discussed in the focus group that is studied, represent the study's objective [30]. In this study, other researchers reviewed the questions before conducting the actual focus group to ensure that they were interpreted in the same way. In addition, data source triangulation was used to strengthen the evidence generated in this study.

External Validity. External validity is concerned with the extent of generalizability [30] and transferability of a study [17]. The study presented here is based on five software development projects in a software company. Providing a detailed description of the context (see Sect. 3) helps in improving the study's external validity [22]. Even though each company and software development is unique, analytical induction helps to determine the generalizability between cases [28]. Hence, we provide an in-depth analysis of each case and carefully describe the context and provide clear insights into a particular context. Practitioners can easily compare the studied context with their own and take into consideration the findings and guidelines that we identified in their processes.

6   Conclusion

In this paper, we presented a study with a software tool that employs NLP to retrieve information from past user stories to support developers through the agile estimation process. The tool has been evaluated in a real setting with a team of six developers from the company estimating user stories for a real project that was about to start. Through the qualitative study, we found that textual similarity alone is not enough for developers to be able to make qualified decisions. The retrieved stories were missing more context, such as categorization, relationship with the referred project, and requirements. Once the developers have the contextual knowledge needed to fully understand a related user story, the actual effort spent on that story can indeed offer a baseline number for developers to use as a starting point for the new estimate. It is then up to them to make an informed decision based on the available data on whether or not the new story at hand would require more or less effort to implement. As the Planning Poker is part of the agile estimation process in the company, the developers will rather keep using it to estimate new projects. The tool has the potential to make the estimation process better and can be used either before or after the Planning Poker session. The tool is oriented towards complementing the sessions rather than replacing them. It can also guide developers on how accurate their estimates are based on the historical data available.

Future work could investigate cross-company historical data to address the low number of stories for NLP training. A partnership with companies around the Atlassian software ecosystem could be a way ahead. An issue that arises, in this case, is data confidentiality, as it would potentially expose business-critical user story information to other companies. In the future, as the collection of data grows, we could also experiment with training our own model in order to check if there are any relevant gains in accuracy and volume of stories retrieved. Another possibility to achieve better results would be replacing USE with other pre-trained models, such as the Infersent model released by Facebook [8], which is also a general-purpose model. This would require additional research since not all models are supported out of the box in the spaCy library. Despite recent replication studies [25] having challenged the performance of specific models targeted at agile estimation, such as Deep-SE, it could also be worthwhile to investigate their performance within our approach.

Acknowledgments. This work was supported by the University of Southern Denmark's Internal Strategic Fund and ELLIIT: the Swedish Strategic Research Area in IT and Mobile Communications.

References

1. Spacy (2021). https://spacy.io
2. Abbas, M., Ferrari, A., Shatnawi, A., Enoiu, E., Saadatmand, M., Sundmark, D.: On the relationship between similar requirements and similar software. Requir. Eng. **28**, 1–25 (2022)
3. Alsaadi, B., Saeedi, K.: Data-driven effort estimation techniques of agile user stories: a systematic literature review. Artif. Intell. Rev. **55**, 1–32 (2022)
4. Barbosa, R., Silva, A., Moraes, R.: Use of similarity measure to suggest the existence of duplicate user stories in the srum process. In: 2016 46th Annual IEEE/IFIP International Conference on Dependable Systems and Networks Workshop (DSN-W), pp. 2–5. IEEE (2016)
5. Cer, D., et al.: Universal sentence encoder. CoRR abs/1803.11175 (2018)
6. Choetkiertikul, M., Dam, H.K., Tran, T., Pham, T., Ghose, A., Menzies, T.: A deep learning model for estimating story points. IEEE Trans. Softw. Eng. **45**(7), 637–656 (2018)
7. Cohn, M.: User Stories Applied: For Agile Software Development. Addison-Wesley Professional, Boston (2004)
8. Conneau, A., Kiela, D., Schwenk, H., Barrault, L., Bordes, A.: Supervised learning of universal sentence representations from natural language inference data. CoRR abs/1705.02364 (2017). http://arxiv.org/abs/1705.02364
9. Cruzes, D.S., Dyba, T.: Recommended steps for thematic synthesis in software engineering. In: 2011 International Symposium on Empirical Software Engineering and Measurement, pp. 275–284. IEEE (2011)

10. Dalpiaz, F.: Requirements data sets (user stories) (2018). https://data.mendeley. com/datasets/7zbk8zsd8y/1
11. De Boer, R.C., Van Vliet, H.: On the similarity between requirements and architecture. J. Syst. Softw. **82**(3), 544–550 (2009)
12. Duszkiewicz, A.G., Sørensen, J.G., Johansen, N., Edison, H., Silva, T.R.: On identifying similar user stories to support agile estimation based on historical data. In: Agil-ISE@CAiSE, pp. 21–26 (2022)
13. Fu, M., Tantithamthavorn, C.: GPT2SP: a transformer-based agile story point estimation approach. IEEE Trans. Softw. Eng. **49**, 611–625 (2022)
14. Gorschek, T., Garre, P., Larsson, S., Wohlin, C.: A model for technology transfer in practice. IEEE Softw. **23**(6), 88–95 (2006)
15. Grenning, J.: Planning poker or how to avoid analysis paralysis while release planning. Hawthorn Woods: Renaissance Softw. Consult. **3**, 22–23 (2002)
16. Haugen, N.C.: An empirical study of using planning poker for user story estimation. In: AGILE 2006 (AGILE 2006), pp. 9-pp. IEEE (2006)
17. Lincoln, Y.S., Cuba, E.G.: Naturalistic Inquiry. Sage Publication, Thousand Oaks (1985)
18. Mahnič, V., Hovelja, T.: On using planning poker for estimating user stories. J. Syst. Softw. **85**(9), 2086–2095 (2012)
19. Miller, R.W.: Schedule, cost, and profit control with pert: a comprehensive guide for program management (1963)
20. Moløkken-Østvold, K., Haugen, N.C., Benestad, H.C.: Using planning poker for combining expert estimates in software projects. J. Syst. Softw. **81**(12), 2106–2117 (2008)
21. Park, S., Kim, H., Ko, Y., Seo, J.: Implementation of an efficient requirements-analysis supporting system using similarity measure techniques. Inf. Softw. Technol. **42**(6), 429–438 (2000)
22. Petersen, K., Wohlin, C.: Context in industrial software engineering research. In: Proceedings of the 2009 3rd International Symposium on Empirical Software Engineering and Measurement, pp. 401–404 (2009)
23. Raharjana, I.K., Siahaan, D., Fatichah, C.: User stories and natural language processing: a systematic literature review. IEEE Access **9**, 53811–53826 (2021)
24. Shepperd, M., Schofield, C.: Estimating software project effort using analogies. IEEE Trans. Softw. Eng. **23**(11), 736–743 (1997)
25. Tawosi, V., Moussa, R., Sarro, F.: Agile effort estimation: have we solved the problem yet? Insights from a replication study. IEEE Trans. Softw. Eng. **49**(4), 2677–2697 (2022)
26. Trendowicz, A., Jeffery, R.: Software Project Effort Estimation. Foundations and Best Practice Guidelines for Success, Springer, Cham (2014). https://doi.org/10.1007/978-3-319-03629-8
27. Usman, M., Mendes, E., Börstler, J.: Effort estimation in agile software development: a survey on the state of the practice. In: Proceedings of the 19th international conference on Evaluation and Assessment in Software Engineering, pp. 1–10 (2015)
28. Wieringa, R.J.: Case study research in information systems engineering. In: Proceedings of the 25th International Conference on Advanced Information Systems Engineering, p. xii (2013)
29. Wieringa, R.J.: Design Science Methodology for Information Systems and Software Engineering. Springer, Heidelberg (2014). https://doi.org/10.1007/978-3-662-43839-8

30. Wohlin, C., Runeson, P., Höst, M., Ohlsson, M.C., Regnell, B., Wesslén, A.: Experimentation in Software Engineering. Springer, Heidelberg (2012). https://doi.org/10.1007/978-3-642-29044-2

31. Zhang, S., Hu, Y., Bian, G.: Research on string similarity algorithm based on levenshtein distance. In: 2017 IEEE 2nd Advanced Information Technology, Electronic and Automation Control Conference (IAEAC), pp. 2247–2251 (2017)

32. Zhao, L., et al.: Natural language processing (NLP) for requirements engineering: a systematic mapping study. ACM Comput. Surv. **54**, 1–41 (2021)

Design Patterns Understanding and Use in the Automotive Industry: An Interview Study

Sushant Kumar Pandey⁽✉⁾ , Sivajeet Chand, Jennifer Horkoff ,
and Miroslaw Staron

Chalmers—University of Gothenburg, Gothenburg, Sweden
{sushant.kumar.pandey,jennifer.horkoff,miroslaw.staron}@gu.se,
sivajeet@student.chalmers.se

Abstract. Automotive software is increasing in complexity, leading to new challenges for designers and developers. Design patterns, which offer reusable solutions to common design problems, are a potential way to deal with this complexity. Although design patterns have received much focus in academic publications, it is not clear how they are used in practice. This paper presents an interview-based study that explores the use of design patterns in the automotive industry. The study findings reveal how automotive practitioners view and use design patterns in their software designs. Our study revealed that industry experts have a view of design patterns which often differs from the academic views. They use design patterns in combination with architecture guidelines, principles, and frameworks. Instead of the academic focus on the design patterns, industry professionals focus on the design, architectural tactics, and standards. Such findings highlight the need for a more nuanced understanding of the concept and practical applications of design patterns within the context of industrial software engineering practices.

Keywords: Design patterns · Automotive industry · Software industry

1 Introduction

From the academic standpoint, design patterns are proven solutions to recurring design problems in the development of software products. The concept of software design patterns was initially introduced by Gang of Four (GoF) [8], who identified a set of pre-defined solutions to common software design challenges. The design patterns can be increasingly useful due to the expanding complexity of modern software, particularly in automotive software, where code bases are rapidly increasing in size and complexity [5]. The GoF design patterns are almost 30 years old, while software engineering has evolved tremendously during that time and therefore, there is a need to a deeper understanding of whether industrial and academic views on using design patterns evolved accordingly.

While significant attention has been given to various aspects of design patterns like detection, verification, and evolution, fewer studies focus on the understanding and use of design patterns in a practice of developing complex software systems, like software for modern vehicles. Previous industrial studies, e.g., [4,15], focused mainly on technical aspects of the use of design patterns, such as evolution over time or new languages. Other studies have a different focus but are relatively dated. For example, Beck et al. [1] explored the implementation of design patterns in real-world industrial settings in the early 1990's, highlighting the benefits and best practices associated with their usage. In addition, most studies do not focus specifically on the automotive domain. In one exception, Mirning et al. [11] on automotive design pattern use, but with a specific focus on user experience design patterns.

The automotive industry poses specific design challenges, such as safety, reliability, and scalability, which require specialized design solutions. These challenges call for using reusable patterns in order to facilitate better communication and understanding of the software design (and architecture). Therefore, understanding how professionals in this domain perceive and utilize design patterns is important for guiding the introduction of design patterns in software designs. By examining the perspectives of architects and developers in the automotive domain, we gain valuable insights into the use of design patterns, helping to identify differences in how industry and academia understand, define, use, and evaluate design patterns.

Our primary objective in this study is to present insights into the understanding and usage of design patterns in the automotive domain, with the focus on automotive companies in Sweden. Through this study, we explore the characteristics and challenges associated with designing automotive software. We conducted an interview study with ten architects and developers within three automotive companies who work in several hierarchical levels: complete vehicle architecture, subsystem architecture and detailed software design [17]. The thematic coding and transcripts of the study can be found here[1].

Our study revealed a notable difference between the academic view of design patterns and the practitioners' view on design patterns. While the existing literature provides a clear definition, industry experts in this domain demonstrate a nuanced and context-specific utilization of these patterns. Their definition and application of the concept of a design pattern is much broader than the academic one. Architects guide design reviews, meetings, and adherence to specific guidelines. The implementation of design patterns is subject to restrictions and constraints, such as limitations from standards such as Autosar and client demands. Design patterns can be validated through manual reviews and code-checking tools, but the effectiveness of these techniques for design pattern validation is uncertain. Our study targets both professionals in the automotive industry and academic researchers, providing practical insights into design patterns usage and understanding in practice, particularly for automotive software.

In this study, we address the following research questions:

---

[1] https://figshare.com/s/b09da53fb12c8e202463.

RQ-1: *How do software architects/engineers in automotive systems understand and use design patterns?*
RQ-2: *How is design pattern guidance given?*
RQ-3: *What level of freedom or autonomy exists when using design patterns?*
RQ-4: *How are design patterns detected/validated?*
RQ-5: *What constitutes a good quality design pattern?*

The paper is organized as follows: Sect. 2 discusses related work, followed by Sect. 3 which presents the methodology. Section 4 reports the study results, and Sect. 4.6 provides a discussion and analysis. Furthermore, Sect. 5 explores the threats to validity, and finally, Sect. 6 concludes the work and discusses future directions.

2   Related Work

Our related work is organized into two parts – technical advances in design patterns (specification, selection, and recognition), and studies of the industrial use of the design patterns.

2.1   Technical Advances in Design Patterns

One of the main ways of detecting design patterns today is to use variations of pattern matching. For example, Tsantali et al. [18] developed a method for detecting design patterns using similarity scoring. They applied their approach to three open-source projects and successfully identified patterns, even in modified versions. Their method demonstrated recall rates ranging from 66.6% to 100%. In a recent study, Xiong et al. [20] introduced a method for detecting design patterns using static analysis and inference techniques. They applied their approach to prototype design patterns from five open-source projects. Their proposed method exhibited improved accuracy, with higher precision (85.7%) and recall (93.8%). All of the above studies focus on the classical GoF patterns.

Nicholson et al. [13] examined design pattern verification, specifically in Java's awt package, utilizing Codecharts for specifying and verifying the *Composite* design pattern. They highlighted the availability of tools for modeling design patterns. Additionally, Blewitt et al. [3] proposed Spine as a verification method for design patterns in evolving Java systems, addressing the absence of formal specifications by considering implementation constraints.

Khawaja et al. [9] conducted a survey and comparative analysis of various design pattern specification languages. They categorized the languages used to specify design pattern (e.g., Java, C++) into different groups and evaluated their strengths and weaknesses. The authors provided an overview of the available tools associated with these languages. They highlighted several unresolved issues that require further investigation in design pattern specification languages.

Parthasarathy et al. [14], who conducted an industrial study on design pattern detection. They employed a pre-trained programming language model

(PLM) and industrial design patterns, specifically controller and handler patterns. Their findings indicated that PLM models could be valuable tools for architects and developers in assessing and addressing violations in automotive software design. The pattern detected is a variation of the GoF publisher-subscriber pattern.

Mayvan et al. [10] provided an extensive overview of research efforts in the field of design patterns. Their study identified research topics, quantified research emphasis, and described research demographics. Through a systematic mapping study of 637 papers, they identified six distinct research topics, with Pattern Development, Pattern Mining, and Pattern Usage emerging as the most active areas in design patterns research. In a recent study, Neghdipour et al. [12] conducted a literature review on design pattern selection. They classified and analysed various approaches, offering criteria for comparison. The study identified key elements, including open issues and available data sets.

While prior research in this area has significantly contributed to automating the process of identifying and applying design patterns, our study engages in qualitative interviews with software professionals in the automotive industry to understand how patterns are perceived and applied in practice.

2.2   Industrial Studies of Design Patterns

In addition to technical advances in design patterns, previous work has looked how design patterns are used in industry. A study by Mirnig et al. [11] focused on user experience design patterns and their applications in the automotive industry. They explored eight newly generated user experience design pattern.

Beck et al. [1] underscored the significance of design patterns in software engineering. They highlighted how design patterns serve as a means of effective communication among designers and as a documentation tool for best practices. Drawing from their collective industrial experiences, the authors described practical experiences in particular design patterns.

In an industrial case study by Bieman et al. [2], 39 versions of an object-oriented system were analyzed to explore the relationship between design patterns, design attributes, and changes. Surprisingly, classes involved in design patterns were found to be highly change-prone, challenging the belief that they are less prone to change.

Bloom et al. [4] explored commonly used I/O design patterns in the IoT industry, specifically focusing on communication protocols and identifying prevalent design patterns for IoT applications. Additionally, Feitosa et al. [7] conducted an industrial case study on the accumulation of pattern grime in GoF design patterns. They found a linear relationship between grime accumulation, pattern type, and developer.

Riehle et al. [15] shared their experiences with design patterns in industry projects, highlighting the advantages of using patterns in software design. They propose the development of a customized design language, along with strategies to encourage use and educate developers on the language. Although related to this study, none of these previous works examine how the general concept of design patterns are understood and use in modern, complex, automotive systems.

In contrast to previous studies, our investigation provides an interview study with qualitative analysis that focuses on design pattern use and understanding in practice, specifically covering the automotive domain. We reported five themes and eighteen codes during our qualitative analysis.

3 Methodology

We opted for a qualitative interview study to address our research questions and gain insights into design patterns in autonomous industries as we wanted to gain insight and understanding of the practice, rather than to study the static use of design patterns (e.g., through repository mining). Our study adhered to the empirical standard set by ACM SIGSOFT Empirical Standard for qualitative surveys[2]. Our study was conducted in collaboration with industry, we had three industrial partners from two automotive companies. These partners were expert architects and software designers who could provide us with detailed knowledge of the practice of software design in the automotive domain, and could direct us to qualified and representative interviewees.

Sampling. We aimed to select interviewees with relevant design pattern experience in software development within the automotive domain. We first received suggestions from our industrial partners regarding potential interview candidates. Then, we snowballed over these participants, asking them to recommend further participants. We also contacted engineers and architects in other automotive companies through our professional network. Ultimately, we conducted ten interviews for this study covering three automotive companies.

Table 1. Demographic information of all interviewees.

ID	Role	Company	Exp. (year)	Programming Language	Level of design (application/-platform)	Responsibilities or Expertise
P_1	Software engineer	C_3	10	C, C++	Platform level	General engineer, designer
P_2	Senior Principal SE engineer	C_1	19	C, python	Both	Infrastructure, designer
P_3	Software architect	C_1	17	Python, C, C++	Platform level	High performance computing, image annotation & segmentation
P_4	Product manager	C_1	13	C, C++, Java	Both	Designer & architecture
P_5	Architect for Software HPC	C_1	16	Python, C++	Platform level	Software design & development
P_6	Solution architect	C_1	29	C, Python, C++	Platform level	Software architect & team lead
P_7	Software Architect at solution level	C_1	15	Python, C, C++, Java, Simulink	Vehicle level	architect work related with task forces.
P_8	Software engineer	C_3	6	Python, C, C++	Application level	Embedded software systems
P_9	Specialist research engineer	C_2	18	C, PROLOG, C++	Both	Software architecture, safety, & development process
P_{10}	System architect	C_1	24	C, Python, C++, Java, tool language	Platform level	Active safety, infotainment, & connectivity

---

[2] tinyurl.com/QualitativeSurveys.

Table 2. Mapping of interview questions to research questions.

Interview Questions	Research Questions
Q1. Demographic questions	N/A
Q2. What role do you play in the company?	N/A
Q3. How many years have you had your role? What is your general experience with software development and architecture?	N/A
Design pattern related questions	-
Q4. How would you define a design pattern in general? And in automotive code?	RQ-1
Q5. To what extent do you use design patterns? In addition to the design pattern, is your design based on some other principles? If yes, then what are those principles?	RQ-1
Q6. How do you prescribe using design patterns to your designers/constructors?	RQ-2
Q7. How do you recognize design patterns in any code? Your code? Other's code?	RQ-4
Q8. How do you validate that you/your organization followed the prescribed design patterns? Q8.1. How do you judge the similarities between the design pattern's skeleton code and the code that implements/instantiates the design pattern?	RQ-1, RQ-2, RQ-4
Q9. Which categories of design pattern do you follow, e.g., GoF, ML-based design patterns, Secure programming design patterns, Safety related design patterns? Q9.1. Which Autosar design patterns do you use generally? Where in the system do you use those?	RQ-1
Q10. At which design/system level do you use design patterns?	RQ-1, RQ-3, RQ-5
Q11. Can you give some examples of design patterns in your system or components?	RQ-1
Q12. Do you want to add any additional comments based on all these questions?	Any

Table 1 shows the demographic information of our interview participants. These interviewees involved individuals with varying roles, seniority, and expertise from companies C_1 to C_3. The interviews took place from October to December 2022 and lasted between 30 and 40 min. Nine interviews were conducted in person, one was conducted online. We used Microsoft Teams to record the in-person interviews and collect transcripts. Prior permission was obtained from the interviewees to record the sessions. Afterward, all interviews were transcribed and anonymized for further analysis. No personal data was collected and stored in this study.

Data Collection. We conducted semi-structured interviews using a specific set of open-ended questions. The interview questions we asked were divided into two main categories, as shown in Table 2. To begin, we provided a brief introduction to our project to the participants. We initiated the interview by gathering demographic information and learning about the participants' professional backgrounds (Q1 to Q3). The second category of questions was centered around design patterns (Q4 to Q12). Some of these questions included examples to provide clarity on the nature of the questions.

Data Analysis. To analyze the qualitative data, we employed a thematic analysis method [16]. Our approach involved a combination of deductive (top-down) and inductive (bottom-up) coding techniques. Initially, we developed high-level codes based on the interview questions and added further codes as we examined the interview transcripts [6]. For the coding process, three authors coded together for the first four participants and collectively validated the codes. Subsequently, the remaining six participants' coding was carried out by two authors, who then sent their coding to the third author for validation. To ensure consistency, three authors validated all the codes twice, increasing consistency.

Additionally, we organized a workshop with our three industrial partners. During the workshop, we shared high-level summaries of our findings, collecting impressions. Our industrial partners generally agreed with our findings regarding design patterns in the automotive industry.

4 Results

In this section, we describe our thematic coding results, giving insights to the state of practice in design pattern understanding and use in the automotive industry. An overview of our themes and codes is shown in Fig. 1. Here, codes refer to findings at the lowest level, while themes are a high-level summary of codes. We summarize the results by themes; these themes address our RQs.

4.1 Design Pattern Usage

Codes within the design pattern usage theme include design pattern definition, design pattern in context, design pattern examples, extent used, and automotive. We will summarize these codes in the following. Codes under this theme address RQ1 - design pattern understanding and usage.

Design Pattern Definition. All of our participants gave us a definition of design patterns. Although most definitions (8/10) were consistent with the academic understanding (e.g., Gamma et al. [8]), they provided definitions which covered wider aspects, including documentation, quality aspects, component responsibility, and matching problems to solutions.

"A design pattern that is a common solution, I would say, to a common problem. So we have a design pattern to solve this in a similar way." -**P**$_5$

Others struggled to give a definition, likely due to implicitly using design patterns through related concepts like architectural patterns or tactics.

"We usually talk about architecture and, not so much, design patterns, maybe. And, we do, I mean. When it comes to code formatting, we run tools for C++. ... Maybe that's a design pattern in source." -**P**$_2$

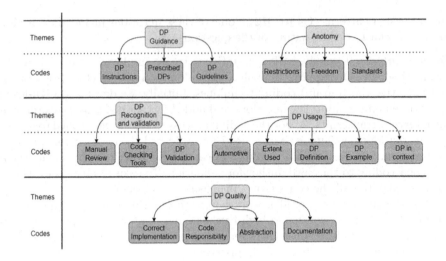

Fig. 1. Overview of Codes/Themes

Design Patterns in Context. As part of our interview questions, we asked several questions about the categories, level, domain, or components in which the design pattern was used. Interviewees provided a wide variety of responses, as it was difficult to differentiate between design pattern categories, domain, and level. Thus, we present these findings together under "context".

When asked about categories, domain or levels, some interviewees gave specific pattern examples, e.g., Simulink patterns, GoF patterns, while some mentioned security patterns, or brought up safety as a domain, with specific patterns. Others focused on layered architecture, or components, or areas. Many participants said that design patterns could be found everywhere. At least half of the participants brought up that the use and needs for design pattern in different areas and level varies. For example:

"For me, it (a pattern) can be all over the place, so it can be component or domain, due to the level of integration of functionality in a single system. So there may be a single system that has perhaps a single function, so maybe a simple embedded computer, to maybe control windshield wipers or a much more complex rich single system that controls multiple other subsystems of the car."- **P₃**

"All levels, but depends on the pattern and depends on the principle."- **P₄**

Design Pattern Examples. During the interviews, participants mentioned several patterns, but the majority of these patterns were not the GoF patterns as are typically studied in academia. Only two participants mentioned GoF patterns explicitly, for example:

"I guess we have used a lot of the design patterns from GoF previously, for example, design patterns that you can read about in books and things. I mean observer, factory, everything. I think it's always a good way; I mean have some

kind of knowledge about common ways of solving problems, but usually, I have not worked with that strictly..."- P_5

Other examples included architecture-like patterns exemplified by Model-View-Controller (MVC), controller–handler, and client–server. Further examples focused on specific frameworks like Autosar patterns, and Simulink patterns. One participant mentioned Android- and Linux-based patterns. Others mentioned general patterns like communication patterns and safety/redundancy patterns.

We can see through these examples that participants use a variety of patterns which are not limited to structured code, but also include aspects of architecture, design frameworks (e.g., Autosar, Simulink), purposive patterns (e.g., communication, redundancy) and operating systems.

Extent Used. The participants' responses revealed a diverse range of design pattern usage. Four out of 10 participants reported not using design patterns directly, these were three software architects and one software engineer. Amongst the six others, two define or advice on the use of design patterns for other teams. These participants hold more senior positions. One participant limited their usage to the patterns defined within the Autosar standard, while three others described usage beyond Autosar.

Amongst these three, one participant employed design patterns by constructing their own patterns, similar to the existing patterns, and used design patterns daily. Notably, five out of 10 participants focused more on architecture and principles than design patterns in their software development practices.

Automotive. In this code, we explored the differences in design patterns in the automotive industry compared to traditional academic definitions. While three participants stated that the definition of design patterns remains the same, the other participants gave reasons why design pattern use in automotive was unique compared to the standard use. The unique characteristics of the automotive industry include standardization (e.g., Autosar, ISO 26262), layered architecture, resource allocation challenges, adherence to MISRA[3] standards, and safety regulations.

Additionally, it was noted that one participant mentioned that certain design patterns may not be compatible with MISRA standards.

RQ-1 Summary: Software architects/developers in the automotive industry have a wider understanding of design patterns compared to academics/scholars. The usage and understanding is tightly interwoven with architecting, following design principles, frameworks, and standards. Most of the examples mentioned by the practitioners are not classical GoF, yet still follow the essential definition of a design pattern – reusable solutions to common software design problems.

4.2   Design Pattern Guidance

This theme covers our findings describing the guidance and instructions given to developers regarding design pattern use and answers RQ-2. The codes within

---

[3] https://www.misra.org.uk/.

this theme include prescribed design patterns, design pattern instruction, and design pattern guidelines, as depicted in Fig. 1.

Prescribed Design Patterns. This code focuses on design patterns that are prescribed, and mandatory to use in some way. Nine out of 10 participants mentioned this code. According to the interviewees, design patterns are not explicitly prescribed but can be implicitly recommended, for example, redundancy patterns. One participant mentioned that well-established patterns might be prescribed within a logical architecture.

"The overall logical architecture is something that has been discussed and defined by a whole range of people are so part of the solution. [...] And those people working in that have discussed the different patterns, which patterns to use, and which cases. So it's fairly well established which patterns to use in which cases."- P_6.

Two interviewees stated that architects decide whether, or which, design patterns to use. One participated said that the use of the design patterns is even mandatory and prescribed by customer requirements.

Although design patterns are not typically prescribed, architectures and developers have specific design guidelines (not necessarily design patterns) that they share. Participants often mention guidelines and documents, but typically the focus is on architectural or modeling guidelines, e.g., from Simulink, and not on design patterns.

Four participants emphasized the importance of code, design, and architecture reviews as a means to follow up on the prescribed practices, but typically the focus of these reviews was not on design patterns explicitly.

Design Pattern Instructions. This code refers to active instruction about design pattern usage. Half of the interviewees made comments classified under this code. Two interviewees (architects) mentioned that architects are responsible for implementing design patterns. Another interviewee, a software engineer, typically does not instruct team members about design patterns. One interviewee, also an engineer, instead talked about having reusable building blocks of software code that developers are instructed to use.

Design Pattern Guidelines. This code captures information about guidelines covering the usage of design patterns. Nine out of 10 interviewees provided information for this code. The interviewees have guidelines to follow, but it is not always clear whether these guidelines require applying design patterns or not. The guidelines, for example, can be about C++ or source code structure, which is related to the use of design patterns, but does not have to use design patterns. P_2 stated in the following paragraph during the interview:

"Basically and then we have guidelines on, How big the functions should be? You know how they should be designed, we have design for classic C, which I worked with when I was a programmer here, [...] We have design documents like 500 pages, which describe how to design things, and we also measured the complexity, and we measured how many data flow you have in a certain function;

we measured those to see [how] could they be broken in better pieces and so have used the Halstead volume for those."-**P**$_2$

One participant mentioned the importance of adhering to and conforming to design patterns during the implementation of the design.

"We find that there is a need for design pattern adherence and conformity at a large scale; due to the different levels of maturity, it can appear as if there are very disparate ways of writing software and systems that may not be that far apart from each other. The methods of development can be very different."- **P**$_3$.

Five participants mention either the use of design pattern guidelines or following a specific design pattern, but given the broad interpretation of design patterns, these participants could be referring to related guidelines. One participant mentioned that design pattern guidelines vary depending on the area. Another interviewee emphasized the need for effective communication between pattern definition and usage across organizations (areas).

"The tricky part [...] is that the organization defining the patterns, like, my organization, needs very tight collaboration with the ones implementing the patterns if we really want them to be followed. So more is needed to look into the measurement results in the end; we need to be there and guide constantly; otherwise, the patterns will be misunderstood."- **P**$_4$

Another participant mentioned that they regularly organize meetings/workshops to guide and suggest implementing patterns and principles. Additionally, one interviewee mentioned the challenge of ensuring that the software developers keep themselves updated about the guidelines.

RQ-2 Summary: Although a selection of design patterns is recommended and guidelines for their implementation are provided, the focus is on implementation, software construction, design, and architecture guidance, rather than explicit usage of the design patterns.

4.3 Autonomy

This theme covers three codes: restrictions, freedom, and standards for implementing design patterns in the automotive industry. It addresses RQ-3.

Restrictions. This code came up in nine interviews. Architects and developers need to consider technical constraints during product development. These limitations primarily involve program code and library selection in C++, which are not directly associated with the design patterns. Two participants mentioned mandatory use of Autosar, due to high-level architectural decisions, and one participant described Autosar-associated patterns that must be used because of this constraint. P$_1$ stated the following statement about this constraint.

"I mean, it comes from a customer. We are requested to use Autosar. So, I don't think there is much option in the project I am involved in... I have always been a supplier, so there is always been requirements of architecture or what type of platform we should use in the project." -P$_1$

One interviewee emphasized the constraints related to domain-specific factors, such as embedded systems, ISO standards, and restrictions originating from suppliers. However, it was not clear in the interview how strongly these constraints related to design patterns. Further investigations should follow up on this point. Other participants mentioned other restrictions such as environments, domains, and compatibility with MISRA.

Freedom. Four interviewees brought up this code, concerning freedom in design pattern use. One participant highlighted the flexibility of using design patterns to fulfill requirements. Another interviewee said that architects are responsible for freely choosing and employing design patterns.

Standards. The interviews' findings highlighted the significance of standards in software development, with all participants mentioning at least one standard and the majority (9) explicitly mentioning Autosar. MISRA, ISO, and ISO safety, also came up in the interviews. Simulink was mentioned often as a standard, even though it is a modeling language, as it is a de-facto standard way of modeling/implementing control systems in the automotive industry [17]. Although the relationship between design patterns and these standards was not always expressed explicitly, it shows that design patterns are considered to be much wider than the GoF design patterns. Autosar was identified as having design patterns as part of the standard, even though these are not called design patterns in the text of the standard.

"Autosar has that sender-receiver and other type of design pattern. We use adaptive Autosar, which is a service-oriented pattern where you have services and users of those services. "-P_1.

One participant mentioned using design patterns from MISRA, while another participant mentioned conflicts between the MISRA standard and design patterns. This suggests that while design patterns are sometimes prescribed within the standards, there are situations where conflicts arise if two (or more) standards need to be followed simultaneously.

"That's only for C++, for C we use a lot of them (design patterns) such as MISRA standards that old ones 2018, 2008. Yeah, I think MISRA is some kind of British organization, they have formed design patterns for security clusters software and we adhere to most of those. "-P_2.

"Some design patterns are not compatible with MISRA guidelines, it's a way to write software code too, you're not allowed to do certain things, in the C language, for example in MISRA, to prevent buggy code. "-P_8.

> **RQ-3 Summary:** The level of freedom in implementing design patterns in the automotive industry varies, with architects having a lot of flexibility that allows them to use design patterns and prescribe their use in detailed design and implementation. A prominent example of this is the use of design patterns from the Autosar standard.

4.4   Design Pattern Recognition and Validation

This theme is related to the recognition or validation of design patterns and will address RQ-4. Manual review, code-checking tools, and design pattern validation are included codes.

Manual Review. This code was mentioned by nine interviewees. Seven participants mentioned that a manual review of design patterns is possible, but it is not clear how frequently this occurs. The others mentioned reviews for source code, quality, or guidelines. Two participants expressed a desire for tools to aid in identifying design patterns if they are not explicitly documented in the design, as manual processes for identifying them can be challenging and time-consuming. One participant also mentioned the need for traceability and deep source code analysis. Two of the participants acknowledged the difficulty of manual reviews and thought that no one would do a deep dive into the source code because of the relation between the size of the code base (tens of millions of lines of code) and the time allotted. One interviewee described manual monitoring of the application of design patterns as follows:

"I don't think we will really check those patterns from my team, [...], but the teams who are developing the functionalities may have a review. So they will have a [source] code review also design reviews."-P_4

Code Checking Tools. This code came up in six interviews. Participants mentioned tools to monitor following good programming practices in source code, including the static analysis tool Clang, Google's coding guidelines, and a tool from MathWorks. Metrics were mentioned for monitoring source code quality, indirectly indicating whether or not design patterns were used correctly. Two participants expressed interest in a dedicated tool for detecting design patterns.

Design Pattern Validation. All interviewees made statements classified under this code. Answers varied, some interviewees did not try to recognize or validate design patterns as part of their role, while others could look manually, and others recommended using tools or metrics. Two participants emphasized that verifying that the source code follows the intended design pattern is difficult to do manually, and this task requires experience. It also requires that the design pattern is somehow explicitly prescribed and that its usage is documented in the source code. Two participants recognized documentation as important for the validation of the use of design patterns. The manual verification is performed during the architecture reviews.

Although tools were mentioned, current tools are not explicitly intended for identifying or validating design patterns, but rather for validating source code quality. One participant said that design patterns were regarded as sources of inspiration rather than used as strict rules, which is aligned with the original intent of the GoF design patterns. At the same time, interviewees mentioned that Autosar prescribes the usage of certain patterns, for example for inter-process communication.

RQ-4 Summary: Design patterns in the automotive industry are detected/validated through manual reviews and the use of these techniques varies. Tools and metrics are used but are not explicitly intended for the detection of design patterns. Tools (or functions in the existing tools) for detecting design patterns would be a desirable help. Since the classical design patterns can be seen as an inspiration, not strict rules, the validation of their usage is often considered optional.

4.5   Design Pattern Quality

This theme focuses on the quality of design patterns, which can help to produce high-quality software, and addresses RQ-5. It contains the codes: correct implementation, source code responsibility, abstraction, and documentation.

Correct Implementation. During the interviews, nine interviewees mentioned the correctness of the implementation, but many statements were not specific to design patterns. Most interviewees were concerned about the correct implementation of design, architecture, functions, and source code, but were less concerned about the correctness of the actual design patterns. Guidelines were frequently mentioned, and following them was seen as a way to achieve high-quality software. One participant underlined the importance of source code adhering to requirements and maintaining traceability. One participant mentioned that some areas needed more education on design patterns.

"I would say that the level at which we're working with design patterns may vary depending on where it looks. Some teams are extremely experienced with software development, and some teams are at the opposite end. But in general, we are still in a phase where [...] education about software development, software architecture, and design patterns would take us [...] forward."-P_6

Source Code Responsibility. Six interviewees mentioned source code responsibility as part of design pattern use. This describes which role the source code plays in the design pattern, or what it is responsible for. For example, one component can be recognized as a director, while another can be recognized as a builder in the builder pattern. Two participants mention source code responsibility as a way to detect the design patterns – detecting patterns by matching to expected roles in a design pattern. One participant highlighted the source code responsibility in the definition of design patterns, i.e. design patterns are about defining responsibilities for code.

One participant said that the code should be aligned with the requirements. However, two participants placed more emphasis on defining the general functionality of code rather than responsibility in terms of design pattern.

Abstraction. Five interviews mentioned abstraction levels of the design to be important for design patterns. One participant said they could recognize design patterns by recognizing the abstraction level of their design. Two more participants mentioned layered architecture, with P_7 describing different design patterns in different abstraction layers.

" We have system design patterns; that is one thing. We have layered architecture from spot two; we have hardware components beneath; we have the controlling software and stuff like that. So that, of course, is a system design pattern. Then beneath that, you are within the processing system, then you have some software and application layer. So that's usually, we have the design patterns within each module."-P_7

Another participant described hardware abstraction layers as rules for design patterns, making a similar point, that rules restrict which design patterns appear at which abstraction levels.

Documentation. Six participants brought up this code. Two participants said that documentation, e.g., of architectural frameworks, prescribe design patterns usage in some way. One participant saw documentation as a valuable resource for validating design patterns, and another saw architecture documentation and code comments as a way to recognize design patterns.

"But of course you can have good comments in the [source] code. Yeah, in the beginning of something from the module they could say this is the model part of the model view controller."-P_{10}

The other two participants mentioned documentation, but not specifically for design patterns. As few participants spoke about design pattern-specific documentation, design pattern-specific documentation may be limited.

> **RQ-5 Summary: Quality of source code, architecture, and design are very important to our participants, but as part of an emphasis on quality, design patterns are not the main focus.**

4.6   Discussion

RQ-1: Design Pattern Understanding and Use. Our interview study finds that design pattern understanding is nuanced, with varying definitions. Design pattern understanding is tightly related to architecture, design principles, frameworks, and standards. We note that when design patterns are taught in educational settings or investigated in research, they are often considered in isolation. While in reality, it is hard to separate design patterns from architecture tactics, design principles, and standards like Autosar or MISRA. Existing design pattern studies overlook this combination of design patterns with other elements in practice.

We find that automotive developers and architects do not typically use GoF patterns, but instead use their own domain- or area-specific patterns. Thus, design pattern studies should focus more on non-classical and flexible patterns. In the automotive domain, we need to study the use of Autosar patterns, and treat MISRA guidelines as design patterns.

The automotive industry has unique characteristics such as resource constraints which affect design pattern use. Although a few papers focus in the automotive domain [11], most studies are domain-independent. Although our study focused on the automotive industry, findings may generalize to other industries with embedded source code and similar characteristics. The effect of domain characteristics on design pattern use should be further investigated.

RQ-2: Design Pattern Guidance. Our study finds that design pattern-specific guidance is limited, and most design pattern guidance is part of artifacts that are intended mainly for other purposes, such as programming, detailed design and architecture guidance, or standards and frameworks (Autosar, MISRA, ISO 26262). It is not clear if industry should have guidance that focuses only on design patterns, or if design patterns guidance as part of other frameworks initiatives is the best option. However, if design pattern guidance is embedded as part of more general artifacts, there should be some initiative to ensure that design patterns are sufficiently covered in these other sources. We are unable to find studies that have findings related to design pattern guidance in practice.

RQ-3: Design Pattern Autonomy. We found a varied level of freedom in design pattern usage in our interviews. Generally, there is a lot of room for flexibility, with restrictions placed via internal architectures or standards such as Autosar. Existing empirical design pattern studies do not typically cover design pattern autonomy in practice, so we do not know if these results are unique or typical.

It is not clear if there should be more restrictions or autonomy in practice. Adherence to design patterns has been identified by our industrial partners as desirable; however, currently, they are able to produce high-quality products with this level of design pattern freedom. Therefore, this raises the question of the importance of design patterns in practice in the automotive domain – maybe they are not as important in practice as the scholarly literature suggests.

RQ-4: Design Pattern Detection and Validation. Techniques for design pattern detection and validation vary, from manual reviews, to use of non-design pattern-specific tooling and metrics. Some participants expressed a desire for tooling to detect design pattern conformance. Much work has been proposed for this purpose, e.g., Xion et al. [20] and Nocholson et al. [13], but typically focuses on GoF patterns. This work may have limited applicability in the context of our study. We believe our results in terms of design patterns used may generalize to other areas, but further studies must be conducted to understand the level of classical GoF pattern use in practice.

RQ-5: Design Pattern Quality. Our interviewees and their companies place much effort on quality, particularly of the source code, architecture, and design. However, not as much effort is placed specifically design pattern quality, which, given the successful software development in the companies, raises important questions of the importance of the explicit role of design patterns in software quality assessments (e.g., as prescribed by ISO 25040).

In addition, most existing studies focus on design pattern detection in a binary way (yes/no), but not explicitly on evaluating design pattern's implementation quality. Future studies could focus more on improving the quality of design pattern, rather than detecting their presence.

5   Threats to Validity

We assess the threats to validity of our study as per Wohlin et al. [19].

Construct Validity. We observed that questions concerning design pattern categories and design/system level were difficult for the interviewees to answer, giving us a wide variety of results. However, we chose to keep these questions in our analysis as the data collected shows the diversity in design pattern use and understanding. We made efforts to use commonly understood terminology as part of our interviews; however, interviewees roles and experiences were varied, so there may have been differing interpretations of terms. Additionally, we acknowledge that the differing interpretations of design patterns between practitioners and academics may threaten construct validity. However, uncovering these differing interpretations was a core motivation for this work, and we believe our results highlight some of these differences.

External Validity. As our study focused on the automotive industry, thus, we cannot claim generalization of our findings to other industries. Although we were able to collect data from multiple companies (three), we cannot generalize our findings to other automotive organizations because of the geographical location of our study. Furthermore, a small sample size (10 participants) may restrict the generalizability of our findings. To mitigate this, we tried to selected interviewees (architects/developers) of different levels and organizations to capture a holistic perspective of an organization, not a specific role.

Internal Validity. Interviews were recorded and transcribed to increase accurate data collection. We analyzed the interviews using thematic coding, which raises standard internal validity threats. However, we tried to increase the reliability of our analysis by including three coders, by reaching a consensus on codes by coding 40% of the interviews together, and then by having the third coder independently check the remaining 60%. All codes were reviewed in at least two iterations as part of merging codes and developing themes.

6   Conclusion and Future Work

In this study, we aimed to gain an understanding of software design pattern use in the automotive industry. The interviews with ten industry professionals across three automotive industries reveal the diverse definitions and contexts in which design patterns are used. We found that although participants focused on software product quality, there as often not a clear and consistent focus on design pattern guidance and usage. The classical GoF design patterns are often not applicable in this domain and the focus is on domain-specific design patterns, for example, those prescribed by the Autosar (and similar) standards. For future research, we recommend a focus on the combination of design pattern, architecture and standards, as well as the detection and quality evaluation of non-classical design patterns. In our next steps, we are focusing on tooling for design pattern detection that works with non-classical industry-defined design patterns.

Acknowledgement. This study was financed by the CHAIR (Chalmers AI Research Center) project "T4AI", Vinnova, Software Center, Volvo Cars, AB Volvo Chalmers, and the University of Gothenburg, Sweden.

References

1. Beck, K., et al.: Industrial experience with design patterns. In: Proceedings of IEEE 18th International Conference on Software Engineering, pp. 103–114. IEEE (1996)
2. Bieman, J.M., Jain, D., Yang, H.J.: OO design patterns, design structure, and program changes: an industrial case study. In: Proceedings IEEE International Conference on Software Maintenance. ICSM 2001, pp. 580–589. IEEE (2001)
3. Blewitt, A., Bundy, A., Stark, I.: Automatic verification of design patterns in java. In: Proceedings of the 20th IEEE/ACM International Conference on Automated Software Engineering, pp. 224–232 (2005)
4. Bloom, G., Alsulami, B., Nwafor, E., Bertolotti, I.C.: Design patterns for the industrial internet of things. In: 2018 14th IEEE International Workshop on Factory Communication Systems (WFCS), pp. 1–10. IEEE (2018)
5. Broy, M.: Challenges in automotive software engineering. In: Proceedings of the 28th International Conference on Software Engineering, pp. 33–42 (2006)
6. Creswell, J.W., Creswell, J.D.: Research Design: Qualitative, Quantitative, and Mixed Methods Approaches. Sage Publications, Thousand Oaks (2017)
7. Feitosa, D., Avgeriou, P., Ampatzoglou, A., Nakagawa, E.Y.: The Evolution of Design Pattern Grime: An Industrial Case Study. In: Felderer, M., Méndez Fernández, D., Turhan, B., Kalinowski, M., Sarro, F., Winkler, D. (eds.) PROFES 2017. LNCS, vol. 10611, pp. 165–181. Springer, Cham (2017). https://doi.org/10.1007/978-3-319-69926-4_13
8. Gamma, E., Helm, R., Johnson, R., Johnson, R.E., Vlissides, J.: Design Patterns: Elements of Reusable Object-oriented Software. Pearson Deutschland GmbH (1995)
9. Khwaja, S., Alshayeb, M.: Survey on software design-pattern specification languages. ACM Comput. Surv. (CSUR) **49**(1), 1–35 (2016)
10. Mayvan, B.B., Rasoolzadegan, A., Yazdi, Z.G.: The state of the art on design patterns: a systematic mapping of the literature. J. Syst. Softw. **125**, 93–118 (2017)
11. Mirnig, A., et al.: Automotive user experience design patterns: an approach and pattern examples. Int. J. Adv. Intell. Syst **9**, 275–286 (2016)
12. Naghdipour, A., Hasheminejad, S.M.H., Barmaki, R.L.: Software design pattern selection approaches: a systematic literature review. Softw. Pract. Experience **53**(4), 1091–1122 (2023)
13. Nicholson, J., Eden, A.H., Gasparis, E., Kazman, R.: Automated verification of design patterns: a case study. Sci. Comput. Program. **80**, 211–222 (2014)
14. Parthasarathy, D., Ekelin, C., Karri, A., Sun, J., Moraitis, P.: Measuring design compliance using neural language models: an automotive case study. In: Proceedings of the 18th International Conference on Predictive Models and Data Analytics in Software Engineering, pp. 12–21 (2022)
15. Riehle, D.: Lessons learned from using design patterns in industry projects. In: Noble, J., Johnson, R., Avgeriou, P., Harrison, N.B., Zdun, U. (eds.) Transactions on Pattern Languages of Programming II. LNCS, vol. 6510, pp. 1–15. Springer, Heidelberg (2011). https://doi.org/10.1007/978-3-642-19432-0_1
16. Runeson, P., Höst, M.: Guidelines for conducting and reporting case study research in software engineering. Empir. Softw. Eng. **14**, 131–164 (2009)
17. Staron, M.: Automotive Software Architectures. Springer, Cham (2021). https://doi.org/10.1007/978-3-030-65939-4

18. Tsantalis, N., Chatzigeorgiou, A., Stephanides, G., Halkidis, S.T.: Design pattern detection using similarity scoring. IEEE Trans. Softw. Eng. **32**(11), 896–909 (2006)
19. Wohlin, C., Runeson, P., Höst, M., Ohlsson, M.C., Regnell, B., Wesslén, A.: Experimentation in software engineering. Springer, Heidelberg (2012). https://doi.org/10.1007/978-3-642-29044-2
20. Xiong, R., Li, B.: Accurate design pattern detection based on idiomatic implementation matching in java language context. In: 2019 IEEE 26th International Conference on Software Analysis, Evolution and Reengineering (SANER), pp. 163–174. IEEE (2019)

Software Testing and Quality Assurance

An Experience in the Evaluation of Fault Prediction

Luigi Lavazza$^{(\boxtimes)}$, Sandro Morasca , and Gabriele Rotoloni

Università degli Studi dell'Insubria, 21100 Varese, Italy
{luigi.lavazza,sandro.morasca,grotoloni}@uninsubria.it

Abstract. *Background.* ROC (Receiver Operating Characteristic) curves are widely used to represent the performance (i.e., degree of correctness) of fault proneness models. *AUC*, the Area Under the ROC Curve is a quite popular performance metric, which summarizes into a single number the goodness of the predictions represented by the ROC curve. Alternative techniques have been proposed for evaluating the performance represented by a ROC curve: among these are *RRA* (Ratio of Relevant Areas) and ϕ (alias Matthews Correlation Coefficient).

Objectives. In this paper, we aim at evaluating *AUC* as a performance metric, also with respect to alternative proposals.

Method. We carry out an empirical study by replicating a previously published fault prediction study and measuring the performance of the obtained faultiness models using *AUC*, *RRA*, and a recently proposed way of relating a specific kind of ROC curves to ϕ, based on iso-ϕ ROC curves, i.e., ROC curves with constant ϕ. We take into account prevalence, i.e., the proportion of faulty modules in the dataset that is the object of predictions.

Results. *AUC* appears to provide indications that are concordant with ϕ for fairly balanced datasets, while it is much more optimistic than ϕ for quite imbalanced datasets. *RRA*'s indications appear to be moderately affected by the degree of balance in a dataset. In addition, *RRA* appears to agree with ϕ.

Conclusions. Based on the collected evidence, *AUC* does not seem to be suitable for evaluating the performance of fault proneness models when used with imbalanced datasets. In these cases, using *RRA* can be a better choice. At any rate, more research is needed to generalize these conclusions.

Keywords: Fault proneness models · Binary classifiers · Fault prediction · Accuracy · Performance metrics · ROC curves · Area under the curve (AUC) · Pearson ϕ · Matthews Correlation Coefficient

1 Introduction

A large research effort has been—and is still being—dedicated to the definition of fault proneness models, i.e., models that estimate the probability that a given

Partly supported by Fondo di Ricerca d'Ateneo dell'Università degli Studi dell'Insubria.

R. Kadgien et al. (Eds.): PROFES 2023, LNCS 14483, pp. 323–338, 2024.
https://doi.org/10.1007/978-3-031-49266-2_22

piece of code is faulty. The evaluation of the degree of correctness of fault proneness models is carried out by measuring several so-called performance metrics,
to choose the ones that provide the most reliable indications.

To this end, several performance metrics have been proposed. Receiver Operating Characteristics (ROC) curves are widely used to represent the performance
of fault proneness models [3]. The area under the ROC curve (AUC) is a quite
popular performance metric [16], which summarizes the goodness of the predictions represented by the ROC curve into a single number.

It is important noting that ROC curves, hence AUC, represent the performance of *families* of fault predictors. In fact, given a fault proneness model,
it is possible to obtain a fault prediction model by setting a threshold: if the
fault proneness of the given software module is greater than the threshold, it is
estimated faulty, otherwise it is estimated not faulty. Therefore, from one fault
proneness model, several faultiness models can be derived, simply by varying
the threshold. Given a fault proneness model, each threshold defines a faultiness
model: when this is applied to the given dataset, we get a set of predictions,
whose accuracy is represented by a point in the ROC space. These points define
a ROC curve, which is a representation of the performance of the fault proneness
model.

The AUC has been widely criticized as a performance metric, especially
because it accounts for thresholds that most probably will not be used in practice: for instance, we would hardly suspect that a software module is faulty only
if its fault proneness is over 95%. Accordingly, alternative techniques have been
proposed for evaluating the performance represented by a ROC curve: among
these is RRA [15], which computes the area under the curve in a "Region of
Interest" (RoI) of the ROC space, comprising only thresholds that are considered
reasonable. Recently, it has been proposed to adapt ϕ (alias Matthews Correlation Coefficient) [14], a performance metric that represents the performance of
a fault prediction, to represent the performance of the entire ROC curve, i.e., of
the fault proneness model [7].

In this paper, we aim at evaluating AUC as a performance metric, also with
respect to the mentioned alternative proposals. To this end, an empirical study
is carried out. We replicate a previously published cross-project fault prediction
study [19] and measure the accuracy of the obtained predictors using AUC,
RRA and a recently proposed way of relating a specific kind of ROC curves to
ϕ [13]. In doing this, we take into account prevalence, i.e., the proportion of
faulty modules in the dataset that is object of predictions.

The contributions of this paper to the current knowledge on performance
metrics consist in providing some empirical evidence that can be useful for the
following purposes:

- Verifying whether or to what extent the criticisms to AUC are justified.
- Understanding the dependence of AUC on the prevalence.
- Evaluating RRA as an alternative to AUC.
- Evaluating whether or to what extent AUC, RRA, and ϕ provide consistent
  performance evaluations, also with respect to varying dataset prevalence.

The paper is organized as follows. Section 2 provides some background material, to make the paper as self-contained as possible. Section 3 describes the empirical study and the obtained result, which are discussed in Sect. 4. Section 5 discusses the threats to the validity of this study. Section 6 accounts for related work. Section 7 draws some conclusions and outlines future work.

2   Background

2.1   Prediction Performance

The extent to which a faultiness model correctly predicts the faultiness of software modules in a dataset is usually assessed based on a confusion matrix, whose general schema is represented in Fig. 1.

Actual

		Negative	Positive	
Estimated	Negative	TN (True Negatives)	FN (False Negatives)	EN= TN+ FN (Estimated Negatives)
	Positive	FP (False Positives)	TP (True Positives)	EP= FP+ TP (Estimated Positives)
		AN= TN+ FP (Actual Negatives)	AP= FN+ TP (Actual Positives)	n = AN+ AP= EN+ EP

Fig. 1. Schema of confusion matrices

Based on confusion matrices, many performance metrics have been defined and used, such as Positive Predictive Value ($PPV = \frac{TP}{EP}$, also known as Precision), True Positive Rate ($TPR = \frac{TP}{AP}$, also known as Recall), F-measure (harmonic mean of PPV and TPR), False Positive Rate ($FPR = \frac{FP}{AN}$, also known as Fall-out), ϕ, and many others. Each of them captures a different aspect of prediction correctness. For instance, PPV quantifies the extent to which a faultiness predictor can be believed reliable when it predicts a module to be faulty, while TPR can be used to assess the extent to which actually faulty modules have been correctly identified. All of the mentioned performance metrics take values in the [0,1] interval, with the exception of ϕ, whose range is $[-1, 1]$ (see Sect. 2.3). Also, for all of them, higher values are desirable, with the exception of FPR, for which lower values are preferable.

From a confusion matrix, it is also possible to derive the proportion of faulty modules, also known as the prevalence $\rho = \frac{AP}{n}$. Prevalence is a an important characteristic of a dataset, as it does not depend on the prediction model. As will be shown in the remainder of the paper, prevalence may influence the values of performance metrics in a substantial way.

2.2   ROC Curves and the *AUC*

A ROC curve [9] illustrates the overall diagnostic ability of a binary scoring classifier, in our case a fault proneness model, i.e., a function that associates a software module with the probability of being faulty. A binary classifier is built by setting a discrimination threshold t and estimating all modules whose score is above t as faulty and the others as non-faulty. Since the value of t is set in a somewhat arbitrary way, many different fault prediction models can be obtained. Each of them will be characterized by different values for the pair of performance metrics $\langle FPR, TPR \rangle$.

A ROC curve plots the values of $y = TPR$ against the values of $x = FPR$ obtained on a dataset by using all possible threshold values t on fault proneness model. A ROC curve is shown in Fig. 4.

At any rate, the ROC curve by itself is simply a visual aid, but a performance metric is needed to have an overall evaluation of the fault proneness model. The so-called Area Under the Curve (*AUC*) has been used to this end in many domains, including Empirical Software Engineering, to evaluate fault proneness models [1,2,4,5,18].

AUC is simply the area below the ROC curve. The longer the ROC curve lingers close to the left side (low *FPR*) and top side (high *TPR*) of the ROC square, the better, and the larger *AUC*. Since the total area of the ROC square is 1, the closer *AUC* is to 1, the better.

Hosmer at al. [11] propose the following intervals as guidelines to interpret the values of *AUC* as a measure of how well a fault proneness model discriminates between faulty and not-faulty modules for all values of threshold t (Table 1):

Table 1. Interpretation of *AUC*

AUC range	Evaluation
$AUC = 0.5$	totally random, as good as tossing a coin
$0.5 < AUC < 0.7$	poor, not much better than a coin toss
$0.7 \leq AUC < 0.8$	acceptable
$0.8 \leq AUC < 0.9$	excellent
$0.9 \leq AUC$	outstanding

2.3 ϕ

The purpose of ϕ, defined in Formula (1), is to assess the strength of the association between estimated and actual values in a confusion matrix

$$\phi = \frac{TP \cdot TN - FP \cdot FN}{\sqrt{EN \cdot EP \cdot AN \cdot AP}} \tag{1}$$

ϕ is in the $[-1, 1]$ range. Specifically, $\phi = 1$ if and only if $FP{=}FN{=}0$, i.e., for perfect predictions. $\phi = 0$ is the expected performance of a perfectly random predictor. $\phi = -1$ if and only if $TP = TN = 0$, i.e., when all predictions are wrong. When $\phi \geq 0$, predictors with higher values of ϕ are preferable.

ϕ truly is an effect size measure, which quantifies how far a prediction is from being random i.e., from the random prediction model that has $\phi = 0$. A commonly cited proposal [8] uses $\phi = 0.1$, $\phi = 0.3$, and $\phi = 0.5$ respectively to denote a weak, a medium, and a large effect size. ϕ is also related to the χ^2 statistic, since $|\phi| = \sqrt{\frac{\chi^2}{n}}$.

2.4   The Prediction Method

Uchigaki et al. proposed a faultiness estimation method based on the "ensembling" of simple Binary Logistic Regression (BLR) models, which they call submodels. In essence, Uchigaki et al. proposed to build simple fault proneness BLR models using a single measure as the independent variable. The "ensemble" fault proneness model is then obtained by performing a weighted sum of the fault proneness values yielded by the sub-models. For details, refer to the original paper [19].

We decided to replicate the work by Uchigaki el al. because it is a relatively simple, well-founded approach, which has received fair acceptance from the research community. At any rate, for our purposes, the fault proneness estimation method being used is not very relevant, since this study focuses on the evaluation of models' performance, rather than how the models were derived.

Note that another reason why we chose to evaluate the method by Uchigaki et al. is that in our previous work [13], we erroneously interpreted the AUC values reported by Uchigaki et al. as ROC AUC, while actually Uchigaki et al. made reference to the area under Alberg diagrams. In this paper, we compute the "proper" AUC, i.e., the area under the ROC curve, which was missing in the paper by Uchigaki et al. [19]. In this way, we not only derive new knowledge concerning AUC and its relationships with other performance metrics, but we also confirm the results concerning AUC given previously [13].

2.5   Relationships Between AUC, RRA and Constant ϕ ROC Curves

Every point of a ROC curve corresponds to a confusion matrix, hence to a specific value of ϕ. To get a value of ϕ, which we call $\overline{\phi}$, that has a meaning comparable with the AUC of an entire ROC curve, we operate as follows [13] .

1. We compute the AUC of the given ROC curve: let it be auc;
2. We define an "iso-ϕ" ROC curve having a constant value of ϕ in all its points having $AUC = auc$.
3. $\overline{\phi}$ is the value of ϕ in all points of the iso-ϕ curve.

For clarity, we note that, since all ROC curves have extreme points $(0,0)$ and $(1,1)$, iso-ϕ curves actually have $\phi = \overline{\phi}$ only where the curve points are not on the $FPR = 0$ or $TPR = 1$ axes. However this is hardly relevant, since the points on the $FPR=0$ axis do not contribute to AUC, and the points on the $TPR=1$ axis provide a contribution that depends only on $\overline{\phi}$ and ρ.

The computations described above are possible because ϕ can be computed using TPR, FPR and ρ. All the points above the diagonal in the ROC space having the same ϕ value form an arc of ellipse, as described by Formula (2) in implicit form. An example of such arc of ellipse is shown in Fig. 4.

$$\phi = \frac{\sqrt{\rho(1-\rho)}(TPR - FPR)}{\sqrt{(\rho TPR + (1-\rho)FPR)(\rho(1 - TPR) + (1-\rho)(1 - FPR))}} \tag{2}$$

Given any $\langle \overline{\phi}, \rho \rangle$ pair, using Formula (2) it is possible to generate the iso-ϕ ROC curve whose points have $\phi = \overline{\phi}$ and then compute its AUC. With a specific range of $\overline{\phi}$ and ρ values, it is possible to generate a table that links each $\langle \overline{\phi}, \rho \rangle$ pair to a value of AUC, as in Table 2. Since any ROC curve has a value of AUC and prevalence ρ of the test dataset, it is possible to use the table to derive a specific value of $\overline{\phi}$ from the two measures. For instance, a ROC curve obtained from a dataset with $\rho= 0.4$ and $AUC= 0.915$ has $\overline{\phi}= 0.6$.

Table 2. AUC for $\overline{\phi}$, depending on ρ.

ρ	$\overline{\phi}$										
	0	0.1	0.2	0.3	0.4	0.5	0.6	0.7	0.8	0.9	1
0.01	0.5	0.824	0.936	0.971	0.985	0.992	0.996	0.998	0.999	1	1
0.1	0.5	0.63	0.745	0.834	0.895	0.936	0.963	0.981	0.992	0.998	1
0.2	0.5	0.598	0.692	0.776	0.845	0.899	0.939	0.967	0.986	0.997	1
0.3	0.5	0.586	0.669	0.748	0.818	0.876	0.923	0.958	0.982	0.996	1
0.4	0.5	0.58	0.659	0.735	0.804	0.865	0.915	0.953	0.98	0.995	1
0.5	0.5	0.578	0.656	0.731	0.8	0.861	0.912	0.951	0.979	0.995	1

Table 2 shows that, for a given $\overline{\phi}$, the value of AUC decreases as ρ increases and that, for balanced datasets (ρ close to 0.5), the values of AUC and $\overline{\phi}$ give concordant information. For example, with $\overline{\phi}=0.3$, which indicates acceptable performance, AUC is slightly greater than 0.7, which indicates acceptable performance as well. Instead, when the dataset is unbalanced, AUC tends to be over-optimistic in relation to $\overline{\phi}$. For instance, with $\rho = 0.01$ and $\overline{\phi}=0.3$, AUC is close to 1, indicating almost perfect performance. This result suggests that AUC is as informative as $\overline{\phi}$ when working with balanced datasets, but when the dataset is unbalanced AUC may be too optimistic, and other metrics, like $\overline{\phi}$, should be considered.

The study of the relationship between $\overline{\phi}$ and AUC can be repeated for alternative performance metrics applicable to a ROC curve. One of these is the Ratio of Relevant Areas (RRA) [15]. The ROC curve considers several thresholds, like those close to (0,0) and (1,1), that are unlikely to be used in practice since they predict almost everything as either negative or positive. Therefore, it can be interesting to focus on a smaller but more significant section of the ROC space, called "Region of Interest" (RoI), which contains only the portion of the ROC curve that is practically relevant. The performance of the curve can be evaluated via the *RRA*, i.e., the ratio between the area under the ROC curve inside the RoI and the area of the RoI itself.

The Region of Interest can be built in different ways, depending on the needs and context. However, a sound definition of the RoI includes the region where both *TPR* and *FPR* indicate performance better than random estimation's: $TPR > \rho$ and $FPR < \rho$. By applying the same procedure described above, but limited to the RoI, we can compute $\overline{\phi}_{RoI}$. Specifically, we can compute the *RRA* for any iso-ϕ curve having $\phi = \overline{\phi}_{RoI}$ and compile a table with different combinations of $\langle \rho, \overline{\phi}_{RoI} \rangle$ pairs. As before, it is possible to use Table 3 to obtain a specific value of $\overline{\phi}_{RoI}$ that corresponds to the iso-ϕ ROC curve having the same ρ and *RRA* of a given ROC curve.

Table 3. *RRA* for $\overline{\phi}_{RoI}$, depending on ρ.

ρ	$\overline{\phi}_{RoI}$										
	0	0.1	0.2	0.3	0.4	0.5	0.6	0.7	0.8	0.9	1
0.01	0	0.068	0.152	0.249	0.359	0.485	0.625	0.781	0.911	0.979	1
0.1	0	0.04	0.122	0.227	0.347	0.482	0.629	0.789	0.912	0.979	1
0.2	0	0.028	0.1	0.203	0.331	0.478	0.635	0.796	0.914	0.979	1
0.3	0	0.023	0.087	0.187	0.317	0.472	0.64	0.801	0.914	0.979	1
0.4	0	0.021	0.081	0.178	0.307	0.466	0.644	0.804	0.915	0.979	1
0.5	0	0.02	0.079	0.175	0.304	0.464	0.647	0.805	0.915	0.979	1

Table 3 shows that, even though the *RRA* value depends on ρ, *RRA* appears less influenced by the nature of the dataset compared to *AUC*, especially for high values of ϕ. *RRA* seems also less optimistic than *AUC* and more aligned with ϕ.

3   The Study

3.1   Organization of the Study

The study was carried out as follows:

1. We built prediction models via the methods proposed by Uchigaki et al.: for each of the datasets of the NASA collection [17] we built a faultiness model, which was applied to the other datasets of the NASA collection. In this way, we obtained 132 ROC curves.
2. For each ROC curve, we computed the *AUC* and *RRA*.

3. For each ROC curve, we identified the iso-ϕ curve having the same AUC as the ROC curve. The obtained iso-ϕ curve has $\phi = \overline{\phi}$.
4. For each ROC curve, we identified the iso-ϕ curve having the same AUC as the ROC curve in the Region of Interest. The obtained iso-ϕ curve has $\phi = \overline{\phi}_{RoI}$.
5. Having a quintuple $\langle \rho, AUC, RRA, \overline{\phi}, \overline{\phi}_{RoI} \rangle$ for each ROC curve, we performed several comparisons, as described below.

3.2   The Dataset

Like Uchigaki et al., we used the NASA collection [17], which includes 12 datasets, each concerning a software application. Every dataset contains, for each module of the application, several code measures, 20 of which are common to all datasets, and a variable that indicates whether the module is defective. These data are used as the independent variables and dependent variable of fault proneness models, respectively. Note that two versions of the NASA collection are available: the original one and a corrected one. We used the latter, available from GitHub (https://github.com/klainfo/NASADefectDataset).

3.3   Method

The first step of the study consisted in building a fault proneness model for each dataset, following Uchigaki et al. [19]):

1. Data were normalized. The normalized value of a measure is performed in two steps: first a logarithmic transformation is applied, then the normalized measure is obtained by subtracting the mean and dividing by the standard deviation.
2. A univariate BLR model is built for each available measure; that is, every available measure is used as the only independent variable to build a fault proneness model. The adjusted R^2 of each model is computed.
3. The "ensemble" model is built. The fault proneness model associated with a given dataset is obtained as the weighted sum of the fault proneness computed by each one of the univariate BLR models previously obtained. The adjusted R^2 is used for weighting each model.

In the second step of the study, we used the obtained fault proneness models to perform cross-project fault prediction: the model obtained from a dataset was used to estimate the faultiness of the other datasets, using all the possible thresholds. In this way, we obtained a ROC curve for each $\langle$training set, test set$\rangle$ pair. Having models from 12 datasets, and each one being applied to the other 11 datasets, we obtained 132 ROC curves.

The third step involved the computation of performance metrics. For each ROC curve, we computed AUC, RRA, $\overline{\phi}$ and $\overline{\phi}_{RoI}$:

1. AUC was computed as usual, i.e., it is the area under the ROC curve in the ROC space.

2. RRA is the area under the ROC curve in the RoI, which is defined as the region of the ROC space above the $TPR = \rho$ horizontal line and to the left of the $FPR = \rho$ vertical line.

3. $\overline{\phi}$ is the value such that the AUC of ROC curve having $\phi = \overline{\phi}$ is equal to the AUC computed at point 1.

4. $\overline{\phi}_{RoI}$ is the value such that the AUC of the considered ROC curve in the RoI is equal to the AUC in the RoI of the iso-ϕ ROC curve having $\phi = \overline{\phi}_{RoI}$.

The values of the computed performance metrics are given in next section.

The final step of the study consisted in analyzing the collected performance metrics, as described in Sect. 4.

3.4   Results of the Study

Table 4 shows the values of the AUC for the obtained fault proneness models. Each column concerns a dataset that is being used as the training set, while each row concerns a dataset that is used as the test sets. For instance, the value in the column labelled "KC3" and the row labelled "CM1" indicates that the fault proneness model obtained from dataset KC3, when applied to estimate the faultiness of CM1's modules, obtained $AUC = 0.709$.

Table 4. AUC of the obtained faultiness models.

AUC		Training											
		CM1	JM1	KC1	KC3	MC1	MC2	MW1	PC1	PC2	PC3	PC4	PC5
Test	CM1 (ρ=0.122)		0.723	0.719	0.709	0.722	0.720	0.728	0.733	0.721	0.737	0.703	0.720
	JM1 (ρ=0.183)	0.698		0.695	0.699	0.699	0.690	0.698	0.700	0.699	0.701	0.697	0.697
	KC1 (ρ=0.155)	0.792	0.794		0.783	0.795	0.790	0.796	0.793	0.787	0.787	0.778	0.797
	KC3 (ρ=0.18)	0.688	0.681	0.672		0.701	0.668	0.683	0.703	0.719	0.718	0.755	0.696
	MC1 (ρ=0.008)	0.892	0.886	0.881	0.905		0.873	0.891	0.898	0.898	0.904	0.915	0.893
	MC2 (ρ=0.352)	0.696	0.690	0.691	0.662	0.681		0.681	0.680	0.682	0.676	0.655	0.685
	MW1 (ρ=0.103)	0.753	0.746	0.739	0.736	0.735	0.728		0.760	0.723	0.762	0.731	0.733
	PC1 (ρ=0.083)	0.766	0.750	0.741	0.779	0.756	0.726	0.760		0.762	0.783	0.787	0.747
	PC2 (ρ=0.011)	0.902	0.875	0.872	0.884	0.889	0.856	0.894	0.897		0.909	0.891	0.881
	PC3 (ρ=0.126)	0.757	0.734	0.724	0.761	0.743	0.711	0.749	0.759	0.752		0.770	0.734
	PC4 (ρ=0.129)	0.691	0.688	0.682	0.756	0.707	0.669	0.687	0.711	0.721	0.728		0.693
	PC5 (ρ=0.03)	0.956	0.956	0.955	0.954	0.955	0.954	0.956	0.956	0.953	0.956	0.951	

Table 5 shows the values of $\overline{\phi}$ for the obtained fault proneness models. For instance, from Table 4 we know that the AUC of the faultiness model trained using KC3 and applied to CM1 is 0.709. Knowing that CM1 has prevalence $\rho = 0.122$, we can find (via the same computations used to define Table 2) the iso-ϕ ROC curve whose AUC is 0.709 when $\rho = 0.122$. This iso-ϕ curve has $\phi = 0.181$, as show in Table 5.

Table 6 shows the values of RRA, for the obtained fault proneness models. Table 7 shows the values of $\overline{\phi}_{RoI}$, for the obtained fault proneness models.

4   Discussion of Results

The left-hand side of Fig. 2 shows the boxplots of the AUC values of the fault proneness models, where the yellow diamonds represent the mean. Every boxplot concerns the application of the models to test datasets having ρ in a specific range. In this way, it is possible to appreciate how prevalence ρ affects AUC. In fact, it is easy to see that (except for a few outliers) AUC appears to grow for decreasing values of ρ. Note that the fault proneness models used are the same across all ρ ranges; hence, the difference of AUC values must be due to the test datasets.

Table 5. $\overline{\phi}$ of the obtained faultiness models.

$\overline{\phi}$		Training											
		CM1	JM1	KC1	KC3	MC1	MC2	MW1	PC1	PC2	PC3	PC4	PC5
Test	CM1 (ρ=0.122)		0.195	0.191	0.181	0.194	0.192	0.200	0.205	0.193	0.209	0.175	0.192
	JM1 (ρ=0.183)	0.200		0.197	0.201	0.201	0.192	0.200	0.203	0.201	0.204	0.199	0.199
	KC1 (ρ=0.155)	0.295	0.298		0.284	0.299	0.292	0.300	0.296	0.289	0.289	0.277	0.301
	KC3 (ρ=0.18)	0.188	0.181	0.171		0.202	0.167	0.183	0.205	0.222	0.221	0.264	0.197
	MC1 (ρ=0.008)	0.131	0.126	0.122	0.142		0.117	0.130	0.136	0.136	0.141	0.153	0.132
	MC2 (ρ=0.352)	0.242	0.235	0.236	0.199	0.223		0.223	0.222	0.224	0.217	0.190	0.228
	MW1 (ρ=0.103)	0.210	0.203	0.196	0.194	0.193	0.186		0.217	0.181	0.219	0.189	0.191
	PC1 (ρ=0.083)	0.204	0.189	0.181	0.217	0.194	0.168	0.198		0.200	0.221	0.225	0.186
	PC2 (ρ=0.011)	0.162	0.138	0.135	0.145	0.150	0.124	0.154	0.157		0.170	0.151	0.143
	PC3 (ρ=0.126)	0.233	0.208	0.198	0.237	0.218	0.185	0.224	0.235	0.227		0.247	0.208
	PC4 (ρ=0.129)	0.168	0.165	0.159	0.234	0.183	0.147	0.164	0.187	0.197	0.204		0.170
	PC5 (ρ=0.03)	0.391	0.391	0.387	0.383	0.387	0.383	0.391	0.391	0.379	0.391	0.372	

Table 6. RRA of the obtained faultiness models.

RRA		Training											
		CM1	JM1	KC1	KC3	MC1	MC2	MW1	PC1	PC2	PC3	PC4	PC5
Test	CM1 (ρ=0.122)		0.113	0.115	0.071	0.103	0.095	0.110	0.109	0.099	0.109	0.043	0.110
	JM1 (ρ=0.183)	0.144		0.140	0.141	0.147	0.135	0.145	0.149	0.143	0.149	0.134	0.143
	KC1 (ρ=0.155)	0.186	0.204		0.159	0.197	0.195	0.201	0.196	0.171	0.179	0.135	0.204
	KC3 (ρ=0.18)	0.133	0.143	0.127		0.162	0.139	0.147	0.169	0.170	0.187	0.255	0.155
	MC1 (ρ=0.008)	0.044	0.031	0.029	0.047		0.019	0.039	0.046	0.042	0.046	0.041	0.037
	MC2 (ρ=0.352)	0.172	0.163	0.150	0.103	0.129		0.129	0.126	0.139	0.121	0.077	0.151
	MW1 (ρ=0.103)	0.190	0.141	0.106	0.066	0.097	0.153		0.193	0.071	0.213	0.061	0.111
	PC1 (ρ=0.083)	0.197	0.144	0.137	0.207	0.170	0.111	0.157		0.218	0.225	0.222	0.140
	PC2 (ρ=0.011)	0.065	0.049	0.046	0.065	0.069	0.046	0.069	0.073		0.070	0.069	0.069
	PC3 (ρ=0.126)	0.092	0.049	0.044	0.087	0.064	0.036	0.071	0.084	0.070		0.098	0.048
	PC4 (ρ=0.129)	0.041	0.038	0.042	0.117	0.056	0.026	0.036	0.056	0.083	0.079		0.040
	PC5 (ρ=0.03)	0.383	0.402	0.404	0.403	0.398	0.393	0.397	0.399	0.380	0.396	0.389	

The right-hand side of Fig. 2 shows the boxplots of $\overline{\phi}$ values of the fault proneness models. Every boxplot concerns the application of the models to test datasets having ρ in a specific range. It can be noticed that $\overline{\phi}$ appears to grow with ρ, hence the behavior of $\overline{\phi}$ with respect to ρ is opposite with respect to the behavior of AUC, which appears to grow when ρ decreases.

It is also possible to note that the indications provided by AUC and $\overline{\phi}$ are coherent when $\rho \in [0.2, 0.4]$; in fact, all the values of AUC are concentrated around 0.7, which indicates barely acceptable performance, and most values of $\overline{\phi}$ are in the $[0.2, 0.25]$ range, which also indicates just acceptable performance. Instead, when $\rho \in [0, 0.1]$, the great majority of the values of AUC are above 0.8, indicating good accuracy, while the great majority of $\overline{\phi}$ values are below 0.2, thus indicating poor performance.

Table 7. $\overline{\phi}_{RoI}$ of the obtained faultiness models.

$\overline{\phi}_{RoI}$		Training											
		CM1	JM1	KC1	KC3	MC1	MC2	MW1	PC1	PC2	PC3	PC4	PC5
Test	CM1 (ρ=0.122)		0.197	0.199	0.148	0.186	0.177	0.193	0.192	0.181	0.192	0.111	0.193
	JM1 (ρ=0.183)	0.243		0.239	0.240	0.246	0.234	0.244	0.248	0.242	0.248	0.233	0.242
	KC1 (ρ=0.155)	0.276	0.292		0.251	0.286	0.284	0.290	0.285	0.263	0.270	0.228	0.292
	KC3 (ρ=0.18)	0.231	0.241	0.225		0.260	0.237	0.245	0.266	0.267	0.282	0.340	0.253
	MC1 (ρ=0.008)	0.068	0.050	0.047	0.072		0.033	0.061	0.071	0.065	0.071	0.064	0.058
	MC2 (ρ=0.352)	0.292	0.284	0.272	0.223	0.251		0.251	0.248	0.261	0.243	0.192	0.273
	MW1 (ρ=0.103)	0.268	0.220	0.183	0.137	0.173	0.232		0.270	0.143	0.289	0.130	0.189
	PC1 (ρ=0.083)	0.269	0.217	0.210	0.278	0.243	0.182	0.230		0.288	0.294	0.292	0.213
	PC2 (ρ=0.011)	0.097	0.076	0.072	0.097	0.102	0.072	0.102	0.107		0.104	0.102	0.102
	PC3 (ρ=0.126)	0.174	0.120	0.113	0.169	0.141	0.101	0.149	0.165	0.148		0.181	0.119
	PC4 (ρ=0.129)	0.110	0.105	0.111	0.203	0.131	0.085	0.102	0.131	0.165	0.160		0.108
	PC5 (ρ=0.03)	0.422	0.437	0.438	0.438	0.434	0.430	0.433	0.434	0.419	0.432	0.426	

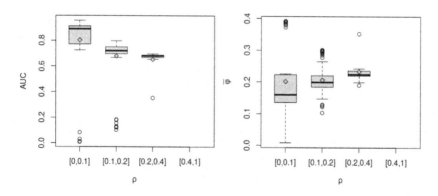

Fig. 2. Boxplots of AUC (left) and $\overline{\phi}$ (right) for estimates of datasets with ρ in the $[0,0.1]$, $[0.1,0.2]$ and $[0.2,0.4]$ ranges.

In conclusion, it seems that AUC and $\overline{\phi}$ agree on the performance of models applied to fairly balanced datasets, while they disagree on the performance obtained with definitely imbalanced datasets.

The left-hand side of Fig. 3 shows the boxplots of RRA values of the fault proneness models. Every boxplot concerns the application of the models to test datasets having ρ in a specific range. It can be seen that—unlike AUC—RRA appears to grow with ρ. At any rate, while there is an increase of the median RRA, the mean RRA appears less sensitive to ρ.

The right-hand side of Fig. 3 shows the boxplots of $\overline{\phi}_{RoI}$. Every boxplot concerns the application of the models to test datasets having ρ in a specific range. It appears that $\overline{\phi}_{RoI}$ depends on ρ like RRA, but with a bigger increase when $\rho \in [0.2, 0.4]$.

In conclusion, we can observe that:

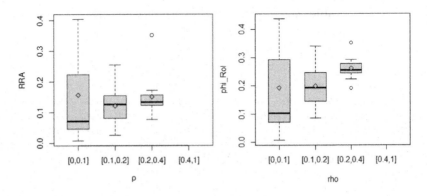

Fig. 3. Boxplots of RRA (left) and $\overline{\phi}_{RoI}$ (right) for estimates of datasets with ρ in the [0,0.1], [0.1,0.2] and [0.2,0.4] ranges.

- AUC seems to be inflated for small values of ρ, i.e., when the test dataset is quite imbalanced. That is, AUC could provide excessively optimistic evaluations for imbalanced datasets.
- RRA seems to be largely independent of ρ, except for median values when datasets are very imbalanced ($\rho \le 0.1$). However, when RRA is around 0.1 or below, its exact value is hardly relevant, since it indicates quite poor performance anyway: therefore, the distribution of such low values of RRA is of little interest. In practice, it seems that RRA can be used with imbalanced datasets as well as with balanced datasets.
- The small values of RRA, $\overline{\phi}$, and $\overline{\phi}_{RoI}$ obtained with imbalanced datasets (small ρ) seem to confirm that AUC is too optimistic when evaluating such datasets.

5   Threats to Validity

In this paper, we used the NASA datasets, which have ρ in the [0.008,0.352] range. Different datasets, also having different ranges of prevalence ρ could be used to study AUC, RRA, and ϕ, resulting in a different set of values. We also used a single fault proneness model, namely the one proposed by Uchigaki et al. [19]; however, AUC and RRA depend only on the structure of the ROC curve itself and not the model that generated it. Similarly, $\overline{\phi}$ and $\overline{\phi}_{RoI}$ are selected based on AUC (or RRA) of the ROC curve and ρ of the test dataset: since none of the metrics depends on the prediction model used and on the properties of the dataset (besides prevalence ρ), and because this test is backed by an analytical study [13], the results obtained with different sets of data and models should lead to similar relationships between the metrics.

Regarding construct validity, there is not a widely accepted way to compare AUC and ϕ: building an iso-ϕ ROC curve with the same AUC of a given ROC curve is only one of the possible techniques, and every method comes with its own limitations. Iso-ϕ curves provide convenient reference values, but most real ROC curves include points with different values of ϕ. For instance, Fig. 4 shows that some points of the ROC curve are above the iso-ϕ curve and some are below. Therefore, iso-ϕ ROC curves are useful to study the behavior of AUC with respect to ρ and ϕ, but additional research is needed to generalize the results reported here to any ROC curve.

In this paper, we compare different performance metrics, which allows us to establish a relationship among them and with ρ. Like any other empirical studies of this type, this study does not give any information about the actual quality of AUC, ϕ and RRA. Instead, this study shows specific quantitative relationships between the metrics, while the consequences have to be drawn, possibly via further investigations. For example, we concluded that AUC is over-optimistic when prevalence ρ is small, but the opposite may be true instead, i.e. ϕ and RRA are over-pessimistic when prevalence ρ is small, or something in between. Regardless of the interpretation, the results give new insights to the relationship between these metrics.

6   Related Work

This paper continues the work started in [13], in which an analytical study of AUC and iso-ϕ ROC curves was carried out.

Several papers have investigated the relationship between different performance metrics for binary classifiers. For instance, [6,12,20,21] compare ϕ with the harmonic mean of Precision and TPR (F-measure), similar to how ϕ, AUC and RRA are compared in this paper. Some of the results of the aforementioned papers are coherent with those described in this paper. For example in [12], an analytical and empirical study showed that F-measure and ϕ give concordant information when ρ is small, and the correlation gets worse as ρ increases.

AUC has been criticized outside the software engineering field. For instance, Hand [10] shows that AUC is a weighted minimum misclassification cost function, and the weights are the unit costs per misclassification. These weights, however, are variables that mainly depend on the binary classifier used. Because of this, AUC is an ill-designed performance metric when interpreted as being related to some kind of cost. Hand concluded that users (software development organizations and software engineering researchers, in our case) should use performance metrics with a more direct correspondence with their objectives.

Other papers have studied the relationship between AUC and ϕ. For instance, Chicco and Jurman have systematically generated tens of thousands of ROC curves considering different prevalence ρ values and computed their AUC and ϕ [7]. The results of their analysis show that, while AUC and ϕ are never on opposite trends, a fairly wide range of ϕ values are possible given a specific value of AUC. They also notice that the spread gets worse as the dataset gets more unbalanced. They justify the results by showing that AUC does not provide any useful informations about Precision $\left(\frac{TP}{EP}\right)$ and Negative Precision $\left(\frac{TN}{EN}\right)$, while ϕ does, questioning the reliability of AUC as a performance metric. Finally, they provide a small empirical study with a model applied on three different datasets. The test shows that the AUC value of these curves is over-optimistic in relation to ϕ because Precision and Negative Precision are quite low and AUC does not take them into account. In their conclusions, they suggest to stop using AUC as a performance metric in favor of ϕ.

The main difference between Chicco and Jurman's study and ours is related to how ϕ is computed. In their paper, they use the ϕ value obtained from the predictor generated using the cut-off threshold $\tau = 0.5$. This approach can be problematic, as this ϕ value is not informative of all the points in the ROC curve, while AUC is, and the selection of this specific τ appears arbitrary. What Chicco and Jurman concluded may not draw a complete picture of the ϕ–AUC relationship, especially if we consider that in our study the two metrics give concordant information when working with balanced datasets.

7   Conclusions

The area under ROC curves (AUC) is widely used for estimating fault proneness models [16]. However, AUC has been criticized because the area under the entire ROC curve takes into account thresholds that are very unlikely to be used for fault prediction.

Alternative approaches have been proposed to summarize via a single performance metric the performance represented by a ROC curve. In this paper we consider RRA, a performance metric that is similar to AUC, but considers only a portion of the ROC space, which excludes unlikely thresholds, and a specific value of ϕ (also known as Matthews Correlation Coefficient) associated to the entire ROC curve, or to the portion of the ROC curve corresponding to feasible thresholds (namely, the same portion considered when computing RRA).

Via an empirical study, we found that AUC, RRA and ϕ tend to provide similar evaluations for relatively balanced datasets, i.e., when actually faulty modules are between 20% and 40% of the total modules (no dataset used in this study accounted for more than 40% faulty modules). Instead, AUC appears excessively optimist for imbalanced datasets, especially when actually faulty modules are less than 10%.

In conclusion, AUC should be used with care. Using RRA or ϕ instead of AUC is an option that should be taken into consideration, to avoid misleading indications due to dataset imbalance.

In general, ROC curves are made of points having different values of ϕ: for instance, Fig. 4 shows that—even though the given ROC curve is similar to its iso-ϕ ROC curve—some points of the ROC curve are above the iso-ϕ curve ($\phi > \overline{\phi} = 0.295$) and some are below ($\phi < \overline{\phi} = 0.295$). Therefore, further investigations are needed, concerning the relationship between AUC and RRA and some value of ϕ computed over the actual given ROC curve, typically characterized by points having various ϕ values. These investigations will be the object of future work.

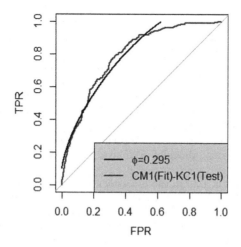

Fig. 4. ROC curve of the model reproduced in this paper using CM1 as the train dataset and KC1 as the test dataset (blue), and the ROC curve having constant $\phi = 0.295$ (black) (Color figure online)

References

1. Arisholm, E., Briand, L.C., Fuglerud, M.: Data mining techniques for building fault proneness models in telecom java software. In: The 18th IEEE International Symposium on Software Reliability, 2007. ISSRE2007, pp. 215–224. IEEE (2007)
2. Beecham, S., Hall, T., Bowes, D., Gray, D., Counsell, S., Black, S.: A systematic review of fault prediction approaches used in software engineering. Technical report Lero-TR-2010-04, Lero (2010)
3. Bradley, A.P.: The use of the area under the roc curve in the evaluation of machine learning algorithms. Pattern Recogn. **30**(7), 1145–1159 (1997)
4. Catal, C.: Performance evaluation metrics for software fault prediction studies. Acta Polytech. Hung. **9**(4), 193–206 (2012)
5. Catal, C., Diri, B.: A systematic review of software fault prediction studies. Expert Syst. Appl. **36**(4), 7346–7354 (2009)

6. Chicco, D., Jurman, G.: The advantages of the Matthews correlation coefficient (MCC) over F1 score and accuracy in binary classification evaluation. BMC Genomics **21**(1), 1–13 (2020)
7. Chicco, D., Jurman, G.: The Matthews correlation coefficient (MCC) should replace the ROC AUC as the standard metric for assessing binary classification. BioData Min. **16**(1), 1–23 (2023)
8. Cohen, J.: Statistical Power Analysis for the Behavioral Sciences Lawrence Earlbaum Associates. Routledge, New York (1988)
9. Fawcett, T.: An introduction to ROC analysis. Pattern Recogn. Lett. **27**(8), 861–874 (2006). https://doi.org/10.1016/j.patrec.2005.10.010
10. Hand, D.J.: Measuring classifier performance: a coherent alternative to the area under the ROC curve. Mach. Learn. **77**(1), 103–123 (2009). https://doi.org/10.1007/s10994-009-5119-5
11. Hosmer, D.W., Jr., Lemeshow, S., Sturdivant, R.X.: Applied Logistic Regression. Wiley, Hoboken (2013)
12. Lavazza, L., Morasca, S.: Comparing ϕ and the F-measure as performance metrics for software-related classifications. EMSE **27**(7), 185 (2022)
13. Lavazza, L., Morasca, S., Rotoloni, G.: On the reliability of the area under the roc curve in empirical software engineering. In: Proceedings of the 24th International Conference on Evaluation and Assessment in Software Engineering (EASE). Association for Computing Machinery (ACM) (2023)
14. Matthews, B.W.: Comparison of the predicted and observed secondary structure of T4 phage lysozyme. Biochim. Biophys. Acta (BBA)-Protein Struct. **405**(2), 442–451 (1975)
15. Morasca, S., Lavazza, L.: On the assessment of software defect prediction models via ROC curves. Empir. Softw. Eng. **25**(5), 3977–4019 (2020)
16. Moussa, R., Sarro, F.: On the use of evaluation measures for defect prediction studies. In: Proceedings of the 31st ACM SIGSOFT International Symposium on Software Testing and Analysis (ISSTA). ACM (2022)
17. Shepperd, M., Song, Q., Sun, Z., Mair, C.: Data quality: some comments on the NASA software defect datasets. IEEE Trans. Software Eng. **39**(9), 1208–1215 (2013)
18. Singh, Y., Kaur, A., Malhotra, R.: Empirical validation of object-oriented metrics for predicting fault proneness models. Softw. Qual. J. **18**(1), 3 (2010)
19. Uchigaki, S., Uchida, S., Toda, K., Monden, A.: An ensemble approach of simple regression models to cross-project fault prediction. In: 2012 13th ACIS International Conference on Software Engineering, Artificial Intelligence, Networking and Parallel/Distributed Computing, pp. 476–481. IEEE (2012)
20. Yao, J., Shepperd, M.: Assessing software defection prediction performance: why using the Matthews correlation coefficient matters. In: Proceedings of the Evaluation and Assessment in Software Engineering, pp. 120–129 (2020)
21. Zhu, Q.: On the performance of Matthews correlation coefficient (MCC) for imbalanced dataset. Pattern Recogn. Lett. **136**, 71–80 (2020)

Is It the Best Solution? Testing an Optimisation Algorithm with Metamorphic Testing

Alejandra Duque-Torres[1]([⊠]), Claus Klammer[2], Stefan Fischer[2], and Dietmar Pfahl[1]

[1] Institute of Computer Science, University of Tartu, Tartu, Estonia
{duquet,dietmar.pfahl}@ut.ee
[2] Software Competence Center Hagenberg (SCCH) GmbH, Hagenberg, Austria
{claus.klammer,stefan.fischer}@scch.at

Abstract. Optimisation algorithms play a vital role in solving complex real-world problems by iteratively comparing various solutions to find the optimal or the best solution. However, testing them poses challenges due to their "non-testable" nature, where a reliable test oracle is lacking. Traditional testing techniques may not directly address whether these algorithms yield the best solution. In this context, Metamorphic Testing (MT) emerges as a promising approach. MT leverages Metamorphic Relations (MRs) to indirectly test the System Under Test (SUT) by examining input-output pairs and revealing inconsistencies based on MRs. In this paper, we apply the MT approach to a black-box industrial optimisation algorithm and present our observations and findings. We identify successful aspects, challenges, and opportunities for further research. The findings from our study are expected to shed light on the practical feasibility of MT for testing optimisation algorithms. The paper provides a formal definition of MT, an overview of related work in optimisation algorithms, and a description of the industrial context, methodology, and results.

Keywords: Software testing · Test Oracle · Metamorphic Testing · Metamorphic Relations · Optimisation Algorithms · Non-Testable Programs

1 Introduction

Optimisation algorithms employ iterative procedures, systematically comparing various solutions until they converge upon an optimal or satisfactory result [2]. This iterative approach allows them to search through large solution spaces, looking for the best or near-optimal solutions to complex problems. Their primary objective is to determine the most favourable values for a set of decision variables, whether it involves maximising or minimising a specific objective function [2]. By doing so, these algorithms play a crucial role in addressing real-world challenges and enhancing decision-making processes across diverse domains.

© The Author(s), under exclusive license to Springer Nature Switzerland AG 2024
R. Kadgien et al. (Eds.): PROFES 2023, LNCS 14483, pp. 339–354, 2024.
https://doi.org/10.1007/978-3-031-49266-2_23

As the practical applications of optimisation algorithms grow in various real-world problems, assessing their quality becomes imperative. Software testing plays a crucial role in this regard. However, testing optimisation algorithms is not a trivial task and involves addressing a more fundamental testing challenge, *i.e.*, the test oracle. Optimisation algorithms fall into the category of "non-testable" programs, where either an oracle does not exist or the tester must expend an extraordinary amount of time to determine it [11]. In the context of optimisation algorithms, if the test oracle were known, there would have been no need for these algorithms in the first place.

Metamorphic Testing (MT) is a software testing approach that has shown promise in alleviating the test oracle problem. The idea behind MT is to examine the relations between input-output pairs of consecutive System Under Test (SUT) executions, known as Metamorphic Relations (MRs). MRs define how the outputs should vary in response to specific changes in the input, enabling testers to indirectly test the SUT by checking whether the inputs and outputs satisfy the MRs [4]. A violated MR suggests a high probability that the SUT has a fault, but the absence of violations does not ensure a fault-free SUT. MT has shown promising results across domains, as it has been demonstrated to be an effective technique for testing in a variety of application domains, such as autonomous driving [14], cloud and networking systems [13], bioinformatic software [9], scientific software [7], as well as for testing a variety of genetic algorithms (GAs), and heuristics such as machine learning (ML) algorithms.

In this paper, we present a comprehensive application of the MT approach to a black-box industrial optimisation algorithm. This paper aims to describe our observations and findings from applying the MT approach in an industrial context. This includes insights into the successful aspects and areas that presented challenges during our study. Additionally, we aim to identify gaps in the current research on MT, highlighting opportunities for further exploration and improvement. Lastly, we share the valuable feedback received from our industry partner. By applying the MT approach to a real-world industrial optimisation algorithm, our research aims to contribute to the advancement of testing methodologies for complex algorithms. The findings from our study are expected to shed light on the practical feasibility of MT in the field of testing optimisation algorithms. Additionally, the industry feedback will provide valuable guidance for future research and industry applications, ultimately enhancing the trust and reliability of optimisation algorithms in industrial settings.

The remainder of this paper is organised as follows. Section 2 presents a formal definition of MT and outlines its basic workflow. Additionally, we provide an overview of related work in the field of testing optimisation algorithms. In Sect. 3, we introduce the industrial context. In Sect. 4, we describe the methodology, including implementation details, MRs used, and the SUT description. Section 5 presents the results of our study and provides a comprehensive discussion of the findings. Finally, in Sect. 6, we conclude the paper.

2   Background and Related Work

This section presents the key concepts utilised in our study. Section 2.1 introduces the MT approach. Additionally, we present an overview of testing techniques used in optimisation algorithms in Sect. 2.2. Furthermore, Sect. 2.3 delves into the related works on MT, focusing on its application in the context of optimisation algorithms.

2.1   Metamorphic Testing

MT is a software testing approach introduced by Chen et al. [3] to address the test oracle problem. This problem arises when a SUT lacks an oracle or creating one to determine the correctness of SUT outputs is practically impossible. MT utilises the internal properties of the SUT to validate expected outputs. It achieves this by examining the relations between inputs and outputs from multiple SUT executions, known as MRs. These MRs define how outputs should change when specific variations occur in the input. The MT process involves at least five steps:

1. Identify a list of MRs that the SUT should satisfy.
2. Create a set of initial test data (*td*).
3. Generate follow-up test data (*ftd*) by applying selected MR-specified transformations to the inputs.
4. Execute the corresponding SUT with *td* and *ftd*.
5. Verify that the changes in the output observed in the *td* and *ftd* match the changes defined by the MR.

The final step requires thorough analysis, as the absence of violations does not guarantee the correctness of the SUT. If an MR is violated, it indicates a potential fault in the SUT, assuming the MR is accurately defined.

2.2   Testing Optimisation Algorithms

Traditionally, optimisation algorithms have been tested in terms of their performance, robustness, and convergence rates using various techniques, including mathematical analysis [1], benchmark or test functions [6], cross-validation [5], and convergence analysis [12]. Mathematical analysis involves exploring the algorithm's mathematical properties to gain insights into its behaviour. While this approach has proven valuable, it may require a strong mathematical background, making it challenging for some practitioners. Benchmark or test functions are employed, where well-defined problems with known optimal solutions serve as a basis for comparison [6].

Cross-validation is particularly useful when optimisation algorithms are applied to ML tasks. It involves dividing the dataset into multiple subsets, training the algorithm on some subsets, and testing its performance on the remaining data. Cross-validation helps to assess the algorithm's generalisation ability and robustness [5]. While effective, this method can incur higher computational costs and time, especially when dealing with large datasets or complex models. Additionally, it may not be suitable for certain data types, such as time series or spatial data. Convergence analysis involves observing how the algorithm's solution approaches the optimal solution over multiple iterations [10]. Its main disadvantage is that it can be computationally intensive and time-consuming, especially for complex optimisation algorithms and large-scale problems.

Although these testing techniques provide valuable insights, they do not directly address the fundamental question of whether an algorithm yields the best solution consistently. As optimisation problems often involve complex and high-dimensional search spaces, ensuring that an algorithm consistently produces optimal or near-optimal solutions remains a challenge.

2.3   Metamorphic Testing and Optimisation Algorithms

Since its introduction in 1998 by Chen et al. [3], MT has proven to be an effective technique for testing in various application domains, including autonomous driving [14], cloud and networking systems [13], bioinformatic software [9], and scientific software [7]. In the context of testing optimisation algorithms using MT, there have been a limited number of studies. However, the existing research demonstrates the effectiveness of MT as a testing technique for optimisation algorithms. For instance, Yoo [11] applied MT to stochastic optimisation algorithms and evaluated its impact on different problem instances, *i.e.,* specific selection of values for the algorithm parameters. The study focused on the Next Release Problem (NRP) and showed that MT could be effective in testing optimisation algorithms, even considering their stochastic nature.

Similarly, Rounds and Kanewala [8] conducted research on testing GAs using MT. They identified 17 MRs and demonstrated that these relations are more effective in detecting defects compared to traditional unit tests based on known outputs. The study also explored system-level relations with various fitness functions and proposed modifications to reduce excessive failure rates. Although there are only a few works specifically focused on MT for testing optimisation algorithms, these studies showcase the potential of MT as a valuable testing approach in this domain.

3   Industry Context

The work has been performed on an industrial use case in the field of machinery and plant engineering. The company's machinery can produce and handle different products for different domains depending on the customers' needs. A huge number of different machine variants and configuration options are available, which specify the size, power, features, and versatility of its different product lines. These machines are part of a larger production process, and their exact use is unknown to the manufacturer. Therefore, there is the need to configure and optimise the machines and the production process by the customer. The machine's ability to easily change for different purposes is an important feature for customers. This makes these machines versatile, and they can be converted for the production of other items in a short time. Although a working machine configuration can be saved and reused later on, there is still room for improvement in the partly manually determined settings. Besides changes in environmental conditions, like temperature, which might require adapting some settings of the production process, there are additional reasons to do so. Sustainability is supported by trying to reduce the energy and resource consumption of the production process without compromising the quality of the resulting products.

The machine vendor incorporates code that supports half-automatic optimisation of parts of the production process. Its goal is to decrease production cycle time and reduce machine resource consumption without compromising product quality. After the machine's initial setup, i.e., once it can produce with the required quality, the operator can initiate the optimisation process. It seeks to refine the production process within the given frame by running cycles and adjusting values that influence the cycle. These settings can be adopted for subsequent use if better values are identified.

It's obvious that supporting the whole range of different machines, machine configurations, and options is a challenge. Especially if there is the need to adapt the algorithm to support specific equipment of a machine, it has to be ensured that the changes do not have any side effects on other plant configurations and still provide valid results. Even the optimisation code has to be reliable, *e.g.*,, when replacing sensors. The optimisation code is currently written as MATLAB scripts and generated to control code during the software build process. Most of the testing activities of the optimisation features are performed manually since it is part of a complex production cycle, which is difficult to automate and realistically simulate currently. In addition to these integration tests, there already existed manually created test scripts in MATLAB that have been used to test some important parts and single functions of the optimisation process.

We could convince our long-lasting company partner to research the potential of MT in the context of this optimisation code. The optimisation algorithm follows some rules which must hold true for all machine types, which, therefore, seemed to be the perfect use case for MT. With the application of MT, we wanted to increase the coverage of some selected central functions of this code and show that the defined assumptions are valid for the specified input space.

4 Methodology

We strictly follow the MT procedure outlined in Sect. 2.1. In this section, we begin by offering a comprehensive overview of the SUT in Sect. 4.1. Afterwards, we proceed to present the formulation of the MRs, which is detailed in Sect. 4.2. Additionally, we provide insights into their implementation in Sect. 4.3.

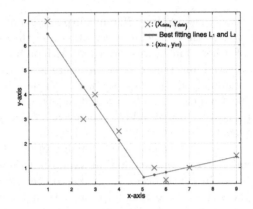

Fig. 1. Graphical representation of the SUT inputs and outputs

4.1   System Under Test

The optimisation algorithm is implemented using MATLAB scripts. The algorithm, hereafter referred to as the SUT, is a black-box system specifically designed to perform the best fitting of two dependent lines and determine their intersection point.

The SUT takes two sets of input data, X_{data} and Y_{data}, representing the x and y coordinates of data points, respectively. By utilising various variables and matrices, it employs linear approximation techniques to represent the lines as shown in Eq. (1) and Eq. (2). The SUT performs its calculations based on the input data, fitting the lines and computing the intersection point of lines L_1 and L_2 (an example is shown in Fig. 1).

$$L_1 : y = a_1 + b_1 * x \ for \ x <= x_i \tag{1}$$

$$L_2 : y = a_2 + b_2 * x \ for \ x > x_i \tag{2}$$

Here, x_i represents the value x of the x-coordinate where the lines L_1 and L_2 intersect. The SUT produces the following outputs:

- x_{int}: This output represents the x-coordinate of the intersection point between lines L_1 and L_2.
- y_{int}: This output represents the y-coordinate of the intersection point between lines L_1 and L_2. It indicates the value of y at the intersection, which is the common output for the given x_{int}.
- PX_{data}: This output is a vector that provides the x-coordinates of the lines L_1 and L_2.
- PY_{data}: This output is a vector that provides the y-coordinates of the lines L_1 and L_2.

– R: This output represents the sum of the root mean squared error (RSME) between the fitted lines L_1 and L_2 and their corresponding y-coordinates. The RSME measures the accuracy of the fitted lines in approximating the input data points (Y_{data}). A lower R-value indicates a better fit between the lines and the data points.

4.2 Formulation of Metamorphic Relations

The process of identifying MRs for the SUT involved conducting several workshops in collaboration with the industrial partner. In these workshops, a comprehensive introduction to the SUT was given, and potential MRs were discussed. Through these collaborative workshops, four MRs were proposed.

The MRs are formulated in an "IF-THEN" format. This format is essentially a logical implication structure where both the antecedent (captured by the 'IF' statement) and the consequent (captured by the 'THEN' statement) are relations defined over the function inputs and outputs. Consequently, each MR comprises two parts: the condition under which the relation holds (the "IF" part) and the expected change in the output when this condition is met (the "THEN" part). Detailed descriptions of the MRs are provided in the following sub-sections.

4.2.1 MR$_1$ - Rotation of Fitted Lines
Let the SUT provide the best fitting lines, denoted as L_1 and L_2, based on the input data X_{data} and Y_{data}. The intersection point of these lines is represented as (x_{int}, y_{int}).

IF the lines L_1 and L_2 are rotated around the intersection point (x_{int}, y_{int}) between the data points X_{data} and Y_{data},

THEN the sum of squared errors (SSE) for the rotated lines ($SSE_{rotated}$) is always larger than the SSE for the original lines ($SSE_{original}$).

4.2.2 MR$_2$ - Shift of the Input Data
Let $X_{data} = x_1, x_2, ..., x_n$ and $Y_{data} = y_1, y_2, ..., y_n$ represent the original input points. Let (x_{int}, y_{int}) be the intersection point of lines L_1 and L_2 calculated by the SUT. $\mathbf{v} = (v_x, v_y)$ is a 2D vector representing the shift in the x and y coordinates, respectively.

IF all input data points in X_{data} and Y_{data} are shifted by a certain vector $\mathbf{v}$, i.e., $X_{shifted} = \{x_i + \mathbf{v}_x| \text{ for all } i\}$, and $Y_{shifted} = \{y_i + \mathbf{v}_y| \text{ for all } i\}$

THEN the resulting intersection point of lines L_1 and L_2 should also be shifted by the same vector $\mathbf{v}$, this is:

$$(x_{int} + \mathbf{v}_x,\ y_{int} + \mathbf{v}_y) = \text{IntersectionPoint}(SUT(X_{shifted}, Y_{shifted}))$$

4.2.3 MR$_3$ - Orthogonal Rotation Invariance Around Intersection Point
Let $X_{data} = x_1, x_2, ..., x_n$ and $Y_{data} = y_1, y_2, ..., y_n$ represent the original input points. Let (x_{int}, y_{int}) be the intersection point of lines L_1 and L_2 calculated by

the SUT. Let $X_{dataROT}$ and $Y_{dataROT}$ represent the orthogonally rotated input points obtained by rotating X_{data} and Y_{data} around (x_{int}, y_{int}) with an angle of rotation θ.

IF $(X_{dataROT}, Y_{dataROT})$ is obtained by orthogonally rotating all input points X_{data} and Y_{data} around (x_{int}, y_{int}) with an angle of rotation θ,

THEN $SUT(X_{dataROT}, Y_{dataROT})$ should produce the intersection point as the original input points; this is:

$$\text{Intersection}(SUT(X_{data}, Y_{data})) = \text{Intersection}(SUT(X_{dataROT}, Y_{dataROT}))$$

4.2.4 MR$_4$ - Permutation of the Input

Let $X_{data} = x_1, x_2, ..., x_n$ and $Y_{data} = y_1, y_2, ..., y_n$ represent the original input points.

Let (x_{int}, y_{int}) be the intersection point of lines L_1 and L_2 calculated by the SUT, *i.e.*, IntersectionPoint$(SUT(X_{data}, Y_{data}))$.

Let $X_{PER} = x_3, x_n, ..., x_1$ and $Y_{PER} = y_3, y_n, ..., y_1$ represent the reordered input points obtained by randomly permuting the elements of (X_{data}, Y_{data}).

Let (x_{intP}, y_{intP}) be the intersection point of lines L_1' and L_2' calculated by the SUT, *i.e.*, IntersectionPoint$(SUT(X_{PER}, Y_{PER}))$.

IF the same set of input points (X_{data}, Y_{data}) is reordered to create a new input data set (X_{PER}, Y_{PER}),

THEN using the reordered input data (X_{PER}, Y_{PER}) should produce the same results as the original input data (X_{data}, Y_{data}).

4.3 Implementation of the Metamorphic Relations

The implementation of each MR is specific to its requirements and characteristics. Consequently, we present a detailed procedure for each MR in the following subsections. However, it is important to note that all MRs share a common initial step, referred to as Step 0:

Step 0 - get the intersection point (x_{int}, y_{int}). The SUT derives the best-fitted lines L_1 and L_2 and calculates the intersection point (x_{int}, y_{int}) based on the provided input data X_{data} and Y_{data}.

4.3.1 MR$_1$– Rotation of Fitted Lines
To apply MR$_1$, two auxiliary programs are needed, one to compute the SSE between the fitted lines and the original data points and another to perform the rotation of lines from 0 to n degrees (where $n < 360°$). The implementation of MR_1 involves the following steps:

1. Compute SSE for the lines L_1 and L_2. The SSE between the fitted lines L_1 and L_2 and the original data *i.e.*, X_{data} and Y_{data}, points is computed. The SSE measures the accuracy of the fitted lines in approximating the input data points (Y_{data}). A lower SSE value indicates a better fit between the lines and the data points.

2. Perform Rotation. The auxiliary program responsible for rotation is executed. It performs orthogonal rotation of lines L_1 and L_2 around the intersection point (x_{int}, y_{int}) with angles ranging from 0 to n degrees. The rotation is performed incrementally in steps of n degree.
3. Compute SSE for Rotated Lines. For each angle of rotation, the SSE between the rotated lines and the original data points is computed. This step quantifies the accuracy of the rotated lines in approximating the input data.
4. Get conclusions. Based on the results, the test concludes whether MR_1 is adhered to or violated. If no violation is detected for any rotation angle, it indicates that the intersection point obtained from the SUT is indeed optimal.

4.3.2 MR_2 - Shift of the Input Data

To apply MR_2, it is necessary to compute a set of shifts $\mathbf{v} = (v_x, v_y)$, which can be randomly generated through n iterations. The implementation of MR_2 involves the following steps:

1. Generate Shift Vectors. The auxiliary program first generates a set of shift vectors $\mathbf{v}$ by randomly computing v_x and v_y for n iterations. These shift vectors represent the amount by which the data points will be shifted in the x and y directions.
2. Shift Data Points. For each generated shift vector $\mathbf{v}$, the program applies the shift to the original data points X_{data} and Y_{data}, creating new sets of data points $X_{shifted}$ and $Y_{shifted}$. The shift is performed by adding v_x to all elements of X_{data} and v_y to all elements of Y_{data}.
3. Fit Lines and Calculate Intersection Point of the shifted data point. The SUT computes the best-fitted lines L_1' and L_2' based on the shifted data points $X_{shifted}$ and $Y_{shifted}$. The SUT then calculates the intersection point (x_{int}', y_{int}') of these fitted lines.
4. Compare Intersection Points. The original intersection point (x_{int}, y_{int}) and the shifted intersection point (x_{int}', y_{int}') are compared. If they are not equal within a certain tolerance, a violation is reported.

4.3.3 MR_3 - Rotation Invariance Around Intersection Point

To apply MR_3, it is necessary to have an auxiliary program that performs the rotation of the input data points X_{data} and Y_{data} by n degrees, where n is less than 360. The implementation of MR_3 involves the following steps:

1. Rotate Data Points. The auxiliary program performs rotation of the original data points X_{data} and Y_{data} around the calculated intersection point (x_{int}, y_{int}) by the angle θ. This rotation is performed by applying standard 2D rotation formulas to each data point.
2. Fit Lines and Calculate Rotated Intersection Point. The SUT computes the best-fitted lines L_1' and L_2' based on the rotated data points $X_{dataROTATED}$ and $Y_{dataROTATED}$. The SUT then calculates the rotated intersection point $(x_{intdataROTATED}, y_{intROTATED})$ of these fitted lines.

3. Compare Intersection Points. The original intersection point (x_{int}, y_{int}) and the rotated intersection point $(x_{intdataROTATED}, y_{intdataROTATED})$ are compared. If they are equal within a certain tolerance, MR$_3$ is considered adhered to. Otherwise, a violation is reported.

4.3.4   MR$_4$ - Permutation of the Input

To apply MR4 (Same Points in Different Order Invariance), it is necessary to have an auxiliary program that generates permutations of the original data points X_{data} and Y_{data}. The implementation of MR4 involves the following steps:

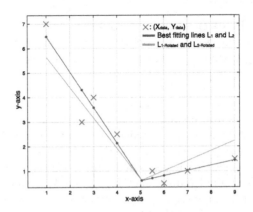

Fig. 2. Graphical representation of MR$_1$. (Color figure online)

1. Generate Permutations. The auxiliary program generates all possible permutations of the original data points X_{data} and Y_{data}. Each permutation represents a different order of the data points.
2. Fit Lines and Calculate Intersection Points. For each permutation of the data points, the SUT computes the best-fitted lines L_1' and L_2' based on the permuted data points X_{PER} and Y_{PER}. The SUT then calculates the intersection point (x_{intPER}, y_{intPER}) of these fitted lines.
3. Compare Intersection Points. The intersection points obtained from the original data points and permuted data points, respectively, are compared. If all the intersection points from different permutations are the same within a certain tolerance, MR$_4$ is considered adhered to. Otherwise, a violation is reported.

5   Results and Discussion

MR$_1$ - Rotation of Fitted Lines. Let's consider the input data (X_{data}, Y_{data}) (red X in Fig. 2). MR$_1$ focuses on the output of the SUT, specifically the best-fitted lines L_1 and L_2 (blue lines in Fig. 2) and their intersection point. Unlike other MRs that typically transform the SUT's input, MR$_1$ uniquely applies a metamorphic transformation to its output, keeping the input data intact. The core concept of MR$_1$ involves orthogonally rotating the output lines, represented in green in Fig. 2. Subsequently, an auxiliary program computes the SSE between the original output of the SUT and the X_{data} and Y_{data}. This process is repeated for all newly rotated lines. MR_1 is not violated when the SSE of the rotated lines will be larger than the SSE of the original lines.

Figure 3 illustrates the analysis of MR_1. In Fig. 3a, we observe the orthogonally rotated lines of L_1 and L_2, covering a range from $-15°$ to $15°$ in steps of $1°$. In Fig. 3b, the graph displays the sum of all error squares resulting from the rotation. The x-axis represents the rotation angle in degrees, ranging from $-15°$ to $15°$, while the y-axis shows the summation of error squares. Notably, at $0°$ rotation, representing the original lines L_1 and L_2, the SSE achieves the lowest value, indicating the minimum error at this point.

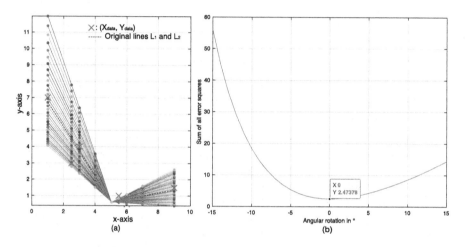

Fig. 3. Analysis of Orthogonal Rotation Invariance MR_1. (a) Rotated lines of L_1 and L_2 from $-15°$ to $15°$ in steps of $1°$. (b) The sum of all error squares from $-15°$ to $15°$

We conducted additional experiments by reducing the rotation degrees to the range $[-2, 2]$ with steps of 0.1. The main goal of this configuration was to investigate the sensitivity and precision of the fitted lines and, consequently, the intersection point. By exploring this narrower rotation range, we aimed to assess how small variations in the rotation angle would affect the accuracy of the fitted lines and their intersection. Despite the variations introduced in the rotation degrees, the results revealed that no violations were registered for MR_1. This finding suggests that the fitted lines and the intersection point remained stable and maintained their accuracy even with minor changes in the rotation angle.

MR_2 - Shift of the Input Data. Figure 4 showcases the element-wise shift of the input data by $\mathbf{v} = (v_x, v_y)$, which is a 2D vector representing the shift in the x and y coordinates, respectively. The red X points indicate the original input data (X_{data}, Y_{data}), while the green X points represent the data after the shift. MR_2 checks whether the new computed lines L_1 and L_2, as well as their intersection point, are shifted by the same vector **v**. Figure 4 visually depicts the concept behind MR_2, where the input data undergoes a controlled shift, and the resulting lines and intersection points are examined for consistency with the shift vector.

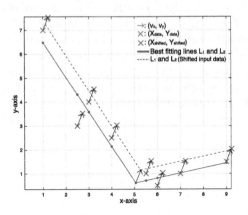

Fig. 4. Graphical representation of MR_2 - Shift of the Input Data (Color figure online)

We utilised the `randperm` MATLAB function to generate random permutations of integers between 1 and 15. These permutations represented the shift in the x and y coordinates, creating a 2D vector for each iteration. We performed 100 iterations using different shift vectors to analyse its behaviour under various conditions thoroughly. To compare floating-point values for equality, we adopted a tolerance approach. In MATLAB, it is common to use a small threshold, typically 0.0001, to check if two floating-point values are close enough to be considered equal. In our code, we used this tolerance to determine if the computed intersection point was within an acceptable range from the original intersection point, shifted by the generated shift-vector. If the difference was within the threshold, we considered the MR_2 as non-violated. However, as we delved deeper into the reported violations for different input data, we noticed that some scenarios required a slightly larger tolerance than the default 0.0001. For certain cases, we found that setting a tolerance of 0.001 was more suitable. This finding emphasised that the choice of tolerance might depend on the specific characteristics of the input data and the SUT being tested. Hence, it's crucial to adjust the tolerance accordingly for accurate and reliable MR_2 results.

MR_3 - Rotation Invariance around Intersection Point. Figure 5a provides is the representation of MR_3, the original points are represented by red x, and the rotate ones are represented by green x. In MR_3, the data points are rotated in 45° increments. In Fig. 5b, the rotated data points are shown, and their respective best-fitted lines, L_1 and L_2, are displayed. MR3 is designed to check the rotation invariance of the SUT around its intersection point between the best-fitted lines. It involves rotating the input points $(Xdata, Y_{data})$ by an angle of rotation θ around the intersection point to obtain the rotated input points $(X_{dataROT}, Y_{dataROT})$. According to MR3, if the SUT is truly rotation invariant when given the rotated input points $(XdataROT, Y_{dataROT})$, it should produce the same results as the intersection points of (X_{data}, Y_{data}).

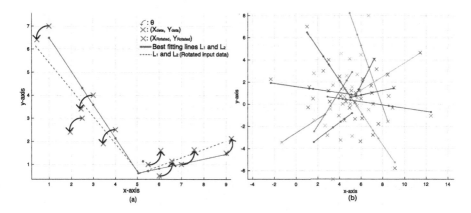

Fig. 5. (a)Graphical representation of MR$_3$; (b) Shows rotated data points every 45°, and their respective L_1 and L_2

As shown in Fig. 5b, MR$_3$ is being violated for all the rotation points. When analysing the reasons behind these violations, we aimed to determine whether they were due to a fault in the system or a mismatch between the SUT, test data, and MR$_3$ itself. Initially, we attributed these violations to differences in floating-point precision during the rotation operation, which might lead to small discrepancies in the results, causing the comparison to fail even though the SUT is theoretically rotation invariant. Additionally, we considered the possibility that the SUT internally performs some sorting of the input data. If the SUT is sensitive to the order of the input data, rotating and then sorting data $(X_{dataROT}, Y_{dataROT})$ could lead to different outcomes compared to the original data (X_{data}, Y_{data}). However, upon further investigation and discussions with the main developer, it was confirmed that the violations were caused by sorting. Therefore, the violations do not necessarily indicate a fault in the code but rather suggest that MR$_3$ may not apply to the SUT. To reuse this MR, it might be necessary to consider how the SUT processes sorted input data and investigate if the sorting operation has any unintended consequences on the SUT's behaviour.

MR4 - Permutation of the Input. To create the new input data sets (X_{PER}, Y_{PER}), we utilised MATLAB's `perms` function, which generated all possible permutations of the input data without repetition. We executed the SUT twice: once with the original input data (X_{data}, Y_{data}) and again with the reordered input data (X_{PER}, Y_{PER}). For each iteration, we calculated the intersection points for both cases and compared the results. The analysis of the results indicates that the SUT exhibits no violation of MR$_4$ for any of the input data sets. This finding result indicates that the SUT remains invariant to the reordering of input data.

5.1   Industry Feedback

Several talks with our industry partner have been held, where we gathered feedback about the current state of the rule check implementations and discussed the next steps. At the end of the project, we organised a meeting to discuss the final results of this industrial evaluation together with the two people from the company involved, the main developer of the optimisation code and the person responsible for the quality of the software stack of the control unit where the resulting optimisation code goes.

The approach has felt valuable to the developer to think about the system limits. It was mentioned that because of this project and the discussions about general valid rules, even for the main developer, the condition space of the observed code has become clearer. In addition, it was confirmed that this approach seems feasible to assure the robustness of the code under test. Besides that, another positive side-effect of the done evaluation was that the topic testing in general could be seen from a different, more abstract angle.

Whether MT approach can provide added value to the investigated use case has been assessed differently. On the one side, we have chosen a function to test with a certain complexity but which is still relatively easy to understand. The size of the underlying codebase is low, and only one additional external code file is used. Hence, and because the code under test is stable and is not intended to be changed in the future anymore, the benefit of providing additional, holistic testing will be low. On the other side, the approach has shown its potential even for this simpler example, and it will provide more benefits for code, which is (a) more difficult to test in isolation, (b) where the functionality cannot be divided into small function units easily, and (c) which is changed more often. We all agreed that we would like to investigate the approach on another use case in another department of the company in the future to see if our assumptions above are confirmed or not.

5.2   Lessons Learned

Throughout this study, we have gained valuable insights and lessons that have contributed to a deeper understanding of the SUT and the overall MT process. Some of the key lessons learned include:

– MT has proven to be a powerful and effective technique for testing complex and black-box systems. By leveraging MRs, we were able to design test cases that validate the SUT's behaviour without the need for an oracle.
– When dealing with floating-point values, it is essential to consider tolerance levels in equality comparisons. Small discrepancies arising from floating-point precision can lead to false violations. We learned to adapt the tolerance threshold to different scenarios to ensure accurate test results.
– Our study highlighted the significance of input order in some cases. In scenarios where the SUT is sensitive to the order of input data, reordering can lead to different outcomes. Understanding such sensitivity can help improve the system's robustness and identify potential areas for optimisation.

- A notable achievement in this study pertains to MR_1, which introduces a novel perspective on MT. By leveraging auxiliary functions and transforming the SUT's output as input for further analysis, MR_1 provides valuable insights into the reliability and correctness of the SUT from a unique angle. Building on this success, the next stage of our research will focus on expanding and refining the definition of MRs using auxiliary functions. We aim to explore how these auxiliary functions can be effectively integrated into other contexts to analyse the reliability and correctness of the SUT from different angles.

5.3 Threats to Validity

In the context of our study, two types of threats to validity are most relevant: threats to internal and external validity. Potential threats to internal validity pertain to MR selection bias, as the specific choice of MRs might unintentionally introduce bias into the study result. Regarding external validity, there are concerns that the chosen SUT may not fully represent all possible software systems, thereby restricting the generalisability of our findings to other applications. The black-box nature of the SUT, coupled with its industrial application, poses further challenges in applying the study's results to different domains.

6 Conclusion

In this paper, we have shared our experience testing a black-box optimisation algorithm using MT. Through the exploration of MRs, we have uncovered a new perspective on MT, particularly with the introduction of MR_1. Unlike other MRs that typically transform the SUT's input, MR_1 instead focuses on transforming the SUT's output and utilising it as input for an auxiliary function. Throughout the study, we encountered and addressed various challenges related to floating-point precision and input order sensitivity. Adapting tolerance levels and carefully considering input order proved vital in achieving accurate test results. These lessons underscore the importance of thorough testing and understanding the intricacies of the SUT to ensure robust and reliable results.

Furthermore, the study engaged with our industry partner, gaining valuable feedback on the MT approach's feasibility and applicability. While the current case study demonstrated the potential of MT even for a relatively simple and stable SUT, it was acknowledged that the approach would offer more significant benefits for more complex, frequently changing systems. The future direction of our research will involve applying MT to other industrial use cases, further validating and refining the approach's efficacy.

Acknowledgement. The research reported in this paper has been partly funded by BMK, BMAW, and the State of Upper Austria in the frame of the SCCH competence center INTEGRATE [(FFG grant no. 892418)] part of the FFG COMET Competence Centers for Excellent Technologies Programme, as well as by the European Regional Development Fund, and grant PRG1226 of the Estonian Research Council.

References

1. Bartz-Beielstein, T., Chiarandini, M., Paquete, L., Preuss, M.: Experimental Methods for the Analysis of Optimization Algorithms. Springer, Heidelberg (2010). https://doi.org/10.1007/978-3-642-02538-9
2. Beiranvand, V., Hare, W., Lucet, Y.: Best practices for comparing optimization algorithms. Optim. Eng. **18**(4), 815–848 (2017)
3. Chen, T.Y., Cheung, S.C., Yiu, S.M.: Metamorphic testing: a new approach for generating next test cases. Department of Computer Science, Hong Kong University of Science and Technology, Hong Kong, Technical report (1998)
4. Duque-Torres, A., Pfahl, D., Klammer, C., Fischer, S.: Bug or not bug? analysing the reasons behind metamorphic relation violations. In: IEEE International Conference on Software Analysis, Evolution and Reengineering (SANER), pp. 905–912 (2023)
5. Hawkins, D.M., Basak, S.C., Mills, D.: Assessing model fit by cross-validation. J. Chem. Inf. Comput. Sci. **43**(2), 579–586 (2003)
6. Jamil, M., Yang, X.S.: A literature survey of benchmark functions for global optimisation problems. Int. J. Math. Model. Numer. Optim. **4**(2), 150–194 (2013)
7. Peng, Z., Kanewala, U., Niu, N.: Contextual understanding and improvement of metamorphic testing in scientific software development. In: 15th ACM/IEEE International Symposium on Empirical Software Engineering and Measurement (ESEM), pp. 1–6 (2021)
8. Rounds, J., Kanewala, U.: Systematic testing of genetic algorithms: a metamorphic testing based approach. arXiv preprint arXiv:1808.01033 (2018)
9. Shahri, M.P., Srinivasan, M., Reynolds, G., Bimczok, D., Kahanda, I., Kanewala, U.: Metamorphic testing for quality assurance of protein function prediction tools. In: IEEE International Conference On Artificial Intelligence Testing (AITest), pp. 140–148. IEEE (2019)
10. Wiesler, S., Ney, H.: A convergence analysis of log-linear training. In: Advances in Neural Information Processing Systems, vol. 24 (2011)
11. Yoo, S.: Metamorphic testing of stochastic optimisation. In: Third International Conference on Software Testing, Verification, and Validation Workshops, pp. 192–201 (2010)
12. Zhang, Y., Gong, D.W., Sun, X.Y., Geng, N.: Adaptive bare-bones particle swarm optimization algorithm and its convergence analysis. Soft. Comput. **18**(7), 1337–1352 (2014)
13. Zhang, Z., Towey, D., Ying, Z., Zhang, Y., Zhou, Z.Q.: MT4NS: metamorphic testing for network scanning. In: 6th IEEE/ACM International Workshop on Metamorphic Testing (MET), MET 2021, pp. 17–23 (2021)
14. Zhou, Z.Q., Sun, L.: Metamorphic testing of driverless cars. Commun. ACM **62**(3), 61–67 (2019). ISSN: 0001-0782

Impacts of Program Structures on Code Coverage of Generated Test Suites

Ryoga Watanabe[✉], Yoshiki Higo, and Shinji Kusumoto

Graduate School of Information Science and Technology, Osaka University, Osaka, Japan
{ryg-wtnb,higo,kusumoto}@ist.osaka-u.ac.jp

Abstract. Unit testing is a part of the process of developing software. In unit testing, developers verify that programs properly work as developers intend. Creating a test suite for a unit test is very time-consuming. For this reason, research is being conducted to generate a test suite for unit testing automatically, and before now, some test generation tools have been released. However, test generation tools may not be able to generate a test suite that fully covers a test target. In our research, we investigate the causes of this problem by focusing on structures of test targets to improve test generation tools. As a result, we found four patterns as the causes of this problem and proposed subsequent research directions for each pattern to solve this problem.

Keywords: Unit testing · Test generation tool · Code coverage · Program structures

1 Introduction

In software development, software testing is conducted in order to verify that programs work properly as developers intend. Software testing is conducted in several phases, depending on the granularity of the test target. Unit testing is a process of testing functions or methods, which are the smallest granular units of the test target. Bugs and problems can be identified early since unit testing is conducted early in software development. Therefore, unit testing is an essential part of software development.

Creating a test suite for a unit test is very time-consuming. For this reason, research is being conducted to generate a test suite for unit testing automatically [8]. Before now, test generation tools such as EvoSuite [2], Randoop [9], and SUSHI [1] have been released. There are several approaches to generating a test suite. For example, EvoSuite uses genetic algorithm, Randoop uses random testing, and SUSHI uses symbolic execution as well as genetic algorithm.

However, test generation tools may not be able to generate a test suite that fully covers a test target. This problem depends on various factors, such as algorithms of generation tools, parameter settings during test generation, and structures of test targets. In our research, we investigate the cause of this problem by focusing on structures of test targets to improve test generation tools.

© The Author(s), under exclusive license to Springer Nature Switzerland AG 2024
R. Kadgien et al. (Eds.): PROFES 2023, LNCS 14483, pp. 355–362, 2024.
https://doi.org/10.1007/978-3-031-49266-2_24

```
1  boolean getBooleanProperty(String prop, boolean defaultValue) {
2      String val = System.getProperty(prop);
3      if ( val == null )
4          return defaultValue;
5      if ( val.equalsIgnoreCase("true") ) {
6          return true ;
7      } else {
8          return false ;
9      }
10 }
```

Fig. 1. An example of the method whose statements are not executed by a test suite generated by EvoSuite

We used EvoSuite to generate test suites from 768 Java methods and then manually picked up the methods whose program statements were not fully covered by the test suites. For these methods, we identified the non-covered program statements. We then considered why these program statements are not covered, and we then classified these methods into patterns that we had created based on the found causes of this problem. As a result, we found four patterns and proposed subsequent research directions for each pattern to solve this problem.

2 Motivating Example

Figure 1 shows a method whose program statements are not covered by a test suite[1] generated by EvoSuite shown in Table 1. The highlighting in Fig. 1 indicates that the **false** branch of the conditional statement **val == null** in line 3 and all the program statements after line 5 are not executed.

Table 1. An example of the test suite from the method shown in Fig. 1 generated by EvoSuite

Input		Assertion
prop	defaultValue	
"Hwiz5]f"	true	returns true
"7G"	false	returns false
null	false	returns false
""	false	throws IllegalArgumentException

We consider the reason why these program statements are not executed by the test suite generated by EvoSuite. The reason is that the condition of line

---

[1] In this paper, the statements partially executed by a generated test suite are presented in yellow . Herein, partially executed means that only a **true** or **false** branch is executed by a generated test suite. The statements never executed by a generated test suite are presented in orange .

3 never becomes **false** with the generated test cases. Then, focusing on the val variable in this conditional statement, this variable is the return value of System.getProperty() in line 2. This means that the condition of line 3 never becomes **false** because System.getProperty() always returns a **null** value. The System.getProperty() method is designed to return the value of a real system property name (such as "**user.dir**") if input; otherwise, it returns a **null** value. Therefore, we can conclude that there are some non-covered program statements by the generated test cases because EvoSuite cannot generate any test case that inputs a real system property name because of the System.getProperty() method.

3 Investigation Settings

3.1 Dataset

We used a dataset [7] consisting of 768 Java methods as the subject of our investigation. These methods have the following characteristics: (1) they do not depend on external variables or methods, (2) they have one or more arguments and a return value, (3) they are described in the Java 8 or earlier specification, and (4) they use only the java.lang or java.util classes.

3.2 Test Generation Tool

We used EvoSuite to generate test suites for the methods in the dataset. EvoSuite generates highly covered JUnit test suites based on genetic algorithm, using techniques such as the hybrid search [6], the dynamic symbolic execution [4], and the testability transformation [5]. EvoSuite is unique among the other test generation tools for Java in its ability to generate test suites with high coverage [11].

EvoSuite has several coverage criteria as coverage targets for generating a test suite. This means that our investigation results will differ depending on which criteria we focus on. We selected to focus on line coverage and branch coverage because they are representative of code coverage and can be measured and visualized by JaCoCo[2].

3.3 Process Steps

We have taken the following steps to prepare for the investigation.

Step.1: for each method from the dataset, we made class definitions that include the method itself. To ensure that all class definition files are compilable, we inserted the import statement import java.util.*; at the beginning of each file.

Step.2: for each class made in Step.1, we generated a test suite using EvoSuite and measured the coverage of the test suite using JaCoCo.

---

[2] https://www.eclemma.org/jacoco/.

```
1  Float parseFloat(String value, float defaultValue) {
2      try {
3          return Float.parseFloat(value) ;
4      } catch (NumberFormatException e) {
5          ...
6      }
7  }
```

Fig. 2. An example of the method that is classified into "Method parameters require specific values"

Step.3: we manually picked up the methods whose line or branch coverage is less than 1.0. Out of 768 methods in the dataset, we picked up 73 methods, which is 9.5% of all the methods. In the steps, we excluded the methods from which EvoSuite cannot generate tests that fail or are incorrectly evaluated as not covered due to the bug in JaCoCo.

Step.4: for the methods we picked up in Step.3, we identified the non-covered program statements by referring to the report generated by JaCoCo. We then classified those methods into patterns that we had created based on the found causes.

4   Investigation Results

As the reasons why the program statements were not covered, we found four patterns:

- "Method parameters require specific values"
- "Method parameters require specific types"
- "Methods include infeasible program statements"
- "Methods include multithreaded program statements"

4.1   "Method Parameters Require Specific Values"

In this pattern, parameters that satisfy some conditions are required in order to cover the non-covered program statements. Fifty-eight out of 73 methods are classified into this pattern. Figure 2 shows an example of the method that is classified into this pattern. This method converts any string representing a float type value (e.g., "10.0f") to an actual float type value. In this method, the normal process of Float.parseFloat() is not covered by the generated test suite. In order to cover this process, a test case is required to input any string representing a float type value into this method.

4.2   "Method Parameters Require Specific Values Types"

In this pattern, parameters of derived classes of the class in the parameter definition are required in order to cover the non-covered program statements. Six out of 73 methods are classified into this pattern. Figure 3 shows an example of

```
1  int uncheckedIntCast(Object x) {
2      if ( x instanceof Number )
3          return ((Number) x).intValue();
4      return ((Character) x).charValue() ;
5  }
```

Fig. 3. An example of the method that is classified into "Method parameters require specific types"

```
1  List<String> splitToList0(String str, char ch) {
2      List<String> result = new ArrayList<>();
3      int ix = 0, len = str.length();
4      for (int i = 0; i < len; i++) {
5          if (str.charAt(i) == ch) {
6              result.add(str.substring(ix, i));
7              ix = i + 1;
8          }
9      }
10     if ( ix >= 0 ) {
11         result.add(str.substring(ix));
12     }
13     return result;
14 }
```

Fig. 4. An example of the method that is classified into "Methods include infeasible program statements"

the method that is classified into this pattern. This method casts the parameter of Object type to int type and returns its value. In this method, the false branch of the condition in line 2 and the statement in line 4 are not covered. The branch in line 3 evaluates whether or not the parameter type is Number. In order to cover them, a test case is required to input a variable other than Number type.

4.3 "Methods Include Infeasible Program Statements"

In this pattern, methods have the program statements that are never executed, no matter what parameters are given. Six out of 73 methods are classified into this pattern. Figure 4 shows an example of the method that is classified into this pattern. This method splits the str string by the ch character and returns the result as a list of strings. The variable ix is initialized with the value 0 in line 3, and there is no program statement to decrease ix below 0, even in the program statement of line 4 to 9, where the value of ix may change. Therefore, the false branch of the if statement in line 10 is never executed, no matter what parameters are given.

4.4 "Methods Include Multithreaded Program Statements"

In this pattern, a test case using multithreading is required to cover the non-covered program statements. Three out of 73 methods are classified into this pattern. Figure 5 shows an example of the method that is classified into this pattern. This method puts the currently running thread to sleep. In this method, the checked exception `InterruptedException` in line 4, thrown by `Thread.sleep()` in line 3, is not caught by the generated test suite. `InterruptedException` is an exception thrown when a thread is in waiting, sleeping, or occupied and the thread is interrupted. In order to catch this exception, a test case is required to throw `InterruptedException` intentionally using multithreading.

```
1  Integer apply(Integer i) {
2      try {
3          Thread.sleep(1);
4      } catch ( InterruptedException e ) {
5          e.printStackTrace() ;
6      }
7      return i;
8  }
```

Fig. 5. An example of the method that is classified into "Methods include multithreaded program statements"

5   Discussion

We propose subsequent research directions to increase coverage for the four patterns we found in our investigation.

5.1   "Method Parameters Require Specific Values" and "Method Parameters Require Specific Types"

The reason why EvoSuite cannot cover program statements classified into the patterns "Method parameters require specific values" or "Method parameters require specific types" is that EvoSuite cannot generate a test case that inputs any string (i.e., any value of `java.lang.String`) to satisfy some conditions to cover them.

EvoSuite uses constants of primitive or `String` type statically embedded in Java bytecode when EvoSuite evolves a test suite in genetic algorithm [2]. Applying this feature, modifying EvoSuite to externally provide the constants and types the user wants EvoSuite to treat while evolving a test suite would improve coverage.

As a simple exploration to demonstrate the effectiveness of this direction, consider inserting a *fake branch* to the test target. A *fake branch* is an `if` statement that does not affect the original method's functionality containing values or types to execute non-covered program statements. For example, suppose the test suite is generated again using EvoSuite for the method shown in Fig. 2 with a *fake branch* inserted, as shown in Fig. 6. In that case, the non-covered program statements (i.e., line 3 in Fig. 2) will be executed because EvoSuite can refer to the value embedded by the *fake branch* (i.e., `"10.0f"`).

```
1    Float parseFloat(String value, float defaultValue) {
2  +      if (value == "10.0f") {}
3         try {
4            return Float.parseFloat(value);
5         } catch (NumberFormatException e) {
6            ...
7         }
8    }
```

Fig. 6. An example of inserting the *fake branch*

5.2 "Methods Include Infeasible Program Statements"

Infeasible program statements can never be executed, regardless of the given parameters. Therefore, it is impossible to solve by adding or modifying test cases. Instead, excluding the infeasible program statements from coverage goals or lower the coverage priority when generating test suites would improve coverage. Evo-Suite uses an approach that optimizes the coverage criteria as a whole rather than each coverage goal of the coverage criteria. This results in a lower coverage priority for infeasible program statements. Integrated development environment features can detect some infeasible program statements. If programmers use this feature to remove infeasible program statements before generating the test suite, these statements can be excluded from the coverage goals. For example, in the method shown in Fig. 4, this corresponds to removing the if statement in line 10.

5.3 "Methods Include Multithreaded Program Statements"

EvoSuite is not compatible with the generation of test suites that use multi-threading [3]. Therefore, from the point of improving program structures, it is impossible to solve this problem. On the other hand, the research [10] has been conducted to develop EvoSuite to generate test suites that support multithreaded processing.

6   Conclusion and Future Work

Our research investigated how program structures affect code coverage of generated test suites. As a result, we found four patterns as the reasons the program statements are not covered. We considered whether a technique exists to solve why program statements are not covered for those patterns and proposed subsequent research directions for each pattern.

Our investigation is conducted in the settings explained in Sect. 3. Therefore, different results may be obtained if another investigation is conducted in different settings. In future work, we will verify what results can be obtained by conducting the same investigation on a different dataset or actual Java projects and on different criteria or test generation tools.

Acknowledgments. This research was supported by JSPS KAKENHI Japan (JP20H04166, JP21K18302, JP21K11829, JP21H04877, JP22H03567, JP22K11985).

References

1. Braione, P., Denaro, G., Mattavelli, A., Pezzè, M.: SUSHI: a test generator for programs with complex structured inputs. In: Proceedings of the International Conference on Software Engineering, pp. 21–24 (2018)
2. Fraser, G., Arcuri, A.: EvoSuite: automatic test suite generation for object-oriented software. In: Proceedings of the European Conference on Foundations of Software Engineering, pp. 416–419 (2011)
3. Fraser, G., Arcuri, A.: Whole test suite generation. IEEE Trans. Softw. Eng. **39**, 276–291 (2013)
4. Godefroid, P., Klarlund, N., Sen, K.: DART: directed automated random testing. In: Proceedings of the ACM SIGPLAN Conference on Programming Language Design and Implementation, pp. 213–223 (2005)
5. Harman, M., et al.: Testability transformation. IEEE Trans. Softw. Eng. **30**, 3–16 (2004)
6. Harman, M., McMinn, P.: A theoretical and empirical study of search-based testing: local, global, and hybrid search. IEEE Trans. Softw. Eng. **36**, 226–247 (2010)
7. Higo, Y., Matsumoto, S., Kusumoto, S., Yasuda, K.: Constructing dataset of functionally equivalent java methods. In: Proceedings of the International Conference on Mining Software Repositories, pp. 682–686 (2022)
8. McMinn, P.: Search-based software test data generation: a survey. Softw. Test. Verif. Reliab. **14**, 105–156 (2004)
9. Pacheco, C., Ernst, M.: Randoop: feedback-directed random testing for Java. In: Proceedings of the Object-Oriented Programming, Systems, Languages and Applications, pp. 815–816 (2007)
10. Steenbuck, S., Fraser, G.: Generating unit tests for concurrent classes. In: Proceedings of the International Conference on Software Testing, Verification and Validation, pp. 144–153 (2013)
11. Vogl, S., Schweikl, S., Fraser, G., Arcuri, A., Campos, J., Panichella, A.: EvoSuite at the SBST 2021 tool competition. In: Proceedings of the International Workshop on Search-Based Software Testing, pp. 28–29 (2021)

Anomaly Detection Through Container Testing: A Survey of Company Practices

Salla Timonen(✉) ⓘ, Maha Sroor ⓘ, Rahul Mohanani ⓘ,
and Tommi Mikkonen ⓘ

University of Jyväskylä, Mattilanniemi 2, Jyväskylä, Finland
{salla.k.timonen,maha.m.sroor,rahul.p.mohanani,tommi.j.mikkonen}@jyu.fi

Abstract. Background: Containers are a commonly used solution for deploying software applications. Therefore, container functionality and security is a concern of practitioners and researchers. Testing is essential to ensure the quality of the container environment component and the software product and plays a crucial role in using containers.

Objective: In light of the increasing role of software containers and the lack of research on testing them, we study container testing practices. In this paper, we investigate the current approaches for testing containers. Moreover, we aim to identify areas for improvement and emphasize the importance of testing in securing the container environment and the final software product.

Method: We conducted a survey to collect primary data from companies implementing container testing practices and the commonly used tools in container testing. There were 14 respondents from a total of 10 different companies with experience using containers and varying work responsibilities.

Findings: The survey findings illustrate the significance of testing, the growing interest in and utilization of containers, and the emerging security and vulnerability concerns. The research reveals variations in testing approaches between companies and the lack of consensus on how testing should be carried out, with advancements primarily driven by industry practices rather than academic research.

Conclusion: In this study, we show the importance of testing software containers. It lays out the current testing approaches, challenges, and the need for standardized container testing practices. We also provide recommendations on how to develop these practices further.

Keywords: Software containers · Testing · Survey

1 Introduction

Containers have become an integral part of modern software engineering (SE) processes, offering numerous benefits such as increased portability, scalability, and flexibility. Like any emerging new technology, containers potentially introduce new risks and vulnerabilities in the development process. With this in

© The Author(s), under exclusive license to Springer Nature Switzerland AG 2024
R. Kadgien et al. (Eds.): PROFES 2023, LNCS 14483, pp. 363–378, 2024.
https://doi.org/10.1007/978-3-031-49266-2_25

mind, testing is fundamental to finding bugs that could impede the progress of containerized software development [1,2].

Containers built using pre-existing images and components can inherit vulnerabilities from dependencies, making testing vital to identify and mitigate risks. The dynamic nature of containers adds complexity, requiring testing to ensure security. Additionally, testing container interactions in distributed systems and their impact on overall security is crucial to prevent breaches [3]. Testing plays a vital role in creating functional and secure software containers.

With the increasing popularity of containers, there is a growing need to address the risks and vulnerabilities associated with their use [4,5]. By addressing these issues, organizations can safeguard sensitive data, prevent unauthorized access, and maintain the integrity of their software environment. However, there is no scientific, empirical consensus on the best practices for testing containers, as advancements in this area are predominantly driven by industry practices rather than academic research [6].

In this paper, we investigate the current status of company practices and tools for detecting anomalies through software container testing. The research focuses on two main aspects – (i) the current approaches employed by companies for testing software containers and (ii) how these approaches can be further developed. As an instrument to study the topic, a survey was conducted, with participation from relevant information technology companies. Hence, the results provide insights into current company practices and identify areas for further research, addressing the gap in the existing literature on testing software containers. Moreover, the results contribute to developing more effective and secure containers by exploring current practices and seeking ways to enhance them.

The structure of the paper is as follows. Section 2 provides some background information regarding what research is currently available on the topic of containers and their testing. Section 3 outlines how the survey was designed and conducted in addition to the tools we used for the analysis. Section 4 presents the results. Section 5 follows with further discussion. Finally, Sect. 6 draws some final conclusions.

2   Background

2.1   Software Containers

Software containers are a critical ingredient in the modern software development context. They enable rapid software updates in cloud context and practices such as DevOps by allowing the packaging of applications and all their necessary dependencies, such as software, configurations, libraries, frameworks, and binaries [7]. Containers isolate and virtualize the operating system, giving each containerized application a separate area of execution within the operating system. This enables multiple applications to run on a single operating system instance, resulting in more lightweight and manageable setups compared to running multiple operating system instances [1,2].

Containers have emerged as a solution to the challenges developers face when migrating applications between different environments, such as from development to testing and production. These migrations often encounter issues due to differences in both hardware and software configurations. To overcome these obstacles and improve flexibility, containers are a commonly used solution [1]. Containers are also widely used to support microservices [8]. Container management systems like Docker and orchestration systems like Kubernetes provide control of applications and provision resources, leading to the development of scalable, reliable, and reactive systems [2].

When using containers, the infrastructure typically consists of a repository for building container images and an image registry for deployment. The container setup can potentially lead to various security breaches, including data theft, denial of service attacks, and unauthorized access. Research has identified threats to containers such as spoofing, tampering, information disclosure, denial of service, and elevation of privilege [5].

Docker Hub, one of the most popular Docker image repositories, distributes official and community images. Security vulnerabilities in these images have been studied, driven by high-profile attacks reported through distribution channels. One study [3], introduces a Docker image vulnerability analysis framework called DIVA for analyzing vulnerabilities in Docker images. Furthermore, [9] identifies three major sources of security risks – sensitive parameters in run commands, malicious Docker images, and unpatched vulnerabilities in contained software.

In an early study in 2015, Docker image security was studied by inspecting images from Docker Hub using an open-source tool, "Banyan" Collector [10]. A more recent article from 2020 highlights that Docker does not offer assurances for recognized security vulnerabilities within container images [11].

2.2   Container Testing Approaches

To address the above concerns, four generalized use cases at the host-container level were proposed to identify threats and provide potential solutions [4]. These use cases include protecting a container from its internal applications, intercontainer protection, host protection from containers, and container protection from the host.

Existing mitigation strategies and their limitations are discussed in [5]. Identified strategies included multi-factor authentication systems, implementing network controls, and security patching, but the need for a reliable and fast patching framework is emphasized as a research gap. Proper isolation is also discussed in the paper. On the other hand, another study suggests that kernel security mechanisms play a more critical role than container isolation methods in preventing privilege escalation attacks [12]. A sandbox mining and enforcing approach was proposed in a study [13] where a mined sandbox confines and restricts a container's access to system calls.

Minimizing administrative privileges is another approach to enhancing container security, with methods like anomaly detection systems [14, 15]. Another article from 2021 [16] investigates the accuracy of container scanning tools and highlights the vulnerability of the container's operating system. Additional mitigation strategies involve implementing strong access controls and ensuring containers remain lightweight [17].

While the mentioned mitigation strategies are valuable for enhancing container security, apart from scanning and monitoring, they focus on preventive measures. Furthermore, if implemented incorrectly, they can create a false sense of security. In addition to these mitigation strategies, there are container security frameworks and testing approaches. One example of anomaly-based detection in containers is from a 2020 article on the implementation of Classical Distributed Learning to detect security attacks in containerized applications [14].

A different approach was outlined in another 2020 article proposing the Docker Image Vulnerability Diagnostics System [11]. It was designed to diagnose Docker images during upload or download, addressing the lack of vulnerability diagnostics in current Docker image distribution. In 2022, the SEAF framework [18] was proposed for scalable, efficient, and application-independent container security detection. Inspecting various security defects and evaluating their impact, it found more than 35 000 security defects from popular repositories.

Other frameworks include the Secure Container Manager Pattern [19] and the Framework to Secure Docker Containers [20], focusing on container management and container security, respectively. CONSERVE is another framework for selecting container monitoring techniques in different application domains [21].

An article dated 2021 [6] highlights the absence of global standards for testing the non-functional part of applications. The authors subsequently developed the Non-Functional Testing Framework for Container-Based Applications [22], emphasizing the crucial role of testing results in determining an application's success. They continue to state that the evolution of containers has been mainly driven by industry adaptation than academic research, particularly in the realm of testing frameworks for container-based applications.

To address the challenges of the unknowns, Siddiqui et al. [22] define four non-functional attributes for container applications, characterizing the surrounding environment and its behaviour: capacity, scalability, stability, and high availability. Although a review of testing approaches was conducted, it focused on cloud-based applications [23].

3   Research Methodology

In this work, we aim to encapsulate current company practices and tools for detecting anomalies in container testing by answering the following research questions:

RQ1: What are the current approaches employed by companies for testing software containers?

RQ2: How can the approaches for testing software containers be improved?

We used an online questionnaire survey instrument to answer the research questions. We followed the standard guidelines for planning and conducting survey studies in SE [24], and empirical standards for SE research [25]. A survey was chosen as the most suitable study method for this research, enabling convenient online distribution and data collection from respondents. Also, it supported collecting valuable insight from participating companies, allowing respondents ample time to review and contemplate the questions without time constraints. You can access the survey questionnaire used to collect data for our research here: https://zenodo.org/record/8378974.

The survey includes a total of 23 questions. The contact form is the only mandatory question. The questions comprised both—multiple-choice questions and open-ended questions. Out of the total, 16 open-ended questions allowed respondents to provide detailed and in-depth responses without being restricted by predefined options. The survey was created with Webropol 3.0[1]—a survey and reporting tool that simplifies creating and distributing online surveys. It also ensures the secure collection, processing, storage, and archiving/destruction of survey data. Moreover, it enables monitoring survey engagement, including the number of opened links, started responses, and completed surveys.

The survey consisted of five sections designed to collect comprehensive information related to the research objectives, as follows:

- *Demographics*: gather data on respondents' roles and experiences.
- *Tools used in the company*: gather data on container-related tools.
- *Testing software containers*: gather data on processes, practices, and future plans for anomaly detection through container testing.
- *Results of testing*: gather data on outcomes, challenges, and assess containerization's influence on testing.
- *Anomaly examples*: gather data on challenges and future implementation plans.

Overall, the survey encompassed a comprehensive examination of respondents' roles, tooling landscape, container testing processes, testing outcomes, and anomaly examples, thereby enabling a thorough exploration of containerization practices and their impact on testing.

The survey gathered a total of fourteen responses from individuals affiliated with ten distinct companies. The work was carried out in industry-academia collaboration, with seven companies contacted directly via email in order to solicit respondents. In addition, other organizations were targeted through a LinkedIn post, seeking respondents interested in the topic of research. The target sample was expected to possess satisfactory knowledge regarding containers and a minimum of one year of experience. Throughout the data collection period, a total of 137 individuals opened the survey (referred to as the "Total"). Out of these participants, 32 initiated the response process (referred to as the "Net Participation"), representing 23.36% of the Total. Of the "net participation" group, 14 individuals successfully completed the survey, accounting for 43.75% of the net participation. The data was collected between January 11th, 2023, and June 13th, 2023.

---

[1] https://webropol.com/.

4   Results

4.1   Demographics

The survey involved a sample of 14 respondents, referred to as P1 through P14. The responses provided insights into a wide array of projects undertaken by these companies, including research and development (R&D), cloud software development, machine learning applications, value stream metrics, web application development, testing activities, back-end services, and development environments. Collectively, the responses reflected the broad spectrum of industries and domains in which containerization practices were implemented.

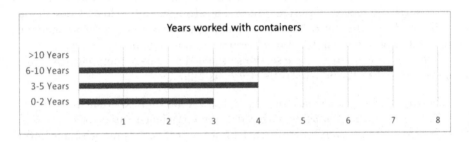

Fig. 1. Respondents' experience with containers

Figure 1 visually presents an overview of the respondents' experience levels. Among the total respondents, seven individuals (50% of the total) reported having 6–10 years of experience with containers. Additionally, four respondents indicated having 3–5 years of experience, while three reported having 0–2 years of experience with containers.

4.2   Tools Used in Companies

Table 1 provides a comprehensive overview of the container platforms the respondents utilize, highlighting the prominent role of various cloud-based platforms. Among the mentioned platforms, Docker emerged as the most widely adopted, with all respondents except one reporting its usage. Kubernetes followed closely with 11 users, while both Azure and Amazon Elastic Container Service (ECS) were utilized by eight respondents each. Another popular platform, AWS Fargate, had a user count of six. Additionally, respondents mentioned other container platforms such as LXC, Nomad, Podman, OCI, Rancher (RKE), OpenShift, and k3s.

The survey respondents mentioned a variety of tools utilized for testing container-based applications. These tools included JUnit, TestContainers (Java), Docker Desktop, Minikube, Robot framework, Spira, Sonarqube, Trivy, Selenium, Protractor, and Jest. Additionally, specific test frameworks like Pact.io

Table 1. Container platforms used by respondents.

Container platform	P1	P2	P3	P4	P5	P6	P7	P8	P9	P10	P11	P12	P13	P14	Total
Docker	x	x	x	x	x	x	x	x	x	x	x	x		x	13
Kubernetes		x	x	x	x	x	x	x	x	x	x				11
Azure		x	x	x		x	x	x			x	x			8
Amazon ECS				x		x	x	x	x	x	x			x	8
AWS Fargate						x	x	x	x			x			x	6
LXC						x	x	x							3
Other(s)			x	x									x		3

and Cucumber were also mentioned. Regarding security and vulnerability testing, respondents identified tools such as Black Duck, AWS Security Hub, Qualys, and Defensics.

The selection of these tools was influenced by factors such as the programming language, the technology stack employed, and the different teams involved within the respondents' respective companies.

4.3   Testing Software Containers

The processes that were used to test containers varied a lot between companies and respondents' roles. However, some common testing practices and tools were mentioned, listed below:

1. Using Github test cases, test containers, continuous integration and continuous deployment (CI/CD) tools, and Robot framework.
2. Conducting tests in a replicated container environment, starting with robot tests on code changes and progressing to deployment in development, staging, and production environments.
3. Performing local testing during development and automated testing in the company's CI/CD platform.
4. Implementing various release trains and CI/CD pipelines, including unit tests, API tests, integration tests, and static code analysis.
5. Incorporating automatic vulnerability scans using tools like Harbor and Trivy in the CI/CD pipeline.
6. Using containers to run full development environments and perform integration tests.
7. Conducting unit tests, functional tests, reliability tests, and security and open-source license scans.
8. Emphasizing integration testing before containerization and occasionally using end-to-end (E2E) tests in cloud-based containerized environments.

In addition to the above, Docker unit tests, container structure tests, and manual functional testing for software within the container were also mentioned by some respondents.

Thirteen respondents mentioned conducting testing before and after containerization, while one respondent was uncertain. Among them, seven stated that testing was specified for the containerized content, five mentioned testing for both the container and the content, and one respondent was unsure.

The answers revealed different approaches to enhancing testability of containerized software. These included running containers in a local development environment, employing loose coupling and abstraction, performing unit testing, using Docker exec commands for output examination, enabling test versions of dependencies, ensuring clear network interfaces between containers, implementing container hardening, focusing on log design, and employing automated pipelines.

Our findings also highlight a wide range of testing methodologies applied to containers and containerized software. These included user interface and user experience tests, database tests, logic tests, security tests, penetration tests, checks for misconfigured containers, manual functional testing, unit tests, functional testing, exploratory testing, test automation, scalability and high availability testing, deployment testing, container structure tests, integration tests, E2E testing, reliability testing, performance testing, and legal testing.

Regarding future testing strategies, emphasis was placed on the automation of various test types, such as unit testing, security testing, integration tests, and quality assurance (QA) steps, including static code analysis and vulnerability scans. Suggestions were made to utilize more tools in vulnerability testing and testing supply chain attacks, incorporate additional scanning tools to enforce best practices, and execute tests within a container as part of the CI/CD pipeline.

Furthermore, the utilization of CI/CD pipelines for managing code changes and the adoption of the MS Azure infrastructure for staging and deployment purposes were also mentioned by some respondents.

4.4   Results of Testing

When asked about the differences observed in testing software before and after containerization, some respondents highlighted positive aspects while others raised concerns about negative aspects. Positive aspects mentioned by respondents included easier automation, consistent software layers, improved execution of full system and E2E tests, more repeatable environments, increased likelihood of production-like environments on development machines, and targeted change testing with isolated environments for each branch.

On the negative side, it was noted that if system logging was not properly implemented before testing, the analysis of error situations required additional effort. Additionally, two respondents mentioned that they either did not observe significant differences or were unaware of any differences in cases where the software had been containerized from the beginning. This suggests that the benefits or challenges associated with containerization may vary depending on the specific context and the extent to which containerization has been integrated into the software development and testing processes.

The responses regarding how the act of containerization affects test results exhibited variability, even among respondents from the same company. While opinions varied, a range of perspectives were expressed.

Four respondents indicated that they did not observe any significant impact of containerization on test results and suggested that containerization did not noticeably alter the outcomes of their testing efforts. On the other hand, two respondents highlighted the positive effects of containerized testing. They emphasized that containerization led to more consistent and faster test results, along with easier maintenance of the testing environment. These individuals found that containerization provided benefits such as improved consistency in test outcomes and enhanced efficiency in maintaining the test infrastructure. Furthermore, multiple respondents emphasized automation capabilities enabled by containers. These varied responses demonstrate that the impact of containerization on test results can differ based on the specific context, company, and individual perspectives.

Another aspect brought up was the need for different configurations in testing, considering that the software environment may impact its behaviour. If tested before containerization, the execution environment may differ from that within a container.

A question about challenges faced when testing containers received numerous answers. The challenges mentioned include the need to have the test environment within the container, longer compilation times, network connectivity issues due to misconfigured containers, difficulties in creating testable environments, complexities in setting up infrastructure for containerized tests, dependencies on additional services for integration or E2E tests (particularly in a microservices architecture), dynamic visualization of results in multi-container environments, synchronization between containers, slow system ramp-up for testing, testers facing challenges in contributing due to managing their settings, difficulty in understanding testing from a container perspective, complexities in debugging tests within complex containerized environments, and more.

4.5 Anomaly Examples

Specific anomalies mentioned to be tested for include regression issues, performance downgrades, load-related anomalies such as session replication issues and bottlenecks, memory leaks, vulnerabilities identified through static code analysis, long-term stable execution on different hardware, smooth dynamic scalability, broken APIs between dependencies, logic issues related to reconnecting and disconnecting, software crashes or hangs, and impacts on functionality, reliability, performance, and supportability.

Regarding what sort of anomalies have been detected through testing, several respondents mentioned that they had not encountered many specific anomalies. However, the anomalies mentioned included errors, regression issues, performance downgrades, session replication issues, critical vulnerabilities such as the log4j bug in 2021 (which was caught through automatic vulnerability scans), challenges with low-level drivers, broken APIs between dependencies, reconnect/disconnect logic issues, failed crash/hang detection, and misconfigurations related to interface definitions and security hardening in containers.

While two respondents mentioned that they had no plans to improve anomaly detection and accuracy, others provided various strategies and approaches:

1. Utilizing static code analysis.
2. Conducting vulnerability scanning.
3. Incorporating the test framework within a container during testing.
4. Developing enhanced testing components that gather more data and can be reused.
5. Increasing knowledge about containerized testing and automation.
6. Implementing daily scans of containers against vulnerability databases.
7. Conducting more testing in development and staging environments.
8. Enhancing health check logic.
9. Isolating changes to identify the specific time when issues occurred.

The question on anomalies that are not yet being tested for but are hoped to implement in the future was answered by only 7 respondents (50%). Although fewer respondents provided answers, several aspects were mentioned:

1. Emphasizing integration testing of the entire architecture in the actual runtime environment rather than focusing solely on individual containers.
2. Automating testing for high-load scenarios.
3. Enhancing the ability to compare resource requirements and performance by analyzing metrics between different releases in CI/CD execution.
4. Increasing the frequency of static scans for container definitions.
5. Addressing the dynamic behaviour of containers in terms of scalability.
6. Conducting stress testing to evaluate system performance under extreme conditions.

5   Discussion

The previous literature has presented approaches to anomaly detection through container testing [6,18,22]. This paper, however, investigates real-world anomaly detection practices in companies and offers improvement approaches. Moreover, it narrows the knowledge gap between industry and academia on container anomaly detection. The survey results comprehensively analyze container testing processes and challenges by leveraging insights from individuals with diverse experiences and roles within our sample. The sample encompasses participants with junior expertise, less than two years of container experience, and those with senior experience, 3 to 10 years of container-related experience. We also ensured variability in the roles and responsibilities of the respondents, incorporating individuals from technical positions such as developers, software architects, testers, and security analysts, as well as managerial positions like heads of R&D, development managers, and team leaders. The diverse composition ensures that our findings encompass technical and managerial perspectives on container testing.

Our findings revealed that Docker and Kubernetes are the most prevalent container platforms. Docker emerged as the leading choice, which corroborates the findings reported in the literature [1]. While Docker and Kubernetes dominated the landscape, we also observed other popular tools, such as Azure, Amazon ECS, and AWS Fargate.

Our survey also uncovered several tools with relatively lower adoption rates. By discerning the prevalence of these diverse software tools, our research contributes valuable insights into the prevailing trends in the domain of container technology. The prominence of Docker and Kubernetes underscores their pivotal roles in shaping contemporary containerization practices.

The survey results further highlight that the selection of container tools is contingent upon several factors, including the software language, technology stack, and the team's preferences within the organization. This finding underscores the importance of tailoring tool choices to align with specific project requirements and team dynamics, reflecting a pragmatic approach to containerization. Participants reported employing multiple testing tools to cater to their respective testing needs. Alongside commercial testing tools, respondents incorporated in-house test platforms, automated CI/CD pipeline tests, and container checker tools into their testing processes. This amalgamation of testing tools underlines the flexibility and adaptability of testing strategies to suit various use cases and testing objectives. By incorporating this comprehensive range of container-related testing tools, our research illuminates the dynamic nature of container testing practices in contemporary software development. This diversity of tooling options underscores the significance of a nuanced and context-aware approach when selecting the most appropriate testing tools.

In the "testing containers" section of the survey, there was a consensus among respondents, indicating that most companies conduct testing both before and after containerization, with a focus on testing the containerized content. The responses also emphasized that current testing techniques are insufficient, and companies are endeavoring to develop procedures to enhance container testability tailored to their specific needs.

The survey results reveal that companies are actively strategizing to enhance their testing solutions, emphasizing automated testing. While the majority of participating companies already utilize automated testing, they view its expansion as a critical defensive measure to augment testing outcomes. Notably, companies exhibited diverse perspectives when asked about their strategies for expanding automated testing. Some companies directed their efforts towards automating testing for pipelines, aiming to streamline the testing process within their CI/CD pipelines. Others concentrated on automating code testing, seeking to automate code functionality and integrity verification. Additionally, some companies expressed their desire for a comprehensive, fully automated testing package, suggesting an overarching approach to automation covering various testing aspects.

These findings indicate the industry's growing inclination towards automation to achieve more efficient, reliable, and comprehensive testing practices. The diversity in companies' approaches highlights the nuanced nature of devising tailored automated testing strategies to address their specific testing requirements and objectives.

The survey addressed the main challenges facing container testing. These challenges include longer compilation times, networking and configuration issues, test environment setup and management difficulties, dependency integration in microservices architecture, visualization and result reporting challenges, and debugging complexities.

The survey results extend the knowledge from industry to literature, adding details about the testing methods used. Moreover, the survey results confirm the common use of tools, diverse needs and corresponding methods and tools [1, 7, 16], concerns about security and vulnerabilities [3–5, 17], the importance of automation and CI/CD implementations and dynamic program analysis [16], and the need for further knowledge and research [6].

5.1   Revisiting Research Questions

RQ1: What Are the Current Approaches Employed by Companies for Testing Software Containers? Currently, companies heavily rely on the tools employed to test containers. Docker stands out as the most utilized container platform, with a mention of 12 different container platforms in total. The tools for testing container-based applications exhibit even greater diversity, often being technology-stack dependent, with 18 tools and test frameworks mentioned and the possibility of many more.

Despite discrepancies in testing approaches, companies share a consensus on multi-phase testing processes. Commonalities among the companies' processes include manual tests, CI/CD pipelines with integrated tests and scans, monitoring, and reporting. Significant differences surface in container testing processes, particularly in two aspects. First is the testing environment, where variations arise depending on whether the test is conducted locally, in a replicated environment, or through other configurations. Second is the extent of testing, ranging from manual functional testing to the more comprehensive multi-container end-to-end setup. The latter involves replicating the production environment, simulation of the staging environment for deployment, verification testing, and, ultimately, production release. One respondent also stated the use of containers was for running development environments allowing the running of complete environments for integration tests.

Our findings also highlight disparities in companies' perspectives regarding conventional testing approaches. Numerous respondents outlined their typical testing approach, encompassing test cases, containers, CI/CD, and automated code change checks. Interestingly, two distinct groups emerged from the responses. The first group focused solely on testing the content within containers. Conversely, the second group stressed the necessity of incorporating additional container-specific testing measures. These measures encompassed container reliability, security assessments, enhanced monitoring capabilities, opensource license scans, input-output comparison validation, and functionality testing in a multi-container setup.

The contrasting viewpoints elucidate the diverse strategies adopted by companies when testing containerized applications. This underscores the significance of tailoring testing practices to suit individual needs and organizational contexts, leading to more robust and comprehensive testing outcomes. While there is shared recognition among companies about the implications of vulnerability testing and its ability to detect misconfiguration issues, not all companies prioritize it. Surprisingly, some companies did not mention vulnerability testing when asked about the types of testing performed.

In summary, the survey results revealed a lack of consensus among companies regarding container testing approaches, the essential phases to be incorporated into the testing process, understanding typical testing practices, and recognizing the significance of security and vulnerability testing. Furthermore, the findings demonstrate the diverse approaches adopted by companies, as discussed in [22].

RQ2: How Can the Approaches for Testing Software Containers Be Improved? Although the results addressed various practices to enhance the testability of containers, companies do not agree on "best practices" for testing containers. Therefore, we collected general recommendations from the survey results to improve testing practices. The provided recommendations are from a managerial perspective to improve the culture around container testing and from a technical perspective to improve the testing practices.

The recommendations for managerial positions include prioritizing learning and staying updated on container testing practices, conducting thorough research to understand the benefits and challenges, reviewing existing testing processes in use to identify areas for improvement, and critically evaluating the suitability of testing tools based on specific project requirements. Managers also recommended fostering a culture of continuous learning and improvement, promoting collaboration, and allocating resources for training and skill development in container testing. Additionally, actively engaging with industry experts and seeking insights from current research and other organizations can provide valuable insights for optimizing container testing strategies.

Our recommendations for technical positions in approaching container testing from a technical standpoint include:

1. Establishing standardized testing processes: establishing standardized testing processes tailored to their specific needs and project requirements can help ensure consistency and efficiency in testing practices.
2. Enhancing tool selection and compatibility: companies should carefully evaluate and select tools that align with their technology stack and testing requirements achieving compatibility, suitability of, and effectiveness of container testing.
3. Incorporating additional types of testing: companies emphasized the importance of incorporating automated tests, integration tests, security testing, and vulnerability scans to enhance the comprehensiveness and accuracy of container testing.

4. Paying attention to misconfiguration issues and anomaly detection: companies recommended focusing on misconfiguration issues and anomaly detection as an essential part of container testing to mitigate potential threats.
5. Combining testing techniques: companies suggested combining testing techniques like running containers in a local development environment, ensuring loose coupling, utilizing abstraction, implementing unit testing, and establishing clear network interfaces could improve the testing results.
6. Integrating testing within CI/CD pipelines: companies emphasised that using CI/CD pipelines for integrated tests and scans can streamline the testing process. Moreover, it ensures continuous monitoring and reporting, which improves the whole container environment's efficiency, reliability, and consistency.
7. Developing the knowledge of challenges and complexities: companies mention that developing the knowledge of container challenges and complexities among practitioners would keep them aware of the possible system vulnerabilities. Also, it would help them choose suitable testing techniques.

5.2   Limitations and Threats to Validity

The research has several limitations that should be considered. First, the survey relied on a relatively small sample size of 14 respondents from 10 different companies, which may limit the generalizability of the findings. Additionally, the data collected in the survey relies on self-reported responses from the respondents, introducing the possibility of response bias. Furthermore, we acknowledge that the lack of existing academic research on container testing practices may restrict the depth of analysis and comparison with prior studies. Obviously, these limitations should be considered when interpreting the results and considering the broader applicability of the findings.

6   Conclusion

This paper studies the current testing practices in the context of the growing interest in software containers and the lack of comprehensive knowledge of testing approaches. It aims to identify the challenges faced in container testing and potential areas for improvement by collecting information from companies that are actively engaged in container testing. The collected data centred on critical areas such as the tools utilized to support containers, prevailing approaches in container testing, challenges encountered during the testing process, and the role of anomaly and vulnerability detection in supporting container testing for improved system security. The findings derived from this research are of utmost significance for companies and practitioners involved in testing software containers. They reveal a lack of consensus on the best practices of container testing, shedding light on the current challenges faced and presenting proposed solutions to elevate testing practices. Moreover, this research offers valuable recommendations based on both technical and managerial experiences, providing valuable insights for improving container testing processes.

In summary, this research contributes with the following major findings:

1. It reveals real-world practices for implementing anomaly detection.
2. It offers actionable guidance to practitioners for implementing anomaly detection in software containers.

To conclude, this work contributes to understanding container testing practices and establishes a solid foundation for future research endeavors and industry advancements in this domain. Despite the limitations of the work, by addressing the complexities and evolving requirements of container testing, this research aims to propel the field forward, bolstering the overall security and reliability of containerized software applications.

Acknowledgement. The research was conducted as part of the Containers as the Quantum Leap in Software Development (QLeap) project, involving the University of Jyväskylä and various industry partners.

References

1. Siddiqui, T., Siddiqui, S., Khan, N.: Comprehensive analysis of container technology. In: 4th International Conference on Information Systems and Computer Networks (ISCON), pp. 218–223 (2019). https://doi.org/10.1109/ISCON47742.2019.9036238
2. Douglis, F., Nieh, J.: Microservices and containers. IEEE Internet Comput. **23**(6), 5–6 (2019). https://doi.org/10.1109/MIC.2019.2955784
3. Shu, R., Gu, X., Enck, W.: A study of security vulnerabilities on docker hub. In: Proceedings of the Seventh ACM on Conference on Data and Application Security and Privacy, pp. 269–280 (2017). https://doi.org/10.1145/3029806.3029832
4. Sultan, S., Ahmad, I., Dimitriou, T.: Container security: issues, challenges, and the road ahead. IEEE Access **7**, 52976–52996 (2019). https://doi.org/10.1109/ACCESS.2019.2911732
5. Wong, A., Chekole, E., Ochoa, M., Zhou, J.: Threat modeling and security analysis of containers: a survey. ArXiv (2021). https://doi.org/10.48550/arXiv.2111.11475
6. Siddiqui, S., Siddiqui, T.: Quantitative data analysis of non functional testing in container applications. In: 2021 9th International Conference on Reliability, Infocom Technologies and Optimization (ICRITO), pp. 1–6 (2021). https://doi.org/10.1109/ICRITO51393.2021.9596457
7. Chen, C., Hung, M., Lai, K., Lin, Y.: Docker and Kubernetes. In: Industry 4.1: Intelligent Manufacturing with Zero Defects, pp. 169–213 (2022). https://doi.org/10.1002/9781119739920.ch5
8. Jamshidi, P., Pahl, C., Mendonça, N., Lewis, J., Tilkov, S.: Microservices: the journey so far and challenges ahead. IEEE Softw. **35**(3), 24–35 (2018). https://doi.org/10.1109/MS.2018.2141039
9. Liu, P., et al.: Understanding the security risks of docker hub. In: Chen, L., Li, N., Liang, K., Schneider, S. (eds.) ESORICS 2020. LNCS, vol. 12308, pp. 257–276. Springer, Cham (2020). https://doi.org/10.1007/978-3-030-58951-6_13
10. Gummaraju, J., Desikan, T., Turner, Y.: Over 30 percent of official images in docker hub contain high priority security vulnerabilities (2015). https://www.banyansecurity.io/blog/over-30-of-official-images-in-docker-hub-contain-high-priority-security-vulnerabilities/. Accessed 20 June 2023

11. Kwon, S., Lee, J.: DIVDS: docker image vulnerability diagnostic system. IEEE Access **8**, 42666–42673 (2020). https://doi.org/10.1109/ACCESS.2020.2976874

12. Lin, X., Lei, L., Wang, Y., Jing, J., Sun, K., Zhou, Q.: A measurement study on linux container security: attacks and countermeasures. In Proceedings of the 34th Annual Computer Security Applications Conference, pp. 418–429 (2018). https://doi.org/10.1145/3274694.3274720

13. Wan, Z., Lo, D., Xia, X., Cai, L.: Practical and effective sandboxing for Linux containers. Empir. Softwa. Eng. **24**(6), 4034–4070 (2019). https://doi.org/10.1007/s10664-019-09737-2

14. Lin, Y., Tunde-Onadele, O., Gu, X.: CDL: classified distributed learning for detecting security attacks in containerized applications. In Annual Computer Security Applications Conference, pp. 179–188 (2020). https://doi.org/10.1145/3427228.3427236

15. Kang, D., Fuller, D., Honavar, V.: Learning classifiers for misuse and anomaly detection using a bag of system calls representation. In Proceedings from the Sixth Annual IEEE SMC Information Assurance Workshop, pp. 118–125 (2005). https://doi.org/10.1109/IAW.2005.1495942

16. Javed, O., Toor, S.: Understanding the quality of container security vulnerability detection tools (2021). https://doi.org/10.48550/arXiv.2101.03844

17. Efe, A., Aslan, U., Kara, A.: Securing vulnerabilities in docker images. Int. J. Innov. Eng. Appl. **4**(1), 31–39 (2020). https://doi.org/10.46460/ijiea.617181

18. Chen, L., et al.: SEAF: a scalable, efficient, and application-independent framework for container security detection. J. Inf. Secur. Appl. **71**, 103351 (2021). https://doi.org/10.1016/j.jisa.2022.103351

19. Syed, M., Fernandez, E.: The secure container manager pattern. In: PLoP 2018. The Hillside Group, Portland (2020). https://dl.acm.org/doi/10.5555/3373669.3373676

20. Abhishek, M., Rajeswara Rao, D.: Framework to secure docker containers. In: 2021 Fifth World Conference on Smart Trends in Systems Security and Sustainability, pp. 152–156 (2021). https://doi.org/10.1109/WorldS451998.2021.9514041

21. Jolak, R., et al.: CONSERVE: a framework for the selection of techniques for monitoring containers security. J. Syst. Softw. **186**, 111158 (2021). https://doi.org/10.1016/j.jss.2021.111158

22. Siddiqui, S., Siddiqui, T.: Non-functional testing framework for container-based applications. Indian J. Sci. Technol. **14**(47), 343–344 (2021). https://doi.org/10.17485/IJST/v14i47.1909

23. Siddiqui, T., Ahmad, R.: A review on software testing approaches for cloud applications. Recent Trends Eng. Mater. Sci. Perspect. Sci. **8**, 689–691 (2016). https://doi.org/10.1016/j.pisc.2016.06.060

24. Molléri, J., Petersen, K., Mendes, E.: Survey guidelines in software engineering: an annotated review. In: Proceedings of the 10th ACM/IEEE ESEM, Article 58 (2016). https://doi.org/10.1145/2961111.2962619

25. Ralph, P., et al.: Empirical standards for software engineering research. In: ACM SIGSOFT Empirical Standards (2020). https://doi.org/10.48550/arXiv.2010.03525

The Effects of Soft Assertion on Spectrum-Based Fault Localization

Kouhei Mihara[✉], Shinsuke Matsumoto, and Shinji Kusumoto

Graduate School of Information Science and Technology, Osaka University,
Osaka, Japan
{k-mihara,shinsuke,kusumoto}@ist.osaka-u.ac.jp

Abstract. This paper investigates the negative effects of soft assertion on the accuracy of Spectrum-based Fault Localization (SBFL). Soft assertion is a kind of test assertion which continues test case execution even after an assertion failure occurs. In general, the execution path becomes longer if the test case fails by a soft assertion. Hence, soft assertion will decrease the accuracy of SBFL which leverages the execution path of failed tests. In this study, we call the change of execution path due to soft assertion as path pollution. Our experimental results show that soft assertion actually reduces the accuracy of SBFL in 35% of faults.

Keywords: fault localization · spectrum-based fault localization · test · assertion · soft assertion · hard assertion

1 Introduction

Spectrum-based Fault Localization (SBFL) has been frequently studied as one of the techniques to support debugging [7,12,13]. SBFL automatically identifies suspicious locations of faults in a source code based on the execution path of test cases. The fundamental idea of SBFL is that the program elements covered by many failed test cases are more likely to be faulty, and those covered by many successful test cases are less likely to be faulty. SBFL has the advantage of high availability, since it uses only automatically measurable information. SBFL is expected to be used not only as supplementary information for debugging [5], but also as pre-processing for automatic debugging [9], and automatic program repair [4,8].

The accuracy of SBFL is affected by various factors, such as the number of faults [14], the structure of test cases [2,10], and the structure of the source code [11]. This study focus on *soft assertion* as one of these factors. In many test frameworks, a test case is immediately aborted and marked as failed when an assertion failure occurs. In contrast, with soft assertion, test case execution continues even if an assertion failure occurs. Therefore, the success or failure of all assertions can be checked at once in a single test execution. The most appropriate scenario for soft assertion is when each assertion in a single test case is independent. In such a scenario, soft assertion enables us to understand whether only one assertion has failed, or if all the other assertions have also failed.

© The Author(s), under exclusive license to Springer Nature Switzerland AG 2024
R. Kadgien et al. (Eds.): PROFES 2023, LNCS 14483, pp. 379–386, 2024.
https://doi.org/10.1007/978-3-031-49266-2_26

It is clear that the use of soft assertion affects the accuracy of SBFL because soft assertion surely changes execution path of failed tests. More specifically, soft assertion will have negative effects on the accuracy of SBFL, since failed tests become to execute more program statements. This paper introduces a concept *path pollution* that represents the increase of coverage of failed tests caused by soft assertion. Basically, a buggy statement is already executed when an assertion failure occurs. Therefore, the rest of program statements should not be executed to accurately locate the buggy statements.

In this study, we investigate the effects of soft assertion on the accuracy of SBFL. As a preliminary investigation, we study on the following two questions. *"RQ1: What libraries support soft assertion?"* and *"RQ2: How much is soft assertion used?"*. It is considered that the decrease in SBFL accuracy occurs in many projects if soft assertion is frequently used in test code of real projects. Therefore, how much soft assertion is used in real projects will become important information when considering the effects of soft assertion on SBFL. As a result of the preliminary investigation, we find that soft assertion is supported by many libraries and frameworks. We also find that 132 out of 1,000 projects are using one or more soft assertions.

Based on the results of the preliminary investigation, we study on the main question: *"RQ3: Does soft assertion decrease the accuracy?"* We compared the SBFL accuracy using a typical assertion and soft assertion by rewriting assert statements in the test code of a bug dataset. As a result of the comparison, a decrease in accuracy is observed in 35% of the faults.

2   Preliminaries

2.1   Spectrum-Based Fault Localization

Spectrum-based Fault Localization is one of the automated fault localization techniques using tests [7,12,13]. In SBFL, the statements executed by test cases are regarded as a spectrum, and the tendency of the spectrum is used to estimate the fault locations. The fundamental idea of SBFL is that the statements executed by many failed test cases are more likely to be faulty, and those executed by many successful test cases are less likely to be faulty.

Here, we explain the specific method of identifying fault locations in SBFL. First, execute all test cases and record the success or failure of each test case and its execution path (spectrum). Next, use the spectrum to calculate a suspicion value for each statement. There are several formulas for calculating suspicion value [3]. Here, we explain the formula called Ochiai [1]. Let $totalFails$ be the total number of failed test cases, s be a statement, $fail(s)$ be the number of failed test cases that execute s, and $pass(s)$ be the number of successful test cases that execute s. Then, the suspicion value is calculated by the following formula.

$$susp(s) = \frac{fail(s)}{\sqrt{totalFails \times (fail(s) + pass(s))}}$$

The $susp(s)$ is calculated for all s, and the higher the value, the more likely that s is faulty. Therefore, what is important is the relative height of $susp(s)$ compared to other statements, rather than the absolute value of $susp(s)$ itself. When discussing the accuracy of SBFL, it is common practice to use a relative indicator of how the faulty statement is ranked in the list of $susp(s)$.

Note that in the calculation of suspicion values, the spectrum of failed test cases is the most important element. This is because the spectrum of failed tests provides strong clues to the fault location, by showing which statements the failed tests executed and which they did not.

2.2 Soft Assertion

The test case is immediately aborted if a single assertion fails in almost all test frameworks, such as JUnit for Java and unittest for Python. In contrast, a soft assertion continues executing a test case even if an assertion fails. In this paper we call the normal assertion as hard assertion, as opposed to soft assertion.

One advantage of soft assertion is that all assertion results can be displayed in a single test execution. Soft assertion is suitable when there are no dependencies between assertion statements, such as checking all fields of a simple Bean class. With hard assertion, it is impossible to distinguish whether only one assertion has failed or whether all the other assertions have also failed. With soft assertion, however, the results of all the assertions can be checked at once.

Soft assertion has a strong meaning for failed test cases, similar to SBFL as mentioned in Sect. 2.1. The behavior is the same for both hard and soft assertion when a test case succeeds, and only when a test case fails, the execution path changes. Therefore, soft assertion is considered to alter SBFL results.

3   Motivating Example

The use of soft assertion may decrease the accuracy of Spectrum-based Fault Localization. This is because the coverage of failed tests increases with soft assertion. When the coverage of failed tests increases, many statements unrelated to the fault are included in the execution path. We call the inclusion as *path pollution* in this paper.

Figure 1 shows an code example where SBFL accuracy decreases due to soft assertion. The example consists of a User class (Fig. 1a) representing a single user and an unit test (Fig. 1b) for the User class. The User class has functions for registering with user information and logging in. The unit test checks the registration function for user information up to line 4 and the login function at lines 5–6. The User class has a fault in the password setter (line 6 in Fig. 1a), where it assigns the password to the this.name property instead of the this.pwd property. As a result, the assertion statement at line 4 fails in Fig. 1b.

The fault is in the password setter of the User class, while the login function checked at lines 5–6 is unrelated to the fault. However, since soft assertion continue to execute the test even after an assertion failure, lines 5–6 are also

```
1  public class User {
2    public void setName(String name) {
3      this.name = name;
4    }
5    public void setPwd(String pwd) {
6      this.name = pwd;
7    }
8    public void login() {
9      if(isLoggedin()) {
         ...
```

```
@Test
1  public void testUser() {
2    User u = new User("mihara", "qwerty123");
3    Soft.assert(u.getName()).isEqualTo("mihara");
4  ❌ Soft.assert(u.getPwd()).isEqualTo("qwerty123");

5    u.login();
6    Soft.assert(u.isLoggedin()).isTrue();
     ...
7  }
```

(a) User class   (b) Unit test with soft assertion

Fig. 1. Code example where SBFL accuracy decreases due to soft assertion

executed. Therefore, login method in Fig. 1a is also included in the execution path of the test. Thus, using soft assertion results in more statements unrelated to faults being executed in failed tests, leading to the pollution of the execution path of failed tests.

When path pollution occurs, the suspicion values of statements unrelated to the fault may increase, and the rank of the suspicion value of faulty statement may decrease. Thus, using soft assertion causes path pollution and decreases the accuracy of SBFL.

4   Research Questions

In this study, we investigate the effects of soft assertion on the accuracy of SBFL. As a preliminary investigation, we study on the actual usage of soft assertion. If soft assertion is frequently used in test code of real projects, SBFL accuracy decreases in many projects. Therefore, understanding actual usage of soft assertion is important to consider its effects on SBFL.

We set RQ1 and RQ2 for preliminary investigation and set RQ3 for the main topic of this research, the effects of soft assertion on SBFL.

RQ1: What libraries support soft assertion?

As one aspect of the actual usage of soft assertion, we investigate what libraries or frameworks support soft assertion. We investigate several libraries and frameworks for their support of soft assertion in various languages.

RQ2: How much is soft assertion used?

Continuing from RQ1, we investigate how much soft assertion is used in real projects. In this investigation, we measure the usage rate of libraries and frameworks that support soft assertion, as discovered in RQ1.

RQ3: Does soft assertion decrease the accuracy?

We investigate whether the accuracy of SBFL actually decreases when soft assertion is used instead of hard assertion in test cases.

5   Methodologies and Results

RQ1: What libraries support soft assertion?

Methodology: We investigate several assertion libraries and testing frameworks to understand how soft assertion is supported. We manually inspect the documentation of each library and framework to determine whether soft assertion is supported. Although the primary language of investigation is Java, we also investigate Kotlin, JavaScript, Python, and C#.

Result: Table 1 shows the result of the investigation. Soft assertion is implemented in two classes in JUnit, the most widely used Java testing framework. Soft assertion is also implemented in other Java test frameworks, such as TestNG and Spock, and assertion libraries such as AssertJ. In addition, many frameworks and libraries implement soft assertion in each of the other languages we investigated. This result suggests that there is a demand for soft assertion in various languages.

RQ2: How much is soft assertion used?

Methodology: To investigate RQ2, we measured the usage rate of soft assertion on GitHub projects. This investigation targets the top 1,000 Java projects in terms of stars. In RQ2, we first search for soft assertion-related keywords in the source code of each project and count the number of projects in which the search hits. The search keywords are the class and method names that are discovered to implement soft assertion in RQ1, specifically "ErrorCollector", "assertAll", "SoftAssert", and "verifyAll". Next, the usage rate of soft assertion is calculated using the formula 1. In the formula, *hit* is the number of projects where the keyword is found and *total* is the total number of projects (1,000).

Table 1. Libraries and frameworks that implement soft assertion

Language	Library name	Type	Class/method name
Java	JUnit	Framework	`ErrorCollector, Assertions`
	TestNG	Framework	`SoftAssert`
	Spock	Framework	`Specification`
	AssertJ	Library	`SoftAssertions, JUnitSoftAssertions`
Kotlin	Kotest	Framework	`assertSoftly`
	Strikt	Library	`expect`
	assertk	Library	`assertAll`
JavaScript	Jasmine	Framework	`expect`
	soft-assert	Library	`jsonAssertion`
Python	softest	Framework	`soft_assert`
	assertpy	Library	`soft_assertions`
C#	Fluent Assertions	Framework	`AssertionScope`
	NUnit	Framework	`Assert.Multiple`

$$\text{Usage rate} = \frac{hit}{total} \times 100\% \tag{1}$$

Result: Table 2 shows the usage rate of soft assertion. The column labelled "Hit count" indicates the number of projects in which soft assertion-related keywords are found. When the usage rate is measured for the libraries as a whole, it is found that 13.2%[1] of projects use soft assertion. This means that more than one in ten projects use soft assertion.

RQ3: Does soft assertion decrease the accuracy?

Methodology: To investigate the effects of soft assertion on the accuracy of SBFL, we conducted an accuracy comparison experiment with soft and hard assertion. The experiment targets 66 faults in the Defects4J [6] dataset, which contains real bugs. The specific experimental procedures are as follows:

Step1:   Apply SBFL and calculate the accuracy.
Step2:   Rewrite all assertions in failed test cases to soft assertions.
Step3:   Apply SBFL again and calculate the accuracy.

We use *rank* as the evaluation metric for the accuracy of SBFL. The *rank* is the rank of the faulty statement when the statements are ranked in descending order of the suspicion values calculated by SBFL. The lower the value of *rank*, the higher the accuracy of SBFL.

Result: The distribution of *rank* scores using hard and soft assertion is shown in Fig. 2. According to the figure, it is observed that there is no significant difference in the distribution between the two assertions. In this analysis, the effects of soft assertion on the accuracy of SBFL is not observed.

For a more detailed analysis, we investigate the proportion of faults as accuracy changes. The result is Fig. 3. The figure shows that about 35% (23 cases) of the faults show a decrease in accuracy, while about 64% (42 cases) show no change in accuracy. In conclusion, although the decrease in accuracy for each fault is small, a significant number of faults showed a decrease in accuracy.

Table 2. Usage rate of soft assertion

Keywords	Library	Hit count	Usage rate(%)
ErrorCollector	JUnit	27	2.7
AssertAll	JUnit	96	9.6
SoftAssert	AssertJ, TestNG	21	2.1
verifyAll	Spock	50	5.0

---

[1] The total sum of the individual usage rates is 19.4%. However, since some projects use multiple libraries, the percentage of unique projects using soft assertion is 13.2%.

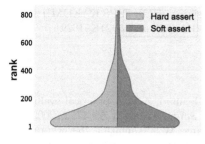

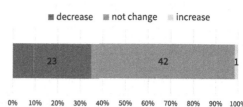

Fig. 2. The distribution of the SBFL accuracy

Fig. 3. The proportion of faults that change in SBFL accuracy

Next, we consider the reason for the changes or lack of changes in the accuracy. In the fault where the accuracy decreases the most, *rank* decreases by 354. The reason for the decreased accuracy in this fault is that the execution path of the failed test case is strongly polluted. In the failed test case of this fault, there are multiple invocations of statements unrelated to the fault after the failed assert. When all the assert statements are replaced with soft assertion, all these statements are executed, and the execution path of the test is polluted. As a result, the rank of the suspicion value of unrelated statements increases, and the rank of the fault statement relatively decreases.

We also consider the reason why the accuracy does not change. In the tests of faults where the accuracy did not change, the failed assert is at the end or near the end of the test case, and there are few subsequent invocations of new statements. Therefore, even when the assert statements are replaced by soft assertion, the execution path of the test case remains almost the same, and the accuracy of SBFL remains unchanged.

We expected that the use of soft assertion would lead to either a decrease or no change in the accuracy of SBFL. However, an improvement in accuracy occurred in one fault. The cause of the improved accuracy for this fault is currently unknown, and investigation of this cause is one of the future tasks.

6   Conclusion and Future Work

We study on the effects of soft assertion on the accuracy of Spectrum-based Fault Localization. As a preliminary investigation, we study on the actual usage of soft assertion. The investigation results revealed the existence of libraries that support soft assertion in several languages. It also showed that 137 of the 1,000 Java projects use soft assertion. Next, we compare the accuracy of SBFL between using hard assertion and soft assertion in test cases. As a result, we confirmed a decrease in accuracy due to soft assertion in 35% of faults.

In future work, we will experiment with a larger number of faults. In this study, only 66 faults of the Defects4J were targeted. Experiments with a larger number of faults are needed.

Acknowledgment. This research was partially supported by JSPS KAKENHI Japan (Grant Number: JP21H04877, JP20H04166, JP21K18302, and JP21K11829).

References

1. Abreu, R., Zoeteweij, P., Golsteijn, R., van Gemund, A.J.: A practical evaluation of spectrum-based fault localization. J. Syst. Softw. **82**(11), 1780–1792 (2009)
2. Ali, S., Andrews, J.H., Dhandapani, T., Wang, W.: Evaluating the accuracy of fault localization techniques. In: Proceedings of the International Conference on Automated Software Engineering, pp. 76–87 (2009)
3. Bagheri, B., Rezaalipour, M., Vahidi-Asl, M.: An approach to generate effective fault localization methods for programs. In: Proceedings of the International Conference on Fundamentals of Software Engineering, pp. 244–259 (2019)
4. Gazzola, L., Micucci, D., Mariani, L.: Automatic software repair: a survey. IEEE Trans. Softw. Eng. **45**(1), 34–67 (2019)
5. Jones, J., Harrold, M., Stasko, J.: Visualization of test information to assist fault localization. In: Proceedings of the International Conference on Software Engineering, pp. 467–477 (2002)
6. Just, R., Jalali, D., Ernst, M.D.: Defects4J: a database of existing faults to enable controlled testing studies for java programs. In: Proceedings of the International Symposium on Software Testing and Analysis, pp. 437–440 (2014)
7. Keller, F., Grunske, L., Heiden, S., Filieri, A., van Hoorn, A., Lo, D.: A critical evaluation of spectrum-based fault localization techniques on a large-scale software system. In: Proceedings of the International Conference on Software Quality, Reliability and Security, pp. 114–125 (2017)
8. Marginean, A., et al.: SapFix: automated end-to-end repair at scale. In: Proceedings of the International Conference on Software Engineering: Software Engineering in Practice, pp. 269–278 (2019)
9. Parnin, C., Orso, A.: Are automated debugging techniques actually helping programmers? In: Proceedings of the International Symposium on Software Testing and Analysis, pp. 199–209 (2011)
10. Qin, Y., Wang, S., Liu, K., Mao, X., Bissyandé, T.F.: On the impact of flaky tests in automated program repair. In: Proceedings of the International Conference on Software Analysis, Evolution and Reengineering, pp. 295–306 (2021)
11. Sasaki, Y., Higo, Y., Matsumoto, S., Kusumoto, S.: SBFL-suitability: a software characteristic for fault localization. In: Proceedings of the International Conference on Software Maintenance and Evolution, pp. 702–706 (2020)
12. de Souza, H.A., Chaim, M.L., Kon, F.: Spectrum-based software fault localization: a survey of techniques, advances, and challenges. arXiv e-prints p. arXiv:1607.04347 (2016)
13. Wong, W.E., Gao, R., Li, Y., Abreu, R., Wotawa, F.: A survey on software fault localization. IEEE Trans. Softw. Eng. **42**(8), 707–740 (2016)
14. Xiaobo, Y., Liu, B., Shihai, W.: An analysis on the negative effect of multiple-faults for spectrum-based fault localization. IEEE Access **7**, 2327–2347 (2019)

Characterizing Requirements Smells

Emanuele Gentili[2]([⊠]) [iD] and Davide Falessi[1] [iD]

[1] University of Rome Tor Vergata, Rome, Italy
falessi@ing.uniroma2.it
[2] MBDA Italy Spa, Rome, Italy
emanuele.gentili@mbda.it

Abstract. Context: Software specifications are usually written in natural language and may suffer from imprecision, ambiguity, and other quality issues, called thereafter, requirement smells. Requirement smells can hinder the development of a project in many aspects, such as delays, reworks, and low customer satisfaction. From an industrial perspective, we want to focus our time and effort on identifying and preventing the requirement smells that are of high interest. **Aim**: This paper aims to characterise 12 requirements smells in terms of frequency, severity, and effects. **Method**: We interviewed ten experienced practitioners from different divisions of a large international company in the safety-critical domain called MBDA Italy Spa. **Results**: Our interview shows that the smell types perceived as most severe are Ambiguity and Verifiability, while as most frequent are Ambiguity and Complexity. We also provide a set of six lessons learnt about requirements smells, such as that effects of smells are expected to differ across smell types. **Conclusions**: Our results help to increase awareness about the importance of requirement smells. Our results pave the way for future empirical investigations, ranging from a survey confirming our findings to controlled experiments measuring the effect size of specific requirement smells.

Keywords: Requirement smells · Requirement quality · Industrial case study

1 Introduction

Software requirements specifications are usually written in natural language [12,19] and may suffer from imprecision, ambiguity, and other quality issues, called thereafter, requirement smells [16]. Requirement smells can hinder the development of a project in many aspects, such as delays, reworks, and low customer satisfaction [1,10].

Researchers identified many types of smells and developed mechanisms, such as tools or regular expressions, for smell identification [18,28]. However, removing all smells is expensive given the high impact of the change on many artefacts such as design, code, testing, or certification [13]. Knowing which smell is important for whom, when, and why reasonably supports the reduction and prevention of smells. Therefore, it is key to gain insights into different types of smells.

© The Author(s), under exclusive license to Springer Nature Switzerland AG 2024
R. Kadgien et al. (Eds.): PROFES 2023, LNCS 14483, pp. 387–398, 2024.
https://doi.org/10.1007/978-3-031-49266-2_27

Fernández et al. [8] reported a survey on the current status and issues in the requirements engineering process. We share with Fernández et al. [8] the need to gather additional empirical evidence about requirements and their quality. However, while they focus on the requirements engineering process, we focus on the requirements as artefacts written in natural language.

Montgomery et al. [18] reported a comprehensive mapping study on defining, improving, or evaluating requirements quality. However, to the best of our knowledge, no study investigated if and how the frequency, severity, or effects change across types of smells. Montgomery et al. [18] acts as our baseline to identify 12 types of smells: Ambiguity, Completeness, Consistency, Correctness, Complexity, Traceability, Reusability, Understandability, Redundancy, Verifiability, Relevancy, and Undefined.

We share the view of Femmer et al. [7] that "Whether a Requirements Smell finding is or is not a problem in a certain context must be individually decided for that context and is subject to reviews and other follow-up quality assurance activities." Thus, this research stems from the industrial need to focus our time and effort on removing and preventing the specific requirement smells that are of high interest.

The aim of this paper is to characterise 12 requirement smells in terms of frequency, severity, and effects. To the best of our knowledge, no previous study analysed how frequency, severity, or effects vary across requirement smells.

We interviewed ten experienced practitioners from different divisions of a large international company in the safety-critical domain called MBDA Italy Spa.

Our interview shows that the smell types perceived as most severe are Ambiguity and Verifiability while as most frequent are Ambiguity and Complexity. We also provide a set of six lessons learned about requirement smells such as that effects of smells are expected to differ across smell types.

The remainder of this paper is structured as follows. Section 2 discusses the related literature, focusing in particular on requirements and their smells. Section 3 reports the design, Sect. 4 the results. Finally, Sect. 5 concludes the paper and outlines directions for future work.

2   Related Work

A "requirement" refers to a specific functionality, constraint or quality that a system must possess in order to meet the needs of its users and stakeholders [19]. Since stakeholders' points of view may differ significantly from each other, and a common language is needed in order to communicate and share information among parties, requirements are usually expressed in natural language [19,20,25].

Kassab et al. [12] report that 61% of users prefer to express requirements in natural language, whereas only 33% use other semi-formal notations like UML. Despite the acquaintance a user can have with natural language, a non-systematic approach, i.e. unstructured, is likely to induce smells on the requirements specification, such as ambiguity, incompleteness, inconsistency and incorrectness [8].

These smells reasonably cause problems during the process stages and, lately, can determine the success or the failure of a project [1,5]. Subramaniam et al. [26] and Mencl [17] propose approaches to prevent undesired effects of smells by means of limiting, i.e. structuring, the natural language syntax, to the extent of automatically generating use cases models for Object Oriented languages. Similarly, Femmer et al. [7] and Ferrari et al. [9] propose tools to automatically identify smells in requirements descriptions according to software requirements definition norms (like CENELEC EN 50128:2011) [9] or standards (like INCOSE or ISO 29184) [7]. These tools aim at driving the requirement elicitation process and assuring higher confidence in the requirement's quality.

In order to gain a deeper insight into Requirement Engineering state-of-the-art, Montgomery et al. [18] conducted a systematic mapping study on 105 relevant primary studies that use "empirical research to define, improve, or evaluate quality attributes". They identified 12 quality attribute themes, specified in 111 attributes sub-types, and reported that most of the studies concentrated on ambiguity, completeness, consistency and correctness quality attribute themes (63%). We share their quality attributes categorization and used them as categories for requirement smells.

2.1 Automated Requirement Smells Detection

Requirement Engineering is acknowledged as an expensive, time-consuming, and error-prone process [2,3]. This is especially true for complex systems with numerous requirements, e.g. thousand of requirements, making it challenging to obtain a comprehensive project specification overview. As a solution, automating smell detection becomes necessary in this context.

As reported by Montgomery et al. [18], a total of 41 distinct tools have been developed to detect requirement smells, and aspects such as ambiguity, incompleteness and inconsistency resulted as the most studied. For instance, Femmer et al. [7] focused on analyzing the syntax of requirements expressed in natural language, providing a tool, called *Smella*, implementing part of the Requirement Engineering standard ISO, IEC, and IEEE. ISO/IEC/IEEE 29148:2011 [11], and assessed the usefulness of the tool in the requirement elicitation process. Similarly, Seki et al. [22] designed a tool for detecting 22 "bad smells" (i.e. requirement smell sub-attributes) in use case description using structured natural language, achieving good performance in terms of precision and recall.

Veizaga et al. [28] developed a tool called *Paska* based on Rimay [27], and conducted an industrial case study on 13 system requirements specification documents from information system in financial domain, achieving a precision and recall in detecting smells of 89%. All the authors agree on the importance of assessing the usefulness of the developed tools through direct feedback from practitioners and on the necessity of a larger empirical evaluation.

2.2 Empirical Evaluation

To the best of our understanding, the closest empirical evaluation to our study is [8]. If, on the one side, we share their need to gather more empirical data about requirements quality, on the other side, we differ in many aspects, such as the approach (survey vs interview) and the object under evaluation. Specifically, they focus on the requirements engineering process, whereas we focus on the requirements artefact as written in natural language. This allows us a way to create a preliminary knowledge base of which smells we should focus on the most.

Regarding the effectiveness of elicitation techniques, Davis et al. [4] conducted a systematic review, reporting that *interview* is the most commonly used elicitation technique, albeit there are no studies assessing that it is the most effective choice. Moreover, across interview strategies, the structured interview is the one gathering more information than unstructured interviews, sorting and ranking or thinking aloud techniques.

This turns out to be even more important if we consider the study conducted by [24], in which it emerges that companies with a "high-maturity rating", i.e. companies claiming to follow the best Requirement Engineering practices as a part of their quality management process, experience the same Requirement Engineering problems of companies with lower scores, remarking the necessity of looking deeply inside Requirement Engineering practices.

3 Methodology

In this section we report on the methodology we use in this work.

3.1 Industrial Context

MBDA Spa is a multinational defence company specialising in the defensive and aerospace domain. We work closely with armed forces and defence organizations to provide advanced defence solutions. Our expertise lies in research, development, and integration of cutting-edge technologies to enhance national security and contribute to the defence capabilities of their client nations. The company comprises four national companies located in Italy, France, Germany, and United Kingdom. To conduct this study, we interviewed ten individuals from MBDA Italy Spa, which serves as the central site for software development supporting all the company's solutions.

3.2 Study Design

In this work we use a qualitative semi-structured interview method, which has been proven to be a flexible instrument for investigating areas of interest whose boundaries are not clear nor complete [21]. Knowing how much a smell is frequent and severe reasonably supports reducing and preventing smells. To investigate

Table 1. Population and project characterization.

Interviewees characteristics			Project characteristics					
Id	Role	#YE	#Req	#Dev	#LOC	#YP	#Exc	Domain
I1	SGL	25	1000	4	300K	3	1	SRT
I2	SGL	22	400	10	100K	2	2	SRT
I3	SPL	7	2000	12	250K	6	18	SRT
I4	Tx	21	300	7	250K	2	15	SRT
I5	SGL	21	750	7	70K	3	10	SRT
I6	SWEng	3	200	3	8K	5	1	HRT
I7	HoD/Tx	23	400	12	50K	4	20	SRT
I8	SWEng	18	2000	12	250K	6	18	SRT
I9	SGL	12	100	6	70k	5	1	HRT
I10	SWEng	16	2000	12	250k	6	18	SRT

which smell is particularly severe or frequent, we used the approach adopted by Fernández et al. [8]. Specifically, we asked about the three top and least severe smells and about the three top and least frequent smells.

Concerning types of smells, we use the categorization proposed by Montgomery et al. [18]: *Ambiguity, Completeness, Complexity, Consistency, Correctness, Traceability, Reusability, Understandability, Redundancy, Verifiability, Relevancy* and *Undefined*. We refer to Montgomery et al. [18] for their definitions. Results about population and project characterization are reported in Table 1. The list of questions is hereafter reported:

- **Interviewee characterization:**
  1. What is your current role? (Role)
     - SW Engineer (SWEng): designs, develops, and maintains software systems for various applications.
     - Technical Expert (Tx): provides specialized knowledge and expertise in software requirements management and architecture modelling.
     - SW Project Leader (SPL): leads a software project, coordinates teams, manages resources, and ensures successful delivery of high-quality software solutions.
     - SW Group Leader (SGL): leads and coordinates a group of projects within a specific field, facilitating Software Project Leaders to ensure successful project execution and delivery.
     - Head of Department (HoD): leads the software department, setting strategic direction, manages SW Group Leaders and Project Leaders, and ensures efficient software development operations.
  2. How many years of experience do you have in software development?(#YE)

- **Project characterization**: we asked information regarding projects that the interviewees are currently engaged in, or, if working on more than one, for a project they perceive as noteworthy in terms of requirement smells analysis.
  1. How many requirements does the project consist of?(#Req)
  2. How many developers does the team consist of?(#Dev)
  3. To which domain does the project belong to?(Domain)
     - Soft Real Time (SRT): refers to systems where meeting timing constraints is important but not critical. Occasional delays or missed deadlines may be tolerable as long as the overall system performance remains acceptable.
     - Hard Real Time (HRT): refers to systems where meeting strict timing constraints is crucial, and failure to do so can result in catastrophic consequences.
  4. How many software components, as the number of executables, does the project consist of?(#Exc)
  5. How many Line Of Code does the project consist of?(#LOC)
  6. How many years does the project last?(#YP)
- **Requirement smells**:
  1. What are the three most and least severe requirement smells?
  2. What are the three most and least frequent requirement smells?
  3. What are the effects of a certain requirement smell?
  4. Are there contexts in which the effects of a certain smell result mitigated/amplified?

3.3   Validity

Since the results rely on a small set of interviews from a single company, we recommend care in generalising results in other contexts.

There might be threats to validity even within our company. For instance, our population might not be representative of the company. To mitigate this threat, we selected subjects with a representative proportion of roles to face this threat.

Another possible threat to validity is selection bias, i.e., that the selected subjects might be biased towards specific answers. We believe this threat is negligible since we had a 100% acceptance rate and subjects with a representative proportion of roles.

An additional possible threat to validity is a wrong interpretation of subjects' answers. To face this threat, we provide no pressure on the time or direction of the answers. We also adopted a semi-structured interview protocol, which allowed us to spot possible misunderstandings while diving deep towards an answer. We also analysed the subjects' answers multiple times to ensure nothing was forgotten or misinterpreted.

4   Study Results

In the following we report the lessons learnt as extracted by analysing our interviews.

LL1: The Perceived Severity Varies Across Types of Smells. Figure 1 reports the frequency distribution of the three most and least severe requirement smells. According to Fig. 1, the perceived most severe smells are Ambiguity (80%), Verifiability (80%), and Consistency (60%). The perceived least severe smells are Relevancy (90%), Reusability (70%) and Redundancy (50%). Interestingly, only Completeness and Correctness have been identified as the most and least three severe by different interviewees.

LL2: The Perceived Severity of the Same Smell Varies Across Project Domains. We know that requirement smells can cause rework and time and cost overruns [1,10], and in some cases, a smell might even be catastrophic. For instance, requirements concerning the performance of the system are key for HRT systems [15]. A single smell in a performance requirement of an HRT system might have a huge impact on the overall project or even people's lives. For instance, regarding Verifiability, "If a performance requirement does not come with clear time constraints, we have a huge verifiability problem. For instance, if a computation task is described with high priority and to be executed fast, this description does not lead to clear tests and therefore, the system might pass the test and eventually create system malfunction since the actual priority and speed constraints required by the production context differ from the tested ones." (cit. I9)

LL3: The Perceived Frequency Varies Across Types of Smells. Figure 2 reports the frequency distribution of the most and least frequent requirement smells. According to Fig. 2, the perceived most frequent smells are Ambiguity (70%), Complexity (70%) and Consistency (40%). The perceived least frequent smells are Understandability (60%), Reusability (40%), and Relevancy (50%). We note that differently from severity, the majority of smells are perceived as most and least frequent by different interviewees; this suggests less agreement among interviewees or, likely, the presence of other factors influencing the frequency of smells, such as roles or phases.

LL4: The Frequency of a Smell is Perceived Differently Across Roles or Phases. The requirements are managed over the development life cycles and get improved over the life cycle. Different companies have a proportion of different roles; each role gets the requirement at a different stage and hence at a different quality. Thus, some smells might not be frequent for a role because another role has already fixed the smell. For instance, "The presence of a SW Requirement Specification expert, who centralizes and pre-filters requirements affected by smells, is fundamental for reducing the frequency of such smells during the Development phase, and helps the whole Team to stay aligned with the given specification." (cit. I8)

LL5: The Perceived Effects May Vary Across Types of Smells. We know that requirements smell can cause rework and time and cost overruns

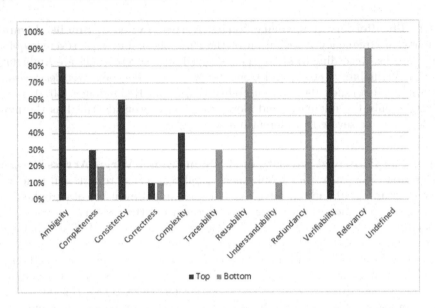

Fig. 1. Distribution of the three most and least severe requirement smells.

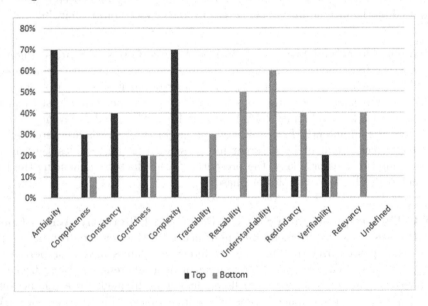

Fig. 2. Distribution of the top three and bottom three requirement smell frequency.

[1,10]. Moreover, reasonably, specific smells cause specific problems. However, the specific effects of specific requirement smells, to the best of our knowledge, are unknown. Let's discuss the examples of the Verifiability, Ambiguity, and Complexity smells.

Regarding Verifiability, if it is unclear how to verify a requirement, then the verification might be incorrect and hence will likely require to be performed multiple times, thus impacting the time and cost of testing. An additional effect of the Verifiability smell is that bugs might not be found during testing, thus leading to decreased customer satisfaction and increased development costs. For instance, "The Verifiability of requirements can determine the success or the failure of a project: scarcely verifiable requirements determine special effort during the Coding phase (it is not clear how to code in order to provide evidence of the desired behaviour) and during the Testing phase (in fact the number and complexity of Test Cases grow significantly)... and a poorly tested SW is likely to exhibit bugs during the Maintenance phase, leading to a high impact in rework, time, extra costs and customer satisfaction, with a general loss of credibility of the Company." (cit. I2)

Regarding Ambiguity, if a requirement is unclear, this will likely need to go back and forth between requirements engineers and developers to identify and formalise a clear version of the content. Thus, an ambiguous requirement is the subject of many change requests. Specifically, "Across all the smells, Ambiguity is the one causing more problems: if evident, it can be addressed and solved at an early stage, before starting to develop code, with relatively little impact in terms of rework; but sometimes, it remains uncaught until Integration Test stage (or even worst, until Maintenance stage) causing bugs whose resolution will have, possibly, a very high impact in term of rework on all process stages, on costs and customer satisfaction." (cit. I2)

Finally, regarding Complexity, it might be that a complex description of functionality leads to a complex implementation of that functionality. Specifically, "When a requirement is too Complex, one of the main effects is that practitioners tend to implement code with the same degree of complexity." (cit. I7)

We note that Verifiability and Ambiguity do not reasonably lead to complex code. Similarly, Complexity does not reasonably lead to decreased customer satisfaction. Thus, the impact of requirement smells is perceived as varying across smells.

LL6: The Severity of a Smell Might Change Across the Stage of the Project. We know that requirement smells can have negative effects on software development [1,10]; however, we realize that the effects of smells might be null or even positive in some circumstances [7]. Let's have an example of how the effect of the underspecification [18], a sub-smell of the Completeness smell, changes across the development process stages and can even be positive. Regarding underspecification, we know from the literature that requirements get more specified over time as the clients get a better understanding of what they want [14]. Thus, some needs that are underspecified at the early stage of the project get specified over time; other needs might remain underspecified since the clients do not (need to) provide more details. Thus, the roles approaching an underspecified requirement at the early stage of the development process are in trouble since they need to make decisions based on assumptions that might change when clients will better specify their needs [6]. Counter-wise, roles approaching an underspecified requirement at a late stage are glad to have many options, knowing that no additional details will invalidate the chosen solution. Specifically, on the one side, "An underspecified functional requirements at an early stage can cause the SW architect to design an incorrect architecture with little-flexibly, not able to satisfy constraints that will come up later during the development stage. So it can potentially bring to the redesign of the whole architecture, at the price of losing time, money and increasing the frustration of the whole development team." (cit. I3) On the other side, "A too-abstract requirement is not necessarily bad news: from Project Leader and Technical Expert points of view, it provides a high degree of freedom in terms of selection of the most convenient software architecture, with the possibility to experiment with newest, and more adequate, SW solutions." (cit. I4) We do not know if this reasoning applies to requirements sub-smells other than underspecification.

5   Conclusions

From an industrial perspective, we want to focus our time and effort on identifying and preventing the requirement smells that are important. Knowing which smell is important for whom, when, and why reasonably supports the reduction and prevention of smells.

Our results rely on ten industrial experts and reveal that the smell types perceived as most important are Ambiguity and Verifiability, while as most frequent are Ambiguity and Complexity. We also provide a set of six lessons learned about requirement smells, such as that effects of smells are expected to differ across types. Our results help increase awareness about the importance of requirement smells.

To our best understanding, this study is the first attempt to characterise requirement smells in terms of severity, frequency and effects. Since the results rely on a small set of interviews from a single company, we recommend care in generalising results in other contexts.

We note that correlation does not imply causation. Smells perceived as important or related to effects are probably only correlated to rather than causing effects. The concept of inherent complexity is something we know for code smells [23] and likely applies to requirement smells too. Specifically, if something is easy to express in natural language, it is likely easy to design, code and test. Counter-wise, if something is complex, it remains complex regardless of how much time we spend improving its description. In other words, spending a lot of effort describing something complex might decrease the requirement smells, but it might not decrease the complexity of developing it. Of course, something easy might become complicated if described in a complex way. Thus, our results pave the way for future empirical investigations, ranging from a survey confirming our findings to mining software repositories to establish correlations between smells and effects on projects to controlled experiments measuring the size of smells effects.

References

1. Ahonen, J.J., Savolainen, P.: Software engineering projects may fail before they are started: post-mortem analysis of five cancelled projects. J. Syst. Softw. **83**(11), 2175–2187 (2010)
2. Boehm, B.W.: Software engineering economics. IEEE Trans. Softw. Eng. **10**(1), 4–21 (1984). https://doi.org/10.1109/TSE.1984.5010193
3. Davis, A.M.: Software Requirements - Analysis and Specification. Prentice Hall, Upper Saddle River (1990). ISBN 978-0-13-824673-0
4. Davis, A.M., Tubío, Ó.D., Hickey, A.M., Juzgado, N.J., Moreno, A.M.: Effectiveness of requirements elicitation techniques: empirical results derived from a systematic review. In: 14th IEEE International Conference on Requirements Engineering (RE 2006), Minneapolis/St.Paul, Minnesota, USA, 11–15 September 2006, pp. 176–185. IEEE Computer Society (2006). https://doi.org/10.1109/RE.2006.17
5. Dick, J., Hull, E., Jackson, K.: Requirements Engineering, 4th edn. Springer, Cham (2017). https://doi.org/10.1007/978-3-319-61073-3. ISBN 978-3-319-61072-6
6. Falessi, D., Cantone, G., Kazman, R., Kruchten, P.: Decision-making techniques for software architecture design: a comparative survey. ACM Comput. Surv. **43**(4):33:1–33:28 (2011). https://doi.org/10.1145/1978802.1978812
7. Femmer, H., Fernández, D.M., Wagner, S., Eder, S.: Rapid quality assurance with requirements smells. CoRR, abs/1611.08847 (2016). http://arxiv.org/abs/1611.08847
8. Fernández, D.M., et al.: Naming the pain in requirements engineering - contemporary problems, causes, and effects in practice. Empir. Softw. Eng. **22**(5), 2298–2338 (2017). https://doi.org/10.1007/s10664-016-9451-7
9. Ferrari, A., et al.: Detecting requirements defects with NLP patterns: an industrial experience in the railway domain. Empir. Softw. Eng. **23**(6), 3684–3733 (2018). https://doi.org/10.1007/s10664-018-9596-7
10. Elizabeth, M., Hull, C., Jackson, K., Dick, J. (eds.): Requirements Engineering, 3rd edn. Springer, Heidelberg (2011). ISBN 978-1-8499-6404-3. https://doi.org/10.1007/978-1-84996-405-0
11. IEC ISO. Ieee. 29148: 2011-systems and software engineering-requirements engineering. Technical report, Technical report (2011)
12. Kassab, M., Neill, C., Laplante, P.: State of practice in requirements engineering: contemporary data. Innov. Syst. Softw. Eng. **10**, 235–241 (2014)
13. Kretsou, M., Arvanitou, E.-M., Ampatzoglou, A., Deligiannis, I.S., Gerogiannis, V.C.: Change impact analysis: a systematic mapping study. J. Syst. Softw. **174**, 110892 (2021). https://doi.org/10.1016/j.jss.2020.110892
14. Kruchten, P.: What do software architects really do? J. Syst. Softw. **81**(12), 2413–2416 (2008). https://doi.org/10.1016/j.jss.2008.08.025
15. Laplante, P.A., et al.: Real-Time Systems Design and Analysis. Wiley, New York (2004)
16. Mavin, A., Wilkinson, P.: Big ears (the return of "easy approach to requirements engineering"). In: 2010 18th IEEE International Requirements Engineering Conference, pp. 277–282. IEEE (2010)
17. Mencl, V.: Deriving behavior specifications from textual use cases. Citeseer (2004)
18. Montgomery, L., Fucci, D., Bouraffa, A., Scholz, L., Maalej, W.: Empirical research on requirements quality: a systematic mapping study. In: Engels, G., Hebig, R., Tichy, M. (eds.) Software Engineering 2023, Fachtagung des GI-Fachbereichs Softwaretechnik, 20–24 February 2023, Paderborn, vol. P-332 of LNI, pp. 91–92. Gesellschaft für Informatik e.V. (2023). https://dl.gi.de/20.500.12116/40098

19. Pohl, K.: Requirements Engineering - Fundamentals, Principles, and Techniques. Springer, Heidelberg (2010). ISBN 978-3-642-12577-5. http://www.springer.com/computer/swe/book/978-3-642-12577-5?changeHeader

20. Robertson, S., Robertson, J.: Mastering the Requirements Process: Getting Requirements Right. Addison-wesley, Boston (2012)

21. Robson, C.: Real world research blackwell. 2ª edição (2002)

22. Seki, Y., Hayashi, S., Saeki, M.: Detecting bad smells in use case descriptions. In: Damian, D.E., Perini, A., Lee, S.W. (eds.) 27th IEEE International Requirements Engineering Conference, RE 2019, Jeju Island, Korea (South), 23–27 September 2019, pap. 98–108. IEEE (2019). https://doi.org/10.1109/RE.2019.00021

23. Sjøberg, D.I.K., Yamashita, A.F., Anda, B.C.D., Mockus, A., Dybå, T.: Quantifying the effect of code smells on maintenance effort. IEEE Trans. Softw. Eng. 39(8), 1144–1156 (2013). https://doi.org/10.1109/TSE.2012.89

24. Solemon, B., Sahibuddin, S., Ghani, A.A.A.: Requirements engineering problems and practices in software companies: an industrial survey. In: Slezak, D., Kim, T., Kiumi, A., Jiang, T., Verner, J., Abrahao, S. (eds.) ASEA 2009. CCIS, vol. 59, pp. 70–77. Springer, Heidelberg (2009). https://doi.org/10.1007/978-3-642-10619-4_9

25. Sommerville, I., Sawyer, P.: Requirements Engineering: A Good Practice Guide. John Wiley & Sons Inc., Hoboken (1997)

26. Subramaniam, K., Liu, D., Far, B.H., Eberlein, A.: UCDA: use case driven development assistant tool for class model generation. In: Maurer, F., Ruhe, G. (eds.) Proceedings of the Sixteenth International Conference on Software Engineering & Knowledge Engineering (SEKE 2004), Banff, Alberta, Canada, 20–24 June 2004, pp. 324–329 (2004)

27. Veizaga, A., Alférez, M., Torre, D., Sabetzadeh, M., Briand, L.C.: On systematically building a controlled natural language for functional requirements. Empir. Softw. Eng. 26(4), 79 (2021). https://doi.org/10.1007/s10664-021-09956-6

28. Veizaga, A., Shin, S.Y., Briand, L.C.: Automated smell detection and recommendation in natural language requirements. CoRR, abs/2305.07097 (2023). https://doi.org/10.48550/arXiv.2305.07097

Do Exceptional Behavior Tests Matter on Spectrum-Based Fault Localization?

Haruka Yoshioka[1]([✉]), Yoshiki Higo[1], Shinsuke Matsumoto[1], Shinji Kusumoto[1], Shinji Itoh[2], and Phan Thi Thanh Huyen[2]

[1] Graduate School of Information Science and Technology, Osaka University, Osaka, Japan
{h-yosiok,higo,shinsuke,kusumoto}@ist.osaka-u.ac.jp
[2] Hitachi, Ltd., Tokyo, Japan
{shinji.itoh.wn,thithanhhuyen.phan.gw}@hitachi.com

Abstract. Debugging is a heavy task in software development. Computer-assisted debugging is expected to reduce these costs. Spectrum-based Fault Localization (SBFL) is one of the most actively studied computer-assisted debugging techniques. SBFL aims to identify the location of faulty code elements based on the execution paths of tests. Previous research reports that the accuracy of SBFL is affected by test types, such as flaky tests. Our research focuses on exceptional behavior tests to reveal the impact of such tests on SBFL. Since separating exceptional handling from normal control flow enables developers to increase program robustness, we think the execution paths of exceptional behavior tests are different from the ones of normal control flow tests, which means that the differences significantly affect the accuracy of SBFL. In this study, we investigated the accuracy of SBFL on two types of faults: faults that occurred in the real software development process and artificially generated faults. As a result, our study reveals that SBFL tends to be more accurate when all failing tests are exceptional behavior tests than when failing tests include no exceptional behavior tests.

Keywords: Spectrum-based Fault Localization · exceptions · exceptional behavior test · exception handling

1 Introduction

Debugging is a heavy task in software development. Previous research reported that the process of identifying and correcting faults during the software development process represents over half of development costs [17]. Computer-assisted debugging can reduce these costs.

Fault localization is one of the computer-assisted debugging techniques. So far, many fault localization techniques have been proposed [6,11]. Spectrum-based Fault Localization (SBFL) is one of the most actively studied techniques [18]. SBFL aims to identify the location of faulty code elements based on the execution paths of tests.

Previous research reports that the accuracy of SBFL is affected by test types, such as flaky tests [16]. In our research, we focus on exceptional behavior tests to

© The Author(s), under exclusive license to Springer Nature Switzerland AG 2024
R. Kadgien et al. (Eds.): PROFES 2023, LNCS 14483, pp. 399–414, 2024.
https://doi.org/10.1007/978-3-031-49266-2_28

reveal the impact of such tests on SBFL. According to the previous investigation [4], separating exceptional handling from normal control flow enables developers to increase program robustness. Therefore, we think the execution paths of exceptional behavior tests are different from the ones of normal control flow tests, which means that the difference significantly affects the accuracy of SBFL. In addition, exceptional behavior tests ensure that their software can handle unexpected situations, recover from errors, and continue to function correctly. From this, we think that exceptional behavior tests can reduce the occurrence of faults, and when faults occur, exceptional behavior tests help developers to identify the causes. Therefore, we hypothesize that exceptional behavior tests are more effective for SBFL.

In this study, we investigated the accuracy of SBFL on two types of faults: faults that occurred in real software development processes and artificially generated faults. Our study revealed that SBFL tended to be more accurate when all failing tests were exceptional behavior tests than when failing tests included no exceptional behavior tests. We confirmed that the number of program statements that need to be checked during debugging was reduced by approximately 33% for faults in real software development processes, and by approximately 66% for artificially generated faults in cases where all failing tests were exceptional behavior tests. Therefore, exceptional behavior tests are important to achieve a higher accuracy of SBFL.

Furthermore, we performed a more detailed categorization of exceptional behavior tests based on the type of exceptions encountered: custom exceptions and standard/third-party exceptions. As a result, we confirmed that SBFL was particularly accurate when all failing tests were exceptional behavior tests that examine the occurrence of standard/third-party exceptions.

The main contributions of our study are as follows.

- This is the first study to investigate the impact of exceptional behavior tests on SBFL.
- We confirmed that SBFL tends to be accurate when all failing tests are exceptional behavior tests.
- We found that SBFL tends to be particularly accurate when all failing tests are exceptional behavior tests that examine standard/third-party exceptions.

2   Preliminaries

2.1   Spectrum-Based Fault Localization (SBFL)

SBFL performs fault localization based on execution paths. SBFL is based on the idea that program statements executed in failing tests are likely to be faulty and those executed in passing tests are likely to be less faulty. Figure 1 shows the procedure for SBFL. The input is a faulty program and its tests. First, the program is run through the tests to obtain the pass or fail of each test and its execution path. From these, the suspicion values are calculated. A suspicion value indicates the likelihood that the program statement includes a fault.

There are many formulae for calculating suspicion values. In previous research, Abreu et al. concluded that Ochiai is the superior formula [1]. Equation (1) shows the definition of Ochiai.

Input   Output

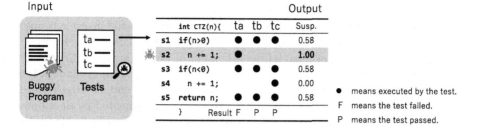

Fig. 1. SBFL flow

```
@Test(expected=ArithmeticException.class)
public void testIncrementToIntegerMaxValue() {
  Math.incrementExact(Integer.MAX_VALUE);
}
```

```
@Test(expected=ArithmeticException.class)
public void testIncrementToIntegerMaxValue() {
  Math.incrementExact(Integer.MAX_VALUE);
}
```

Fig. 2. Exceptional behavior tests   **Fig. 3.** Non-exceptional behavior tests

$$susp(s) = \frac{fail(s)}{\sqrt{totalfails \times (fail(s) + pass(s))}} \qquad (1)$$

s: a program statement.
$susp(s)$: suspicion value of s.
$totalfails$: the number of failing tests.
$fail(s)$: the number of failing tests that execute s.
$pass(s)$: the number of passing tests that execute s.

2.2 Exceptional Behavior Tests

Exceptional behavior tests verify whether exceptions occur as intended. We investigate a project written in Java. In accordance with previous studies [3], we define exceptional behavior tests as tests that use the methods listed in Table 1.

Figure 2 shows an example of exceptional behavior test: the test verifies whether an `ArithmeticException` occurs as intended using `expected` attribu-

Table 1. The test frameworks and methods for examining exception handling used in previous research [3].

Framework	Methods for detecting exceptions
JUnit	Using `assertThrows`. Specification of `expected` in @Test. Using `ExpectedException`.
TestNG	Specification of `expectedExceptions` in @Test.
AssertJ	Using `assertThatThrownBy`. Using `assertThatExceptionOfType`. Using `assertThatIOException`.
Common to all frameworks	Using a `fail` call right before a `catch` block.

tion in @Test from JUnit. The method under test, Math.incrementExact(int a), returns an incremented value of its argument, int a. If the increment operation results in an overflow, it throws an ArithmeticException. In Fig. 2, Integer.MAX_VALUE is specified as the argument of Math.incrementExact(int a). This causes an overflow and triggers the throwing of an ArithmeticException.

Exceptions can be classified into custom exceptions and standard/third-party exceptions. Custom exceptions are exceptions implemented by developers themselves, while standard/third-party exceptions are exceptions implemented in standard/third-party libraries. Among exceptional behavior tests, we call tests that inspect custom exceptions as *custom exceptional behavior tests* (hereinafter referred to as CETest), and tests that inspect standard/third-party exceptions as *standard/third-party exceptional behavior tests* (hereinafter referred to as STETest).

Tests that examine aspects other than exception handling are referred to as non-exceptional behavior tests. All tests other than exceptional behavior tests are non-exceptional behavior tests. An example of a non-exceptional behavior test is shown in Fig. 3. The test provides 10 as an argument to Math.incrementExact(int a) and expects the return value to be 11.

3   Research Questions

In this study, we set the following research questions to investigate whether exceptional behavior tests matter on SBFL.

RQ1: Do exceptional and non-exceptional behavior tests have different effects on SBFL?

We investigate how the ratio of exceptional behavior tests in passing/failing tests affects SBFL. If the ratio significantly affects the accuracy of SBFL, this research enables developers to make preliminary judgments about its reliability.

RQ2: Are there any differences in the length of execution paths between exceptional and non-exceptional behavior tests?

We examine the number of statements executed in exceptional behavior tests and non-exceptional behavior ones. In SBFL, statements executed in failing tests are considered potential candidates for faults. Therefore, the number of statements executed in failing tests is strongly related to the accuracy of the SBFL.

RQ3: Do custom exceptional behavior tests and standard/third party exceptional behavior ones have different effects on SBFL?

We investigate whether CETests and STETests have different impacts on SBFL. If the accuracy of SBFL differs significantly between these two types of tests, our study can suggest to developers which type of tests they should make proactively.

4   Experimental Setup

4.1   Tools

We use the following tools.

kGenProg[1]. kGenProg is an automated program repair tool developed in Higo et al.'s study [5]. We use kGenProg to calculate suspicion values of SBFL.

ExceptionHunter[2]. ExceptionHunter is a static analysis tool for Java programs developed in Francisco et al.'s study [3]. ExceptionHunter identifies whether a test is an exceptional behavior test or not.

Mutanerator[3]. Mutanerator is a mutant generation tool for Java programs. It applies mutant operators described in Table 2.

4.2   Benchmarks

We take the following benchmarks.

- Faults occurred in the real-world software development process (hereafter referred to as *real faults*).
- Faults artificially generated using Mutanerator (hereafter referred to as *artificial faults*).

We use Defects4J [7] as real faults. Defects4J is a dataset that collects faulty Java programs that occurred in real development processes. Many previous studies use Defects4J as a benchmark [10,12]. Our experiment focuses on six projects within Defects4J: Math, Chart, Lang, Jsoup, JacksonCore, and Codec. kGenProg does not work well with the other projects, so we select these six projects. We exclude some faults due to their inability to be within our environment.

Table 2. Mutation operators that are used in Mutanerator.

Mutation operators	Description
Conditional Boundary	Changing the bounds of relational operators
Increments	Swapping of increment/decrement
Invert Negatives	Rewriting of negative numbers to positive numbers
Math	Rewriting arithmetic operators
Negate Conditionals	Rewriting relational operators
Void Method Calls	Removing method calls of type void
Primitive Returns	Rewriting the return value of primitive types to 0

---

[1] https://github.com/kusumotolab/kGenProg.
[2] https://github.com/easy-software-ufal/exceptionhunter.
[3] https://github.com/kusumotolab/Mutanerator.

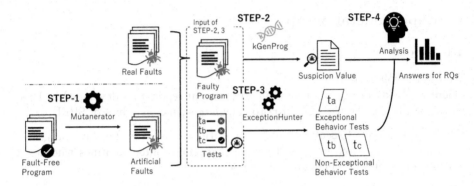

Fig. 4. Workflow of our research

To introduce artificial faults, we apply a two-step process. Initially, we fix faults in Defects4J. Subsequently, we employ Mutanerator to generate new faults. This approach allows us to incorporate artificial faults into our benchmarks.

Artificial faults have been used as benchmarks in previous studies [2, 9] Previous research reported that real and artificial faults have different effects on fault localization effectiveness [14]. However, Yan et al. reported that artificial faults including seeded faults simulate the real scenarios, and may still happen in practice [9]. Therefore, we include artificial faults as a benchmark in this study.

4.3   Workflow

Figure 4 shows the overall workflow of our experiment. The workflow consists of 4 steps. STEP-1 to STEP-3 are performed automatically by the tools: Mutanerator, kGenProg, and ExceptionHunter. In STEP-4, we manually analyze the impact of exceptional behavior tests on SBFL.

STEP-1. Mutanerator is applied to fault-free programs to generate artificial faults. A fault-free program passes all tests. Mutanerator changes fault-free programs into artificial faults that fail one or more tests.

STEP-2. We input a faulty program and its tests to kGenProg. kGenProg runs the program through its tests and calculates the suspicion values.

STEP-3. ExceptionHunter classifies tests into exceptional behavior tests or not. ExceptionHunter can further classify exceptional behavior tests into CETest and STETest.

STEP-4. Based on the results of STEP-2 and STEP-3, we investigate whether exceptional behavior tests matter on SBFL.

4.4   Evaluation Metrics

This research uses Rank and rTop-N as evaluation metrics.

Rank

Rank is the position of a faulty statement when arranging program statements in the descending order of suspicion values. If multiple statements share the same suspicion value, Rank takes the average rank of their ties. For a fault with multiple faulty statements, Rank takes the ranking of the first faulty statement, because the localization of the first faulty statement is critical to debugging [10,12,18]. For example, if three faulty statements in a given fault are ranked 2, 5, and 10, Rank of the fault becomes 2.

rTop-N

We create rTop-N with reference to Top-N. Top-N is the number of faults that Rank within N. Top-N is an effective evaluation metric for SBFL and has been used in many previous studies [10,12]. However, Top-N is inappropriate for comparing faults with different sample sizes. For example, there is a difference in meaning between Top-N being 100 out of 200 faults and Top-N being 100 out of 1000 faults. In this study, faults are classified according to the ratio of exceptional behavior tests. Because the number of faults varies after classification, we need to compare faults with different sample sizes. Therefore, we use rTop-N, which is Top-N normalized by the sample size. Equation (2) shows the definition of rTop-N.

$$\text{rTop-N} = \frac{\text{The number of faults that Rank is within N.}}{\text{The total number of faults.}} \qquad (2)$$

For example, suppose that Rank of two faults are 2 and 10, respectively. In this case, we calculate rTop-5. For the two faults, only the first fault has Rank within 5. Therefore, rTop-5 $= 1/2 = 0.5$.

In this study, we use a value of 5 for N. Previous study [8] reports that 73.58% of developers check only the top 5 elements returned by fault localization techniques.

5   Results and Discussion

We answer RQ1–RQ3 with the experimental results.

5.1   RQ1: Do exceptional and non-exceptional behavior tests have different effects on SBFL?

In RQ1, we investigate whether the ratio of exceptional behavior tests in passing/failing tests affects SBFL. Hereafter, we describe the ratio of exceptional behavior tests in failing tests as `rEFail`, and the one in passing tests as `rEPass`. For example, in Fig. 4, the failing tests are t_a and t_b, and the exceptional behavior tests are t_a. Since the failing exceptional behavior test is only t_a, `rEFail` is $1/2 = 0.5$.

Does rEFail affect SBFL?

First, we investigate the impact of rEFail on SBFL. In this experiment, faults are classified as follows.

- **rEFail = 0**
  Failing tests have no exceptional behavior test.
- **0 < rEFail < 1**
  Failing tests have both exceptional and non-exceptional behavior tests.
- **rEFail = 1**
  All failing tests are exceptional behavior tests.

Table 3 shows the number of faults corresponding to each case. The upper part shows real faults and the lower part shows artificial ones. Most of the faults belong to rEFail = 0. Regarding real faults, there are only six faults with 0 < rEFail < 1 in total. Therefore, for real faults, we compare rTop-5 and Rank only for rEFail = 0 and rEFail = 1.

First, we examine the effect of rEFail on rTop-5. Table 4 shows the results of rTop-5. The hyphenation "—" indicates no fault corresponding to the condition of rEFail. The bold letters mean the best rTop-5 for each project. Regarding real faults, only Math, Lang, and JacksonCore have faults with rEFail = 1. For all these three projects, the faults with rEFail = 1 achieve better rTop-5 than the ones with rEFail = 0. As for artificial faults, four projects have faults with rEFail = 1: Math, Lang, Jsoup, and Codec. Among these projects, Math, Lang, and Codec have the best rTop-5 with rEFail = 1. While Jsoup shows the worst rTop-5 with rEFail = 1, we think this is because there is only one fault with rEFail = 1. From the results, we conclude that faults with rEFail = 1 tend to achieve better rTop-5 than ones with rEFail = 0 or 0 < rEFail < 1.

Second, we examine the impact of rEFail on Rank. Figure 5 and Fig. 6 show Rank for real and artificial faults, respectively. The horizontal axis represents the Rank, and each fault's Rank is denoted as a black dot overlaid on the box-and-whisker plot. The outliers of Rank are excluded from the plots to make them easier to read. The red diamond in the figure represents the mean of Rank.

We initially focus on real faults in Fig. 5. Three projects contain rEFail = 1: Math, Lang, and JacksonCore. For Math and JacksonCore, the faults with

Table 3. The number of faults categorized by rEFail.

Real faults

	Math	Chart	Lang	Jsoup	JacksonCore	Codec	Total
rEFail = 0	67	13	20	14	14	13	141
0 < rEFail < 1	1	0	2	1	2	0	6
rEFail = 1	12	0	3	0	1	0	16

Artificial faults

	Math	Chart	Lang	Jsoup	JacksonCore	Codec	Total
rEFail = 0	399	488	277	166	307	272	1909
0 < rEFail < 1	93	0	566	1	33	150	843
rEFail = 1	39	0	7	1	0	4	51

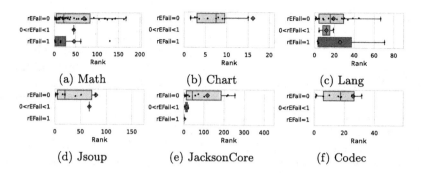

(a) Math   (b) Chart   (c) Lang

(d) Jsoup   (e) JacksonCore   (f) Codec

Fig. 5. The distribution of Rank in real faults categorized by rEFail.

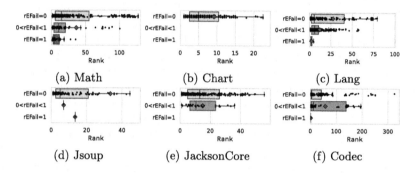

(a) Math   (b) Chart   (c) Lang

(d) Jsoup   (e) JacksonCore   (f) Codec

Fig. 6. The distribution of Rank in artificial faults categorized by rEFail.

rEFail = 1 achieve better Rank than the ones with rEFail = 0 in terms of the first quartile, median, third quartile, and mean values in the box-and-whisker plots. In the case of Lang, however, the faults with rEFail = 1 yield the worse mean and third quartile than those with rEFail = 0, while showing better first quartile and median values with rEFail = 1 than with rEFail = 0. From the results, we conclude that rEFail = 1 tends to achieve better Rank than rEFail = 0 for real faults.

Turning our attention to artificial faults in Fig. 6. Four projects have faults with rEFail = 1: Math, Lang, Jsoup, and Codec. Among these projects, Math, Lang, and Codec exhibit the best mean, first quartile, median, and third quartile values when rEFail = 1. As Jsoup does not take the best Rank when rEFail =

Table 4. rEFail and rTop-5

	Real faults						Artificial faults					
	Math	Chart	Lang	Jsoup	JacksonCore	Codec	Math	Chart	Lang	Jsoup	JacksonCore	Codec
rEFail = 0	0.30	**0.38**	0.35	**0.29**	0.07	**0.23**	0.22	**0.52**	0.49	**0.51**	0.25	0.51
0 < rEFail < 1	0.00	—	0.50	0.00	0.50	—	0.38	—	0.34	0.00	0.18	0.43
rEFail = 1	**0.50**	—	**0.67**	—	**1.00**	—	**0.54**	—	**1.00**	0.00	—	**1.00**

1, which could be attributed to the fact that Jsoup has only one fault with rEFail = 1. Overall, these results indicate that rEFail = 1 tends to achieve better Rank than rEFail = 0 and 0 < rEFail < 1 for artificial faults. Then we compare rEFail = 0 and 0 < rEFail < 1. From Fig. 6, Math, Lang, and JacksonCore have a better Rank with rEFail = 0 than with 0 < rEFail < 1, while Codec has better Rank when rEFail = 0. Therefore, it remains unclear which of rEFail = 0 or 0 < rEFail < 1 tends to be better.

To confirm our observation, we performed the Mann-Whitney U test at a significance level of 0.01. Since the results of the Shapiro-Wilk test confirmed that the distribution of Rank did not follow a normal distribution for both real and artificial faults, we used the Mann-Whitney U test. First, we focus on real faults. Regarding real faults, we do not distinguish the faults by projects due to the small number of faults with rEFail = 1. For real faults, the p-value between rEFail = 0 and rEFail = 1 is 0.083, which is not statistically significant. We think the lack of statistical significance is likely due to the limited number of faults with rEFail = 1. Next, we focus on artificial faults, and Table 5 shows the results. We exclude projects without any faults with rEFail = 1 or 0 < rEFail < 1 from the table. The bold letters indicate p-values that are below the 0.01 significance level. We focus on the p-values between rEFail = 0 and rEFail = 1. We confirmed that the p-values for Math and Codec are below the 0.01 significance level. Although there is no significant difference for Jsoup, we think this is because there is only one fault with rEFail = 1. As for Lang, while the p-value is not less than the significance level, the mean of Rank with rEFail = 1 is 24.93 better than with rEFail = 0. Based on these results, we conclude that Rank tends to be better when rEFail = 1 than when rEFail = 0 for artificial faults. Then we focus on the p-values between 0 < rEFail < 1 and rEFail = 1. No statistically significant difference is found in Math and Codec, even though they have 39 and 4 faults with rEFail = 1, respectively. Therefore, we conclude that it is unclear which Rank tends to be better between rEFail = 1 and 0 < rEFail < 1.

From these results, we can conclude that SBFL tends to be more accurate when rEFail = 1 than when rEFail = 0. When comparing rEFail = 1 with rEFail = 0, the average of Rank with rEFail = 1 is about 33% better for real faults and 66% better for artificial faults. We discuss the reason for this in Sect. 5.2.

Table 5. The p-value in artificial faults

	0 < rEFail < 1 rEFail = 0	0 < rEFail < 1 rEFail = 1	rEFail = 0 rEFail = 1
Math	**3.8E-04**	5.6E-02	**1.9E-06**
Lang	5.5E-02	**4.6E-03**	1.8E-02
Jsoup	7.6E-01	1.0	5.3E-01
Codec	5.1E-02	1.5E-02	**2.3E-03**

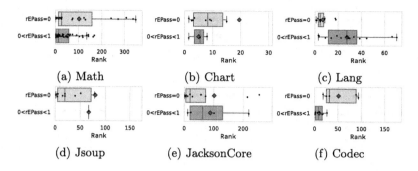

Fig. 7. The distribution of Rank in real faults categorized by `rEPass`.

Does rEPass affect SBFL?

As in the case of `rEFail`, we classify faults into three categories based on `rEPass`: `rEPass = 0`, `0 < rEPass < 1`, and `rEPass = 1`. Table 6 shows the distribution of faults for each case. There is no fault with `rEPass = 1`, both in real and artificial faults.

Table 7 shows the results of rTop-5. Regarding real faults, while `Math` and `Codec` achieve better rTop-5 with `0 < rEPass < 1`, `Chart`, `Lang`, `Jsoup`, and `JacksonCore` achieve better rTop-5 with `rEPass = 0`. For artificial faults, the superiority of rTop-5 with `0 < rEPass < 1` or `rEPass = 0` varies depending on the projects. Therefore, no clear regularity regarding the impact of `rEPass` on rTop-5 is revealed in this experiment.

Figure 7 and Fig. 8 show box-and-whisker plots of Rank for real and artificial faults, respectively. Regarding real faults, `Math`, `Chart`, and `Codec` exhibit better Rank when `0 < rEPass < 1` than when `rEPass = 0`. Conversely, for `Lang` and `JacksonCore`, Rank with `rEPass = 0` is distributed in a better range than with `0 < rEPass < 1`. Therefore, it remains uncertain which category yields better Rank for real faults. As for artificial faults, the superiority of either Rank, `rEPass = 0` or `0 < rEPass < 1`, depends on the projects. Consequently, we cannot say which of `rEPass = 0` or `0 < rEPass < 1` tends to be better.

Table 6. The number of faults categorized by `rEPass`.

Real Faults

	Math	Chart	Lang	Jsoup	JacksonCore	Codec	Total
rEPass = 0	21	11	11	14	16	5	78
0 < rEPass < 1	59	2	14	1	1	8	85
rEPass = 1	0	0	0	0	0	0	0

Artificial faults

	Math	Chart	Lang	Jsoup	JacksonCore	Codec	Total
rEPass = 0	81	325	8	105	202	13	734
0 < rEPass < 1	450	163	842	63	138	413	2069
rEPass = 1	0	0	0	0	0	0	0

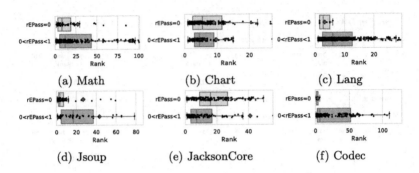

Fig. 8. The distribution of Rank in artificial faults categorized by rEPass.

> **Answer for RQ1**: Our findings indicate that when all failing tests are exceptional behavior tests, SBFL results are significantly more accurate compared to scenarios where failing tests have no exceptional behavior tests. The number of statements that must be examined before identifying the first faulty location is reduced by approximately 33% for real faults and 66% for artificial faults when all failing tests are exceptional behavior tests. Therefore, we conclude that exceptional behavior tests matter on SBFL.

5.2 RQ2: Are there any differences in the length of execution paths between exceptional and non-exceptional behavior tests?

In RQ2, we focus on rEFail since we revealed that rEFail significantly affects the accuracy of SBFL in RQ1. Table 8 shows the results. We find that when rEFail = 1, the number of program statements executed in failing tests is smaller than when rEFail = 0 for both real and artificial faults. The reason for this can be attributed to how programs handle abnormal processes. When a program encounters an abnormal process, it throws an exception to deal with the abnormal process. The thrown exception is caught in an appropriate lower-layer class during propagating to higher-layer classes. Therefore, exceptional behavior tests tend to examine the behavior of relatively lower-layer classes that throw exceptions. Since lower-layer classes generally invoke a smaller number of state-

Table 7. rEPass and rTop-5

	Real faults						Artificial faults					
	Math	Chart	Lang	Jsoup	JacksonCore	Codec	Math	Chart	Lang	Jsoup	JacksonCore	Codec
rEPass = 0	0.19	0.45	0.64	0.29	0.19	0.00	0.40	0.49	0.88	0.63	0.12	0.85
0 < rEPass < 1	0.37	0.00	0.21	0.00	0.00	0.38	0.25	0.58	0.39	0.30	0.43	0.48
rEPass = 1	—	—	—	—	—	—	—	—	—	—	—	—

ments than higher-layer classes, the number of statements executed in exceptional behavior tests tends to be smaller than in non-exceptional behavior tests. Therefore, it can be inferred that failing tests tend to execute fewer statements when rEFail = 1.

As discussed earlier, SBFL considers statements executed in failing tests as potential fault candidates. Consequently, the shorter the execution paths of failing tests, the higher the accuracy achieved by SBFL. Thus, the result of RQ1 can be attributed to the smaller number of statements executed in exceptional behavior tests.

> **Answer for RQ2**: When all failing tests are exceptional behavior tests, the number of program statements executed in failing tests tends to be small. We think this fact gives better SBFL results when rEFail=1, because the number of candidates for faulty locations is relatively small.

5.3   RQ3: Do custom exceptional behavior tests and standard/third party exceptional behavior ones have different effects on SBFL?

In this RQ, we focus on the ratio of CETests and STETests in failing tests. The ratio of CETests in failing tests is denoted as rCEFail, and the ratio of STETests is denoted as rSTEFail. As in RQ1, we categorize the faults based on rCEFail and rSTEFail. Due to space constraints, we do not show the distribution of Rank as it is in RQ1. Instead, we utilize the mean of Rank, which is denoted as ave(Rank), for our discussions.

Table 9 shows the results of rTop-5 and ave(Rank). The left side of the table shows rTop-5 and the right side shows ave(Rank). rTop5-All and ave(Rank)-All are rTop-5 and ave(Rank) obtained from the entire set of subjects.

First, we focus on the real faults in the upper part of Table 9. The column rTop5-All indicates that rTop-5 with rCEFail = 1 is almost the same as rCEFail = 0 and 0 < rCEFail < 1. In addition, the column ave(Rank)-All indicates that the faults with rCEFail = 1 yield the worst ave(Rank) compared to the ones in the other categories. On the contrary, faults with rSTEFail = 1 achieve better rTop-5 and Rank than the others. Therefore, for real faults, SBFL is particularly accurate when rSTEFail = 1. Next, we focus on the artificial faults in the lower part of Table 9. From rTop5-All and ave(Rank)-All, rTop-5 is 0.21 and ave(Rank) is 4.98 better when rSTEFail = 1 than when rCEFail = 1.

Table 8. rEFail and the number of statements executed in failing tests.

	Real faults						Artificial faults					
	Math	Chart	Lang	Jsoup	JacksonCore	Codec	Math	Chart	Lang	Jsoup	JacksonCore	Codec
rEFail = 0	252	73	62	477	328	89	327	74	87	400	292	109
0 < rEFail < 1	290	—	32	134	373	—	685	—	97	14	1582	159
rEFail = 1	112	—	39	—	16	—	150	—	8	17	—	3

For both real and artificial faults, we can conclude that $\texttt{rSTEFail} = 1$ achieves better rTop-5 and ave(Rank) than those with $\texttt{rCEFail} = 1$.

The reason why rTop-5 and Rank with $\texttt{rSTEFail} = 1$ is better than $\texttt{rCEFail} = 1$ lies in shorter execution paths of failing tests. As previously described in Sect. 5.2, the accuracy of SBFL tends to be high when failing tests have shorter execution paths. Specifically, for $\texttt{rSTEFail} = 1$, the length of the execution paths of failing tests is 47.40, whereas, for $\texttt{rCEFail} = 1$, it is significantly longer, at 168.33.

We now discuss why the execution paths of CETests are longer than that of STETests. One of the reasons developers create custom exceptions is to handle exceptions related to business logic or workflow. In order to raise a custom exception, it is necessary to invoke a program that implements the business logic or workflow, replicating the situation where the custom exception occurs. On the other hand, standard/third-party exceptions may occur more frequently during program developments and can even occur from simple actions, such as improper method calls or referring null objects. Therefore, we think that reproducing the situation where custom exceptions occur is more complex than standard/third-party exceptions. Exceptional behavior tests reproduce a situation where an exception occurs to verify that the intended exceptions are appropriately thrown. Therefore, the complexity of reproducing situations leads CETests to achieve a higher number of program statements being executed.

> **Answer for RQ3**: When all failing tests are STETests, SBFL tends to be more accurate than when all failing tests are CETests. Therefore, CETests and STETests have different effects on SBFL.

6   Threats to Validity

As evaluation metrics, we used Rank and rTop-N based on Top-N. Top-N is widely used in previous studies [10,12] Other evaluation metrics may yields different results. In addition, we used real and artificial faults as benchmarks. For the

Table 9. rCEFail/rSTEFail and rTop-5, ave(Rank)

Real faults	rTop-5							ave(Rank)						
	Math	Chart	Lang	Jsoup	JacksonCore	Codec	rTop5-All	Math	Chart	Lang	Jsoup	JacksonCore	Codec	ave(Rank)-All
rCEFail = 0	0.33	0.38	0.40	0.27	0.13	0.23	0.31	63.97	16.12	19.24	78.93	109.8	25.88	55.37
0 < rCEFail < 1	0.00	—	—	—	0.50	—	0.33	45.50	—	—	—	13.25	—	24.00
rCEFail = 1	0.33	—	—	—	—	—	0.33	86.50	—	—	—	—	—	86.50
rSTEFail = 0	0.30	0.38	0.35	0.29	0.13	0.23	0.29	70.58	16.12	19.00	79.79	104.5	25.88	59.51
0 < rSTEFail < 1	0.00	—	0.50	0.00	—	—	0.25	45.50	—	11.75	67.00	—	—	34.00
rSTEFail = 1	0.67	—	0.67	—	1.00	—	0.70	6.08	—	25.83	—	1.00	—	11.50

Artificial faults	rTop-5							ave(Rank)						
	Math	Chart	Lang	Jsoup	JacksonCore	Codec	rTop5-All	Math	Chart	Lang	Jsoup	JacksonCore	Codec	ave(Rank)-All
rCEFail = 0	0.23	0.52	0.39	0.51	0.26	0.53	0.49	38.88	9.23	16.75	33.08	32.24	29.38	23.42
0 < rCEFail < 1	0.37	—	—	—	0.13	0.39	0.36	42.92	—	—	—	16.17	62.96	51.99
rCEFail = 1	0.54	—	—	—	—	1.00	0.59	11.28	—	—	—	—	1.50	10.33
rSTEFail = 0	0.27	0.52	0.49	0.51	0.26	0.48	0.52	38.62	9.23	27.36	33.35	32.65	41.07	29.76
0 < rSTEFail < 1	0.39	—	0.34	0.00	0.13	0.85	0.34	9.25	—	11.74	7.00	15.75	3.23	11.67
rSTEFail = 1	0.50	—	1.00	0.00	—	—	0.80	11.50	—	2.43	13.50	—	—	5.35

real faults, we used only six Defects4J projects. For artificial faults, we used faults generated from the six projects used as real faults. Our analysis is based on projects as the unit of analysis, and six projects is a very small number. Larger scale experiments may yield different results.

7 Related Works

Francisco et al. surveyed Java projects to assess the prevalence of exceptional behavior tests [3]. Their results showed that approximately 60.91% of projects have at least one test method that examines the behavior of exceptions, and the percentage of exceptional behavior tests is less than 10% in 76.02% of projects. This study also revealed a tendency among developers to prioritize testing for custom exceptions over standard/third-party exceptions. They reported that more focus should be placed on creating exceptional behavior tests. We think the results of our research motivate developers to make exceptional behavior tests.

8 Conclusion

We examined the impact of exceptional behavior tests on SBFL. Our experiments revealed that SBFL was able to localize faulty code elements more accurately when all failing tests were exceptional behavior tests than when failing tests did not include any exceptional behavior tests. Therefore, we concluded that exceptional behavior tests matter on SBFL. In addition, we examined whether the ratio of CETests or STETests in the failing tests affects SBFL, and found that SBFL was particularly accurate when all failing tests were STETests. The results of our study enable developers to make a preliminary assessment of the reliability of SBFL, which is expected to improve the efficiency of debugging.

SBFL is also a technique used in Automated Program Repair (APR) [5,13, 19]. Previous research have shown that fault localization techniques affect the effectiveness of APR [15]. Therefore, future research includes an investigation of the effect of exceptional behavior tests on APR.

Acknowledgements. This research was supported by JSPS KAKENHI Japan (JP20H04166, JP21K18302, JP21K11829, JP21H04877, JP22H03567, JP22K11985)

References

1. Abreu, R., Zoeteweij, P., Golsteijn, R., van Gemund, A.J.: A practical evaluation of spectrum-based fault localization. J. Syst. Softw. **82**(11), 1780–1792 (2009)
2. Ali, S., Andrews, J.H., Dhandapani, T., Wang, W.: Evaluating the accuracy of fault localization techniques. In: Proceedings of International Conference on Automated Software Engineering, pp. 76–87 (2009)

3. Dalton, F., Ribeiro, M., Pinto, G., Fernandes, L., Gheyi, R., Fonseca, B.: Is exceptional behavior testing an exception? an empirical assessment using java automated tests. In: Proceedings of International Conference on Evaluation and Assessment in Software Engineering, pp. 170–179 (2020)

4. Garcia, A.F., Rubira, C.M., Romanovsky, A., Xu, J.: A comparative study of exception handling mechanisms for building dependable object-oriented software. J. Syst. Softw. **59**(2), 197–222 (2001)

5. Higo, Y., et al.: kGenProg: a high-performance, high-extensibility and high-portability APR system. In: Proceedings of Asia-Pacific Software Engineering Conference, pp. 697–698 (2018)

6. Jin, W., Orso, A.: BugRedux: reproducing field failures for in-house debugging. In: Proceedings of International Conference on Software Engineering, pp. 474–484 (2012)

7. Just, R., Jalali, D., Ernst, M.D.: Defects4j: a database of existing faults to enable controlled testing studies for java programs. In: Proceedings of International Symposium on Software Testing and Analysis, pp. 437–440 (2014)

8. Kochhar, P.S., Xia, X., Lo, D., Li, S.: Practitioners' expectations on automated fault localization. In: Proceedings of International Symposium on Software Testing and Analysis, pp. 165–176 (2016)

9. Lei, Y., Xie, H., Zhang, T., Yan, M., Xu, Z., Sun, C.: Feature-FL: feature-based fault localization. IEEE Trans. Reliab. **71**(1), 264–283 (2022)

10. Li, X., Li, W., Zhang, Y., Zhang, L.: Deepfl: integrating multiple fault diagnosis dimensions for deep fault localization. In: Proceedings of International Symposium on Software Testing and Analysis, pp. 169–180 (2019)

11. Liu, C., Yan, X., Fei, L., Han, J., Midkiff, S.P.: SOBER: statistical model-based bug localization. In: Proceedings of European Software Engineering Conference Held Jointly with International Symposium on Foundations of Software Engineering, pp. 286–295 (2005)

12. Lou, Y., et al.: Can automated program repair refine fault localization? a unified debugging approach. In: Proceedings of International Symposium on Software Testing and Analysis, pp. 75–87 (2020)

13. Martinez, M., Martin, M.: Ultra-large repair search space with automatically mined templates: the cardumen mode of astor. In: Proceedings of International Symposium on Search Based Software Engineering, pp. 65–86 (2017)

14. Pearson, S., et al.: Evaluating and improving fault localization. In: Proceedings of International Conference on Software Engineering, pp. 609–620 (2017)

15. Qi, Y., Mao, X., Lei, Y., Wang, C.: Using automated program repair for evaluating the effectiveness of fault localization techniques. In: Proceedings of International Symposium on Software Testing and Analysis, pp. 191–201 (2013)

16. Qin, Y., Wang, S., Liu, K., Mao, X., Bissyandé, T.F.: On the impact of flaky tests in automated program repair. In: International Conference on Software Analysis, Evolution and Reengineering, pp. 295–306 (2021)

17. Tassey, G.: The economic impacts of inadequate infrastructure for software testing (2002)

18. Wong, W.E., Gao, R., Li, Y., Abreu, R., Wotawa, F.: A survey on software fault localization. IEEE Trans. Softw. Eng. **42**(8), 707–740 (2016)

19. Yuan, Y., Banzhaf, W.: Arja: automated repair of java programs via multi-objective genetic programming. Trans. Softw. Eng. **46**(10), 1040–1067 (2020)

On Deprecated API Usages: An Exploratory Study of Top-Starred Projects on GitHub

Pietro Cassieri[1], Simone Romano[2($\boxtimes$)] , and Giuseppe Scanniello[2]

[1] Fisciano, Italy
[2] University of Salerno, Fisciano, Italy
{siromano,gscanniello}@unisa.it

Abstract. A deprecated *Application Programming Interface (API)* is one that is no longer recommended to use by its original developers. While deprecated APIs (*i.e.,* deprecated fields, methods, and classes) are still implemented, they can be removed in future implementations. Therefore, developers should not use deprecated APIs in newly written code and should update existing code so that it does not use deprecated APIs anymore. In this paper, we present the results of an exploratory *Mining-Software-Repository* study to gather preliminary empirical evidence on deprecated API usages in open-source Java applications. To that end, we quantitatively analyzed the commit histories of 14 applications whose software projects were top-starred on GitHub. We found that deprecated APIs usages are pretty widespread in the studied software applications; and only in half of these applications, developers remove deprecated API usages after few commits and days. Also, half of the studied applications mostly use deprecated APIs declared in their own source code, rather than using deprecated APIs that lie in third-party software. Finally, we noted that the introductions and removals of deprecated API usages are mostly the result of changes made by senior developers, rather than newcomer ones.

Keywords: GitHub · Code Smell · Deprecated API Usage · Java

1 Introduction

Application Programming Interfaces (APIs) allow software components (*e.g.,* libraries and frameworks) to make their features available to other software components/applications. By using APIs, developers can save time and effort, and reuse well-tested features [16]. To remain useful in a changing development environment, APIs must evolve over time—while new features are introduced, existing ones are modified or removed. Changes to APIs can be substantial; as a consequence, API consumers (*i.e.,* software applications using/consuming APIs) might be forced to update their code. And, the migration process from the old

---

P. Cassieri—Independent Researcher.

R. Kadgien et al. (Eds.): PROFES 2023, LNCS 14483, pp. 415–431, 2024.
https://doi.org/10.1007/978-3-031-49266-2_29

API to the new one might require time and effort. To let API consumers gradually migrate toward a new API, the developers of that API use the *deprecation* mechanism. In other words, by deprecating an API (*e.g.*, a field, a method, or even a class[1]), the developers warn API consumers that such an API is no longer recommended to use and can be removed in future implementations. The deprecation period allows, therefore, API consumers to have a gradual migration from the deprecated API to the new one (*i.e.*, the API to be used in place of the deprecated one). Replacing deprecated API usages (*e.g.*, calls to deprecated methods, accesses to deprecates field, *etc.*) is an established process in software development; however, it is still unclear how long this migration takes.

Code smells (also known as *Bad Smells in Code*) are indicators of potential problems in source code [21]. In the last two decades, the Software Engineering community has displayed an increasing interest in code smells and several code-smell catalogs have been proposed (*e.g.*, [6,21]). Among them, the catalog by *SonarSource*[2] includes deprecated API usages [2]. Also, in the Android ecosystem, the usages of a deprecated API can introduce a *forward compatibility* smell [18]. Such a code smell arises when an Android application uses an API without any compatibility check and, although this API exists in the latest version of Android, it is deprecated. Thus, this API could be deleted in the future resulting in a bug in the Android application that uses it.

In this paper, we present the results of an exploratory *Mining-Software-Repository* study on deprecated API usages in open-source Java applications. More in detail, we quantitatively analyzed the commit histories of 14 applications, whose software projects were top-starred on GitHub in order to gather preliminary empirical evidence on (*i*) the spread of deprecated API usages, (*ii*) their lifespan, (*iii*) where consumed deprecated APIs lie (*i.e.*, internally or externally to software applications being analyzed), and (*iv*) who (*i.e.*, newcomer or senior developers) introduces and removes deprecated API usages.

Our results suggest that deprecated APIs usages are pretty widespread in the studied software applications even though not all applications suffer in the same way from this code smell. Only in half of these applications, deprecated API usages are removed after few commits and days. Also, half of the studied applications mostly use deprecated APIs declared in their own source code, rather than using deprecated APIs that lie in third-party software. Finally, the introductions and removals of deprecated API usages are mostly the result of changes made by senior developers, rather than newcomer ones.

The main contributions of this paper follow.

1. We bring preliminary empirical evidence on deprecated API usages in open-source Java applications whose software projects are top-starred on GitHub.
2. We provide a curated dataset on deprecated API usages for increasing the credibility of our findings as well as the replicability of our study. Data extraction and analysis scripts are provided together with the dataset [15].

The remainder of the paper is organized as follows. In Sect. 2, we provide background information and summarize research work related to ours. The

---

[1] In this paper, we use the term "class" to also refer to interfaces and enums.

[2] It is the company that owns *SonarQube, SonarLint*, and *SonarCloud*.

design of our mining study is presented in Sect. 3, while the obtained results are reported in Sect. 4. We discuss the obtained results, as well as the threats that might affect their validity, in Sect. 5. Final remarks conclude the paper in Sect. 6.

2   Related Work

In this section, we first report background information and then related work.

2.1   Background Information

According to the official Java documentation, a deprecated API (*e.g.,* a field, a method, or even a class) is one that is today deemed unimportant, to the extent that it should no longer be utilized as it has been superseded and may potentially cease to exist in the future [1]. The inclusion of deprecation as a language feature serves as a means for API producers to signal that a particular feature is no longer recommended for use [17]. Also, the deprecation mechanism grants API consumers the flexibility to gradually adapt to the changes in the APIs. Indeed, over time, APIs evolve and certain features may be substituted with newer ones that offer increased performance, reliability, maintainability, or security. Suddenly eliminating outdated features (*i.e.,* without using the deprecation mechanism) would negatively impact API consumers who should adapt to the changes in the APIs shortly without allowing them a smooth transition.

API deprecation still presents challenges because deprecating an API can disrupt the software development of its API consumers, requiring the developers of API consumers to update their codebase. Although the migration process from the old to the new API is gradual when using the deprecation mechanism, such a process might still require time and effort, and be risky. Furthermore, API deprecation requires API producers to properly adjust documentation to help any developer to understand the deprecation process and migrate to alternative solutions effectively.

According to Sawant *et al.* [16], the reasons behind API deprecation are the following: avoiding bad coding practices, design pattern introduction, presence of unimplemented methods, presence of functional defects, merging of existing methods, new feature introduction, updating dependencies, presence of redundant methods, renaming of features, presence of security flaws, separation of concerns, and presence of temporary features. Sawant *et al.* [16] also observed that the most frequent reason behind API deprecation is *new feature introduction*, but there are cases where API deprecation is due to the presence of functional defects—this is the second most recurring reason—and security flaws. Accordingly, it seems important to study not only the life cycle of deprecated APIs from the point of view of the producer but also from that of the consumer.

2.2   Studies on Deprecated APIs

Researchers have studied deprecated APIs from the perspectives of producers and consumers. For example, Zhou and Walker [22] investigated API deprecation from the perspective of producers. In particular, they analyzed the *deprecate-replace-remove* cycle in the APIs of producers (Java applications, in particular), and observed that such a cycle is often not followed: many APIs are removed without prior deprecation, many deprecated APIs are subsequently un-deprecated, and some removed APIs are even resurrected. Also, the reason behind the deprecation of an API is often not provided within the deprecation message; thus, API consumers are not properly helped to make informed decisions on whether and how promptly to remove deprecated API usages. Another study taking the producer's perspective is that by Brito *et al.* [3], who observed that, in most cases, the message of deprecated APIs indicates the recommended replacement API.

As for the consumer's perspective, Sawant *et al.* [17] studied how consumers react to API deprecation in Java applications. To do so, they qualitatively analyzed 380 API usages and found seven reaction patterns, namely: no reaction; deletion of the deprecated API usage without any replacement; substitution with a recommended replacement; substitution with an in-house replacement; substitution with a replacement from the *Java Development Kit*; substitution with another third-party API; and rollback to a previous version, un-deprecated, of that API. Among these patterns, the most common one resulted to be "no reaction", namely: in most cases, API consumers continue using deprecated APIs.

Li *et al.* [12] studied Android's deprecated APIs. In particular, they focused on the deprecation of APIs in Android's codebase as well as how consumers (*i.e.*, Android applications) react to Android's deprecated APIs. They reported that Android's codebase is regularly cleaned-up from deprecated APIs, often in a short time frame; the deprecation message of Android's deprecated APIs usually includes the recommended replacement API; and Android applications usually retain deprecated API usages, rather than removing them.

Finally, Qiu *et al.* [14] by examining the general utilization of APIs stumbled upon interesting findings regarding the usage of deprecated APIs in the Java ecosystem. In particular, the authors discovered that deprecated APIs are widely used despite some of them being deprecated a long time ago.

The key differences between our study and those mentioned just before above can be summarized as follows. First, unlike the studies by Brito *et al.* [3], Sawant *et al.* [16], and Zhou and Walker [22], who investigated deprecated APIs from the producer's perspective, we took the consumer's perspective (*i.e.*, we looked at deprecated API usages). Second, we specifically investigated deprecated API usages, while Qiu *et al.* [14] focused on API usages in general. Third, we did not study Android's deprecated APIs as done by Li *et al.* [12]. And fourth, we investigated facets related to deprecated API usages not previously investigated—*e.g.*, the study by Sawant *et al.* [17], which is the most similar to ours, did not consider where consumed deprecated APIs lie (*i.e.*, internally or externally to software applications being analyzed) or did not perform survival analysis to understand how long deprecated API usages survive in terms of both commits and days.

3   Study Design

The *goal* of our mining study is to quantitatively analyze the commit histories of software applications with the *purpose* of understanding: *(i)* the spread of deprecated API usages (*i.e.*, usages of deprecated fields, methods, and classes), *(ii)* their lifespan, *(iii)* where consumed deprecated APIs lie (*i.e.*, internally or externally to software applications being analyzed), and *(iv)* who (*i.e.*, newcomer or senior developers) introduces and removes deprecated API usages. The *perspective* of our study is that of practitioners and researchers. The former might be interested in improving their knowledge of deprecated API usages in order to make more-informed decisions on how to manage them. The latter might be interested in conducting future research on deprecated API usages in light of our results. The *context* consists of open-source Java applications whose software projects were (hosted and) top-starred on GitHub.

3.1   Research Questions

Consistent with our study goal, we formulated and then investigated the following Research Questions (RQs):

RQ1. *How widespread are deprecated API usages?* The study of this RQ aims
   to discover whether and to what extent open-source Java applications, whose
   software projects were top-starred on GitHub, are affected by deprecated API
   usages. We can postulate that the higher the spread of this code smell, the
   higher the likelihood for software applications to be exposed to problems,
   including functional defects and security flaws [16].

RQ2. *How long deprecated API usages survive before being removed?*
   This RQ is to comprehend how long deprecated API usages remain in open-
   source Java applications having software projects top-starred on GitHub—
   i.e., from when deprecated API usages appear up to when they are removed.
   If deprecated API usages survive for a long time, this might suggest that API
   deprecation per se is not perceived as a good enough reason to change the
   source code of API consumers.

RQ3. *Where are consumed deprecated APIs?*
   Given a software application, consumed deprecated APIs can be declared in
   third-party software (*i.e.*, in the dependencies of that application) or in its
   own source code. With this RQ, we want to study this phenomenon, thus
   improving our body of knowledge on deprecated API usage in open-source
   Java applications with software projects top-starred on GitHub.

RQ4. *Who introduces and removes deprecated API usages?*
   Here, we aim to complete our study by focusing on whether and to what
   extent different kinds of developers deal with deprecated API usages. More
   specifically, the goal of this RQ is to understand if newcomer developers introduce and remove deprecated API usages differently from senior ones—to discern between newcomer and senior developers, we used the same approach
   as Tufano *et al.* [20]. If newcomer and senior developers differently deal with
   deprecated API usages, it might mean that they differently approach code
   cleaning practices or have different responsibilities in software projects.

3.2   Study Context and Execution

We focused our study on open-source Java applications whose software projects were hosted on GitHub and listed among the top-starred ones. We based our study on GitHub because it is the most popular version-control platform according to the *2022 Stack Overflow Developer Survey* [19]. We took into account top-starred projects since GitHub's stars are indicators of projects' popularity [9] and we wanted to take a picture of the phenomenon of deprecated API usage within very-popular software projects.

To gather applications with software projects top-starred on GitHub, we searched through the *GitHub Advanced Search Page* [7] those projects that:

- were developed in Java and contained `pom.xml` files, to select Java applications that used *Maven* as the build-automation tool;
- were not forks,[3] to avoid selecting duplicated applications;
- were not archived and for which the last push date was within one month from the query date (December 30th, 2022), to avoid selecting applications whose development was ceased;
- had at least one fork, to select applications with more than one contributor.

We sorted the found projects by stars and planned to study the top 20. Since GitHub can host projects not related to software development (*e.g.,* tutorials, books, students' assignments, *etc.*) [10], we inspected each project and had to discard one project in the top 20 because it provided Java implementations of algorithms intended for learning purposes.

To detect deprecated API usages, we performed the following steps.

1. We locally cloned each software application.
2. We got the name of the default branch by using the `git symbolic-ref` command.
3. We retrieved the list of commits in the default branch by means of the `git log` command.
4. We traversed the commits of the default branch from the first to the last commit by executing a `git checkout` command each time.
5. We retrieved the list of deprecated API usages—in particular, the usages of deprecated methods, fields, and classes—by running the `mvn clean install` command on each commit with the `showDeprecation` and `showWarnings` options enabled. To speed up the analysis process, we also enabled the `skipTests` and `maven.javadoc.skip` options —the former allows avoiding the test execution, the latter is to disable the Javadoc generation.

When detecting deprecated API usages, we bumped into software applications having both very long building times and commit histories. In particular, we were forced to discard five projects (plus one project intended for learning purposes

---

[3] In GitHub, a fork is a copy of an existing project that allows the fork's owner to suggest changes from his/her fork to the original project (via pull requests) as well as bring changes from the original project.

Table 1. Some information on the selected applications.

Application[*]	# Stars	# Classes[†]	# Methods[†]	# Fields[†]	LOC[†]
ANTLR	13.9k	655	4,382	1,489	40,495
Apollo	27.8k	624	3,352	1,838	26,851
Arthas	31.7k	776	4,867	2,006	40,277
Bytecode Viewer	13.5k	369	1,527	981	18,589
canal	25k	1,010	8,193	3,724	107,662
EasyExcel	26.8k	526	2,194	1,355	19,019
HikariCP	17.8k	163	1,315	362	10,639
Hutool	25.4k	2,138	16,132	4,059	114,506
JEECG BOOT	33.5k	637	3,311	2,062	33,357
litemall	17.7k	617	11,845	1,939	90,876
mall	63.7k	754	14,152	2,237	100,638
MyBatis	18.2k	1,564	7,553	3,166	53,926
Spring Cloud Alibaba	24.8k	238	1,049	458	7,107
Zipkin	16k	776	4,444	1,509	37,250

[*] The link to the software project on GitHub can be found in our replication package [15].
[†] Computed on the last analyzed commit.

as mentioned above) from the top 20 most-starred ones because the execution of the above-mentioned steps required, according to our estimations, at least three months. Summing up, we took into account 14 applications whose software projects were among the top 20 most-starred ones on GitHub. In Table 1, we provide some information on the studied applications.

4 Results

In this section, we present the results of our study arranged by RQ.

4.1 RQ1: How Widespread Are Deprecated API Usages?

In Fig. 1, we show the boxplots depicting the distributions of deprecated API usages across the commit history of each application. In Table 2, we report the values of some descriptive statistics—*i.e.,* mean, Standard Deviation (SD), minimum (min), median, maximum (max), and percentage of zeros (% Zeros)—we used to have a complete view of these distributions.

By looking at Fig. 1, we can notice that, although the distributions of deprecated API usages are not the same across the software applications, such a code smell is pretty widespread in all applications except one, HikariCP, whose commits never contain deprecated API usages.

The results in Table 2 allow confirming that deprecated API usages are pretty widespread in the studied applications. The maximum values are all greater

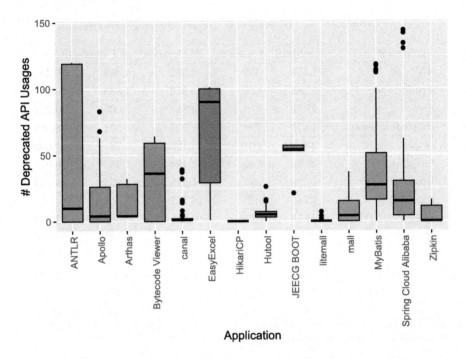

Fig. 1. Boxplots showing the number of deprecated API usages across the commit history of each application.

Table 2. Values of the descriptive statistics we used to summarize the distribution of deprecated API usages across the commit history of each application.

Application	Mean	SD	Min	Median	Max	% Zeros
ANTLR	57.8	58.434	0	10	120	32.989
Apollo	16.443	22.713	0	4	83	26.861
Arthas	10.264	10.722	3	4	32	0
Bytecode Viewer	30.206	28.056	0	36	64	26.425
canal	5.975	11.737	0	1	39	14.068
EasyExcel	63.353	37.261	1	90	101	0
HikariCP	0	0	0	0	0	100
Hutool	5.419	3.325	0	5	26	4.055
JEECG BOOT	53.281	6.711	21	54	57	0
litemall	0.359	0.935	0	0	7	84.137
mall	6.898	7.523	0	4	37	30.659
MyBatis	36.367	27.552	0	27	118	0.039
Spring Cloud Alibaba	22.228	27.755	0	15	144	2.379
Zipkin	3.865	5.75	0	0	16	64.918

than zero with the only exception of HikariCP. This means that almost all the applications have at least one commit with a deprecated API usage. We can also notice that the percentage of zeros is lower than 50% in 11 out of 14 applications. In other words, in most applications, deprecated API usages affect more than half of their commits. On average, the number of deprecated API usages per commit ranges from 0 (HikariCP) to 63.353 (EasyExcel).

> **Answer to RQ1:** *Deprecated API usages are pretty widespread in the studied applications whose projects are top-starred on GitHub, thus potentially exposing those applications to problems.*

4.2 RQ2: How Long Deprecated API Usages Survive Before Being Removed?

To answer this RQ, we followed the evolution of each deprecated API usage along the commit history of each application. In particular, given a deprecated API usage, we computed its survival time in terms of commits and days. The former is defined as the interval of consecutive commits in the default branch in which that deprecated API usage was present (*i.e.*, from the first commit that introduced the deprecated API usage, referred to as *introducing commit*,[4] up to the last commit in which that deprecated API usage was present). Similarly, the survival time in terms of days is defined as the interval of consecutive days in which that deprecated API usage was present (*i.e.*, from the introducing-commit day up to the day of the last commit in which that deprecated API usage was present). We ran the survival analysis in terms of both commits and days because they can provide different and complementary views about the event of interest (*e.g.*, there could be differences among applications in terms of the number of commits per day) [20].

When running survival analyses on commit histories, researchers are forced to analyze finite commit histories although the studied software applications continue to evolve with time [4,13]. In other words, the removal of a deprecated API usage (*i.e.*, the event of interest) can occur outside the analyzed commit history. Therefore, based on the terminology used in survival-analysis studies, we can distinguish between two kinds of deprecated API usages: *complete* and *censored*. A deprecated API usage is complete when we know the introducing commit and the *removing one* (*i.e.*, the commit in which that deprecated API usage was removed).[5] On the other hand, a deprecated API usage is censored when we know the introducing commit, but not the removing one—this is because nobody has removed yet that deprecated API usage by the last analyzed commit.

To estimate how long deprecated API usages survive, by taking into account both complete and censored deprecated API usages, we leveraged survival analysis. In particular, we built the *Kaplan-Meier survival curve* [11], which depicts

---

[4] A commit introduces a deprecated API usage when: *(i)* a developer writes a piece of source code that uses a deprecated API; *(ii)* a developer performs a dependency update that makes an already-used API deprecated; and *(iii)* a developer deprecates an API in its codebase but this API is currently used in that codebase.

[5] We considered a deprecated API as removed in any case it disappears from the source code (*i.e.*, deletion of the deprecated API usage without any substitution; replacement of it with another API usage; rollback to a previous version, un-deprecated, of that API; and un-deprecation of an API consumed internally).

Table 3. Survival analysis results. We do not report HikariCP because it is not affected by any deprecated API usage.

Application	#	# Events	Median Survival Time	
			By Commits	By Days
ANTLR	794	675 (85%)	10 [7, 10]	1.023 [0.876, 1.02]
Apollo	307	269 (88%)	72 [57, 85]	153.114 [108.139, 182.64]
Arthas	62	32 (52%)	493 [396, –]	607.251 [296.934, –]
Bytecode Viewer	271	207 (76%)	87 [78, 125]	33.869 [13.347, 44.45]
canal	114	76 (67%)	19 [5, 49]	6.639 [3.494, 155.75]
EasyExcel	1,325	1,296 (98%)	15 [8, 18]	19.984 [13.435, 21.85]
Hutool	230	224 (97%)	7 [5, 26]	3.026 [2.459, 6.4]
JEEC BOOT	161	104 (65%)	36 [36, 59]	41.067 [41.067, 58.88]
litemall	15	13 (87%)	9 [2, 14]	2.723 [0.623, 4.52]
mall	104	100 (96%)	17.5 [5, 64]	44.731 [8.995, 112.03]
MyBatis	1,082	1,053 (97%)	8 [8, 17]	4.939 [4.081, 10.45]
Spring Cloud Alibaba	2,036	2,019 (99%)	4 [2, 4]	2.726 [0.962, 2.73]
Zipkin	195	195 (100%)	3 [2, 9]	0.902 [0.486, 1.78]

the survival probability of deprecated API usages at any point in time with respect to commits (and days). From this curve, we then computed the *median survival time*, defined as the time for which the survival probability is equal to 0.5 [8]. In our case, the median survival time estimates how long deprecated API usages survive in terms of commits (and days).

In Table 3, we show the results of the survival analysis on deprecated API usages. In particular, this table reports the median survival time values (with the corresponding 95% confidence intervals) in terms of commits and days, as well as the number of (distinct) deprecated API usages (see the # column) and how many of them are removed in absolute and percentage terms (see the # *Events* column).

First of all, we can notice that most deprecated API usages are then removed. In particular, the percentage of deprecated API usages removed in the analyzed time span ranges from 52% (Arthas) to 100% (Zipkin). Furthermore, in nine out of 13 software applications (*i.e.*, excluding HikariCP, which is not affected by deprecated API usages), such a percentage is never lower than 85%.

If we consider the median survival time in terms of commits, we can observe that deprecated API usages tend to survive for few commits in half the applications. In particular, in six out of 13 software applications, deprecated API usages survive for less than or up to ten commits. On the remaining seven software applications, the median survival time ranges from 15 (EasyExcel) to 493 (Arthas).

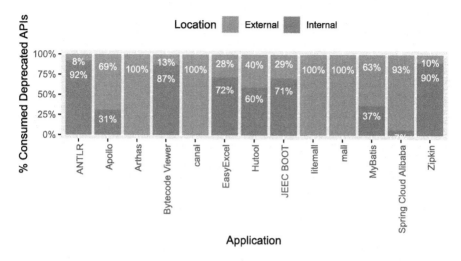

Fig. 2. Barplots showing the percentage of consumed deprecated APIs that are internal or external to a given software application. We do not report HikariCP because it is not affected by any deprecated API usage.

As for the median survival time in terms of days, we can observe a trend similar to that mentioned above, namely: in half of the cases, deprecated API usages tend to survive for few days. Indeed, the median survival time is less than ten days in seven (out of 13) software applications. On the remaining six, deprecated API usages tend to survive for 19.984 (EasyExcel) to 607.251 days (Arthas).

> **Answer to RQ2:** *In the studied applications, the greater part of deprecated API usages is removed. Also, in half of these applications, deprecated API usages tend to survive for a while, in terms of both commits and days, before being removed. In the other half, it seems that developers take care of removing deprecated API usages as soon as possible since such a code smell tends not to survive for a long time.*

4.3 RQ3. Where Are Consumed Deprecated APIs?

To answer this RQ, we first extracted the list of packages of each software application. Later, for each deprecated API consumed by a given software application, we checked if the deprecated API package was listed among the packages of that software application. If so, we classified the deprecated API as *internal*; otherwise, it was classified as *external*.

In Fig. 2, we graphically describe, through a barplot, the percentage of consumed deprecated APIs that are internal or external to studied software applications. Interestingly, in half the studied applications, most usages refer to deprecated APIs that are declared internally to these applications. More specifically, in six (out of 13) software applications, the percentage of consumed deprecated APIs that are internal to a given application ranges from 60% (Hutool) to 92%

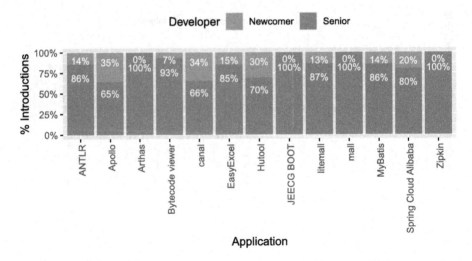

Fig. 3. Barplots showing the percentage of introductions of deprecated API usages by newcomer and senior developers. We do not report HikariCP because it is not affected by any deprecated API usage.

(ANTLR). Finally, we can notice that, only for four applications, there is no usage of deprecated APIs declared internally.

> **Answer to RQ3:** *Consuming their own deprecated APIs is a common phenomenon in the studied software applications—indeed, half of the studied applications mostly use deprecated APIs declared in their own source code.*

4.4   RQ4. Who Introduces and Removes Deprecated API Usages?

To answer this RQ, we first retrieved the contributors that performed each introducing or removing commit. Later, we classified each contributor as either *newcomer* or *senior* by using the same approach as Tufano *et al.* [20]. In particular, if a contributor had performed less than four commits at the time of the introducing (or removing) commit, we classified that contributor as a newcomer developer; otherwise, we classified him/her as a senior one.

In Fig. 3, we depict, through a barplot, the percentage of introductions of deprecated API usages by newcomer and senior developers. We can observe that, whatever the software application is, the percentage of introductions of deprecated API usages by senior developers is higher than that of newcomer ones. More in detail, the number of introductions of deprecated API usages by senior developers accounts for 65% (Apollo) to 100% (Arthas, JEECG BOOT, mall, Zipkin) of introductions.

In Fig. 4, we show the barplot regarding the percentage of deprecated API usages removed by newcomer and senior developers. We can observe that, regardless of the software application, most of the removals of deprecated API usage

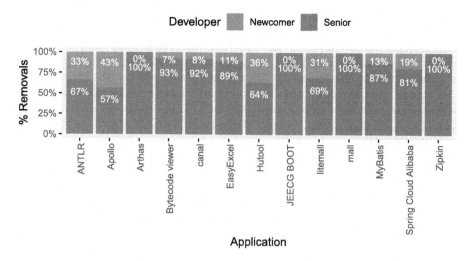

Fig. 4. Barplots showing the percentage of removals of deprecated API usages by newcomer and senior developers. We do not report HikariCP because it is not affected by any deprecated API usage.

are performed by senior developers. In particular, the percentage of deprecated API usages removed by senior developers ranges from 57% (Apollo) to 100% (Arthas, JEECG BOOT, mall, Zipkin).

> **Answer to RQ4:** *The introductions of deprecated API usages are mostly the result of changes made by senior developers, rather than newcomer ones. This is probably due to the fact that senior developers are usually responsible for dependency updates, which make an already-used API deprecated. However, we cannot exclude a second hypothesis, namely: novice developers try to avoid writing pieces of source code that use deprecated APIs. As for the removals of deprecated API usages, they are mostly performed by senior developers. The possible reasons for such a finding are: (i) senior developers are conscious to have introduced deprecated APIs in past commits and thus take care of removing the previously-introduced code smells and (ii) one of the roles of senior developers is to periodically clean source code.*

5   Overall Discussion

In this section, we first discuss our results, including possible implications and research future directions. Then, we highlight possible threats to validity.

5.1   Implications and Future Extensions

Deprecated API usages are pretty widespread in the studied applications, specifically open-source Java applications having software projects top-starred on

GitHub. This finding confirms those from past research that highlighted the presence of deprecated API usages in open-source Java applications whose software projects were available on GitHub (*i.e.*, projects non-top-starred) [14,17]. Such a spread of deprecated API usages potentially exposes those applications to problems, including functional defects and security flaws [16]. Therefore, it is of utmost importance that developers of API producers provide the reasons behind deprecated APIs so that developers of API consumers can make informed decisions on whether and how promptly to remove deprecated API usages. Unfortunately, the evidence gathered so far shows that the reasons behind API deprecation are often not disclosed within deprecation messages [22].

Our research reveals the virtuous attitudes of developers who, even after a long time and several commits, eventually remove the greater part of deprecated API usage. This finding is in contrast with that by Sawant *et al.* [17], who observed that API consumers mostly continue using deprecated APIs. These contrasting findings might be due to the different samples—*i.e.*, software applications having top-starred projects on GitHub seem to have a greater attention to removing deprecated API usages. Our research also shows that, in half of the studied applications, developers take care of removing deprecated API usages as soon as possible; while, in the other half, deprecated API usages tend to survive for a while before developers remove them. In other words, in these applications, API deprecation per se is not perceived as a good enough reason to change the source code of API consumers. Again, we highlight the importance of providing the reasons behind deprecated APIs so that developers of API consumers can make informed decisions on whether and how promptly to remove deprecated API usages. In this regard and similar to Sawant *et al.* [17], we support the introduction of a severity level for API deprecation (*e.g.*, the higher the severity level, the more promptly API consumers should remove deprecated API usages). As a future research direction, we want to also deepen why some deprecated API usages are promptly removed while others are not.

We also show that deprecated APIs are consumed by the same applications that declare them. Indeed, half of the studied applications mostly use deprecated APIs declared in their own source code, rather than those declared in third-party software. This finding is quite surprising and justifies an in-depth study.

Our study highlights the significant role of senior developers in removing deprecated API usage. This remarks how important is to have developers working on a software project for a long time in open-source communities, where experienced developers can support newcomer ones. The study also shows how senior developers introduce deprecated API usage much more than those novice. We can postulate that this is due to the fact that senior developers are usually responsible for dependency updates, which make an already-used API deprecated. However, it is also possible that novice developers try to avoid writing pieces of source code that use deprecated APIs—after all, there is empirical evidence showing that code smells are mostly introduced by senior developers [20]. Our study justifies future research on this matter.

5.2   Threats to Validity

In the following of this section, we discuss the threats to external, conclusion, and construct validity that might have affected our results.

External Validity. When datasets are relatively small and empirical research relies on them, generalizing the outcomes poses a threat to external validity. This is why caution is needed when generalizing the results presented in this paper. In this respect, we would like to recall that our study is exploratory and, as such, it aims to gather preliminary empirical evidence on deprecated API usages in open-source Java applications. Therefore, we advise further studies on a higher number of software applications.

Construct Validity. When a commit did not compile, we skipped that commit. Although we relied on a popular build automation tool (*i.e.,* Maven) to automate the compilation process of the applications, the lack of ability to compile open-source applications at the commit level in GitHub is an inherent limitation to any study similar to ours (*e.g.,* [4]). To study the phenomenon of interest, we automatically detected deprecated API usages through Maven on each commit of the default branch, and this might have affected the results. As for the classification of senior and newcomer developers, we used the same approach as Tufano *et al.* [20], which still poses a threat to the construct validity. Finally, the metrics we used to answer our RQs might have affected the obtained results—however, there is no accepted metric to quantitatively study our RQs.

Conclusion Validity. Despite the Kaplan-Mayer method is one of the best options in studies like ours where censored data points need to be taken in account (*e.g.,* [5,20]), its use might have affected the results concerning RQ2.

6   Conclusion

In this paper, we present the results of an exploratory study on deprecated API usages in 14 open-source Java applications whose software projects were top-starred on GitHub. The most important takeaway results of our study can be summarized as follows: *(i)* deprecated APIs usages are pretty widespread in the studied software applications; *(ii)* only in half of these applications, developers remove deprecated API usages after few commits and days; *(iii)* half of the studied applications use deprecated APIs declared in their source code, rather than in third-party software; and *(iv)* the introductions and removals of deprecated API usages are mostly the result of changes made by senior developers, rather than newcomer ones.

Funding Information. This study has been partially supported by "MSR4SBOM-Mining Software Repositories for enhanced Software Bills of Materials" (code: P20224HSZE), a research project funded by the Italian Ministry for Universities and Research (MUR).

References

1. Java deprecation. https://docs.oracle.com/javase/8/docs/technotes/guides/javadoc/deprecation/deprecation.html. Accessed 31 July 2023
2. Sonarsource's rules. https://rules.sonarsource.com/. Accessed 31 July 2023
3. Brito, G., Hora, A., Valente, M.T., Robbes, R.: On the use of replacement messages in API deprecation: an empirical study. J. Syst. Softw. **137**, 306–321 (2018)
4. Caivano, D., Cassieri, P., Romano, S., Scanniello, G.: An exploratory study on dead methods in open-source java desktop applications. In: Proceedings of International Symposium on Empirical Software Engineering and Measurement, pp. 10:1–10:11. ACM (2021)
5. Caivano, D., Cassieri, P., Romano, S., Scanniello, G.: On the spread and evolution of dead methods in java desktop applications: an exploratory study. Empir. Softw. Eng. **28**(64), 1–28 (2023)
6. Fowler, M.: Refactoring: Improving the Design of Existing Code, 1st edn. Addison-Wesley, Boston (1999)
7. GitHub: Github advanced search page. https://github.com/search/advanced. Accessed 31 July 2023
8. Goel, M.K., Khanna, P., Kishore, J.: Understanding survival analysis: Kaplan-Meier estimate. IJAR **1**(4), 274 (2010)
9. Borges, H., Valente, M.T.: What's in a github star? understanding repository starring practices in a social coding platform. J. Syst. Softw. **146**, 112–129 (2018)
10. Kalliamvakou, E., Gousios, G., Blincoe, K., Singer, L., German, D., Damian, D.: The promises and perils of mining github. In: Proceedings of Mining Software Repositories, pp. 92–101. ACM (2014)
11. Kaplan, E.L., Meier, P.: Nonparametric estimation from incomplete observations. JASA **53**(282), 457–481 (1958)
12. Li, L., Gao, J., Bissyandé, T.F., Ma, L., Xia, X., Klein, J.: CDA: characterising deprecated android APIs. Empir. Softw. Eng. **25**(3), 2058–2098 (2020)
13. Nocera, S., Romano, S., Francese, R., Scanniello, G.: A large-scale fine-grained empirical study on security concerns in open-source software. In: Proceedings of Euromicro Conference on Software Engineering and Advanced Applications, pp. 418–425. IEEE (2023)
14. Qiu, D., Li, B., Leung, H.: Understanding the API usage in java. Inf. Softw. Technol. **73**, 81–100 (2016)
15. Romano, S.: Replication package. https://figshare.com/s/2d66e96eb099e4c32b4f
16. Sawant, A.A., Huang, G., Vilen, G., Stojkovski, S., Bacchelli, A.: Why are features deprecated? an investigation into the motivation behind deprecation. In: Proceedings of International Conference on Software Maintenance and Evolution, pp. 13–24. IEEE (2018)
17. Sawant, A.A., Robbes, R., Bacchelli, A.: To react, or not to react: patterns of reaction to API deprecation. Empir. Softw. Eng. **24**(6), 3824–3870 (2019)
18. Scalabrino, S., Bavota, G., Linares-Vásquez, M., Piantadosi, V., Lanza, M., Oliveto, R.: API compatibility issues in Android: causes and effectiveness of data-driven detection techniques. Empir. Softw. Eng. **25**(6), 5006–5046 (2020)
19. Stack Overflow: Stack overflow developer survey 2022. https://survey.stackoverflow.co/2022. Accessed 31 July 2023

20. Tufano, M., et al.: When and why your code starts to smell bad (and whether the smells go away). IEEE Trans. Softw. Eng. **43**(11), 1063–1088 (2017)
21. Wake, W.C.: Refactoring Workbook, 1st edn. Addison-Wesley, Boston (2003)
22. Zhou, J., Walker, R.J.: API Deprecation: a retrospective analysis and detection method for code examples on the web, pp. 266–277. ACM (2017)

Security, Vulnerabilities, and Human Factors

Evaluating Microservice Organizational Coupling Based on Cross-Service Contribution

Xiaozhou Li[1]([✉])(iD), Dario Amoroso d'Aragona[2](iD), and Davide Taibi[1,2](iD)

[1] University of Oulu, Oulu, Finland
{xiaozhou.li,davide.taibi}@oulu.fi
[2] Tampere University, Tampere, Finland
{dario.amorosodaragona,davide.taibi}@tuni.fi

Abstract. For traditional modular software systems, "high cohesion, low coupling" is a recommended setting while it remains so for microservice architectures. However, coupling phenomena commonly exist therein which are caused by cross-service calls and dependencies. In addition, it is noticeable that teams for microservice projects can also suffer from high coupling issues in terms of their cross-service contribution, which can inevitably result in technical debt and high managerial costs. Such organizational coupling needs to be detected and mitigated in time to prevent future losses. Therefore, this paper proposes an automatable approach to evaluate the organizational coupling by investigating the microservice ownership and cross-service contribution. Furthermore, we validate the feasibility of the approach using a case study of a popular microservice project. The results show that, with sufficient software repository data, we can not only evaluate the organizational coupling in microservice system projects but also continuously monitor its evolution.

Keywords: Microservice · Organizational Coupling · Service Ownership · Cross-service contribution

1 Introduction

Together with the advance of software engineering theories and practice, modularization has long been considered a mechanism to enhance a system's flexibility and comprehensibility system as well as its development efficiency [25]. Meanwhile, coupling and cohesion are the two critical concepts for modularized systems that characterize the interdependence amongst the modules when one well-recognized software design principle is "high cohesion low coupling". In particular, microservice, as one of the most dominantly popular modularized architectures for cloud-native systems, is also required to comply with the principle in order to guarantee the architecture quality [32]. Regarding the coupling of microservices, d'Aragona et al. define logical coupling between two microservices as the phenomenon where both are changed by a single commit [12]. Zhong et al. define microservices coupling as the mutual influence therein caused by their calling and dependencies in between [34].

Despite the importance of the issue, limited studies have been conducted on handling the couplings in microservice architecture. For example, Zhong et al. propose the Microservice Coupling Index (MCI) based on relative measurement theory which measures the dependence of the target microservices relative to the possible couplings between them [34]. d'Aragona et al. propose to use commit data as a metric to statically calculate logical coupling between microservices and validate the existence of such couplings in a large number of open-source microservices projects [12]. Especially, these studies propose microservice couplings from dynamic analysis or static analysis perspectives, as well as the temporal and deployment perspectives [32]. However, limited studies have taken into account the couplings on the organizational level, though organization-related issues are usually as important as technology issues if not more so [27].

For large software projects, properly structured organization shall contribute to effective collaboration with reduced communication, which is critical for the project's success [8]. For microservice-based projects, stakeholders shall be aware of and able to handle critical organizational issues, e.g., coupling, for the migration from monolith to microservices [23]. As microservice promotes and benefits from "strong module boundaries", the communication structure of the organization building it shall mirror such structure with the boundaries [10,13]. After all, a module, in many contexts, is considered more than just a subprogram but rather a responsibility assignment [25]. It implies that the organizational structure of microservice projects shall also establish boundaries amongst different teams where developers within a team shall closely collaborate (i.e., high cohesion) while developers across teams shall be highly independent (i.e., low coupling). Therefore, it is not surprising that the notion of "One Microservice per Developer" has been promoted by many practitioners and companies [3,11,29,30]. Though several studies have investigated microservice projects' organizational structure [4,20], studies on the coupling of microservices in terms of their organization structures are still limited.

Therefore, in this study, we propose the metric to assess the coupling on organizational structure level for microservice projects, named *organizational coupling*. A prerequisite step of evaluating such coupling is to identify the team for each microservice of the target project. Therefore, the degree to which two microservices are coupled in terms of developers' "cross-boundaries" contribution can be determined by that of those developers simultaneously belonging to both teams. To such an end, our work here can answer the following research question (RQ): *How to evaluate the organizational coupling between microservices in terms of cross-service contribution?*

The remainder of this paper is organized as follows. Section 2 introduces the related studies regarding coupling in microservice and microservice organizational structure. Section 3 presents the method to evaluate the organizational coupling between microservices. Section 4 uses a case study to validate the method in terms of its operationality. Section 5 provides a discussion on the implications and future work. Section 6 discusses the threats to validity. Section 7 concludes the article.

2   Related Work

The organizational structure of software projects has long been a critical factor determining the projects' success [8]. Many studies have proposed approaches to analyze or improve software projects' organizational structure. Nagappan et al. propose a metric scheme to quantify organizational complexity regarding the product development process checking if the metrics impact failure-proneness where the level of organizational code ownership is a key metric [22]. Mockus studies the relationship between developer-centric measures of organizational change and the probability of customer-reported defects with the results showing organizational change is associated with lower software quality [21]. Isern et al. investigate the popular agent-oriented methodologies in terms of their support and possibilities for modeling organizational structures with different levels of complexity [18].

Regarding the organizational structure of microservice projects, Li et al. propose an approach using social network analysis (SNA) to reconstruct the organizational structure of microservice-based software projects in terms of contributor collaboration [20]. d'Aragona et al. investigate the application of the "one microservice per developer" principle in OSS microservice projects and propose an approach of using exploratory factor analysis (EFA) to establish the different team specialty profiles [11]. Ashraf et al. conducted an empirical study and found that developer communities change considerably through projects' lifetime and that their alignment with the pre-defined microservice (or subsystem) teams is mostly low [2].

On the other hand, many studies have proposed methods to measure the coupling between software modules. Allen et al. propose related information theory-based measures of coupling and cohesion of a module based on the properties proposed by Briand et al. [1,7]. Poshyvanyk and Marcus also propose a new set of coupling measures for object-oriented systems, named conceptual coupling, based on the semantic information shared between elements of the source code [28]. Other methods are also proposed to measure the coupling between packages or classes [16,17]. All such coupling metrics and proposed measuring methods focus on the dependency relations within the source code without considering the connections among developers or latent teams.

Regarding the coupling in microservice-based systems, Zhong et al. propose the Microservice Coupling Index (MCI) derived from the relative measurement theory, which measures how the coupled microservices are relative to the possible couplings between them [34]. Pedraza-Coello and Valdés-Souto propose a method to measure the coupling between microservices in early phases based on COSMIC method concepts regarding the data movements in functional processes [26]. d'Aragona et al. propose a metric to statically calculate logical coupling between microservices based on commits [12]. Though these studies have addressed the issue of coupling in microservice-based systems, limited have yet considered the couplings on the organizational level.

3   Organizational Coupling

Here we introduce the concept of organizational coupling and the methodology to evaluate the organizational coupling in any particular microservice-based system, which answers the proposed research question.

3.1   Identify Microservice Teams

As the initial step of evaluating the coupling between microservice teams, it is necessary to have a method to identify the team for each microservice in the target project. To do so, we adapt the method proposed by Bird et al. regarding the ownership profile of a particular software component [6], which, herein, is the microservices.

Let M be the target microservice of a particular software product where file set F is identified in the folder (or the repository) of M located in the project. Thus, we see all the contributors that have committed to any of those n files establishing the team of microservice M, denoted as T_M.

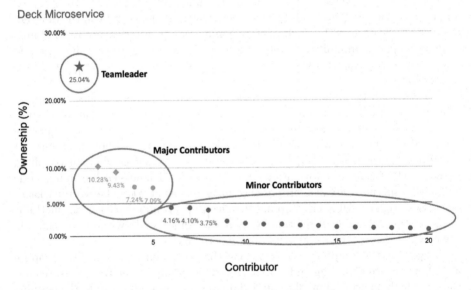

Fig. 1. Ownership Proportion Example

Herein, we calculate the quantified contribution of any developer $D \in T_M$ to M as the sum of all the number of changes to each file $f \in F$. Furthermore, we calculate D's ownership (i.e., the proportion of ownership) of M as the ratio of the number of commit changes that D has made relative to the total number of commit changes (in terms of lines of code) for M. To be noted, compared to the original study of Bird et al. [6], we use the number of commit changes instead of the number of commits due to the consideration that commits vary largely between one and another in terms of the exerted effort from the developers.

Therefore, based on the calculated ownership proportion of each $D \in T_M$, we see the developer(s) who has the highest proportion of ownership for M as the *Teamleader(s)*. According to the definitions by Bird et al. [6], we also define 1) *Major* contributors as the developers whose contribution reach at least 5% proportion level, and 2) *Minor* contributors as the developers whose contribution does not reach 5% proportion level. An example of a microservice team with ownership proportion is shown in Fig. 1. In this way, for each microservice in a given microservice-based architecture, based on the commits data, we can identify the team, i.e., all the developers who have contributed to it, and the ownership proportion of each developer, i.e., how much contribution ratio his/her is to the whole team.

3.2   Contribution Switch as Weight

Herein, we also take into account the phenomenon of the developer's contribution switch as an important factor influencing the organizational coupling between microservices. On the organizational level, we consider two individual microservices (as well as their teams) are more heavily coupled when the developers from either team more frequently commit to the other.

Given two microservices M_a and M_b, assume a developer $D \in T_{M_a}$ or $D \in T_{M_b}$ whose *contribution switch weight* between these two microservices is denoted as $S_D(M_a, M_b)$. Therefore, whenever D commits to M_a and then commits to M_b afterward (e.g., Commit 1 and 2 in Fig. 2), we consider such an incidence as a *contribution switch* of developer D from M_a to M_b. Similarly, developer D also switches from M_b back to M_a via Commit 3 shown in Fig. 2. To be noted, herein we only take into account the sequential relation of the commit series without considering the time intervals in between.

Therefore, given the sequence of commits of D in terms of M_a and M_b, we can simply count the number of contribution switches therein. In addition, regarding the situation of logically coupled commits [12] where both microservices are changed in a single commit (e.g., Commit 3 and 4), we consider this situation as two contribution switches.

To generalize, given the previously described situation where k contribution switches are performed by D between M_a and M_b while D has in total n commits for both microservices, the contribution switch weight can be calculated as follows.

$$S_D(M_a, M_b) = \frac{k}{2 \times (n - 1)} \tag{1}$$

Taking Fig. 2 as an example where $n = 8$, as we can observe eight contriution switches (i.e., $k = 8$), $S_D(M_1, M_2) = 8/(2 \times (8 - 1)) = 0.571$. Considering the situation where every commit from the developer changes both microservices (i.e., logical coupling [12]), $S_D(M_1, M_2) = 14/(2 \times (8 - 1)) = 1$. On the contrary, when the developer only contributes to one microservice, $S_D(M_1, M_2) = 0/(2 \times (8 - 1)) = 0$. It means the two microservices are not coupled in terms of the

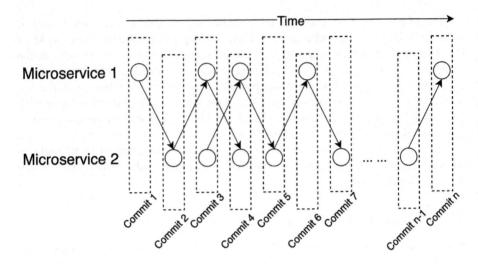

Fig. 2. Contribution Switch between Microservices

contribution of D on the organizational level. Therefore, we can easily conclude that $S_D(M_a, M_b) \in [0, 1]$. To be noted, the contribution switch weight is only to influence the organizational coupling in terms of individual developers.

3.3 Measure Organizational Coupling

Given any two microservices M_a and M_b, T_{M_a} and T_{M_b} are the teams for each microservice respectively, which are identified by the method proposed in Sect. 3.1. Therein, we can simply identify the p developers who have contributed in both microservices, denoted as $T_{(M_a \cap M_b)} = \{D_1, D_2, ...D_p\}$. For any particular developer $D_i \in T_{(M_a \cap M_b)}$, all the commits he/she has conducted in temporal sequence are denoted as C_{D_i}. For each $c \in C_{D_i}$, we can identify on which microservice it commits to. Therefore, by finding the ones that are committed to M_a or M_b or both, we obtain a sub-sequence of commits, denoted as $C_{D_i}(M_a, M_b)$. Such a commit sequence can be depicted as a figure similar to Fig. 2 where all the contribution switches can be identified with the contribution switch weight, $S_{D_i}(M_a, M_b)$, calculated based on the method described in Sect. 3.2.

To investigate the coupled contribution of D_i on M_a and M_b, we adopt the harmonic mean of D_i's contribution in them, considering the reason that the more equally any developer commits to multiple microservices, the more organizationally coupled the two microservices are, regarding this developer's contribution.

Let $\{ca_1, ca_2, ...ca_m\}$ be the corresponding contribution value sequence for the m commits in $C_{D_i}(M_a)$ while $\{cb_1, cb_2, ...cb_n\}$ be that for the n commits in $C_{D_i}(M_b)$. Herein, the contribution value of each commit is calculated by the sum of all the number of changes to each file in the target microservices.

Let $OC(D_i, M_a, M_b)$ be the organizational coupling (OC) caused by developer D_i's cross-service contribution on microservices M_a and M_b, we can calculate $OC(D_i, M_a, M_b)$ as follows.

$$OC(D_i, M_a, M_b) = (\frac{2\sum_{j=1}^{m} ca_j \sum_{k=1}^{n} cb_j}{\sum_{j=1}^{m} ca_j + \sum_{k=1}^{n} cb_j}) \times S_{D_i}(M_a, M_b) \qquad (2)$$

Thus, the overall organizational coupling between M_a and M_b, denoted as $OC(M_a, M_b)$, can be calculated as follows.

$$OC(M_a, M_b) = \sum_{i=1}^{p} OC(D_i, M_a, M_b) = \sum_{i=1}^{p} (\frac{2\sum_{j=1}^{m} ca_j \sum_{k=1}^{n} cb_j}{\sum_{j=1}^{m} ca_j + \sum_{k=1}^{n} cb_j}) \times S_{D_i}(M_a, M_b) \qquad (3)$$

The value of $OC(M_a, M_b)$ can range from 0 to infinity, as there is no limit on either the volume of contribution between services or the number of developers therein.

4   Case Study

In this study, we demonstrate the applicability of the proposed organizational coupling evaluation method with a case study. We select, *Spinnaker*[1], a microservice-based application management and deployment system supporting software change releases. Spinnaker is an open-source, multi-cloud continuous delivery platform that combines a powerful and flexible pipeline management system with integrations to the major cloud providers. Herein, we use the Spinnaker project as a proof-of-concept to demonstrate and validate how to identify and evaluate the organizational coupling within microservice-based systems.

4.1   Data Collection

Spinnaker contains 12 independent microservices[2]. The dependencies of the microservices are shown in Fig. 3.

The 12 microservices include *CloudDriver, Deck, Echo, Fiat, Front50, Gate, Halyard, Igor, Kayenta, Keel, Orca,* and *Rosco*. The detailed functionality and responsibility of each microservice are introduced in the Spinnaker official documentation as well as its GitHub repositories[3]. To be noted, different from other popular microservice-based projects, e.g., eShopOnContainers[4], Spinnaker project is organized as a polyrepo architecture instead of monorepo [9]. Therefore, we shall gather data from the 12 corresponding repositories of the project.

---

[1] https://spinnaker.io/.
[2] https://spinnaker.io/docs/reference/architecture/microservices-overview/.
[3] https://github.com/spinnaker.
[4] http://github.com/dotnet-architecture/eShopOnContainers.

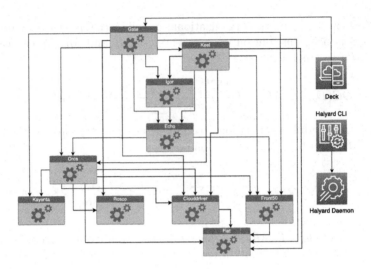

Fig. 3. Spinnaker Architecture Overview

By using the GitHub REST API[5], we are able to collect all the commit data for the target 12 microservices of the Spinnaker project. We collected 43,654 commits from all 12 microservice repositories between 2012-03-18 and 2023-07-06. 801 different developers contributed to all these commits, with 241,828 file changes.

The distribution of 1) the number of commits for each microservice and 2) the number of different developers for each microservice are shown in Fig. 4 and Fig. 5. To be noted, in the original dataset, for each individual commit, the contributor is identified by *author_email*. However, considering the situation where multiple emails can belong to the same user, e.g., *lwander@users.noreply.github.com* and *lwander@google.com*, we preprocess the author identity by dropping the email extension and combining such accounts.

4.2   Results

Identify Microservice Teams. Firstly, we identify the developer team for each microservice using the method introduced in Sect. 3.1. Due to the fact that the Spinnaker project is structured as poly-repo, each microservice is an independent repository. Therefore, the team of each microservice shall contain all the contributors of each repository, which is comparatively easier to identify compared to mono-repo projects, e.g., eShopOnContainer. The number of developers in each microservice team is shown in Fig. 5.

In addition, we can further specify the team structure of each microservice team by identifying the team leaders, major contributors, and minor contributors of each team. Figure 6 shows the Top 20 contributors of each microservice team

---

[5] https://docs.github.com/en/rest?apiVersion=2022-11-28.

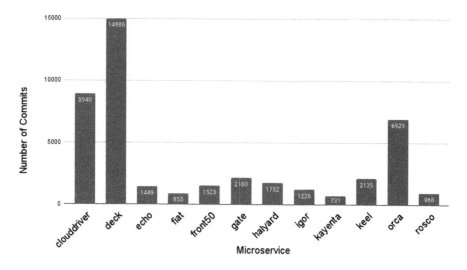

Fig. 4. Number of Commits for each Microservice

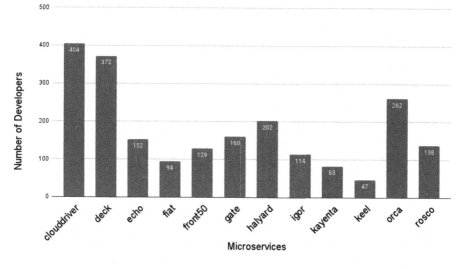

Fig. 5. Number of Developers for each Microservice

in terms of their ownership proportion. It is easy to observe that all microservice teams have at least one team leader and one major contributor. Meanwhile, no team has more than six major contributors (including the team leader).

Specifically, we list the team leader and major contributors of each microservice team in Table 1. Considering the privacy reason, we only show the first four letters of each contributor's identity. We can observe that the majority of the team leaders have a 20%–30% ownership proportion. The team leader of the Halyard microservice has the highest ownership of the service (52.39%), while the team leader of the CloudDriver microservice has the lowest (7.72%). Meanwhile,

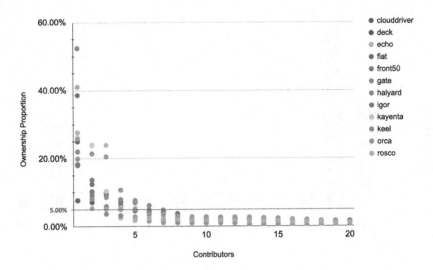

Fig. 6. Ownership Proportion of Spinnaker Microservices

Table 1. Microservice Teamleaders and Major Contributors

Microservice	Teamleader	Major Contributor(s)
CloudDriver	cfiexxx (7.72%)	duftxxx (7.12%), lwanxxx (5.47%), camexxx (5.18%)
Deck	chrixxx (25.04%)	vmurxxx (10.28%), benjxxx (9.43%), githxxx (7.24%), zantxxx (7.09%)
Echo	clinxxx (27.65%)	ajorxxx (23.98%), adamxxx (23.94%)
Fiat	ttomxxx (38.60%)	devexxx (12.46%), cfiexxx (10.15%), rziexxx (6.19%), adamxxx (5.39%)
Front50	adamxxx (18.35%)	rziexxx (13.70%), ajorxxx (9.82%), danixxx (7.22%), cfiexxx (5.12%)
Gate	danixxx (22.08%)	adamxxx (9.04%), jacoxxx (8.61%), builxxx (7.99%), ajorxxx (7.65%), cfiexxx (6.16%)
Halyard	lwanxxx (52.39%)	ezimxxx (9.06%)
Igor	rziexxx (18.00%)	jorgxxx (10.03%), ezimxxx (5.88%), clinxxx (5.56%), tomaxxx (5.31%)
Kayenta	duftxxx (26.25%)	fielxxx (23.84%), explxxx (10.42%), asmixxx (5.55%), chrixxx (5.48%)
Keel	1323xxx (25.69%)	lhocxxx (21.47%), rflexxx (20.56%), robfxxx (10.71%), emjexxx (7.31%)
Orca	rflexxx (20.00%)	robfxxx (8.11%), clinxxx (5.32%), robxxx (5.14%), adamxxx (5.01%)
Rosco	duftxxx (41.03%)	ezimxxx (5.41%), ttomxxx (5.16%), andexxx (5.00%)

we can also observe that the majority of the microservice teams have one clear team leader whose ownership proportion is at least 5% higher than that of the second major contributor. Five microservice teams have at least two contributors who share a similar ownership proportion.

Moreover, it is also noticeable that developer *duftxxx* is the team leader of both *Kayenta* service and *Rosco* service. He/she is also the major contributor of *CloudDriver* service. Meanwhile, 11 out of the 12 microservice team leaders are also major contributors to at least one other team.

Organizational Couplings and Evolution. With the team of each microservice identified, we can then calculate the organizational coupling between each pair by adopting the method introduced in Sect. 3.3. According to the version log of Spinnaker[6], the latest stable version (1.30.2) was released on June 1st, 2023. We select all the commit data until this date and calculate all the organizational couplings. We set the coloring criteria as follows: 1) Red (Very Highly Coupled): $OC \geq 10,000$; 2) Orange (Highly Coupled): $1,000 \leq OC < 10,000$; 3) Yellow (Loosely Coupled): $100 \leq OC < 1,000$; 4) Green (Very Loosely Coupled): $OC < 100$. To be noted, the threshold setting here is only proposed as proof-of-concept. A universally applicable setting shall be verified with a sufficiently representative number of cases.

The results are shown in Fig. 7.

	clouddriver	deck	echo	fiat	front50	gate	halyard	igor	kayenta	keel	orca	rosco
clouddriver		78585.98	13011.88	5427.89	16136.81	18870.45	20307.99	9160.67	2385.83	4052.30	84837.13	8599.75
deck	78585.98		14757.72	1955.46	9763.35	10148.37	9443.25	8511.54	1403.65	662.18	46389.44	6186.84
echo	13011.88	14757.72		4474.11	15186.57	13012.91	5450.21	12873.03	1340.65	1984.78	24376.66	3237.72
fiat	5427.89	1955.46	4474.11		4802.92	4967.14	1788.99	3511.84	943.64	1307.55	5062.67	1625.67
front50	16136.81	9763.35	15186.57	4802.92		15648.10	3011.38	8799.82	1198.09	2225.38	17656.63	3177.98
gate	18870.45	10148.37	13012.91	4967.14	15648.10		3562.55	8086.81	1028.37	1965.20	22652.99	2652.88
halyard	20307.99	9443.25	5450.21	1788.99	3011.38	3562.55		4198.37	2126.06	627.41	10771.22	4996.74
igor	9160.67	8511.54	12873.03	3511.84	8799.82	8086.81	4198.37		1106.74	3108.80	13987.61	3698.48
kayenta	2385.83	1403.65	1340.65	943.64	1198.09	1028.37	2126.06	1106.74		642.38	2628.45	1264.86
keel	4052.30	662.18	1984.78	1307.55	2225.38	1965.20	627.41	3108.80	642.38		7757.00	772.94
orca	84837.13	46389.44	24376.66	5062.67	17656.63	22652.99	10771.22	13987.61	2628.45	7757.00		7490.00
rosco	8599.75	6186.84	3237.72	1625.67	3177.98	2652.88	4996.74	3698.48	1264.86	772.94	7490.00	

Fig. 7. Organizational Coupling between Services (Version 1.30.2)

We can observe that the majority of the 12 microservices of Spinnaker are at least highly coupled in terms of developers' cross-service contribution. The most severely high coupling is the one between *Orca* service and *CloudDriver* service (84837.13). Meanwhile, both these services are also heavily coupled with all other services. On the contrary, *Keel* is loosely coupled with several services, including *Deck*, *Halyard*, *Kayenta* and *Rosco* when *Kayenta* and *Fiat* are also loosely coupled.

Such a phenomenon likely results from the fact that the Spinnaker project had the first initial release in late 2015 with the earliest service repository created in May 2014. It is only reasonable that in the early development phase, a limited number of developers were heavily involved in nearly all the services. Therefore, we can also investigate the changes in such organizational coupling between services through the project timeline. The first stable version (Version 1.0.0) of Spinnaker was released on June 5th, 2017. We select six commit datasets of six consecutive years from 2017-06-05 to 2023-06-04. By adopting the same method for each dataset, we can obtain six different heatmaps regarding the organizational coupling between services in the specific one-year period and observe the changes (shown in Fig. 8). For the purpose of display, the 12 microservices are named S1 - S12 in alphabetical order while the decimal numbers are limited to zero.

---

[6] https://spinnaker.io/docs/releases/versions/.

1st Year (2017-06-05 to 2018-06-04)

	S1	S2	S3	S4	S5	S6	S7	S8	S9	S10	S11	S12
S1		6849	1361	213	547	1897	3659	947	572	1179	7085	227
S2	6849		1167	95	462	1216	1583	415	111	78	4066	294
S3	1361	1167		97	351	1224	362	408	3	173	1440	162
S4	213	95	97		142	279	135	100	6	2	146	77
S5	547	462	351	142		642	70	224	22	282	565	86
S6	1897	1216	1224	279	642		702	504	94	183	1083	178
S7	3659	1583	362	135	70	702		179	763	0	1243	256
S8	947	415	408	100	224	504	179		3	798	876	78
S9	572	111	3	6	22	94	763	3		0	521	6
S10	1179	78	173	2	282	183	0	798	0		2441	3
S11	7085	4066	1440	146	565	1083	1243	876	521	2441		395
S12	227	294	162	77	86	178	256	78	6	3	395	

4th Year (From 2020-06-05 to 2021-06-04)

	S1	S2	S3	S4	S5	S6	S7	S8	S9	S10	S11	S12
S1		2641	1243	1055	1290	1062	484	680	241	280	4932	539
S2	2641		393	86	286	147	313	295	71	77	1101	248
S3	1243	393		439	1748	698	209	724	172	243	1549	305
S4	1055	86	439		426	436	127	393	195	215	567	171
S5	1290	286	1748	426		885	223	684	114	202	1616	225
S6	1062	147	698	436	885		209	409	158	225	1347	221
S7	484	313	209	127	223	209		249	83	108	340	188
S8	680	295	724	393	684	409	249		150	331	810	228
S9	241	71	172	195	114	158	83	150		129	225	102
S10	280	77	243	215	202	225	108	331	129		271	149
S11	4932	1101	1549	567	1616	1347	340	810	225	271		378
S12	539	248	305	171	225	221	188	228	102	149	378	

2nd Year (From 2018-06-05 to 2019-06-04)

	S1	S2	S3	S4	S5	S6	S7	S8	S9	S10	S11	S12
S1		13231	3695	1115	2207	1811	5691	3263	159	456	12912	707
S2	13231		1450	283	541	723	2098	2545	63	40	4586	564
S3	3695	1450		1851	2866	1164	2649	3455	253	623	4920	120
S4	1115	283	1851		2505	560	255	2401	100	572	1232	135
S5	2207	541	2866	2505		1242	396	3975	194	294	2057	184
S6	1811	723	1164	560	1242		808	1121	248	51	1805	102
S7	5691	2098	2649	255	396	808		1392	164	2	3708	1322
S8	3263	2545	3455	2401	3975	1121	1392		224	646	3124	104
S9	159	63	253	100	194	248	164	224		87	297	79
S10	456	40	623	572	294	51	2	646	87		366	5
S11	12912	4586	4920	1232	2057	1805	3708	3124	297	366		486
S12	707	564	120	135	184	102	1322	104	79	5	486	

5th Year (From 2021-06-05 to 2022-06-04)

	S1	S2	S3	S4	S5	S6	S7	S8	S9	S10	S11	S12
S1		681	154	244	195	349	327	158	122	119	738	282
S2	681		111	68	98	138	65	101	87	197	166	82
S3	154	111		145	213	175	151	185	101	121	190	138
S4	244	68	145		135	188	206	137	106	118	179	203
S5	195	98	213	135		165	157	176	115	107	208	157
S6	349	138	175	188	165		145	169	113	132	163	136
S7	327	65	151	206	157	145		185	104	130	289	258
S8	158	101	185	137	176	169	185		106	139	163	151
S9	122	87	101	106	115	113	104	106		105	123	89
S10	119	197	121	118	107	132	130	139	105		137	86
S11	738	166	190	179	208	163	289	163	123	137		184
S12	282	82	138	203	157	136	258	151	89	86	184	

3rd Year (From 2019-06-05 to 2020-06-04)

	S1	S2	S3	S4	S5	S6	S7	S8	S9	S10	S11	S12
S1		7164	1570	1095	2305	1856	4053	1904	305	643	7561	2696
S2	7164		626	214	644	561	1738	1144	231	215	3302	888
S3	1570	626		818	1422	1966	921	2040	361	688	2138	570
S4	1095	214	818		975	996	446	659	281	484	908	470
S5	2305	644	1422	975		2578	745	2087	377	768	2453	663
S6	1856	561	1966	996	2578		688	1994	297	1359	2557	584
S7	4053	1738	921	446	745	688		1063	667	289	2791	1468
S8	1904	1144	2040	659	2087	1994	1063		410	947	3525	730
S9	305	231	361	281	377	297	667	410		207	289	361
S10	643	215	688	484	768	1359	289	947	207		1841	427
S11	7561	3302	2138	908	2453	2557	2791	3525	289	1841		1847
S12	2696	888	570	470	663	584	1468	730	361	427	1847	

6th Year (From 2022-06-05 to 2023-06-04)

	S1	S2	S3	S4	S5	S6	S7	S8	S9	S10	S11	S12
S1		1007	352	343	702	110	111	107	118	31	1153	165
S2	1007		119	83	150	30	25	99	75	35	694	66
S3	352	119		166	620	111	96	120	247	42	313	224
S4	343	83	166		217	100	74	108	104	33	379	115
S5	702	150	620	217		128	99	108	128	38	555	170
S6	110	30	111	100	128		85	83	64	31	133	92
S7	111	25	96	74	99	85		84	43	21	113	95
S8	107	99	120	108	108	83	84		80	39	216	78
S9	118	75	247	104	128	64	43	80		44	170	180
S10	31	35	42	33	38	31	21	39	44		38	20
S11	1153	694	313	379	555	133	113	216	170	38		241
S12	165	66	224	115	170	92	95	78	180	20	241	

Fig. 8. Evolution of Organizational Coupling between Services

Observing the service organizational coupling from 2017-06-05 to 2018-06-04, we find that *Kayenta* and *Keel* are very loosely coupled with the majority of the others. The reason is likely that *Kayenta* was created in January 2017 while *Keel* in October 2017. *CloudDriver* and *Orca* are still highly coupled with many other services. Thereafter, the organizational coupling among nearly all services increased in the 2nd year (from 2018-06-05 to 2019-06-04). However, in the 3rd year (from 2019-06-05 to 2020-06-04), we can observe the decrease of the coupling amongst all services except *Kayenta* and *Keel*, whose coupling with other services still increased. It implies that there are still developers from other service teams contributing to these two newly established services. From 2020-06-05, we can easily observe the organizational coupling among all services decreases in the last three years.

5   Discussion

In this study, we propose the organizational coupling between microservices as a measure to evaluate how much any two microservices are coupled by the cross-service contribution behaviors of the developers. Such coupling is also damaging to the quality of microservice architecture because spontaneous and unregulated contributions across will inevitably result in an increase in unnecessary communication costs, mismatch between developers and code, and risks in deteriorating system architecture [8,10,14]. Here, we define the organizational coupling of two different microservices as the degree to which the developers cross-contribute between them. The method of evaluating the organizational coupling between two given microservices includes three steps: 1) identifying the contributor team of each microservice and finding the developers who contribute in both; 2) calculating the contribution switch of each common developer and using it as the weight on his/her mean contribution on both microservices; 3) summing all the common developers' weighted cross-service contribution of both microservices as the organizational coupling value. This answers the research question.

When considering the organizational coupling between microservices, we consider that the switching behavior of the developers is a key factor. The reason is that people need to stop thinking about one task in order to fully transition their attention and perform well on another [19]. Therefore, the more frequently developers switch between different microservices, the more difficult it is for them to concentrate and perform well on any. Thus, it is reasonable to consider the two microservices organizationally coupled when developers contribute across them, as such switching behaviors can influence the quality of both. However, the current calculation is more to take this factor into account as a proof-of-concept rather than accurately calculate the values. So herein, we conceptualize the contribution switch as the switch times between two services within a given time without considering the timespan between the switches. Furthermore, we shall also consider other factors when calculating the contribution switch, e.g., microservice priority [5], project roles [15], and so on.

For future work, we shall continue to enrich the concept of organization coupling by taking into account more factors as parameters. On the other hand, strategies and mechanisms to monitor and handle such organizational couplings are also required in order to continue promoting the principle of "one microservice per developer". For example, we can adopt time series approaches to monitor the changes in organizational coupling networks together with anomaly detection techniques to identify the severe coupling whenever it occurs [31]. Furthermore, we shall also investigate techniques to reduce organizational coupling by encouraging developers to reduce contribution switching frequency or developer number.

6   Threats to Validity

In this section, we discuss the threats to the validity of the proposed approach and the measures for mitigating them by following the guidelines provided by Wohlin [33], including the threats to internal validity, external validity, construct validity and conclusion validity.

Internal Validity. Though we take into account the contribution switch as the weight of the organizational coupling, it is possible that other factors can also influence the evaluation. For example, the collaboration and communication between developers from different microservices, e.g., working on the same files or services, communications via issue comments, mailing lists or Internet Relay Chat, etc., can also affect the intensiveness of the connection between them [20,24]. This study simplifies the calculation by considering only the committing behavior as contribution while the above-mentioned perspectives can be integrated in the future.

External Validity. Towards the generalization of the proposed approach, we select one of the commonly adopted microservice projects as the target case. Though the proposed approach is validated only by this case study, it still shows that for any microservice projects managed in GitHub with contribution data accessible, we can replicate the approach easily. Nonetheless, it still requires sufficient evidence to validate whether the approach can provide a legitimate assessment with more projects and, especially, more industrial cases. Industry surveys will also be conducted in the future to validate the approach further.

Construct Validity. The categorization of different coupling severity is provided for proof-of-concept, where the threshold setting is guided based on an expert's opinion. On the other hand, the calculation of the contribution switch can also take into account the influence of its time span as well as other potential factors. Herein, we simplify the model by considering the time spans between sequential commits are equal. On the other hand, regarding the contribution calculation of the two microservices, it is very likely the developer contributes very little to one when largely to the other. We shall consider such a situation less coupled than one where the developer equally contributes to both. To mitigate such a threat, we adopt the harmonic mean of the contribution instead of the arithmetic mean and the geometric mean.

Conclusion Validity. The results of the case study can be influenced by the potential situation if the amount of committing behavior of the entire project decreases annually. In such a situation, the conclusion of the organizational coupling of this project decreasing through these years might not stand. The threat is mitigated by the selection of an active project as a case when a significant and continuous decrease in developers' contribution across all microservices is nearly impossible.

7   Conclusion

In this study, we propose the concept of organizational coupling as a measure to evaluate how much any two microservices are coupled by the cross-service contribution behaviors of the developers. Such organizational coupling needs to be detected and mitigated in time to prevent future losses. For such a purpose, we also propose an automatable approach to evaluate the organizational coupling by investigating the microservice ownership and cross-service contribution and validating its usefulness with a case study. Organizational coupling is a critical issue for microservice-based systems on the organizational structural level. Such issues can potentially impact the deterioration of system architecture, which needs to be detected and addressed in time. Continuously tracking the changes and evolution in the organizational coupling shall facilitate the monitoring and maintenance of the system architecture and the detection of potential degradation and anomalies on the organizational level.

References

1. Allen, E.B., Khoshgoftaar, T.M., Chen, Y.: Measuring coupling and cohesion of software modules: an information-theory approach. In: Proceedings Seventh International Software Metrics Symposium, pp. 124–134. IEEE (2001)
2. Ashraf, U., Mayr-Dorn, C., Mashkoor, A., Egyed, A., Panichella, S.: Do communities in developer interaction networks align with subsystem developer teams? An empirical study of open source systems. In: 2021 ICSSP and ICGSE, pp. 61–71. IEEE (2021)
3. Balalaie, A., Heydarnoori, A., Jamshidi, P.: Microservices architecture enables DevOps: migration to a cloud-native architecture. IEEE Softw. 33(3), 42–52 (2016). https://doi.org/10.1109/MS.2016.64
4. Baškarada, S., Nguyen, V., Koronios, A.: Architecting microservices: Practical opportunities and challenges. J. Comput. Inf. Syst. (2018)
5. Bendoly, E., Swink, M., Simpson, W.P., III.: Prioritizing and monitoring concurrent project work: effects on switching behavior. Prod. Oper. Manag. 23(5), 847–860 (2014)
6. Bird, C., Nagappan, N., Murphy, B., Gall, H., Devanbu, P.: Don't touch my code! examining the effects of ownership on software quality. In: Proceedings of the 19th ACM SIGSOFT Symposium and the 13th European Conference on Foundations of Software Engineering, pp. 4–14 (2011)
7. Briand, L.C., Morasca, S., Basili, V.R.: Property-based software engineering measurement. IEEE Trans. Softw. Eng. 22(1), 68–86 (1996)
8. Brooks Jr., F.P.: The Mythical Man-Month: Essays on Software Engineering. Pearson Education, London (1995)
9. Brousse, N.: The issue of monorepo and polyrepo in large enterprises. In: Companion Proceedings of the 3rd International Conference on the Art, Science, and Engineering of Programming, pp. 1–4 (2019)
10. Conway, M.E.: How do committees invent. Datamation 14(4), 28–31 (1968)
11. d'Aragona, D.A., Li, X., Cerny, T., Janes, A., Lenarduzzi, V., Taibi, D.: One microservice per developer: is this the trend in OSS? In: Papadopoulos, G.A., Rademacher, F., Soldani, J. (eds.) ESOCC 2023. LNCS, vol. 14183, pp. 19–34. Springer, Cham (2023). https://doi.org/10.1007/978-3-031-46235-1_2
12. d'Aragona, D.A., Pascarella, L., Janes, A., Lenarduzzi, V., Taibi, D.: Microservice logical coupling: a preliminary validation. In: 2023 IEEE 20th International Conference on Software Architecture Companion (ICSA-C), pp. 81–85. IEEE (2023)
13. Fowler, M.: Microservice trade-offs (2015). https://martinfowler.com/articles/microservice-trade-offs.html
14. Fowler, M.: Conway's law (2022). https://martinfowler.com/bliki/ConwaysLaw.html
15. Grotto, A.R., Mills, M.J., Eatough, E.M.: Switching gears: a self-regulatory approach and measure of nonwork role re-engagement following after-hours work intrusions. J. Bus. Psychol. 37(3), 491–507 (2022)

16. Gupta, V., Kumar Chhabra, J.: Package coupling measurement in object-oriented software. J. Comput. Sci. Technol. **24**, 273–283 (2009)
17. Hammad, M., Rawashdeh, A.: A framework to measure and visualize class coupling. Int. J. Softw. Eng. Appl. **8**(4), 137–146 (2014)
18. Isern, D., Sánchez, D., Moreno, A.: Organizational structures supported by agent-oriented methodologies. J. Syst. Softw. **84**(2), 169–184 (2011)
19. Leroy, S.: Why is it so hard to do my work? The challenge of attention residue when switching between work tasks. Organ. Behav. Hum. Decis. Process. **109**(2), 168–181 (2009)
20. Li, X., Abdelfattah, A.S., Yero, J., d'Aragona, D.A., Cerny, T., Taibi, D.: Analyzing organizational structure of microservice projects based on contributor collaboration. In: 2023 IEEE International Conference on Service-Oriented System Engineering (SOSE), pp. 1–8. IEEE (2023)
21. Mockus, A.: Organizational volatility and its effects on software defects. In: Proceedings of the Eighteenth ACM SIGSOFT International Symposium on Foundations of Software Engineering, pp. 117–126 (2010)
22. Nagappan, N., Murphy, B., Basili, V.: The influence of organizational structure on software quality: an empirical case study. In: Proceedings of the 30th International Conference on Software Engineering, pp. 521–530 (2008)
23. Newman, S.: Building Microservices. O'Reilly Media, Inc. (2021)
24. Panichella, S., Bavota, G., Di Penta, M., Canfora, G., Antoniol, G.: How developers' collaborations identified from different sources tell us about code changes. In: 2014 IEEE ICSME, pp. 251–260. IEEE (2014)
25. Parnas, D.L.: On the criteria to be used in decomposing systems into modules. Commun. ACM **15**(12), 1053–1058 (1972)
26. Pedraza-Coello, R., Valdés-Souto, F.: Measuring coupling in microservices using COSMIC measurement method. In: ICSEA 2021, p. 26 (2021)
27. Perry, D.E., Staudenmayer, N.A., Votta, L.G.: People, organizations, and process improvement. IEEE Softw. **11**(4), 36–45 (1994)
28. Poshyvanyk, D., Marcus, A.: The conceptual coupling metrics for object-oriented systems. In: 2006 22nd IEEE International Conference on Software Maintenance, pp. 469–478. IEEE (2006)
29. Reinfurt, M.: The horror of microservices in small teams - and why you shouldn't build them (2021). https://shorturl.at/bgHKR
30. Richardson, C.: Dark energy, dark matter and the microservices patterns? (2022). https://shorturl.at/etHM5
31. Shaukat, K., et al.: A review of time-series anomaly detection techniques: a step to future perspectives. In: Arai, K. (ed.) FICC 2021. AISC, vol. 1363, pp. 865–877. Springer, Cham (2021). https://doi.org/10.1007/978-3-030-73100-7_60
32. Walpita, P.: Coupling and cohesion in microservices (2020). https://priyalwalpita.medium.com/coupling-and-cohesion-in-microservices-235ed9203843
33. Wohlin, C., Runeson, P., Höst, M., Ohlsson, M.C., Regnell, B., Wesslén, A.: Experimentation in Software Engineering. Springer, Heidelberg (2012). https://doi.org/10.1007/978-3-642-29044-2
34. Zhong, C., Zhang, H., Li, C., Huang, H., Feitosa, D.: On measuring coupling between microservices. J. Syst. Softw. **200**, 111670 (2023)

On Fixing Bugs: Do Personality Traits Matter?

Simone Romano[1](✉), Giuseppe Scanniello[1], Maria Teresa Baldassarre[2],
Danilo Caivano[2], and Genoveffa Tortora[1]

[1] University of Salerno, Fisciano, Italy
{siromano,gscanniello,tortora}@unisa.it
[2] University of Bari, Bari, Italy
{mariateresa.baldassarre,danilo.caivano}@uniba.it

Abstract. We present the results of a prospective observational study aimed to understand whether there is a relationship between personality traits (*i.e.,* agreeableness, conscientiousness, extroversion, neuroticism, and openness) and the performance of undergraduates in Computer Science while accomplishing bug fixing. We involved 62 undergraduates, who took part in eight laboratory sessions. The experimental sessions took place over a period of seven weeks. In each session, the participants were asked to fix bugs either in a C or in a Java program. We collected a relevant number of observations (496, in total) so making our study the largest (quantitative) one on the impact of personality on individual performance while executing an SE task. We observed that the lower the neuroticism level of a student, the better his/her performance in fixing bugs is.

Keywords: Bug fixing · personality traits · FFM

1 Introduction

When software systems grow in size and complexity, or when developers have to work under pressure to meet frequent deadlines, the introduction of bugs is unavoidable [1]. End-users lose trust in a software system when they experience problems due to bugs. Also, their presence has financial impacts—*e.g.,* an industrial survey by the Cambridge Judge Business School shows that: (*i*) developers spend 620 million hours a year debugging software failures (caused by bugs) and (*ii*) bugs cost the enterprise software market $61 billion annually [2].

Bug fixing is a critical Software Engineering (SE) task and inherently has strong dynamics at play, especially in how to find the developer to handle a bug report [3]. For example, when a bug is assigned to someone, he/she could reassign it to someone else for several reasons (*e.g.,* lack of time to investigate deeply the problem or an attempt to find a person with better expertise). If the optimal bug fixer was not identified (even in the case of a few reassignments), this could lead to a low-quality or faulty bug fix [3].

R. Kadgien et al. (Eds.): PROFES 2023, LNCS 14483, pp. 451–467, 2024.
https://doi.org/10.1007/978-3-031-49266-2_31

Empirical investigations have been conducted to study the effect of personality while executing SE tasks [4]. Most of these investigations have been conducted in the context of team performance, building, and climate [4–6]. Few studies have investigated the role of developers' personalities on individual performance in SE tasks [6]. These studies share a common goal: to understand which personality traits/types are ideal (or not) when executing a given SE task. So far, no study has focused on bug fixing despite it being recognized as financially critical [2].

In this paper, we present the results of a prospective observational study with 62 undergraduates in Computer Science (CS)—each involved in eight laboratory sessions for a total of 496 observations—to understand whether, or not, there is a relationship between the personality traits of individuals and their performance in fixing bugs. To assess the personality traits of the participants, we used the *Five-Factor Model (FFM)* [7]—also known as the *Big Five* or *OCEAN* model—, which suggests a taxonomy for personality traits that includes five factors: *agreeableness, conscientiousness, extroversion, neuroticism,* and *openness (to experience)*. Our study is *observational* since we monitored the effect (if any) of explanatory variables (*i.e.,* personality traits) on response ones (*i.e.,* performance in fixing bugs) without manipulating the former—as opposed to interventional studies, such as experiments, where researchers administer treatments to participants to manipulate explanatory variables and assess their effect on response ones [8]. An observational study can be either prospective or retrospective: if researchers collect data from the present time to the future, the study is prospective; if researchers exploit existing data, the study is retrospective [8]. Our study is *prospective* because we gathered observations over time from a group of participants executing a series of bug-fixing tasks.

Paper Structure. In Sect. 2, we provide background information and outline motivations and related work. We present our study in Sect. 3. We discuss our results in Sect. 4, together with possible limitations. Final remarks and a discussion of practical implications for our results conclude the paper.

2   Motivation, Background, and Related Work

An understanding of human factors in software development is clearly of interest to project managers, and not only [9]. In particular, project managers need to learn about human factors because they frequently deal with negotiations and personality conflicts, and value having the right developers for a given SE task (*e.g.,* bug fixing) [10]. Among human factors, developers' personality (along with its influence on individual and team performance) has attracted the interest of the SE research community since the 1960s [4,5]. For example, Weinberg [11] in his book emphasized the effect of developers' personalities on the completion of programming tasks with success: "Because of the complex nature of the programming task, the programmer's personality—his individuality and identity—are far more important factors in his success than is usually recognized." Although empirical investigations have been conducted to study the effect of personality while executing SE tasks [4], these investigations have been mostly conducted in the context of team performance, building, and climate [4–6]. For example, Cruz *et al.* [6] in their Systematic Literature Review (SLR) observed that, from the data extracted from 90 studies, pair programming and team building were among the most recurring research topics. That is, the existing literature on the developers' personality mostly concerns group work and only a few have investigated the role of developers' personalities on individual performance in SE tasks [6]. For example, Cruz *et al.* [6] reported that researchers focusing on individual performance consider that personality can be more important than development technologies, processes, or tools. Therefore, it seems important to study developers' personality traits and the impact they can have on software development and its related tasks. It is also worth mentioning that no study has focused on bug fixing despite being financially critical [2].

Various personality-assessment models exist, among which the most accredited ones are: *(i)* FFM [7]; *(ii)* MBTI [12]; *(iii)* KTS [13]; and *(iv)* HEXACO [14]. The FFM arranges personality traits based on the following five factors: **agreeableness** (it points out how an individual treats relationships and interacts with others), **conscientiousness** (it highlights a personality that is careful, scrupulous, hardworking, and persevering), **extraversion** (it represents to what extent an individual seeks social interaction in his/her environment), **neuroticism** (it concerns how an individual is inclined to experience negative emotions and mood changes), and **openness** (it indicates to what extent an individual is open to new ideas and willing to learn). In the FFM, each personality trait is a spectrum and thus individuals are ranked on a scale between the two extremes. To quantify the FFM personality traits, self-report psychometric questionnaires (also known as personality inventories) are typically used—an example is the *IPIP-NEO-120* [15]. According to McCrae and Costa [16], the FFM provides an alternative means for interpreting MBTI findings within a broader, more commonly shared conceptual framework. Also, Jia *et al.* [17] in their comparative study of personality-assessment models (including the FFM, MBTI, and KTS) recommended the use of the FFM in SE work. This is because the FFM provides a more comprehensive description of human personality and it is the most used personality-assessment model in research fields different from SE. More recently, Anglim and O'Connor [18] delineated recommendations to help researchers choose between the HEXACO and FFM. In particular, they recommended using the HEXACO when studying morally-relevant behaviors (it is not our case); otherwise, they recommend the use of the FFM. Based on the considerations above, we founded our research on the FFM.

The impact of personality on individual performance has been investigated in research fields different from SE. For example, Cubel *et al.* [19] conducted a laboratory study to directly test the relationship between the FFM personality traits and individual performance within the labor market context. Individual performance was measured by asking the study participants to answer as many additions as possible in ten minutes. The authors observed that the participants who were more neurotic (*i.e.*, those characterized by a higher level of neuroticism) performed worse, while those who were more conscientious performed better. Although studies like the one by Cubel *et al.* [19] show that there is a relationship between personality traits and individual performance, this does not imply that such a relationship exists in the SE context. As for the SE research field, few studies have investigated the impact of personality on individual performance while executing SE tasks—e.g., in the SLR by Cruz et al. [6], only 12% of the papers focused on individual performance. Also, most of these studies focused on programming tasks. Da Cunha et al. [20] investigated the relationship between the personality types of undergraduates and their individual performance in a code-review task consisting of 282 lines of Java code (containing 16 bugs). The authors used the MBTI and observed that the students with the NT (iNtuition and Thinking) personality type were the best at reviewing code. Shoaib et al. [21] studied whether the personality of graduates influenced their individual performance in an exploratory-testing task. The authors showed that extrovert individuals—the MBTI was used—had the best performance in exploratory testing. Kanij et al. [22] investigated, through a web-based survey, whether the FFM personality traits of (software) testers differed from the ones of non-testers, and found that testers were more conscientious as compared to non-testers. Similarly, Sturdee et al. [23] investigated whether the FFM personality traits of game developers were different from those of non-game developers, and observed that game developers had a higher neuroticism level. Russo and Stol [24] investigated how HEXACO personality traits differed in men and women in the software industry and found some differences (e.g., women are more open to experience than men). Finally, some researchers [25,26] have investigated the relationship between FFM personality traits and programming-related factors—e.g., Romano et al. [25] found correlations between some personality traits (e.g., neuroticism) of undergraduates and software quality (e.g., cyclomatic complexity).

Summing up, only a few studies have investigated the effect of personality on individual performance in SE tasks and no study has focused on bug-fixing tasks. We would like to point out that, while the study by Da Cunha et al. [20] focused on a single code-review task (i.e., on identifying bugs in a piece of Java code, without bug reports, during a single experimental session), our study focuses on fixing bugs (in C and Java programs), equipped with bug reports, across eight experimental sessions. Furthermore, we used a different personality-assessment model (FFM vs. MBTI).

3   Study

We planned and executed our study, following Wohlin et al.'s guidelines [27], in order to answer the following research question:

RQ. *Do personality traits affect individual performance in fixing bugs in C and Java programs?*

This RQ aims to study whether, and to what extent, the personality traits (estimated by the FFM) of an individual have an effect on his/her performance when fixing bugs. RQ is grounded on the empirical evidence gathered in research fields different from SE, where researchers have shown that some personality traits affect individual performance (e.g., [19]).

3.1   Participants

The participants were undergraduates attending the SE course at the University of Basilicata (Italy). The course was scheduled in the first semester of the third (and last) year of the CS program. The study had both research and educational goals: on one hand, we conceived the study to answer RQ; on the other hand, the study allowed the students to experience bug fixing in an unfamiliar codebase. Participation in the study was voluntary; that is, we did not pay the students for their participation. However, as suggested by Carver *et al.* [28], we rewarded the students who accepted to participate in the study with a bonus—*i.e.*, two points to be added to their final mark of the SE course.[1] By following Carver *et al.*'s suggestions [28], we informed the students that: *(i)* they would receive the bonus regardless of their performance in the study; *(ii)* they could drop out from the study at any time without being negatively judged; *(iii)* the highest mark of the SE course could be reached even without participating in the study; and *(iv)* the gathered data would be treated confidentially and anonymously shared for research purposes only. 62 students participated in the study. The participants were skilled at programming in C and Java, based on their answers to a pre-questionnaire, and had followed the Procedural Programming (PP) and Object-Oriented Programming (OOP) courses (where they had learned to program in C and Java, respectively). Both courses were practice-oriented and the students had to take both writing and practical tests. Both PP and OOP courses were scheduled before the SE one. We focused our study on C and Java because both languages were taught at the University of Basilicata and choosing two (instead of one) gave us an opportunity to mitigate threats to internal validity.

3.2   Experimental Material

To estimate personality traits, we used the IPIP-NEO-120 personality inventory [15]. It allows measuring the FFM personality traits through 120 items—24 items for each personality trait. An item is a statement (*e.g.,* "I get stressed out easily") to be rated on a five-point rating scale from very inaccurate (*i.e.,* one) to very accurate (*i.e.,* five). We also asked the participants to fill in a pre-questionnaire where they stated: *(i)* whether they were skilled at programming in C and Java; and *(ii)* the marks they had achieved in the PP and OOP courses (*i.e.,* "None", "18–21", "22–24", "25–27", or "28–30").[2] The information gathered through the pre-questionnaire allowed for characterizing the participants and analyzing the effect of confounders, namely variables associated with the explanatory one that might affect the response variable so hiding the true relationship between the explanatory and response variables [27].

---

[1] While it is forbidden to pay students for participating in research studies in our country, it is allowed to reward them with a bonus in their final mark.

[2] "None" indicated that the student had not passed (or never sit) the exam of the course while, for example, "28–30" indicates that the student had passed the exam of the course with the highest marks.

Our study consisted of eight tasks—*i.e.*, bug-fixing tasks on eight different programs, four implemented in C and four in Java. These programs, with the only exceptions of two Java programs (*i.e.*, PacMan and SQuiz), were used as experimental objects by Scanniello *et al.* [29] in their family of experiments. The researchers seeded bugs by applying mutation operators. The rationale behind the application of mutation operators was to simulate errors that developers usually make. When seeding bugs, the researchers avoided the bugs interacting with one another—with real bugs, this could not be possible (*i.e.*, they could interact with one another). Also, the researchers sought to seed bugs that presumably had a similar complexity to be fixed. A bug report—consisting of an ID, title, and problem description—accompanied each bug. With the only exceptions of PacMan and SQuiz, we used the bug reports by Scanniello *et al.* [29]. As for PacMan and SQuiz, these programs were available on the web, *i.e.*, in the teaching material of an OOP course held at a university different from those of the authors. We added these two programs to get a balanced number of C and Java programs. The codebase of these programs was sufficiently complex without being obvious as the codebase of the programs used by Scanniello *et al.* [29]. We seeded bugs into PacMan and SQuiz by applying the same approach as Scanniello *et al.* [29] and then created bug reports similar to those used in the other programs. The bug reports, bug location, and codebase of each program are available in our replication package [30]. Finally, to homogenize the bug-fixing experience of the participants (before executing the tasks), we asked them to accomplish a warm-up (bug-fixing) task on a Java program and another one on a C program. This design choice allowed simplifying our data analysis by avoiding taking into account the bug-fixing experience of the students.

3.3 Tasks

Each bug-fixing task required fixing two or more bugs (see Table 1). The bug reports, each associated with a bug to be fixed, were presented one at a time (*i.e.*, the participants did not know the next bug reports). When fixing a bug, the participants had to delimit the patch (*i.e.*, the code they changed to fix the bug) by using code comments as follows: /*Start <BUG REPORT ID>*/ just before the patch and /*End <BUG REPORT ID>*/ just after the patch. This procedure was the same as Scanniello *et al.* [29]. The participants were allowed to skip a bug when they could not fix it. Once a bug was fixed or skipped, the participants could not go back.

3.4 Variables

The response variable of our study was **PRF** (PeRFormance), which was computed as $PRF = \frac{\#BugsCorrectlyFixed}{\#Bugs} * 100$, where $\#BugsCorrectlyFixed$ was the number of bugs the participant had fixed correctly during the bug-fixing task on a given program, while $\#Bugs$ was the total number of bugs in that program. To determine whether a bug was correctly fixed or not, we inspected the patch

Table 1. Summary of the programs used in the bug-fixing tasks.

Program	Language	#Files	KLOC*	#Bugs	Bug Density**
AveCalc	Java	8	1.437	6	4.175
Agenda	C	4	0.594	4	6.734
LaTazza	Java	16	1.079	6	5.561
GAS-station	C	1	0.502	4	7.968
PacMan	Java	4	1.397	4	2.863
Hotel-reservation	C	1	0.394	2	5.076
SQuiz	Java	3	0.601	3	4.992
Financial	C	3	0.222	2	9.009

*It stands for Kilo Lines Of Code (without blank and comment lines).
**It is computed as the number of bugs per KLOC.

provided by the participant. If the patch for a bug was the same as our *ground-truth* patch, the bug was correctly fixed. If the patch was different, two of the authors independently evaluated (*e.g.,* by debugging the program) whether or not the patch was equivalent to our ground-truth patch. In no case, we observed disagreement between the evaluations of the two authors. The values of the PRF variable range between 0% and 100%. The higher the value of this variable, the better the participant's performance is. The strategy we used to define the performance in fixing bugs was *time-fixed*, which is defined as follows: use a brief time limit and let the participants solve a task in predetermined steps; the number of successful steps within the time limit defines performance [31]. Consistent with such a definition, we used a brief time limit for each task, let the participants fix bugs in a predetermined order, and then defined their performance as the percentage of bugs correctly fixed within the time limit. We estimated this time limit through a pilot study with a student having a similar background to that of the participants in our study.

The explanatory variables were the FFM personality traits, namely: **A** (Agreeableness), **C** (Conscientiousness), **E** (Extraversion), **N** (Neuroticism), and **O** (Openness). We quantified these variables by converting the answers to the IPIP-NEO-120 into scores as suggested by Goldberg *et al.* [32]. The values of the explanatory variables range from 24 to 120—the higher the value, the greater the level of the corresponding personality trait is. The mid value for all explanatory variables is 72. This means that, for example, if a student has an A value greater than this threshold, he/she is more agreeable than disagreeable.

We identified two confounders: **C.Mark** and **Java.Mark**. The former indicates the exam mark of the PP course (so assuming that it reflects the C experience/knowledge of the participant) while the latter indicates the exam mark of the OOP course (so reflecting the Java experience/knowledge of the participant). The C.Mark and Java.Mark confounders assume the following values: *None, 18–21, 22–24, 25–27,* or *28–30* (see Sect. 3.2).

3.5   Design

The study was conducted as follows:

1) Filling in IPIP-NEO-120 and pre-questionnaire. The participants filled in the IPIP-NEO-120 and pre-questionnaire alone but in person—this was to provide clarifications if needed. We measured the personality traits only once because personality traits are relatively stable over time [33]—*i.e.,* personality traits do not change in a short time frame like the one in our study.

2) Running training sessions. On two different days, all the participants together took part in two training sessions in a laboratory: the former focused on bug fixing in Java code; the latter concerned bug fixing in C code. At the beginning of each session, one of the authors showed how to fix some sample bugs given the corresponding bug reports. Later, the participants carried out the warm-up bug-fixing task on a Java or C program. No participant missed the training sessions.

3) Running experimental sessions. In the eight experimental sessions, we alternated a bug-fixing task on a Java program with one on a C program (to mitigate a *maturation* threat [27]). We scheduled the experimental sessions based on the availability of the participants. This was to mitigate a threat of *mortality* [27]—no participant dropped out of the study.[3] The participants agreed on scheduling the tasks at 18:00 on Mondays, from October to December. The time span of the experimental sessions was constrained by their execution within the SE course. The participants carried out the tasks in the same laboratory as the training sessions. To prevent the exchange of information in the experimental sessions, two of the authors monitored the participants. To allow the participants to carry out the tasks and easily collect the experimental data, we implemented the experimental procedure with the support of Google Forms. As for the Java programs, the participants used *NetBeans* to accomplish the task while, for the C programs, the IDE was *Dev-C++*. We opted for these IDEs because the students were familiar with them—they had used these IDEs in the OOP and PP courses, respectively.

3.6   Data Analysis

We characterized the gathered data by using descriptive statistics. We then built *Linear Mixed Models* (*LMMs*) to study the effect of the explanatory variables (*i.e.,* the personality traits), with and without the adjustment for the confounders, on the response variable (*i.e.,* the performance in fixing bugs). LMMs extend *Linear Models* (*LMs*) because they incorporate both fixed- and random-effects terms in a linear predictor expression [34]. We used LMMs, rather

---

[3] On a few occasions, some participants informed us that they were unable to take part in an experimental session. When this happened, we arranged an ad-hoc experimental session, before the next one (if any).

than LMs, to overcome the problem related to the non-independence of data—based on the study design, we had multiple measures for each participant and each task. For all built LMMs, the random-effect terms were $(1|Participant)$ and $(1|Task)$, which read as: "one random intercept for each participant" and "one random intercept for each task," respectively. Modeling the participants and bug-fixing tasks as the random variables within the aforementioned random-effects terms allowed us to: *(i)* overcome the problem related to the non-independence of data (*i.e.*, LMMs will be aware that there are multiple measures per each participant and each task); and *(ii)* take into account the by-participant and by-task variations (*e.g.*, LMMs will take into account the variation due to the different tasks). The formula of the first built model, **LMM$_1$**, is: $PRF \sim A + C + E + N + O + (1|Participant) + (1|Task)$. LMM$_1$ allowed studying the effect of the personality traits (modeled as fixed-effects terms) on the performance in fixing bugs without adjusting for the confounders (*i.e.*, C.Mark and Java.Mark). It is worth mentioning that the FFM personality traits are orthogonal to one another [35]. This is why we did not consider any interaction between the explanatory variables in LMM$_1$.

We built a second model, **LMM$_2$**, to study the effect of the personality traits, adjusted for C.Mark and Java.Mark (modeled as fixed-effects terms), on the performance in fixing bugs. That is, LMM$_2$ allowed us to take into account the possible influence of the confounders on the relationship between the explanatory and response variables. Also, by comparing LMM$_1$ and LMM$_2$, we can better understand the extent to which the confounders would affect such a relationship. The formula of LMM$_2$ is: $PRF \sim A + C + E + N + O + C.Mark + Java.Mark + (1|Participant) + (1|Task)$. In LMM$_2$, we did not consider any interaction between the confounding and explanatory variables because when adding any interaction to LMM$_2$, the model suffered from high multicollinearity. High multicollinearity is a serious problem since it makes the estimates (of regression coefficients) of LMMs inaccurate so affecting the ability to draw a correct conclusion about the relationships between the explanatory variables and the response one [36].

To determine both the magnitude and direction of the relationships between the explanatory and the response variables, we leveraged the estimates of LMMs, which are unstandardized effect sizes. As suggested by Bates *et al.* [34], we used 95% (profile) *Confidence Intervals (CIs)* of those estimates as a method of statistical inference—*i.e.*, if a CI did not cross the null value (*i.e.*, 0), the effect of the explanatory variable was deemed (statistically) significant. We also computed the *t-test p-value* for each estimate, by using the Kenward-Roger approximation for *denominator degrees of freedom (ddf)*, as a complementary method for statistical inference. The ddf to compute t- and F-test p-values is unknown for LMMs; therefore, approximations like the Kenward-Roger one are used to overcome that issue [34]. The use of two methods of statistical inference allows for mitigating threats to conclusion validity. We fixed the α significance level at 0.05—*i.e.*, if the p-value was less than 0.05, the effect was deemed (statistically) significant.

For each LMM, we computed *Nakagawa's marginal and conditional R^2* to provide an indication of the variance explained in that LMM [37]. Also, we checked for multicollinearity of fixed-effects terms by using the *Variance Inflation Factor (VIF)* and assumed high multicollinearity when a VIF value was greater than 10 [36]. To face multicollinearity, we planned to exclude any problematic variable [36]—this is why, as mentioned above, we excluded any interaction between the confounding and explanatory variables in LMM$_2$. Finally, we used diagnostic plots (see the replication package [30]) to check LMM assumptions.

Table 2. Some descriptive statistics for the response and explanatory variables.

Variable	Mean	SD	Min	Median	Max
PRF	50.319	32.068	0	50	100
A	93.694	11.358	55	95.5	117
C	85.258	11.387	65	86.5	111
E	78.71	10.44	57	79	100
N	66.871	12.78	39	65.5	99
O	85.371	11.613	51	86	113

4   Results and Threats to Validity

Below, we show the data characterization and results from the LMM analysis. Finally, we discuss the threats that could affect the validity of our results.

4.1   Data Characterization and LMM Analysis Results

In Table 2, we summarize the data of the response and explanatory variables by using mean, Standard Deviation (SD), Minimum (Min), median, and Maximum (Max). The participants correctly fixed, on average, about 50% of the bugs (since the mean value for PRF is 50.319%). The min value of PRF is 0%, which indicates very bad performance in bug fixing (*i.e.,* no bug correctly fixed). As for the A, C, E, and O explanatory variables, we can observe that the mean and median values are higher than 72 (*i.e.,* the mid value, see Sect. 3.4) so suggesting that most participants were: more agreeable than disagreeable; more conscientious than non-conscientious; more extrovert than introvert; and more open to experience than closed. Instead, the mean and median values of the N explanatory variable were both lower than 72; namely, most participants were more non-neurotic than neurotic.

The results from the analysis of LMM$_1$ and LMM$_2$ (*i.e.,* without and after adjusting for confounders, respectively) are shown in Table 3. The lower part of this table shows some information on the built LMMs, including the highest VIF values. In that respect, the VIF values were never greater than 10 (see Sect. 3.6). The diagnostic plots—which did not suggest critical violations of LMM assumptions—along with other information on the built LMMs (*e.g.*, standard errors, estimates for the confounders in LMM_2, *etc.*) are available in our replication package [30].

If we consider the results concerning LMM_1, we can notice a significant effect of neuroticism: the CI for N does not cross 0 and the corresponding p-value (0.032) is less than $\alpha = 0.05$. The estimate for N is -0.408, meaning that when the neuroticism level decreases by one unit, the performance in fixing bugs increases by 0.408 on average (with all other variables held constant). The question that now arises is whether the observed significant effect of neuroticism is actually caused by the confounders. Namely, we need to know whether the performance in bug fixing of the less-neurotic participants was better just because the less-neurotic participants had more C and Java programming experience/knowledge (*i.e.*, higher marks in the PP and OOP courses). The analysis of LMM_2 goes towards answering that question and seems to suggest a significant of neuroticism—indeed, the effect of N on PRF is borderline significant (*i.e.*, the CI indicates a significant effect, while the p-value is slightly greater than α).

Table 3. Results from the analysis of LMM_1 and LMM_2. In bold, p-values and CIs indicating significant effects.

	LMM_1			LMM_2		
	Estimate	CI	p-value	Estimate	CI	p-value
Intercept	79.393	**[12.069, 146.717]**	**0.029**	48.591	[-2.096, 99.277]	0.096
A	−0.4	[−0.81, 0.01]	0.068	−0.052	[−0.36, 0.257]	0.768
C	0.386	[−0.024, 0.796]	0.078	0.012	[−0.281, 0.305]	0.943
E	0.024	[−0.402, 0.451]	0.914	−0.05	[−0.361, 0.26]	0.776
N	−0.408	**[−0.761, −0.055]**	**0.032**	−0.258	**[−0.506, −0.01]**	0.072
O	0.01	[−0.379, 0.398]	0.962	0.065	[−0.199, 0.328]	0.667
	Conditional (Marginal) $R^2 = 0.493\ (0.049)$			Conditional (Marginal) $R^2 = 0.496\ (0.203)$		
	Max VIF $= 1.13$			Max VIF $= 5.44$		

If we compare the estimates for N with and without adjusting for the confounders, we can observe a clear increase (36.76%) in the estimate of N—it passes from -0.408 (without the adjustment in LMM_1) to -0.258 (with the adjustment in LMM_2)—so indicating that the confounders affect the relationship between neuroticism and performance in bug fixing. Nevertheless, the effect of neuroticism is still borderline significant (*i.e.*, only the CI indicates a significant effect).

Further Analysis. Although all students stated to be skilled in C and Java programming, the reader might question that the students who have not passed the exam of the PP course and/or OOP course might not be sufficiently skilled in these programming languages and, therefore, might not be representative of a population of novice developers. This is why we repeated the LMM analysis by considering two data-cleaning scenarios: *ScenarioB*, where we used the observations from the participants who had passed at least the exam of the PP course (392 observations); and *ScenarioC*, where we used the observations *(i)* from the participants who executed the tasks on the C programs and had also passed the exam of the PP course and *(ii)* from the participants who executed the tasks on the Java programs and had also passed the exam of the OOP course (324 observations). These two scenarios allowed us to confirm, according to both CIs and p-values for N, that there is a significant effect of neuroticism with and without adjusting for the confounders—the interested reader can find details in the technical report available in our replication package [30].

Summing up, the significant effect of neuroticism on the performance in bug fixing is quite consistent across the three scenarios even when adjusting for the confounders. We can exclude that the observed significant effect of neuroticism on the performance in fixing bugs is actually caused by the C and Java programming experience/knowledge the participants had. This is because the effect of neuroticism is significant after taking into account the effect of the confounders. Therefore, we can answer RQ as follows: *neuroticism has a detrimental effect on the individual performance in fixing bugs—i.e., the lower the neuroticism level, the better the individual performance is.*

4.2   Threats to Validity

Despite our effort to lessen or avoid as many threats to validity as possible, some of them are unavoidable. This is because reducing or avoiding a kind of threat may intensify or introduce another kind of threat [27]. Since we conducted the first study on the effect of (FFM) personality traits when fixing bugs, we preferred to reduce threats to internal validity (*i.e.*, making sure that the relationship between personality traits and individual performance was correctly identified), rather than being in favor of external validity (*e.g.*, generalizing the results to industrial practices). Accordingly, we prioritized the threats to validity as follows: internal, construct, conclusion, and external [27].

Threats to Internal Validity. Our study might be affected by a *selection threat* since the participants were volunteers—volunteers might be more motivated than the whole population [27]. The participants might also have reacted differently as time passed (*maturation threat*). To mitigate learning effects, we performed the following actions: *(i)* we conceived two warm-up tasks before the experimental ones; *(ii)* we considered, as experimental objects, programs from different problem domains, differing in size, type, and density of seeded bugs; and *(iii)* interleaved C and Java programs. Finally, each bug-fixing task lasted at most 60 min so mitigating tiredness and boredom effects. In studies like ours, the effect of confounders might cause spurious cause-effect relationships (*threat of ambiguity about the direction of causal influence*). To deal with this kind of threat, we properly analyzed the gathered data and homogenized the participants' bug-fixing experience through warm-up tasks.

Threats to Construct Validity. Using a single measure involves the risk that if the measure gave a measurement bias, the study would be misleading [27] (*threat of mono-method bias*). Although we used a single kind of measure to quantify the performance in fixing bugs, the used strategy (*i.e.*, time-fixed) is well-known [31]. Also, we collected more observations per participant. Finally, to mitigate an *evaluation-apprehension threat*, we made clear to the participants that their performance in the study would not have affected their exam marks.

Threats to Conclusion Validity. There is always heterogeneity in a study group (*threat of random heterogeneity of participants*) [27]. To reduce this threat, we considered a group of undergraduates in CS taking the same university course. Also, when analyzing the data, we took into account the by-participant variation (through a random-effects term) and the effect of the C.Mark and Java.Mark confounders. We also homogenized the experience of the participants in bug fixing by means of warm-up tasks. Another potential threat is *reliability of measures*. The basic principle behind the reliability of measures is that when a phenomenon is measured twice (or more), the outcome shall be the same [27]. Accordingly, we used an objective measure to estimate the performance in fixing bugs. Also, we opted for C.Mark and Java.Mark (representing the marks of the exams of the PP and OOP courses, respectively) because these measures should be more reliable than other measures like the self-declared experience in C and Java programming. To measure the participants' personality traits, we employed a highly-used and validated self-report psychometric questionnaire [15].

Threats to External Validity. CS students can be considered proxies of novice developers in certain circumstances—*e.g.*, when they are adequately trained to accomplish a given kind of task [38]. Also, as past work suggests [38], it does not matter whether CS students perform as well as novice developers in absolute terms, what matters is the effect of personality traits and whether that effect is similar with CS students and with novice developers. Finally, it is worth noting that the use of students as participants in the early stage of research brings a number of advantages, as compared to professionals [28,38]. For example, reaching a higher sample size (so mitigating threats to conclusion validity) or having the opportunity of obtaining initial empirical evidence. There might also be a threat of *interaction of setting and treatment* since the used programs and bugs might not be representative of real-world applications and bugs.

5   Final Remarks

In this paper, we presented the results of a prospective observational study to investigate if personality traits impact the individual performance of undergraduates when fixing bugs. The results of our study have practical implications for researchers, practitioners (project managers and developers), and educators.

Implications for Educators. We observed that neuroticism has a detrimental effect on individual performance in fixing bugs. This finding is consistent with that by Cubel *et al.* [19] who observed, in a context different from SE, that more-neurotic people perform worse. That is, this finding allows stating that neuroticism has a detrimental effect on individual performance and, specifically, when fixing bugs. It is also worth mentioning that past research, in the labor market field, has shown that neuroticism is negatively associated with earnings (*i.e.,* the less neurotic employees are, the greater their earnings) [39]. Also, researchers have found that less-neurotic employees experience less stress at work [40], and acute stress in the workplace is related to poor health outcomes [41]. Therefore, CS educators should leverage the above-mentioned empirical evidence to help CS students to work at the best of their possibility and then succeed in their future job. Mindfulness[4] represents a promising means to reach these goals. For example, Krasner *et al.* [43] observed that practicing mindfulness made medical students less neurotic. Despite further research is needed, we can postulate that arranging mindfulness workshops in the university setting is beneficial to any CS student and, especially, to those that are more neurotic.

Implications for Practitioners. Our results, along with past ones (*e.g.,* [40, 41]) suggest project managers that pay attention to the personality traits of developers. In particular, project managers should allow more-neurotic developers to reach their best in SE tasks and, specifically, in fixing bugs. Project managers could be also interested in assigning bugs to the most suitable developers, based on their personality traits. In this regard, our results suggest that, when there is time pressure to fix a bug (like in our experimental setting), the most suitable developer is low in neuroticism. For example, critical or blocker bugs have higher time pressure than major or minor bugs; therefore it would be better to assign the former to less-neurotic developers.

Implications for Researchers. Replicated studies are needed to confirm or contradict our results. To ease researchers to carry out replications and/or aggregate our results into a wider study, we made our replication package publicly available [30], which includes bug reports, bug location, and codebase of the used programs, as well as raw data, R notebooks, and a technical report. We confide that our initial evidence can represent the premise for further investigations with software companies and professionals—after all, it is easier to involve software companies and professionals in empirical studies when initial evidence is available [28]. This would fill the chasm between research and industry and would improve our body of knowledge on the relationship between personality traits and developers' performance in fixing bugs.

Funding Information. This study has been partially supported by "MOOD-Mindfulness fOr sOftware Developers" (CUP: D53D23008880006), a research project funded by the Italian Ministry for Universities and Research (MUR).

---

[4] It is a meditation technique that, through breathing, aims to keep the mind calm and educate attention by focusing only on one thing at a time [42].

References

1. Catolino, G., Palomba, F., Zaidman, A., Ferrucci, F.: Not all bugs are the same: understanding, characterizing, and classifying bug types. J. Syst. Softw. **152**, 165–181 (2019)
2. C. J. B. School: The business value of optimizing CI pipelines (2020). https://info.undo.io/ci-research-report
3. Guo, P.J., Zimmermann, T., Nagappan, N., Murphy, B., Nagappan, N., Zimmermann, T.: "Not my bug!" and other reasons for software bug report reassignments. In: Proceedings of the ACM Conference on Computer Supported Cooperative Work (2011)
4. Soomro, A.B., Salleh, N., Mendes, E., Grundy, J., Burch, G., Nordin, A.: The effect of software engineers' personality traits on team climate and performance: a systematic literature review. Inf. Softw. Technol. **73**, 52–65 (2016)
5. Cruz, S.S.J.O., da Silva, F.Q.B., Monteiro, C.V.F., Santos, P., Rossilei, I., dos Santos, M.T.: Personality in software engineering: preliminary findings from a systematic literature review. In: Proceedings of Annual Conference on Evaluation Assessment in Software Engineering, pp. 1–10 (2011)
6. Cruz, S.S.J.O., da Silva, F.Q.B., Capretz, L.F.: Forty years of research on personality in software engineering: a mapping study. Comput. Hum. Behav. **46**, 94–113 (2015)
7. McCrae, R.R., John, O.P.: An introduction to the five-factor model and its applications. J. Pers. **60**(2), 175–215 (1992)
8. Saarimäki, N., Lenarduzzi, V., Vegas, S. Juristo, N., Taibi, D.: Cohort studies in software engineering: a vision of the future. In: Proceedings of International Symposium on Empirical Software Engineering and Measurement, pp. 33:1–33:6. ACM (2020)
9. Constantine, L.: Constantine on Peopleware, 3rd edn. Prentice Hall, Hoboken (1995)
10. Capretz, L.F.: Bringing the human factor to software engineering. IEEE Softw. **31**(2), 104 (2014)
11. Weinberg, G.M.: The Psychology of Computer Programming. Wiley, Hoboken (1985)
12. Myers, I.B., McCaulley, M.H., Quenk, N.L., Hammer, A.L.: MBTI Manual (A Guide to the Development and Use of the Myers Briggs Type Indicator, 3rd edn. Consulting Psychologists Press (1998)
13. Keirsey, D., Bates, M.M.: Please Understand Me II. Prometheus Nemesis Book Co. (1988)
14. Ashton, M.C., Lee, K.: The HEXACO model of personality structure and the importance of the H factor. Soc. Pers. Psychol. Compass **2**(5), 1952–1962 (2008)
15. Johnson, J.A.: Measuring thirty facets of the five factor model with a 120-item public domain inventory: development of the IPIP-NEO-120. J. Res. Pers. **51**, 78–89 (2014)
16. McCrae, R.R., Costa, P.T.: Reinterpreting the Myers-Briggs type indicator from the perspective of the five-factor model of personality. J. Pers. **57**(1), 17–40 (1989)
17. Jia, J., Zhang, P., Zhang, R.: A comparative study of three personality assessment models in software engineering field. In: Proceedings of International Conference on Software Engineering and Service Science, pp. 7–10. IEEE (2015)
18. Anglim, J., O'connor, P.: Measurement and research using the big five, HEXACO, and narrow traits: a primer for researchers and practitioners. Aust. J. Psychol. **71**(1), 16–25 (2019)

19. Cubel, M., Nuevo-Chiquero, A., Sanchez-Pages, S., Vidal-Fernandez, M.: Do personality traits affect productivity? Evidence from the laboratory. Econ. J. **126**(592), 654–681 (2016)
20. Da Cunha, A., Greathead, D.: Does personality matter?: an analysis of code-review ability. Commun. ACM **50**(5), 109–112 (2007)
21. Shoaib, L., Nadeem, A., Akbar, A.: An empirical evaluation of the influence of human personality on exploratory software testing. In: Proceedings of International Multitopic Conference, pp. 1–6. IEEE (2009)
22. Kanij, T., Merkel, R., Grundy, J.: An empirical investigation of personality traits of software testers. In: Proceedings of International Workshop on Cooperative and Human Aspects of Software Engineering, pp. 1–7. IEEE (2015)
23. Sturdee, M., Ivory, M., Ellis, D., Stacey, P., Ralph, P.: Personality traits in game development. In: Proceeding of International Conference on Evaluation and Assessment in Software Engineering, pp. 221–230. ACM (2022)
24. Russo, D., Stol, K.-J.: Gender differences in personality traits of software engineers. IEEE Trans. Softw. Eng. **48**(3), 819–834 (2022)
25. Romano, S., Scanniello, G., Dionisio, P.: On the role of personality traits in implementation tasks: a preliminary investigation with students. In: Proceeding of Euromicro Conference on Software Engineering and Advanced Applications, pp. 189–196. IEEE (2022)
26. Karimi, Z., Baraani-Dastjerdi, A., Ghasem-Aghaee, N., Wagner, S.: Links between the personalities, styles and performance in computer programming. J. Syst. Softw. **111**, 228–241 (2016)
27. Wohlin, C., Runeson, P., Höst, M., Ohlsson, M.C., Regnell, B., Wessln, A.: Experimentation in Software Engineering. Springer, Heidelberg (2012). https://doi.org/10.1007/978-3-642-29044-2
28. Carver, J., Jaccheri, L., Morasca, S., Shull, F.: Issues in using students in empirical studies in software engineering education. In: Proceedings of International Software Metrics Symposium, pp. 239–249. IEEE (2003)
29. Scanniello, G., Risi, M., Tramontana, P., Romano, S.: Fixing faults in C and java source code: abbreviated vs. full-word identifier names. ACM Trans. Softw. Eng. Methodol. **26**(2), 1–43 (2017)
30. Romano, S., Scanniello, G., Baldassarre, T., Caivano, D., Tortora, G.: Replication package (2022). http://figshare.com/s/cf5d568f0515c12aff6d
31. Bergersen, G.R., Sjøberg, D.I.K., Dybå, T.: Construction and validation of an instrument for measuring programming skill. IEEE Trans. Softw. **40**(12), 1163–1184 (2014)
32. Goldberg, L.R., et al.: The international personality item pool and the future of public-domain personality measures. J. Res. Pers. **40**(1), 84–96 (2006)
33. Bleidorn, W., et al.: The policy relevance of personality traits. Am. Psychol. **74**, 1056–1067 (2019)
34. Bates, D., Mächler, M., Bolker, B., Walker, S.: Fitting linear mixed-effects models using lme4. J. Stat. Softw. **67**(1), 1–48 (2015)
35. McCrae, R.R., Costa, P.T.: Personality in Adulthood: A Five-Factor Theory Perspective, 2nd edn. Guilford Press (2003)
36. James, G., Witten, D., Hastie, T., Tibshirani, R.: An Introduction to Statistical Learning: With Applications in R. Springer, Heidelberg (2014). https://doi.org/10.1007/978-1-4614-7138-7
37. Nakagawa, S., Johnson, P.C.D., Schielzeth, H.: The coefficient of determination R2 and intra-class correlation coefficient from generalized linear mixed-effects models revisited and expanded. J. R. Soc. Interface **14**(134), 20170213 (2017)

38. Falessi, D., et al.: Empirical software engineering experts on the use of students and professionals in experiments. Empir. Softw. Eng. **23**(1), 452–489 (2018)
39. Nyhus, E.K., Pons, E.: The effects of personality on earnings. J. Econ. Psychol. **26**(3), 363–384 (2005)
40. Ebstrup, J.F., Eplov, L.F., Pisinger, C., Jørgensen, T.: Association between the five factor personality traits and perceived stress: is the effect mediated by general self-efficacy? Anxiety Stress Coping **24**, 407–419 (2011)
41. Garfin, D.R., Thompson, R.R., Holman, E.A.: Acute stress and subsequent health outcomes: a systematic review. J. Psychosom. Res. **112**, 107–113 (2018)
42. Bernardez, B., Duran Toro, A., Parejo Maestre, J.A., Juristo, N., Ruiz-Cortes, A.: Effects of mindfulness on conceptual modeling performance: a series of experiments. IEEE Trans. Softw. 1 (2020)
43. Krasner, M.S., et al.: Association of an educational program in mindful communication with burnout, empathy, and attitudes among primary care physicians. JAMA **302**, 1284–1293 (2009)

A Rapid Review on Software Vulnerabilities and Embedded, Cyber-Physical, and IoT Systems

Alessandro Marchetto[1]([✉])[iD] and Giuseppe Scanniello[2][iD]

[1] University of Trento, Trento, Italy
alessandro.marchetto@unitn.it
[2] University of Salerno, Salerno, Italy
gscanniello@unisa.it

Abstract. This paper presents a Rapid Review (RR) conducted to identify and characterize existing approaches and methods that discover, fix,
and manage vulnerabilities in Embedded, Cyber-Physical, and Internet-
Of-Things systems and software (ESs hereafter). In the last years, a growing interest concerned the adoption of ESs in different domains (e.g.,
automotive, healthcare) and with different purposes. Modern ESs are
heterogeneous, computationally powerful, connected, and intelligent systems characterized by many technologies, devices, and an extensive use
of embedded software (SW). Adopting software that could emulate or
substitute hardware (HD) components makes the ESs flexible, tunable,
and less costly but demands attention to security aspects such as SW
vulnerabilities. Vulnerabilities can be exploited by attackers and compromise entire systems. The findings of our RR emerge from 61 papers
and can be summarized as follows: (i) complex and connected ESs are
studied especially for autonomous vehicles and robots; (ii) new methods
and approaches are proposed mainly to discover software-vulnerabilities
related to memory management in ES firmware software; and (iii) most
of the proposed methods apply fuzzy-based dynamic analysis to binary
and executable files of ES software.

Keywords: Cybersecurity · Embedded systems · Rapid Review ·
Software Vulnerability

1 Introduction

A growing popularity, pervasiveness, and ubiquitousness is characterizing
Embedded, Cyber-Physical, and Internet-of-Things Systems (ESs hereafter) in
several application domains, e.g., automotive, aerospace, consumer electronics,
railways, telecommunications, and healthcare, just to cite a few. The global ES
market is expected to grow again in the next years[1], due to new technologies

---

[1] https://www.transparencymarketresearch.com.

such as virtualization, embedded AI/ML, automation, high-performing devices and GPU, and 5G/6G low-latency communication. An *ES* is a computing system designed for specific functions and composed of a combination of hardware (HD), software (SW), mechanical and communication parts. *ES* is a quite generic term used to identify any computing systems other than general purpose computers and servers [7]. Modern ESs are heterogeneous, computationally powerful, connected, and intelligent systems based on many technologies, devices, and an extensive use of embedded software. New technologies, high connectivity, and an extensive adoption and reuse of SW, that could substitute HD components, make ESs flexible, tunable, and less costly but increase the attack surface and demand an increased attention to security aspects, such as SW vulnerabilities (e.g., collected in the National Vulnerability Database by means of the Common Vulnerabilities and Exposures). SW vulnerabilities, if exploited by attackers, can lead to security breaches and cause dramatic damage. Even if this field is still in its infancy, the community is developing new techniques for ES SW vulnerability detection, fixing, and management.

In this work, we report the results of a Rapid Review (RR) conducted to identify what are: (i) the type of ESs studied, (ii) the studied security aspects, concerning ES SW vulnerabilities; and (iii) the proposed solutions. Differently from traditional Systematic Literature Review (SLR), Evidence-Based Practice (EBP) is mainly applied to provide the current best evidence from the literature research in a given domain of expertise, aiming at supporting the integration of such an evidence in decision-making processes. Recent work [10] highlights that EBP can suffer from the lack of connection with practice. Hecem Rapid Reviews (RRs) have been proposed [2,10] for taking into account constraints related to practical environments and cases, e.g., delivering evidence promptly, with lower costs, and reporting the evidence through a clear and simple way. RRs are emerging as a streamlined approach to derive, synthesize and present research evidences for supporting emergent decisions. We opted for a RR, instead of a traditional SLR, since it better fits our needs: (i) deliver evidence promptly with limited resources, e.g., focus on a single source and involve a single researcher for the literature analysis; (ii) conduct a practice-oriented secondary studies [1]; (iii) show the emerging results clearly and simply by focusing on evidences [2]. Nevertheless, our results can be of interest to any researchers and engineers who want to know the state-of-the-art in the field of embedded software vulnerabilities, for supporting ES development processes.

2 Planning and Execution

Following [2], we: (1) defined our research questions (RQs); (2) defined the search strategy and the paper selection procedure (e.g., source database); (3) defined the search query, as well as filtering, inclusion, and exclusion criteria; (4) identified a set of criteria to be used to characterize and analyze the selected papers; and (5) identified the threats to validity that could have affected our study.

Research Questions With the goal of identifying and characterizing the existing approaches that discover, fix, and manage vulnerabilities in ES software, our RR has been driven by the following RQs.

RQ1. *What are the types of ES investigated in existing literature?* RQ1 aims at identifying what types of ESs are investigated in the literature by focusing on the SW's security vulnerabilities and on existing approaches to discover, fix, and manage such vulnerabilities. By starting from the high-level categorization of ESs (i.e., ES, IoT, CPS), we then identified different categories of ESs, based on functional requirements and performance (i.e., standalone ESs, real-time ESs, network ESs, mobile ESs), and based on both performance and complexity of the ES (i.e., small, medium, large). RQ1 can help researchers in identifying the type of non-adequately investigated ESs that could be object of further investigation. Furthermore, RQ1 can help practitioners by acting as a proxy for the information needed to identify security problems and solutions about the ES they are adopting.

RQ2. *What are the security aspects, concerning ES software vulnerabilities, in which existing studies focus?* RQ2 aims at going in-depth into the security aspect, concerning ES software vulnerabilities, investigated in the literature. To drive the analysis of the literature, we identified the following factors:

- **Vulnerability management phase**: we aim at delineating which phase of vulnerability management is investigated for ES software, i.e., vulnerability discovery, vulnerability assessment, and vulnerability fixing.
- **Type of the vulnerability**: we aim at identifying the type of ES software vulnerabilities (e.g., buffer overflow, SQL injection, and weak access control or authentication) analyzed by the existing literature.
- **Cybersecurity attacks that can exploit the vulnerabilities**: we aim at identifying the potential effect of the vulnerabilities by starting from the identification of the target (i.e., HD, software -SW, communication) and type of cyber-attacks (e.g., denial of service -DoS, control hihacking attacks) that could exploit such vulnerabilities.

RQ2 can help researchers in getting a quick insight about the vulnerabilities that could affect ES SW. Furthermore, RQ2 can help practitioners in the identification of security vulnerabilities and issues that could affect the ES they are adopting.

RQ3. *What are the proposed solutions to address (discover, fix, etc.) vulnerabilities in ES software?* RQ3 aims at inspecting methods and approaches presented in the literature to deal with vulnerabilities in ES SW. We analyzed the goal of each paper, the type of the proposed solution (e.g., static analysis, dynamic analysis, hybrid analysis, ML/Deep Learning-based analysis, manual analysis), as well as the main object of the solution (e.g., source code, binary code, executable file, software artifact). RQ3 can help researchers in getting a quick insight into the existing methods and approaches for ES SW. Furthermore, RQ3 can help practitioners in identifying potential solutions that can be adopted to improve the security of the ES they are adopting.

Search Strategy and Selection Procedure In-line with [2], we searched on *Scopus* as a single database since it is recognized to be a large source of peer-reviewed literature [9] and it captures the literature of different editors. To build the query string, we started from the main terms and phrases related to our RQs, such as: "Embedded system", "Software", "Source Code", and "Vulnerability" and combined them with AND and OR operators. We hence obtained a list of 524 papers published. We then applied filtering, inclusion and exclusion criteria [2], thus we: (i) filtered out papers published before the year 2000, since we observed that only a few papers have been published on the topic before; and (ii) limited our search to papers written in English and published in conference and journals. We hence obtained a list of 479 papers published. We decided to refine again the initial query string with terms and phrases related to the different phases of the vulnerability management process, the resulting query string, in the Scopus syntax, is the following one:

TITLE-ABS-KEY ("EMBEDDED SYSTEM") **AND** (TITLE-ABS-KEY ("SOFTWARE") **OR** TITLE-ABS-KEY ("SOURCE CODE")) **AND** TITLE-ABS-KEY ("VULNERABILITY") **AND** (TITLE-ABS-KEY ("VULNERABILITY DISCOVERY") **OR** TITLE-ABS-KEY ("VULNERABILITY DETECTION") **OR** TITLE-ABS-KEY ("VULNERABILITY IDENTIFICATION") **OR** TITLE-ABS-KEY ("VULNERABILITY UNDERST**AND** ING") **OR** TITLE-ABS-KEY ("VULNERABILITY ANALYSIS") **OR** TITLE-ABS-KEY ("VULNERABILITY ASSESSMENT") **OR** TITLE-ABS-KEY ("VULNERABILITY REPAIR") **OR** TITLE-ABS-KEY ("VULNERABILITY PREVENTION") **OR** TITLE-ABS-KEY ("VULNERABILITY FIX") **OR** TITLE-ABS-KEY ("VULNERABILITY MANAGEMENT") **OR** TITLE-ABS-KEY ("VULNERABILITY EXPLOITATION") **OR** TITLE-ABS-KEY ("VULNERABILITY EXPLOITS") **OR** TITLE-ABS-KEY ("VULNERABILITY REDUCTION") **OR** TITLE-ABS-KEY ("VULNERABILITY DEMONSTRATION"))

In Scopus, "TITLE-ABS-KEY" is the operator to search for terms and phrases on titles, abstracts, or keywords. It is worth noticing that the used query included plurals and variants of the used terms and phrases. With this query, we obtained a list of 61 papers. Those papers have been further manually analyzed for, on the one hand, include the ones that present or discuss any aspects related to the security vulnerability of ES SW, using ES SW for IoT devices, firmware images, and any other works on devices that can contribute to answering our RQs. While, on the other hand, excluding such papers that: (i) are not related to ES SW; (ii) investigate topics such as risk assessment, attack and threat modeling; and (iii) extend another paper; (iv) we could not find. These criteria have been checked by one of the authors in two rounds: the author screened both title and abstract of each paper to determine whether it met the inclusion/exclusion criteria, and then the author analyzed the full text of each paper to decide whether to apply inclusion/exclusion criteria. Finally, 50 papers have been selected to be fully analyzed and characterized.

Analysis Criteria. In-line with [2], we did not conduct an in-depth quality appraisal of the selected papers but rather we conducted a thematic analysis [1] by classifying each paper according to some predefined criteria identified from our RQs. Table 1 summarizes the four groups of criteria used for collecting the evidences with the thematic analysis and expressed in terms of considered aspects and examples of values:

- **Goal**: aspects related to the goal of the work, e.g., presenting a new approach for discovering vulnerabilities of an ES SW;
- **Target embedded system**: aspects devoted to describe the ES target of the presented work, e.g., IoT industrial device, robotic autonomous systems.
- **Investigated security aspects**: aspects characterizing the vulnerability analyzed in the work, such as the vulnerability's type (e.g., memory corruption via buffer overflow), the target artifacts where the vulnerability is located (e.g., HD, software -SW or the communication -COM), type and expected impact of the attack that could exploit the vulnerability (respectively, e.g., injecting of corrupted inputs and unexpected code execution).
- **Proposed solution**: aspects related to the proposed solution, e.g., a new vulnerability discovery method based on static ES SW analysis, a reverse engineering technique for binary ES firmwares.

Table 1. Analysis criteria for the detailed analysis

Id	Aspect	Example of possible values
Goal		
c1	Goal	New method or approach, assessment, tool presentation
c2	Goal description	One-sentence text description of the paper's goal
Target embedded system		
c3	Involved ES architecture	E.g., (pure) ES, ES for IoT, CPS
c4	Type of ES - functional reqs	Standalone ES, real-time ES, network ES, mobile ES
c5	Type of ES - micro-controller	Small ES, medium ES, large ES
c6	Application domain	E.g., aviation, automotive, manufacturing, security
Investigated security aspects		
c7	Vulnerability mgmn. phase	E.g., discovery, assessment, prevention, fix
c8	Attack target	HD, SW, COM (communication), devices
c9	Attack target details	Free text to describe the type target attacked
c10	Affected HD device	IoT device, memory, processor, FPGA, PLC
c11	SW vulnerability	E.g., buffer overflow, command injection, SQL injection
c12	Type of the attack	E.g., hijacking attacks, injecting packets or input, malware
c13	Attack's impact	E.g., denial of service, code execution, integrity violation
Proposed solution		
c14	Object of the analysis	E.g., source code, binary, software image, executable file
c15	Object of the analysis: detail	Free text description of the analysis's object
c16	Analysis method	E.g., static/dynamic analysis, ML/Deep Learning, Manual
c17	Analysis method: detail	Free text description about the analysis method

These criteria have been defined by a three-step procedure: (1) an initial set of criteria has been defined by one of the authors and applied to a few papers; (2) the output of this preliminary analysis has been used, by both authors, to refine and finalize the initial set. Finally, (3) all papers have been (re)analyzed with this refined criteria by one of the authors. Therefore, these criteria have been used to characterize each paper and capture the evidences needed to answer to our RQs. In detail, **Target embedded system** is used to answer **RQ1**, **Investigated security aspects** for answering **RQ2**, and both **Goal** and **Proposed solution** are used to answer **RQ3**.

Threats to Validity. The main threats to validity concern: (i) the analysis of the literature conducted only by one of the authors, which might introduce a bias, and (ii) the adoption of only one source of peer-reviewed papers, which might limit the set of literature papers considered. Another threat to validity concerns the detailed analysis, (iii) it has been conducted only by one author by analyzing the full text of all selected papers and without applying a structured quality appraisal of the papers, so possibly limiting the reliability of the gathered evidence. A threat to validity concerns also the (iv) analysis criteria adopted to collect enough evidence to answer our RQs. Different sets of criteria can be defined and can potentially let emerge different evidences. We are conscious that these threats can have limited the validity of our work, but they are in line with the ones typically expected for a RR [2]. We opted for a RR because it better fits our current needs but we believe that our work can be the starting point to identify and characterize existing methods for vulnerabilities discovery, management, exploiting and fixing in ES SW, as well as for identifying new research areas to be further investigated.

3   Results

We report and discuss our findings, results and references are online[2]. With the aim of communicating evidence to practitioners, we focus on evidence briefing [2].

Table 2 (RQ1) presents the evidence related to the **Target embedded system** criterion. **RQ1**: (i) Most of the papers investigate vulnerabilities related to ES SW, without specifically defining the target ES. (ii) Among the specified ones, complex and connected ESs are the most investigated type of ESs. (iii) In terms of domain, autonomous vehicles and robots attract most of the attention and effort of the community.

Table 2 (RQ2) presents the evidence related to the **Investigated security aspects** criterion. **RQ2**: (i) The large majority of papers investigate methods to discover software vulnerabilities in ES firmware software and software related to connected devices. (ii) The large majority of papers investigate vulnerability related to memory management and, in particular, buffer overflow and

---

[2] https://tinyurl.com/4rfbzc2w.

segmentation faults. (iii) significant number of papers investigates (D)DoS attacks that lead to service interruption but also side-channel attacks and code injection are largely explored.

Table 2 (RQ3) and Fig. 1 present the evidences related to **Proposed Solution** and **Goal** (RQ3). The figure presents examples of collocated graphs built by grouping the one-sentence paper's goal descriptions related to the vulnerability management phase criterion, A collocates graph[3] represents terms that occur in close proximity as a force-directed network graph; dark boxes in the graph are the most frequent terms, while edges are relations between contextual terms. The graphs highlight the relationship among relevant terms used in the work's goals, i.e., their commonality. Figure 1 (**Analysis**) shows, e.g., that *fault-injection* on *code* is largely investigated in vulnerability Analysis. **RQ3**: (i) The large majority of papers present a new approach/technique to deal with vulnerabilities in ES, while a few papers present validation experiments and topic-specific literature reviews. (ii) Binary and executable are the most frequently investigated type of ES SW. (iii) Dynamic analysis, in particular, based on fuzzing is the mostly applied type of analysis proposed in the papers for vulnerability discovery, assessment, analysis, and fix.

4   Related Work

A few literature reviews has been conducted in the ES-related field. For instance, [7] reports on a systematic literature review for ESs threats and vulnerabilities and present a taxonomy of attacks. Some works, e.g., [8], focus on HD vulnerabilities, but our interest is related to ES SW vulnerabilities. For instance, [3] presents a taxonomy of vulnerabilities and attacks for aerospace on-board systems. [4,5] focus on IoT devices vulnerability detection. [6] focuses on automatic methods to discover vulnerabilities in ES binary firmware code. Existing reviews are related to our RR but do not fit our RQs, they are limited to a specific technology (e.g., IoT) or application domain (e.g., aerospace). Conversely, we did not limit our work to specific technologies or domains. Furthermore, to the best of our knowledge, this paper is the first one that presents a RR to vulnerability for ES SW and that focuses on emerged evidences to report the results.

---

[3] Voyant tool: https://voyant-tools.org, online 2023.

Table 2. RR Findings

RQ1: *What are the types of ES considered in existing literature studies?*
Involved ES architecture: ES - "not specified" (21), ES to implement IoT systems (5), Industrial ES (3), ES for connected devices (2), Cyber-Physical Systems for IoT (2), Legacy ES devices (1), ES for robotic autonomous systems (1), ES for critical systems (1), Cyber-Physical Systems (1), Computer (1), EE for Vehicular E/E architecture (1), ES for Smart Grid (1), specific ES: DMA input device (1), RISC-V-based ES (1), ARM-based ES (1), PLC (1), System-on-Chip (1)
Type of ES based on functional requirements: Network/connected ES (17), Standalone ES (9), Real-time ES (9), and Mobile ES (2)
Type of ES based on micro-controller: Complex ES (17), Small ES (8), and Medium ES (6)
Application domain: Automotive (8), Electric power management (3), Autonomous vehicle (1) Aviation, Aerospace, Aircraft (7), Transportation (3), electric charging system (2), healthcare (2), LTE/5/6G communication (2), Security (2), Industrial control systems - e.g., Nuclear systems, Air conditioning control systems (2), System automation (2), Intelligence (1), Localization (1), Manufacturing (1), Network devices (1), Printer devices (1), Reconnaissance and surveillance (1), Rovers (1), Smart grid (1), Space (1)
RQ2: *What are the studied vulnerability management phases?*
Vulnerability mgmt. phase: Discovery/ detection (22), Assessment (11), Analysis (10), Exploitation (9), Prevention (7), Fixing (4), Managing (2)
Attack target: SW (26), Devices (11), COM (8), HD (6)
[t]5*Attack target: detail: Device software update (1), software for connected devices (6), e.g., smartcard, connected IoT, printer, smartphone, software code - "generic" (6), software implementing security algorithm and protocols (2), firmware software (2), e.g., control algorithms, legacy software, software for memory management, software for device/ECU, generated software code (1), software for communication protocols (6), e.g., for robots, vehicle networks, PLCs, devices, real-time operating system (1), software code variants (1), software for industrial components (1), software for Cyber-physical systems - "generic" (2), the software supply chain for ES (1), web interfaces for ES (1)
Affected HD device: ES architecture, e.g., micro, vehicle E/E, autonomous systems, smart grid, aerospace (7), Connected/Network devices (6), e.g., routers, DSL/cable modems, VoIP phones, IP/ CCTV cameras, Individual ECU, e.g., vehicle, aerospace (4), PLC-based (1), printers (1), RISC-V-based ES (3), smartcard (1), smartphone (2), ARM architecture and devices (3), DMA/ memory-access-based peripherals (3), ES processors with memory access (3), Cyber-Physical Systems 'generic' (1), FPGA-based board (2)
SW vulnerability: Buffer overflow (11), Memory corruption vulnerabilities (5), e.g., Buffer-related overflows, Stack and heap overflows, Memory leak, Segmentation fault, Misconfiguration (1), Software errors or transient faults, e.g., Electronic noise (4), Web-related vulnerabilities: SQL injection, XSS, Cross-site request forgery, Command injection (4) Remote command injection (3), Race conditions (2), Authentication (2), Buffer over-read (2), Buffer underflow (2), Communication-based vulnerabilities, e.g., interface/APIs (2), design vulnerability (2), Insecure data input (2), String format vulnerability (2), Buffer overflow, Variants based on jumps via return address changes (1), Integer overflow (1), Vulnerable update mechanism (1), The vulnerability in module dependency management (1)
Type of the attack: (D)DoS (7), (Timing) Side-channel attacks (7), Code injection (5), Data spoofing (4), False data injection (4), Power analysis attack (4), Data sniffing (3), Replay attack (3), Unauthorized changes/access (3), Data corruption (2), Jamming (2), malware injection (2), MitM (2), Software supply chain attacks (2), Session hijacking (2), Clock glitching attack (1), Dallas attack (1), Model backdoor injections (1), Rowhammer attack (1)
Attack's impact: Interruption of service (7), Sensitive data leakage (4), Remote code execution (3), Illegitimate access (2)
RQ3: *What are the proposed solutions to address (discover, fix etc.) vulnerabilities in ES SW?*
Goal: Present a new approach/technique (44), report validation experiments (4), SOTA review (2)
Goal description: Collocates graphs (e.g., Fig. 1) built by starting from the one-sentence paper's goal descriptions grouped for vulnerability management phase
Object: SW binary (17), Executable SW (11), SW source code (6), traces and logs (4), e.g., Execution traces, Communications, Signal traces, including Memory usage profile, and other SW artifacts (3), SW design and model (2)
Object: detail: Programming language: C/C++ (5). Binary code, e.g., Encrypted code (2), Docker images and third-party software (2), binary bytecode (1). Execution traces: Traces of communication (2), Traces of execution (2), Traces of memory usage profile (1), Traces of power signals (1), Network services (1), Vehicular architecture design (1)
Investigated method: Static (11), Dynamic (8), Hybrid: static + dynamic (8), Manual (6), Hybrid: manual + dynamic (4), Machine Learning (ML) (4) Hybrid: dynamic + ML (2), Hybrid: simulation + ML (1), Hybrid: static + simulation (1)
Investigate method: detail: Dynamic: Fuzzing (8), testing (4), Symbolic execution (3), Taint analysis (1), Fuzzing and memory check (1). Manual: Design-time analysis (7). Static: Symbolic execution (4), Compiler-based (3), Abstract interpretation (2), Data flow (1), Code differentiation (1), Dependency analysis (1). ML: DeepLearning (2), DeepLearning and kernel methods (1), Active inference (1)

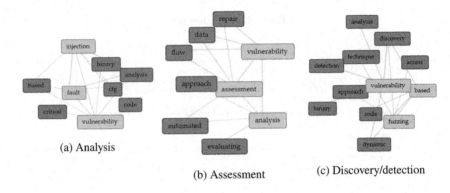

(a) Analysis

(b) Assessment

(c) Discovery/detection

Fig. 1. Examples of collocates graphs for goal descriptions

5   Final Remarks

Our RR is the starting point to identify existing methods for vulnerabilities management in ES SW, as well as for identifying new research areas. We observed that: (i) modern ESs for autonomous vehicles and robots have largely attracted the attention, even if most works did not clearly focus on specific ES types; (ii) new methods for vulnerability discovering are often presented, while only a few work exists for method assessment; (iii) such new methods frequently target vulnerabilities related to memory management (buffer overflow) and (iv) apply fuzz testing to binary and executable ES SW.

References

1. Braun, V., Clarke, V.: Using thematic analysis in psychology. Qual. Res. Psychol. **3**(2), 77–101 (2006)
2. Cartaxo, B., Pinto, G., Soares, S.: Rapid reviews in software engineering. In: Contemporary Empirical Methods in Software Engineering, pp. 357–384. Springer, Cham (2020). https://doi.org/10.1007/978-3-030-32489-6_13
3. Dessiatnikoff, A., Deswarte, Y., Alata, E., Nicomette, V.: Potential attacks on onboard aerospace systems. IEEE Secur. Priv. **10**(4), 71–74 (2012)
4. Eceiza, M., Flores, J.L., Iturbe, M.: Fuzzing the internet of things: a review on the techniques and challenges for efficient vulnerability discovery in embedded systems. IEEE Internet Things J. **8**(13), 10390–10411 (2021)
5. Feng, X., Zhu, X., Han, Q.-L., Zhou, W., Wen, S., Xiang, Y.: Detecting vulnerability on IoT device firmware: a survey. IEEE/CAA J. Automatica Sin. **10**(1), 25–41 (2023). https://doi.org/10.1109/JAS.2022.105860
6. Fournaris, A.P., Pocero Fraile, L., Koufopavlou, O.: Exploiting hardware vulnerabilities to attack embedded system devices: a survey of potent microarchitectural attacks. Electron. **6**(3) (2017). ISSN 2079-9292
7. Papp, D., Ma, Z., Buttyan, L.: Embedded systems security: threats, vulnerabilities, and attack taxonomy, pp. 145–152. IEEE, Turkey (2015)

8. Qasem, A., Shirani, P., Debbabi, M., Wang, L., Lebel, B., Agba, B.L.: Automatic vulnerability detection in embedded devices and firmware: survey and layered taxonomies. ACM Comput. Surv. **54**(2) (2021). https://doi.org/10.1145/3432893. ISSN 0360-0300

9. Schotten, M., M'hamed., E., Meester, W., Steiginga, S., Ross, C.: A Brief History of Scopus: The World's Largest Abstract and Citation Database of Scientific Literature, pp. 31–58. CRC Press, January 2017

10. Speckemeier, C., Niemann, A., Wasem, J., Buchberger, B., Neusser, S.: Methodological guidance for rapid reviews in healthcare: a scoping review. Res. Synth. Methods **13**(4), 394–404 (2022)

Social Sustainability Approaches for Software Development: A Systematic Literature Review

Ana Carolina Moises de Souza[✉], Daniela Soares Cruzes, Letizia Jaccheri, and John Krogstie

Norwegian University of Science and Technology, 7491 Trondheim, Norway
{ana.c.m.de.souza,daniela.s.cruzes,letizia.jaccheri,
john.krogstie}@ntnu.no

Abstract. Social aspects in software sustainability refer to the impact of the software on the broader social and societal context. These aspects involve considerations such as accessibility, equity, inclusion, diversity, ethical and human values. While achieving software sustainability requires developers to embrace approaches that support the three dimensions of sustainability, there remains a lack of concrete approaches to address social aspects during software development. This literature review aims to facilitate the integration of social aspects into the software development process by identifying approaches related to social sustainability in software engineering. We extracted and analyzed data from 19 studies through thematic syntheses. The results of our analysis provide a list of recommended tools and practices to support social aspects and attain software sustainability goals. By incorporating these approaches into software development, we ensure that the software is not only technically sustainable but also socially responsible from a human perspective.

Keywords: Social Sustainability · Social Aspects · Agile Software Development · Software Sustainability · Sustainable Software

1 Introduction

Sustainability is an important area of concern in modern software engineering due to the significant environmental and social consequences resulting from the increasing use of technology. Since 1987, sustainable development has been under discussion, and much has been done in society to preserve the same resources we have today for future generations [5]. This definition of sustainability encompasses three interrelated dimensions: economic, social, and environmental. Littig and Grießler [11] argue that all three dimensions of sustainability should be equally considered: "Human needs cannot be sufficiently met just by providing an ecologically stable and healthy environment, but that - if a society is indeed committed to sustainability - the equally legitimate social and cultural needs

R. Kadgien et al. (Eds.): PROFES 2023, LNCS 14483, pp. 478–494, 2024.
https://doi.org/10.1007/978-3-031-49266-2_33

ought to be taken care of as well. Economic, social, and cultural conditions, efforts, and values are deemed to be resources that also need to be preserved for future generations." In software engineering and other sectors, there has been a focus on the environmental dimension of sustainability, evidenced by [13,16]. However, there is a growing need to investigate the social dimension, combined with the individual and human dimensions, to achieve sustainability in software engineering [6,20,23].

Social sustainability can be achieved when software is designed to promote social aspects of the community, such as equality, diversity, community building, and a sense of belonging [4,20,32]. These aspects also relate to individuals' aspirations for an equal society [4]. But the question still remains: how can we develop software to minimize negative societal impacts? To address this question, we aim to review the existing literature on software development and social sustainability to identify tools, approaches, or methods that software developers can use to integrate social sustainability into their software development practices.

Moreover, we are motivated by the assumption that some organizations struggle to apply social sustainability principles effectively in the context of software development [6]. With this context in mind, we have followed SLR guidelines to identify relevant studies on social sustainability approaches in software development. After executing the SLR guidelines [18], we selected 19 out of 5858 papers from the search results. We extracted information, such as the type of study, sustainability dimensions, and empirical validation, from the selected papers. After the data extraction, we conducted a data synthesis using thematic analysis. The approaches contributing to social sustainability were categorized into social aspects and goals. Our contribution demonstrates how these approaches, tools, and practices can help integrate social sustainability concerns into software development. This paper is organized as follows: Sect. 2 introduces our theoretical framework and related work in software sustainability. Section 3 outlines our systematic literature review protocol. Section 4 presents the SLR findings and addresses each question. Section 5 discusses social aspects of software engineering, along with limitations, opportunities, and future work. Finally, Sect. 6 summarizes our study.

2 Background

This section provides an overview of the scoping, mapping, or systematic literature reviews we selected during the exploratory phase and through our search string as related work. We will also describe the theoretical framework that supported our higher themes and guided our synthesis analysis.

2.1 Reviews in Software Sustainability

While numerous studies have been conducted in the field of sustainable software engineering, there is a relative lack of focus on social sustainability and the software development process. Secondary studies collectively emphasize the importance of considering both product and process sustainability, highlight the neglect of social aspects in software sustainability, and call for developing tools and frameworks that address social dimensions alongside environmental and economic considerations. In Table 1, we summarized each secondary paper's outcome and the gap they identified in their study. These identified gaps formed the basis for defining the research questions in our systematic literature review.

Table 1. Recent Reviews on Software Sustainability

Authors	Outcome	Identified Gap in the Studies
McGuire, S. et al. [21]	A multisystemic nature of sustainability is suggested considering micro and macro levels of each sustainability dimension	Lack of empirical validation and experiments in social sustainability
Swacha, J. [30]	Reference and evaluation models used to address software sustainability	Lack of verification or validation of the models
Gustavsson, J. et al. [14]	Sustainability should be addressed in a holistic manner and should consider social aspects during software development	Need for tools to assist in social sustainability adoption
Khalifeh, A. et al. [17]	A framework for incorporating economic considerations, environmental concerns, and social responsibilities into software product projects	Incorporation of social sustainability into software projects
Alharthi, A.D. et al. [3]	Meta-requirements for addressing sustainability in e-Learning systems	Diversify the social sustainability aspects of a product

2.2 Theoretical Framework on Social Sustainability

Interdisciplinary research related to society, human values, and sustainability is a traditional combination in software engineering, as it reflects the growing recognition of the need for a more holistic approach to software development and its impact on the world [11,24]. Incorporating perspectives from fields such as sociology, psychology, and philosophy is essential for understanding the societal impact of software systems and the ethical implications of their development and use [1,22]. Figure 1 shows the perspectives of society towards social sustainability inspired by [22] and adapted from Ajmal et al. [1]. The External Societal Perspectives contribute to the definition of social sustainability.

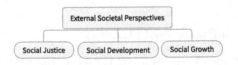

Fig. 1. Theoretical Framework adapted from [1]

Social Growth refers to an individual's ability to thrive in society through community engagement, autonomy in decision-making, and contributing to the well-being of others [1]. In our study, we incorporate human and individual dimensions within the concept of Social Growth, which we call "Personal Growth."

Social Development involves building a community that promotes the well-being of its members. It is a collective responsibility shared by government, companies, agencies, and individuals [1]. Social Development encompasses creating supportive policies and programs, providing resources for individual social development, and actively participating in community initiatives for sustainable development [27].

Social Justice is based on the principle that everyone should have equal access to rights and opportunities, regardless of their background [1]. Achieving social justice requires addressing aspects such as equality, diversity, trust, fairness, transparency, and security. The Covid-19 pandemic has emphasized the need for innovative approaches in various sectors to safeguard sustainability and human security [31].

3   Review Method

The Systematic Literature Review (SLR) [18] was performed to investigate studies addressing social aspects during software development. To achieve this goal, we addressed three research questions that range from broad to specific, aligned with the gaps presented in Table 1:

- RQ1 - What are the characteristics of the literature addressing social sustainability in software development?
- RQ2 - How do the proposed support tools address social aspects in software engineering?
- RQ3 - How can social sustainability be concretely addressed in software development practice?

3.1   Studies Selection

In this study, the search string focused on sustainability and its relationship with software development. The term 'sustainability' was intentionally chosen to avoid narrowing or refining the dimensions, allowing for the selection of various dimensions. The refinement of the social dimension occurred after a thorough review of the literature. It is worth mentioning that some authors introduced new dimensions, such as 'human', which is related to the social aspect. Therefore, specifying social in the search string would remove the papers that covered related dimensions. To ensure a comprehensive range of results, we tested multiple versions of the search string and refined it through several rounds of testing. Eventually, we settled on the current search string as the most appropriate and relevant for our study:

> ((Abstract="sustainable software" OR Abstract=sustainability)
> AND
> (Any field=software OR Any field=mobile))

To ensure the validity and reliability of our search results, we conducted the search using the Web of Science database, which covers a wide range of well-known scientific databases. Our search strategy allowed us to collect relevant data to address the research questions of our study, resulting in a total of 5858 papers that needed to be screened. The filtering process involved three main activities, as shown in Fig. 2. Firstly, we applied a search string and conducted a title reading to exclude duplicates and papers unrelated to software engineering based on the defined exclusion criteria. Secondly, we performed an abstract reading to identify papers that addressed social aspects of software engineering and also applied exclusion criteria, such as non-peer-reviewed papers, papers under six pages, and those not related to software engineering. The final activity involved a full reading of the selected papers to refine our results and identify those that proposed activities, practices, guidelines, frameworks, or models to address social sustainability in software development. After completing the selection phase, we proceeded to synthesize and assess the quality of the studies from the chosen papers.

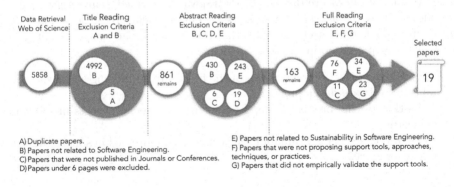

A) Duplicate papers.
B) Papers not related to Software Engineering.
C) Papers that were not published in Journals or Conferences.
D) Papers under 6 pages were excluded.

E) Papers not related to Sustainability in Software Engineering.
F) Papers that were not proposing support tools, approaches, techniques, or practices.
G) Papers that did not empirically validate the support tools.

Fig. 2. Filtering steps, exclusion criteria and results numbering.

3.2   Data Extraction, Quality Assessment and Data Synthesis

A protocol was developed to identify the answers to the questions and better understand the chosen studies. Table 2 shows the extracted information proposed in the studies and discussed in the results Sect. 4. Each study was assessed based on the criteria derived from two sources: Dybå and Dingsøyr [10] and Hernandez et al. [15]. To help assess the quality of the studies, we created a set of questions. The answer for each question was either Yes (1) or No (0). The sum of the answers provides the quality score of the studies (see Fig. 3). This score helps identify a research's relevance, rigor, and credibility. Thematic synthesis was performed

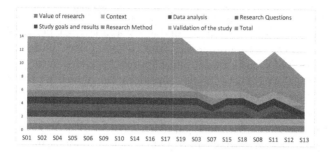

Fig. 3. Quality Assessment Results.

to synthesize the findings. In this method, researchers typically read through the data and identify recurring ideas, concepts, or themes [8]. These themes are then grouped together into higher-order categories or themes that capture the overall essence of the data. Four steps were performed during data synthesis in the MAXQDA tool (https://www.maxqda.com/literature-review): 1) Identified and coded the keywords related to social aspects (e.g. equality, diversity, etc.) explicitly in the text; 2) Selected and synthesized from the text the relevant practices that connected with the social aspects; 3) Categorized the practices-related codes into software life cycle phases or organizational practices; and 4) Grouped these codes into higher themes (social aspects) based on the theoretical framework. To better visualize the connections between social aspects, social goals, software life cycle phases, and practices, we created three maps for each social dimension, which are available in this research package.

4   Results

In this study, we identified practices in 19 papers that proposed support tools to address sustainability in software. The studies are mostly published at conferences resulting in 12 papers. Only 7 papers were published in Journal. Further results are discussed in the following sections.

4.1   RQ 1 - Social Sustainability Studies in Software Development

To answer this question, we will go through the data extraction protocol and explain how we extracted and summarized the findings of studies that address social sustainability. The extracted data and the corresponding number of findings are presented in Table 2. The **Business Domain** information was extracted from the papers to determine the applicability of the approaches proposed in the studies based on the specific context. 15 out of 19 papers did not specify a particular business domain and conducted their studies across various domains. The **Software Life Cycle** was collected to identify which phases of the software development life cycle were addressed by studies. The studies primarily focused on the Software Requirements (10 out of 19), with no coverage of other areas

such as construction, maintenance, and testing. Within the software requirements domain, there is a clear focus on sustainability as it pertains to the purpose of the software, its functionalities, and the associated business constraints.
The incorporation of social sustainability approaches helps in the development of
software that takes social aspects into consideration right from the requirements
stage. The **Study Type** was extracted to understand the research method and
its empirical validation. Various study types were identified, in which case studies research method was the most popular (3 out of 19). A case study involves
analysis of a particular situation to gain a better understanding of complex

Table 2. Results of the extracted data from the studies.

Data Extraction	S01	S02	S03	S04	S05	S06	S07	S08	S09	S10	S11	S12	S13	S14	S15	S16	S17	S18	S19	#
Business Domain																				
Not specified	•	•	•	•	•	•	•	•		•	•	•	•	•		•			•	15
Health															•		•			2
Energy																		•		1
OSS							•													1
Phase of the Software Life Cycle (SLC)																				
Requirements	•		•	•					•	•	•	•	•		•				•	10
Overall SLC								•						•		•	•	•		5
Design					•	•														2
Not specified		•					•													2
Study Type																				
Case study				•								•							•	3
Documental														•	•					2
Action Research						•											•			2
Delphi									•			•								2
Design Science									•	•										2
Survey	•				•															2
Pilot Study			•											•						2
Experience Report																	•			1
Experiment																•				1
Grounded theory		•																		1
Mixed Methods													•							1
Sustainability Dimensions																				
Social	•	•	•	•	•	•	•	•	•	•	•	•		•	•	•	•	•	•	18
Environmental		•	•	•	•	•		•	•	•		•	•	•			•		•	13
Technical	•	•	•	•	•	•		•	•	•		•	•	•					•	13
Economic		•	•	•	•			•	•	•		•	•				•		•	12
Individual									•	•		•		•					•	5
Human														•						1
Purpose														•						1
Legal														•						1
Integrative														•						1
Design-aesthetics														•						1
Types of support tool																				
Models		•	•	•	•						•					•		•	•	8
Awareness							•	•			•			•						3
Maps						•											•			2
Catalog	•														•					2
Value Pattern												•	•							2
Reports							•							•						2
Empirical validation																				
Industry		•		•	•	•	•	•			•	•		•	•	•	•	•	•	14
Pilot validated			•										•							2
Academic	•							•	•											3

phenomena. On the **Sustainability Dimensions**, we observed that studies on software engineering and sustainability often encompass multiple dimensions of sustainability. 5 out of 19 studies exclusively investigated the social dimension. The category of **Support Tool Type** was created to group studies that present tools with similar or related functionalities. The categorization was based on how the tools were described in the studies. When a clear definition was not provided, we categorized the tools ourselves. In this category, 8 out of 19 papers were classified as models. More detail about the tools description and related studies is explained in the results Sect. 4 for RQ2. The **Empirical Validation** was performed in the industrial setting in 14 of the studies, providing valuable real-world perspectives from developers and companies.

4.2 RQ2 - Proposed Tools to Address Social Sustainability

The tools identified in this SLR consist of various resources such as practices, questions, checklists, visualization tools, diagrams, and frameworks that assist developers in understanding, implementing, discussing, or testing sustainability dimensions. We grouped the tools into six main types of tools (Table 3): awareness, catalog, maps, models, values patterns, and reports.

Models simplify complex real-world concepts and can be used for structured decision-making and implementing new concepts within existing processes. The tools categorized as "models" describe guidelines for considering sustainability in the software development phases.

- **How**: Models were divided into organizational models S02, S018 and product-oriented model S03, S04, S05, S06, S16 S19. Organizational models analyze the overall influence of the organization on sustainability, including how system purchases align with sustainability and business strategy. Product-oriented models focus on the product's impact on sustainability, addressing requirements, development stages, and involving stakeholders. Sustainability is considered a quality aspect of the software in some of these models, mapping it to existing software engineering quality attributes.
- **Similarities**: One commonality is that all the tools categorized into models intentionally addressed social aspects in their proposals.
- **Differences**: S02 outlines the dimensions, practices, and stakeholders related to social sustainability in software product lines. S018 is designed to support decisions in procurement systems. S03 focuses on defining a software sustainability model for software-intensive systems and supporting decision-making tasks such as prioritizing requirements and analyzing trade-offs. S04, S05, S06, propose sustainability models for quality requirements prioritization and software sustainability assessment. It covers 17 qualities from ISO/IEC 25010:2011. S16 proposes a model for a rapid prototyping solution that involves older adults as participants in the process. S19 maps stakeholder profiles onto sustainability dimensions.

In Table 3, we summarized the remaining support tools due to space limitations in this paper. These tools' focus and key features were extracted from the selected studies.

Table 3. Summary of Support Tools for Social Sustainability

Type	Focus...	Key Features	Studies
Awareness	On creating awareness towards the social aspects of a software product	Can be utilized during the conceptual phase and for continuous review of software requirements	S09, S10, S13
Catalog	On a pre-defined and ready-to-use catalog for software requirements addressing sustainability dimensions	Useful for eliciting software requirements and reviewing business needs	S01 S15
Maps	On mapping existing software engineering practices into sustainability and human values	Map software engineering best practices to integrate sustainability goals into a product. Map software requirements into human values	S08 S17
Models	On providing a structure to simplify complex concepts	Approaches to achieving sustainability at the organizational level or product level	S02, S03, S04, S05, S06, S16, S19
Reports	On giving guidance on how and what information to report	Sustainability indicators measure initiatives and are reported in Corporate Social Responsibilities reports	S07 S14
Value Patterns	On describing common themes in language related to social aspects. Patterns consist of values, activities, and indicators	Help software developers understand patterns and relationships of social aspects	S11 S12

While we have identified promising tools for addressing social sustainability in software development in this SLR, three tools stand out due to their significant practical contributions. One such tool is the Sustainability Quality Model S04, S05, and S06. These studies incorporated feedback from sustainability experts and software developers, enhancing the model's credibility. Another noteworthy tool is the Sustainability Awareness Framework S09 and S010, which falls under the awareness support tool type. The selected studies have demonstrated the validation and applicability of this framework in the industry. The Sustainability Catalog Webtool S01 is a tool that facilitates the visualization and relationship between different dimensions of sustainability, thus categorized as a catalog. Therefore the contribution of RQ2 is to recommend support tools that can assist developers and organizations in integrating social sustainability practices into their software development process.

4.3   RQ3 - Social Sustainability in Software Engineering

The investigation for this question was conducted to identify the software development practices that impact social sustainability by examining primary studies, coding information for social connections, and aligning with the theoretical framework described in Sect. 2. It was identified that social sustainability in software engineering focuses on the social aspects related to development, justice, and personal growth. These social aspects encompass social goals such as equality, human rights, security, etc. (see Fig. 4). For each goal, we summarized a practice identified in the studies. These synthesized practices are related to human factors that serve as motivators to address social sustainability in software development.

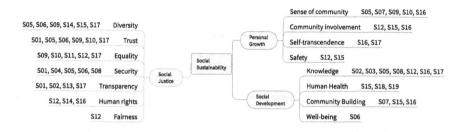

Fig. 4. Social Goals identified in the studies based on the Theoretical Framework.

Social Justice refers to social goals of diversity, trust, equality, security, transparency, human rights and fairness.

Diversity is important for software products and agile teams [2,19]. Practices like designing accessible software (S05 S06) and considering cultural diversity (S15) promote inclusion. In S14, organizations could address the gender gap in software engineering, exploring reasons and proposing initiatives to increase women's participation in computer science. Evaluating software's impact on perception and discriminatory behavior, S09 and involving diverse stakeholders help mitigate negative effects on diversity S17.

Trust is crucial in society, and designing software that instills confidence and meets stakeholders' expectations promotes trust S05, S06. Assessing the software's impact on trust and mitigating potential issues are important practices S09 S10. Security requirements can also enhance trust S01. S17 addresses identifying security options that users can rely on to establish trust.

Equality ensures equal opportunities for individuals to maximize their potential in life and talents [12]. In Information Communication Technology (ICT), we can promote equal access to digital services, infrastructure, hardware, and software. As such, software should provide access to its resources regardless of personal characteristics or beliefs. S05 proposes that during the software requirements, identifying inclusive requirements and implementing accessibility features contributes to addressing equality. In S09 S10, the software's impact on bias and inequality should be assessed throughout development. S11 S12 mentioned that Stakeholders' profiles should be considered to ensure equal opportunities. S17 identifies that using a common language promotes equal participation and collaboration among project stakeholders. Respecting diverse attributes, identities, and capabilities contributes to an equal society.

Software *Security* encompasses technical and social aspects of sustainability. One practice recommended in S08 is to design software that enables quick and easy security updates. The social dimension of security involves preserving user information, identity, privacy, and integrity, with confidentiality, authenticity, accountability, and integrity emphasized in S01, S04, S05 and S06. Considering these aspects during software requirements ensures they are prioritized alongside other requirements.

Transparency empowers end-users, builds trust, and enables informed decision-making. In S01 and S02, designing software that provides timely feedback and guides users might enhance transparency. Developing software following regulatory standards with legal backing also increases transparency S13. Transparency can be achieved by ensuring data ownership, transparent data handling, and storage and adopting values-conscious practices for personal data S17.

Human rights, regardless of race or religion, should be respected in software design S16. Identifying and addressing requirements that uphold human rights prevent violations S12. In S14, organizational actions, such as non-discrimination policies, contribute to a safe workplace.

Fairness means treating individuals impartially and equitably, without discrimination or favoritism based on arbitrary factors [25]. In software requirements engineering, a practice in S12 involves identifying software needs through a fair selection of stakeholders without favoritism.

Social Development refers to social goals of knowledge, human health, community building, and well-being.

Knowledge is promoted by access to educational systems. S16 discussed ICT Literacy, which enhances people's knowledge. It helps people overcome their fear of technology and effectively use the software. In S08, participatory design aligns with the goal of designing easy-to-learn and user-friendly software. In the studies S02, S05 and S17, organizations should align technical and social skills to create a shared purpose for software under development. S12 describes the understanding of how technology is accepted and can help developers create accessible functionalities. S03 highlighted a practice to identify stakeholders knowledgeable about sustainability during the software requirements.

Human health refers to the condition of an individual's physical, mental, and social state. S15 indicated designing solutions that promote healthy lifestyles and offer predefined sustainability-related requirements applicable across various domains. According to S18, software should prioritize end-user health and avoid causing harm. S19 provides a stakeholder list for sustainability, including advocates for human health.

Community Building is primarily addressed in open-source communities. In S07, reporting the quality of the code and offering training to the community can be adopted by organizations. S15 proposed implementing solutions that promote social solidarity and are related to community building. S16 recommended promoting inter-generational interaction within software development teams to address bias and foster innovative solutions.

Well-being refers to optimal physical, mental, and emotional health and happiness. S06 revealed that software helps users achieve their goals and can reduce stress and frustration. Adopting this practice in projects from a software design perspective can address wellness concerns.

Personal Growth: refers to social goals of a sense of community, community involvement, self-transcendence, and safety.

Sense of Community refers to the individual's concern regarding the potential negative consequences of software on society. In S5, S6 one of the quality attributes proposed is freedom from risk to mitigate the negative impacts on the environment that can also impact the social dimension. In S07, users can rank their experiences when using a software or service. S09 S10 introduced a question to identify how the system affects a person's sense of belonging. S016 proposed inviting potential users to co-design solutions.

Community Involvement refers to how the software can motivate individuals to participate in the community. S12 discussed the indicators to measure community participation, such as social interaction activities, volunteer work, and decision-making, which help establish social ties and networks. S15 emphasized the importance of social interaction between users and developers as a practice that facilitates personal growth. S16 proposed the integration of individuals into agile processes, enabling their participation throughout the entire lifecycle.

Self-transcendence in human values theory refers to surpassing individual needs and desires to engage in actions that benefit others and the larger community [26]. In S16, practicing self-transcendence can involve assisting older adults in becoming familiar with technology and encouraging their feedback on solutions. Self-transcendence can also be linked to collaborative work practices. S17 recognized the importance of treating stakeholders as peers and fostering non-hierarchical communication to promote harmonious interactions between developers and stakeholders.

Safety enables personal growth by focusing on prevention. From a software perspective, it entails creating requirements that protect end-users against crimes such as cyberattacks. S12 identified secure features to protect user property from crimes. S15 identified features that ensure user safety by respecting their privacy and preventing data breaches.

5 Discussion

This review emphasized the underexplored nature of social sustainability in software engineering and the lack of clear definitions and boundaries in the field [3,14,17]. The need for a consensus on the definition of social sustainability and the importance of establishing a common language that resonates with software developers are emphasized in the selected studies. To better handle this definition, we used a theoretical framework to understand social sustainability through the lens of social science.

Throughout the review, we noticed that the studies either focused on one specific social goal or did not investigate a selected one. Therefore, a more holistic approach to investigating social sustainability in software development is needed. By doing so, we can avoid situations where these goals may not be explicitly linked to social sustainability [7]. Moreover, this review identified social aspects and goals that trigger a topic to be investigated: corporate digital responsibility [7].

To gain insight into our study, we examined its implications through two lenses: socially sustainable software and societal issues and threats. While the software is designed to benefit society by solving real-world problems and facilitating tasks, people involved in software development often overlook the potential negative consequences of this software. Therefore, designing socially sustainable software requires knowledge of societal issues, threats, social aspects, and goals, thus encompassing social sustainability. A recent societal issue observed is: the negative impacts of Generative Pre-processed Transformers (GPTs) and the wider field of Artificial Intelligence (AI) [9]. Although the main focus of this discussion is not artificial intelligence per se, we acknowledge that when developing AI tools is necessary to adhere to the software engineering process. Best practices of software engineering cannot be dissociated from AI solutions development. Eventually, the social sustainability practices cannot be dissociated either.

In the search for concrete practices for the software development team, we highlight the following types of support tools as ready to be used: awareness, model and catalog. These support tools offer practical adoption, such as detailed guidelines, online resources, and plugins. For instance, the Sustainability Awareness Framework (S09, S10), classified as an awareness tool, provides online material with questionnaires templates and workshop facilitation guidance [29]. Anyhow, it is essential to acknowledge a general lack of empirical evidence regarding the impact of adopting these tools on the final product and the long-term effects of software on society. Likewise, continuous software development brings to light additional challenges inherent to modern non-functional aspects of software. A key aspect is prioritizing sustainability throughout the software development phases [28].

6   Conclusion

As we move forward to address social issues related to the impact of software on human life, we increasingly recognize the importance of practical and scientific research on socially sustainable software. As software and society evolve over time, what will be the impact of this software if it maintains the same functionalities without paying attention to human factors and societal behavior?

This research aimed to discover relevant approaches to address social issues during software development. The studies in this review have discussed social issues and threats in their papers and suggested addressing them in software development. We have provided a list of recommended support tools and practices to allow software developers to explore the societal issues and threats of the software under construction.

The practices and tools identified in this review require validation through experiments or focus groups with software developers to ensure the identified practices' practicality and effectiveness. Further validation and testing of the identified support tools provide insights into their efficacy, enabling informed decisions on their adoption in software development. Exploring how these tools assist in the decision-making process for adopting social sustainability practices offers an opportunity to incorporate social sustainability considerations into software development processes effectively.

As with other reviews, this research has limitations. The restriction to searching only on the Web of Science potentially overlooks relevant studies from other sources. Studies need to be done for further empirical validation of the synthesized practices' efficiency, usefulness, and contribution to improving social sustainability. There is a possible theoretical limitation since we did not explore practices that might be found in social science papers, limiting the investigation of social aspects in software engineering.

SLR References List

1. S01 - Albuquerque, D., et al.: A sustainability requirements catalog for the social and technical dimensions. In: Conceptual Modeling 40th Inter. Conf. (2021).
2. S02 - Chitchyan, et al.: Uncovering sustainability concerns in software product lines. Journal of Software: Evolution and Process (2017).
3. S03 - Condori-Fernandez, et al.: A nichesourcing framework applied to software sustainability requirements. In: 13th Inter. Conf. on Research Challenges in Information Science (2019).
4. S04 - Condori-Fernandez, N., Lago, P.: Towards a software sustainability-quality model: Insights from a multi-case study. In: 13th Inter. Conf. on Research Challenges in Information Science (2019).
5. S05 - Condori-Fernandez, N., Lago, P.: Characterizing the contribution of quality requirements to software sustainability. Journal of Systems and Software (2018).
6. S06 - Condori-Fernandez, N., et al.: An action research for improving the sustainability assessment framework instruments. Sustainability (2020).
7. S07 - de Magdaleno, M.I.A., Garcia-Garcia, J.: Sustainability and social responsibility reporting in open source software. Inter. Journal of the Commons (2015).
8. S08 - Poth, A., Nunweiler, E.: Develop sustainable software with a lean ISO 14001 setup facilitated by the EFIS® framework. In: Lean and Agile Software Development: 6th Inter. Conf. (2022).

9. S09 - Duboc, L., et al.: Do we really know what we are building? Raising awareness of potential sustainability effects of software systems in requirements engineering. In: 27th Inter. Requirements Engineering Conf. (2019).

10. S10 - Duboc, L., et al.: Requirements engineering for sustainability: an awareness framework for designing software systems for a better tomorrow. Requirements Engineering (2020).

11. S11 - Al Hinai, M., Chitchyan, R.: Building social sustainability into software: Case of equality. In: 2015 IEEE Fifth Inter. Workshop on Requirements Patterns (2015).

12. S12 - Al Hinai, M., Chitchyan, R.: Engineering requirements for social sustainability. In: ICT for Sustainability (2016).

13. S13 - Pham, Y.D., et al.: Towards a multi-dimensional representation for requirements of sustainable software. In: 28th Inter. Requirements Engineering Conf. (2020).

14. S14 - Calero, C., et al.: Is software sustainability considered in the csr of software industry? Inter. Journal of Sustainable Development and World Ecology (2019).

15. S15 - Ouhbi, S., et al.: Sustainability requirements for connected health applications. Journal of Software: Evolution and Process (2018).

16. S16 - Kopeć, W., et al.: Guidelines towards better participation of older adults in software development processes using a new spiral method and participatory approach. In: 11th Inter. Work. on Cooperative and Human Aspects of Software Engineering (2018).

17. S17 - Ferrario, M.A., et al.: Values-first SE: research principles in practice. In: Proceedings of the 38th Inter. Conf. on Software Engineering Companion. (2016).

18. S18 - Bomfim, C., et al.: Modelling sustainability in a procurement system: An experience report. In: 22nd Inter. Requirements Engineering Conf. (2014).

19. S19 - Penzenstadler, et al.: Who is the advocate? Stakeholders for sustainability. In: 2nd Inter. Workshop on Green and Sustainable Software (2013).

References

1. Ajmal, M.M., Khan, M., Hussain, M., Helo, P.: Conceptualizing and incorporating social sustainability in the business world. Int. J. Sustain. Dev. World Ecol. **25**(4), 327–339 (2018)

2. Albusays, K., et al.: The diversity crisis in software development. IEEE Softw. **38**(2), 19–25 (2021)

3. Alharthi, A.D., Spichkova, M., Hamilton, M.: Sustainability requirements for eLearning systems: a systematic literature review and analysis. Requir. Eng. **24**, 523–543 (2019)

4. Becker, C., et al.: The Karlskrona manifesto for sustainability design. arXiv preprint arXiv:1410.6968 (2014)

5. Brundtland, G.H.: Report of the world commission on environment and development: our common future (1987). https://sustainabledevelopment.un.org/content/documents/5987our-common-future.pdf. Accessed 18 June 2022

6. Calero, C., Guzmán, I.G.R.D., Moraga, M.A., García, F.: Is software sustainability considered in the CSR of software industry? J. Sustain. Dev. World Ecol. **26**(5). 439–459 (2019)
7. Cheng, C., Zhang, M.: Conceptualizing corporate digital responsibility: a digital technology development perspective. Sustainability **15**(3), 3 (2023)
8. Cruzes, D.S., Dyba, T.: Recommended steps for thematic synthesis in software engineering. In: 2011 International Symposium on Empirical Software Engineering and Measurement, pp. 275–284. IEEE (2011)
9. Dwivedi, Y.K.: Opinion paper: so what if ChatGPT wrote it? Multidisciplinary perspectives on opportunities, challenges and implications of generative conversational AI for research, practice and policy. Int. J. Inf. Manag. **71**, 1–63 (2023)
10. Dybå, T., Dingsøyr, T.: Empirical studies of agile software development: a systematic review. Inf. Softw. Technol. **50**(9–10), 833–859 (2008)
11. Eizenberg, E., Jabareen, Y.: Social sustainability: a new conceptual framework. Sustainability **9**(1), 68 (2017)
12. Government, U.K.: Equality act 2013 (2013). https://www.legislation.gov.uk/ukpga/2010/15/part/2. Accessed 2 June 2023
13. Guldner, A., Kern, E., Kreten, S., Naumann, S.: Criteria for sustainable software products: analyzing software, informing users, and politics. Softw. Sustain. 17–42 (2021)
14. Gustavsson, J.L., Penzenstadler, B.: Blinded by simplicity: locating the social dimension in software development process literature. In: 7th International Conference on ICT for Sustainability, pp. 116–127 (2020)
15. Hernandez Gonzalez, A., Calero, C., Perez Parra, D., Mancebo, J.: Approaching green bpm characterisation. J. Softw. Evol. Process **31**(2), e2145 (2019)
16. Higón, D.A., Gholami, R., Shirazi, F.: ICT and environmental sustainability: a global perspective. Telemat. Inform. **34**(4), 85–95 (2017)
17. Khalifeh, A., Farrell, P., Alrousan, M., Alwardat, S., Faisal, M.: Incorporating sustainability into software projects: a conceptual framework. Int. J. Manag. Projects Bus. **13**(6), 1339–1361 (2020)
18. Kitchenham, B., Charters, S.M.: Guidelines for performing systematic literature reviews in software engineering. EBSE Technical report EBSE-2007-01, Keele University and University of Durham (2007)
19. Kohl Silveira, K., Prikladnicki, R.: A systematic mapping study of diversity in software engineering: a perspective from the agile methodologies. In: 12th International Workshop on Cooperative and Human Aspects of Software Engineering (CHASE), pp. 7–10 (2019)
20. Lago, P., Koçak, S.A., Crnkovic, I., Penzenstadler, B.: Framing sustainability as a property of software quality. Commun. ACM **58**(10), 70–78 (2015)
21. McGuire, S., Shultz, E., Ayoola, B., Ralph, P.: Sustainability is stratified: toward a better theory of sustainable software engineering. arXiv preprint arXiv:2301.11129 (2023)
22. Partridge, E.: Social sustainability': a useful theoretical framework. In: Australasian Political Science Association Annual Conference, pp. 28–30 (2005)
23. Penzenstadler, B., Femmer, H.: A generic model for sustainability with process-and product-specific instances. In: The Workshop on Green in/by Software Engineering, pp. 3–8 (2013)
24. Perera, H., et al.: A study on the prevalence of human values in software engineering publications, 2015–2018. In: 42nd International Conference on Software Engineering, pp. 409–420 (2020)

25. Rescher, N.: Fairness, 1st edn. Routledge, Abingdon-on-Thames (2002)
26. Schwartz, S.H., et al.: An overview of the Schwartz theory of basic values. Online Read. Psychol. Cult. **2**(1), 2307–0919 (2012)
27. Sen, A., Anand, S.: Sustainable human development: concepts and priorities. UNDP United Nations Development Programme (1994)
28. de Souza, A.C.M., Cruzes, D.S., Jaccheri, L.: Sustainability-driven meetings as a way to incorporate sustainability into software development phases. In: 18th International Conference on Evaluation of Novel Approaches to Software Engineering, ENASE, pp. 597–604 (2023)
29. SUSO: Sustainability awareness framework (2022). https://www.suso.academy/en/sustainability-awareness-framework-susaf/. Accessed 23 June 2023
30. Swacha, J.: Models of sustainable software: a scoping review. Sustainability **14**(1), 1 (2022)
31. UNDP: Human development report 2021–22. UNDP United Nations Development Programme (2022). http://report.hdr.undp.org
32. Winkler, T.: Human values as the basis for sustainable software development. In: 2018 IEEE International Symposium on Technology and Society (ISTAS), pp. 37–42. IEEE (2018)

The Testing Hopscotch Model – Six Complementary Profiles Replacing the Perfect All-Round Tester

Torvald Mårtensson[1,2](✉) ⓘ and Kristian Sandahl[3] ⓘ

[1] Linköping University, Linköping, Sweden
torvald.martensson@liu.se
[2] Saab AB, Linköping, Sweden
torvald.martensson@saabgroup.com
[3] Linköping University, Linköping, Sweden
kristian.sandahl@liu.se

Abstract. Contrasting the idea of a team with all-round testers, the Testing Hopscotch model includes six complementary profiles, tailored for different types of testing. The model is based on 60 interviews and three focus groups with 22 participants. The validation of the Testing Hopscotch model included ten validation workshops with 58 participants from six companies developing large-scale and complex software systems. The validation showed how the model provided valuable insights and promoted good discussions, helping companies identify what they need to do in order to improve testing in each individual case. The results from the validation workshops were confirmed at a cross-company workshop with 33 participants from seven companies and six universities. Based on the diverse nature of the seven companies involved in the study, it is reasonable to expect that the Testing Hopscotch model is relevant to a large segment of the software industry at large. The validation of the Testing Hopscotch model showed that the model is novel, actionable and useful in practice, helping companies identify what they need to do to improve testing in their organization.

Keywords: Software Testing · Tester · Knowledge · Skills · Large-Scale

1 Introduction

Testing of a large-scale and complex software system spans from automated testing of software modules to testing of the complete system with end-user representatives. Test activities are generally conducted in a pipeline for continuous integration and delivery [1], including testing on different levels, different test techniques and in different types of test environments [2]. A multi-vocal literature review for our previous work [3] revealed that academic publications, books and popular web sites provide extensive lists of skills, knowledge and abilities that are described as important for testing of software systems, but generally do not include adaptations or tailoring for different types of test activities. As one example, Sánchez-Gordón et al. [4] presents 35 skills in seven categories: cognitive skills, communication skills, social skills, being open and adaptive to change, technical knowledge, testing skills, and knowledge of tools.

© The Author(s), under exclusive license to Springer Nature Switzerland AG 2024
R. Kadgien et al. (Eds.): PROFES 2023, LNCS 14483, pp. 495–510, 2024.
https://doi.org/10.1007/978-3-031-49266-2_34

As testing of large-scale and complex software systems is a demanding task, the idea of an all-round tester (mastering all types of testing) sets expectations that are difficult to meet for most engineers, leading to a higher risk that problems could be missed or overlooked. In the companies we work with as researchers, we have observed a need for complementary profiles that are more feasible to reach for engineers working with testing, and a model or a method that could help companies identify where and how they need to improve. Companies need a structured way to identify and visualize strengths and weaknesses in the organization with regard to different types of test activities, and a way to support engineers specializing in all necessary types of testing. Based on this, the topic of this research paper is to answer the following research question: *How can a model be constructed to support practitioners in the industry to optimize knowledge, skills and personality traits for the engineers working with testing of large-scale and complex software systems?*

The contribution of this paper is two-fold. First, it presents the validation of the Testing Hopscotch model, showing how the model is actionable and useful in practice, helping companies to improve testing in each individual case. Second, it presents results from interviews with teachers at six universities, revealing the gap between teaching at the universities and the needs described by practitioners in large-scale companies.

The remainder of this paper is organized as follows. In the next section we present the research method, including a description of the studied companies. Section 3 presents the validation of the Testing Hopscotch model, including a description of the model. Section 4 summarizes a series of interviews with teachers at six universities. The results from the cross-company workshop are described in Sect. 5, and threats to validity are discussed in Sect. 6. The paper is then concluded in Sect. 7.

2   Research Method

2.1   A Study in Three Steps

An overview of the steps in the study and the companies and universities involved in each step is presented in Fig. 1.

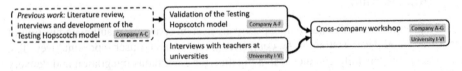

Fig. 1. An overview of the steps in the reported research study.

This study builds on our *previous work*, including a review of related literature, a series of interviews with practitioners, and the development of the Testing Hopscotch model [3]. The Testing Hopscotch model (further described in Sect. 3) was developed primarily based on thematic coding analysis [5] of the results from 60 interviews with participants from three large-scale companies (Company A-C) and confirmed in three focus groups [6] with a total of 22 participants from the same companies.

The *validation of the Testing Hopscotch model* included ten validations workshops with 58 participants from six companies (Company A-F) selected based on the guidelines from Robson and McCartan [5] and Sagoe [6]. Company D-F had not been involved in our previous work with the model, purposely selected in order to provide external validation and data triangulation [7].

This was followed by a series of *interviews with teachers at six universities* (University I–IV), conducted as semi-structured interviews [8] using an interview guide with pre-defined specific questions, and analyzed using thematic coding analysis [5].

The study was then concluded with a *cross-company workshop* with 33 participants from seven companies (Company A–G) and six universities (University (I–IV), with the purpose of confirming and complementing the findings from the previous steps, and discussing limitations of the findings in order to enable analytic generalization [7, 9].

2.2   A Study with Seven Companies and Six Universities

The study included seven large-scale industry companies (referred to as Company A–G) and six universities (referred to as University I–VI). The companies were purposely selected as suitable for the study, as they have similar characteristics, but at the same time operate in different industry segments: *Automotive products and services, Communications systems and services, Development, manufacturing and maintenance of pumps, Heavy trucks, buses, engines and services, Services and solutions for military defense, Transport solutions for commercial use,* and *Video surveillance cameras and systems.* The universities were purposely selected as they were located in the same geographical areas as the companies in the study.

Due to non-disclosure agreements, we do not reveal the identities of the companies or universities in the study. The companies included in the study are all multinational organizations with more than 4,000 employees. The size of the universities ranged from 6,000 to 50,000 students. All of the companies develop large-scale and complex software systems for products, which also include a significant amount of mechanical and electronic systems (including standard components as well as bespoke hardware).

3   Validation of the Testing Hopscotch Model

3.1   A Description of the Testing Hopscotch Model

Testing of a large-scale and complex software system requires many types of knowledge, skills and personality traits. Contrasting the idea of a team with all-round testers, the Testing Hopscotch model (Fig. 2) visualizes a fellowship of good testing with six complementary profiles, tailored for different types of test activities. The model is based on our previous work [3], with a series of interviews with 60 participants from three companies developing large-scale software systems (Company A-C), followed by three focus groups with 22 participants from the same three companies.

Our previous work showed that, according to practitioners in industry, the idea of a perfect all-round tester is not a feasible approach for engineers working with testing of large-scale software systems. In response to this, the Testing Hopscotch model proposes

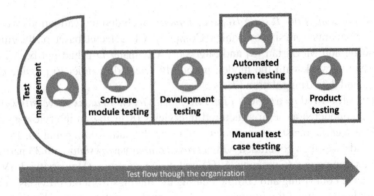

Fig. 2. The six complementary profiles in the Testing Hopscotch model

six complementary profiles, including the key characteristics for each of the six profiles, i.e. the knowledge, skills and personality traits considered to be most relevant for each profile:

- *The Software Module Testing profile*: Knows the structure of the software module, and how the software is designed (testing the software with focus on the software module). Good programming skills and knowledge and experience from software development (often a developer). Can use test techniques such as boundary value analysis or equivalence partitioning in a systematic way.
- *The Development Testing profile*: Well-informed on the status of the ongoing development in the team (testing continuously in parallel with development). Flexible and open-minded, adapting to changing plans and functional scope. User-focused and function-oriented, finding the right functions for the user (including complicated combinations).
- *The Manual Test Case Testing profile*: Testing for compliance with requirements or user scenarios, with an independent perspective. Optimizes planning of test suites and execution of test cases for efficiency. Structured and detail-oriented to cover all relevant corner cases, and to report relevant information from the test.
- *The Automated System Testing profile*: Knows how to automate, and how the test framework should interact with the system under test (scripting automated test cases and working with the framework). Good programming and scripting skills. Knows how to use tools for testing and test frameworks for automation, and how to design generic functions and components for test automation.
- *The Product Testing profile*: Domain expert with end-user focus, including performance, usability or other types of system-wide characteristics. Knows how to test like the end-user uses the product, and knows if a problem is a problem. Good knowledge of all functions and sub-systems, including limitations and weak spots.
- *The Test Management profile*: Planning and coordination of large test activities, involving the right individuals in planning, execution and analysis of test results. Can define a pipeline with different types of test activities, based on knowledge and experience with different test techniques and test environments. Knows how to improve and optimize testing in the organization.

In the analysis of the interview results, we also identified a set of characteristics (Fig. 3) described by the 60 interviewees as important for all types of testing, but with different meanings for each of the six profiles in the Testing Hopscotch model: To *know the system and its design/architecture* is important for all engineers working with testing, but means different things for different types of testing. For example, the design and architecture for the units and components is more interesting for the Software Module Testing profile, whereas someone in the Product Testing profile is interested in the architecture of the complete system. To *know how the system is used by the end-user* is primarily interesting if you test e.g. usability of the complete product, but is also important input for the unit tester (is the software for a web page or is it part of a critical flight control system). You must also be able to actually be *working with testing* and know relevant test techniques, tools and test environments, and communication and reporting: the Software Module Testing profile uses test techniques such as all pairs or domain border analysis, whereas the Development Testing profile can use exploratory testing. Similarly, tools and test environments are different for the different profiles. Communication and reporting are often more focused on statistics for particularly the Manual Test Case Testing profile, and more on a textual description for the Product Testing profile. The most important *soft skills* as described by the 60 interviewees are to be curious and want to learn, to be meticulous and well-organized, and to be critical and assertive. To be curious and want to learn was primarily described as important for the Development Testing profile, but also for the other profiles as everyone must be able to learn new test techniques and understand new types of products.

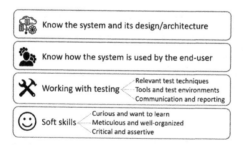

Fig. 3. Characteristics important for all types of testing (knowledge, skills and personality traits), but with different meanings for the six profiles in the Testing Hopscotch model

3.2 Using the Testing Hopscotch Model

In focus groups arranged with Company A–C (described in Sect. 2), the companies expressed a need for a model or a method that could help companies identify and visualize strengths and weaknesses in the organization with regards to different types of test activities, and how to support engineers specializing in all necessary types of testing. Based on input from the companies, a two-step process was developed to help companies identify what they need to do to improve testing in their organization.

In the first step, the participants at a workshop are asked to *evaluate the status of each of the Testing Hopscotch profiles* in their organization. Before the self-assessment, the participants are asked to define the context of their evaluation (e.g. their team or the whole company) and to agree on if all of the complementary profiles are within their area of responsibility. For example, if the participants evaluate their own development team, the team might not be responsible for testing of the complete product (and therefore the Product Testing profile would be excluded from the evaluation). For each of the remaining profiles, the participants were asked to respond (on a six-point Likert scale from Strongly Disagree to Strongly Agree) to the following statements:

- We have *good engineers like this profile* in our organization (e.g. team, department).
- We have an established *competence/career path* for this profile (e.g. expectations, competence levels, recommended courses, training programs).
- We have established *ways of working* and/or best practices for this profile (e.g. good test cases, relevant data).
- We have *test environments* supporting this profile (e.g. debugging tools, test worthiness for requirement closure).

The factors that are evaluated (competence/career path, ways of working and test environments) correspond to three of the four components of the Test System defined by Rex Black [10] (where the fourth component is the actual test cases). An example of a self-assessment using the complementary profiles in the Testing Hopscotch model is shown in Fig. 4. The self-assessment uses a six-point Likert scale from 1 to 6 (Strongly Disagree, Disagree, Somewhat Disagree, Somewhat Agree, Agree, Strongly Agree).

	Software Module Testing	Development Testing	Manual Test Case Testing	Automated System Testing	Product Testing	Test Management
Engineers We have good engineers like this profile in our organization	5	2	3	6	3	6
Competence path We have an established career/competence path for this profile	6	2	2	5	6	5
Ways of working We have established ways of working and/or best practices for this profile	4	3	5	5	5	5
Test environments We have test environments supporting this profile	4	4	4	6	4	-

Fig. 4. An example (not related to the companies participating in the study) of a self-assessment using the complementary profiles in the Testing Hopscotch model

In the second step, the participants in the workshop are asked to *prioritize the most important problem areas and identify improvement initiatives*. The participants are encouraged not to produce long lists of problems that need to be fixed, but instead to define between three and five improvement initiatives that they consider to be most urgent. To emphasize the areas with low ratings (1, 2 or 3) these are colored in red (visualized in Fig. 4). The visualization of the self-assessment should not be seen as a perfect template for defining the most important improvement initiatives, but instead as a catalyst for good discussions within the group of workshop participants.

3.3 Validation with Six Companies

To validate the Testing Hopscotch Model as actionable and useful in practice, a series of validation workshops were arranged. The workshops were purposely arranged to validate the model on different levels of integration in a large-scale system: single sub-system, a system with many sub-systems (but not a complete product) and a complete product (also in one case several products). Ten validation workshops were arranged with a total of 58 participants from six companies (Company A–F). Three of the companies (Company D–F) had not been involved in our previous work with the Testing Hopscotch model (external validation). All validation workshops are listed in Table 1, including the number of participants at each of the workshops.

Table 1. The ten validation workshops and the number of participants

Workshop	Context	Participants
#1	Company A, development team for a sub-system	8
#2	Company A, development team for a sub-system	8
#3	Company A, the company (many products)	7
#4	Company B, development team for a sub-system	3
#5	Company B, development team for a sub-system	3
#6	Company C, system with many sub-systems	4
#7	Company D, system with many sub-systems	7
#8	Company D, system with many subsystems	6
#9	Company E, a large project for one of the products	8
#10	Company F, the company (one of the products)	4
	Summary	58

The validation workshops lasted for two hours and followed the two-step process described in Sect. 3.2. The results from each workshop were strengths and weaknesses visualized in a matrix similar to the example in Fig. 4, and a list of improvement initiatives based on the problems emphasized in the visualization. Suggestions for improvement initiatives could be described as for example "We need more Product testers (some are really good but we need more)" or "Define competence path for the Test Case Testing profile".

At the workshops, one of the researchers focused on leading the workshop and the other focused on documenting how the participants used the model, and their comments and responses. In order to validate the model as actionable with the two-step process (and not depending on detailed guidance from the researchers) four of the workshops were held without the researchers present. For workshops #1, #2, #4 and #5 material were provided for the line manager leading each workshop and a follow-up meeting was held after the workshop to collect the same information as from the other workshops. At the follow-up meeting, we noted that workshop groups #1, #2 and #4 had spent more time on the assessment of the engineers, but that group #5 on the other hand had focused more on the assessment of how the organization supported the profiles with test environments etc. However, all four groups saw benefits from the assessment of strengths and weaknesses, exemplified by quotes like "using the model helped us to see where we have single-points or where we need to be better" (Company A) and "the model gave us a good overview of strengths and weaknesses in the group" (Company B). All four groups also described benefits from evaluating the support for the profiles, exemplified by quotes like "here we can see where we lack support from other parts of the organization" (Company B) or "this model is very good for discussions on a company-level, but also in each of the teams, to talk about career paths" (Company A).

Results from each of the validation workshops are not presented in this paper due to non-disclosure agreements with the companies. We are careful about jumping to conclusions based on the results from the validation workshops, but we believe two things can be seen as indications of problem areas important for all of the companies: All workshop groups described problems related to competence paths for at least two profiles, indicating that the lack of competence levels, recommended courses and training programs et cetera is seen as a problem in all of the participating companies. Similarly, all workshop groups described problems related to the Development Testing profile. This indicates that testing in parallel with development might be an undervalued type of testing: on one hand a large part of the test effort in most organizations, but on the other hand in the need for much more support and attention from management.

3.4 Evaluating the Model

As a final step of the validation workshops, the participants were asked to respond on a Likert scale (same as in Sect. 3.2) to the statements "The Testing Hopscotch model can help you find what you need to do in order to improve testing in our company" and "The Testing Hopscotch model generated useful discussions on how to improve testing in our company", and were encouraged to provide comments and improvement ideas. The participants were also asked if there was anything important that was not covered by the profiles in the model, and if there was anything else that should be changed. The model was well received by nine of the ten workshop groups, who responded either "Agree" or "Strongly Agree" to the first two questions.

The model was described as *actionable and helping the companies*, exemplified by quotes like "The matrix clarified what we as a company must need to do to improve our testing" (Company A), "It highlights the parts we need to improve" (Company F) and "We knew it was something there, this model helped us to articulate it" (Company E). The model was also described as *useful in practice* in the companies: "For sure, this could be useful!" (Company F), "We discussed if it should be mandatory for all teams in the company to use this model. We recommend the other teams to use the model. This was valuable." (Company A).

The workshop participants also described how the model worked as *a catalyst for discussions* at the workshop, for example "A simple model, but we had surprising discussions on questions that needed to be discussed" (Company E) or "Now we have more awareness of the Development Testing profile" (Company E). The model also provided *new perspectives*: "Ways of working for the Development Testing profile is missing – I did not know that" (Company D) and "I was surprised, this was news to me" (Company F). Other comments also support the completeness of the model, such as "A good model, it resonates across different types of test activities" (Company E) and "I like the Hopscotch model, it is testing structured in a good way" (Company B).

Two of the workshop groups wanted the Product Testing profile to be better described (which was particularly interesting as these two groups were among the ones using the model without the researchers present). One participant at another workshop asked for better definitions of what a module is, and what a system is. Three of the groups discussed how some of their engineers were a combination of the Development Testing profile and the Manual Test Case Testing profile. The names of the profiles in the model were discussed by five of the groups, especially the Development Testing profile. For this reason, this was also discussed with all participating companies at the cross-company workshop (described in Sect. 5.2). One of the workshop groups (#6) clearly did not like the model. The participants in group #6 described how "other things are more important for us", and how they focused on "coaching the teams" instead of individuals. One participant argued that focus should be on a general "tester mindset" instead of the profiles. However, we also noticed how all participants described in different ways how different competences, skills and types of personalities are important for different types of testing (which was also confirmed by the participants).

3.5 Summary and Discussion

In summary, we find that nine of the ten workshop groups described how the model provided valuable insights and promoted good discussions (Sect. 3.4), which showed in comments such as "I think it is a very interesting approach" (Company F) or "I now see that it is important to distinguish between these roles" (Company D). Ten validation workshops were arranged with a total of 58 participants from six companies (Sect. 3.3). The groups at the validation workshops used the two-step process (Sect. 3.2) to validate the model on different levels of integration and testing in a large-scale system. Feedback and comments from the workshop participants were used by the researchers to further improve the presentation of the model.

We find the responses from the tenth group (#6) to be a particularly interesting and relevant part of the validation of the Testing Hopscotch model, related to the problem with "the Agile blind spot" described by Jurgen Appelo [11]. Appelo describes how "Agile is great only when the team is great. [...] And that's what most Agile development methods assume. It's their blind spot. But the world isn't perfect, and neither are most employees. Therefore, management has to figure out how to address the blind spot". According to Appelo, if the members of the team do not have the knowledge and skills they need, "no amount of coaching can help a team like that to magically self-organize and to deliver a successful product". We argue that as development of a large-scale and complex software system requires many types of knowledge and skills, focusing only on "coaching the team" is based on expectations that are difficult to meet for most employees. Paraphrasing the words of Jurgen Appelo, we can say that the idea of the perfect all-round tester is great. But the world isn't perfect, and neither are most employees. Therefore, we need the Testing Hopscotch profiles.

4 Testing in Teaching at Universities

4.1 Background Information

In order to investigate how knowledge and skills related to testing of software systems are described in courses taught at universities, we conducted a series of interviews with representatives from six universities, located in the same geographical areas as the companies in the study. The interviewees were all teaching testing courses at their universities and had senior roles at the universities as professor or associate professor.

The interviewed teachers described how the universities included testing in software engineering courses (programming courses and project courses) and in separate courses focused on testing. Three of the universities also had advanced testing courses, including one course on automated testing and one course on model-based testing. The teachers described how the courses were based primarily on elements from books on software testing, on the teachers' own research and the teachers' own experience. Teachers at two of the universities described how they included guest lectures from industry and also frequently introduced recent research papers in their courses.

4.2 Testing in Teaching at the Six Universities

The main question in the interview guide was "In the courses for MSc students, how do you describe knowledge, skills and personality for a good engineer who works with testing?" Extracts from the interview responses were coded and collated into themes, and a thematic network was constructed [5], resulting in a thematic map representing the responses from the interviewees.

Teachers at all of the universities described in different ways how they talked in their lectures about the importance of *understanding the context and understanding the system.* Testing is conducted differently in different contexts or domains (such as safety critical systems or web applications). How much testing is needed and which test techniques are most relevant for different types of contexts. It is also important to be able to understand the system you are testing (functions, design and architecture) in order to test in a good way. All teachers included some type of *test fundamentals and test techniques* in their courses. This includes basic terminology, how to define test cases, test and requirements, and testing as a part of quality assurance. Testing is conducted on different levels, with different types of testing and test techniques. In various ways, the teachers also include the purpose of testing, prioritizing in testing, and planning of test activities. All teachers also included one or more aspects of *soft skills* in their teaching. This included various types of soft skills, but primarily skills related to communication. Other skills were being structured and detail-oriented ("pickiness") and having the ability to work under pressure. The teachers also included collaboration in an Agile context, creativity, motivation, and problems related to bias.

In the analysis we identified some elements that were only described by one or two universities: One of the teachers described the need to test with an end-user perspective. Another teacher described the need for the ability to communicate well with the stakeholders for the test activities. Teachers from two universities described or touched upon the need for testing with different perspectives, in particular testing in close collaboration with the development team in contrast to independent testers.

4.3   Challenges Related to Teaching

Some of the teachers also described challenges or problems related to teaching. Two of the teachers described difficulties in finding time to cover testing in different types of products and organizations, spanning from testing in a small start-up company to testing of large-scale and complex products in an organization with thousands of employees. One of the teachers described this in the following words: "Testing is shaped around the development process, not the other way. It's challenging to teach a testing course […]. You never know what the students will get in touch with, what development process, so you do not know what they need." Another teacher described how the universities were only able "to provide the students with a general toolbox for testing, and allow them to use the things they need".

One teacher described a different type of challenge, related to the students at the universities. "In one of the courses I talk about the need for independent testers and how close should you be to the development team. However, I am not sure how many of the students that really understand this." We interpret this as an example of how some aspects of testing are more difficult to teach to students at a university, who often lack experience of working in the industry.

Finally, during the interview one of the teachers questioned the idea of discussing personality traits for engineers working with testing: "I do not focus such on personality. We are all able to communicate, but it is not a requirement to communicate in a certain way." The teacher explained further: "When we define the tester, we risk to be discriminating and risk to miss out perspectives. […] We must avoid homogeneous teams if everyone converges to one type of personality."

4.4   Summary and Discussion

The interviews with the teachers at the six universities showed that teaching at the universities covered different aspects of knowledge and skills for an engineer working with testing: understanding the context and the system, test fundamentals and test techniques, and different types of soft skills (Sect. 4.2). To a large extent, this is similar to the set of general characteristics described by the 60 interviewees (Sect. 3.1) but some things are missing. Knowledge and skills related to tools and test environments were described as important by the practitioners, but the teachers did not emphasize these things in the same way. The need for different types of knowledge and skills for different types of testing was touched upon by two of the teachers, but the perspective was generally to "provide the students with a general toolbox" (to quote one of the teachers).

However, the challenges described by some of the teachers (Sect. 4.3) suggest an explanation for the differences between the results from the interviews with the teachers and the practitioners in industry: As the universities should prepare the students for anything from a small start-up to a large-scale organization with complex products, it is not feasible to find room for more than the basic "toolbox" of fundamentals and test techniques (as described by one of the teachers). Additionally, some aspects of testing seem to be difficult to teach to students who lack experience with industry. This means that the gap between teaching at the universities and the needs described by practitioners in large-scale companies is not likely to disappear. Instead, it is the companies in industry who must define competence paths and best practices for the complementary profiles for engineers working with testing.

5 Cross-Company Workshop

5.1 Background Information

As a complement to the validation workshops, a cross-company workshop was arranged with the six companies from the validation workshops (Company A–F) and the six universities from the interview series (University I–VI). A seventh company (Company G) was also invited to provide new perspectives. The cross-company workshop included 33 participants, with three to six representatives from each of the seven companies and one participant from each of the six universities. The cross-company workshop was arranged as a hybrid event with 25 participants present on site (including the two researchers) and another eight participants virtually on a Teams meeting.

5.2 Discussions at the Cross-Company Workshop

At the cross-company workshop, the researchers presented the results from the study, including the results from the validation of the Testing Hopscotch model (Sect. 3) and the results from the interview series with the universities (Sect. 4). The presentations worked as a catalyst, promoting good discussions among the workshop participants. Two topics in particular generated longer discussions: One of the professors argued that the focus should be on other aspects, and gave examples such as focus on test automation or on the test activities instead of on personas. Building on this, another participant representing one of the universities emphasized the importance of describing the purpose and needs motivating the model ("who should use the model and why"). The workshop participants also discussed the results from the validation of the Hopscotch model, and in particular the responses from workshop group #6. One participant said that he recognized problems with teams that were very focused on Agile methodology as such. Another participant argued the model might work better with a more mature organization, where general ways of working for system and software development have been established.

Based on the feedback from some of the validation groups (Sect. 3.4) the researchers asked the participants at the cross-company workshop to discuss whether the profiles should be described as "tester" profiles or "testing" profiles. The participants were also asked to discuss different names for the profiles, especially the profile for testing in parallel with development, referred to by participants at the validation workshops as "Agile testing", "integration testing", "feature testing" and "concurrent testing". The participants at the cross-company workshop seemed to prefer "testing" profiles over "tester" profiles, and found that the name "Development Testing profile" corresponded in the best way to the terminology used in most companies.

5.3 Is the Testing Hopscotch Model for Everyone?

The participants in the cross-company workshop were split into five groups, with four of the groups located in separate rooms and one group for the participants in the Teams meeting. All groups were arranged to include participants from as many companies and universities as possible. The groups were asked to discuss if the Testing Hopscotch model is valid for all types of systems/products, and for all types of ways of working:

- If the system-under-test is not large and/or complex?
- If the system is a very large system of systems?
- If everything is automated?
- If there are no requirements and no test cases?

The breakout sessions in smaller groups were followed by a summarizing session with all participants, discussing the findings from each group. None of the groups had identified any limitations for the Testing Hopscotch model with regards to small or large systems. Three of the groups concluded that in a smaller project or smaller context one person covers all of the profiles. However, the model was still seen as relevant as "the model describes the perspectives that need to be covered". In a similar way, in a very large context "one person is fully occupied with just one of the profiles". More automated testing was not described as a problem for the Testing Hopscotch model by any of the groups. However, two of the groups directly questioned the idea of automating everything, as "there is always something manual". One of the groups specifically pointed to troubleshooting as a manual test activity, and emphasized the need for manual testing in order to preserve the engineers' knowledge of the system. The scenario with no requirements and no test cases was not seen as relevant by the groups, as there is always some kind of specification or description of the desired behavior for the system. One participant commented that sometimes the specification is "in our heads", which is "a problem if the employees change jobs".

In addition to the questions from the researchers, two of the groups also discussed additional questions. One group discussed feedback cycles, and came to the conclusion that the Testing Hopscotch model works if you have longer feedback cycles from the end user, or if you deliver more frequently. The same group stated that it is important to understand what is the system of interest, "where are you in this [system] hierarchy". Another group discussed levels of details in a model such as the Testing Hopscotch model: if a model is too detailed it is too specific, if it is too abstract it does not mean anything. One participant stated that "there is a problem with specific profiles or pre-scribed ways of working, but if everyone does what they want there are a lot of parallel tools and ways of working that drive costs".

5.4 Summary and Discussion

In summary, we find that the presentation of the validation of the Testing Hopscotch model was well received by the participants at the cross-company workshop. The cross-company workshop provided good discussions and comments from the participants (Sect. 5.2) used by the researcher to further improve the presentations of the model.

During the breakout sessions in smaller groups (Sect. 5.3) the participants discussed possible limitations for the Testing Hopscotch model, but none of the groups presented any identified limitations at the summarizing session. However, previously one of the participants at the cross-company workshop argued that the model might work better with a more mature organization (Sect. 5.2). We consider this to be a reasonable consideration, valuable for future application of the Testing Hopscotch model.

6 Threats to Validity

6.1 Threats to Construct Validity

It is plausible that a different set of questions or a different context for the study would lead to a different focus in the participants' responses at the interviews, the validation workshops or the cross-company workshop. In order to handle these threats to construct validity, the interview guides and the workshops were designed with open-ended questions, and the workshop participants were selected as good informants with appropriate roles in the companies (following the guidelines from Robson and McCartan [5]).

6.2 Threats to Internal Validity

Of the 12 threats to internal validity listed by Cook, Campbell and Day [12], we con-sider Selection, Ambiguity about causal direction and Compensatory rivalry to be relevant to this work:

- *Selection*: All interviewees and workshop participants were purposely sampled in line with the guidelines for qualitative data appropriateness given by Robson and McCartan [5]. The selection of workshop participants was informed by senior experts on testing in each company. Based on the rationale of these samplings and supported by Robson and McCartan who consider this type of sampling superior for this type of study in order to secure appropriateness, we consider this threat to be mitigated.
- *Ambiguity about causal direction*: While in some cases we discuss relationships in this study, we are very careful about making statements regarding causation. Statements that include cause and effect are collected from the interviews and the focus groups, and are not introduced in the interpretation of the data.
- *Compensatory rivalry*: The questions for the interviews, the validation workshops and the cross-company workshop were deliberately designed to be value neutral for the participants, and not judging performance or skills of the individual interviewee.

6.3 Threats to External Validity

It is conceivable that the findings from this study are only valid for the seven companies involved in the study, or for companies that operate in the same industry segments and have similar characteristics (presented in Sect. 2.2). Because of the diverse nature of the seven companies, the companies included in the study represent a good cross-section of the industry. Based on analytical generalization [7, 9] it is reasonable to expect that the results from the study are also relevant to a large segment of the software industry at large.

7 Conclusions and Further Work

7.1 Conclusions

Contrasting the idea of a team with all-round testers, *the Testing Hopscotch model* visualizes a fellowship of good testing with six complementary profiles, tailored for different types of test activities. The model is based on a series of interviews with 60 participants from three companies developing large-scale software systems, followed by three focus groups with 22 participants in total from the same three companies.

The *validation of the Testing Hopscotch model* (Sect. 3) included ten validation workshops with a total of 58 participants from six companies. The groups at the validation workshops used a two-step process to validate the model at different levels of integration in a large-scale system. The validation of the Testing Hopscotch model showed how the model provided valuable insights and promoted good discussions, helping companies identify what they need to do to improve testing in their organization. According to the participants at the validation workshops, the model also provided new perspectives and insights.

The *interviews with teachers at six universities* (Sect. 4) showed that their teaching at the universities covered different aspects of knowledge and skills for an engineer working with testing, in many ways similar to the characteristics described by the 60 interviewees, but also revealing some missing elements (important for testing of large-scale software systems). As it is difficult for the teachers to find room in the courses for more than fundamentals and test techniques, the gap between teaching at the universities and the needs described by practitioners in large-scale companies is not likely to disappear. Instead, it is the companies in industry who must define competence paths and best practices for the complementary profiles for engineers working with testing.

The *cross-company workshop* (Sect. 5) with 33 participants from seven companies and six universities provided good discussions and comments, which were used by the researchers to further improve the presentations of the model. At the breakout sessions in five separate groups, the participants did not identify any limitations for the Testing Hopscotch model with regard to type of system under test or ways of working, which strengthens the generalizability of the model. We find that the validation workshops and the cross-company workshop showed that the Testing Hopscotch model is novel, actionable and useful in practice – helping companies identify what they need to do to improve testing in their organization.

7.2 Further Work

The validation of the Testing Hopscotch model showed how the model can help companies identify what they need to do to improve testing in their organization. Further work could investigate how the model can also be a catalyst to improve test efficiency and effectiveness in an organization (although this can be difficult to measure).

At the validation workshops we observed how at first the workshop participants sometimes interpreted the profiles as more static roles. Another observation was that some of the workshop participants started by talking about test activities instead of competence profiles for engineers working with testing (the long-term cultivation of knowledge that resides in the individuals). In response to this, we recognize that improvements to the description and the visualization of the model could be further investigated as a part of future studies related to the Testing Hopscotch model.

At the discussions at the cross-company workshop, one of the participants argued that the model might work better with a more mature organization, where general ways of working for system and software development have been established. We consider this to be a reasonable consideration, that could be investigated in further work. Further validation could also continue to investigate the limitations of the applicability of the Testing Hopscotch model, as this has not been fully defined in this study.

References

1. Ståhl, D., Mårtensson, T., Bosch, J.: Continuous practices and devops: beyond the buzz, what does it all mean? In: 43rd Euromicro Conference on Software Engineering and Advanced Applications (SEAA 2017), pp. 440–448 (2017)
2. Mårtensson, T., Ståhl, D., Bosch, J.: Test activities in the continuous integration and delivery pipeline. J. Softw. Evol. Process **31**(4) (2019)
3. Mårtensson, T., Sandahl, K.: Stop looking for the perfect all-round tester. In: 49th Euromicro Conference on Software Engineering and Advanced Applications (SEAA 2023). In press
4. Sánchez-Gordón, M., Rijal, L., Colomo-Palacios, R.: Beyond technical skills in software testing: automated versus manual testing. In: 42nd International Conference on Software Engineering Workshops (ICSEW 2020), pp. 161–164 (2020)
5. Robson, C., McCartan, K.: Real World Research, 4th edn. Wiley (2016)
6. Sagoe, D.: Precincts and prospects in the use of focus groups in social and behavioral science research. Qualit. Rep. **17**(15) (2012)
7. Runeson, P., Höst, M.: Guidelines for conducting and reporting case study research in software engineering. Empir. Softw. Eng. **14**(2), 131–164 (2009)
8. Drever, E.: Using Semi-structured Interviews in Small-scale Research: A Teacher's Guide. The SCRE Centre (2003)
9. Wieringa, R., Daneva, M.: Six strategies for generalizing software engineering theories. Sci. Comput. Program. **101**, 136–152 (2015)
10. Black, R.: Pragmatic Software Testing: Becoming an Effective and Efficient Test Professional. Wiley Publishing (2007)
11. Appelo, J.: Management 3.0: Leading Agile Developers, Developing Agile Leaders. Pearson Education (2011)
12. Cook, T.D., Campbell, D.T., Day, A.: Quasi-experimentation: Design and Analysis Issues for Field Settings, vol. 351. Houghton Mifflin Boston (1979)

Continuous Experimentation and Human Factors
An Exploratory Study

Amna Pir Muhammad[1]([✉]) [iD], Eric Knauss[1] [iD], Jonas Bärgman[2] [iD],
and Alessia Knauss[3] [iD]

[1] Dept. of Computer Science and Eng., Chalmers | University of Gothenburg,
Gothenburg, Sweden
`amnap@chlamers.se`
[2] Department of Mechanics and Maritime Sciences,
Chalmers University of Technology, Gothenburg, Sweden
[3] Zenseact AB, Gothenburg, Sweden

Abstract. In today's rapidly evolving technological landscape, the success of tools and systems relies heavily on their ability to meet the needs and expectations of users. User-centered design approaches, with a focus on human factors, have gained increasing attention as they prioritize the human element in the development process. With the increasing complexity of software-based systems, companies are adopting agile development methodologies and emphasizing continuous software experimentation. However, there is limited knowledge on how to effectively execute continuous experimentation with respect to human factors within this context. This research paper presents an exploratory qualitative study for integrating human factors in continuous experimentation, aiming to uncover distinctive characteristics of human factors and continuous software experiments, practical challenges for integrating human factors in continuous software experiments, and best practices associated with the management of continuous human factors experimentation.

Keywords: Continuous Experimentation · Human Factors · Human Factors Experiments · Continuous Human Factors Experimentation

1 Introduction

In today's fast-paced software development environments, characterized by competitive and unpredictable markets, there is a need to deliver and improve products rapidly [31]. This urgency is intensified by complex customer requirements and rapid technological advancements. Consequently, many software companies have embraced or are transitioning toward continuous experimentation [25,35].

Continuous software experimentation[1] involves iteratively gathering user feedback and observing user interactions [6]. With the growing significance of

---

[1] Key terms of this study are defined in Table 1.

© The Author(s), under exclusive license to Springer Nature Switzerland AG 2024
R. Kadgien et al. (Eds.): PROFES 2023, LNCS 14483, pp. 511–526, 2024.
https://doi.org/10.1007/978-3-031-49266-2_35

software in complex and automated systems, continuous experimentation has become increasingly prevalent across various industries. These systems require robust and continuously evolving software [19]. Researchers have acknowledged that the design for such systems is inherently complex and that a more comprehensive understanding of the real world can be achieved by actively looking at the system from a human factors perspective and not only a technical perspective [2,11].

In order to ensure the effectiveness, safety, and reliability of systems, particularly complex software systems, it is desirable to provide more holistic knowledge on human factors in continuous experimentation. Especially for safety-critical systems, a human factors perspective may provide crucial in-depth insights. Therefore, integrating human factors experimentation into the continuous experimentation process promises to be a game changer [16,30]. Human factors refer to the various aspects of individuals, including their physical, cognitive, social, and emotional elements, all of which can significantly influence their performance and interactions with systems [12]. Human factors experiments prioritize studying user behavior and involve experiments with humans as participants [8]. We acknowledge that the concepts of continuous software experimentation and human factors experiments overlap to some extent (i.e., the latter can be a component of the former, and vice versa), but in this study, we discuss them as separate entities as they come from different domains and are likely to complement each other. However, to understand whether HF experiments fit the continuous software experiment practices, one needs to understand in detail where they differ, where they overlap, and in what they can be integrated.

While the significance of human factors has been widely recognized [24,32] and continuous software experimentation methodologies are widespread in industry and have received extensive research attention [7,13], there remains a research gap when it comes to incorporating human factors experiments into the well established continuous software experimentation processes [30]. Consequently, further investigation is required to bridge this gap [22].

This research aims to address differences, associated challenges, and best practices for integration of human factors experiments within the context of continuous experimentation. The following research questions (RQs) are used to guide our research:

RQ1: What are main differences when comparing human factors experiments with continuous software experimentation?
RQ2: What are main practical challenges when managing human factors experiments in continuous software experimentation?
RQ3: What are best practices for managing human factors in continuous experimentation?

The findings for RQ1 reveal that while both human factors and software experimentation emphasize the significance of understanding user behavior and needs, they differ in their approach. RQ2 highlights the challenges in managing human factors experiments, pointing to complexities like GDPR compliance, data collection issues, additional costs, and an industry scarcity of experts.

RQ3 focuses on best practices in this domain, emphasizing the need to prioritize research based on product timelines, invest in actionable metrics, maintain robust experimental infrastructure and documentation, and including or transferring human factors knowledge.

The rest of this paper is structured as follows: We start with an overview of definitions for key terms used in this paper in Sect. 2, which covers background knowledge and related work as well. Section 3 presents the research methodology, and Sect. 4 outlines the findings. Section 5 presents the discussion and potential threats to validity. Finally, Sect. 6 concludes the paper.

2 Background and Related Work

Key terms of this study can be interpreted differently depending on the domain. Hence, for the scope of this study, we use the definitions provided in Table 1.

Table 1. Definitions of key terms used in this study

Term	Definition
Continuous (software) experimentation	An approach to support software development, where research and development activities are guided by iteratively conducting experiments, collecting user feedback, and observing the interaction of users with the system or services under development. The goal of continuous software experimentation is to evaluate features, assess risks, and drive evolution [6,13,35]
Human factors in development	The field that aims to inform developers by providing fundamental knowledge about human capabilities and limitations throughout the design cycle so that products will meet specific quality objectives. These capabilities and limitations include cognitive, physical, behavioral, psychological, social, effective, and motivational aspects [12,21]
Human factors experiments	Investigations that focus on how human capabilities and limitations affect specific quality objectives during the interaction between humans and the system, service, or product under development. Thus, humans are part of human factors experiments and their behavior and perception/opinions (of, e.g., the system, service, or product under assessment) can impact the result and consequently the design of the system [9,28]
Continuous human factors experimentation	An iterative approach in software development that evaluates how human capabilities and limitations impact specific quality objectives during user interactions. It involves ongoing experiments, user feedback, and observations to inform the design process and enhance user experience

Continuous Software Experimentation. Agile development methodologies have gained widespread popularity in software development due to their iterative and collaborative nature [1]. These methodologies emphasize continuous experimentation, which involves constantly testing and validating hypotheses to make data-driven decisions throughout development [35]. This approach has proven effective in optimizing software products and services.

Continuous experimentation is primarily applied in web-based systems, allowing developers to analyze and deploy changes based on real-world data and user preferences, rather than relying solely on simulations or the opinion of the highest-paid person's opinion (HiPPO) [14]. Leading technology companies like Microsoft, Google, Facebook, and Booking.com utilize online controlled experiments, also known as A/B tests, to evaluate the impact of changes made to their software products and services [5,7,13].

Despite the numerous advantages of wide-ranging continuous software experimentation, there are still several challenges that need to be addressed during its implementation. Some of the major hurdles include cultural shifts within development teams, slow development cycles, product instrumentation, and the identification of appropriate metrics for measuring user experience [15,17]. Rissanen and Münch [26] confirmed these challenges and also found that capturing and transferring user data becomes challenging due to legal agreements.

Human Factors and Experimentation. By including human factors experiments from the outset, it becomes possible to ensure system reliability and evaluate the system considering real-world human constraints [28]. Human factors experiments aim to understand how people interact with technology, products, and systems to optimize usability, user experience, and overall performance [12]. They commonly evaluate aspects such as user interface design, cognitive workload, situation awareness, and user behavior [10,27,29,33].

Continuous Human Factors Experimentation. In terms of testing and experiments, there have been some initial efforts to integrate usability testing and user-centered design practices into agile development, like for example the approach proposed by Nakao et al. [23] to incorporate usability testing throughout the agile development process. Despite these efforts, research has emphasized the need for new processes and tools that empower practitioners of human factors to promote usable and effective products in the agile development environment [30] and the integration of human factors into the well established continuous software experimentation practices used in agile development [22].

Note that our research does not center around the impact of human factors on employees or developers involved in the development processes, as mentioned in [34]. Instead, our focus is primarily on the product itself. By conducting and analyzing a series of semi-structured interviews, we aim to explore the integration of human factors experiments within the context of continuous experimentation in software development.

3   Methodology

Sampling: We conducted interviews with eight professionals (P1-P8). We aimed for a broad sample of expert participants with high experience in human factors, continuous experimentation, ideally in both fields. This criteria however limits the number of available subjects. Thus, we accepted lower participant numbers than initially planned and focused on interviewing a smaller selection of leading experts in their respective fields for this exploratory study.

We focused on recruiting industry participants from renowned organizations such as Microsoft. Targeting those known for their impactful success stories, to ensure a significant impact and obtain high-quality input. Our academic interviewees have extensive experience collaborating closely with industry, and their credentials include thousands of citations (h-index > 35 in four cases), providing them with a good overview of practices in the field that supports our exploratory study goal.

Table 2 presents each participant's role and experience level.

Data Collection: To gather comprehensive information for our study, we used a qualitative study design inspired by Maxwell [20]. Our data collection involved conducting a series of semi-structured interviews, following a predefined set of open-ended questions while allowing flexibility to include additional follow-up questions when necessary. The interview questions used can be found here.

The interviews were conducted online through Zoom, with each session lasting around one hour. We obtained permission from the interviewees to record the sessions, which we later transcribed and anonymized for analysis.

The interview questions were organized into three main categories. The first set aimed to collect demographic information from the interviewees, as well as confirming their experience working with continuous experimentation and human factors. The second set focused on exploring the management of experimentation in both software and human factors contexts. We used these question to get a better understanding of the participants background, how and which experiments they use and generally of the topic under study. Finally, we asked specific questions related to human factors in continuous experimentation. We used the entire data in our analysis and to answer our research questions.

Table 2. Interviewees' roles and relevant work experience (Experience level: Low = 0–5 years, Medium = 5–10 years, High = More than 10 years).

ID	Role	Main Domain	Continuous experimentat. experience	Human Factors experience
P1	SE Researcher	Academia	High	Low
P2	Human Factors Researcher	Academia	Low	High
P3	Human factors Engineer	Industry	High	High
P4	UX Expert	Industry	High	High
P5	Data Scientist	Industry	High	Low
P6	SE/Human Factors Researcher	Academia	High	High
P7	CS Researcher and IT Consultant	Industry & Academia	High	High
P8	Human Factors Researcher	Academia	Low	High

We initiated each interview by providing a brief overview of the study to establish a shared understanding and create a comfortable environment. We also presented the basic terms and definitions relevant to the study topic, seeking agreement from the interviewees. This approach aimed to establish a common foundation for our discussions, minimize potential confusion, and ensure a consistent standpoint when gathering participants' perspectives. Notably, all participants expressed agreement with our definitions, offering no suggestions for improvement or indicating any discrepancies between their own understanding and our proposed definitions as outlined in Table 1.

Data Analysis: For the qualitative analysis, we employed the thematic analysis approach [4] to identify themes and analyze the content. This approach consists of six key steps. Initially, we comprehensively reviewed all the interview notes and generated research-related memos. To facilitate the process, we employed Nvivo initially and later transitioned to using the Miro board for enhanced visualization. These tools allowed us to assign codes or labels to the text. Through an iterative process, we refined the coding scheme to uncover significant ideas and viewpoints. The codes were then analyzed and grouped together to identify common patterns, thereby defining the themes. Subsequently, we thoroughly reviewed and verified the themes that emerged from the coding process, ensuring clarity, consistency, and addressing any ambiguities, contradictions, or omissions.

4   Findings

We present our findings for each research question with primary themes and their related sub-themes. Figure 1 gives an overview of the main themes.

RQ1: What are main differences when comparing human factors experiments with continuous software experimentation?

F1.1: Contextual Factors

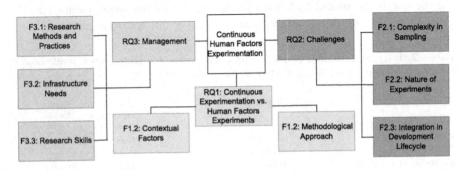

Fig. 1. Overview of key high-level themes identified from the interview analyses.

Human Behavior vs. Technical Aspects: Both software developers and human factors professionals recognize the importance of an intuitive user perspective. They acknowledge that users have varying levels of technical proficiency and may not be inclined to explore complex features. However, human factors experts go a step further by emphasizing the need to understand the underlying reasons for potential user challenges. For example, these challenges could include over-trusting software or avoiding it altogether due to fear or apprehension. To address these concerns, human factors experiments are conducted to gain insights into human behaviors, needs, and experiences. These experiments prioritize the user perspective and strive to optimize user satisfaction and safety. On the other hand, software experiments typically have a more technical development-centric focus. This discrepancy in approach highlights the importance of adopting a human-centric understanding of user behavior and needs, which may differ from the primary focus of developers on technical functionalities.

"They can develop and test and design and maybe it doesn't need to involve human, then it works fine, as soon as you add human, a whole set of questions & requirements come into place which needs to be considered." — P8

Human factors experts primarily focus on observing and analyzing human behaviors to collect data using different interaction metrics. Such an environment poses inherent challenges due to numerous uncontrollable variables at play. For instance, humans exhibit a learning effect that can significantly impact the experimental results. Moreover, interpersonal communication and feedback loops among participants may also influence their responses to the experiments.

Conversely, continuous software experimentation primarily focuses on monitoring system behavior rather than directly observing human behavior. Such experiments collect data from performance indicators, system logs, issue reports, or user interactions documented by the software. They are often conducted under controlled conditions, emphasizing variables like reaction time, resource usage, scalability, or software stability. We believe that these differences are brought to a point by the following exemplary quote:

"The main difference between human factor and traditional experiments, for instance, is that humans have much more of a learning effect." — P7

F1.2: Methodological Approach

Diverse Approaches in Experimentation: The methodology for both human factors and continuous software experiments varies depending on the nature and scope of the feature being tested. Various techniques can be employed for both software and human factors experiments.

"If it's a very small audience, then product teams can also choose actually to do some surveys and interviews they invite customers in. So it really depends on like what is the scope of the feature that you're testing." — P5

While some methodologies, such as surveys and interviews, can be utilized for both software and human factors experiments, there are some notable differences in how the results are analyzed and interpreted. We found that while A/B experimentation is a dominant method in continuous software experimentation, it is often only one of many methods used in human factors experiments.

Qualitative and Quantitative: Much like software experiments, human factors involve qualitative and quantitative data analysis. However, the analysis of human factors experiments leans more towards qualitative methods due to the complexity of measuring and interpreting human behavior. Therefore, conducting effective human factors experiments necessitates practitioners with a strong foundation in qualitative methodologies and empirical work involving human participants. Such practitioners are able to capture the rich and nuanced aspects of human behavior and user experience. In contrast, continuous software experiments often adopt a more quantitative approach, aiming to establish causal relationships between independent and dependent variables, allowing for statistical analysis. That said, a substantial part of human factors experiments still involve collecting quantitative data, such as eye-tracking data and performance data (e.g., in the automotive domain in terms of measures of lane keeping, time gaps, etc., or task completion times considering desktop software tools).

> *"If you have a background in quantitative experiments with technical systems, I would think you cannot do [human factors experiments] in a good way. You need some kind of background in doing empirical work with humans."* — P6

RQ2: What are main practical challenges when managing human factors experiments in continuous software experimentation?

F2.1: Complexity in Sampling

Controlled vs. Uncontrolled Variables: One aspect is the presence of a higher amount of uncontrolled variables in human factors experiments. Numerous contextual factors cannot be fully controlled, which poses challenges in ensuring comparability and measuring variables. Lack of control over contextual factors also complicates the analysis, as there may be numerous variables that cannot be fully controlled or accounted for in the experiment.

> *"The other issue is control. I think you will look at situations where there are just a lot of context factors, there is just no way to control everything."* — P1

Statistical Analysis: One challenge lies in the statistical analysis of the data. In certain cases, conducting a rigorous statistical analysis may not be feasible due to the nature of the human factors experiment. For instance, the research goal might involve observing how people react in a particular situation without quantifiable metrics, so conducting a traditional statistical analysis becomes challenging.

> *"It might not be possible to do a proper statistical analysis because you might want to expose people to a certain situation and see what happens."* — P2

Participant Scarcity: Another challenge in human factors experiments is the limited availability of participants. Getting enough people to participate can be difficult, and the scarcity of eligible participants further complicates the process. In contrast, continuous software experiments, especially those conducted online, can be performed on a larger scale. While involving as many participants as possible is generally advised, practical limitations may hinder this goal.

> *"Often these studies are fairly small regarding the number of subjects."* — P6

F2.2: Nature of Experiments

Personal Information and GDPR Issues: When conducting experiments, the collection of personal information can be crucial for understanding human behavior and software performance. In experimental research, collecting personal information is pivotal for understanding both human behavior and software performance. This is particularly evident in human factors experiments, where insights into how individuals from varied backgrounds interact with technology are essential. However, collecting this in-depth personal information presents challenges, mainly due to privacy and ethical issues. The requirements of GDPR regulations amplify these concerns, necessitating meticulous attention. While software experiments might occasionally need such information, the emphasis is much greater in human factors experiments.

> *"It is a bit hard. Like with the GDPR and everything. How to store stuff actually? It makes it a bit more complicated."* — P4

Prototype vs. Real Environment: Our interviewees mentioned that, although experiments are typically carried out using prototypes or simulators, human factors experts also advocate for conducting experiments in the actual environment where the product will be finally be used. Experiments conducted in real environments offer a more realistic and authentic representation of how participants interact with the product or system in their natural settings. Unlike prototype experiments, where external factors can be tightly controlled, real environment experiments expose participants to multiple variables and contextual factors that can significantly impact human performance and behavior.

> *"Having design prototypes is one approach so that people get the vision behind. But testing in real cars, it makes it so difficult, which is, but also important, to go in that direction or to get more research done."* — P3

Expensive: Human factors experiments are often perceived as more costly compared to continuous software experiments. This perception stems from the direct involvement of real humans participating in real-time scenarios. For instance, experts in human factors often need to recruit participants for their studies, compensating them for their time and effort, which can be a significant expense. On the other hand, many continuous software experiments can gather data online, reducing the need for physical presence and direct human interaction, and direct payment. While continuous software experiments do have associated costs-such as development, deployment, and server infrastructure-these expenses are generally lower than those of human factors experiments.

"We have to pay for this for facilities, we have to pay participants because we get people from the real world, and the preparations is quite prolonged." — P8

F2.3: Integration in Development Lifecycle

Execution Time: Managing and executing human factors experiments in agile development can be challenging due to their inherent time-consuming nature. Unlike continuous software experiments that typically run for at least a week, human factors experiments often require more time to obtain meaningful results. The duration of such experiments is influenced by the desired change in a metric being measured. Obtaining timely results from human factors, that can be integrated into ongoing projects without significant delays can be difficult, especially in agile, short sprint-based, work flows.

"You do a sprint and then you need results to run it and assume you need these kind of results quickly. So not in three months. And that's, I would say that's the problem for integrating these kind of things." — P2

Infrastructure Needs: One challenge involves obtaining the necessary tools and setup to conduct the desired tests. Ensuring that the basic infrastructure is in place to facilitate the experiments can be a significant hurdle.

"If there's getting the right tools and right setup, like the basics in place to even be able to test what you wanna test. That could be a challenge." — P4

Too Few Human Factors Experts: Many companies struggle with insufficient human factors expertise and limited resources, which can hinder their ability to improve user experience. This deficiency often leads to a few outliers (or even the development team itself) having a disproportionate impact on the final product design. This concern arises from the fact that there are too few human factors experts available, which limits comprehensive evaluations and increases the risk of biased results.

"So I think that's what, what other companies are lacking actually: Enough human factors, people doing that kind of work." — P3

Lack of Motivation: Another challenge is that many individuals with a technical mindset often overlook the importance of understanding human behaviors. This lack of motivation can hinder the collection of relevant data and make it difficult to address the complexities involved in studying human subjects.

"How can you influence people? I think that's the number one thing." — P1

RQ3: What are best practices for managing human factors in continuous experimentation?

F3.1: Research Methods and Practices

Prioritizing Hypotheses/Research Questions: Prioritizing research questions and hypotheses based on the product timetable and development sprints is a crucial aspect in agile development. By identifying the experiments that have the most impact on design decisions and user experience improvement, organizations can allocate resources efficiently and gain valuable insights.

> *"The number of experiments that you can do is basically infinite. So the hardest part in running experiments is how do I prioritize running the most valuable experiments first. And, I think that's where many companies struggle."* — P7

Metrics and Measurement Instrumentation: Based on our interviewees, to enable informed decision-making it is essential to invest in the development of meaningful metrics that align with the desired outcomes. While simple interaction metrics like clicks or selections are useful, it is important to go beyond them and capture success metrics related to user sessions and product features. As one of our interviewees pointed out, the value of experiments ultimately relies on having good metrics and making significant investments in their development. Without such metrics, experiments become less valuable as they fail to provide actionable results for decision-making. It was also emphasised that developing and validating such metrics can (and must be allowed to) take substantial time.

Another critical aspect is the measurement of various metrics that provide insights into different aspects of the product under evaluation. It is worth noting that interviewees stressed the significance of using proper measurement methods to obtain valuable results for making informed decisions. To measure different aspects of the product or system being evaluated, multiple metrics should be computed simultaneously. These metrics should align with the goals of the experiment and help determine what is reasonable to measure and what constitutes a good outcome.

> *"But at the end of the day about experiments, it all boils down to metrics. If you don't have good metrics and you don't invest significantly into metrics, your experiments will not be valuable."* — P5

Results and Lessons Learned: When determining whether to reuse or evolve experiments, the organization may take several factors into consideration. These factors include the importance of the findings, potential influencing factors, and information indicating changes in the validity of previous results. The relevance of the results and their impact on decision-making are carefully evaluated when planning subsequent experiments. It was also mentioned that the decision to reuse experiments is often driven by the interest and initiative of individuals involved in the projects, rather than being a formalized process.

> *"There are sometimes factors that are influencing what's factors that may confound the outcomes from one experiment such that we need to rerun it in order to make sure that the thing is still true."* — P7

F3.2: Infrastructure Needs

Experimental Setup: The infrastructure should support the setup and integration of different components required for the experiment. This includes ensuring that the necessary tools and setups are in place to conduct the experiments effectively. It may involve creating prototypes, simulating scenarios, or integrating various hardware and software components to enable the desired testing environment. Careful planning of the experiment is crucial.

> "If there's getting the right tools and getting the right setup or the right HMI, like the basics in place even to be able to test what you wanna test." — P4

Traceability and Documentation: Maintaining traceability and documentation throughout the experimental process is important. This includes preserving initial design proposals that led to the ideas being tested. Having a clear traceability trail helps in understanding the decision-making process during the experiment and provides valuable insights for product teams. Utilizing an experimentation platform that incorporates this traceability is essential.

> "So having some traceability on the decisions that led to what is being tested would be very helpful, I think, for product teams. And that should be part of the experimentation platform." — P5

Collaboration and Management Support: Our interviewees highlighted that infrastructure should facilitate collaboration among different teams involved in the experiments. It should provide a platform for coordinating activities, managing participants, and ensuring the smooth execution of the experiments. Additionally, management buy-in, support, and drive are also important factors to overcome obstacles and successfully implement the infrastructure needed for human factors experiments.

> "Main obstacle is kind of like management, high management buy-in, and support and then like knowledge on how to design and collect it. So, to me, infrastructure would be something they [practitioners] would know how to solve that." — P6

F3.3: Research Skills

Roles and Responsibilities: Our findings indicate that experiment management becomes a collaborative effort within cross-functional teams in an agile environment. These teams typically include data scientists, engineers, product managers, program managers, and user researchers. Our findings also highlight the pivotal role of data scientists in continuous software experiments and the need for technical support from engineers in human factors experiments. Moreover, considering a single role for responsibility, product managers are crucial in deciding which experiments to run and ensuring that relevant metrics are effectively measured. We learned that while the responsibility for managing continuous human factors experiments can be shared within a team or primarily held by the manager, it is crucial to recognize that specialized knowledge and expertise are often necessary. Having human factors specialists in human factors experimentation can greatly benefit the planning and management of human factors experiments. Human factors specialists bring specialized knowledge and expertise in research methodology, data analysis, and experimental design to guide the team and ensure precise and accurate experiments.

"I really think that it should be less of a single responsibility and more of a team responsibility." — P7

Knowledge and Training: A solid foundation of knowledge, theory, and models is essential to design and evolve effective human factors experiments. Furthermore, establishing an infrastructure to disseminate this knowledge and provide comprehensive training to researchers and teams is crucial. Agile teams can conduct human factors experiments with appropriate training and methodologies.

"A bit with training. If you follow a specific procedure, then I think it's not a problem." — P4

The training should cover experimental design, research methodology, human factors principles, biases, usability evaluation methods, and research methods. Although individuals inherently possess some understanding of human behavior, training will help broaden their perspective.

5 Discussion

Continuous experimentation for web-based systems has received extensive research attention [7,13], however, the human factors aspect remains relatively underexplored. This study explores the idea to bridge this gap by discussing the integration of human factors experiments with continuous experimentation. This promises to enable continuous experimentation even in the domain of safety critical systems to a larger extent. Integrating human factors experiments into continuous experimentation presents both benefits and challenges [18]. For instance, these experiments can shed light on usability, user experience, and decision-making [28]. Yet, they also pose challenges, such as the need to execute experiments in real environments with real human participants [3].

We confirm challenges highlighted by previous studies [15,17,26] that have investigated challenges in continuous experimentation in general (e.g., cultural shifts and appropriate identification of metrics) also for the integration of human factors into continuous experimentation. On top of that, our findings introduce additional complexities when human factors are integrated into the mix.

Moreover, our findings indicate that the integration of human factors in continuous experimentation is currently lacking. One of the contributing factors to this gap is the shortage of human factors experts available to collaborate with teams engaged in continuous experimentation [21]. While these teams conduct experiments tailored to their specific system components, they often lack input from human factors specialists. Another factor is the usually higher complexity of human factors experiments. On the fast pace of continuous experimentation, this affects options for data collection and appears to cause human factors experiments leaning towards qualitative data collection in this context.

To effectively integrate human factors experiments into continuous experimentation, companies should consider including human factors experts within teams and raising awareness among developers about the importance of incorporating human factors. The successful execution of human factors experiments by teams requires developers to be skilled in empirical study methods, enabling them to conduct impactful human factors experiments.

Threats to Validity: The interdisciplinary nature and vast scope of the fields involved introduces a threat to **Construct Validity** in that various definitions exist for the same terms, such as "human factors". Consequently, different individuals may have different interpretations. We have included clear definitions of the key concepts in interviews and report to mitigate this threat and ensure a common understanding of the fundamental concepts used in this study. Additionally, experienced authors were involved in the study to address the risk of construct validity. Their expertise assisted the first author in developing an interview guide that effectively aligned with the study's research objectives. For **Internal Validity**, we implemented measures to reduce bias and confounding variables, such as having multiple authors conduct each interview to minimize personal bias. Due to the specialized scope and high demands on participant expertise (human factors and continuous experimentation), we had to rely on convenience sampling, taking into account both the profile and availability of potential subjects. Consequently, the low number of participants introduces a threat to **External Validity**. We aimed to mitigate this threat by aiming for covering a wide range of roles, domains, and cultural backgrounds. Finally, to ensure **Reliability,** we implemented various measures. Throughout the interviews, we had multiple researchers present to enhance the reliability of our data. Additionally, we provided used materials and a detailed analysis process, enabling other researchers to replicate our methodology in diverse contexts. Moreover, the authors actively engaged in discussions to maintain consistency in the coding results. However, despite our efforts, we acknowledge the possibility of some subjectivity in our analysis.

6   Conclusion

This qualitative exploratory study investigates the integration of human factors with continuous experimentation. To effectively integrate human factors experiments in continuous experimentation, there's a pressing need for upgraded infrastructure, improved developers' awareness about the importance of human factors, and training developers in empirical study methods essential for effective human-centric experimentation.

By fostering interdisciplinary collaboration and promoting the integration of human factors considerations into continuous experimentation, organizations can enhance the user experience, and improve the quality of software and systems. Future research should focus on developing frameworks and detailed guidelines for effectively incorporating human factors into continuous experimentation processes, leading to the creation of more user-centric, safe, and acceptable systems.

Acknowledgements. The authors express their gratitude to the interviewees for their valuable time and insights. The project has received funding from the Marie Skłodowska-Curie grant agreement 860410 under the European Union's Horizon 2020 research and innovation program.

References

1. Abrahamsson, P., Salo, O., Ronkainen, J., Warsta, J.: Agile software development methods: review and analysis. arXiv preprint arXiv:1709.08439 (2017)
2. Boy, G.A.: Human-centered design of complex systems: an experience-based approach. Design Sci. **3**, e8 (2017)
3. Charlton, S.G., O'Brien, T.G.: Handbook of Human Factors Testing and Evaluation. CRC Press, Boca Raton (2019)
4. Clarke, V., Braun, V., Hayfield, N.: Thematic analysis. Qual. Psychol.: Pract. Guide Res. Methods **3**, 222–248 (2015)
5. Fabijan, A., Dmitriev, P., Olsson, H.H., Bosch, J.: The evolution of continuous experimentation in software product development: from data to a data-driven organization at scale. In: 2017 IEEE/ACM 39th International Conference on Software Engineering (ICSE), pp. 770–780. IEEE (2017)
6. Fagerholm, F., Guinea, A.S., Mäenpää, H., Münch, J.: The right model for continuous experimentation. J. Syst. Softw. **123**, 292–305 (2017)
7. Feitelson, D.G., Frachtenberg, E., Beck, K.L.: Development and deployment at Facebook. IEEE Internet Comput. **17**(4), 8–17 (2013)
8. Franklin, A.D.: What makes a 'good' experiment? Br. J. Philos. Sci. **32**(4), 367–374 (1981)
9. Gandevia, S.: A human factor in 'good' experiments. Br. J. Philos. Sci. **37**(4), 463–466 (1986)
10. Hancock, P., Caird, J.K.: Experimental evaluation of a model of mental workload. Hum. Factors **35**(3), 413–429 (1993)
11. Hancock, P.A.: Some pitfalls in the promises of automated and autonomous vehicles. Ergonomics **62**(4), 479–495 (2019)
12. Human Factors and Ergonomics Society: Definitions of human factors and ergonomics (2023). https://www.hfes.org/About-HFES/What-is-Human-Factors-and-Ergonomics. Accessed 17 Feb 2023
13. Kevic, K., Murphy, B., Williams, L., Beckmann, J.: Characterizing experimentation in continuous deployment: a case study on bing. In: 39th International Conference on Software Engineering (ICSE-SEIP). IEEE (2017)
14. Kohavi, R., Henne, R.M., Sommerfield, D.: Practical guide to controlled experiments on the web: listen to your customers not to the hippo. In: Proceedings of the 13th ACM SIGKDD, pp. 959–967 (2007)
15. Kohavi, R., et al.: Online experimentation at Microsoft. Data Min. Case Stud. **11**(2009), 39 (2009)
16. Lee, J.D., Seppelt, B.D.: Human factors in automation design. In: Nof, S. (ed.) Springer Handbook of Automation. Springer Handbooks, pp. 417–436. Springer, Heidelberg (2009). https://doi.org/10.1007/978-3-540-78831-7_25

17. Lindgren, E., Münch, J.: Software development as an experiment system: a qualitative survey on the state of the practice. In: Lassenius, C., Dingsøyr, T., Paasivaara, M. (eds.) XP 2015. LNBIP, vol. 212, pp. 117–128. Springer, Cham (2015). https://doi.org/10.1007/978-3-319-18612-2_10

18. Madni, A.M.: Integrating humans with and within complex systems. CrossTalk **5** (2011)

19. Maruping, L.M., Matook, S.: The evolution of software development orchestration: current state and an agenda for future research. Eur. J. Inf. Syst. **29**(5), 443–457 (2020)

20. Maxwell, J.A.: Qualitative Research Design: An Interactive Approach. Sage Publications (2012)

21. Muhammad, A.P., Knauss, E., Bärgman, J.: Human factors in developing automated vehicles: a requirements engineering perspective. J. Syst. Softw. 111810 (2023)

22. Muhammad, A.P., Knauss, E., Bärgman, J., Knauss, A.: Towards challenges and practices with managing human factors in automated vehicle development. In: 31st IEEE International Requirements Engineering Conference (RE 2023). IEEE (2023)

23. Nakao, Y., Moriguchi, M., Noda, H.: Using agile software development methods to support human-centered design. NEC Tech. J. **8**(3), 37–40 (2014)

24. Norman, D.: Design of Everyday Things, Revised and Expanded. Basic books (2013)

25. Olsson, H.H., Alahyari, H., Bosch, J.: Climbing the "stairway to heaven"-a mulitiple-case study exploring barriers in the transition from agile development towards continuous deployment of software. In: 2012 38th Euromicro Conference on Software Engineering and Advanced Applications, pp. 392–399. IEEE (2012)

26. Rissanen, O., Münch, J.: Continuous experimentation in the b2b domain: a case study. In: 2015 IEEE/ACM 2nd International Workshop on Rapid Continuous Software Engineering, pp. 12–18. IEEE (2015)

27. Royer, M., Houser, K., Durmus, D., Esposito, T., Wei, M.: Recommended methods for conducting human factors experiments on the subjective evaluation of colour rendition. Light. Res. Technol. **54**(3), 199–236 (2022)

28. Sætren, G.B., Hogenboom, S., Laumann, K.: A study of a technological development process: human factors-the forgotten factors? Cogn. Technol. Work **18**, 595–611 (2016)

29. Shneiderman, B.: Human factors experiments in designing interactive systems. Computer **12**(12), 9–19 (1979)

30. Steinberg, R., Grumman, N.: Human factors at the speed of relevance for agile engineering. In: Proceedings of the Human Factors and Ergonomics Society Annual Meeting, vol. 66. SAGE Publications, Los Angeles (2022)

31. Verhoef, P.C., et al.: Digital transformation: a multidisciplinary reflection and research agenda. J. Bus. Res. **122**, 889–901 (2021)

32. Wickens, C.D., Gordon, S.E., Liu, Y., Lee, J.: An Introduction to Human Factors Engineering, vol. 2. Pearson Prentice Hall, Upper Saddle River (2004)

33. Williams, K.W.: Impact of aviation highway-in-the-sky displays on pilot situation awareness. Hum. Factors **44**(1), 18–27 (2002)

34. Yaman, S.G.: Initiating the transition towards continuous experimentation: empirical studies with software development teams and practitioners. Ser. Publ. A (2019)

35. Yaman, S.G., et al.: Introducing continuous experimentation in large software-intensive product and service organisations. J. Syst. Softw. **133**, 195–211 (2017)

Author Index

Printed in the United States
by Baker & Taylor Publisher Services